C000164393

THE BOOK

Vauxhall Astra and Zafira Diesel
Service and Repair Manual

Martynn Randall and A K Legg LAE MIMI

Models covered

(3797-376-1AJ3)

Astra Hatchback, Saloon & Estate and Zafira MPV models with turbo-diesel engines, including special/limited editions
1.7 litre (1686 & 1700cc) & 2.0 litre (1995cc)

For coverage of petrol models, see manual no. 3758
Does NOT cover 1.7 litre CDTi (common rail) engine, or automatic transmission variants

© Haynes Publishing 2006

ABCDE
FG

A book in the **Haynes Service and Repair Manual Series**

ISBN **978 1 78521 288 8**

British Library Cataloguing in Publication Data
A catalogue record for this book is available from the British Library.

Printed in the USA

Haynes Publishing
Sparkford, Yeovil, Somerset BA22 7JJ, England

Haynes North America, Inc
861 Lawrence Drive, Newbury Park, California 91320, USA

Haynes Publishing Nordiska AB
Box 1504, 751 45 UPPSALA, Sverige

Printed using 33-lb Resolute Book 65 4.0 from Resolute Forest Products Calhoun, TN mill. Resolute is a member of World Wildlife Fund's Climate Savers programme committed to significantly reducing GHG emissions. This paper uses 50% less wood fibre than traditional offset. The Calhoun Mill is certified to the following sustainable forest management and chain of custody standards: SFI, PEFC and FSC Controlled Wood.

Contents

LIVING WITH YOUR VAUXHALL ASTRA/ZAFIRA

Contents

REPAIRS AND OVERHAUL

Advanced driving

Many people see the words 'advanced driving' and believe that it won't interest them or that it is a style of driving beyond their own abilities. Nothing could be further from the truth. Advanced driving is straightforward safe, sensible driving - the sort of driving we should all do every time we get behind the wheel.

An average of 10 people are killed every day on UK roads and 870 more are injured, some seriously. Lives are ruined daily, usually because somebody did something stupid. Something like 95% of all accidents are due to human error, mostly driver failure. Sometimes we make genuine mistakes - everyone does. Sometimes we have lapses of concentration. Sometimes we deliberately take risks.

For many people, the process of 'learning to drive' doesn't go much further than learning how to pass the driving test because of a common belief that good drivers are made by 'experience'.

Learning to drive by 'experience' teaches three driving skills:

☐ Quick reactions. (Whoops, that was close!)
☐ Good handling skills. (Horn, swerve, brake, horn).
☐ Reliance on vehicle technology. (Great stuff this ABS, stop in no distance even in the wet...)

Drivers whose skills are 'experience based' generally have a lot of near misses and the odd accident. The results can be seen every day in our courts and our hospital casualty departments.

Advanced drivers have learnt to control the risks by controlling the position and speed of their vehicle. They avoid accidents and near misses, even if the drivers around them make mistakes.

The key skills of advanced driving are **concentration,** effective all-round **observation, anticipation** and **planning.** When **good vehicle handling** is added to

these skills, all driving situations can be approached and negotiated in a safe, methodical way, leaving nothing to chance.

Concentration means applying your mind to safe driving, completely excluding anything that's not relevant. Driving is usually the most dangerous activity that most of us undertake in our daily routines. It deserves our full attention.

Observation means not just looking, but seeing and seeking out the information found in the driving environment.

Anticipation means asking yourself what is happening, what you can reasonably expect to happen and what could happen unexpectedly. (One of the commonest words used in compiling accident reports is 'suddenly'.)

Planning is the link between seeing something and taking the appropriate action. For many drivers, planning is the missing link.

If you want to become a safer and more skilful driver and you want to enjoy your driving more, contact the Institute of Advanced Motorists at www.iam.org.uk, phone 0208 996 9600, or write to IAM House, 510 Chiswick High Road, London W4 5RG for an information pack.

Working on your car can be dangerous. This page shows just some of the potential risks and hazards, with the aim of creating a safety-conscious attitude.

General hazards

Scalding

• Don't remove the radiator or expansion tank cap while the engine is hot.
• Engine oil, automatic transmission fluid or power steering fluid may also be dangerously hot if the engine has recently been running.

Burning

• Beware of burns from the exhaust system and from any part of the engine. Brake discs and drums can also be extremely hot immediately after use.

Crushing

• When working under or near a raised vehicle, always supplement the jack with axle stands, or use drive-on ramps. *Never venture under a car which is only supported by a jack.*

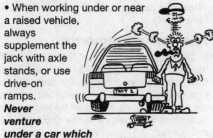

• Take care if loosening or tightening high-torque nuts when the vehicle is on stands. Initial loosening and final tightening should be done with the wheels on the ground.

Fire

• Fuel is highly flammable; fuel vapour is explosive.
• Don't let fuel spill onto a hot engine.
• Do not smoke or allow naked lights (including pilot lights) anywhere near a vehicle being worked on. Also beware of creating sparks (electrically or by use of tools).
• Fuel vapour is heavier than air, so don't work on the fuel system with the vehicle over an inspection pit.
• Another cause of fire is an electrical overload or short-circuit. Take care when repairing or modifying the vehicle wiring.
• Keep a fire extinguisher handy, of a type suitable for use on fuel and electrical fires.

Electric shock

• Ignition HT voltage can be dangerous, especially to people with heart problems or a pacemaker. Don't work on or near the ignition system with the engine running or the ignition switched on.

• Mains voltage is also dangerous. Make sure that any mains-operated equipment is correctly earthed. Mains power points should be protected by a residual current device (RCD) circuit breaker.

Fume or gas intoxication

• Exhaust fumes are poisonous; they often contain carbon monoxide, which is rapidly fatal if inhaled. Never run the engine in a confined space such as a garage with the doors shut.
• Fuel vapour is also poisonous, as are the vapours from some cleaning solvents and paint thinners.

Poisonous or irritant substances

• Avoid skin contact with battery acid and with any fuel, fluid or lubricant, especially antifreeze, brake hydraulic fluid and Diesel fuel. Don't syphon them by mouth. If such a substance is swallowed or gets into the eyes, seek medical advice.
• Prolonged contact with used engine oil can cause skin cancer. Wear gloves or use a barrier cream if necessary. Change out of oil-soaked clothes and do not keep oily rags in your pocket.
• Air conditioning refrigerant forms a poisonous gas if exposed to a naked flame (including a cigarette). It can also cause skin burns on contact.

Asbestos

• Asbestos dust can cause cancer if inhaled or swallowed. Asbestos may be found in gaskets and in brake and clutch linings. When dealing with such components it is safest to assume that they contain asbestos.

Special hazards

Hydrofluoric acid

• This extremely corrosive acid is formed when certain types of synthetic rubber, found in some O-rings, oil seals, fuel hoses etc, are exposed to temperatures above 400°C. The rubber changes into a charred or sticky substance containing the acid. *Once formed, the acid remains dangerous for years. If it gets onto the skin, it may be necessary to amputate the limb concerned.*
• When dealing with a vehicle which has suffered a fire, or with components salvaged from such a vehicle, wear protective gloves and discard them after use.

The battery

• Batteries contain sulphuric acid, which attacks clothing, eyes and skin. Take care when topping-up or carrying the battery.
• The hydrogen gas given off by the battery is highly explosive. Never cause a spark or allow a naked light nearby. Be careful when connecting and disconnecting battery chargers or jump leads.

Air bags

• Air bags can cause injury if they go off accidentally. Take care when removing the steering wheel and/or facia. Special storage instructions may apply.

Diesel injection equipment

• Diesel injection pumps supply fuel at very high pressure. Take care when working on the fuel injectors and fuel pipes.

⚠ *Warning: Never expose the hands, face or any other part of the body to injector spray; the fuel can penetrate the skin with potentially fatal results.*

Remember...

DO

• Do use eye protection when using power tools, and when working under the vehicle.

• Do wear gloves or use barrier cream to protect your hands when necessary.

• Do get someone to check periodically that all is well when working alone on the vehicle.

• Do keep loose clothing and long hair well out of the way of moving mechanical parts.

• Do remove rings, wristwatch etc, before working on the vehicle – especially the electrical system.

• Do ensure that any lifting or jacking equipment has a safe working load rating adequate for the job.

DON'T

• Don't attempt to lift a heavy component which may be beyond your capability – get assistance.

• Don't rush to finish a job, or take unverified short cuts.

• Don't use ill-fitting tools which may slip and cause injury.

• Don't leave tools or parts lying around where someone can trip over them. Mop up oil and fuel spills at once.

• Don't allow children or pets to play in or near a vehicle being worked on.

Vauxhall Astra 5-door Saloon . . .

. . . and Estate models

The Vauxhall Astra-G model was introduced in the UK in February 1998 as a replacement for the previous Astra, the 'F' model. It was available in Saloon, Hatchback and Estate versions with 1.7 and 2.0 litre diesel engines and various petrol engines (not covered in this Manual). The 1.7 litre diesel engines are in either single overhead camshaft (SOHC) 8-valve or double overhead camshaft (DOHC) 16-valve form; the 2.0 litre engine is of single overhead camshaft (SOHC) 16-valve type. The models in this Manual are fitted with a five-speed manual transmission mounted on the left-hand side of the engine. The automatic transmission fitted to certain diesel Van models is not covered in this Manual.

All models have front-wheel-drive with fully-independent front suspension, and semi-independent rear suspension with a torsion beam and trailing arms.

Electro/Hydraulic power steering (PAS) is fitted as standard to all models, whilst Anti-Lock Braking (ABS) is available as an option.

The Zafira range was launched in June 1999, and was available with the 2.0 litre engine. Whilst the Zafira shares the same drivetrain and suspension as the Astra, the body is that of a Multi Personnel Vehicle (MPV). Not only does the Zafira have 7 seats arranged in three rows, it quickly converts to a spacious load carrier – thanks to the 'Flex 7' system, which allows the rear seats to fold completely flat into the floor giving an uninterrupted load space.

Both models have a full-sized driver's side airbag fitted as standard, and side impact airbags available as an option. Passenger's side airbags became standard equipment from January 1999.

Cruise control is available as an option on certain models.

For the home mechanic, the Vauxhall Astra/Zafira is a straightforward vehicle to maintain and repair since design features have been incorporated to reduce the cost of ownership to a minimum, and most of the items requiring frequent attention are easily accessible.

Your Vauxhall Astra and Zafira manual

The aim of this manual is to help you get the best value from your vehicle. It can do so in several ways. It can help you decide what work must be done (even should you choose to get it done by a garage), provide information on routine maintenance and servicing, and give a logical course of action and diagnosis when random faults occur. However, it is hoped that you will use the manual by tackling the work yourself. On simpler jobs, it may even be quicker than booking the car into a garage and going there twice, to leave and collect it. Perhaps most important, a lot of money can be saved by avoiding the costs a garage must charge to cover its labour and overheads.

The manual has drawings and descriptions to show the function of the various components, so that their layout can be understood. Then the tasks are described and photographed in a clear step-by-step sequence.

References to the 'left' or 'right' are in the sense of a person in the driver's seat, facing forward.

Acknowledgements

Certain illustrations are the copyright of Vauxhall Motors Limited, and are used with their permission. Thanks are also due to Draper Tools Limited, who provided some of the workshop tools, and to all those people at Sparkford who helped in the production of this manual.

We take great pride in the accuracy of information given in this manual, but vehicle manufacturers make alterations and design changes during the production run of a particular vehicle of which they do not inform us. No liability can be accepted by the authors or publishers for loss, damage or injury caused by any errors in, or omissions from, the information given.

Project vehicles

The main vehicle used in the preparation of this manual, and which appears in many of the photographic sequences, was a 1.7 litre Vauxhall Astra DTI.

Vauxhall Zafira

The following pages are intended to help in dealing with common roadside emergencies and breakdowns. You will find more detailed fault finding information at the back of the manual, and repair information in the main chapters.

If your car won't start and the starter motor doesn't turn

☐ Open the bonnet and make sure that the battery terminals are clean and tight.
☐ Switch on the headlights and try to start the engine. If the headlights go very dim when you're trying to start, the battery is probably flat. Get out of trouble by jump starting (see next page) using a friend's car.

If your car won't start even though the starter motor turns as normal

☐ Is there fuel in the tank?
☐ Is there moisture on electrical components under the bonnet? Switch off the ignition, then wipe off any obvious dampness with a dry cloth. Spray a water-repellent aerosol product (WD-40 or equivalent) on visible electrical connectors under the bonnet.

A Check the condition and security of the battery connections.

B Check the engine wiring harness at the left-hand rear of the engine compartment.

C Check the wiring to the charge pressure sensor (engine top cover removed)

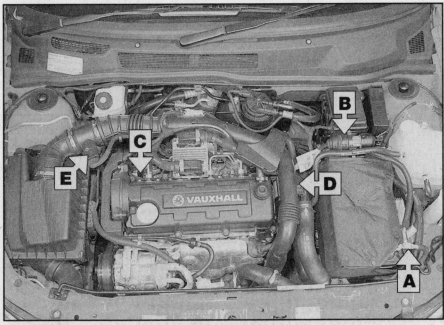

Check that electrical connections are secure (with the ignition switched off) and spray them with a water dispersant spray like WD-40 if you suspect a problem due to damp.

D Check the wiring to the coolant temperature sensor (engine top cover removed)

E Check the wiring to the airflow meter

Jump starting

When jump-starting a car using a booster battery, observe the following precautions:

☐ Before connecting the booster battery, make sure that the ignition is switched off.

☐ Ensure that all electrical equipment (lights, heater, wipers, etc) is switched off.

☐ Take note of any special precautions printed on the battery case.

☐ Make sure that the booster battery is the same voltage as the discharged one in the vehicle.

☐ If the battery is being jump-started from the battery in another vehicle, the two vehicles MUST NOT TOUCH each other.

☐ Make sure that the transmission is in neutral (or PARK, in the case of automatic transmission).

HAYNES HiNT

Jump starting will get you out of trouble, but you must correct whatever made the battery go flat in the first place. There are three possibilities:

1 *The battery has been drained by repeated attempts to start, or by leaving the lights on.*

2 *The charging system is not working properly (alternator drivebelt slack or broken, alternator wiring fault or alternator itself faulty).*

3 *The battery itself is at fault (electrolyte low, or battery worn out).*

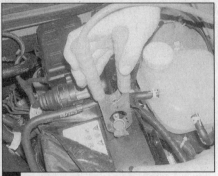

1 Connect one end of the red jump lead to the positive (+) terminal of the flat battery

2 Connect the other end of the red lead to the positive (+) terminal of the booster battery.

3 Connect one end of the black jump lead to the negative (-) terminal of the booster battery

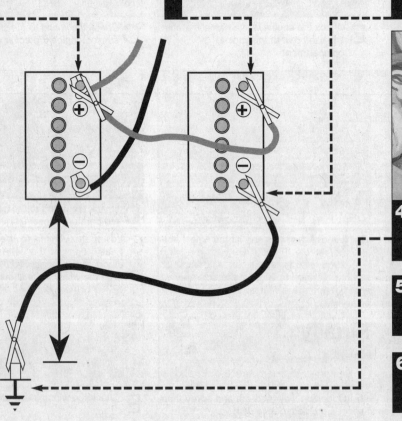

4 Connect the other end of the black jump lead to a bolt or bracket on the engine block, well away from the battery, on the vehicle to be started.

5 Make sure that the jump leads will not come into contact with the fan, drive-belts or other moving parts of the engine.

6 Start the engine using the booster battery and run it at idle speed. Switch on the lights, rear window demister and heater blower motor, then disconnect the jump leads in the reverse order of connection. Turn off the lights etc.

Wheel changing

Some of the details shown here will vary according to model. For instance, the location of the spare wheel and jack is not the same on all cars. However, the basic principles apply to all vehicles.

⚠️ *Warning: Do not change a wheel in a situation where you risk being hit by another vehicle. On busy roads, try to stop in a lay-by or a gateway. Be wary of passing traffic while changing the wheel – it is easy to become distracted by the job in hand.*

Preparation

☐ When a puncture occurs, stop as soon as it is safe to do so.
☐ Park on firm level ground, if possible, and well out of the way of other traffic.

☐ Use hazard warning lights if necessary.
☐ If you have one, use a warning triangle to alert other drivers of your presence.
☐ Apply the handbrake and engage first or reverse gear.

☐ Chock the wheel diagonally opposite the one being removed – a couple of large stones will do for this.
☐ If the ground is soft, use a flat piece of wood to spread the load under the jack.

Changing the wheel

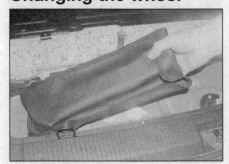

1 On Astra models the jack and wheelbrace are stowed under the spare wheel beneath the luggage compartment floor. On Zafira models they are beneath a cover at the rear of the luggage compartment floor.

2 The spare wheel is stored beneath a cover in the luggage compartment on Astra models. Raise the cover, remove the securing screw and lift out the spare wheel. Place it beneath the sill as a precaution against the jack failing. On Zafira models, the spare wheel is located under the rear of the vehicle. Lift the rear of the luggage compartment floor, and slacken the hexagon bolt in the compartment floor, using the wheelbrace. Unhook the catch, lower the spare wheel, and detach the safety cable. The spare wheel can now be lifted out. Place it beneath the sill as a precaution against the jack failing.

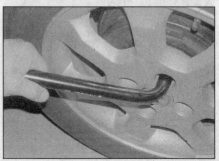

3 On models with steel wheels, use the special tool to pull the wheel trim from the wheel. On models with alloy wheels, use the screwdriver provided inserted at the wheel bolt holes, to prise off the trim. Where an anti-theft device is fitted, use the tool provided to remove the trim. Loosen each wheel bolt by half a turn.

4 All models have depressions in the sill vertical web, which indicate the points at which the jack head is to be attached. On Astra models, the depressions are concealed by flaps in the outer sill bodywork. Prise out the flaps to access the jacking points. Position the jack head under the jacking point and make sure that the slot in the head engages correctly with the vertical web of the sill. Turn the handle until the base of the jack touches the ground then make sure that the base is located directly below the sill. Raise the vehicle until the wheel is clear of the ground. If the tyre is flat make sure that the vehicle is raised sufficiently to allow the spare wheel to be fitted.

5 Remove the bolts and lift the wheel from the vehicle. Place it beneath the sill in place of the spare as a precaution against the jack failing. Fit the spare wheel and tighten the bolts moderately with the wheelbrace.

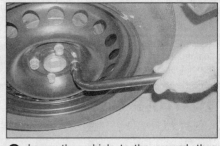

6 Lower the vehicle to the ground, then finally tighten the wheel bolts in a diagonal sequence. Refit the wheel trim. Note that the wheel bolts should be tightened to the specified torque at the earliest opportunity.

Finally...

☐ Remove the wheel chocks.
☐ Stow the jack and tools in the correct locations in the car.
☐ Check the tyre pressure on the wheel just fitted. If it is low, or if you don't have a pressure gauge with you, drive slowly to the nearest garage and inflate the tyre to the right pressure.
☐ Have the damaged tyre or wheel repaired as soon as possible.

Identifying leaks

Puddles on the garage floor or drive, or obvious wetness under the bonnet or underneath the car, suggest a leak that needs investigating. It can sometimes be difficult to decide where the leak is coming from, especially if the engine bay is very dirty already. Leaking oil or fluid can also be blown rearwards by the passage of air under the car, giving a false impression of where the problem lies.

 Warning: Most automotive oils and fluids are poisonous. Wash them off skin, and change out of contaminated clothing, without delay.

 HAYNES HiNT *The smell of a fluid leaking from the car may provide a clue to what's leaking. Some fluids are distinctively coloured. It may help to clean the car carefully and to park it over some clean paper overnight as an aid to locating the source of the leak.*
Remember that some leaks may only occur while the engine is running.

Sump oil

Engine oil may leak from the drain plug...

Oil from filter

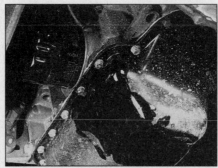

...or from the base of the oil filter.

Gearbox oil

Gearbox oil can leak from the seals at the inboard ends of the driveshafts.

Antifreeze

Leaking antifreeze often leaves a crystalline deposit like this.

Brake fluid

A leak occurring at a wheel is almost certainly brake fluid.

Power steering fluid

Power steering fluid may leak from the pipe connectors on the steering rack.

Towing

When all else fails, you may find yourself having to get a tow home – or of course you may be helping somebody else. Long-distance recovery should only be done by a garage or breakdown service. For shorter distances, DIY towing using another car is easy enough, but observe the following points:

☐ Use a proper tow-rope – they are not expensive. The vehicle being towed must display an ON TOW sign in its rear window.
☐ Always turn the ignition key to the 'on' position when the vehicle is being towed, so that the steering lock is released, and that the direction indicator and brake lights will work.
☐ Before being towed, release the handbrake and select neutral on the transmission.

☐ Note that greater-than-usual pedal pressure will be required to operate the brakes, since the vacuum servo unit is only operational with the engine running.
☐ The driver of the car being towed must keep the tow-rope taut at all times to avoid snatching.
☐ Make sure that both drivers know the route before setting off.
☐ Only drive at moderate speeds and keep the distance towed to a minimum. Drive smoothly and allow plenty of time for slowing down at junctions.
☐ A towing eye is provided with the warning triangle and first aid kit in the luggage compartment.
☐ To fit the towing eye, prise the cover

from the front bumper, then screw in the towing eye anti-clockwise as far as it will go using the handle of the wheelbrace to turn the eye. **Note that the towing eye has a left-hand thread (see illustration).** A rear towing eye is provided beneath the rear of the vehicle.

The towing eye has a left-hand thread

Introduction

There are some very simple checks which need only take a few minutes to carry out, but which could save you a lot of inconvenience and expense.

These 'Weekly checks' require no great skill or special tools, and the small amount of time they take to perform could prove to be very well spent, for example;

☐ Keeping an eye on tyre condition and pressures, will not only help to stop them wearing out prematurely, but could also save your life.

☐ Many breakdowns are caused by electrical problems. Battery-related faults are particularly common, and a quick check on a regular basis will often prevent the majority of these.

☐ If your car develops a brake fluid leak, the first time you might know about it is when your brakes don't work properly. Checking the level regularly will give advance warning of this kind of problem.

☐ If the oil or coolant levels run low, the cost of repairing any engine damage will be far greater than fixing the leak, for example.

Underbonnet check points

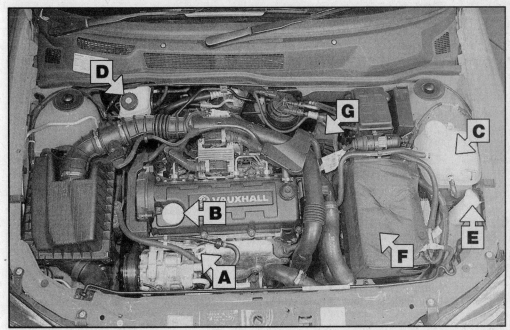

◀ **1.7 litre DOHC 16-valve (Isuzu engine)**

A *Engine oil level dipstick*

B *Engine oil filler cap*

C *Coolant reservoir (expansion tank)*

D *Brake fluid reservoir*

E *Washer fluid reservoir*

F *Battery*

G *Power steering fluid reservoir*

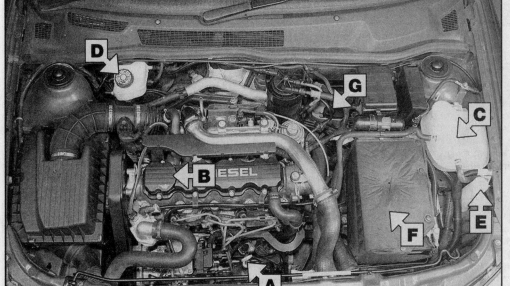

◀ **1.7 litre SOHC 8-valve (GM engine)**

A *Engine oil level dipstick*

B *Engine oil filler cap*

C *Coolant reservoir (expansion tank)*

D *Brake fluid reservoir*

E *Washer fluid reservoir*

F *Battery*

G *Power steering fluid reservoir*

Engine oil level

Before you start

☐ Make sure that your car is on level ground.
☐ Check the oil level before the car is driven, or at least 5 minutes after the engine has been switched off.

If the oil is checked immediately after driving the vehicle, some of the oil will remain in the upper engine components, resulting in an inaccurate reading on the dipstick!

The correct oil

Modern engines place great demands on their oil. It is very important that the correct oil for your car is used (See 'Lubricants and fluids').

Car Care

☐ If you have to add oil frequently, you should check whether you have any oil leaks. Place some clean paper under the car overnight, and check for stains in the morning. If there are no leaks, the engine may be burning oil.

☐ Always maintain the level between the upper and lower dipstick marks (see photo 3). If the level is too low, severe engine damage may occur. Oil seal failure may result if the engine is overfilled by adding too much oil.

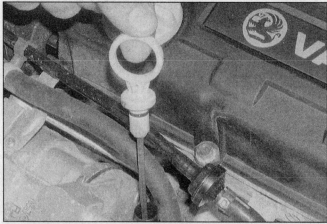

1 The dipstick is located on the front of the engine (see *Underbonnet Check Points* for exact location). Withdraw the dipstick.

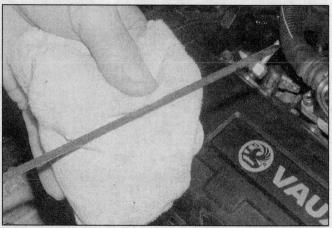

2 Using a clean rag or paper towel remove all oil from the dipstick. Insert the clean dipstick into the tube as far as it will go, then withdraw it again.

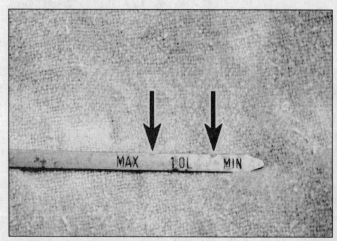

3 Note the oil level on the end of the dipstick, which should be between the upper (MAX) mark and lower (MIN) mark. Approximately 1.0 litre of oil will raise the level from the lower mark to the upper mark.

4 Oil is added through the filler cap. Rotate the cap through a quarter-turn anti-clockwise and withdraw it. Top-up the level; a funnel may help to reduce spillage. Add the oil slowly, checking the level on the dipstick often. Do not overfill.

Coolant level

Warning: DO NOT attempt to remove the expansion tank pressure cap when the engine is hot, as there is a very great risk of scalding. Do not leave open containers of coolant about, as it is poisonous.

Car Care

☐ With a sealed-type cooling system, adding coolant should not be necessary on a regular basis. If frequent topping-up is required, it is likely there is a leak. Check the radiator, all hoses and joint faces for signs of staining or wetness, and rectify as necessary.

☐ It is important that antifreeze is used in the cooling system all year round, not just during the winter months. Don't top-up with water alone, as the antifreeze will become too diluted.

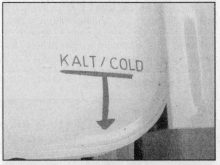

1 The coolant level varies with the temperature of the engine. When the engine is cold, the coolant level should be slightly above the KALT/COLD mark on the side of the tank. When the engine is hot, the level will rise.

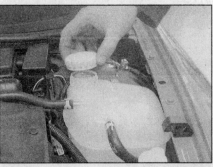

2 If topping-up is necessary, **wait until the engine is cold**. Slowly unscrew the expansion tank cap, to release any pressure present in the cooling system, and remove it.

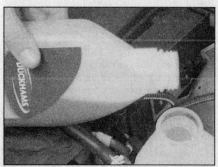

3 Add a mixture of water and antifreeze to the expansion tank until the coolant is up to the MAX level mark. Refit the cap and tighten it securely.

Brake (and clutch) fluid level

Warning:
☐ Brake fluid can harm your eyes and damage painted surfaces, so use extreme caution when handling and pouring it.
☐ Do not use fluid that has been standing open for some time, as it absorbs moisture from the air, which can cause a dangerous loss of braking effectiveness.

HAYNES HINT
• *Make sure that your car is on level ground.*
• *The fluid level in the reservoir will drop slightly as the brake pads wear down, but the fluid level must never be allowed to drop below the MIN mark.*

Safety First!

☐ If the reservoir requires repeated topping-up this is an indication of a fluid leak somewhere in the system, which should be investigated immediately.
☐ If a leak is suspected, the car should not be driven until the braking system has been checked. Never take any risks where brakes are concerned.

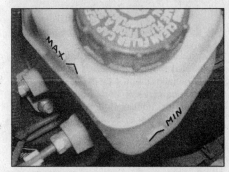

1 The MAX and MIN marks are indicated on the front of the reservoir. The fluid level must be kept between the marks at all times. **Note:** *On Zafira models, first remove the plastic water deflector from in front of the windscreen.*

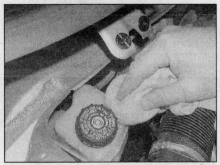

2 If topping-up is necessary, first wipe clean the area around the filler cap to prevent dirt entering the hydraulic system.

3 Carefully add fluid, taking care not to spill it onto the surrounding components. Use only the specified fluid; mixing different types can cause damage to the system. After topping-up to the correct level, securely refit the cap and wipe off any spilt fluid.

Tyre condition and pressure

It is very important that tyres are in good condition, and at the correct pressure - having a tyre failure at any speed is highly dangerous. Tyre wear is influenced by driving style - harsh braking and acceleration, or fast cornering, will all produce more rapid tyre wear. As a general rule, the front tyres wear out faster than the rears. Interchanging the tyres from front to rear ("rotating" the tyres) may result in more even wear. However, if this is completely effective, you may have the expense of replacing all four tyres at once! Remove any nails or stones embedded in the tread before they penetrate the tyre to cause deflation. If removal of a nail does reveal that the tyre has been punctured, refit the nail so that its point of penetration is marked. Then immediately change the wheel, and have the tyre repaired by a tyre dealer.

Regularly check the tyres for damage in the form of cuts or bulges, especially in the sidewalls. Periodically remove the wheels, and clean any dirt or mud from the inside and outside surfaces. Examine the wheel rims for signs of rusting, corrosion or other damage. Light alloy wheels are easily damaged by "kerbing" whilst parking; steel wheels may also become dented or buckled. A new wheel is very often the only way to overcome severe damage.

New tyres should be balanced when they are fitted, but it may become necessary to re-balance them as they wear, or if the balance weights fitted to the wheel rim should fall off. Unbalanced tyres will wear more quickly, as will the steering and suspension components. Wheel imbalance is normally signified by vibration, particularly at a certain speed (typically around 50 mph). If this vibration is felt only through the steering, then it is likely that just the front wheels need balancing. If, however, the vibration is felt through the whole car, the rear wheels could be out of balance. Wheel balancing should be carried out by a tyre dealer or garage.

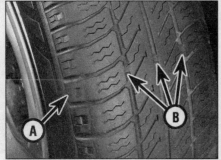

1 Tread Depth - visual check
The original tyres have tread wear safety bands (B), which will appear when the tread depth reaches approximately 1.6 mm. The band positions are indicated by a triangular mark on the tyre sidewall (A).

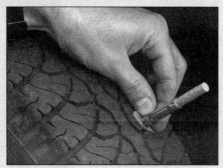

2 Tread Depth - manual check
Alternatively, tread wear can be monitored with a simple, inexpensive device known as a tread depth indicator gauge.

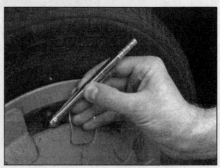

3 Tyre Pressure Check
Check the tyre pressures regularly with the tyres cold. Do not adjust the tyre pressures immediately after the vehicle has been used, or an inaccurate setting will result.

Tyre tread wear patterns

Shoulder Wear

Underinflation (wear on both sides)
Under-inflation will cause overheating of the tyre, because the tyre will flex too much, and the tread will not sit correctly on the road surface. This will cause a loss of grip and excessive wear, not to mention the danger of sudden tyre failure due to heat build-up.
Check and adjust pressures
Incorrect wheel camber (wear on one side)
Repair or renew suspension parts
Hard cornering
Reduce speed!

Centre Wear

Overinflation
Over-inflation will cause rapid wear of the centre part of the tyre tread, coupled with reduced grip, harsher ride, and the danger of shock damage occurring in the tyre casing.
Check and adjust pressures

If you sometimes have to inflate your car's tyres to the higher pressures specified for maximum load or sustained high speed, don't forget to reduce the pressures to normal afterwards.

Uneven Wear

Front tyres may wear unevenly as a result of wheel misalignment. Most tyre dealers and garages can check and adjust the wheel alignment (or "tracking") for a modest charge.
Incorrect camber or castor
Repair or renew suspension parts
Malfunctioning suspension
Repair or renew suspension parts
Unbalanced wheel
Balance tyres
Incorrect toe setting
Adjust front wheel alignment
Note: *The feathered edge of the tread which typifies toe wear is best checked by feel.*

Screen washer fluid level

Screenwash additives not only keep the windscreen clean, they also prevent the washer system freezing in cold weather – which is when you are likely to need it most. Don't top up using plain water as the screenwash will become too diluted, and will freeze during cold weather. *On no account use coolant antifreeze in the washer system – this could discolour or damage paintwork.*

1 The reservoir for the windscreen and rear window (where applicable) washer systems is located on the front left-hand side of the engine compartment. If topping-up is necessary, open the cap.

2 When topping-up the reservoir(s) a screenwash additive should be added in the quantities recommended on the bottle. Use of a funnel may be useful.

Power steering fluid level

Before you start

☐ Park the vehicle on level ground.
☐ With the engine idling, turn the steering wheel slowly from lock to lock 2 or 3 times and set the front wheels at the straight-ahead position, then stop the engine.

HAYNES HiNT *For the check to be accurate, the steering must not be turned once the engine has been stopped.*

Safety First!

☐ The need for frequent topping-up indicates a leak, which should be investigated immediately.

1 The power steering fluid reservoir is located on RHD vehicles on the left-hand side of the engine compartment between the transmission and the bulkhead. On LHD vehicles, the reservoir is located between the engine and bulkhead on the right-hand side of the engine compartment. The fluid level should be checked with the engine stopped.
Note: *On Zafira models, first remove the plastic water deflector from in front of the windscreen.*

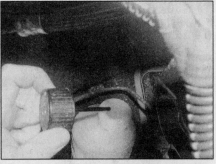

2 Unscrew the filler cap from the top of the reservoir. On TRW manufactured units, the dipstick is incorporated into the filler cap, whilst Delphi manufactured units have the dipstick incorporated into the filter immediately below the filler cap. Wipe all fluid from the dipstick with a clean rag. Refit the dipstick, then remove it again. Note the fluid level on the dipstick.

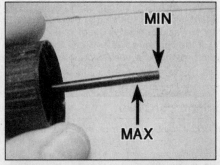

3 When the engine is cold, the fluid level should be between the upper and lower marks on the dipstick. Top up the fluid level using the specified type of fluid (do not overfill the reservoir), then refit and tighten the filler cap.

Wiper blades

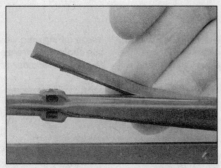

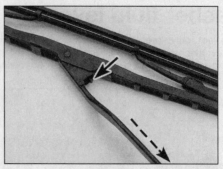

1 Check the condition of the wiper blades; if they are cracked or show any signs of deterioration, or if the glass swept area is smeared, renew them. Wiper blades should be renewed annually.

2 To remove a wiper blade, pull the arm fully away from the glass until it locks. Swivel the blade through 90º, then squeeze the locking clip, and detach the blade from the arm. When fitting the new blade, make sure that the blade locks securely into the arm, and that the blade is orientated correctly.

Battery

Caution: Before carrying out any work on the vehicle battery, read the precautions given in 'Safety first!' at the start of this manual.

☐ Make sure that the battery tray is in good condition, and that the clamp is tight. Corrosion on the tray, retaining clamp and the battery itself can be removed with a solution of water and baking soda. Thoroughly rinse all cleaned areas with water. Any metal parts damaged by corrosion should be covered with a zinc-based primer, then painted.

☐ Periodically (approximately every three months), check the charge condition of the battery as described in Chapter 5A.

☐ If the battery is flat, and you need to jump start your vehicle, see *Roadside Repairs*.

1 The battery is located on the left-hand side of the engine compartment. Unclip the fabric cover from the top of the battery (if fitted) for access to the terminals. The exterior of the battery should be inspected periodically for damage such as a cracked case or cover.

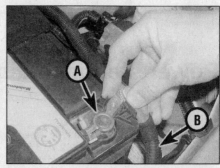

2 Check the tightness of battery clamps (A) to ensure good electrical connections. You should not be able to move them. Also check each cable (B) for cracks and frayed conductors.

Battery corrosion can be kept to a minimum by applying a layer of petroleum jelly to the clamps and terminals after they are reconnected.

3 If corrosion (white, fluffy deposits) is evident, remove the cables from the battery terminals, clean them with a small wire brush, then refit them. Automotive stores sell a tool for cleaning the battery post . . .

4 . . . as well as the battery cable clamps

Electrical systems

☐ Check all external lights and the horn. Refer to the appropriate Sections of Chapter 12 for details if any of the circuits are found to be inoperative.

☐ Visually check all accessible wiring connectors, harnesses and retaining clips for security, and for signs of chafing or damage.

 HAYNES HiNT *If you need to check your brake lights and indicators unaided, back up to a wall or garage door and operate the lights. The reflected light should show if they are working properly.*

1 If a single indicator light, stop-light or headlight has failed, it is likely that a bulb has blown and will need to be replaced. Refer to Chapter 12 for details. If both stop-lights have failed, it is possible that the switch has failed (see Chapter 9).

2 If more than one indicator light or headlight has failed, it is likely that either a fuse has blown or that there is a fault in the circuit (see Chapter 12). On Zafira models, the main fuses are located beneath a cover on the driver's side of the facia between the steering column and the drivers' door. Pull out and remove the cover, then pull out the bottom of the fusebox. On Astra models, the main fuses are located next to the steering column behind the storage compartment. Open the compartment, squeeze the lugs at each side, pull the compartment down to its full extent and detach it. Remove the fixing screws and remove the storage compartment frame, then pull out the bottom of the fusebox. Additional fuses and relays are located in the left-hand side of the engine compartment.

3 To replace a blown fuse, remove it, where applicable, using the plastic tool provided. Fit a new fuse of the same rating, available from car accessory shops. It is important that you find the reason that the fuse blew (see *Electrical fault finding* in Chapter 12).

Lubricants and fluids

Engine	Multigrade engine oil, viscosity SAE 5W/40, 10W/40 or 15W/40, to ACEA A3/B3 or higher
Cooling system	
Up to Model Year 2001	'Blue' antifreeze, Vauxhall part number 90 297 545
From Model Year 2001	'Red' antifreeze, Vauxhall part number 09 194 431
Manual gearbox	Gear oil, Vauxhall part number 09 120 541
Power steering reservoir	Special steering fluid, Vauxhall part number 90 544 116
Brake and clutch fluid reservoir	Hydraulic fluid to SAE J1703, DOT 4

Choosing your engine oil

Engines need oil, not only to lubricate moving parts and minimise wear, but also to maximise power output and to improve fuel economy.

HOW ENGINE OIL WORKS

• Beating friction

Without oil, the moving surfaces inside your engine will rub together, heat up and melt, quickly causing the engine to seize. Engine oil creates a film which separates these moving parts, preventing wear and heat build-up.

• Cooling hot-spots

Temperatures inside the engine can exceed 1000° C. The engine oil circulates and acts as a coolant, transferring heat from the hot-spots to the sump.

• Cleaning the engine internally

Good quality engine oils clean the inside of your engine, collecting and dispersing combustion deposits and controlling them until they are trapped by the oil filter or flushed out at oil change.

OIL CARE - FOLLOW THE CODE

To handle and dispose of used engine oil safely, always:

- • **Avoid skin contact with used engine oil. Repeated or prolonged contact can be harmful.**
- • **Dispose of used oil and empty packs in a responsible manner in an authorised disposal site. Call 0800 663366 to find the one nearest to you. Never tip oil down drains or onto the ground.**

Tyre pressures (cold)

Note: *Pressures apply to original-equipment tyres, and may vary if any other make or type of tyre is fitted; check with the tyre manufacturer or supplier for correct pressures if necessary. The pressures are given on the inside of the fuel filler flap.*

	Front	Rear
1.7 litre engine Astra models		
Up to 3 persons	2.2 bar (32 psi)	2.0 bar (29 psi)
Full load	2.3 bar (33 psi)	3.2 bar (46 psi)
2.0 litre engine Astra models		
Up to 3 persons	2.4 bar (34 psi)	2.5 bar (36 psi)
Full load	2.5 bar (36 psi)	2.8 bar (41 psi)
Zafira models		
Up to 3 persons	2.2 bar (32 psi)	2.2 bar (32 psi)
Full load	2.6 bar (38 psi)	3.0 bar (44 psi)

Chapter 1:
Routine maintenance and servicing

Contents

Degrees of difficulty

| Easy, suitable for novice with little experience | | Fairly easy, suitable for beginner with some experience | | Fairly difficult, suitable for competent DIY mechanic | | Difficult, suitable for experienced DIY mechanic | | Very difficult, suitable for expert DIY or professional | |

Cooling system

Antifreeze mixture:
50% antifreeze .... Protection down to –37°C
55% antifreeze .... Protection down to –45°C
Note: *Refer to antifreeze manufacturer for latest recommendations.*

Brakes

Friction material minimum thickness:
Front brake pads .... 2.0 mm
Rear brake pads .... 2.0 mm
Rear brake shoes .... 1.0 mm

Torque wrench settings

	Nm	lbf ft
1.7 litre SOHC engine		
Alternator:		
Alternator-to-bracket bolts – M10	46	34
Alternator-to-bracket bolts – M8	25	18
Alternator bracket-to-cylinder block bolts	35	26
Alternator lock bolt to tension rail	35	26
Compressor drivebelt tensioner centre bolt	45	33
Fuel filter mounting plate nuts	25	18
Oil filter	15	11
Roadwheel bolts	110	81
Sump drain plug	10	7
1.7 litre DOHC and 2.0 litre engine		
Balance weight to driveshaft	10	7
Engine mounting to body	45	33
Engine mounting to subframe	55	41
Fuel filter housing cover centre bolt	6	4
Oil filter housing cover	25	18
Roadwheel bolts	110	81
Sump drain plug:		
1.7 litre	78	58
2.0 litre	18	13

Lubricants and fluids

Refer to *Weekly checks*

Capacities

Engine oil
Including oil filter .... 5.0 litres
Excluding oil filter .... 5.4 litres
Difference between MIN and MAX on dipstick .... 1.0 litre

Cooling system
1.7 litre DOHC engine .... 7.1 litres
1.7 litre SOHC engine .... 8.7 litres
2.0 litre engines .... 7.9 litres

Transmission
1.7 litre engine .... 1.6 litres
2.0 litre engine .... 1.8 litres

Washer fluid reservoir
Without headlight washers .... 2.3 litres
With headlight washers .... 4.5 litres

Fuel tank
Astra models .... 52 litres
Zafira models .... 58 litres

Note: *From Model Year 2001 the 10 000 mile (15 000 km) service interval is extended to 20 000 miles (30 000 km). The time interval remains the same at 12 months.*

1 The maintenance intervals in this manual are provided with the assumption that you, not the dealer, will be carrying out the work. These are the minimum maintenance intervals recommended by us for vehicles driven daily. If you wish to keep your vehicle in peak condition at all times, you may wish to perform some of these procedures more often. We encourage frequent maintenance, because it enhances the efficiency, performance and resale value of your vehicle.

2 If the vehicle is driven in dusty areas, used to tow a trailer, or driven frequently at slow speeds (idling in traffic) or on short journeys, more frequent maintenance intervals are recommended.

3 When the vehicle is new, it should be serviced by a factory-authorised dealer service department, in order to preserve the factory warranty.

Every 5000 miles (7500 km) or 6 months, whichever comes first

☐ Renew the engine oil and filter (Section 4)

Note: *Vauxhall recommend that the engine oil and filter are changed every 10 000 miles (15 000 km) or 12 months. However, oil and filter changes are good for the engine and we recommend that the oil and filter are renewed more frequently, especially if the vehicle is used on a lot of short journeys.*

Every 10 000 miles (15 000 km) or 12 months, whichever comes first

☐ Check the condition and tension of the auxiliary drivebelts (Section 5)*
☐ Drain water from the fuel filter (Section 6)
☐ Idle speed and exhaust emission check (Section 7)
☐ Check the operation of all electrical systems (Section 8)
☐ Check and if necessary adjust the headlight beam alignment (Section 9)*
☐ Check the body and underbody for corrosion protection (Section 10)*
☐ Check the front brake pads and discs for wear (Section 11)
☐ Check the rear brake pads and discs (where applicable) for wear (Section 12)
☐ Check and if necessary adjust the handbrake (Section 13)*
☐ Check all components, pipes and hoses for fluid leaks (Section 14)*
☐ Check the roadwheel bolts are tightened to the specified torque (Section 15)
☐ Check the rear suspension level control system (where applicable) (Section 16)
☐ Renew the pollen filter (Section 17)

Note: *If the vehicle is used in dusty conditions, the pollen filter should be renewed more frequently.*

☐ Carry out a road test (Section 18)

* *On vehicles covering a high mileage (more than 20 000 miles/ 30 000 km annually) carry out the items marked with an asterisk every 20 000 miles (30 000 km).*

Every 20 000 miles (30 000 km) or 2 years, whichever comes first

☐ Renew the air cleaner element (Section 19)
☐ Renew the fuel filter (Section 20)
☐ Lubricate all door locks and hinges, door stops, bonnet lock and release, and tailgate lock and hinges (Section 21)
☐ Check the rear brake shoes and drums for wear (Section 22)
☐ Check the steering and suspension components for condition and security (Section 23)
☐ Check the condition of the driveshaft gaiters (Section 24)

Every 40 000 miles (60 000 km)

☐ Renew the timing belt – 1.7 litre engines (Section 25)

Note: *Although the normal interval for timing belt renewal is 80 000 miles (120 000 km), it is strongly recommended that the interval is halved to 40 000 miles (60 000 km) on vehicles which are subjected to intensive use, ie, mainly short journeys or a lot of stop-start driving. The actual belt renewal interval is therefore very much up to the individual owner, but bear in mind that severe engine damage will result if the belt breaks.*

Every 80 000 miles (120 000 km)

☐ Check and, if necessary, adjust the valve clearances – 1.7 litre DOHC engine (Section 26)

Every 2 years, regardless of mileage

☐ Renew the brake fluid (Section 27)
☐ Renew the remote control batteries (Section 28)
☐ Renew the coolant (Section 29)
☐ Renew the coolant (Section 29)

Note: *Vehicles using Vauxhall antifreeze do not need the coolant renewed on a regular basis.*

Underbonnet view of a 1.7 litre DOHC 16-valve model

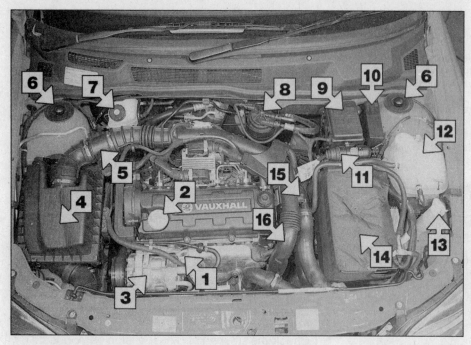

1 Engine oil level dipstick
2 Engine oil filler cap
3 Air conditioning compressor
4 Air cleaner assembly
5 Airflow meter
6 Front suspension strut upper mountings
7 Brake fluid reservoir
8 Fuel filter
9 Engine related fusebox
10 Main electrical fusebox
11 Engine wiring harness connection
12 Coolant expansion tank
13 Windscreen/headlamp washer fluid
    reservoir
14 Battery
15 Thermostat housing
16 Air inlet duct to intercooler

Front underbody view of a 1.7 litre DOHC 16-valve model

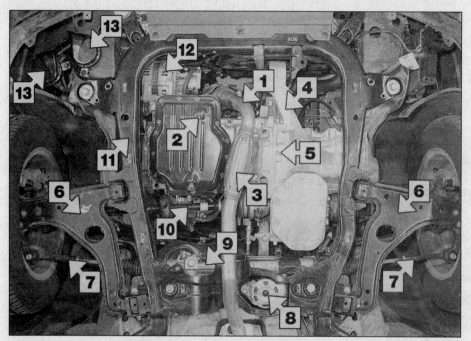

1 Oil filter
2 Engine oil drain plug
3 Exhaust downpipe with flexible section
4 Front engine mounting
5 Manual transmission
6 Front suspension lower arms
7 Track rod ends
8 Rear engine mounting
9 Steering gear
10 Driveshaft
11 Subframe
12 Alternator
13 Horns

Rear underbody view of a 1.7 litre DOHC 16-valve model

1 Rear exhaust silencer and tailpipe
2 Rear suspension torsion beam and trailing arms
3 Brake proportioning valve
4 Fuel tank
5 Handbrake cables
6 Spare wheel well
7 Rear coil springs
8 Rear shock absorber lower mountings

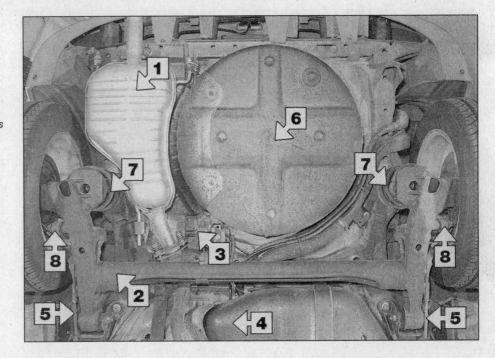

Underbonnet view of a 1.7 litre SOHC 8-valve model

1 Engine oil level dipstick
2 Engine oil filler cap
3 Thermostat housing
4 Radiator top hose
5 Air cleaner assembly
6 Front suspension strut upper mountings
7 Brake fluid reservoir
8 Airflow meter
9 Fuel filter
10 Engine related fusebox
11 Main electrical fusebox
12 Power steering hydraulic fluid reservoir
13 Air inlet duct to intercooler
14 Engine wiring harness connection
15 Coolant expansion tank
16 Windscreen/headlamp washer fluid reservoir
17 Battery

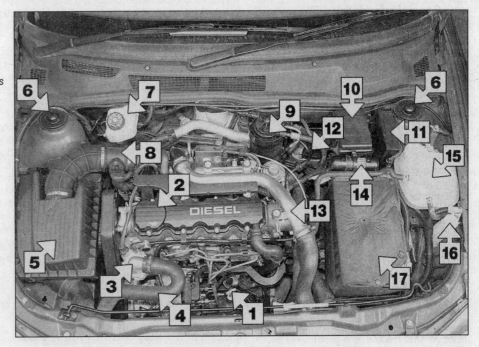

Front underbody view of a 1.7 litre SOHC 8-valve model

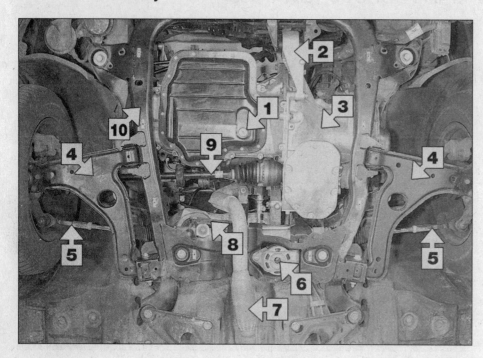

1 Engine oil drain plug
2 Front engine mounting
3 Manual transmission
4 Front suspension lower arms
5 Track rod ends
6 Rear engine mounting
7 Exhaust downpipe with flexible section
8 Steering gear
9 Driveshaft
10 Subframe

Maintenance procedures

1 General information

1 This Chapter is designed to help the home mechanic maintain his/her vehicle for safety, economy, long life and peak performance.
2 The Chapter contains a master maintenance schedule, followed by Sections dealing specifically with each task in the schedule. Visual checks, adjustments, component renewal and other helpful items are included. Refer to the accompanying illustrations of the engine compartment and the underside of the vehicle for the locations of the various components.
3 Servicing your vehicle in accordance with the mileage/time maintenance schedule and the following Sections will provide a planned maintenance programme, which should result in a long and reliable service life. This is a comprehensive plan, so maintaining some items but not others at the specified service intervals, will not produce the same results.
4 As you service your vehicle, you will discover that many of the procedures can – and should – be grouped together, because of the particular procedure being performed, or because of the proximity of two otherwise-

unrelated components to one another. For example, if the vehicle is raised for any reason, the exhaust can be inspected at the same time as the suspension and steering components.
5 The first step in this maintenance programme is to prepare yourself before the actual work begins. Read through all the Sections relevant to the work to be carried out, then make a list and gather all the parts and tools required. If a problem is encountered, seek advice from a parts specialist, or a dealer service department.

2 Regular maintenance

1 If, from the time the vehicle is new, the routine maintenance schedule is followed closely, and frequent checks are made of fluid levels and high-wear items, as suggested throughout this manual, the engine will be kept in relatively good running condition, and the need for additional work will be minimised.
2 It is possible that there will be times when the engine is running poorly due to the lack of regular maintenance. This is even more likely if a used vehicle, which has not received regular and frequent maintenance checks, is

purchased. In such cases, additional work may need to be carried out, outside of the regular maintenance intervals.
3 If engine wear is suspected, a compression test (refer to Chapter 2A, 2B or 2C, as applicable) will provide valuable information regarding the overall performance of the main internal components. Such a test can be used as a basis to decide on the extent of the work to be carried out. If, for example, a compression test indicates serious internal engine wear, conventional maintenance as described in this Chapter will not greatly improve the performance of the engine, and may prove a waste of time and money, unless extensive overhaul work is carried out first.
4 The following series of operations are those most often required to improve the performance of a generally poor-running engine:

Primary operations

a) Clean, inspect and test the battery (refer to 'Weekly checks').
b) Check all the engine-related fluids (refer to 'Weekly checks').
c) Check the condition and tension of the auxiliary drivebelt (Section 5).
d) Check the condition of the air filter, and renew if necessary (Section 19).
e) Renew the fuel filter (Section 20).

f) Check the condition of all hoses, and check for fluid leaks (Section 14).

5 If the above operations do not prove fully effective, carry out the following secondary operations:

Secondary operations

All items listed under *Primary operations*, plus the following:

a) Check the charging system (refer to Chapter 5A).

b) Check the preheating system (refer to Chapter 5B).

c) Check the fuel system (refer to Chapter 4A).

3 Service indicator reset

1 Astra & Zafira models are equipped with a Service Interval Display (SID), mounted in the lower half of the speedometer in the instrument panel. The liquid crystal display will change to INSP when a service is due within one week or 300 miles. After having carried out the required service, the SID can be reset using the following procedure.

2 With the ignition turned off, press and hold-in the odometer trip reset button.

3 Switch the ignition on. Continue to hold-in the trip reset button for at least 3 seconds.

4 The SID will flash a few times and reset. Release the button.

Every 5000 miles (7500 km) or 6 months

4 Engine oil and filter renewal

1 Frequent oil and filter changes are the most important preventative maintenance procedures which can be undertaken by the DIY owner. As engine oil ages, it becomes diluted and contaminated, which leads to premature engine wear.

2 Before starting this procedure, gather together all the necessary tools and materials. Also make sure that you have plenty of clean rags and newspapers handy, to mop up any spills. Ideally, the engine oil should be warm, as it will drain more easily, and more built-up sludge will be removed with it. Take care not to touch the exhaust or any other hot parts of the engine when working under the vehicle. To avoid any possibility of scalding, and to protect yourself from possible skin irritants and other harmful contaminants in used engine oils, it is advisable to wear gloves when carrying out this work.

3 Firmly apply the handbrake then jack up the front of the vehicle and support it on axle stands (see *Jacking and vehicle support*). Remove the undertray from under the engine compartment.

4 Remove the oil filler cap **(see illustration)**.

5 Using a spanner, or preferably a suitable socket and bar, slacken the drain plug about half a turn **(see illustration)**. Position the draining container under the drain plug, then remove the plug completely **(see Haynes Hint)**.

6 Allow some time for the oil to drain, noting that it may be necessary to reposition the container as the oil flow slows to a trickle.

1.7 litre SOHC engine

7 After all the oil has drained, wipe the drain plug and the sealing washer with a clean rag. Examine the condition of the sealing washer, and renew it if it shows signs of scoring or other damage which may prevent an oil-tight seal. Clean the area around the drain plug opening, and refit the plug complete with the washer and tighten it to the specified torque.

8 Move the container into position under the oil filter which is located on the rear, right-hand side of the cylinder block.

9 Use an oil filter removal tool to slacken the filter initially, then unscrew it by hand the rest of the way. Empty the oil from the old filter into the container.

10 Use a clean rag to remove all oil, dirt and sludge from the filter sealing area on the engine.

11 Apply a light coating of clean engine oil to the sealing ring on the new filter, then screw the filter into position on the engine. Tighten the filter firmly by hand only – **do not** use any tools. If a genuine filter is being fitted and the special oil filter tool (a socket which fits over the end of the filter) is available, tighten the filter to the specified torque.

12 Remove the old oil and all tools from under the vehicle then lower the vehicle to the ground.

13 Fill the engine through the filler hole, using the correct grade and type of oil (refer to *Weekly Checks* for details of topping-up). Pour in half the specified quantity of oil first, then wait a few minutes for the oil to drain into the sump. Continue to add oil, a small quantity at a time, until the level is up to the lower mark on the dipstick. Adding approximately a further 1.0 litre will bring the level up to the upper mark on the dipstick.

14 Start the engine and run it for a few minutes, while checking for leaks around the oil filter seal and the sump drain plug. Note that there may be a delay of a few seconds before the low oil pressure warning light goes out when the engine is first started, as the oil circulates through the new oil filter and engine oil galleries before the pressure builds up.

15 Stop the engine, and wait a few minutes for the oil to settle in the sump once more. With the new oil circulated and the filter now completely full, recheck the level on the dipstick, and add more oil as necessary.

16 Dispose of the used engine oil safely with reference to *General repair procedures*.

4.4 Removing the oil filler cap – 1.7 litre engine

4.5 Sump drain plug – 1.7 litre engine

HAYNES HINT

As the drain plug threads release, move it sharply away so the stream of oil issuing from the sump runs into the container, not up your sleeve.

4.17 The oil filter is located on the rear of the cylinder block on the 1.7 litre DOHC engine

4.18 On 2.0 litre engines undo the retaining screws and remove the cover from the top of the engine

4.19a Unscrew the cover . . .

4.19b . . . and remove the filter element – 2.0 litre engine

4.20 Fitting the element to the cover – 1.7 litre DOHC engine

4.21 Sealing rings on the cover and pin – 1.7 litre DOHC and 2.0 litre engines

1.7 litre DOHC and all 2.0 litre engines

17 On the 1.7 litre DOHC engine, the oil filter is located on the rear of the cylinder block **(see illustration)**. On 2.0 litre engines it is located on the front of the cylinder head.
18 To gain access to the oil filter on 2.0 litre engines, undo the retaining screws and remove the plastic cover from the top of the engine **(see illustration)**.

19 Using a large socket, unscrew the cover and remove it from the top of the oil filter housing **(see illustrations)**. Lift out the old filter element.
20 Fit the new filter element to the housing or cover **(see illustration)**.
21 Renew the sealing rings then refit the oil filter cover and tighten it to the specified torque **(see illustration)**. Where necessary, refit the plastic cover to the engine and securely tighten its screws.

22 After all the oil has drained, wipe the drain plug and the sealing washer with a clean rag. Examine the condition of the sealing washer, and renew it if it shows signs of scoring or other damage which may prevent an oil-tight seal. Clean the area around the drain plug opening, and refit the plug complete with the washer and tighten it to the specified torque.
23 Fill the engine with oil as described in paragraphs 12 to 16.

Every 10 000 miles (15 000 km) or 12 months

5 Auxiliary drivebelt check and renewal

Checking

1 Drivebelts are prone to failure after a long period of time and should therefore be inspected regularly.
2 With the engine stopped, inspect the full length of the drivebelt for cracks and separation of the belt plies. It will be necessary to turn the engine (using a spanner or socket and bar on the crankshaft pulley bolt) in order to move the belt from the pulleys so that the belt can be inspected thoroughly. Twist the belt between the pulleys so that

both sides can be viewed. Also check for fraying, and glazing which gives the belt a shiny appearance. Check the pulleys for nicks, cracks, distortion and corrosion.
3 If the belt shows signs of wear or damage, it must be renewed.

Renewal

1.7 litre DOHC engine

4 Remove the air cleaner assembly together with the air ducts and airflow meter with reference to Chapter 4A.
5 If the drivebelt is to be re-used, mark the direction of travel to ensure it is refitted the same way round. Note the run of the drivebelt around the pulleys **(see illustration)**.
6 Using a socket on the centre bolt, turn the drivebelt tensioner clockwise to release the

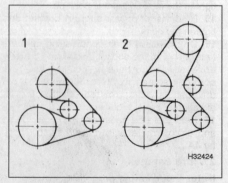
5.5 Auxiliary drivebelt arrangements – 1.7 litre DOHC engine
1 Models without air conditioning
2 Models with air conditioning

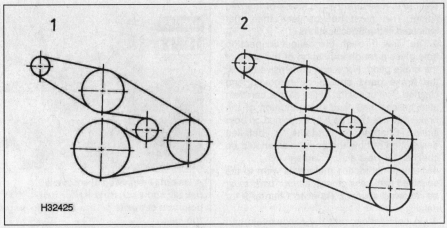

H32425

5.22 Auxiliary drivebelt arrangements – 2.0 litre engines

1 Models without air conditioning *2 Models with air conditioning*

6.3 Draining water from the fuel filter – 2.0 litre engines

tension, then slip the drivebelt from the pulleys.

7 Manoeuvre the new drivebelt into position and seat it on the pulley grooves. Release the tensioner and check again that the drivebelt is correctly seated.

8 Refit the air cleaner assembly, air ducts and airflow meter with reference to Chapter 4A.

1.7 litre SOHC engine

9 Remove the air cleaner assembly together with the air ducts and airflow meter with reference to Chapter 4a.

10 If the drivebelt is to be re-used, mark the direction of travel to ensure it is refitted the same way round. Note the run of the drivebelt around the pulleys.

11 On models with air conditioning, use a socket on the tensioner bolt to release the tension, then slip the multi-groove drivebelt from the pulleys.

12 Unbolt and remove the alternator support bracket.

13 Loosen the lock bolt, then turn the adjustment nut to release the belt tension. Remove the belt from the pulleys.

14 Locate the new belt on the pulleys, then apply a torque of 450 N (new belts) or 250 to 400 N (used belts) to the adjustment nut and tighten the lock bolt in this position.

15 Refit the alternator support bracket and tighten the bolts.

16 On models with air conditioning, turn the tensioner with the socket, and locate the new drivebelt on the pulleys, making sure it is correctly seated in the grooves. If the old drivebelt is being refitted, make sure its direction of travel is correct.

17 Refit the air cleaner assembly, air ducts and airflow meter with reference to Chapter 4A.

2.0 litre engines

Note: *The following procedure requires the engine to be supported while removing the right-hand engine mounting.*

18 Remove the air cleaner assembly together with the air ducts and airflow meter with

reference to Chapter 4A.

19 Apply the handbrake, then jack up the front of the vehicle and support it on axle stands (see *Jacking and vehicle support*). Remove the undertray from under the engine compartment.

20 Mark the position of the engine mounting.

21 Place a block of wood between a trolley jack and the sump. Raise the jack to support the weight of the engine.

22 Before removing the mounting, if the drivebelt is to be re-used, mark it for the direction of travel to ensure it is refitted the correct way round. Note the run of the drivebelt around the pulleys **(see illustration)**.

23 Using a socket on the tensioner bolt, turn it anti-clockwise to release the tension, then slip the multi-groove drivebelt from the pulleys.

24 Unbolt and remove the right-hand engine mounting, then withdraw the drivebelt.

25 With the tensioner bolt turned anti-clockwise, fit the new drivebelt onto the pulleys making sure that it is correctly located in the pulley grooves, then release the tensioner. If the old drivebelt is being refitted, make sure its direction of travel is correct.

26 Refit the engine bracket and lower the trolley jack supporting the engine.

27 Refit the undertray and lower the vehicle to the ground.

28 Refit the air cleaner assembly, air ducts and airflow meter with reference to Chapter 4A.

6 Fuel filter water draining

Caution: Before starting any work on the fuel filter, wipe clean the filter assembly and the area around it; it is essential that no dirt or other foreign matter is allowed into the system. Obtain a suitable container into which the filter can be drained and place rags or similar material under the filter

assembly to catch any spillages. Do not allow diesel fuel to contaminate components such as the alternator and starter motor, the coolant hoses and engine mountings, and any wiring.

1 The fuel filter is located on the left-hand side of the bulkhead at the rear of the engine compartment, next to the fusebox.

2 In addition to taking the precautions noted above to catch any fuel spillages, connect a tube to the drain screw on the base of the fuel filter/filter housing. Place the other end of the tube in a clean jar or can.

3 Unscrew the drain screw and allow the filter to drain until clean fuel, free of dirt or water, emerges from the tube (approximately 100 cc is usually sufficient) **(see illustration)**. Note that it maybe necessary to slacken the bleed screw or filter housing cover bolt (as applicable) to allow the fuel to drain.

4 Securely close the drain screw and remove the tube, containers and rag, mopping up any spilt fuel. Where necessary, securely tighten the bleed screw or tighten the housing cover screw.

5 On completion, dispose safely of the drained fuel. Check carefully all disturbed components to ensure that there are no leaks (of air or fuel) when the engine is restarted.

6 Start the engine and bleed the fuel system as described in Chapter 4A.

7 Idle speed and exhaust emission check

1 Vauxhall specify that this check should be carried out annually on vehicles which are subject to intensive use (eg, taxis and hire cars) and every 3 years on other vehicles. The check involves checking the engine management system operation by plugging an electronic tester into the system diagnostic socket to check the electronic control unit (ECU) memory for faults. This work should be entrusted to a Vauxhall dealer or a suitably-equipped garage. In reality, if the vehicle is running correctly and no problems have been noticed then this check need not be carried out. In the UK, if the vehicle is over 3 years old, the exhaust emissions will be checked as part of the MOT test anyway.

8 Electrical systems check
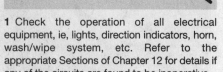

1 Check the operation of all electrical equipment, ie, lights, direction indicators, horn, wash/wipe system, etc. Refer to the appropriate Sections of Chapter 12 for details if any of the circuits are found to be inoperative.
2 Visually check all accessible wiring connectors, harnesses and retaining clips for security, and for signs of chafing or damage. Rectify any faults found.

9 Headlight beam alignment check

Refer to Chapter 12.

10 Body corrosion check

This work should be carried out by a Vauxhall dealer in order to validate the vehicle warranty. The work includes a thorough inspection of the vehicle paintwork and underbody for damage and corrosion.

11 Front brake pad and disc check

1 Firmly apply the handbrake, then jack up the front of the vehicle and support it securely on axle stands (see *Jacking and vehicle support*). Remove the front roadwheels.
2 For a quick check, the pad thickness can be carried out via the inspection hole on the front of the caliper **(see Haynes Hint)**. Using a

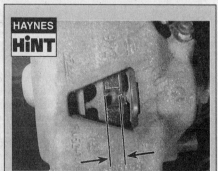

For a quick check, the thickness of friction material remaining on the inner brake pad can be measured through the aperture in the caliper body.

steel rule, measure the thickness of the pad lining. This must not be less than that indicated in the Specifications.
3 The view through the caliper inspection hole gives a rough indication of the state of the brake pads. For a comprehensive check, the brake pads should be removed and cleaned. The operation of the caliper can then also be checked, and the condition of the brake disc itself can be fully examined on both sides. Chapter 9 contains a detailed description of how the brake disc should be checked for wear and/or damage.
4 If any pad's friction material is worn to the specified thickness or less, *all four pads must be renewed as a set*. Refer to Chapter 9 for details.
5 On completion, refit the roadwheels and lower the vehicle to the ground.

12 Rear brake pad and disc check

1 Chock the front wheels, then jack up the rear of the vehicle and support it securely on axle stands (see *Jacking and vehicle support*). Remove the rear roadwheels.
2 For a quick check, the pad thickness can be carried out via the inspection hole on the rear of the caliper. Using a steel rule, measure the thickness of the pad lining including the backing plate. This must not be less than that indicated in the Specifications.
3 A view through the caliper inspection hole gives a rough indication of the state of the brake pads. For a comprehensive check, the brake pads should be removed and cleaned. The operation of the caliper can then also be checked, and the condition of the brake disc itself can be fully examined on both sides. Chapter 9 contains a detailed description of how the brake disc should be checked for wear and/or damage.
4 If any pad's friction material is worn to the specified thickness or less, *all four pads must be renewed as a set*. Refer to Chapter 9 for details.
5 On completion, refit the roadwheels and lower the vehicle to the ground.

13 Handbrake adjustment check

Refer to Chapter 9.

14 Hose and fluid leak check

1 Visually inspect the engine joint faces, gaskets and seals for any signs of water or oil

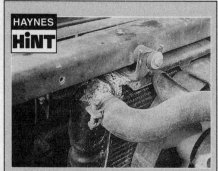

A leak in the cooling system will usually show up as white- or rust-coloured deposits on the area adjoining the leak.

leaks **(see Haynes Hint)**. Pay particular attention to the areas around the cylinder head cover, cylinder head, oil filter and sump joint faces. Bear in mind that, over a period of time, some very slight seepage from these areas is to be expected – what you are really looking for is any indication of a serious leak. Should a leak be found, renew the offending gasket or oil seal by referring to the appropriate Chapters in this manual.
2 Also check the security and condition of all the engine-related pipes and hoses, and all braking system pipes and hoses and fuel lines. Ensure that all cable ties or securing clips are in place, and in good condition. Clips which are broken or missing can lead to chafing of the hoses, pipes or wiring, which could cause more serious problems in the future.
3 Carefully check the radiator hoses and heater hoses along their entire length. Renew any hose which is cracked, swollen or deteriorated. Cracks will show up better if the hose is squeezed. Pay close attention to the hose clips that secure the hoses to the cooling system components. Hose clips can pinch and puncture hoses, resulting in cooling system leaks. If the crimped-type hose clips are used, it may be a good idea to replace them with standard worm-drive clips.
4 Inspect all the cooling system components (hoses, joint faces, etc) for leaks.
5 Where any problems are found on system components, renew the component or gasket with reference to Chapter 3.
6 With the vehicle raised, inspect the fuel tank and filler neck for punctures, cracks and other damage. The connection between the filler neck and tank is especially critical. Sometimes a rubber filler neck or connecting hose will leak due to loose retaining clamps or deteriorated rubber.
7 Carefully check all rubber hoses and metal fuel lines leading away from the fuel tank. Check for loose connections, deteriorated hoses, crimped lines, and other damage. Pay particular attention to the vent pipes and hoses, which often loop up around the filler neck and can become blocked or crimped.

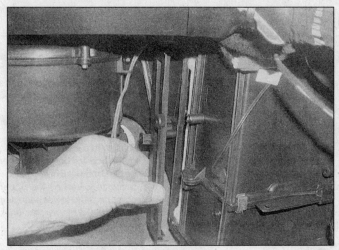

17.2a Remove the cover . . .

17.2b . . . and pull out the pollen filter

Follow the lines to the front of the vehicle, carefully inspecting them all the way. Renew damaged sections as necessary. Similarly, whilst the vehicle is raised, take the opportunity to inspect all underbody brake fluid pipes and hoses.

8 From within the engine compartment, check the security of all fuel, vacuum and brake hose attachments and pipe unions, and inspect all hoses for kinks, chafing and deterioration.

9 Check the condition of the power steering fluid pipes and hoses.

15 Wheel bolt tightness check

1 Remove the wheel trims and check the tightness of all the wheel bolts, using a torque wrench.

2 Refit the wheel trims on completion.

16 Rear suspension level control system check

Where fitted on Estate models, check that the rear suspension level control system operates correctly with reference to Chapter 10. In the event of a fault, have the system checked by a Vauxhall dealer.

17 Pollen filter renewal

1 With reference to Chapter 11, remove the passenger side glovebox and lower facia panel. Remove the passenger side footwell air duct.

2 The pollen filter is built into the heater distribution housing. Two types of filter housing are fitted: one has the filter cover secured by two locking pins, and on the other housing the cover is secured by two bolts and two clamps. Release the clamps/pin and bolts where applicable and open the cover. Pull the filter from the housing **(see illustrations)**.

3 Fit the new filter using a reversal of the removal procedure; some filters have an arrow marking visible on the end of the filter. Make sure that this arrow points to the front of the car with the cover open.

18 Road test

Instruments and electrical equipment

1 Check the operation of all instruments and electrical equipment.

2 Make sure that all instruments read correctly, and switch on all electrical equipment in turn, to check that it functions properly.

Steering and suspension

3 Check for any abnormalities in the steering, suspension, handling or road 'feel'.

4 Drive the vehicle, and check that there are no unusual vibrations or noises.

5 Check that the steering feels positive, with no excessive 'sloppiness', or roughness, and check for any suspension noises when cornering and driving over bumps.

Drivetrain

6 Check the performance of the engine, clutch, transmission and driveshafts.

7 Listen for any unusual noises from the engine, clutch and transmission.

8 Make sure that the engine runs smoothly when idling, and that there is no hesitation when accelerating.

9 Check that the clutch action is smooth and progressive, that the drive is taken up smoothly, and that the pedal travel is not excessive. Also listen for any noises when the clutch pedal is depressed.

10 Check that all gears can be engaged smoothly without noise, and that the gear lever action is smooth and not abnormally vague or 'notchy'.

11 Listen for a metallic clicking sound from the front of the vehicle, as the vehicle is driven slowly in a circle with the steering on full-lock. Carry out this check in both directions. If a clicking noise is heard, this indicates wear in a driveshaft joint (see Chapter 8).

Check the operation and performance of the braking system

12 Make sure that the vehicle does not pull to one side when braking, and that the wheels do not lock prematurely when braking hard.

13 Check that there is no vibration through the steering when braking.

14 Check that the handbrake operates correctly, without excessive movement of the lever, and that it holds the vehicle stationary on a slope.

15 Test the operation of the brake servo unit as follows. Depress the footbrake four or five times to exhaust the vacuum, then start the engine. As the engine starts, there should be a noticeable 'give' in the brake pedal as vacuum builds up. Allow the engine to run for at least two minutes, and then switch it off. If the brake pedal is now depressed again, it should be possible to detect a hiss from the servo as the pedal is depressed. After about four or five applications, no further hissing should be heard, and the pedal should feel considerably harder.

Every 20 000 miles (30 000 km) or 2 years

19 Air cleaner element renewal

1 The air cleaner is located in the front right-hand corner of the engine compartment.
2 Release the securing clips, and lift up the air cleaner cover **(see illustration)**. On 2.0 litre engines take care not to strain the wiring for the airflow meter/intake air temperature sensor wiring (as applicable) as the cover is lifted.
3 Lift out the filter element **(see illustration)**.

4 Wipe out the casing and the cover. Fit the new filter, noting that the rubber locating flange should be uppermost, and secure the cover with the clips.

20 Fuel filter renewal

1 Drain the fuel filter as described in Section 6.
2 Disconnect the wiring from the temperature switch and heating element which are fitted between the fuel filter and mounting bracket **(see illustration)**.
3 Slightly loosen the filter central bolt, then disconnect the quick-release hoses from the filter **(see illustration)**.
4 Unclip the filter housing from the bracket **(see illustration)**.
5 With the filter housing in a suitable container, unscrew and remove the central bolt and recover the bottom nut **(see illustration)**. Drain the fuel.
6 Remove the cover, followed by the upper seal, filter element, spring and lower seal **(see illustrations)**. Discard the seals as new ones must be fitted.

19.2 Release the securing clips . . .

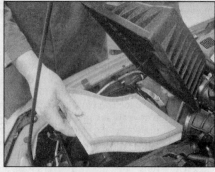

19.3 . . . then lift the cover and remove the air filter element

20.2 Disconnecting the wiring from the fuel filter temperature switch and heating element

20.3 Disconnecting the hoses from the fuel filter

20.4 Unclipping the filter housing from the bracket

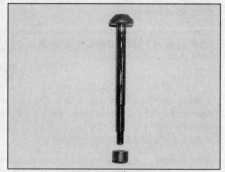

20.5 Central bolt and nut

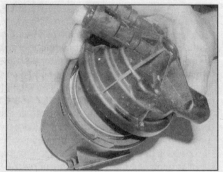

20.6a Remove the cover . . .

20.6b . . . upper seal . . .

20.6c . . . and filter element

7 Clean the filter housing thoroughly.

8 Fit the bottom seal and spring inside the housing, and where applicable locate the bottom nut in the filter housing. One type of nut locates in the lower seal whereas the other type is simply screwed onto the end of the central bolt.

9 Insert the new filter element, then if possible fill the filter housing with fresh fuel in order to assist the self-purging process. Ideally the fuel level should be just below the rim of the body.

10 Refit the cover to the housing together with a new upper seal, then refit the centre bolt, ensuring the seals are in position, and tighten it to the specified torque. **Do not** overtighten the cover screw as the housing is easily damaged.

11 Start the engine and bleed the fuel system as described in Chapter 4A.

21 Hinge and lock lubrication

1 Work around the vehicle and lubricate the hinges of the bonnet, doors and tailgate with a light machine oil.

2 Lightly lubricate the bonnet release mechanism and exposed section of inner cable with a smear of grease.

3 Check the security and operation of all hinges, latches and locks, adjusting them where required. Check the operation of the central locking system.

4 Check the condition and operation of the tailgate struts, renewing them both if either is leaking or no longer able to support the tailgate securely when raised.

22 Rear brake shoe and drum check

Refer to the detailed description given in Chapter 9.

23 Suspension and steering check

Front suspension and steering check

1 Raise the front of the vehicle, and securely support it on axle stands (see *Jacking and vehicle support*).

2 Visually inspect the balljoint dust covers and the steering rack-and-pinion gaiters for splits, chafing or deterioration. Any wear of these components will cause loss of lubricant, together with dirt and water entry, resulting in rapid deterioration of the balljoints or steering gear.

3 Check the power steering fluid hoses for chafing or deterioration, and the pipe and hose unions for fluid leaks. Also check for signs of fluid leakage under pressure from the steering gear rubber gaiters, which would indicate failed fluid seals within the steering gear.

4 Grasp the roadwheel at the 12 o'clock and 6 o'clock positions, and try to rock it **(see illustration)**. Very slight free play may be felt, but if the movement is appreciable, further investigation is necessary to determine the source. Continue rocking the wheel while an assistant depresses the footbrake. If the movement is now eliminated or significantly reduced, it is likely that the hub bearings are at fault. If the free play is still evident with the footbrake depressed, then there is wear in the suspension joints or mountings.

5 Now grasp the wheel at the 9 o'clock and 3 o'clock positions, and try to rock it as before. Any movement felt now may again be caused by wear in the hub bearings or the steering track-rod balljoints. If the outer balljoint is worn, the visual movement will be obvious. If the inner joint is suspect, it can be felt by placing a hand over the rack-and-pinion rubber gaiter and gripping the track-rod. If the wheel is now rocked, movement will be felt at the inner joint if wear has taken place.

6 Using a large screwdriver or flat bar, check for wear in the suspension mounting bushes by levering between the relevant suspension component and its attachment point. Some movement is to be expected, as the mountings are made of rubber, but excessive wear should be obvious. Also check the condition of any visible rubber bushes, looking for splits, cracks or contamination of the rubber.

7 With the car standing on its wheels, have an assistant turn the steering wheel back-and-forth, about an eighth of a turn each way. There should be very little, if any, lost movement between the steering wheel and roadwheels. If this is not the case, closely observe the joints and mountings previously described. In addition, check the steering column universal joints for wear, and also check the rack-and-pinion steering gear itself.

Rear suspension check

8 Chock the front wheels, then jack up the rear of the vehicle and support securely on axle stands (see *Jacking and vehicle support*).

9 Working as described previously for the front suspension, check the rear hub bearings, the suspension bushes and the shock absorber mountings for wear.

Shock absorber check

10 Check for any signs of fluid leakage around the shock absorber body, or from the rubber gaiter around the piston rod. Should any fluid be noticed, the shock absorber is defective internally, and should be renewed. **Note:** *Shock absorbers should always be renewed in pairs on the same axle.*

11 The efficiency of the shock absorber may be checked by bouncing the vehicle at each corner. Generally speaking, the body will return to its normal position and stop after being depressed. If it rises and returns on a rebound, the shock absorber is probably suspect. Also examine the shock absorber upper and lower mountings for any signs of wear.

24 Driveshaft gaiter check

1 With the vehicle raised and securely supported on stands, turn the steering onto full lock then slowly rotate the roadwheel. Inspect the condition of the outer constant velocity (CV) joint rubber gaiters while squeezing the gaiters to open out the folds **(see illustration)**. Check for signs of cracking, splits or deterioration of the rubber which may allow the grease to escape and lead to water and grit entry into the joint. Also check the security and condition of the retaining clips. Repeat these checks on the inner CV joints. If any damage or deterioration is found, the gaiters should be renewed as described in Chapter 8.

2 At the same time, check the general condition of the CV joints themselves by first holding the driveshaft and attempting to rotate the wheel. Repeat this check by holding the inner joint and attempting to rotate the driveshaft. Any appreciable movement indicates wear in the joints, wear in the driveshaft splines or loose driveshaft retaining nut.

23.4 Check for wear in the hub bearings by grasping the wheel and trying to rock it

24.1 Check the condition of the driveshaft gaiters (1) and retaining clips (2)

Every 40 000 miles (60 000 km)

**25 Timing belt renewal
(1.7 litre engines)**

Note: *Vauxhall recommend that the interval for timing belt renewal is 80 000 (120 000 km), regardless of time. However, if the vehicle is used mainly for short journeys or a lot of stop-start driving it is recommended that the renewal* *interval is shortened. The actual belt renewal interval is very much up to the individual owner, but bear in mind that severe engine damage will result if the belt breaks in use.*
1 Refer to Chapter 2A or 2B.

Every 80 000 miles (120 000 km)

**26 Valve clearance check and adjustment
(1.7 litre DOHC engine)**

Refer to Chapter 2B.

Every 2 years, regardless of mileage

27 Brake fluid renewal

⚠ **Warning: Brake hydraulic fluid can harm your eyes and damage painted surfaces, so use extreme caution when handling and pouring it. Do not use fluid that has been standing open for some time, as it absorbs moisture from the air. Excess moisture can cause a dangerous loss of braking effectiveness.**

1 The procedure is similar to that for the bleeding of the hydraulic system as described in Chapter 9.
2 Working as described in Chapter 9, open the first bleed screw in the sequence, and pump the brake pedal gently until nearly all the old fluid has been emptied from the master cylinder reservoir. Top-up to the MAX level with new fluid, and continue pumping until only the new fluid remains in the reservoir, and new fluid can be seen

emerging from the bleed screw. Tighten the screw, and top the reservoir level up to the MAX level line.

> **HAYNES HiNT** *Old hydraulic fluid is invariably much darker in colour than the new, making it easy to distinguish the two.*

3 Work through all the remaining bleed screws in the sequence until new fluid can be seen at all of them. Be careful to keep the master cylinder reservoir topped-up to above the MIN level at all times, or air may enter the system and greatly increase the length of the task.
4 When the operation is complete, check that all bleed screws are securely tightened, and that their dust caps are refitted. Wash off all traces of spilt fluid, and recheck the master cylinder reservoir fluid level.
5 Check the operation of the brakes before taking the car on the road.

28 Remote control battery renewal

Note: *The following procedure must be performed within 3 minutes, otherwise the remote control unit will have to be re-programmed.*
1 Using a screwdriver inserted as shown prise the key section from the remote control unit. Then prise the battery cover from the remote control unit **(see illustrations)**.
2 Note how the battery is fitted, then carefully remove it from the contacts.
3 Fit the new battery and refit the cover making sure that it clips fully onto the base. Refit the key section.

29 Coolant renewal

Refer to Chapter 3.

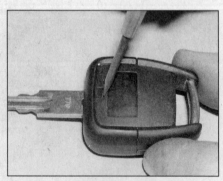

28.1a Prise the key section away . . .

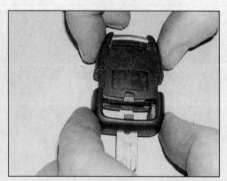

28.1b . . . from the remote control . . .

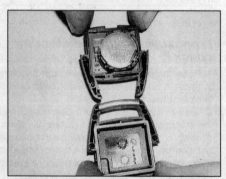

28.1c . . . and open the battery cover

Chapter 2 Part A:
1.7 litre SOHC engine in-car repair procedures

Contents

Degrees of difficulty

Easy, suitable for novice with little experience	Fairly easy, suitable for beginner with some experience	Fairly difficult, suitable for competent DIY mechanic	Difficult, suitable for experienced DIY mechanic	Very difficult, suitable for expert DIY or professional

Specifications

Note: *Where specifications are given as N/A, no information was available at the time of writing. Refer to your Vauxhall dealer for the latest information available.*

General

Engine type	Four-cylinder, in-line, water-cooled. Belt-driven single overhead camshaft, 8 valves
Manufacturer's engine code	X17DTL
Bore	82.5 mm
Stroke	79.5 mm
Capacity	1700 cc
Firing order	1-3-4-2 (No 1 cylinder at timing belt end)
Direction of crankshaft rotation	Clockwise (viewed from timing belt end of engine)
Compression ratio	22:1
Maximum power	50 kW at 4500 rpm
Maximum torque	132 Nm at 1800 to 3250 rpm

Compression pressures

Standard	22.0 to 30.0 bar
Maximum difference between any two cylinders	1.0 bar

Camshaft

Endfloat	0.05 to 0.20 mm
Maximum permissible radial run-out	0.05 mm
Cam lift:	
Inlet valve	9.40 mm
Exhaust valve	9.40 mm
Bearing running clearance:	
Standard	N/A
Service limit	N/A

Lubrication system

Oil pump type . . . . Rotor-type, driven by the crankshaft
Minimum permissible oil pressure at idle speed, with engine
  at operating temperature (oil temperature of at least 80°C) . . . . 3.9 bar (57 psi)

Oil pump clearances:	Standard	Service limit
Outer rotor-to-body clearance	0.24 to 0.36 mm	0.40 mm
Inner-to-outer rotor clearance	0.10 mm	0.145 mm
Rotor endfloat	0.035 to 0.100 mm	0.150 mm

Torque wrench settings

	Nm	lbf ft
Air conditioning compressor bracket bolts	40	30
Air conditioning compressor	20	15
Alternator upper support bracket	18	13
Alternator lower mounting bolt	25	18
Auxiliary belt tensioner to compressor bracket	25	18
Camshaft cover bolts	8	6
Camshaft sprocket bolt*:		
Stage 1	75	55
Stage 2	Angle-tighten a further 60°	
Coolant pipe to cylinder block	20	15
Coolant pump:		
Pump retaining bolts	25	18
Pulley retaining bolts	10	7
Connecting rod big-end bearing cap bolts*:		
Stage 1	35	26
Stage 2	Angle-tighten a further 45°	
Stage 3	Angle-tighten a further 15°	
Crankshaft pulley bolts	20	15
Crankshaft pulse pick-up bolt	8	6
Crankshaft sprocket bolt*:		
Stage 1	130	96
Stage 2	Angle-tighten a further 45°	
Cylinder head bolts*:		
Stage 1	25	18
Stage 2	Angle-tighten a further 90°	
Stage 3	Angle-tighten a further 90°	
Stage 4	Angle-tighten a further 45°	
Stage 5 (after a test-run)	Angle-tighten a further 45°	
Engine/transmission mounting bolts:		
Right-hand mounting:		
Mounting-to-bracket bolt	55	41
Bracket-to-support bolts	55	41
Mounting-to-body bolts	35	26
Support-to-cylinder block bolts	50	37
Left-hand mounting:		
Mounting bracket-to-adapter bolts	55	41
Mounting-to-bracket bolt	55	41
Mounting-to-body bolts	20	15
Adapter-to-transmission bolts	35	26
Battery support-to-body bolts	15	11
Front mounting:		
Mounting-to-transmission bolts	60	44
Mounting-to-body bolt	55	41
Rear mounting:		
Mounting-to-bracket bolts	55	41
Mounting-to-subframe bolts	55	41
Bracket-to-transmission bolts	80	59
Engine-to-transmission unit bolts	60	44
Engine transport shackle bolts	25	18
Exhaust front pipe bolts	20	15
Exhaust gas recirculation valve-to-inlet manifold	8	6
Exhaust manifold-to-cylinder head nuts*	22	16
Exhaust manifold-to-cylinder head bolts	22	16
Exhaust manifold support bracket	25	18
Flywheel bolts*:		
Stage 1	65	48
Stage 2	Angle-tighten a further 30°	
Stage 3	Angle-tighten a further 15°	

Injection pump sprocket bolts	25	18
Injector pipe unions	25	18
Main bearing bridge-to-cylinder block bolts*:		
Stage 1	20	15
Stage 2	Angle-tighten a further 45°	
Main bearing cap bolts*:		
Stage 1	50	37
Stage 2	Angle-tighten a further 45°	
Stage 3	Angle-tighten a further 15°	
Oil cooler bracket	5	4
Oil cooler pipe union	30	22
Oil dipstick guide tube bracket-to-cylinder block bolt	25	18
Oil filter	15	11
Oil pressure relief valve bolt	50	37
Oil pressure switch	40	30
Oil pump to cylinder block	8	6
Oil pump cover retaining bolts	10	7
Oil pump pick-up/strainer bolts*:		
Stage 1	8	6
Stage 2	Angle-tighten a further 30°	
Oil temperature sensor to main sump casting	18	13
Sump bolts:		
Main casting-to-block/oil pump cover nuts/bolts	20	15
Main casting-to-transmission bolts	40	30
Sump pan-to-main casting bolts:		
Stage 1	8	6
Stage 2	Angle-tighten a further 30°	
Drain plug	10	7
Roadwheel bolts	110	81
Thermostat housing	15	11
Timing belt cover bolts	8	6
Timing belt idler pulley bolt	40	30
Timing belt tensioner pulley bolts	25	18
Turbocharger oil feed pipe to cylinder block	20	15
Turbocharger oil feed pipe to turbocharger	30	22
Turbocharger oil return pipe to sump	45	33
Vacuum pump to camshaft housing	28	21

*Use new fasteners

1 General information

1 This Part of Chapter 2 describes those repair procedures that can reasonably be carried out on the 1.7 litre SOHC 8V engine while it remains in the car. If the engine has been removed from the car and is being dismantled as described in Part D, any preliminary dismantling procedures can be ignored.

2 Note that, while it may be possible physically to overhaul items such as the piston/connecting rod assemblies while the engine is in the car, such tasks are not normally carried out as separate operations. Usually, several additional procedures (not to mention the cleaning of components and of oilways) have to be carried out. For this reason, all such tasks are classed as major overhaul procedures, and are described in Part D of this Chapter.

3 Part D describes the removal of the engine/transmission unit from the vehicle, and the full overhaul procedures that can then be carried out.

Engine description

4 The 1.7 litre engine is of the eight-valve, in-line four-cylinder, single overhead camshaft (SOHC) type, mounted transversely at the front of the car with the transmission attached to its left-hand end.

5 The crankshaft runs in five main bearings. Thrustwashers are fitted to No 3 main bearing (upper half) to control crankshaft endfloat.

6 The connecting rods rotate on horizontally-split bearing shells at their big-ends. The pistons are attached to the connecting rods by gudgeon pins, which are a sliding fit in the connecting rod small-end eyes and retained by circlips. The aluminium-alloy pistons are fitted with three piston rings – two compression rings and an oil control ring.

7 The cylinder block is made of cast iron and the cylinder bores are an integral part of the block. On this type of engine the cylinder bores are sometimes referred to as having dry liners.

8 The inlet and exhaust valves are each closed by coil springs, and operate in guides pressed into the cylinder head.

9 The camshaft is driven by the crankshaft via a timing belt and rotates directly in the head. The camshaft operates the valves through followers which are situated directly below the camshaft. Valve clearances are automatically adjusted by hydraulic tappets.

10 Lubrication is by means of an oil pump, which is driven by the crankshaft. It draws oil through a strainer located in the sump, and then forces it through an externally-mounted filter into galleries in the cylinder block/crankcase. From there, the oil is distributed to the crankshaft (main bearings) and camshaft. The big-end bearings are supplied with oil via internal drillings in the crankshaft, while the camshaft bearings also receive a pressurised supply. The camshaft lobes and valves are lubricated by splash, as are all other engine components. In order to cool the piston crowns, oil spray jets are fitted into the cylinder block at the base of each cylinder. An oil cooler is fitted to keep the oil temperature stable under arduous operating conditions.

Repair operations possible with the engine in the car

11 The following work can be carried out with the engine in the car:
  a) Compression pressure testing.
  b) Camshaft cover – removal and refitting.

c) Timing belt cover – removal and refitting.
d) Timing belt – removal and refitting.
e) Timing belt tensioner and sprockets – removal and refitting.
f) Camshaft and followers – removal, inspection and refitting.
g) Cylinder head – removal and refitting.
h) Connecting rods and pistons – removal and refitting*.
i) Sump – removal and refitting.
j) Oil pump – removal, overhaul and refitting.
k) Oil cooler – removal and refitting.
l) Crankshaft oil seals – renewal.
m) Engine/transmission mountings – inspection and renewal.
n) Flywheel – removal, inspection and refitting.

* Although the operations marked with an asterisk can be carried out with the engine in the car after removal of the sump, it is better for the engine to be removed, in the interests of cleanliness and improved access. For this reason, the procedure is described in Chapter 2D.

2 Compression test – description and interpretation

Compression test

Note: A compression tester specifically designed for diesel engines must be used for this test.

1 When engine performance is down, or if misfiring occurs which cannot be attributed to the fuel system, a compression test can provide diagnostic clues as to the engine's condition. If the test is performed regularly, it can give warning of trouble before any other symptoms become apparent.
2 A compression tester specifically intended for diesel engines must be used, because of the higher pressures involved. The tester is connected to an adapter which screws into the glow plug or injector hole. On these models, an adapter suitable for use in the glow plug holes will be required, due to the design of the injectors. It is unlikely to be worthwhile buying such a tester for occasional use, but it may be possible to borrow or hire one – if not, have the test performed by a garage.
3 Unless specific instructions to the contrary are supplied with the tester, observe the following points:
a) The battery must be in a good state of charge, the air filter must be clean, and the engine should be at normal operating temperature.
b) All the glow plugs should be removed before starting the test (see Chapter 5B).
c) Release the retaining clip and disconnect the wiring connector from the fuel injection pump control unit (see Chapter 4A) to prevent the engine from running or fuel from being discharged.
4 There is no need to hold the accelerator pedal down during the test, because the diesel engine air inlet is not throttled.
5 Crank the engine on the starter motor; after one or two revolutions, the compression pressure should build up to a maximum figure, and then stabilise. Record the highest reading obtained.
6 Repeat the test on the remaining cylinders, recording the pressure in each.
7 All cylinders should produce very similar pressures; any difference greater than that specified indicates the existence of a fault. Note that the compression should build-up quickly in a healthy engine; low compression on the first stroke, followed by gradually-increasing pressure on successive strokes, indicates worn piston rings. A low compression reading on the first stroke, which does not build-up during successive strokes, indicates leaking valves or a blown head gasket (a cracked head could also be the cause). Deposits on the undersides of the valve heads can also cause low compression. **Note:** *The cause of poor compression is less easy to establish on a diesel engine than on a petrol one. The effect of introducing oil into the cylinders ('wet' testing) is not conclusive, because there is a risk that the oil will sit in the recess on the piston crown instead of passing to the rings.*
8 On completion of the test, reconnect the injection pump wiring connector then refit the glow plugs as described in Chapter 5B.

Leakdown test

9 A leakdown test measures the rate at which compressed air fed into the cylinder is lost. It is an alternative to a compression test, and in many ways it is better, since the escaping air provides easy identification of where pressure loss is occurring (piston rings, valves or head gasket).
10 The equipment needed for leakdown testing is unlikely to be available to the home mechanic. If poor compression is suspected, have the test performed by a suitably-equipped garage.

3 Top dead centre (TDC) for No 1 piston – locating
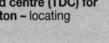

1 In its travel up and down its cylinder bore, Top Dead Centre (TDC) is the highest point that each piston reaches as the crankshaft rotates. While each piston reaches TDC both at the top of the compression stroke and again at the top of the exhaust stroke, for the purpose of timing the engine, TDC refers to the piston position (usually number 1) at the top of its compression stroke.
2 Number 1 piston (and cylinder) is at the right-hand (timing belt) end of the engine, and its TDC position is located as follows. Note that the crankshaft rotates clockwise when viewed from the right-hand side of the car.
3 Disconnect the battery negative terminal. To improve access to the crankshaft pulley,

3.6 Align the notch on the crankshaft sprocket rim with the mark on the base of the oil pump cover (arrowed)

apply the handbrake, then jack up the front of the vehicle and support it on axle stands and remove the right-hand front wheel, and engine undertray where fitted.
4 Remove the camshaft cover as described in Section 4.
5 With reference to Section 5, undo the retaining bolts and remove the crankshaft pulley.
6 Using a socket and extension bar on the crankshaft sprocket bolt, rotate the crankshaft until the notch on the crankshaft sprocket rim is aligned with the mark on the base of the oil pump cover (see illustration). Once the mark is correctly aligned, No 1 and 4 pistons are at TDC.
7 To determine which piston is at TDC on its compression stroke, observe the position of the exhaust camshaft lobe for No 1 cylinder. The exhaust lobe is the one nearest the timing belt. When No 1 piston is at TDC on its compression stroke, the lobe will be pointing almost vertically away from the cylinder head. If the lobe is pointing down, then No 4 cylinder is at TDC on its compression stroke; rotate the crankshaft through a further complete turn (360º) to bring No 1 cylinder to TDC on its compression stroke.
8 With No 1 piston at TDC on its compression stroke, lock the crankshaft in position by inserting Vauxhall tool KM951 into the opening in the transmission casing. If Vauxhall tool KM951 is not available, use an 8mm bolt ground to a point. The lower steering column pinch-bolt is ideal for this task, as it is the correct diameter, and already ground to the correct shape (see illustrations).

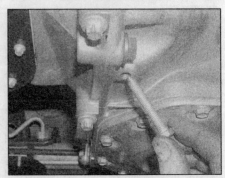

3.8a Insert the crankshaft locking pin through the hole . . .

3.8b . . . and into the flywheel rim

4.2 Disconnect the breather hoses from the front and rear of the camshaft cover

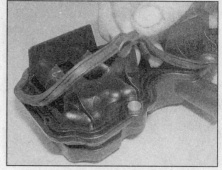

4.4 Fit the seal to the camshaft cover

4 Camshaft cover –
removal and refitting

Removal

1 With reference to Chapter 4A, remove the air cleaner housing, and air intake ducting complete with the hot film air mass meter.
2 Release the retaining clips and disconnect the breather hoses from the front and rear of the camshaft cover (see illustration). It is necessary to remove the two bolts securing the wiring trough to the camshaft cover, and lift the wiring trough in order to gain access to the rear breather hose.
3 Slacken and remove the camshaft cover retaining bolts, and lift the camshaft cover and seal away from the camshaft housing.

Refitting

4 Ensure the cover and cylinder head surfaces are clean and dry then fit the seal to the camshaft housing (see illustration).
5 Carefully lower the cover into position, ensuring the seal remains correctly seated. Refit the retaining bolts and tighten them to the specified torque.
6 Reconnect the breather hoses to the front and rear of the cover and secure in position with the retaining clips.
7 Refit the air intake ducts and air cleaner housing.

5 Crankshaft pulley –
removal and refitting

Removal

1 Apply the handbrake, then jack up the front of the car and support it on axle stands. Remove the right-hand roadwheel and engine compartment undertray.
2 Remove the auxiliary drivebelt(s) as described in Chapter 1. Prior to removal, mark the direction of rotation on the belt(s) to ensure the belt is refitted the same way around.
3 Slacken and remove the small retaining bolts securing the pulley to the crankshaft sprocket and remove the pulley from the engine. If necessary, prevent crankshaft rotation by holding the sprocket retaining bolt with a suitable socket.

Refitting

4 Refit the pulley to the crankshaft sprocket, tightening the pulley retaining bolts to the specified torque (see illustration).
5 Refit the auxiliary drivebelt(s) as described in Chapter 1 using the mark made prior to removal to ensure the belt is fitted the correct way around.
6 Refit the roadwheel and engine undertray, then lower the car to the ground and tighten the wheel bolts to the specified torque.

6 Timing belt covers –
removal and refitting

Removal

Upper cover

1 With reference to Chapter 4A, remove the air cleaner housing and intake ducts, complete with hot film mass air flow meter.
2 Undo the two retaining bolts and remove the upper timing belt cover (see illustration).

Lower cover

3 Remove the upper cover as described in paragraphs 1 to 2.
4 Remove the crankshaft pulley as described in Section 5.
5 Undo the retaining bolts and remove the lower cover from the engine unit, along with its rubber sealing strips. Inspect the sealing strips for signs of damage or deterioration and renew if necessary (see illustration).

Rear cover

6 Remove the timing belt as described in Section 7.
7 Remove the camshaft sprocket, the fuel injection pump sprocket, the timing belt idler pulley and the tensioner assembly as described in Section 8.
8 Mark the position of the right-hand engine

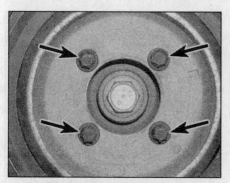

5.4 Crankshaft pulley retaining bolts (arrowed)

6.2 Timing belt upper cover bolts

6.5 Timing belt lower cover bolts

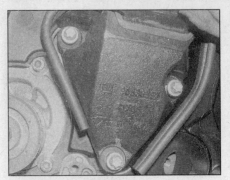

6.8 Undo the three right-hand engine mounting bolts

7.5 Mark the position of the three bolt heads relative to the bracket prior to removing the bolts

7.10 Use an open-ended spanner on the hexagonal section of the camshaft to prevent rotation

mounting to the support bracket, and undo the three securing bolts (see illustration).

9 Unbolt the six rear cover retaining bolts from the cylinder head/block and remove the cover from the engine unit.

Refitting

10 Refitting is the reverse of removal, ensuring the cover sealing strips are correctly fitted and all retaining bolts are tightened to the specified torque.

7 Timing belt – removal and refitting

Note: The timing belt must be removed and refitted with the engine cold. A new camshaft sprocket retaining bolt will be required. Ideally, this procedure requires access to special Vauxhall tools.

Removal

1 Position No 1 cylinder at TDC on its compression stroke as described in Section 3.
2 Remove the crankshaft pulley as described in Section 5.
3 With reference to Section 6, remove the upper and lower timing belt covers.
4 Support the weight of the engine using a trolley jack with a block of wood placed on its head.
5 Mark the position of the right-hand engine mounting to the support bracket, and undo the three securing bolts (see illustration).

6 Undo the three retaining bolts and remove the engine mounting damper block and bracket from the right-hand side inner wing.
7 Slacken the timing belt tensioner retaining bolt. Using an Allen key, rotate the tensioner arm clockwise until the roller is as far away from the belt as possible to relieve the tension in the timing belt, hold it in position and securely tighten the retaining bolt.
8 Slide the timing belt from its sprockets and remove it from the engine. If the belt is to be re-used, use white paint or similar to mark the direction of rotation on the belt. Do not rotate the crankshaft or camshafts until the timing belt has been refitted.
9 Check the timing belt carefully for any signs of uneven wear, splitting or oil contamination, and renew it if there is the slightest doubt about its condition. If the engine is undergoing an overhaul and is approaching the specified interval for belt renewal (see Chapter 1) renew the belt as a matter of course, regardless of its apparent condition. If signs of oil contamination are found, trace the source of the oil leak and rectify it, then wash down the engine timing belt area and all related components to remove all traces of oil.

Refitting

10 Prevent the camshaft from rotating by using an open-ended spanner on the hexagonal section of the camshaft, and undo the camshaft sprocket retaining bolt. Discard the old bolt and fit the new one. Only finger-tighten the bolt at this stage – it must be possible to rotate the pulley independently of the camshaft (see illustration).

11 Slacken the injection pump sprocket retaining bolts. It must be possible to rotate the pulley independently of the injection pump shaft (see illustration).
12 Ensure that the crankshaft is still positioned at TDC and the locking pin is still in place.
13 Fit the timing belt over the crankshaft, injection pump and camshaft sprockets, ensuring that the belt rear run is taut (ie, all slack is on the tensioner pulley side of the belt). Do not twist the belt sharply while refitting it. Ensure that the belt teeth are correctly seated centrally in the sprockets. If a used belt is being refitted, ensure that the arrow mark made on removal points in the normal direction of rotation, as before.
14 Temporarily tension the timing belt by releasing the belt tensioner retaining bolt and, using an Allen key, rotate the tensioner arm anti-clockwise so that the pointer is aligned with the cut-out on the backplate (see illustration). Hold the tensioner in the correct position and tighten its retaining bolt securely.
15 It is now necessary to set the position of the camshaft using a DTI (Dial Test Indicator) gauge. Vauxhall specify the use of tool No KM 661-1 to support the DTI and allow it to move across the camshaft housing without changing height relative to the housing top surface. The tool has locating pins on the underside, which engage with the threaded holes in the housing top surface. There are two sets of pins set 10 mm apart, so that the tool can be accurately in one of two positions, in order to take two readings with the DTI (see illustration). The

7.11 Injection pump pulley retaining bolts (arrowed)

7.14 Align the tensioner pointer with the cut-out on the backplate

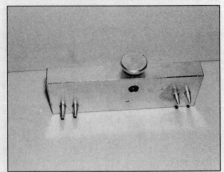

7.15 DTI support tool for camshaft setting

7.16 Position the DTI foot directly over the centre line of No 1 cylinder inlet camshaft lobe

7.23 Insert the injection pump locking pin (see text)

8.7 Vauxhall tool inserted into the injection pump flange and retaining bore (sprocket removed for clarity)

DTI 'foot' should have a flat bottom and be 7 to 10 mm in diameter. Proceed as follows:

16 Insert the DTI into tool KM 661-1, and attach the 7 to 10 mm foot to the DTI probe.

17 Position KM 661-1 over the No 1 cylinder inlet camshaft lobe (second lobe from the timing belt end), with the arrow on the tool pointing towards the timing end of the engine **(see illustration)**.

18 When viewed from the timing belt end of the engine, the left-hand positioning pins of KM 661-1 must engage in the threaded holes in the camshaft housing upper face. In this position the foot of the DTI should be directly over the centre of the camshaft, and touching the base circle of the camshaft lobe.

19 Preload the DTI by no more than 0.5 mm, and zero the gauge.

20 Now move the support (KM 661-1) 10 mm to the left, so that the right-hand set of locating pins engage with the threaded holes in the upper face of the camshaft housing.

21 Check that the crankshaft locking pin (Tool No KM 951 or an 8 mm bolt ground to a point) is still in place in the transmission casing, and the crankshaft is still at TDC. In this position the locking pin should engage with a V-shaped notch in the flywheel rim, and the mark on the crankshaft sprocket should align with the mark on the oil pump cover.

22 Read off the measurement displayed on the DTI gauge. If the timing is correct, the reading should be 0.55 mm. If this is not the case, tun the camshaft using an open-ended spanner on the camshaft flats until the correct reading is achieved.

23 Using an open ended spanner, turn the injection pump flange bolt until the recess in the pump pulley aligns with the recess in the pump flange and the pump retaining bore. Insert retaining pin KM 6011 to lock the position of the pulley/flange/bore. If tool KM 6011 is not available, use rod 9.5 mm in diameter and approximately 75 mm long **(see illustration)**.

24 Tighten the camshaft sprocket bolt to the specified torque, preventing the camshaft from rotating by counter-holding the shaft with an open-ended spanner on the flats of the camshaft.

25 Tighten the injection pump sprocket bolts

to the specified torque, and remove the locking pin.

26 Remove the crankshaft locking pin.

27 Rotate the crankshaft smoothly through two complete turns (720°) in the normal direction of rotation to settle the timing belt in position. Realign the crankshaft sprocket timing mark and check that the injection pump sprocket locking pin can be refitted, and the camshaft DTI reading is within specification.

28 Check the position of the timing belt tensioner pointer. For a new belt, the pointer should align with the cut-out on the backplate. If a used belt has been refitted, the pointer should be aligned to a position approximately 4mm to the left of the cut-out. If necessary, slacken the tensioner retaining bolt, and using an Allen key, move the tensioner arm until the pointer is in the correct position.

29 Remove the DTI and holder, refit the following components, tightening the retaining bolts to the correct torque where specified:

a) *Timing belt covers.*
b) *Right hand engine mounting (aligning the previously made marks).*
c) *Crankshaft pulley.*
d) *Camshaft cover.*
e) *Air inlet trunking.*
f) *Air cleaner housing.*
g) *Engine undertray.*
h) *Roadwheel.*

8 Timing belt tensioner and sprockets – removal and refitting

Camshaft sprocket

Note: A new camshaft sprocket retaining bolt will be required.

Removal

1 Remove the timing belt as described in Section 7.

2 Remove the camshaft cover as described in Section 4.

3 Prevent the camshaft from turning by

counter-holding the shaft with an open-ended spanner on the hexagon section of the camshaft, and remove the sprocket retaining bolt. Remove the sprocket.

Refitting

4 Refit the sprocket to the end of the camshaft and fit the new retaining bolt, but only finger-tighten it at this stage.

5 It is now necessary to carry out the camshaft timing procedure as described in Section 7, paragraphs 11 to 29.

Injection pump sprocket

Removal

6 Remove the timing belt as described in Section 7.

7 Insert Vauxhall tool No KM 6011 in through the sprocket recess into the pump flange and retaining bore to prevent the sprocket from rotating. In the absence of the special Vauxhall tool, a suitable alternative can be made using a steel rod 75 mm long and 9.5 mm in diameter **(see illustration)**.

8 Unscrew the three retaining bolts and remove the sprocket.

Refitting

9 Refit the sprocket to the pump shaft, aligning the recess in the sprocket with the recess in the pump flange and retaining bore **(see illustration 7.23)**.

10 Fit the sprocket retaining bolts, but only finger-tighten the bolts at this stage.

11 It is now necessary to carry out the camshaft timing procedure as described in Section 7, paragraphs 11 to 29.

Crankshaft sprocket

Removal

12 Remove the crankshaft pulley as described in Section 5.

13 Slacken the crankshaft sprocket retaining bolt. To prevent crankshaft rotation, have an assistant select top gear and apply the brakes firmly. If the engine is removed from the vehicle it will be necessary to lock the flywheel (see Section 16).

14 Remove the timing belt as described in Section 7.

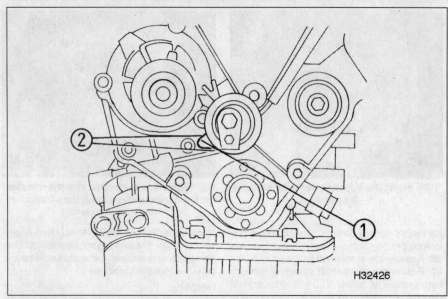

8.21 Ensure that the tensioner locating lever (1) engages in the guide webs on the oil pump (2)

15 Unscrew the retaining bolt and washer and remove the crankshaft sprocket from the end of the crankshaft. If the sprocket is a tight fit, draw it off of the crankshaft using a suitable puller. If the Woodruff key is a loose fit in the crankshaft, remove it and store it with the sprocket for safe-keeping.

Refitting

16 Ensure the Woodruff key is correctly fitted then slide on the crankshaft sprocket aligning its groove with the key.
17 Refit the retaining bolt and washer then lock the crankshaft by the method used on removal, and tighten the sprocket retaining bolt to the specified torque setting.
18 Refit the timing belt as described in Section 7.

Tensioner assembly

Removal

19 Remove the timing belt as described in Section 7.
20 Unscrew the retaining bolt and remove the tensioner assembly from the engine.

Refitting

21 Fit the tensioner assembly, ensuring that the locating lever engages in the guide webs in the oil pump cover **(see illustration)**. Finger tighten the tensioner retaining bolt only at this stage.
22 Refit the timing belt as described in Section 7.

Idler pulley

Removal

23 Remove the timing belt as described in Section 7.
24 Slacken and remove the retaining bolt and remove the idler pulley complete with spacer sleeve from the engine **(see illustration)**.

Refitting

25 Refit the idler pulley and spacer sleeve. Tighten the retaining bolt to the specified torque.
26 Refit the timing belt as described in Section 7.

9 Camshaft oil seal – renewal

1 Remove the camshaft sprocket as described in Section 8.
2 Carefully punch or drill a small hole in the oil seal. Screw in a self-tapping screw, and pull on the screw with pliers to extract the seal **(see illustration)**.
3 Clean the seal housing, and polish off any burrs or raised edges which may have caused the seal to fail in the first place.
4 Lubricate the lips of the new seal with clean engine oil, and press it into position using a suitable tubular drift (such as a socket) which bears only on the hard outer edge of the seal. The outside face of the seal should be flush with the outside edge of the housing. Take care not to damage the seal lips during fitting; note that the seal lips should face inwards.
5 Refit the camshaft sprocket as described in Section 8.

10 Camshaft and followers – removal, inspection and refitting

Note: *Vauxhall tool No KM 890 is required to remove the camshaft without disturbing the cylinder head gasket. If this tool is not available, the cylinder head will have to be removed – see Section 11.*

Removal

1 Disconnect and remove the battery. **Note:** *Before disconnecting the battery, refer to 'Disconnecting the battery' in the reference section at the rear of this manual.*
2 Remove the camshaft sprocket as described in Section 8. Turn the crankshaft 90° backwards (anti-clockwise) to prevent accidental contact between the pistons and valves.
3 Release the retaining clips and remove the turbocharger-to-intercooler air pipe and the intercooler-to-inlet manifold pipe. These pipes are also secured to various supporting brackets – refer to Chapter 4A if necessary.
4 Disconnect the brake servo pipe and the

8.24 Unscrew the bolt and remove the idler pulley

9.2 Pull on the screw to extract the seal

10.4 Depress the retaining clip and disconnect the brake servo hose from the vacuum pump

10.5 Unscrew the vacuum pump retaining bolts (arrowed)

10.6 The camshaft thrust plate is retained by two Allen screws

10.14 Refit the hydraulic adjusters, thrust pieces and rocker arms

vacuum pipe from the vacuum pump (see illustration).

5 Slacken and remove the vacuum pump retaining bolts and remove the pump complete with the turbocharger air pipe bracket (see illustration).

6 Undo the two Allen screws and remove the camshaft thrust plate from the left-hand side of the camshaft (see illustration).

7 If available fit Vauxhall tool No KM 890 by means of which the camshaft can be removed without disturbing the camshaft housing. The tool consists of a series of plates carrying adjustable feet which bolt to the camshaft housing so that the feet depress the rocker arms. The camshaft can then be withdrawn from the housing. In the absence of this tool, the camshaft housing will have to be removed. As the bolts that retain the camshaft housing also secure the cylinder head, it will be necessary to remove the cylinder head and replace the gasket. Follow the procedure as described in Section 11.

8 With the camshaft removed, obtain eight small, clean plastic containers, and label them for identification. Alternatively, divide a larger container into compartments. Lift the rocker arms, thrust pads and hydraulic adjusters out from the top of the cylinder head and store each one in its respective fitted position.

Inspection

9 Examine the camshaft bearing surfaces and cam lobes for signs of wear ridges and scoring. Renew the camshaft if any of these conditions are apparent. Examine the

condition of the bearing surfaces both on the camshaft journals and in the camshaft housing. If the housing bearing surfaces are worn excessively, replacement parts may be available – check with your Vauxhall dealer.

10 Support the camshaft end journals on V-blocks, and measure the run-out at the centre journal using a dial gauge. If the run-out exceeds the specified limit, the camshaft should be renewed.

11 Always renew the camshaft oil seal prior to camshaft replacement – see Section 9.

12 The camshaft thrust plate should appear unworn and without grooves. Renew the thrust plate if the camshaft endfloat is excessive.

13 Examine the hydraulic adjusters and their bores in the cylinder head for signs of wear or damage. If any adjuster is visibly worn, or has a history of noisy operation, it should be renewed.

Refitting

14 Where removed, lubricate each of the hydraulic adjusters, thrust pads and rocker arms, and refit them to their original positions (see illustration). Coat the thrust faces of the rocker arms with MoS_2 (Molybdenum Disulphide) paste.

15 With tool KM 890 installed, carefully slide the camshaft into the housing, through the new oil seal and secure in place with the thrust plate. Tighten the thrust plate retaining bolts to the specified torque (see illustration 10.6).

16 Ensure that the rocker arms and thrust

pads are correctly located, and carefully remove tool KM 890.

17 Refit the camshaft sprocket, only finger-tighten the new retaining bolt at this stage.

18 Turn the camshaft so that the exhaust camshaft lobe of No. 1 cylinder (nearest the timing belt end) is pointing vertically away from the cylinder head. Rotate the crankshaft 90° to TDC, and refit the timing belt as described in Section 7, paragraphs 11 to 29.

19 Refit the vacuum pump to the left-hand end of the camshaft housing, note the turbocharger air pipe bracket is secured by the upper pump retaining bolt. Ensure that the vacuum pump drive engages with the groove in the end of the camshaft (see illustration), and tighten the retaining bolts to the specified torque.

20 Reconnect the brake servo pipe and vacuum pipe to the vacuum pump.

21 Connect the intercooler-to-inlet manifold air pipe, and the turbocharger-to-intercooler air pipe. Refit the pipe retaining clips and securely tighten the bolts/nuts of the pipes retaining brackets.

22 Refit and reconnect the battery.

11 Cylinder head – removal and refitting

Caution: Be careful not to allow dirt into the fuel injection pump or injector pipes during this procedure.
Note: New cylinder head bolts will be required on refitting.

Removal

1 Disconnect and remove the battery – refer to Chapter 5A if necessary. Note: Before disconnecting the battery, refer to 'Disconnecting the battery' in the reference section at the rear of this manual.

2 Drain the cooling system as described in Chapter 3. Undo the retaining screw and remove the air filter housing, complete with hot film mass air flow sensor and ducting.

3 Detach the alternator from the tension rail and top-rear support bracket. Slacken the lower alternator mounting bolt, remove the alternator drivebelt, and swing the alternator to the rear (see illustration).

10.19 The vacuum pump drive engages with the groove in the end of the camshaft

11.3 Alternator top-rear support bracket (arrowed)

11.10 Unclip the fuel supply and return hoses

11.13 Disconnect the fuel leak-back pipe from the No 1 cylinder injector

11.17 Turbocharger oil return pipe

4 With reference to Section 6, remove the rear timing belt cover.

5 Release the pipe retaining clips and bracket retaining bolts, release the cable loom clips, and remove the turbocharger-to-intercooler air pipe, and the intercooler-to-inlet manifold air pipe – refer to Chapter 4A if necessary.

6 Disconnect the brake servo pipe and vacuum pipe from the vacuum pump at the left-hand end of the camshaft housing.

7 Disconnect the wiring connectors from the coolant temperature sensor, charge pressure sensor, and the EGR (Exhaust Gas Recirculation) solenoid valve.

8 Detach the wiring harness trough from the camshaft housing and position it to one side.

9 Release the retaining clips and disconnect the upper radiator hose from the coolant flange and radiator.

10 Unclip the fuel supply and return lines from the brackets by the camshaft housing **(see illustration)**.

11 Release the retaining clips and disconnect the expansion tank coolant hose from the front-top of the thermostat housing and camshaft housing. Move the hose to one side.

12 Remove the fastening clips holding the injector pipes together. Prior to removal note the fitted location of the clips.

13 Wipe clean the pipe unions then slacken the union nuts securing the injector pipes to the top of each injector and the four union nuts securing the pipes to the rear of the injection pump; as each pump union nut is slackened, retain the adapter with a suitable

open-ended spanner to prevent it being unscrewed from the pump. With all the union nuts undone, remove the injector pipes from the engine unit and mop up any spilt fuel. Disconnect the fuel leak-back pipe from the No 1 cylinder injector **(see illustration)**.

14 Undo the two nuts and disconnect the wiring from the top of No 2 and 3 cylinder glow plugs.

15 Unscrew the union, and disconnect the turbocharger oil feed pipe from the cylinder block – refer to Chapter 4A.

16 Disconnect the oil feed pipe from the turbocharger – refer to Chapter 4A.

17 Undo the union bolt, and disconnect the turbocharger oil return pipe from the upper section of the oil sump. Recover the sealing washers **(see illustration)**.

18 Detach the exhaust manifold support bracket from the cylinder block and exhaust manifold **(see illustration)**. Unscrew the retaining nuts and detach the exhaust front pipe from the exhaust manifold.

19 Undo the bolt and remove the wiring loom/fuel pipe retaining bracket from the left-hand end of the cylinder head.

20 Undo the two retaining bolts and remove the thermostat housing from the right-hand end of the cylinder head. Disengage the housing from the metal coolant pipe at the rear of the cylinder block – note the two sealing rings. Lay the housing to one side complete with the heater hose **(see illustration)**.

21 Working in the **reverse** of the sequence shown in illustration 11.43, progressively

slacken the ten main cylinder head bolts by half a turn at a time, until all bolts can be unscrewed by hand.

22 Remove the cylinder head bolts and recover the washers.

23 Lift the camshaft housing away from the cylinder head and obtain eight small, clean plastic containers, and label them for identification. Alternatively, divide a larger container into compartments. Lift the rocker arms, thrust pads and hydraulic adjusters out from the top of the cylinder head and store each one in its respective fitted position.

24 With the help of an assistant, as it is a heavy assembly, lift the cylinder head away from the cylinder block. Remove the gasket, noting the two locating dowels fitted to the top of the cylinder block. If they are a loose fit, remove the locating dowels and store them with the head for safe-keeping. Keep the head gasket for identification purposes (see paragraph 31).

25 If the cylinder head is to be dismantled for overhaul, then refer to Part D of this Chapter.

Preparation for refitting

26 The mating faces of the cylinder head and cylinder block/crankcase must be perfectly clean before refitting the head. Use a hard plastic or wood scraper to remove all traces of gasket and carbon; also clean the piston crowns. Take particular care, as the surfaces are damaged easily. Also, make sure that the carbon is not allowed to enter the oil and water passages – this is particularly important for the lubrication system, as carbon could block the oil supply to any of the engine's components. Using adhesive tape and paper, seal the water, oil and bolt holes in the cylinder block/crankcase. To prevent carbon entering the gap between the pistons and bores, smear a little grease in the gap. After cleaning each piston, use a small brush to remove all traces of grease and carbon from the gap, then wipe away the remainder with a clean rag. Clean all the pistons in the same way.

27 Check the mating surfaces of the cylinder block/crankcase and the cylinder head for nicks, deep scratches and other damage. If slight, they may be removed carefully with a file, but if excessive, machining may be the only alternative to renewal.

28 Ensure that the cylinder head bolt holes in the crankcase are clean and free of oil.

11.18 Exhaust manifold support bracket

11.20 Undo the two thermostat housing bolts

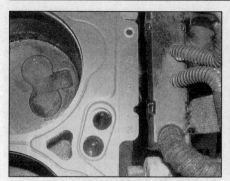

11.31 Cylinder head gasket identification notch

11.32 Mount a dial test indicator (DTI) on the cylinder block and zero the gauge

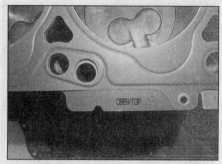

11.36 Position the gasket over the locating dowels with the mark OBEN/TOP facing upwards

Syringe or soak up any oil left in the bolt holes. This is most important in order that the correct bolt tightening torque can be applied and to prevent the possibility of the block being cracked by hydraulic pressure when the bolts are tightened.

29 The cylinder head bolts must be discarded and renewed, regardless of their apparent condition.

30 If warpage of the cylinder head gasket surface is suspected, use a straight-edge to check it for distortion. Refer to Part D of this Chapter if necessary.

31 On this engine, the cylinder head-to-piston clearance is controlled by fitting different thickness head gaskets. The gasket thickness can be determined by looking at the left-hand front corner of gasket and checking on the number of notches **(see illustration)**.

Notches in gasket	Gasket thickness
No notch	1.30 mm
One notch	1.40 mm
Two notches	1.50 mm

The correct thickness of gasket required is selected by measuring the piston protrusions as follows.

32 Ensure that the crankshaft is correctly positioned in the TDC position. Mount a dial test indicator securely on the block so that its pointer can be easily pivoted between the piston crown and block mating surface. Zero the dial test indicator on the gasket surface of the cylinder block then carefully move the indicator over No 1 piston and measure its protrusion at the three points

shown **(see illustration)**. Repeat this procedure on No 4 piston.

33 Rotate the crankshaft half a turn (180°) to bring No 2 and 3 pistons to TDC. Ensure the crankshaft is accurately positioned then measure the protrusions of No 2 and 3 pistons at the specified points. Once both pistons have been measured, rotate the crankshaft through a further one and a half turns (540°) to bring No 1 and 4 pistons back to TDC.

34 Find out the average piston protrusion by adding up the 12 different measurements taken (three for each piston) and dividing the total by 12. Using this average measurement, select the correct thickness of head gasket required using the following table.

Piston protrusion measurement	Gasket thickness required
up to 0.80 mm	no notch
0.80 to 0.90 mm	1 notch
Over 0.90 mm	2 notches

Note: *If any one of the piston protrusion measurements taken exceeds the average protrusion by more than 0.05 mm, select the gasket from the next available thickness up from the average. For example, if the average protrusion is 0.79 mm but one of the protrusion measurements taken was 0.85 mm (a difference of 0.06 mm) then use a 'one notch' gasket instead of a 'no notch' gasket.*

Refitting

35 Wipe clean the mating surfaces of the cylinder head and cylinder block/crankcase.

36 Check that the two locating dowels are in position then fit a new gasket to the cylinder block, with the mark OBEN/TOP facing upwards and on the front side of the engine **(see illustration)**.

37 In order to prevent any accidental contact between the pistons and valves, turn the crankshaft approximately 90° backwards (anti-clockwise).

38 With the aid of an assistant, carefully refit the cylinder head assembly to the block, aligning it with the locating dowels.

39 Lubricate the hydraulic adjusters, thrust pads and rocker arms, and refit them into their original locations. Coat the thrust faces of the rocker arms with MoS₂ (Molybdenum Disulphide) paste **(see illustration)**.

40 Apply a bead of suitable sealant (available from your Vauxhall dealer) to the upper mating surface of the cylinder head **(see illustration)**.

41 Carefully replace the camshaft housing (with camshaft still installed) onto the cylinder head.

42 Apply a smear of oil to the threads and the underside of the heads of the new cylinder head bolts and carefully enter each bolt into its relevant hole (do not drop them in). Screw all bolts in, by hand only, until finger-tight.

43 Working progressively and in the sequence shown, tighten the cylinder head bolts to their Stage 1 torque setting, using a torque wrench and suitable socket **(see illustration)**.

44 Once all bolts have been tightened to the Stage 1 torque, working again in the specified

11.39 Apply a smear of MoS₂ (Molybdenum Disulphide) paste to the rocker arm thrust faces

11.40 Apply a bead of sealant to the upper mating surface of the cylinder head

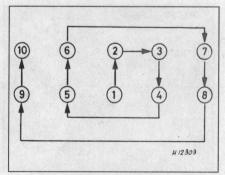

11.43 Cylinder head bolt tightening sequence

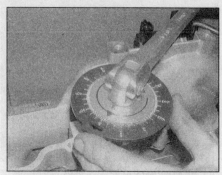

11.44 Use an angle gauge to tighten the cylinder head bolts to Stages 2, 3 & 4

11.45 Refit the coolant pipe seals prior to refitting the thermostat housing

sequence, go around and tighten all bolts through the specified Stage 2 angle. It is recommended that an angle-measuring gauge is used to ensure accuracy **(see illustration)**. If a gauge is not available, use white paint to make alignment marks prior to tightening; the marks can then be used to check that the bolt has been rotated through the correct angle. Tighten the bolts in the same sequence through the angles specified for Stages 3 and 4.

45 Refit the thermostat housing to the right-hand end of the cylinder head, using new seal rings on the end of the coolant pipe at the rear of the cylinder block and between the thermostat housing and cylinder head. Ensure that the metal coolant pipe at the rear of the cylinder block engages correctly with the housing. Tighten the bolts to the specified torque **(see illustration)**.

46 Reconnect the turbocharger oil feed pipe to the cylinder block and turbocharger, tightening the union bolts to the specified torque.

47 Fit the support bracket to the alternator and turbocharger, tightening the bolts to the specified torque.

48 Apply a smear of exhaust sealing paste to the mating surface and gasket of the exhaust front pipe, and reconnect it to the exhaust manifold. Tighten the bolts to the specified torque.

49 Re-attach the exhaust manifold support bracket to the manifold and cylinder block, and tighten the bolts to the specified torque.

50 Connect the turbocharger oil return pipe

to the upper part of the oil sump using new sealing washers. Tighten the bolt to the specified torque.

51 Refit the timing belt rear cover, engine mounting bracket, idler pulley, camshaft sprocket and timing belt as described in Sections 6, 8 and 7 respectively.

52 With reference to Section 6, refit the right-hand engine mounting, and the lower and upper timing belt covers.

53 Refit the crankshaft pulley as described in Section 5. Refit the front right roadwheel and lower the vehicle to the ground.

54 Re-attach the wiring connections to the glow plugs. Tighten the retaining nuts securely.

55 Refit the injector pipes to the injectors and injection pump and tighten the union nuts to the specified torque setting. Refit the injector pipe clamp into its original location.

56 Reconnect the coolant hoses to the outlet flange and camshaft housing cover.

57 Clip the injection pump fuel lines back into their brackets by the camshaft housing.

58 Refit the coolant hose to the radiator top connection and the thermostat housing. Secure the retaining clips.

59 Re-attach the wiring trough to the camshaft housing.

60 Reconnect the wiring plugs to the coolant temperature sensor, charge pressure sensor and EGR (Exhaust Gas Recirculation) solenoid valve.

61 Fit the engine breather hoses to the camshaft housing cover, and secure the retaining clips.

62 Attach the vacuum pipe and brake servo pipe to the vacuum pump.

63 Refit the air pipe from the inlet manifold to the intercooler. Note the bolt securing the pipe to the retaining bracket.

64 Reconnect the air pipe from the intercooler to the turbocharger. Secure the retaining clips.

65 Re-attach the alternator to the tension rail and tighten the alternator lower mounting bolt to the specified torque.

66 Refit the auxiliary drivebelt(s) as described in Chapter 1.

67 Re-install the air cleaner housing, and air intake ducting complete with hot film mass air meter. Refer to Chapter 4A if necessary.

68 Top up the cooling system as described in Chapter 3.

69 Check the engine oil level and top up if necessary.

70 Tighten the roadwheel bolts to the specified torque.

71 Refit and reconnect the battery.

72 After starting the engine check for leaks. After a test run, tighten the cylinder head bolts to the specified angle for Stage 5.

12 Sump – removal and refitting

Removal

Note: *In order to completely remove the upper sump casting with the engine in place, the main bearing bridge must be removed. New bolts will be required to refit the bearing bridge.*

1 Firmly apply the handbrake then jack up the front of the car and support it on axle stands. Where necessary, undo the retaining screws and remove the engine undertray.

2 Drain the engine oil as described in Chapter 1, then fit a new sealing washer and refit the drain plug, tightening it to the specified torque.

3 Slacken and remove the bolts securing the sump lower pan to the main casting then remove the sump pan from underneath the vehicle.

4 To remove the main casting from the engine, disconnect the wiring plug from the oil temperature sensor fitted into the front side of the casting.

5 Undo the bolt securing the oil dipstick guide tube to the cylinder block.

6 Pull the oil dipstick guide tube up and out from the main sump casting **(see illustration)**.

7 Unscrew the union bolt and disconnect the turbocharger oil return pipe from the sump casting. Recover the sealing washers **(see illustration)**.

8 Undo the two bolts securing the oil pick-up pipe to the sump casting and remove the pipe. Note the two sealing rings on the pump end of the pipe.

9 Progressively slacken and remove the nuts

12.6 Pull the dipstick guide tube from the sump casting

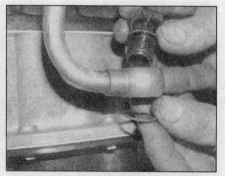

12.7 Turbocharger oil return pipe sealing washers

12.11 Apply a bead of sealant to the oil pump cover and rear main bearing areas of the gasket mating face

12.13 Refit the main bearing bridge

12.20 Note the rubber seals on the oil pick-up pipe

and bolts securing the main casting to the base of the cylinder block/oil pump cover/transmission. Break the joint by striking the casting with the palm of the hand, then set it aside on the front subframe.

10 Undo the main bearing bridge retaining bolts, and remove the sump casting along with the bearing bridge.

Refitting

11 Remove all traces of dirt and oil from the mating surfaces of the sump main casting and pan. Apply a bead of suitable sealant to the areas of the oil pump cover and rear main bearing mating surfaces **(see illustration)**.

12 Place a new gasket on the sump main casting and place the casing on the front subframe.

13 Using new bolts, refit the main bearing bridge to the cylinder block and tighten the bolts to the specified torque **(see illustration)**.

14 Offer up the main casting and finger tighten all the retaining bolts.

15 Tighten the bolts securing the sump casting to the cylinder block and oil pump to the specified torque. **Note:** *If the sump casting is being refitted with the engine remove from the vehicle and separated from the transmission, it is necessary to ensure that the flange of the casting at the flywheel end is flush with the corresponding flange of the cylinder block.*

16 Tighten the bolts securing the sump casting to the transmission to the specified torque.

17 Re-attach the turbocharger oil return pipe to the sump casting, using new sealing washers where applicable. Tighten the union bolt to the specified torque.

18 Insert the oil dipstick guide tube into the main sump casting, with new seal rings if needed, and attach the guide tube to the cylinder block. Tighten the guide tube-retaining bracket bolt to the specified torque.

19 Reconnect the crankshaft pulse pick-up, and oil temperature sensor wiring plugs. Clip the wiring loom to the retaining bracket.

20 Replace the sealing rings on the end of the oil pick-up pipe and refit the pipe to the main sump casting. Tighten the new bolts to the specified torque **(see illustration)**.

21 Remove all traces of dirt and oil from the mating surfaces of the sump lower pan and the main casting.

22 Using a new gasket, refit the pan to the base of the main casting and tighten its retaining bolts to the specified torque.

23 Refit the engine undertray, lower the vehicle to the ground, then fill the engine with fresh oil with reference to Chapter 1.

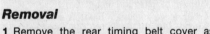

13 Oil pump – removal, inspection and refitting

Removal

1 Remove the rear timing belt cover as described in Section 6.

2 Remove the sump main casting as described in Section 12.

3 With reference to Section 8 remove the timing belt idler pulley and tensioner.

4 Undo the crankshaft sprocket retaining bolt, and remove the sprocket from the crankshaft. To prevent crankshaft rotation, have an assistant select top gear and apply the brakes firmly. If the engine is removed from the vehicle it will be necessary to lock the flywheel (see Section 16).

5 Undo the oil cooler pipe unions from the oil filter housing, and lay the pipes, complete with bracket, to one side.

6 Disconnect the oil pressure switch wiring plug **(see illustration)**.

7 Undo the six pump retaining bolts, and pull the pump from its locating dowels **(see illustration)**.

8 Using a flat-bladed screwdriver, prise out the sealing ring which is fitted into the pump housing and discard it.

Inspection

9 With the pump removed from the vehicle, unscrew the cross-head screws and remove the oil pump inner cover.

10 Check the clearance between the inner and outer rotor teeth, and the outer rotor and the pump body.

11 Using a straight-edge across the pump body flange, measure the rotor endfloat **(see illustration)**.

12 If any of the clearances are outside the

13.6 Disconnect the oil pressure warning light switch

13.7 Oil pump retaining bolts (arrowed)

13.11 Use a straight-edge and feeler gauges to measure the rotor endfloat

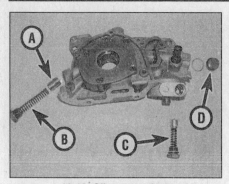

13.13 Oil pump valves

a) *Pressure regulator valve piston*
b) *Pressure regulator valve spring*
c) *Thermostatic valve*
d) *Blanking plug*

specified tolerance, renew the components as necessary. Note that the outer rotor face is marked for position.

13 The pressure regulator valve can be unscrewed from the pump body and the components cleaned and examined **(see illustration)**.

14 The oil pressure warning light switch is screwed into the rear of the pump. If it is defective it should be renewed as described in Chapter 5A.

15 The oil cooler thermostatic valve/filter bypass valve is screwed into the oil filter housing.

Refitting

16 Where removed, fit a new sealing ring to the oil pressure relief valve then refit the valve assembly to the cylinder block and tighten it to the specified torque setting.

17 Fit a new pump body oil seal, ensuring that the sealing lip is facing inwards, and press it squarely into the body using a tubular drift (such as a socket), which bears only on the hard outer edge of the seal. Press the seal into position so that it is flush with the body, then lubricate the oil seal lips with clean engine oil **(see illustration)**.

18 Lubricate the pump rotors with clean engine oil and refit them to the pump housing. Make sure that the marks on the faces of the

rotor are pointing rearwards away from the pump body **(see illustration)**.

19 Apply a smear of suitable sealant (available from your Vauxhall dealer) to the oil pump inner cover mating surface, and position the cover on the oil pump body.

20 Fit the inner cover retaining screws and tighten them to the specified torque.

21 Ensure the mating surfaces of the oil pump body and cylinder block are clean and dry and the locating dowels are in position. Remove all traces of sealant from the threads of the pump cover bolts.

22 Using a new gasket, refit the oil pump to the cylinder block, taking care not to damage the oil seal lips on the end of the crankshaft, and align the slots in the oil pump rotor with the corresponding drive lugs of the crankshaft **(see illustration)**. Tighten the retaining bolts to the specified torque.

23 The remainder of the refitting procedure is a reversal of the removal procedure, noting the following points:

a) *Tighten all bolts to the correct torques where specified.*
b) *Use new sealing washers when refitting the oil cooler pipe unions.*
c) *Check and if necessary top up the engine oil as described in Chapter 1.*
d) *The original crankshaft sprocket retaining bolt must not be re-used.*

14 Oil pump seal – renewal

1 Remove the crankshaft sprocket as described in Section 8.

2 Carefully punch or drill two small holes opposite each other in the oil seal. Screw a self-tapping screw into each, and pull on the screws with pliers to extract the seal.

Caution: Great care must be taken to avoid damage to the oil pump.

3 Clean the seal housing, and polish off any burrs or raised edges which may have caused the seal to fail in the first place.

4 Lubricate the lips of the new seal with clean engine oil, and press it into position using a

suitable tubular drift (such as a socket) which bears only on the hard outer edge of the seal. Take care not to damage the seal lips during fitting; note that the seal lips should face inwards.

5 Refit the crankshaft sprocket as described in Section 8.

15 Oil cooler – removal and refitting

Removal

1 With reference to Chapter 11, remove the front bumper.

2 Detach the oil pipes from the top and bottom of the oil cooler. Be prepared for oil spillage.

3 Undo the fastening bolt at the top of the cooler, and pull the assembly down and out of the bracket.

Refitting

4 Insert the cooler into the bracket, and tighten the retaining bolt to the specified torque.

5 Reconnect the upper and lower oil cooler pipes, tightening the unions to the specified torque.

6 Refit the front bumper as described in Chapter 11.

7 Check and if necessary top up the engine oil level as described in Chapter 1.

16 Flywheel – removal, inspection and refitting

Note: *New flywheel retaining bolts will be required on refitting.*

Removal

1 Remove the transmission as described in Chapter 7 then remove the clutch assembly as described in Chapter 6.

13.17 Position the oil seal so that the edge of the seal is flush with the oil pump body

13.18 The marks on the oil pump rotors must face away from the pump body

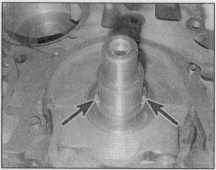

13.22 Align the slots in the oil pump rotor with the corresponding drive lugs of the crankshaft (arrowed)

2 Prevent the flywheel from turning by locking the ring gear teeth **(see illustration)**. Alternatively, bolt a strap between the flywheel and the cylinder block/crankcase. Make alignment marks between the flywheel and crankshaft using paint or a suitable marker pen.

3 Slacken and remove the retaining bolts then remove the flywheel. Do not drop it, as it is very heavy.

Inspection

4 Examine the flywheel for wear or chipping of the ring gear teeth. Renewal of the ring gear is possible but is not a task for the home mechanic; renewal requires the new ring gear to be heated (up to 180° to 230°C) to allow it to be fitted.

5 Examine the flywheel for scoring of the clutch face. If the clutch face is scored, the flywheel may be surface-ground, but renewal is preferable.

6 If there is any doubt about the condition of the flywheel, seek the advice of a Vauxhall dealer or engine reconditioning specialist. They will be able to advise if it is possible to recondition it or whether renewal is necessary.

Refitting

7 Clean the mating surfaces of the flywheel and crankshaft.

8 Apply a drop of locking compound to the threads of each of the new flywheel retaining bolts then refit the flywheel and install the new bolts. Note that one mounting hole in the flywheel is very slightly smaller than the other five. Consequently, only one of the flywheel bolts has a reduced diameter, and will fit into the hole. If the original flywheel is being refitted align the marks made prior to removal.

9 Lock the flywheel using the method employed on dismantling then, working in a diagonal sequence, evenly and progressively tighten the retaining bolts to the specified Stage 1 torque setting.

10 Once all bolts have been tightened to the Stage 1 torque, go around and tighten all bolts through the specified Stage 2 and Stage 3 angles. It is recommended that an angle-measuring gauge is used during the

16.2 Fabricate a locking tool to retain the flywheel

final stages of the tightening, to ensure accuracy. If a gauge is not available, use white paint to make alignment marks prior to tightening; the marks can then be used to check that the bolt has been rotated through the correct angle.

11 Refit the clutch as described in Chapter 6 then remove the locking tool and refit the transmission as described in Chapter 7.

17 Crankshaft oil seals – renewal

Right-hand (timing belt end) oil seal

1 Refer to Section 14.

Left-hand (flywheel end) oil seal

2 Remove the flywheel as described in Section 16.

3 Carefully punch or drill two small holes opposite each other in the oil seal. Screw a self-tapping screw into each and pull on the screws with pliers to extract the seal.

4 Clean the seal housing and polish off any burrs or raised edges which may have caused the seal to fail in the first place.

5 Lubricate the lips of the new seal with clean engine oil and ease it into position on the end of the shaft. Press the seal squarely into position until it is flush with the housing **(see illustration)**. If necessary, a suitable tubular

drift, such as a socket, which bears only on the hard outer edge of the seal can be used to tap the seal into position. Take great care not to damage the seal lips during fitting and ensure that the seal lips face inwards.

6 Wash off any traces of oil, then refit the flywheel as described in Section 16.

18 Engine/transmission mountings – inspection and renewal

Inspection

1 If improved access is required, raise the front of the car and support it securely on axle stands. Where necessary, undo the retaining bolts and remove the undertray from beneath the engine/transmission unit.

2 Check the mounting rubber to see if it is cracked, hardened or separated from the metal at any point; renew the mounting if any such damage or deterioration is evident.

3 Check that all the mountings' fasteners are securely tightened; use a torque wrench to check if possible.

4 Using a large screwdriver or a pry bar, check for wear in the mounting by carefully levering against it to check for free-play; where this is not possible, enlist the aid of an assistant to move the engine/transmission unit back-and-forth, or from side-to-side, while you watch the mounting. While some free-play is to be expected even from new components, excessive wear should be obvious. If excessive free-play is found, check first that the fasteners are correctly secured, then renew any worn components as described below.

Renewal

Note: *Before slackening any of the engine mounting bolts/nuts, the relative positions of the mountings to their various brackets should be marked to ensure correct alignment upon refitting.*

Right-hand mounting

5 With reference to Chapter 4A, remove the air cleaner housing.

6 Support the weight of the engine using a trolley jack with a block of wood placed on its head.

7 Remove the three bolts securing the right-hand engine mounting to the engine mounting support bracket **(see illustration)**.

8 Undo the bolts securing the mounting to the body, and withdraw the bracket with the mounting **(see illustration 18.7)**.

9 If required, the mounting can be separated by undoing the single bolt in the centre of the rubber element.

10 Refitting is a reversal of removal. Tighten the bolts to the specified torque.

Front mounting

11 Firmly apply the handbrake then jack up the front of the vehicle and support it on axle stands.

17.5 Position the oil seal so that its outer face is flush with the cylinder block

18.7 Remove the three bolts securing the engine mounting to the mounting support bracket

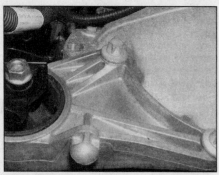

18.13 Withdraw the front engine mounting bolt

18.21 Remove the two bolts securing the mounting to the subframe

18.28 Unscrew the six bolts and remove the mounting bracket

12 Support the weight of the engine/transmission using a trolley jack with a block of wood placed on its head.

13 Slacken and remove the nut and washer securing the mounting to the bracket. Withdraw the bolt **(see illustration)**

14 Undo the bolts securing the mounting bracket to the transmission, then manoeuvre the mounting and bracket out of position. **Note:** *Take great care not to place any excess stress on the exhaust system when raising or lowering the engine. If necessary, disconnect the front pipe from the manifold (see Chapter 4A).*

15 Check all components for signs of wear or damage, and renew as necessary.

16 On reassembly, refit the mounting bracket and tighten its bolts to the specified torque.

17 Locate the mounting in the subframe, ensuring it is fitted the correct way up, and manoeuvre the engine/transmission into position. Refit the mounting bolts and new nuts. Tighten them to the specified torque.

18 Lower the vehicle to the ground.

Rear mounting

19 Firmly apply the handbrake then jack up the front of the vehicle and support it on axle stands.

20 Support the weight of the engine/transmission using a trolley jack with a block of wood placed on its head. Position the jack underneath the transmission and raise the transmission slightly to remove all load from the rear mounting.

21 Slacken and remove the two bolts securing the rear mounting to the subframe, and the nut securing the mounting to the transmission bracket, then manoeuvre the assembly out from underneath the vehicle **(see illustration)**.

22 On refitting, manoeuvre the mounting into position and refit the bolts/nuts securing it to the subframe. Ensure that the mounting is correctly engaged with the transmission bracket and fit the mounting-to-bracket retaining nut. Tighten the mounting bolts/nuts to their specified torque settings. Remove the jack from underneath the engine/transmission.

23 Lower the vehicle to the ground.

Left-hand mounting

24 Release the retaining clips and screws, and remove the engine undertray.

25 Remove the battery as described in Chapter 5A. **Note:** *Before disconnecting the battery, refer to 'Disconnecting the battery' in the reference section at the rear of this manual.*

26 Undo the retaining bolts, and remove the battery tray from the body.

27 Support the weight of the transmission using a trolley jack with a block of wood placed on its head.

28 Undo the six retaining bolts, and withdraw the mounting bracket from the transmission **(see illustration)**.

29 Slacken and remove the four Torx screws and manoeuvre the mounting out from the inner wing **(see illustration)**.

30 If required, separate the rubber element from the bracket by unscrewing the single retaining bolt **(see illustration)**.

31 Refitting is a reversal of removal. Ensure all bolts/nuts are tightened to their specified torques.

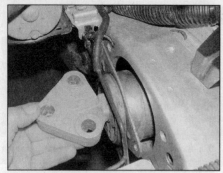

18.29 Remove the four Torx screws and withdraw the mounting

18.30 To separate the mounting, unscrew the single bolt

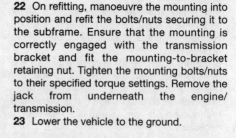

Chapter 2 Part B:
1.7 litre DOHC engine in-car repair procedures

Contents

Degrees of difficulty

| Easy, suitable for novice with little experience | | Fairly easy, suitable for beginner with some experience | | Fairly difficult, suitable for competent DIY mechanic | | Difficult, suitable for experienced DIY mechanic | 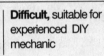 | Very difficult, suitable for expert DIY or professional | |

Specifications

Note: *Where specifications are given as N/A, no information was available at the time of writing.*
Refer to your Vauxhall dealer for the latest information available.

General

Engine type	Four-cylinder, in-line, water-cooled. Belt-driven double overhead camshaft, 16 valves
Manufacturer's engine code	Y17DT
Bore	79.0 mm
Stroke	86.0 mm
Capacity	1686 cc
Firing order	1-3-4-2 (No 1 cylinder at timing belt end)
Direction of crankshaft rotation	Clockwise (viewed from timing belt end of engine)
Compression ratio	18.4:1
Maximum power	55 kW at 4400 rpm
Maximum torque	165 Nm at 2400 rpm

Compression pressures

Standard	26.0 to 30.0 bar (377 to 435 psi)
Maximum difference between any two cylinders	1.5 bar (22 psi)

Valve clearances

Engine cold:	
Inlet and exhaust	0.4 ± 0.05 mm

Camshaft

Endfloat	N/A
Maximum permissible radial run-out	0.05 mm
Camshaft lift:	
Inlet valve	7.8 to 7.68 mm
Exhaust valve	7.95 to 7.77 mm
Bearing running clearance:	
Standard	N/A
Service limit	N/A

Lubrication system

Oil pump type	Rotor-type, driven by timing belt
Minimum permissible oil pressure at idle speed, with engine at operating temperature (oil temperature of at least 80°C)	1.27 bar (18 psi)

Oil pump clearances:

	Standard	Service limit
Outer rotor-to-body clearance	0.24 to 0.36 mm	0.40 mm
Inner-to-outer rotor clearance	0.13 to 0.15 mm	0.20 mm
Rotor endfloat	0.035 to 0.100 mm	0.150 mm

Torque wrench settings

	Nm	lbf ft
Alternator to alternator support bracket:		
M8 bolt:	19	14
M10 bolt:	46	34
Auxiliary belt tensioner to alternator support	50	37
Auxiliary belt guide roller to alternator support	38	28
Baffle plate-to-cylinder block bolts	19	14
Camshaft bearing cap nuts:		
M8 nuts:	21	15
M10 nuts:	43	32
Camshaft cover bolts	10	7
Camshaft housing	22	16
Camshaft sprocket	64	47
Camshaft thrust plate	8	6
Coolant pump:		
Pump retaining bolts	24	18
Pulley retaining bolts	10	7
Coolant pipe to cylinder block	95	70
Coolant temperature sensor	22	16
Connecting rod big-end bearing cap nuts*:		
Stage 1	25	18
Stage 2	Angle-tighten a further 100°	
Stage 3	Angle-tighten a further 15°	
Crankshaft pulse pickup	10	7
Crankshaft pulley bolts	20	15
Crankshaft oil seal housing bolts	10	7
Crankshaft sprocket bolt	196	145
Cylinder head bolts*:		
Stage 1	40	30
Stage 2	Angle-tighten a further 60°	
Stage 3	Angle-tighten a further 15°	
Stage 4	Angle-tighten a further 60°	
Stage 5	Angle-tighten a further 15°	
Engine/transmission mounting bolts:		
Right-hand mounting:		
Bracket-to-engine bolts	50	37
Mounting-to-body nuts	45	33
Mounting-to-bracket bolt	55	41
Left-hand mounting:		
Mounting-to-body bolts	20	15
Bracket-to-transmission bolts	35	26
Mounting-to-bracket bolts	55	41
Rear mounting:		
Mounting-to-bracket bolts	55	41
Mounting-to-subframe bolts	55	41
Bracket-to-transmission bolts	60	44
Front mounting:		
Mounting-to-transmission bolts	60	44
Mounting to subframe	55	41
Engine-to-transmission unit bolts:		
M10 bolts	40	30
M12 bolts	60	44
Engine control unit bracket to camshaft housing	10	7
Engine control unit to bracket	6	4
Engine transport shackles	25	18
Exhaust gas recirculation pipe bracket to camshaft housing	8	6
Exhaust gas recirculation valve to manifold	25	18
Flywheel bolts*:		
Stage 1	30	22
Stage 2	Angle-tighten a further 45 to 60°	

	Nm	lbf ft
Fuel return line to camshaft housing	15	11
Glow plug	20	15
Heat exchanger to oil filter housing	12	8
Injection pump control unit	10	7
Injection pump control unit bracket to cylinder block	48	35
Injection pump to bracket	19	14
Injection pump bracket to cylinder block	54	40
Injection pump to cylinder block	20	15
Injection pump sprocket nut	69	51
Injector nozzle bracket to camshaft housing	22	16
Injector pipe unions	23	17
Main bearing cap bolts	88	65
Oil dipstick guide tube bolts	10	7
Oil feed line to turbocharger	10	7
Oil filter housing cover	25	18
Oil filter housing to cylinder block	25	18
Oil pressure relief valve bolt	30	22
Oil pressure switch	20	15
Oil pump cover retaining bolts	10	7
Oil pump drive gear to pump	44	32
Oil pump pick-up/strainer bolts	19	14
Sump bolts:		
Main casting-to-block bolts	10	7
Sump pan-to-main casting bolts	10	7
Drain plug	78	58
Roadwheel bolts	110	81
Thermostat housing to cylinder head	24	18
Thermostat housing cover	24	18
Timing belt cover bolts	10	7
Timing belt idler pulley bolt	76	56
Timing belt tensioner pulley to cylinder block	38	28
Timing belt tensioner spring retainer to rear cover	10	7
Turbocharger to bracket	26	19
Turbocharger to manifold	26	19
Turbocharger oil feed line to cylinder block	10	7
Wiring tray to cylinder head	6	4

*Use new fasteners

1 General information

1 This Part of Chapter 2 describes those repair procedures that can reasonably be carried out on the 1.7 litre DOHC diesel engine while it remains in the car. If the engine has been removed from the car and is being dismantled as described in Part D, any preliminary dismantling procedures can be ignored.

2 Note that, while it may be possible physically to overhaul items such as the piston/connecting rod assemblies while the engine is in the car, such tasks are not normally carried out as separate operations. Usually, several additional procedures (not to mention the cleaning of components and of oilways) have to be carried out. For this reason, all such tasks are classed as major overhaul procedures, and are described in Part D of this Chapter.

3 Part D describes the removal of the engine/transmission unit from the vehicle, and the full overhaul procedures that can then be carried out.

Engine description

4 The 1.7 litre (1686 cc) diesel engine is of the sixteen-valve, in-line four-cylinder, double overhead camshaft (DOHC) type, mounted transversely at the front of the car with the transmission attached to its left-hand end.

5 The crankshaft runs in five main bearings. Thrustwashers are fitted to No 2 main bearing shell (upper half) to control crankshaft endfloat.

6 The connecting rods rotate on horizontally-split bearing shells at their big-ends. The pistons are attached to the connecting rods by gudgeon pins, which are a sliding fit in the connecting rod small-end eyes and retained by circlips. The aluminium-alloy pistons are fitted with three piston rings – two compression rings and an oil control ring.

7 The cylinder block is made of cast iron and the cylinder bores are an integral part of the block. On this type of engine the cylinder bores are sometimes referred to as having dry liners.

8 The inlet and exhaust valves are each closed by coil springs, and operate in guides pressed into the cylinder head.

9 The inlet camshaft is driven by the crankshaft by a timing belt and rotates directly in the camshaft housing. The exhaust camshaft is driven by the inlet camshaft via a spur gear. The camshafts operate the valves via followers, which are situated directly below the camshafts. Valve clearances are adjusted using shims which are fitted between the camshafts and followers.

10 Lubrication is by means of an oil pump, which is driven by the timing belt. It draws oil through a strainer located in the sump, and then forces it through an externally-mounted filter into galleries in the cylinder block/crankcase. From there, the oil is distributed to the crankshaft (main bearings) and camshaft. The big-end bearings are supplied with oil via internal drillings in the crankshaft, while the camshaft bearings also receive a pressurised supply. The camshaft lobes and valves are lubricated by splash, as are all other engine components. An oil cooler is fitted to keep the oil temperature stable under arduous operating conditions.

Repair operations possible with the engine in the car

11 The following work can be carried out with the engine in the car:

a) Compression pressure testing.
b) Camshaft cover – removal and refitting.
c) Timing belt cover – removal and refitting.
d) Timing belt – removal and refitting.
e) Timing belt tensioner and sprockets – removal and refitting.
f) Valve clearances – checking and adjustment.

g) Camshaft and followers – removal, inspection and refitting.

h) Cylinder head – removal and refitting.

i) Connecting rods and pistons – removal and refitting*.

j) Sump – removal and refitting.

k) Oil pump – removal, overhaul and refitting.

l) Oil cooler – removal and refitting.

m) Crankshaft oil seals – renewal.

n) Engine/transmission mountings – inspection and renewal.

o) Flywheel – removal, inspection and refitting.

p) Camshaft housing – removal and refitting.

* Although the operation marked with an asterisk can be carried out with the engine in the car after removal of the sump, it is better for the engine to be removed, in the interests of cleanliness and improved access. For this reason, the procedure is described in Chapter 2D.

2 Compression test – description and interpretation

Compression test

Note: A compression tester specifically designed for diesel engines must be used for this test.

1 When engine performance is down, or if misfiring occurs which cannot be attributed to the fuel system, a compression test can provide diagnostic clues as to the engine's condition. If the test is performed regularly, it can give warning of trouble before any other symptoms become apparent.

2 A compression tester specifically intended for diesel engines must be used, because of the higher pressures involved. The tester is connected to an adapter which screws into the glow plug or injector hole. On these models, an adapter suitable for use in the glow plug holes will be required, due to the design of the injectors. It is unlikely to be worthwhile buying such a tester for occasional use, but it may be possible to borrow or hire one – if not, have the test performed by a garage.

3 Unless specific instructions to the contrary are supplied with the tester, observe the following points:

a) The battery must be in a good state of charge, the air filter must be clean, and the engine should be at normal operating temperature.

b) All the glow plugs should be removed before starting the test (see Chapter 5B).

c) Release the retaining clip and disconnect the wiring connector from the fuel injection pump control unit (see Chapter 4A) to prevent the engine from running or fuel from being discharged.

4 There is no need to hold the accelerator pedal down during the test, because the diesel engine air inlet is not throttled.

5 Crank the engine on the starter motor; after one or two revolutions, the compression pressure should build up to a maximum figure, and then stabilise. Record the highest reading obtained.

6 Repeat the test on the remaining cylinders, recording the pressure in each.

7 All cylinders should produce very similar pressures; any difference greater than that specified indicates the existence of a fault. Note that the compression should build-up quickly in a healthy engine; low compression on the first stroke, followed by gradually-increasing pressure on successive strokes, indicates worn piston rings. A low compression reading on the first stroke, which does not build-up during successive strokes, indicates leaking valves or a blown head gasket (a cracked head could also be the cause). Deposits on the undersides of the valve heads can also cause low compression.

Note: The cause of poor compression is less easy to establish on a diesel engine than on a petrol one. The effect of introducing oil into the cylinders ('wet' testing) is not conclusive, because there is a risk that the oil will sit in the recess on the piston crown instead of passing to the rings.

8 On completion of the test, reconnect the injection pump wiring connector then refit the glow plugs as described in Chapter 5B.

Leakdown test

9 A leakdown test measures the rate at which compressed air fed into the cylinder is lost. It is an alternative to a compression test, and in many ways it is better, since the escaping air provides easy identification of where pressure loss is occurring (piston rings, valves or head gasket).

10 The equipment needed for leakdown testing is unlikely to be available to the home mechanic. If poor compression is suspected, have the test performed by a suitably-equipped garage.

3 Top dead centre (TDC) for No 1 piston – locating

Note: If the engine is to be locked in position with No 1 piston at TDC on its compression stroke then a M6 and M8 bolt will be required.

1 In its travel up and down its cylinder bore, Top Dead Centre (TDC) is the highest point that each piston reaches as the crankshaft rotates. While each piston reaches TDC both at the top of the compression stroke and again at the top of the exhaust stroke, for the purpose of timing the engine, TDC refers to the piston position (usually number 1) at the top of its compression stroke.

2 Number 1 piston (and cylinder) is at the right-hand (timing belt) end of the engine, and its TDC position is located as follows. Note that the crankshaft rotates clockwise when viewed from the right-hand side of the car.

3 Disconnect the battery negative terminal. **Note:** Before disconnecting the battery, refer to 'Disconnecting the battery' in the reference section at the rear of this manual. To improve access to the crankshaft pulley, apply the handbrake, then jack up the front of the vehicle and support it on axle stands. Remove the right-hand front wheel and where necessary, undo the retaining screws/clips and remove the undertray from beneath the engine/transmission unit.

4 Remove the timing belt upper cover as described in Section 6.

5 Using a socket and extension bar on the crankshaft sprocket bolt, rotate the crankshaft until the notch on the crankshaft pulley rim is aligned with the pointer on the base of the oil pump cover **(see illustration)**. Once the mark is correctly aligned, No 1 and 4 pistons are at TDC.

6 To determine which piston is at TDC on its compression stroke, check the position of the timing holes in the camshaft and injection pump sprockets. When No 1 piston is at TDC on its compression stroke, both sprocket holes will be aligned with the threaded holes in the cylinder head/block, and both exhaust camshaft lobes for cylinder No 1 are pointing upwards if viewed through the oil filler hole. If the timing holes are 180° out of alignment then No 4 cylinder is at TDC on its compression stroke; rotate the crankshaft through a further complete turn (360°) to bring No 1 cylinder to TDC on its compression stroke.

7 With No 1 piston at TDC on its compression stroke, if necessary, the camshaft and fuel injection pump sprockets can be locked in position. Secure the camshaft sprocket in position by screwing a M6 bolt into the hole in the cylinder head and lock the injection pump sprocket in position by screwing a M8 bolt into the cylinder block **(see illustrations)**.

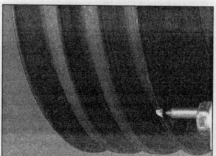

3.5 Align the timing mark on the crankshaft pulley with the pointer on the oil pump cover to bring No 1 piston to TDC

3.7a The camshaft sprocket can be locked using a 6 mm bolt . . .

3.7b . . . and the injection pump sprocket by an 8 mm bolt

4.5 Slacken the fuel injector pipe unions

4.12a Fit the seal to the cover groove

4 Camshaft cover –
removal and refitting

Removal

1 With reference to Chapter 4A, remove the air cleaner housing and air intake trunking complete with the hot film air mass meter.

2 Remove the engine control unit from above the camshaft cover, as described in Chapter 4A, Section 8.

3 Unclip the wiring loom cable tie, undo the retaining screws/nut and remove the engine control unit bracket.

4 Undo the bolt, release the wiring loom retaining clip, and remove the engine transport shackle from the right-hand rear of the cylinder head. Slacken the bolt securing the left-hand rear shackle.

5 Slacken the fuel injector pipe unions located at the fuel injection pump (see illustration). Access to the unions on the pump is limited. We found it necessary to remove the oil cooler/filter housing retaining bolt, and prise the foam filling from between the injection pump and filter housing.

6 Undo the injector pipe unions at the injectors.

7 Remove the retaining bolts, and lift away the injector outer seals.

8 Undo the wiring tray retaining bolt from the end of the cylinder head, release the two

4.12b Check the O-ring on the underside of the cover

retaining clips, and lift the tray out of the way (see illustration 6.7).

9 Unscrew the bolts securing the timing belt upper cover to the camshaft housing.

10 Remove the retaining bolts and lift away the camshaft cover, complete with seal.

11 Examine the cover seal for signs of damage or deterioration and renew if necessary.

Refitting

12 Ensure the cover and cylinder head surfaces are clean and dry then fit the seal to the cover groove. Check the condition of the O-ring seal on the underside of the cover and renew if necessary (see illustrations).

13 Apply sealant to the mating surfaces. Ensure that the oil borehole at the right-hand end of the exhaust camshaft is not covered in sealant (see illustrations).

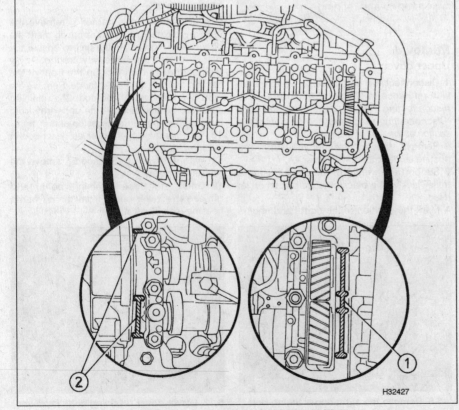

H32427

4.13a Apply sealant to areas (1) and (2)

4.13b Ensure the borehole is not covered in sealant

4.15 The injector seals are marked 'upper' and 'outside'

5.3 Remove the small bolts securing the pulley to the sprocket

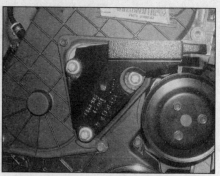

6.5 Undo the bolts and separate the engine mounting support bracket from the mounting adapter

14 Carefully lower the cover into position, ensuring the seal remains correctly seated. Refit the timing belt upper cover and camshaft cover retaining bolts and tighten them to the specified torque.

15 The remainder of the reassembly procedure is a reversal of removal, noting the following points:

a) Ensure all bolts are tightened to the correct torque setting where specified.

b) The injector outer seals are marked 'upper' and 'outer'. Fit the seals and make sure that the centre of the seal is pushed over the injector taper (see illustration).

c) After starting the engine, check for leaks.

5 Crankshaft pulley – removal and refitting

Removal

1 Apply the handbrake, then jack up the front of the car and support it on axle stands. Remove the right-hand roadwheel and where necessary, undo the retaining screws and remove the undertray from beneath the engine/transmission unit.

2 Remove the auxiliary drivebelt as described in Chapter 1. Prior to removal, mark the direction of rotation on the belt to ensure the belt is refitted the same way around.

3 Slacken and remove the small retaining bolts securing the pulley to the crankshaft sprocket and remove the pulley from the

engine (see illustration). If necessary, prevent crankshaft rotation by holding the sprocket retaining bolt with a suitable socket.

Refitting

4 Refit the pulley to the crankshaft sprocket, aligning the pulley hole with the sprocket locating pin. Refit the pulley retaining bolts, tightening the to the specified torque.

5 Refit the auxiliary drivebelt as described in Chapter 1 using the mark made prior to removal to ensure the belt is fitted the correct way around.

6 Refit the engine undertray and roadwheel, then lower the car to the ground and tighten the wheel bolts to the specified torque.

6 Timing belt covers – removal and refitting

Removal

Upper cover

1 Disconnect the battery negative terminal, with reference to Chapter 5A. Note: Before disconnecting the battery, refer to 'Disconnecting the battery' in the reference section at the rear of this manual.

2 Remove the air cleaner housing and ducting as described in Chapter 4A.

3 Support the weight of the engine using a trolley jack with a block of wood placed on its head.

4 Mark the position of the right-hand engine

mounting to the support bracket, and undo the three securing bolts (see illustration 20.7).

5 Undo the retaining bolts and separate the engine mounting support bracket from the engine block mounting adapter (see illustration).

6 With reference to Chapter 5A if necessary, disconnect the wiring plug and connection from the alternator.

7 Undo the Torx retaining bolt, release the wiring tray and loom retaining clips by squeezing the tangs of the retaining clips, and remove the wiring tray from the right-hand end of the cylinder head (see illustration).

8 Release the hoses from the upper cover clips, remove the eight upper cover retaining bolts and withdraw the cover. Note the cover bolts are of different lengths (see illustration).

Lower cover

9 With reference to Chapter 1, remove the auxiliary drivebelt. Prior to removal, mark the direction of rotation on the belt to ensure the belt is refitted the same way around. Apply the handbrake, then jack up the front of the car and support it on axle stands. Remove the right-hand roadwheel and undo the retaining screws/clips and remove the undertray from beneath the engine/transmission unit.

10 Remove the upper cover as described in paragraphs 1 to 8.

11 With reference to Section 5, remove the crankshaft pulley.

12 Undo the three retaining bolts, and remove the lower cover from the oil pump housing (see illustration).

6.7 Undo the Torx bolt and release the wiring tray retaining clips (arrowed)

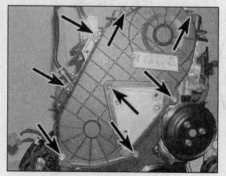

6.8 Remove the eight upper timing belt cover retaining bolts (arrowed)

6.12 Lower cover retaining bolts (arrowed)

6.13a Manoeuvre the engine mounting adapter from the timing belt area (arrowed)

6.13b Temporarily refit the timing belt tensioner lower retaining bolt (arrowed)

6.17 Rear timing belt cover bolts

13 Manoeuvre the engine mounting adapter out from the timing belt area. Temporarily refit the bolt retaining the timing belt tensioner pulley bracket **(see illustrations)**.

Rear cover

14 Remove timing belt as described in Section 7.

15 With reference to Section 8, remove the timing belt tension and guide rollers, camshaft sprocket and injection pump sprocket.

16 Detach the tensioner spring retainer.

17 Undo the four retaining bolts, and remove the rear timing belt cover **(see illustration)**.

Refitting

18 Refitting is the reverse of removal, ensuring all retaining bolts are tightened to the specified torque.

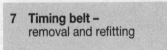

7   Timing belt –
removal and refitting

Note: The timing belt must be removed and refitted with the engine cold.

Removal

1 Position No 1 cylinder at TDC on its compression stroke as described in Section 3. Lock the camshaft and injection pump sprockets in position by screwing the bolts into the threaded holes in the cylinder head/block.

2 Remove the crankshaft pulley as described in Section 5.

3 Unbolt and remove the timing belt upper and lower covers with reference to Section 6.

4 Slacken the timing belt tensioner retaining bolt then carefully unhook the tensioner spring from its locating pins **(see illustration)**.

5 Slide the timing belt off its sprockets and remove it from the engine. If the belt is to be re-used, use white paint or similar to mark the direction of rotation on the belt. **Do not** rotate the crankshaft until the timing belt has been refitted.

6 Check the timing belt carefully for any signs of uneven wear, splitting or oil contamination, and renew it if there is the slightest doubt about its condition. If the engine is undergoing an overhaul and is approaching the specified interval for belt renewal (see Chapter 1) renew the belt as a matter of course, regardless of its apparent condition. If signs of oil contamination are found, trace the source of the oil leak and rectify it, then wash down the engine timing belt area and all related components to remove all traces of oil.

Refitting

7 On reassembly, thoroughly clean the timing belt sprockets and ensure the camshaft and injection pump sprockets are locked correctly in position. Temporarily refit the crankshaft pulley to the sprocket and check that the pulley cut-out is still aligned with the pointer on the oil pump cover; the mark on the

crankshaft sprocket should also be aligned with the mark on the oil pump cover **(see illustration)**.

8 Remove the pulley and fit the timing belt over the crankshaft, oil pump, injection pump and camshaft sprockets, ensuring that the belt rear run is taut (ie, all slack is on the tensioner pulley side of the belt). Do not twist the belt sharply while refitting it. Ensure that the belt teeth are correctly seated centrally in the sprockets, and that the timing marks remain in alignment. If a used belt is being refitted, ensure that the arrow mark made on removal points in the normal direction of rotation, as before **(see illustration)**.

9 Tension the belt by refitting the tensioner pulley spring, ensuring it is correctly located on its pins.

10 Check that the crankshaft sprocket timing mark is still correctly positioned then unscrew the locking bolts from the injection pump and camshaft sprockets.

11 Slacken the tensioner pulley retaining bolt then rotate the crankshaft pulley approximately 60° **backwards** (anti-clockwise) to automatically adjust the timing belt tension. Hold the crankshaft pulley stationary and securely tighten the tensioner pulley retaining bolt.

12 Rotate the crankshaft smoothly through two complete turns (720°) in the normal direction of rotation to settle the timing belt in position. Realign the crankshaft sprocket timing mark and check that the camshaft and

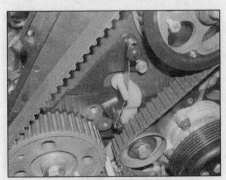

7.4 Unhook the tensioner spring

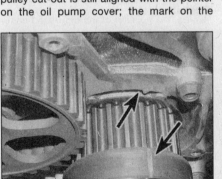

7.7 Align the notch on the crankshaft sprocket with the pointer on the oil pump cover (arrowed)

7.8 Timing belt routing

injection pump sprocket locking bolts can be refitted.

13 Slacken the tensioner pulley retaining bolt then rotate the crankshaft pulley approximately 60° **backwards** (anti-clockwise) to automatically adjust the timing belt tension. Hold the crankshaft pulley stationary and tighten the tensioner pulley retaining bolts to the specified torque.

14 Return the crankshaft to TDC and make a final check that the sprocket timing mark/holes are correctly positioned.

15 Refit the timing belt covers and the crankshaft pulley as described in Sections 5 and 6.

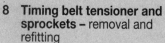

8 Timing belt tensioner and sprockets – removal and refitting

Camshaft sprocket

Removal

1 Remove the timing belt as described in Section 7. Prior to attempting to unscrew the sprocket retaining bolt, turn the crankshaft 60° **backwards** (anti-clockwise) to prevent any accidental piston-to-valve contact.

2 Screw the sprocket locking bolt fully into position then slacken and remove the sprocket retaining bolt, using the locking bolt to prevent rotation.

3 Unscrew the locking bolt and remove the sprocket from the end of the camshaft, noting which way around it is fitted **(see illustration)**. If the sprocket locating pin is a loose fit, remove it from the camshaft end and store it with the sprocket for safe-keeping.

Refitting

4 Ensure the locating pin is in position then refit the sprocket to the camshaft end aligning its locating hole with the pin.

5 Refit the sprocket retaining bolt then align the timing hole with the cylinder head hole and screw in the locking bolt. Use the locking bolt to retain the sprocket and tighten the sprocket bolts to the specified torque. Rotate the crankshaft 60° **forwards** (clockwise) until the groove in the crankshaft timing belt

8.3 Remove the camshaft sprocket

sprocket is at '12 o'clock' and aligns with the cast-in mark on the oil pump cover.

6 Refit the timing belt as described in Section 7.

Injection pump sprocket

Removal

7 Remove the timing belt as described in Section 7.

8 Screw the sprocket locking bolt fully into position to prevent rotation. Alternatively, a suitable tool can be made using two lengths of steel strip (one long, the other short), and three nuts and bolts; one nut and bolt forms the pivot of a forked tool, with the remaining two nuts and bolts at the tips of the 'forks' to engage with the sprocket spokes **(see illustration)**.

9 Slacken and remove the sprocket retaining nut.

10 Remove the sprocket from the injection pump shaft, noting which way around it is fitted. If the Woodruff key is a loose fit in the pump shaft, remove it and store it with the sprocket for safe-keeping. **Note:** *The sprocket is a tapered-fit on the injection pump shaft and in some cases a suitable puller may be needed to free it from the shaft* **(see illustration)**.

Refitting

11 Ensure the Woodruff key is correctly fitted to the pump shaft then refit the sprocket, aligning the sprocket groove with the key **(see illustration)**.

8.8 Using a sprocket holding tool to prevent rotation as the injection pump sprocket nut is slackened

12 Refit the retaining nut and tighten it to the specified torque whilst using the holding tool/locking bolt to prevent rotation.

13 If not already done, align the sprocket timing hole with the threaded hole in the cylinder block and screw in the locking bolt.

14 Refit the timing belt as described in Section 7.

Crankshaft sprocket

Removal

15 Remove the timing belt as described in Section 7.

16 Slacken the crankshaft sprocket retaining bolt. To prevent crankshaft rotation, have an assistant select top gear and apply the brakes firmly. If the engine is removed from the vehicle it will be necessary to lock the flywheel (see Section 18).

17 Unscrew the retaining bolt and washer and remove the crankshaft sprocket from the end of the crankshaft. If the sprocket is a tight fit, draw it off of the crankshaft using a suitable puller **(see illustration)**. If the Woodruff key is a loose fit in the crankshaft, remove it and store it with the sprocket for safe-keeping.

18 Slide the flanged spacer off of the crankshaft, noting which way around it is fitted.

Refitting

19 Refit the flanged spacer to the crankshaft

8.10 Using a puller to remove the injection pump sprocket

8.11 Align the keyway in the sprocket with the Woodruff key in the shaft

8.17 Slide the sprocket from the shaft

8.19 Fit the flanged spacer with the convex side away from the oil pump cover

8.21 Refit the sprocket retaining bolt and washer

8.26 Use a socket and extension bar on one of the oil pump cover bolts to prevent the sprocket from turning

with its convex surface facing away from the oil pump housing **(see illustration)**.
20 Ensure the Woodruff key is correctly fitted then slide on the crankshaft sprocket aligning its groove with the key.
21 Refit the retaining bolt and washer then lock the crankshaft by the method used on removal, and tighten the sprocket retaining bolt to the specified torque setting **(see illustration)**.
22 Refit the timing belt as described in Section 7.

Oil pump sprocket

Removal

23 Remove the timing belt as described in Section 7.
24 Prevent the oil pump sprocket from rotating using a socket and extension bar

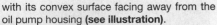

fitted to one of the oil pump cover bolts then slacken and remove the sprocket retaining nut.
25 Remove the sprocket from the oil pump shaft, noting which way around it is fitted.

Refitting

26 Refit the sprocket, aligning it with the flat on the pump shaft, and fit the retaining nut. Tighten the sprocket retaining nut to the specified torque, using the socket and extension bar to prevent rotation **(see illustration)**.
27 Refit the timing belt as described in Section 7.

Tensioner assembly

Removal

28 Remove the timing belt as described in Section 7.
29 Carefully unhook the tensioner spring, unscrew the retaining bolts and remove the tensioner assembly from the engine **(see illustration)**.

Refitting

30 Fit the tensioner assembly to the engine tightening its retaining bolts by hand only. Refit the tensioner spring.
31 Refit the timing belt as described in Section 7.

Idler pulley

Removal

32 Remove the timing belt as described in Section 7.

33 Slacken and remove the retaining bolt and remove the idler pulley from the engine **(see illustration)**.

Refitting

34 Refit the idler pulley and tighten the retaining bolt to the specified torque.
35 Refit the timing belt as described in Section 7.

9 Camshaft oil seal – renewal

1 Remove the camshaft sprocket as described in Section 8.
2 Carefully punch or drill a small hole in the oil seal. Screw in a self-tapping screw, and pull on the screw with pliers to extract the seal **(see illustration)**.
3 Clean the seal housing, and polish off any burrs or raised edges which may have caused the seal to fail in the first place.
4 Lubricate the lips of the new seal with clean engine oil, and press it into position using a suitable tubular drift (such as a socket) which bears only on the hard outer edge of the seal. Take care not to damage the seal lips during fitting; note that the seal lips should face inwards **(see illustration)**.
5 Refit the camshaft sprocket as described in Section 8.

8.29 Timing belt tensioner spring

8.33 Timing belt idler pulley retaining bolt

9.2 Pull the screw to extract the seal

9.4 Press the oil seal into position using a tubular drift such as a socket

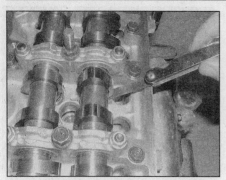

10.7 With the camshaft lobe pointing away from the follower measure the clearance

10.14 Carefully depress the follower and slide the shim out

10.15 The thickness of each shim should be stamped on one of its surfaces

10 Valve clearances – checking and adjustment

Checking

1 The importance of having the valve clearances correctly adjusted cannot be overstressed, as they vitally affect the performance of the engine. The engine must be cold for the check to be accurate. The clearances are checked as follows.

2 Apply the handbrake, then jack up the front of the car and support it on axle stands. Remove the right-hand front roadwheel to gain access to the crankshaft pulley. Where fitted release the retaining clips/screws and remove the engine undertray.

3 Remove the camshaft cover as described in Section 4, and with reference to Chapter 4A, remove the fuel injectors.

4 Using a socket and extension on the crankshaft sprocket bolt, rotate the crankshaft in the normal direction of rotation (clockwise when viewed from the right-hand end of the engine) until the notch on the crankshaft pulley is correctly aligned with the pointer on the base of the oil pump cover.

5 Now rotate the crankshaft in the normal direction (clockwise) until the inlet camshaft lobes for No 1 cylinder (nearest the timing belt end of the engine) and the exhaust camshaft lobes for No 3 cylinder are pointing away from the followers. This indicates that these valves are completely closed, and the clearances can be checked.

6 On a piece of paper, draw the outline of the engine with the cylinders numbered from the timing belt end. Show the position of each valve, together with the specified valve clearance. Note that the clearance for both the inlet and exhaust valves is the same.

7 With the cam lobes positioned as described in paragraph 5, using feeler blades, measure the clearance between the base of both No 1 cylinder inlet cam lobes and No 3 cylinder exhaust cam lobes and their followers. Record the clearances on the paper (see illustration).

8 Rotate the crankshaft pulley through a half a turn (180°) to position No 3 cylinder inlet camshaft lobes and No 4 cylinder exhaust camshaft lobes pointing away from their followers. Measure the clearance between the base of the camshaft lobes and their followers and record the clearances on the paper.

9 Rotate the crankshaft pulley through a half a turn (180°) to position No 2 cylinder exhaust camshaft lobes and No 4 cylinder inlet camshaft lobes pointing away from their followers. Measure the clearance between the base of the camshaft lobes and their followers and record the clearances on the paper.

10 Rotate the crankshaft pulley through a half a turn (180°) to position No 1 cylinder exhaust camshaft lobes and No 2 cylinder inlet camshaft lobes pointing away from their followers. Measure the clearance between the base of the camshaft lobes and their followers and record the clearances on the paper.

11 If all the clearances are correct, refit the cylinder head cover (see Section 4), and injectors (see Chapter 4A), then refit the roadwheel and lower the vehicle to the ground and tighten the wheel bolts to the specified torque. If any clearance measured is not correct, adjustment must be carried out as described in the following paragraphs.

Adjustment

12 Rotate the crankshaft pulley until the lobe of the valve to be adjusted is pointing directly away from the follower. Note: Ensure that the crankshaft is **not** positioned at TDC, as when a valve follower is depressed to remove the shim, the valve will strike the piston.

13 Rotate the follower until the groove on its upper edge is facing towards the front of the engine (exhaust followers), or rear of the engine (inlet followers).

14 In the absence of the special Vauxhall tool (KM-6090), position a large flat-bladed screwdriver between the edge of the follower and the base of the camshaft. Use the screwdriver to carefully depress the follower until there is enough clearance to allow the shim to be slid out from between the follower and camshaft (a magnetic tool is particularly useful for this task) (see illustration).

15 Clean the shim, and measure its thickness with a micrometer. The shims carry thickness markings, but wear may have reduced the original thickness, so be sure to check (see illustration).

16 Add the measured clearance of the valve to the thickness of the original shim then subtract the specified valve clearance from this figure. This will give you the thickness of the shim required. For example:

Clearance measured of valve	0.35 mm
Plus thickness of the original shim	2.70 mm
Equals	3.05 mm
Minus clearance required	0.40 mm
Thickness of shim required	2.65 mm

17 Obtain the correct thickness of shim required and lubricate it with clean engine oil. Carefully depress the follower and slide the shim into position, with the thickness number downwards, ensuring it is correctly located.

> **HAYNES HINT** *It may be possible to correct the clearances by moving the shims around between the valves. Keep a note of all the shim thicknesses to assist valve clearance adjustment when they need to be done again.*

18 Repeat the procedure given in paragraphs 12 to 17 on the remaining valves which require adjustment.

19 Rotate the crankshaft a few times to settle all shims in position the recheck the valve clearances before refitting the camshaft cover (see Section 4), and fuel injectors (Chapter 4A)

20 Refit the roadwheel then lower the vehicle to the ground and tighten the wheel bolts to the specified torque.

11 Camshaft and followers – removal, inspection and refitting

Removal

1 Remove the camshaft cover as described in Section 4.

2 Remove the fuel injectors as described in Chapter 4A.

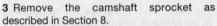

11.5 Insert a screw through the fixed gear and into the backlash compensating gear (arrowed)

11.9 Lift out the cam followers and shims

11.13 Ensure each shim is correctly located

3 Remove the camshaft sprocket as described in Section 8.

4 Undo the nuts and remove the No 5 bearing cap from the left-hand (gearbox) end of the camshafts.

5 The exhaust camshaft gear incorporates a backlash compensating gear. This must now be locked to the fixed exhaust camshaft gear by inserting a suitably-sized bolt/rod into the hole on the inboard face of the fixed gear, and through into the backlash compensating gear. This prevents the spring preload of the compensating gear being lost when either camshaft is removed **(see illustration)**.

6 Working in a spiral pattern from the outside in, slacken the remaining camshaft bearing cap retaining nuts by one turn at a time, to relieve the pressure of the valve springs on the bearing caps gradually and evenly. Once the valve spring pressure has been relieved, the nuts can be fully unscrewed and removed. *Caution: If the bearing cap nuts are carelessly slackened, the bearing caps might break. If any bearing cap breaks then the complete cylinder head assembly must be renewed; the bearing caps are matched to the head and are not available separately.*

7 Remove the bearing caps, noting each caps correct fitted location. The bearing caps are numbered 1 to 5 and the arrow on each cap points towards the timing belt end of the engine.

8 Lift the camshafts out of the cylinder head.

9 Obtain sixteen small, clean plastic containers, and label them for identification. Alternatively, divide a larger container into compartments. Lift the followers and shims out from the top of the cylinder head and store each one in its respective fitted position. Make sure the followers and shims are not mixed to ensure the valve clearances remain correctly adjusted on refitting **(see illustration)**.

Inspection

10 Examine the camshaft bearing surfaces and camshaft lobes for signs of wear ridges and scoring. Renew the camshaft if any of these conditions are apparent. Examine the condition of the bearing surfaces both on the camshaft journals and in the cylinder head. If the head bearing surfaces are worn excessively, the cylinder head will need to be renewed.

11 Support the camshaft end journals on V-blocks, and measure the run-out at the centre journal using a dial gauge. If the run-out exceeds the specified limit, the camshaft should be renewed.

12 Examine the followers and their bores in the cylinder head for signs of wear or damage. If any follower is visibly worn it should be renewed.

Refitting

13 Where removed, lubricate the followers with clean engine oil and carefully insert each one into its original location in the cylinder head. Ensure each shim is correctly located in the top of the its relevant follower **(see illustration)**.

14 Rotate the crankshaft approximately 60° **backwards** (anti-clockwise) as a precaution against accidental piston-to-valve contact. Lubricate the camshaft followers with clean engine oil then lay the camshafts in position. Check that the exhaust camshaft backlash compensating gear is still locked to the fixed gear. Ensure that the mark on the outer face exhaust camshaft gear lies between the two marks on the outer face of the inlet camshaft gear, and that the marks are approximately level with the upper edge of the camshaft housing **(see illustration)**. **Note:** *If the exhaust camshaft is being renewed, it will be necessary to obtain Vauxhall tool No KM 6092, and pre-tension the backlash compensating gear prior to installation.*

15 Ensure the mating surfaces of the bearing caps and camshaft housing are clean and dry and lubricate the camshaft journals and lobes with clean engine oil.

16 Apply a smear of suitable sealant (available from Vauxhall dealers) to the areas of the camshaft housing No 1 bearing cap mating surface **(see illustration)**.

17 Refit the No 1 to 4 camshaft bearing caps in their original locations on the cylinder head. The caps are numbered 1 to 5 (No 1 cap being at the timing belt end of the engine) and the arrow cast onto the top of each cap should point towards the timing belt end of the engine **(see illustration)**.

18 Refit the No 1 to 4 bearing cap nuts, tightening them by hand only.

11.14 Align the camshaft gear marks (arrowed)

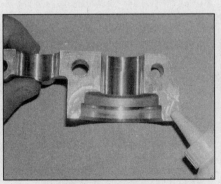

11.16 Apply a smear of sealant to the No 1 camshaft-bearing cap

11.17 The arrows on the camshaft bearing caps should point towards the timing belt end of the engine

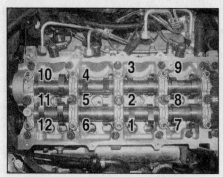

11.20 Camshaft bearing cap tightening
sequence

12.1 Remove the two bolts securing the rear
timing belt cover to the camshaft housing

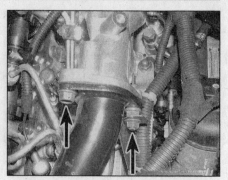

12.3 Undo the charge air pipe bolts
(arrowed)

19 Remove the bolt/rod locking the backlash compensating gear to the exhaust camshaft fixed gear, and refit the No 5 camshaft bearing cap.

20 Working in the specified sequence, tighten the nuts by one turn at a time to gradually impose the pressure of the valve springs evenly on the bearing caps (see illustration). Repeat this sequence until all bearing caps are in contact with the cylinder head then go around in the specified sequence and tighten them to the specified torque.

Caution: If the bearing cap bolts are carelessly tightened, the bearing caps might break. If any bearing cap breaks then the complete cylinder head assembly must be renewed; the bearing caps are matched to the head and are not available separately.

21 Fit a new camshaft oil seal as described in Section 9.

22 Refit the camshaft sprocket and timing belt as described in Sections 7 and 8.

23 Check the valve clearances as described in Section 10, then refit the camshaft cover as described in Section 4, and the fuel injectors as described in Chapter 4A.

12 Camshaft housing – removal and refitting

Removal

1 Remove the camshaft sprocket as described in Section 8, and the camshaft cover as described in Section 4. Remove the

two bolts securing the rear timing belt cover to the camshaft housing (see illustration).

2 With reference to Chapter 4A, remove the fuel injectors.

3 Remove the bolts securing the charge air pipe and bracket to the left-hand end of the camshaft housing and inlet manifold. Undo the retaining clips and release the pipe from the inlet trunking (see illustration).

4 Undo the bolts securing the EGR (exhaust gas recirculation) pipe to the exhaust manifold and the left-hand end of the camshaft housing. Undo the large union at the EGR valve, and remove the pipe (see illustrations). It should now be possible to remove the left-hand rear transport eye from the camshaft housing.

5 Detach the hose from the leak-back pipe, and disconnect the heater plug wiring connectors (see illustration).

6 Release the refrigerant hoses from the retaining clip on the right-hand side inner wing. Without undoing the refrigerant pipes, disconnect the wiring plug, unbolt the air conditioning compressor from its support bracket (3 bolts), and position it clear of the engine. Use a cable tie or similar to tie the compressor to the bonnet slam panel out of the way. Undo the three bolts and remove the air conditioning support bracket (see illustrations).

7 Slacken the camshaft housing retaining bolts 1/2 turn at a time in the reverse of the sequence shown in illustration 12.11.

12.4a Recover the EGR pipe gasket

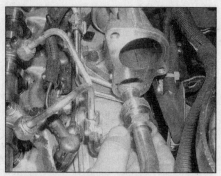

12.4b Undo the large EGR union nut

12.5 Disconnect the fuel leak-back pipe

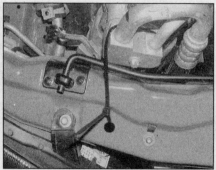

12.6a Tie the compressor to the slam
panel . . .

12.6b . . . and remove the compressor
mounting bracket

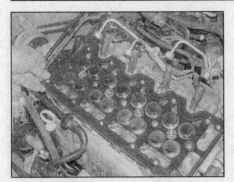

12.8 Remove the gasket

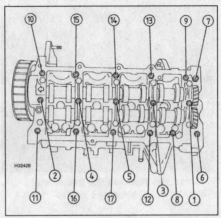

12.11 Camshaft housing bolts tightening sequence

13.4 Store the followers the correct way up

8 Undo the bolts completely and remove the camshaft housing. Remove and discard the gasket **(see illustration)**.

Refitting

9 Ensure all mating surfaces are clean and free from any gasket or sealant residue.
10 Prior to refitting the housing, check that the camshaft gears are correctly aligned, with the mark on the outer face of the exhaust gear between the marks on the outer face of the inlet gear (see Section 11, paragraph 14)
11 With a new gasket in place, position the camshaft housing on to the cylinder head, and tighten the housing bolts evenly and gradually to the specified torque, in the sequence shown **(see illustration)**.
12 Refitting is a reversal of removal. noting the following points:
a) *Check the valve clearances and adjust if necessary (Section 10).*
b) *Tension the timing belt as described in Section 7.*
c) *Check the fuel leak-back pipe and hose for leaks.*

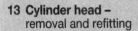

13 Cylinder head –
   removal and refitting

Caution: *Be careful not to allow dirt into the fuel injection pump or injector pipes during this procedure.*
Note: *New cylinder head bolts will be required on refitting.*

Removal

1 Drain the cooling system as described in Chapter 3.
2 Remove the camshaft sprocket as described in Section 8.
3 Slacken and remove the bolts securing the timing belt rear cover to the end of the cylinder head/camshaft housing.
4 With reference to Section 12, remove the camshaft housing. As a precaution, obtain sixteen small, clean plastic containers, and label them for identification. Alternatively, divide a larger container into compartments. Lift the followers out from the top of the

cylinder head and store each one in its respective fitted position **(see illustration)**.
5 Undo the three retaining bolts and manoeuvre the exhaust manifold heatshield out of the engine compartment.
6 Remove the nuts and bolts securing the exhaust manifold to the cylinder head, and recover the washers. Using a Torx socket, slacken and remove the two manifold retaining studs, and gently pull the manifold away from the engine. Alternatively, remove the exhaust manifold as described in Chapter 4A.
7 Unscrew the retaining bolts, disconnect the vacuum pipe, and remove the EGR (exhaust gas recirculation) valve **(see illustration)**.

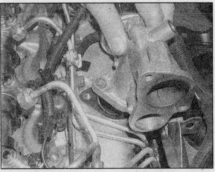

13.7 Remove the EGR valve

13.10 Release the retaining clip and disconnect the fuel leak-back pipe from the injection pump

8 With reference to Chapter 4A, remove the injector supply pipes. Wipe clean the pipe unions then slacken the union nuts securing the injector pipes to the rear of the injection pump; as each pump union nut is slackened, retain the adapter with a suitable open-ended spanner to prevent it being unscrewed from the pump. With all the union nuts undone, remove the injector pipes from the engine unit and mop up any spilt fuel.
9 Detach the vacuum hose and wiring plug from the EGR (exhaust gas recirculation) valve solenoid **(see illustration)**.
10 Disconnect the fuel leak-back hose from the injection pump **(see illustration)**.
11 Unplug the charge pressure sensor, located next to the EGR solenoid on the inlet manifold **(see illustration)**.

13.9 Detach the EGR solenoid valve vacuum hose and wiring plug

13.11 Unplug the charge pressure sensor

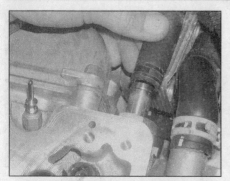

13.13 Disconnect the coolant pipe from the cylinder head

13.14a Remove the thermostat housing . . .

13.14b . . . and wastegate vacuum pipe bracket

12 Disconnect the wiring harness from the heater plugs (see Chapter 5B).

13 Release the retaining clip and disconnect the coolant hose from the left-hand rear of the cylinder head **(see illustration)**.

14 Disconnect the coolant temperature sensor, unscrew the retaining bolts and pull the thermostat housing and wastegate vacuum pipe bracket away from the left-hand end of the cylinder head **(see illustrations)**.

15 Working in the **reverse** of the sequence shown in illustration 13.33, progressively slacken the cylinder head bolts by half a turn at a time, until all bolts can be unscrewed by hand.

16 Lift out the cylinder head bolts and recover the washers.

17 Lift the cylinder head away; seek assistance if possible, as it is a heavy assembly **(see illustration)**. Remove the gasket, noting the two locating dowels fitted to the top of the cylinder block. If they are a loose fit, remove the locating dowels and store them with the head for safe-keeping. Keep the head gasket for identification purposes (see paragraph 24).

18 If the cylinder head is to be dismantled for overhaul, then refer to Part D of this Chapter.

Preparation for refitting

19 The mating faces of the cylinder head and cylinder block/crankcase must be perfectly clean before refitting the head. Use a hard plastic or wood scraper to remove all traces of

gasket and carbon; also clean the piston crowns. Take particular care, as the surfaces are damaged easily. Also, make sure that the carbon is not allowed to enter the oil and water passages – this is particularly important for the lubrication system, as carbon could block the oil supply to any of the engine's components. Using adhesive tape and paper, seal the water, oil and bolt holes in the cylinder block/crankcase. To prevent carbon entering the gap between the pistons and bores, smear a little grease in the gap. After cleaning each piston, use a small brush to remove all traces of grease and carbon from the gap, then wipe away the remainder with a clean rag. Clean all the pistons in the same way.

20 Check the mating surfaces of the cylinder block/crankcase and the cylinder head for nicks, deep scratches and other damage. If slight, they may be removed carefully with a file, but if excessive, machining may be the only alternative to renewal.

21 Ensure that the cylinder head bolt holes in the crankcase are clean and free of oil. Syringe or soak up any oil left in the bolt holes. This is most important in order that the correct bolt tightening torque can be applied and to prevent the possibility of the block being cracked by hydraulic pressure when the bolts are tightened.

22 The cylinder head bolts must be discarded and renewed, regardless of their apparent condition.

23 If warpage of the cylinder head gasket surface is suspected, use a straight-edge to check it for distortion. Refer to Part D of this Chapter if necessary.

24 On this engine, the cylinder head-to-piston clearance is controlled by fitting different thickness head gaskets. The gasket thickness can be determined by looking at the left-hand front corner of gasket and checking on the number of holes **(see illustration)**.

Holes in gasket	Gasket thickness
No holes	1.45 mm
One hole	1.50 mm
Two hole	1.55 mm

The correct thickness of gasket required is selected by measuring the piston protrusions as follows.

25 Ensure that the crankshaft is still correctly positioned in the TDC position. Mount a dial test indicator securely on the block so that its pointer can be easily pivoted between the piston crown and block mating surface. Zero the dial test indicator on the gasket surface of the cylinder block then carefully move the indicator over No 1 piston and measure the its protrusion at its highest point between the valve cut-outs, and then again at its highest point between the valve cut-outs at 90° to the first measurement **(see illustration)**.

26 Rotate the crankshaft half a turn (180°) to bring No 2 and 3 pistons to TDC. Ensure the crankshaft is accurately positioned then measure the protrusions of No 2 and 3 pistons

13.17 Lift the cylinder head away

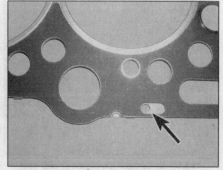

13.24 Cylinder head gasket identification hole (arrowed)

13.25 Measure the piston projection at the highest points between the valve cut-outs

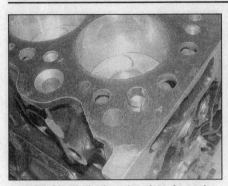

13.29 Check the locating dowels are in place

13.33 Tighten the bolts to the Stage 1 setting . . .

13.34 . . . then to the Stage 2 setting

at the specified points. Once both pistons have been measured, rotate the crankshaft through a further one and a half turns (540°) to bring No 1 and 4 pistons back to TDC.

27 Select the correct thickness of head gasket required by determining the largest amount of piston protrusion, and using the following table.

Piston protrusion measurement	Gasket thickness required
0.630 to 0.696 mm	1.45 mm (no holes)
0.697 to 0.763 mm	1.50 mm (one hole)
0.764 to 0.830 mm	1.55 mm (two holes)

Refitting

28 Wipe clean the mating surfaces of the cylinder head and cylinder block/crankcase.
29 Check that the two locating dowels are in position then fit a new gasket to the cylinder block (see illustration).
30 If not already positioned at TDC, rotate the crankshaft so that No 1 piston is at its highest point in the cylinder. Now turn the crankshaft 60° **backwards** (anti-clockwise). This is to ensure that whist the cylinder head and camshafts are being refitted, there is little chance of accidental piston-to-valve contact.
31 With the aid of an assistant, carefully refit the cylinder head assembly to the block, aligning it with the locating dowels.
32 Carefully enter each new cylinder head bolt into its relevant hole (*do not drop them*

in). Screw all bolts in, by hand only, until finger-tight.
33 Working progressively and in the sequence shown starting from the centre, tighten the cylinder head bolts to their Stage 1 torque setting, using a torque wrench and suitable socket (see illustration).
34 Once all bolts have been tightened to the Stage 1 torque, working again in the specified sequence, go around and tighten all bolts through the specified Stage 2, 3, 4 and 5 angles. It is recommended that an angle-measuring gauge is used to ensure accuracy (see illustration). If a gauge is not available, use white paint to make alignment marks prior to tightening; the marks can then be used to check that the bolt has been rotated through the correct angle.
35 Refitting is a reversal of removal, bearing in mind the following points:
a) *Prior to refitting the timing belt, turn the crankshaft 60° in the normal direction of rotation (clockwise) to TDC on No 1 cylinder until the groove in the crankshaft sprocket aligns with the cast-in mark on the oil pump housing (see illustration 7.7).*
b) *After refitting the injectors and pipes, check all unions for leaks (see Chapter 4A).*
c) *Ensure all wiring is correctly routed secured*
d) *Check the valve clearances as described in Section 10.*

e) *On completion, top up the coolant system as described in Chapter 3.*

14 Sump –
removal and refitting

Removal

1 Disconnect the battery negative terminal.
Note: *Before disconnecting the battery, refer to 'Disconnecting the battery' in the reference section at the rear of this manual.*
2 Firmly apply the handbrake then jack up the front of the car and support it on axle stands. Where necessary, undo the retaining screws and remove the engine undertray.
3 Drain the engine oil as described in Chapter 1, then fit a new sealing washer and refit the drain plug, tightening it to the specified torque.
4 Slacken and remove the bolts securing the sump lower pan to the main casting then remove the sump pan from underneath the vehicle (see illustration).
5 To remove the main casting from the engine, remove the exhaust system front pipe as described in Chapter 4A.
6 Undo the two bolts securing the oil dipstick guide tube to the main sump casting.
7 Progressively slacken and remove the nuts and bolts securing the main casting to the base of the cylinder block/oil pump cover and transmission. Break the joint by striking the casting with the palm of the hand, or using a wide plastic spatula carefully inserted in the joint between the sump and cylinder block. Lower the casting away from the engine and withdraw it from underneath the vehicle.
8 While the sump main casting is removed, take the opportunity to check the oil pump pick-up/strainer for signs of clogging or splitting. If necessary, unbolt the pick-up/strainer and remove it from the engine along with its sealing ring (see illustration). The strainer can then be cleaned easily in solvent or renewed.

Refitting

9 Remove all traces of dirt, oil and sealant from the mating surfaces of the sump main

14.4 If the lower pan is stuck to the main casting, carefully ease it away using a wide-bladed scraper

14.8 Remove the oil pick-up pipe and strainer

14.10 Fit a new oil pick-up pipe sealing ring

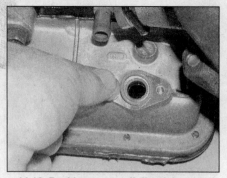

14.12 Position a new oil dipstick guide tube sealing ring

14.13 Refit the sump main casting

casting and pan, the cylinder block and (where removed) the pick-up/strainer.

10 Where necessary, fit a new sealing ring to the oil pump pick-up/strainer and fit the strainer to the base of the cylinder block (see illustration). Refit the strainer retaining bolt and tighten it to the specified torque.

11 Ensure the main casting and cylinder block mating surfaces are clean and dry, and apply a coat of suitable sealant (available from Vauxhall dealers) to the upper mating surface of the casting.

12 Position a new dipstick guide tube rubber seal on the main casting (see illustration).

13 Offer up the main casting and loosely refit all the retaining nuts and bolts (see illustration). Note that the four long bolts correspond with the bolts holes at the rear of the casting. If the sump is being fitted with the engine removed from the vehicle and separated from the transmission, ensure that the rear face of the casting is flush with the transmission mounting face of the cylinder block. Working out from the centre in a diagonal sequence, progressively tighten the main casting retaining bolts to the specified torque setting.

14 Refit the bolts securing the main casting to the transmission housing and tighten them to the specified torque.

15 Ensure that the oil dipstick guide tube is correctly positioned, refit the retaining bolts, and tighten to the specified torque.

16 Refit the exhaust front pipe as described in Chapter 4A.

17 Ensure the main casting and sump pan mating surfaces are clean and dry and apply a coat of suitable sealant (available from Vauxhall dealers) to the upper mating surface of the pan. Refit the pan to the base of the main casting and tighten its retaining bolts to the specified torque (see illustration).

18 Where removed, refit the engine undertray, lower the vehicle to the ground then fill the engine with fresh oil, with reference to Chapter 1.

15 Oil pump – removal, inspection and refitting

Removal

Note: The oil pressure relief valve is screwed into the cylinder block and cannot be removed without disturbing the fuel injection pump (see paragraph 7).

1 Remove the timing belt as described in Section 7.

2 Remove the oil pump and crankshaft timing belt sprockets as described in Section 8.

3 Remove the sump main casting as described in Section 14.

4 Slacken and remove the retaining bolts then slide the oil pump cover off of the end of the crankshaft, taking great care not to lose the locating dowels. Remove the sealing ring, which is fitted around the oil pump housing section of the cover, and discard it.

5 Using a suitable marker pen, mark the surface of the pump outer rotor; the mark can then be used to ensure the rotor is refitted the correct way around.

6 Remove the oil pump inner and outer rotors from the cylinder block (see illustrations).

7 If necessary, remove the fuel injection pump as described in Chapter 4A, and unscrew the oil pressure relief valve assembly from the rear of the cylinder block, where it is located on the right-hand side of the injection pump lower mounting bracket. Remove the sealing ring.

Inspection

8 Clean the components, and carefully examine the rotors, pump housing and cover for any signs of scoring or wear. Renew any component which shows signs of wear or damage. If the pump housing in the cylinder block is marked then seek the advice of a Vauxhall dealer on the best course of action.

9 If the components appear serviceable, fit the rotors into the housing and measure the clearance between the outer rotor and pump housing, and the inner rotor tip-to-outer rotor clearance using feeler blades (see illustration). Also measure the rotor endfloat, and check the flatness of the end cover. If the clearances exceed the specified tolerances, renew the worn components.

10 If the relief valve has been removed, check that the valve piston is free to move easily and return smoothly under spring pressure. If not renew the valve assembly.

14.17 Apply a bead of sealant and refit the pan to the sump main casting

15.6a Remove the oil pump inner rotor . . .

15.6b . . . and outer rotor

15.9 Measure the inner rotor tip-to-outer rotor clearance

15.13 The seal fits flush with the housing

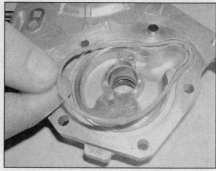

15.15 Fit a new seal to the oil pump cover

Refitting

11 Where removed, fit a new sealing ring to the oil pressure relief valve then refit the valve assembly to the cylinder block and tighten it to the specified torque setting.

12 Lubricate the pump rotors with clean engine oil and refit them to the pump housing, using the mark made prior to removal to ensure the outer rotor is fitted the correct way around.

13 Prior to refitting, carefully lever out the crankshaft and oil pump oil seals using a flat-bladed screwdriver. Fit the new oil seals, ensuring that each seals sealing lip is facing inwards, and press them squarely into the housing using a tubular drift which bears only on the hard outer edge of the seal. Press each seal into position so that it is flush with the housing then lubricate the oil seal lips with clean engine oil **(see illustration)**.

14 Ensure the mating surfaces of the oil pump and cylinder block are clean and dry and the locating dowels are in position. Remove all traces of sealant from the threads of the pump cover bolts.

15 Fit a new seal into the groove around the oil pump housing section of the cover, and apply a bead of suitable sealant (available from Vauxhall dealers) to the pump cover mating surface **(see illustration)**.

16 Carefully manoeuvre the oil pump cover into position, taking great care not to damage

the oil seal lips on the crankshaft and inner rotor shaft. Locate the cover on the dowels making sure the pump sealing ring remains correctly positioned.

17 Apply a smear of sealant to the threads of each cover retaining bolt then refit all bolts and tighten them to the specified torque. Note that the longer bolt corresponds to the lower left-hand bolt hole in the cover.

18 Refit the timing belt sprockets and belt as described in Sections 7 and 8 then refit the sump as described in Section 13.

19 On completion refill the engine with clean oil as described in Chapter 1.

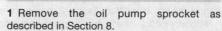

16 Oil pump seal – renewal

1 Remove the oil pump sprocket as described in Section 8.

2 Carefully punch or drill a small hole in the oil seal. Screw a self-tapping screw into the seal, and pull on the screw with pliers to extract the seal **(see illustration)**.

Caution: Great care must be taken to avoid damage to the oil pump.

3 Clean the seal housing, and polish off any burrs or raised edges which may have caused the seal to fail in the first place.

4 Lubricate the lips of the new seal with clean engine oil, and press it into position using a

suitable tubular drift (such as a socket) which bears only on the hard outer edge of the seal. Take care not to damage the seal lips during fitting; note that the seal lips should face inwards.

5 Refit the oil pump sprocket as described in Section 8.

17 Oil cooler –
removal and refitting

Removal

1 Firmly apply the handbrake, then jack up the front of the vehicle and support it on axle stands. Where necessary, undo the retaining screws and remove the undertray to gain access to the oil cooler which is situated on the rear left-hand of the cylinder block.

2 Drain the cooling system as described in Chapter 3. Alternatively, clamp the oil cooler coolant hoses directly above the cooler, and be prepared for some coolant loss as the hoses are disconnected. To improve access to the coolant hoses, remove the charge air pipe/hose (see Chapter 4A).

3 Position a suitable container beneath the oil filter. Undo the oil cooler return hose union/release the retaining clip and disconnect the return hose.

4 Release the clips and disconnect the coolant hoses from the oil cooler, and release the wiring loom retaining clip.

5 Remove the single bolt securing the oil filter housing to the cylinder block. Discard the sealing ring; a new one must be used on refitting.

Refitting

6 Fit a new sealing ring to the recess in the rear of the cooler, then offer the cooler to the cylinder block **(see illustration)**.

7 Ensure that the oil cooler return hose union is correctly positioned, ensure that the lug of the oil filter housing engages correctly in the groove of the injection pump bracket, then

16.2 Pull the screw to extract the seal

17.6 Fit a new sealing ring to the recess in the cooler

17.7 Ensure that the lug of the oil filter housing engages in the groove of the injection pump bracket, then refit the centre bolt

18.2 Fabricate a locking tool to retain the flywheel

18.3 Remove the flywheel bolts and recover the plate

refit the centre bolt and tighten it to the specified torque **(see illustration)**.

8 Reconnect the coolant hoses to the cooler and secure them in position with the retaining clips.

9 Lower the vehicle to the ground. Top-up the engine oil level as described in Chapter 1.

10 If removed, refit the air intake duct.

11 Refill or top-up the cooling system as described in Chapter 3 (as applicable). Start the engine, and check the oil cooler for signs of leakage.

18 Flywheel – removal, inspection and refitting
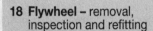

Note: *New flywheel retaining bolts will be required on refitting.*

Removal

1 Remove the transmission as described in Chapter 7 then remove the clutch assembly as described in Chapter 6.

2 Prevent the flywheel from turning by locking the ring gear teeth **(see illustration)**. Alternatively, bolt a strap between the flywheel and the cylinder block/crankcase. Make alignment marks between the flywheel and crankshaft using paint or a suitable marker pen.

3 Slacken and remove the retaining bolts and plate, then remove the flywheel **(see illustration)**. Do not drop it, as it is very heavy.

Inspection

4 Examine the flywheel for wear or chipping of the ring gear teeth. Renewal of the ring gear is possible but is not a task for the home mechanic; renewal requires the new ring gear to be heated (up to 180° to 230°C) to allow it to be fitted.

5 Examine the flywheel for scoring of the clutch face. If the clutch face is scored, the flywheel may be surface-ground, but renewal is preferable.

6 If there is any doubt about the condition of the flywheel, seek the advice of a Vauxhall

dealer or engine reconditioning specialist. They will be able to advise if it is possible to recondition it or whether renewal is necessary.

Refitting

7 Clean the mating surfaces of the flywheel and crankshaft.

8 Apply a drop of locking compound to the threads of each of the new flywheel retaining bolts then refit the flywheel and retaining plate and install the new bolts. If the original is being refitted align the marks made prior to removal.

9 Lock the flywheel using the method employed on dismantling then, working in a diagonal sequence, evenly and progressively tighten the retaining bolts to the specified Stage 1 torque setting.

10 Once all bolts have been tightened to the stage 1 torque, go around and tighten all bolts through the specified Stage 2 angle. It is recommended that an angle-measuring gauge is used during the final stages of the tightening, to ensure accuracy. If a gauge is not available, use white paint to make alignment marks prior to tightening; the marks can then be used to check that the bolt has been rotated through the correct angle.

11 Refit the clutch as described in Chapter 6 then remove the locking tool and refit the transmission as described in Chapter 7.

19 Crankshaft oil seals – renewal

Right-hand (timing belt end) oil seal

1 Remove the crankshaft sprocket as described in Section 8.

2 Carefully punch or drill two small holes opposite each other in the oil seal. Screw a self-tapping screw into each and pull on the screws with pliers to extract the seal.

3 Clean the seal housing and polish off any burrs or raised edges which may have caused the seal to fail in the first place.

4 Lubricate the lips of the new seal with clean

engine oil and ease it into position on the end of the shaft. Press the seal squarely into position until it is flush with the housing. If necessary, a suitable tubular drift which bears only on the hard outer edge of the seal can be used to tap the seal into position. Take great care not to damage the seal lips during fitting and ensure that the seal lips face inwards.

5 Wash off any traces of oil, then refit the crankshaft sprocket as described in Section 8.

Left-hand (flywheel end) oil seal

6 Remove the flywheel as described in Section 18.

7 Renew the seal as described in paragraphs 2 to 4 **(see illustration)**.

8 Refit the flywheel as described in Section 18.

20 Engine/transmission mountings – inspection and renewal

Inspection

1 If improved access is required, raise the front of the car and support it securely on axle stands. Where necessary, undo the retaining bolts and remove the undertray from beneath the engine/transmission unit.

2 Check the mounting rubber to see if it is cracked, hardened or separated from the metal at any point; renew the mounting if any such damage or deterioration is evident.

19.7 The seal fits flush with the housing

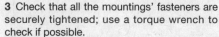

20.7 Remove the bolts securing the right-hand mounting to the support bracket

20.13 Front engine mounting bolts

20.21 Unscrew the two rear engine mounting retaining bolts

3 Check that all the mountings' fasteners are securely tightened; use a torque wrench to check if possible.

4 Using a large screwdriver or a pry bar, check for wear in the mounting by carefully levering against it to check for free-play; where this is not possible, enlist the aid of an assistant to move the engine/transmission unit back-and-forth, or from side-to-side, while you watch the mounting. While some free-play is to be expected even from new components, excessive wear should be obvious. If excessive free-play is found, check first that the fasteners are correctly secured, then renew any worn components as described below.

Renewal

Note: *Before slackening any of the engine mounting bolts/nuts, the relative positions of the mountings to their various brackets should be marked to ensure correct alignment upon refitting.*

Right-hand mounting

5 With reference to Chapter 4A, remove the air cleaner housing.

6 Support the weight of the engine using a trolley jack with a block of wood placed on its head.

7 Remove the three bolts securing the right-hand engine mounting to the engine mounting support bracket (see illustration).

8 Undo the bolts securing the mounting to the body, and withdraw the bracket with the mounting.

9 If required, the mounting can be separated by undoing the single bolt in the centre of the rubber element.

10 Refitting is a reversal of removal. Tighten the bolts to the specified torque.

Front mounting

11 Firmly apply the handbrake then jack up the front of the vehicle and support it on axle stands.

12 Support the weight of the engine/transmission using a trolley jack with a block of wood placed on its head.

13 Slacken and remove the nut and washer securing the mounting to the bracket. Withdraw the bolt (see illustration)

14 Undo the bolts securing the mounting bracket to the transmission, then manoeuvre the mounting and bracket out of position.

Note: *Take great care not to place any excess stress on the exhaust system when raising or lowering the engine. If necessary, disconnect the front pipe from the manifold (see Chapter 4A).*

15 Check all components for signs of wear or damage, and renew as necessary.

16 On reassembly, refit the mounting bracket (aligning the previously made marks) and tighten its bolts to the specified torque.

17 Locate the mounting in the subframe, ensuring it is fitted the correct way up, and manoeuvre the engine/transmission into position. Refit the mounting bolts and new nuts. Tighten them to the specified torque.

18 Lower the vehicle to the ground.

Rear mounting

19 Firmly apply the handbrake then jack up the front of the vehicle and support it on axle stands.

20 Support the weight of the engine/transmission using a trolley jack with a block of wood placed on its head. Position the jack underneath the transmission and raise the transmission slightly to remove all load from the rear mounting.

21 Slacken and remove the two bolts securing the rear mounting to the subframe, and the nut securing the mounting to the transmission bracket, then manoeuvre the assembly out from underneath the vehicle (see illustration).

22 On refitting, manoeuvre the mounting into position and refit the bolts/nuts securing it to the subframe. Ensure that the mounting is correctly engaged with the transmission bracket and fit the mounting-to-bracket retaining nut. Tighten the mounting bolts/nuts to their specified torque settings. Remove the jack from underneath the engine/transmission.

23 Lower the vehicle to the ground.

Left-hand mounting

24 Release the retaining clips and screws and remove the engine undertray.

25 Remove the battery as described in Chapter 5A. **Note:** *Before disconnecting the battery, refer to 'Disconnecting the battery' in the reference section at the rear of this manual.*

26 Undo the retaining bolts, and remove the battery tray from the body.

27 Support the weight of the transmission using a trolley jack with a block of wood placed on its head.

28 Undo the six retaining bolts, and withdraw the mounting bracket from the transmission (see illustration).

29 Slacken and remove the four Torx screws and manoeuvre the mounting out from the inner wing (see illustration).

30 If required, separate the rubber element from the bracket by unscrewing the single retaining bolt.

31 Refitting is a reversal of removal. Ensure all bolts/nuts are tightened to their specified torques.

20.28 Undo the six bolts and remove the mounting bracket

20.29 Remove the four Torx bolts and manoeuvre the mounting out from the inner wing

Chapter 2 Part C:
2.0 litre engine in-car repair procedures

Contents

Degrees of difficulty

Easy, suitable for novice with little experience	Fairly easy, suitable for beginner with some experience	Fairly difficult, suitable for competent DIY mechanic	Difficult, suitable for experienced DIY mechanic	Very difficult, suitable for expert DIY or professional

Specifications

Note: *Where specifications are given as N/A, no information was available at the time of writing. Refer to your Vauxhall dealer for the latest information available.*

General

Engine type	Four-cylinder, in-line, water-cooled. Chain-driven single overhead camshaft, acting on hydraulic tappets, 16 valves
Manufacturer's engine code:	
Low-pressure turbo model	X20DTL or Y20DTL
High-pressure turbo model	Y20DTH
Bore	84 mm
Stroke	90 mm
Capacity	1994 cc
Injection sequence	1-3-4-2 (No 1 cylinder at timing chain end of engine)
Direction of crankshaft rotation	Clockwise (viewed from timing chain end of engine)
Compression ratio	18.5:1
Maximum power:	
Low-pressure turbo model	60 kW at 4300 rpm
High-pressure turbo model	74 kW at 4300 rpm
Maximum torque:	
Low-pressure turbo models:	
X20DTL	185 Nm at 1800 to 2500 rpm
Y20DTL	185 Nm at 1500 to 2750 rpm
High-pressure turbo model	230 Nm at 1950 to 2500 rpm

Compression pressures

Standard	25 to 28 bar (363 to 406 psi)
Maximum difference between any two cylinders	1 bar (15 psi)

Camshaft

Endfloat	0.04 to 0.14 mm
Maximum permissible radial run-out	0.06 mm
Cam lift (inlet and exhaust)	8.0 mm

Lubrication system

Oil pump type	Gear-type, driven directly from crankshaft
Minimum permissible oil pressure at idle speed, with engine at operating temperature (oil temperature of at least 80°C)	1.5 bar (22 psi)

Torque wrench settings

	Nm	lbf ft
Auxiliary drivebelt tensioner assembly bolts:		
Pulley backplate pivot bolt	42	31
Strut mounting bolts	23	17
Camshaft bearing cap bolts:		
X20DTL/Y20DTL	20	15
Y20DTH	15	11
Camshaft cover bolts	8	6
Camshaft sprocket bolt*:		
Stage 1	90	66
Stage 2	Angle-tighten a further 60°	
Stage 3	Angle-tighten a further 30°	
Connecting rod big-end bearing cap bolt*:		
Stage 1	35	26
Stage 2	Angle-tighten a further 45°	
Stage 3	Angle-tighten a further 15°	
Crankshaft pulley bolt*:		
Stage 1	150	111
Stage 2	Angle-tighten a further 45°	
Stage 3	Angle-tighten a further 15°	
Cylinder head bolts*:		
Stage 1	25	18
Stage 2	Angle-tighten a further 65°	
Stage 3	Angle-tighten a further 65°	
Stage 4	Angle-tighten a further 65°	
Stage 5	Angle-tighten a further 65°	
Stage 6	Angle-tighten a further 15°	
Cylinder head-to-timing chain cover/block bolts:		
X20DTL/Y20DTL	20	15
Y20DTH*:		
Stage 1	20	15
Stage 2	Angle-tighten a further 30°	
Stage 3	Angle-tighten a further 5°	
Engine/transmission mounting bolts:		
Right-hand mounting:		
Mounting-to-body nuts	45	33
Mounting-to-bracket bolt	55	41
Left-hand mounting:		
Mounting-to-body bolts	20	15
Bracket-to-transmission bolts	35	26
Mounting-to-bracket bolts	55	41
Rear mounting:		
Mounting-to-bracket bolts	55	41
Mounting-to-subframe bolts	55	41
Bracket-to-transmission bolts	60	44
Front mounting:		
Mounting-to-transmission bolts	60	44
Mounting to subframe	55	41
Engine-to-transmission unit bolts:		
M10 bolts	40	30
M12 bolts	60	44
Flywheel bolts*:		
Stage 1	45	33
Stage 2	Angle-tighten a further 30°	
Stage 3	Angle-tighten a further 15°	
Injection pump sprocket bolts:		
X20DTL/Y20DTL	20	15
Y20DTH	28	21
Injection pump sprocket cover bolts	6	4
Main bearing cap bolts*:		
Stage 1	90	66
Stage 2	Angle-tighten a further 60°	
Stage 3	Angle-tighten a further 15°	

Main bearing cap bridge bolts	20	15
Oil cooler-to-oil filter housing bolts	15	11
Oil pump:		
Oil pressure relief valve bolt	60	44
Pump cover screws	8	6
Pump pick-up/strainer bolts	8	6
Safety valve bolt	45	33
Cylinder block oil spray nozzle bolts	22	16
Sump bolts:		
Sump to cylinder block/timing chain cover bolts	20	15
Sump flange-to-transmission bolts:		
M8 bolts	20	15
M10 bolts	40	30
Drain plug	18	13
Roadwheel bolts	110	81
Timing chain cover bolts	20	15
Timing chain guide bolts	8	6
Timing chain tensioner blade pivot bolt	20	15
Timing chain tensioner cap	60	44

*Use new fasteners

1 General information

How to use this Chapter

1 This Part of Chapter 2 describes those repair procedures that can reasonably be carried out on the 2.0 litre engine while it remains in the car. If the engine has been removed from the car and is being dismantled as described in Part D, any preliminary dismantling procedures can be ignored.

2 Note that, while it may be possible physically to overhaul items such as the piston/connecting rod assemblies while the engine is in the car, such tasks are not normally carried out as separate operations. Usually, several additional procedures (not to mention the cleaning of components and of oilways) have to be carried out. For this reason, all such tasks are classed as major overhaul procedures, and are described in Part D of this Chapter.

3 Part D describes the removal of the engine/transmission unit from the vehicle, and the full overhaul procedures that can then be carried out.

Engine description

4 The 2.0 litre (1994 cc) engine is a completely new engine designed by Vauxhall. It is of the sixteen-valve, in-line four-cylinder, single overhead camshaft (SOHC) type, mounted transversely at the front of the car with the transmission attached to its left-hand end.

5 The crankshaft runs in five main bearings. Thrustwashers are fitted to No 3 main bearing to control crankshaft endfloat.

6 The connecting rods rotate on horizontally-split bearing shells at their big-ends. The pistons are attached to the connecting rods by gudgeon pins, which are a sliding fit in the connecting rod small-end eyes and retained by circlips. The aluminium-alloy pistons are fitted with three piston rings – two compression rings and an oil control ring.

7 The cylinder block is made of cast iron and the cylinder bores are an integral part of the block. On this type of engine the cylinder bores are sometimes referred to as having dry liners.

8 The inlet and exhaust valves are each closed by coil springs, and operate in guides pressed into the cylinder head.

9 The camshaft is driven by the crankshaft via a dual timing chain arrangement; the lower timing chain links the crankshaft to the fuel injection pump and the upper chain links the injection pump to the camshaft. The camshaft rotates directly in the head and operates the sixteen valves via followers and hydraulic tappets. The followers are situated directly below the camshaft, each one operating two valves. Valve clearances are automatically adjusted by the hydraulic tappets.

10 Lubrication is by means of an oil pump, which is driven off the right-hand end of the crankshaft. It draws oil through a strainer located in the sump, and then forces it through an externally-mounted filter into galleries in the cylinder block/crankcase. From there, the oil is distributed to the crankshaft (main bearings) and camshaft. The big-end bearings are supplied with oil via internal drillings in the crankshaft, while the camshaft bearings also receive a pressurised supply. The camshaft lobes and valves are lubricated by splash, as are all other engine components. An oil cooler is fitted to keep the oil temperature stable under arduous operating conditions.

11 The high-pressure turbo model (Y20DTH) is fitted with an intercooler.

Repair operations possible with the engine in the car

12 The following work can be carried out with the engine in the car:

a) *Compression pressure testing.*
b) *Camshaft cover – removal and refitting.*
c) *Timing chain cover – removal and refitting.*
d) *Timing chains – removal and refitting.*
e) *Timing chain tensioners, guides and sprockets – removal and refitting.*
f) *Camshaft and followers – removal, inspection and refitting.*
g) *Cylinder head – removal and refitting.*
h) *Connecting rods and pistons – removal and refitting*.*
i) *Sump – removal and refitting.*
j) *Oil pump – removal, overhaul and refitting.*
k) *Oil cooler – removal and refitting.*
l) *Crankshaft oil seals – renewal.*
m) *Engine/transmission mountings – inspection and renewal.*
n) *Flywheel – removal, inspection and refitting.*

* *Although the operation marked with an asterisk can be carried out with the engine in the car after removal of the sump, it is better for the engine to be removed, in the interests of cleanliness and improved access. For this reason, the procedure is described in Chapter 2D.*

2 Compression test – description and interpretation

Compression test

Note: *A compression tester specifically designed for diesel engines must be used for this test.*

1 When engine performance is down, or if misfiring occurs which cannot be attributed to the fuel system, a compression test can provide diagnostic clues as to the engine's condition. If the test is performed regularly, it can give warning of trouble before any other symptoms become apparent.

2 A compression tester specifically intended for diesel engines must be used, because of the higher pressures involved. The tester is connected to an adapter which screws into the glow plug or injector hole. On these models, an adapter suitable for use in the glow plug holes will be required, due to the design of the injectors. It is unlikely to be worthwhile buying such a tester for occasional use, but it may be possible to borrow or hire one – if not, have the test performed by a garage.

3 Unless specific instructions to the contrary are supplied with the tester, observe the following points:

a) *The battery must be in a good state of charge, the air filter must be clean, and the engine should be at normal operating temperature.*

b) *All the glow plugs should be removed before starting the test (see Chapter 5B).*

c) *Release the retaining clip and disconnect the wiring connector from the fuel injection pump control unit (see Chapter 4A) to prevent the engine from running or fuel from being discharged.*

4 There is no need to hold the accelerator pedal down during the test, because the diesel engine air inlet is not throttled.

5 Crank the engine on the starter motor; after one or two revolutions, the compression pressure should build up to a maximum figure, and then stabilise. Record the highest reading obtained.

6 Repeat the test on the remaining cylinders, recording the pressure in each.

7 All cylinders should produce very similar pressures; any difference greater than that specified indicates the existence of a fault. Note that the compression should build-up

quickly in a healthy engine; low compression on the first stroke, followed by gradually-increasing pressure on successive strokes, indicates worn piston rings. A low compression reading on the first stroke, which does not build-up during successive strokes, indicates leaking valves or a blown head gasket (a cracked head could also be the cause). Deposits on the undersides of the valve heads can also cause low compression.

Note: *The cause of poor compression is less easy to establish on a diesel engine than on a petrol one. The effect of introducing oil into the cylinders ('wet' testing) is not conclusive, because there is a risk that the oil will sit in the swirl chamber or in the recess on the piston crown instead of passing to the rings.*

8 On completion of the test, reconnect the injection pump wiring connector then refit the glow plugs as described in Chapter 5B.

Leakdown test

9 A leakdown test measures the rate at which compressed air fed into the cylinder is lost. It is an alternative to a compression test, and in many ways it is better, since the escaping air provides easy identification of where pressure loss is occurring (piston rings, valves or head gasket).

10 The equipment needed for leakdown testing is unlikely to be available to the home mechanic. If poor compression is suspected, have the test performed by a suitably-equipped garage.

3 Top dead centre (TDC) for No 1 piston – locating

1 In its travel up and down its cylinder bore, Top Dead Centre (TDC) is the highest point that each piston reaches as the crankshaft rotates. While each piston reaches TDC both at the top of the compression stroke and again at the top of the exhaust stroke, for the purpose of timing the engine, TDC refers to the piston position (usually number 1) at the top of its compression stroke.

2 Number 1 piston (and cylinder) is at the right-hand (timing chain) end of the engine, and its TDC position is located as follows. Note that the crankshaft rotates clockwise when viewed from the right-hand side of the car.

3 Disconnect the battery negative terminal. *Note: Before disconnecting the battery, refer to 'Disconnecting the battery' in the reference section at the rear of this manual.* To improve access to the crankshaft pulley, apply the handbrake, then jack up the front of the vehicle and support it on axle stands. Remove the retaining screws/clips and remove the engine undertray.

4 To check the position of the camshaft either remove the camshaft cover (Section 5), so that the position of the cam lobes can be seen, or remove the braking system vacuum pump (Chapter 9) so the timing hole on the camshaft end can be seen.

5 Using a socket and extension bar on the crankshaft pulley bolt, rotate the crankshaft until the notch on the crankshaft pulley rim is aligned with the mark on the timing chain cover. Once the mark is correctly aligned, No 1 and 4 pistons are at TDC.

6 To determine which piston is at TDC on its compression stroke, check the position of the camshaft lobes/timing hole (as applicable). When No 1 piston is at TDC on its compression stroke, No 1 cylinder camshaft lobes will be pointing upwards and the timing hole on the left-hand of the camshaft will be at the top (12 o'clock position) with the camshaft slot parallel with the head surface **(see illustrations)**. If No 1 cylinder camshaft lobes are pointing downwards and the camshaft end timing mark is at the bottom (6 o'clock position) then No 4 cylinder is at TDC on its compression stroke; rotate the crankshaft through a further complete turn (360°) to bring No 1 cylinder to TDC on its compression stroke.

7 With No 1 piston at TDC on its compression stroke, if necessary, the crankshaft can be locked in position by inserting a pin in through the crankshaft sensor bore on the front of the cylinder block. If access to the special Vauxhall tool (KM-929) cannot be gained, a home-made alternative will have to be manufactured (see Section 4). Remove the crankshaft sensor and insert the pin, making sure it is correctly located in the crankshaft web slot **(see illustrations)**.

3.6a When No 1 cylinder is at TDC on its compression stroke, its camshaft lobes (arrowed) will be pointing upwards . . .

3.6b . . . and the timing hole (arrowed) on the left-hand end of the camshaft will be at the top

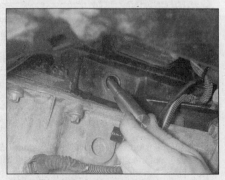

3.7a Remove the crankshaft sensor from the cylinder block and insert the locking pin . . .

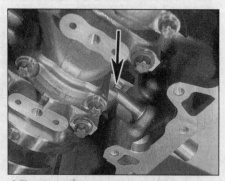

3.7b . . . making sure it correctly engages with the crankshaft cut-out (arrowed – shown with the sump removed)

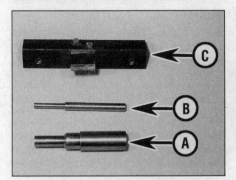

4.0a Home made tools necessary to check/adjust the valve timing

A   Crankshaft locking pin
B   Injection pump flange locking pin
C   Camshaft locking tool

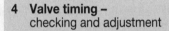

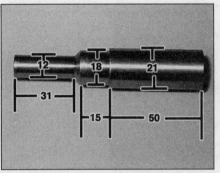

4.0b Crankshaft locking pin dimensions (in mm)

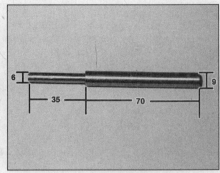

4.0c Injection pump flange locking pin dimensions (in mm)

4 Valve timing – checking and adjustment

Note: *To check the valve (and fuel injection pump) timing, it will be necessary to use the following Vauxhall special tools (or suitable equivalents); the camshaft locking tool (KM-932), the injection pump flange locking pin (KM-927), the crankshaft locking pin (KM-929) and the camshaft sprocket wrench (KM-933). If access to these tools cannot be gained, this task must be entrusted to a Vauxhall dealer. If the necessary facilities are available to manufacture home-made tools, the dimensions of the locking pins are given in the accompanying illustrations* (see illustrations). *The camshaft locking tool (also pictured) ensures that the camshaft remains correctly positioned by keeping the camshaft slot parallel to the cylinder head surface.*

1 Remove the auxiliary drivebelt as described in Chapter 1. Undo the auxiliary drivebelt tensioner pulley strut lower mounting bolt and the pulley backplate pivot bolt and remove the tensioner assembly from the engine. **Note:** *Store the assembly so the tensioner strut is the correct way up; if the strut is not stored properly it will have to be primed once it is refitted.*

2 Remove the braking system vacuum pump as described in Chapter 9.

3 To improve access to the injection pump sprocket cover and the pump, carry out the following.

a) *Remove the air cleaner housing and exhaust system front pipe (see Chapter 4A).*

b) *Mark the position of the right-hand engine mounting bracket in relation to the cylinder head bracket. Undo the three bolts securing the right-hand engine mounting to the cylinder head bracket, and the three bolts securing the right-hand engine mounting to the inner wing, then raise the right-hand end of the engine using a jack/engine support bar (see Section 17). Raise the engine as high as possible without placing any excess strain on the remaining mountings or any pipes/hoses or wiring.*

4 Remove the camshaft cover and position No 1 cylinder at TDC on its compression stroke as described in Section 3.

5 Remove the crankshaft sensor as described in Chapter 4A, Section 8.

6 Undo the retaining screws and remove the injection pump sprocket cover from the timing chain cover.

7 Ensure the crankshaft pulley notch is correctly aligned with the timing chain cover mark then insert the crankshaft locking pin into the crankshaft sensor aperture and engage it with the slot in the crankshaft web **(see illustrations 3.7a and 3.7b)**.

8 With the crankshaft locked in position, insert the injection pump flange locking pin into the hole in the flange and engage it with

hole in the pump body, then slide the camshaft locking tool into position on the left-hand end of the camshaft **(see illustrations)**.

9 If all the locking tools can be correctly fitted the valve timing is correctly set and no adjustment is necessary, proceed as described in paragraphs 21 to 26. If either of the tools can not be inserted, adjust the timing as follows noting that a new camshaft sprocket bolt and tensioner bolt sealing ring will be required.

10 Remove the camshaft/injection pump sprocket locking tool (as applicable) then unbolt the right-hand mounting bracket assembly from the cylinder head.

11 Unscrew the upper timing chain tensioner cap from the rear of the cylinder head and remove the plunger, noting which way around it is fitted. Remove the sealing ring from the cap and discard it, a new one should be used on refitting.

12 Hold the camshaft, using an open-ended spanner on the flats provided, then slacken and remove the camshaft sprocket retaining bolt. Fit the new bolt, tightening it finger-tight only at this stage.

13 Slacken the bolts securing the injection pump sprocket to the pump flange.

14 With the crankshaft locked in position, ensure the timing mark on the injection pump upper timing chain sprocket is correctly aligned with the pump flange timing hole. Insert the flange locking pin making sure it is correctly seated then tighten the sprocket retaining bolts to the specified torque **(see illustration)**.

4.8a Insert the locking pin through the flange cut-out and engage it in the pump body hole

4.8b Engage the camshaft locking tool with the camshaft cut-out (arrowed)

4.14 Ensure the pump sprocket timing mark (arrowed) is correctly positioned then tighten the sprocket bolts to the specified torque

4.18 Adjust the upper timing chain tension as described in the text then tighten the camshaft sprocket bolt to the Stage 1 torque setting

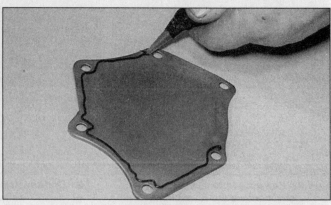

4.21 Apply a bead of sealant to the mating surface of the injection pump sprocket cover

15 Slide the camshaft locking tool into position making sure its pin engages centrally in the camshaft bore.

16 With all locking tools in position, fit the sprocket wrench to the camshaft sprocket; in the absence of the special wrench, pass two bolts through the sprocket holes and use a screwdriver to lever on the bolts. Have an assistant keep the timing chain taut on its guide (upper) side by applying **slight** pressure to the sprocket; this will ensure all slack in the chain is on the tensioner side of chain.

17 With the upper timing chain tensioned as described, check that the injection pump locking pin slides in and out of position with only a slight amount of drag. If excessive force is needed to move the pin, have your assistant decrease the pressure on the sprocket or, if the pin moves easily, increase the pressure.

18 Once the upper timing chain is correctly tensioned, retain the camshaft with an open-ended spanner and tighten the camshaft sprocket retaining bolt to the specified Stage 1 torque setting **(see illustration)**. Check the injection pump pin action then tighten the bolt through the specified Stage 2 angle and finally through the specified Stage 3 angle. It is recommended that an angle-measuring gauge is used during the final stages of the tightening, to ensure accuracy. If a gauge is not available, use white paint to make alignment marks between the bolt head and pulley prior to tightening; the marks can then be used to check that the bolt has been rotated through the correct angle.

19 Remove all the locking tools and fit a new sealing ring to the upper timing chain tensioner cap. Insert the plunger into the cylinder head, ensuring its closed end is facing the timing chain, then install the cap and tighten it to the specified torque. Note: *If a new tensioner is being fitted, release it by pushing the cap centre pin fully in until it is heard to 'click', the tensioner pin should then be able to be easily depressed and return smoothly.*

20 Rotate the crankshaft through two complete rotations (720º) in the correct direction of rotation (to bring number 1 piston back to TDC on its compression stroke) and check that all the locking tools can be inserted correctly.

21 Ensure the mating surfaces of the pump sprocket cover and timing chain cover are clean and dry. Where the cover was originally fitted with a gasket, fit the cover with a new gasket and tighten the retaining bolts to the specified torque. If no gasket was fitted, apply a bead of sealant (approximately 2 mm thick) to the cover mating surface then refit the cover and tighten its retaining bolts to the specified torque **(see illustration)**.

22 Refit the auxiliary drivebelt tensioner assembly to the engine unit, tightening the strut and backplate pivot bolts to their specified torque settings. If a new tensioner strut is being fitted, or the original was not stored properly, prime the strut by repeatedly compressing it using a socket on the backplate hexagonal section. Once the strut is functioning correctly, refit the auxiliary drivebelt as described in Chapter 1.

23 Refit the right-hand mounting bracket assembly to the cylinder head (where removed) then lower the engine/transmission unit back down. Refit the right-hand engine mounting to the inner wing and align the mounting with the previously made marks on the cylinder head bracket, fit and tighten the bolts to the specified torque. Refit the camshaft cover (see Section 5).

5.3 On low-pressure turbo models remove the metal pipe and intake duct linking the turbocharger to the manifold

24 Refit the exhaust front pipe and air cleaner housing as described in the Chapter 4A.

25 Refit the vacuum pump to the cylinder head (see Chapter 9).

26 Fit the crankshaft sensor to the cylinder block (see Chapter 4A) and reconnect the battery.

5 Camshaft cover – removal and refitting

Removal

1 Undo the retaining screws and remove the plastic cover from the top of the camshaft cover.

2 Slacken the retaining clip and disconnect the breather hose from the rear of the cover. On Zafira models, remove the engine compartment seal and water deflector cover from in front of the windscreen.

3 On low-pressure turbo (X20DTL and Y20DTL engines) models slacken the clamp securing the metal pipe to the turbocharger, and the clamp securing the intake duct to the manifold. Undo the two retaining bolts and remove the duct assembly from the engine along with the sealing ring which is fitted between the pipe and turbocharger **(see illustration)**. On high-pressure turbo (Y20DTH) models, release the retaining clips and bracket bolts, and remove the charge air pipe from the turbocharger to the intercooler.

4 On all models, release the glow plug wiring guide from the rear of the cover. Undo the bolt securing the inlet manifold wiring harness tray to the cover. Unclip the vacuum pipe from the right-hand end of the cover.

5 Slacken and remove the camshaft cover retaining bolts along with their sealing washers then lift the camshaft cover and seal away from the cylinder head **(see illustration)**. Examine the cover seal and retaining bolt sealing washers for signs of damage or deterioration and renew if necessary.

Refitting

6 Ensure the cover and cylinder head

5.5 Slacken and remove the camshaft cover retaining bolts noting the sealing washer (arrowed) which is fitted to each bolt

5.6 Fit the seal to the camshaft cover groove

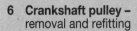

6 Crankshaft pulley – removal and refitting

Note: *A new pulley retaining bolt will be required on refitting.*

Removal

1 Apply the handbrake, then jack up the front of the car and support it on axle stands. Remove the right-hand roadwheel.
2 Undo the retaining screws/clips and remove the engine undertray.
3 Remove the auxiliary drivebelt as described in Chapter 1. Prior to removal, mark the direction of rotation on the belt to ensure the belt is refitted the same way around.
4 Slacken the crankshaft pulley retaining bolt. To prevent crankshaft rotation whilst the retaining bolt is slackened, have an assistant select top gear and apply the brakes firmly; if the engine is removed from the vehicle it will be necessary to lock the flywheel (see Section 16).
5 Unscrew the retaining bolt and washer and remove the crankshaft pulley from the end of the crankshaft. Whilst the pulley is removed check the oil seal for signs of wear or damage and, if necessary, renew as described in Section 15.

Refitting

6 Carefully locate the crankshaft pulley on the crankshaft end, aligning the pulley slot with the crankshaft key. Slide the pulley fully into position, taking great care not to damage the oil seal, then fit the washer and new retaining bolt **(see illustrations)**.
7 Lock the crankshaft by the method used on removal, and tighten the pulley retaining bolt to the specified Stage 1 torque setting then angle-tighten the bolt through the specified Stage 2 angle, using a socket and extension bar, and finally through the specified Stage 3 angle. It is recommended that an angle-measuring gauge is used during the final stages of the tightening, to ensure accuracy **(see illustration)**. If a gauge is not available, use white paint to make alignment marks between the bolt head and pulley prior to tightening; the marks can then be used to check that the bolt has been rotated through the correct angle.

5.8a Apply a smear of sealant to the semi-circular cut-out on the right-hand end of the cylinder head . . .

5.8b . . . and to the areas of the cylinder head surface on each side of the left-hand end camshaft cap

surfaces are clean and dry then fit the seal to the cover groove **(see illustration)**.
7 Fit the sealing washers to the retaining bolts, ensuring they are fitted the correct way up. Fit the retaining bolts to the cover making sure the cover seal is held firmly in position by the lower shoulder on each bolt.
8 Apply a smear of sealant to the circular cut-out on the right-hand end of the cylinder head mating surface and the areas of the cylinder head mating surface on either side of the left-hand end of the camshaft **(see illustrations)**.
9 Carefully lower the cover into position and screw in the retaining bolts. Once all bolts are hand-tight, go around and tighten them all to

the specified torque setting.
10 Clip the vacuum pipe and wiring back into position and reconnect the breather hose to the rear of the cover.
11 On low-pressure turbo models refit the intake duct and pipe, using a new sealing ring, and tighten its retaining clamps and bolts securely. On high-pressure models, refit the turbocharger-to-intercooler hose, tighten the mounting bracket bolt and retaining clips securely.
12 On all models, refit the plastic cover and securely tighten its retaining bolts. On Zafira models, refit the engine compartment seal and water deflector cover from in front of the windscreen.

6.6a Slide the crankshaft pulley carefully into position engaging its slot (arrowed) with the Woodruff key . . .

6.6b . . . then fit the retaining bolt and washer

6.7 Lock the crankshaft then tighten the pulley retaining bolt

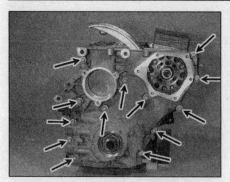

7.8 Timing chain cover retaining bolt locations (arrowed)

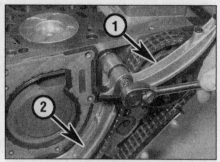

7.10 Unscrew the pivot bolt and remove the upper (1) and lower (2) timing chain tensioner blades

7.11 Undo the retaining bolts (arrowed) and remove the lower timing chain guide

8 Refit the auxiliary drivebelt as described in Chapter 1 using the mark made prior to removal to ensure the belt is fitted the correct way around.

9 Position the engine undertray and refit the retaining clips/screws.

10 Refit the roadwheel then lower the car to the ground and tighten the wheel bolts to the specified torque.

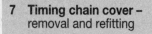

7 Timing chain cover – removal and refitting

Removal

1 Remove the upper timing chain and sprockets as described in Section 9.

2 Remove the cylinder head as described in Section 11. **Note:** *In theory it is possible to remove the timing chain cover without disturbing the cylinder head. However, this procedure carries a high risk of damaging the head gasket, resulting in oil/coolant leakage once the cover is refitted. If you wish to attempt this, leave the cylinder head in position and just undo the retaining bolts securing the head to the top of the timing chain cover. Be warned though that, after refitting, you may find the head gasket will need renewing, meaning that the cylinder head will have to be removed after all. The decision is yours as to whether this is a chance worth taking.*

3 Remove the water pump as described in Chapter 3.

4 Remove the crankshaft pulley as described in Section 6. Prior to slackening the pulley bolt, temporarily remove the locking pin from the crankshaft to prevent damage. Refit the pin once the bolt is loose.

5 Remove the sump as described in Section 12.

6 Remove the alternator as described in Chapter 5A.

7 Unscrew the lower timing chain tensioner cap from the rear of the timing chain cover and remove the tensioner plunger, noting which way around it is fitted. Remove the sealing ring from the cap and discard it, a new one should be used on refitting.

8 Noting each bolt's correct fitted location (the bolts are not all the same length), slacken and remove all the bolts securing the timing chain cover to the cylinder block **(see illustration)**.

9 Carefully ease the timing cover squarely away from the cylinder block and manoeuvre it out of position, noting the correct fitted positions of its locating dowels. If the locating dowels are a loose fit, remove them and store with the cover for safe-keeping.

10 Undo the pivot bolt and remove the upper and lower timing chain tensioner blades from the cylinder block **(see illustration)**.

11 Undo the retaining bolts and remove the lower timing chain guide from the cylinder block, noting which way around the guide is fitted **(see illustration)**.

12 Temporarily free the lower timing chain sprocket from the injection pump and manoeuvre the timing chain cover gasket away from the cylinder block. Once the gasket has been removed, seat the sprocket back on the injection pump flange **(see illustration)**.

Refitting

13 Prior to refitting the cover, it is recommended that the crankshaft oil seal should be renewed. Carefully lever the old seal out of the cover using a large flat-bladed screwdriver. Fit the new seal to the cover, making sure its sealing lip is facing inwards. Press/tap the seal into position until it is flush with the cover, using a suitable tubular drift, such as a socket, which bears only on the hard outer edge of the seal.

14 Ensure the mating surfaces of the cover and cylinder block are clean and dry and the locating dowels are in position.

15 Temporarily free the sprocket from the injection pump flange then manoeuvre the gasket into position and locate it on the dowels. Locate the sprocket back on the injection pump flange.

16 Refit the lower timing chain guide to the cylinder block and tighten its retaining bolts to the specified torque. Ensure the guide is fitted the correct way around with its stepped face on the inside **(see illustration)**.

17 Manoeuvre the timing chain tensioner blades into position and refit the pivot bolt, tightening it to the specified torque setting **(see illustration)**.

7.12 Free the sprocket from the injection pump and remove the timing chain cover gasket

7.16 Refit the lower timing chain guide and tighten its retaining bolts to the specified torque

7.17 Refit the pivot bolt to the tensioner blades and tighten to the specified torque

8.3a Unscrew the tensioner cap from the rear of the cylinder head . . .

8.3b . . . and withdraw the plunger, noting which way around it is fitted

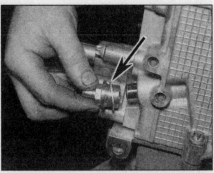

8.6a Insert the plunger, making sure its closed end is facing the timing chain, then fit the tensioner cap and sealing washer (arrowed)

18 Manoeuvre the timing cover into position. Align the oil pump drive gear with the crankshaft sprocket and slide the cover into position, locating it on the dowels.
19 Refit the timing chain cover retaining bolts, ensuring each one is fitted in its original location, and tighten them evenly and progressively to the specified torque.
20 Fit a new sealing ring to the lower timing chain tensioner cap. Insert the plunger, ensuring its closed end is facing the timing chain, then fit the cap to the timing chain cover and tighten to the specified torque. **Note:** *If a new tensioner is being fitted, release it by pushing the cap centre pin fully in until it is heard to 'click', the tensioner pin should then be able to be easily depressed and return smoothly.*
21 Refit the crankshaft pulley as described in Section 6.
22 Refit the cylinder head as described in Section 11.
23 Refit the upper timing chain and sprockets as described in Section 9.
24 Refit the sump as described in Section 12.
25 Refit the water pump, alternator (see Chapter 3 and 5A) and refit the auxiliary drivebelt (see Chapter 1).
26 On completion refill the engine with oil and coolant as described in Chapters 1 and 3. Start the engine and check for signs of oil leaks.

8 Timing chain tensioners – removal and refitting

Upper timing chain tensioner

Removal

1 Remove the air cleaner housing as described in Chapter 4A.
2 Referring to Section 17, support the engine/transmission unit and unbolt the right-hand mounting assembly from the cylinder head.
3 Unscrew the tensioner cap from the rear of the cylinder head and remove the plunger, noting which way around it is fitted **(see illustrations)**. Remove the sealing ring from the cap and discard it, a new one should be used on refitting.
Caution: Do not rotate the engine whilst the tensioner is removed.
4 Inspect the tensioner plunger for signs of wear or damage and renew if necessary.

Refitting

5 Lubricate the tensioner plunger with clean engine oil and insert it into the cylinder head. Ensure the plunger is fitted the correct way around with its closed end facing the timing chain.
6 Fit a new sealing ring to the tensioner cap then fit the cap to the cylinder head,

tightening it to the specified torque. **Note:** *If a new tensioner is being fitted, release it by pushing the cap centre pin fully in until it is heard to 'click', the tensioner pin should then be able to be easily depressed and return smoothly* **(see illustrations)**.
7 Refit the engine/transmission right-hand mounting assembly (see Section 17).
8 Refit the air cleaner housing as described in Chapter 4A.

Lower timing chain tensioner

Removal

9 Firmly apply the handbrake then jack up the front of the vehicle and support it on axle stands.
10 Undo the retaining bolts/clips and remove the engine undertray (where fitted).
11 Unscrew the tensioner cap from the rear of the timing chain cover and remove the plunger, noting which way around it is fitted. Remove the sealing ring from the cap and discard it, a new one should be used on refitting **(see illustrations)**.
Caution: Do not rotate the engine whilst the tensioner is removed.
12 Inspect the tensioner plunger for signs of wear or damage and renew if necessary.

Refitting

13 Lubricate the tensioner plunger with clean

8.6b If a new tensioner is being fitted, release it by depressing the cap centre pin until it is heard to click

8.11a Slacken and remove the lower timing chain tensioner cap and sealing washer from the rear of the timing chain cover . . .

8.11b . . . then withdraw the tensioner plunger

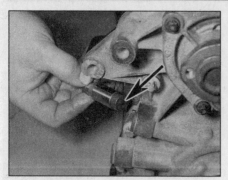

8.13 Ensure the plunger is fitted the correct way around with its closed end (arrowed) facing the timing chain

8.14 If a new tensioner is being fitted, release it by depressing the cap centre pin until it is heard to click

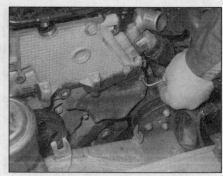

9.6a Undo the retaining screws . . .

engine oil and insert it into the timing chain cover. Ensure the plunger is fitted the correct way around with its closed end facing the timing chain (see illustration).

14 Fit a new sealing ring to the tensioner cap then fit the cap to the cover, tightening it to the specified torque. **Note:** *If a new tensioner is being fitted, release it by pushing the cap centre pin fully in until it is heard to 'click', the tensioner pin should then be able to be easily depressed and return smoothly (see illustration).*

15 Refit the undertray (where fitted) then lower the vehicle to the ground.

Upper and lower timing chain tensioner blades

16 Tensioner blade removal and refitting is part of the timing chain cover removal and refitting procedure (see Section 7). The blades must be renewed if they show signs of wear or damage on their chain surfaces.

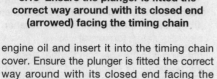

9 Timing chains and sprockets – removal, inspection and refitting

Note: *In order to set the valve timing accurately, several special Vauxhall service tools (or suitable alternatives) are required (see Section 4). If access to suitable tools cannot be gained then it*

is recommended that this task is entrusted to a Vauxhall dealer or suitably-equipped garage. If the task is to be carried out without the tools then accurate alignment marks must be made between the sprocket(s), chain(s) and the shaft(s) prior to removal to ensure the valve timing is correctly set on refitting.
Note: A new camshaft sprocket retaining bolt and new upper timing chain guide retaining bolts will be required on refitting.

Removal

Upper timing chain and sprockets

1 Disconnect the battery negative lead then remove the camshaft cover (see Section 5). **Note:** *Before disconnecting the battery, refer to 'Disconnecting the battery' in the reference section at the rear of this manual*

2 Position No 1 cylinder at TDC on its compression stroke as described in Section 3 and lock the crankshaft in position.

3 To improve access to the injection pump sprocket cover, carry out the following.
  a) Remove the air cleaner housing and exhaust system front pipe (see Chapter 4A).
  b) Remove the auxiliary drivebelt (Chapter 1).
  c) Mark the position of the right-hand engine mounting bracket in relation to the cylinder head bracket. Undo the three bolts securing the right-hand engine mounting to the cylinder head bracket, and the three bolts securing the right-hand engine mounting to

the inner wing, then raise the right-hand end of the engine using a jack/engine support bar (see Section 17). Raise the engine as high as possible without placing any excess strain on the remaining mountings or any pipes/hoses or wiring.

4 Remove both the upper and lower timing chain tensioners as described in Section 8.

5 Undo the auxiliary drivebelt tensioner pulley strut lower mounting bolt and the pulley backplate pivot bolt and remove the tensioner assembly from the engine. **Note:** *Store the assembly so the tensioner strut is the correct way up; if the strut is not stored properly it will have to be primed once it is refitted.*

6 Undo the retaining bolts and remove the injection pump sprocket cover from the timing chain cover (see illustrations).

7 If the special locking tools are available, lock the injection pump sprockets and camshaft in position (see Section 4). If the tools are not being used, make accurate alignment marks between the chain and sprockets, and the sprockets and the camshaft/pump flange.

8 Undo the retaining bolts then lift the upper chain guide out from the top of the cylinder head. **Note:** *The upper timing chain guide bolts should be heated with a hot air gun prior to removal; this loosens the locking compound on the bolt head and significantly eases removal of the bolts (see illustrations).*

9.6b . . . and remove the injection pump sprocket cover from the engine

9.8a To ease removal, heat up the upper timing chain guide bolts with a hot air gun prior to removal

9.8b Unscrew the retaining bolts . . .

9.8c . . . and lift the upper guide out from the top of the cylinder head

9.9 Retain the camshaft with an open-ended spanner and unscrew the sprocket retaining bolt

9.10 Unbolt the sprocket from the injection pump then free it from the chain and remove it through the cover aperture

9.14 Free the sprocket from the injection pump flange and remove it complete with the lower timing chain

9 Hold the camshaft using an open-ended spanner on the flats provided, then slacken and remove the camshaft sprocket retaining bolt **(see illustration)**. To ensure the camshaft sprocket and chain remain correctly mated, cable tie the chain to the sprocket. **Note:** *If the locking tools are being used, remove them prior to slackening the sprocket bolt and refit them once the bolt is loose.*

10 Remove the injection pump locking tool (where fitted) then slacken and remove the bolts securing the injection pump sprockets to the pump flange. Manoeuvre the injection pump upper chain sprocket out of position then free the camshaft sprocket from the camshaft end and lift the sprocket and upper timing chain out from the top of the cylinder head **(see illustration)**.

Lower timing chain and sprockets

11 Remove the upper timing chain and sprockets as described in paragraphs 1 to 10.

12 Remove the timing chain cover as described in Section 7.

13 Make alignment marks between the chain and sprockets and the injection pump sprocket and pump flange.

14 Free the pump sprocket from its flange and remove the sprocket and timing chain from the engine, noting which way around the sprocket is fitted **(see illustration)**.

15 Slide the crankshaft sprocket off from the crankshaft end and recover the Woodruff key from the crankshaft groove **(see illustrations)**.

Inspection

16 Examine the teeth on the sprockets for any sign of wear or damage such as chipped, hooked or missing teeth. If there is any sign of wear or damage on either sprocket, both sprockets and the relevant chain should be renewed as a set.

17 Inspect the links of each timing chain for signs of wear or damage on the rollers. The extent of wear can be judged by checking the amount by which the chain can be bent sideways; a new chain will have very little sideways movement. If there is an excessive amount of side play in a timing chain, it must be renewed.

18 Note that it is a sensible precaution to renew the timing chains, regardless of their apparent condition, if the engine has covered a high mileage, or if it has been noted that the chain(s) have sounded noisy when the engine running. Although not strictly necessary, it is always worth renewing the chains and sprockets as a matched set, since it is false economy to run a new chain on worn sprockets and *vice-versa*. If there is any doubt about the condition of the timing chains and sprockets, seek the advice of a Vauxhall dealer service department, who will be able to advise you as to the best course of action, based on their previous knowledge of the engine.

19 Examine the chain guide(s) and tensioner blade(s) for signs of wear or damage to their chain contact faces, renewing any which are badly marked.

Refitting

Upper timing chain and sprockets

20 If any new components are being fitted, transfer the alignment marks from the original components to aid refitting. Ensure the crankshaft is still locked in the TDC position.

21 Engage the camshaft sprocket with the chain and lower the assembly into position.

22 Manoeuvre the injection pump sprocket into position and engage it with the timing chain.

23 Ensure the marks made prior to removal are all correctly aligned then engage the sprockets with the camshaft and injection pump flange. Where necessary, remove the cable tie from camshaft sprocket.

24 Align the injection pump sprocket timing mark with the hole in the pump flange then refit the retaining bolts tightening them by hand only at this stage **(see illustration)**.

25 Fit the new sprocket retaining bolt to the

9.15a Slide the sprocket off from the end of the crankshaft . . .

9.15b . . . and remove the Woodruff key

9.24 Align the injection pump sprocket timing mark (arrowed) with the pump flange hole and refit the retaining bolts

9.25 Fit the new camshaft sprocket retaining bolt and tighten it by hand only

9.27 Refit the upper timing chain guide to the cylinder head making sure its locating lug (arrowed) is uppermost

camshaft end, tightening by hand only at this stage **(see illustration)**.

26 Refit the lower timing chain tensioner as described in Section 8.

27 Slide the upper timing chain guide into position, ensuring its locating lug is uppermost, then fit the new retaining bolts and tighten them to the specified torque **(see illustration)**.

28 If the special tools are available, fit all the tools to ensure the pump, camshaft and crankshaft are correctly positioned. If the tools are not being used, ensure the marks made prior to removal are realigned.

29 If the special tools are available, adjust the valve timing as described in Section 4, paragraphs 14 to 18. Remove all the locking tools.

30 If the tools are not available, align the marks made prior to removal then tighten the injection pump sprocket bolts to the specified torque. Tighten the camshaft sprocket bolt to the specified Stage 1 torque setting, whilst preventing the camshaft from rotating. Ensure the marks remain in alignment then tighten the bolt through the specified Stage 2 angle and finally through the specified Stage 3 angle. It is recommended that an angle-measuring gauge is used during the final stages of the tightening, to ensure accuracy. If a gauge is not available, use white paint to make alignment marks prior to tightening; the marks can then be used to check that the bolt has been rotated through the correct angle.

31 Refit the upper timing chain tensioner as described in Section 8.

32 Ensure the mating surfaces of the pump sprocket cover and timing chain cover are clean and dry. Where the cover was originally fitted with a gasket, fit the cover with a new gasket and tighten the retaining bolts to the specified torque. If no gasket was fitted, apply a bead of sealant (approximately 2 mm thick) to the cover groove then refit the cover and tighten its retaining bolts to the specified torque.

33 Refit the auxiliary drivebelt tensioner assembly to the engine unit, tightening the strut and backplate pivot bolts to their specified torque settings. If a new tensioner strut is being fitted, or the original was not

stored properly, prime the strut by repeatedly compressing it using a socket on the backplate hexagonal section. Once the strut is functioning correctly, refit the auxiliary drivebelt as described in Chapter 1.

34 Refit the right-hand mounting assembly to the cylinder head then lower the engine/transmission unit back down. Refit the right-hand engine mounting to the inner wing and align the mounting with the previously made marks on the cylinder head bracket, fit and tighten the bolts to the specified torque.

35 Refit the camshaft cover as described in Section 5.

36 Refit the exhaust front pipe, air cleaner housing and crankshaft sensor (see Chapter 4A). Where the camshaft timing tool has have been used, refit the vacuum pump to the cylinder head (see Chapter 9).

Lower timing chain and sprockets

37 If any new components are being fitted transfer the alignment marks from the original components to aid refitting.

38 Refit the Woodruff key to the crankshaft then slide on the crankshaft sprocket, aligning the sprocket groove with the key.

39 Ensure the injection pump flange is still correctly positioned with the flange timing cut-out aligned with the hole in the pump body and the crankshaft is still locked at TDC.

40 Aligning the marks made prior to removal, engage the pump sprocket with the chain and manoeuvre the assembly into position. Engage the chain with the crankshaft

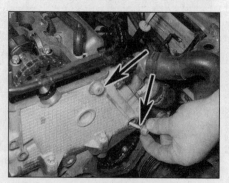

10.9 Remove the retaining bolts (arrowed) and lift out the upper timing chain guide

sprocket and seat the pump sprocket on the flange, ensuring the sprocket is fitted the correct way around. Check that all the marks made prior to removal are correctly aligned and that the injection pump flange timing cut-out is correctly position in the oblong slot in the sprocket.

41 Refit the timing cover as described in Section 7 then refit the upper timing chain as described earlier in this Section.

10 Camshaft and followers – removal, inspection and refitting

Note: *A new camshaft sprocket retaining bolt and new upper timing chain guide retaining bolts will be required on refitting.*

Removal

1 Disconnect the battery negative lead then remove the camshaft cover as described in Section 5. **Note:** *Before disconnecting the battery, refer to 'Disconnecting the battery' in the reference section at the rear of this manual.*

2 Remove the braking system vacuum pump as described in Chapter 9.

3 Position No 1 cylinder at TDC on its compression stroke as described in Section 3 and lock the crankshaft in position.

4 To improve access to the injection pump sprocket cover, carry out the following.
   a) Remove the air cleaner housing and exhaust system front pipe (see Chapter 4A).
   b) Remove the auxiliary drivebelt (see Chapter 1).
   c) Mark the position of the right-hand engine mounting bracket in relation to the cylinder head bracket. Undo the three bolts securing the right-hand engine mounting to the cylinder head bracket, and the three bolts securing the right-hand engine mounting to the inner wing, then raise the right-hand end of the engine using a jack/engine support bar (see Section 17). Raise the engine as high as possible without placing any excess strain on the remaining mountings or any pipes/hoses or wiring.

5 Remove the upper timing chain tensioner as described in Section 8.

6 Undo the auxiliary drivebelt tensioner pulley strut lower mounting bolt and the pulley backplate pivot bolt and remove the tensioner assembly from the engine. **Note:** *Store the assembly so the tensioner strut is the correct way up; if the strut is not stored properly it will have to be primed once it is refitted.*

7 Undo the retaining bolts and remove the injection pump sprocket cover from the timing chain cover.

8 Make accurate alignment marks between the upper timing chain and sprockets, and the camshaft sprocket and camshaft.

9 Undo the retaining bolts then lift the upper chain guide out from the top of the cylinder head **(see illustration)**. **Note:** *The upper*

10.11a Free the camshaft sprocket from the timing chain . . .

10.11b . . . then pass a screwdriver or extension bar through the chain to prevent it falling down into the engine

10.12 Each camshaft bearing cap should be stamped with an identification number (arrowed)

timing chain guide bolts should be heated with a hot air gun prior to removal; this loosens the locking compound on the bolt head and significantly eases removal of the bolts.

10 Hold the camshaft, using an open-ended spanner on the flats provided, then slacken and remove the camshaft sprocket retaining bolt. Remove the crankshaft locking tool prior to slackening the sprocket bolt and refit it once the bolt is loose.

11 Disengage the camshaft sprocket from the upper timing chain and remove it from the engine. Pass a screwdriver or extension bar through the upper chain, to prevent it falling down into the cylinder head, and rest it on the head upper surface **(see illustrations)**.

12 Note the identification markings on the camshaft bearing caps. The caps are numbered 1 to 5 with all numbers being the right way up when viewed from the front of the engine; number 1 cap being at the timing chain end of the engine and number 5 at the flywheel end **(see illustration)**. If the markings are not clearly visible, make identification marks to ensure each cap is fitted correctly on refitting.

13 Working in a spiral pattern from the outside inwards, slacken the camshaft bearing cap retaining bolts by one turn at a time, to relieve the pressure of the valve springs on the bearing caps gradually and

evenly. Once the valve spring pressure has been relieved, the bolts can be fully unscrewed and removed, along with the caps. Take care not to loose the locating dowels which are fitted to the left-hand end (No 5) bearing cap and lift the camshaft out from the head.

Caution: If the bearing cap bolts are carelessly slackened, the bearing caps might break. If any bearing cap breaks then the complete cylinder head assembly must be renewed; the bearing caps are matched to the head and are not available separately.

14 Obtain eight (twenty-four if the tappets are also to be removed) small, clean plastic containers, and label them for identification. Alternatively, divide a larger container into compartments. Lift the followers out from the top of the cylinder head and store each one in its respective fitted position **(see illustration)**.

15 If the hydraulic tappets are also to be removed, remove the injector crossover pipes as described in Chapter 4A, Section 12. Using a rubber sucker or magnet, withdraw each hydraulic tappet and place it in its container.

Inspection

16 Examine the camshaft bearing surfaces and cam lobes for signs of wear ridges and scoring. Renew the camshaft if any of these conditions are apparent. Examine the

condition of the bearing surfaces both on the camshaft journals and in the cylinder head. If the head bearing surfaces are worn excessively, the cylinder head will need to be renewed.

17 Support the camshaft end journals on V-blocks, and measure the run-out at the centre journal using a dial gauge. If the run-out exceeds the specified limit, the camshaft should be renewed.

18 Examine the follower bearing surfaces which contact the camshaft lobes for wear ridges and scoring. Renew any followers on which these conditions are apparent.

19 Check the hydraulic tappets (where removed) and their bores in the cylinder head for signs of wear or damage. If any tappet is thought to be faulty it should be renewed.

Refitting

20 Where removed, lubricate the hydraulic tappets with clean engine oil and carefully insert each one into its original location in the cylinder head **(see illustration)**. Refit the injector crossover pipes as described in Chapter 4A.

21 Refit the camshaft followers to the cylinder head. Ensure each follower is fitted in its original location and the punch marks on the follower upper surface are facing the injector crossover pipe **(see illustration)**.

22 Lubricate the camshaft followers with

10.14 Removing a camshaft follower

10.20 Lubricate the hydraulic tappets with clean engine oil and install them in the cylinder head

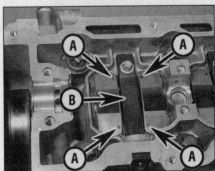

10.21 On refitting ensure that all followers are correctly positioned and that the punch marks (A) are facing towards the injector crossover pipe (B)

10.22a Refit the camshaft, positioning it so that No 1 cylinder lobes are pointing upwards (arrowed) . . .

10.22b . . . and the slot in the left-hand end is parallel to the cylinder head with the timing hole (arrowed) at the top

10.24 Apply sealant to the areas shown on the left-hand end of the cylinder head (arrowed)

10.25 Refit the camshaft bearing caps using the identification markings to ensure each is correctly positioned

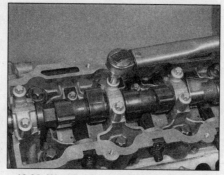

10.26 Working as described in the text, tighten the bearing cap bolts to the specified torque

10.27 Refit the camshaft sprocket and install a new retaining bolt

clean engine oil then lay the camshaft in position. Ensure the crankshaft is still locked in position and position the camshaft so that the lobes of No 1 cylinder are pointing upwards and the slot on the left-hand end of the camshaft is parallel with the cylinder head surface (timing hole at the top) **(see illustrations)**.

23 Ensure the mating surfaces of the bearing caps and cylinder head are clean and dry and lubricate the camshaft journals and lobes with clean engine oil.

24 Apply a smear of sealant to the cylinder head mating surface of the left-hand (No 5) bearing cap and fit the cap locating dowels to the cylinder head **(see illustration)**.

25 Refit the camshaft bearing caps and the retaining bolts in their original locations on the cylinder head **(see illustration)**. The caps are numbered 1 to 5 from timing chain end of the cylinder head and all numbers should be the right way up when viewed from the front of the engine.

26 Tighten all bolts by hand only then, working in a spiral pattern from the centre outwards, tighten the bolts by one turn at a time to gradually impose the pressure of the valve springs on the bearing caps. Repeat this sequence until all bearing caps are in contact with the cylinder head then go around and tighten the camshaft bearing cap bolts to the specified torque **(see illustration)**.
Caution: If the bearing cap bolts are

carelessly tightened, the bearing caps might break. If any bearing cap breaks then the complete cylinder head assembly must be renewed; the bearing caps are matched to the head and are not available separately.

27 Using the marks made on removal, ensure that the upper timing chain is still correctly engaged with the injection pump sprocket then refit the camshaft sprocket to the chain. Seat the sprocket on the end of the camshaft and fit the new retaining bolt **(see illustration)**.

28 Slide the upper timing chain guide into position, ensuring its locating lug is

10.30a If the timing tools are not available, align the marks made prior to removal then tighten the sprocket bolts to the Stage 1 torque setting . . .

uppermost, then fit the retaining bolts and tighten them to the specified torque.

29 If the special tools are available, adjust the valve timing as described in Section 4, paragraphs 14 to 18. Remove all the locking tools.

30 If the tools are not available, align the marks made prior to removal on the camshaft and sprocket. Hold the camshaft with an open-ended spanner and tighten the sprocket bolt to the specified Stage 1 torque setting. Ensure the marks have remained in alignment then tighten the bolt through the specified Stage 2 angle and finally through the specified Stage 3 angle. It is recommended that an angle-measuring gauge is used during the final stages of the tightening, to ensure accuracy **(see illustrations)**. If a gauge is not

10.30b . . . and then through the specified Stage 2 and 3 angles

available, use white paint to make alignment marks prior to tightening; the marks can then be used to check that the bolt has been rotated through the correct angle.

31 Refit the upper timing chain tensioner as described in Section 8.

32 Ensure the mating surfaces of the pump sprocket cover and timing chain cover are clean and dry. Where the cover was originally fitted with a gasket, fit the cover with a new gasket and tighten the retaining bolts to the specified torque. If no gasket was fitted, apply a bead of sealant (approximately 2 mm thick) to the cover groove then refit the cover and tighten its retaining bolts to the specified torque.

33 Refit the auxiliary drivebelt tensioner assembly to the engine unit, tightening the strut and backplate pivot bolts to their specified torque settings. If a new tensioner strut is being fitted, or the original was not stored properly, prime the strut by repeatedly compressing it using a socket on the backplate hexagonal section. Once the strut is functioning correctly, refit the auxiliary drivebelt as described in Chapter 1.

34 Refit the right-hand mounting assembly to the cylinder head. then lower the engine/transmission unit back down. Refit the right-hand engine mounting to the inner wing and align the mounting with the previously made marks on the cylinder head bracket, fit and tighten the bolts to the specified torque.

35 Refit the camshaft cover as described in Section 5.

36 Refit the exhaust front pipe, air cleaner housing and crankshaft sensor (see Chapter 4A).

37 Refit the vacuum pump as described in Chapter 9.

11 Cylinder head – removal and refitting

Caution: Be careful not to allow dirt into the fuel injection pump or injector pipes during this procedure.

Note: New cylinder head bolts, upper timing chain guide bolts and a camshaft sprocket retaining bolt will be required on refitting.

11.3a Unscrew the union bolts (arrowed) then disconnect the fuel feed and return hose unions from the injection pump ...

Removal

1 Drain the cooling system as described in Chapter 3.

2 Carry out the operations described in paragraphs 1 to 11 of Section 10, noting that it will be necessary to raise the engine on a jack. Support the engine by inserting stout block of wood in between the right-hand end of the sump and the subframe.

3 Wipe clean the area around the fuel hose unions on the injection pump then slacken and remove the union bolts and sealing washers. Disconnect the return pipe from the pump union then releasing the hoses from their retaining clips, and position them clear of the cylinder head **(see illustrations)**.

4 Remove the inlet and exhaust manifolds as described in Chapter 4A. If no work is to be carried out on the cylinder head, the head can be removed complete with manifolds once the following operations have been carried out (see Chapter 4A).

a) On high-pressure turbo models, remove the intake ducts and metal pipe from the turbocharger.

b) Unbolt the wiring harness tray from the top of the inlet manifold, disconnect the wiring connectors and position it clear of the engine. Unclip the crankshaft sensor wiring from the manifold.

c) Remove the injector pipes linking the pump to the injectors.

d) Disconnect the vacuum hoses from the

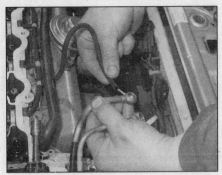

11.3b ... and disconnect the return pipe

inlet manifold switchover valve and the EGR valve.

e) Disconnect/unbolt the wiring connectors from the glow plugs then remove the turbocharger heatshields.

f) Disconnect the turbocharger oil pipes from the cylinder block. Disconnect the wastegate diaphragm vacuum hose.

g) Remove the starter motor heatshield and unbolt the wiring harness guide and exhaust manifold support bracket from the rear of the block.

5 Release the retaining clips and disconnect the coolant hoses from the front and rear of the right-hand end of the cylinder head **(see illustrations)**.

6 Slacken and remove the alternator upper mounting bolt, and pivot the alternator to the rear to position it clear of the cylinder head.

7 Slacken and remove the three bolts securing the right-hand end of the cylinder head to the top of the timing chain cover and the single bolt securing the head to the block **(see illustration)**.

8 Working in the **reverse** of the sequence shown in illustration 11.26, progressively slacken the ten main cylinder head bolts by half a turn at a time, until all bolts can be unscrewed by hand.

9 Lift out the cylinder head bolts and recover the washers.

10 Lift the cylinder head away; seek assistance if possible, as it is a heavy assembly (especially if complete with manifolds). Remove the gasket, noting the

11.5a Disconnect the coolant hoses (arrowed) from the front of the cylinder head ...

11.5b ... and the hose from the rear of the cylinder head

11.7 Unscrew the bolts (arrowed) securing the right-hand end of the cylinder head to the timing chain cover/block

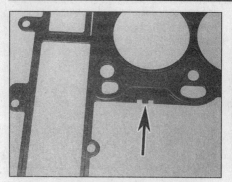

11.17 Cylinder head gasket thickness identification cut-outs

11.18 Measuring piston protrusion using a dial gauge

two locating dowels fitted to the top of the cylinder block. If they are a loose fit, remove the locating dowels and store them with the head for safe-keeping. Keep the head gasket for identification purposes (see paragraph 17).
Caution: Do not lay the head on its lower mating surface; support the head on wooden blocks, ensuring each block only contacts the head mating surface not the glow plugs or injector nozzles. The glow plugs and injector nozzles protrude from the bottom of the head and they will be damaged if the head is placed directly onto a bench.
11 If the cylinder head is to be dismantled for overhaul, then refer to Part D of this Chapter.

Preparation for refitting

12 The mating faces of the cylinder head and cylinder block/crankcase must be perfectly clean before refitting the head. Use a hard plastic or wood scraper to remove all traces of gasket and carbon; also clean the piston crowns. Take particular care, as the surfaces are damaged easily. Also, make sure that the carbon is not allowed to enter the oil and water passages – this is particularly important for the lubrication system, as carbon could block the oil supply to any of the engine's components. Using adhesive tape and paper, seal the water, oil and bolt holes in the cylinder block/crankcase. To prevent carbon entering the gap between the pistons and bores, smear a little grease in the gap. After cleaning each piston, use a small brush to remove all traces of grease and carbon from the gap, then wipe away the remainder with a clean rag. Clean all the pistons in the same way.
13 Check the mating surfaces of the cylinder block/crankcase and the cylinder head for nicks, deep scratches and other damage. If slight, they may be removed carefully with a file, but if excessive, machining may be the only alternative to renewal.
14 Ensure that the cylinder head bolt holes in the crankcase are clean and free of oil. Syringe or soak up any oil left in the bolt holes. This is most important in order that the correct bolt tightening torque can be applied and to prevent the possibility of the block being cracked by hydraulic pressure when the bolts are tightened.

15 The cylinder head bolts must be discarded and renewed, regardless of their apparent condition.
16 If warpage of the cylinder head gasket surface is suspected, use a straight-edge to check it for distortion. Refer to Part D of this Chapter if necessary.
17 On this engine, the cylinder head-to-piston clearance is controlled by fitting different thickness head gaskets. The gasket thickness can be determined by looking at the tab situated directly in front of No 1 cylinder **(see illustration)**.

Notches on tab	Gasket thickness
No notches	1.2 mm
One notch	1.3 mm
Two notches	1.4 mm

The correct thickness of gasket required is selected by measuring the piston protrusions as follows.
18 Ensure that the crankshaft is still locked in the TDC position. Mount a dial test indicator securely on the block so that its pointer can be easily pivoted between the piston crown and block mating surface. Zero the dial test indicator on the gasket surface of the cylinder block then carefully move the indicator over No 1 piston and measure its protrusion **(see illustration)**. Repeat this procedure on No 4 piston.
19 Remove the crankshaft locking tool and rotate the crankshaft half a turn (180°) to bring No 2 and 3 pistons to TDC. Ensure the crankshaft is accurately positioned then measure the protrusions of No 2 and 3 pistons. Once both pistons have been measured, rotate the crankshaft through a

11.22 Ensure the locating dowels are in position (arrowed) and fit the new gasket

further one and a half turns (540°) to bring No 1 and 4 pistons back to TDC and lock the crankshaft in position again.
Caution: When rotating the crankshaft, keep the upper timing chain taut to prevent the chain jamming around the injection pump sprocket.
20 Using the largest protrusion measurement of the four pistons, select the correct thickness of head gasket required using the following table.

Piston protrusion measurement	Gasket thickness required
0.40 to 0.50 mm	1.2 mm
0.51 to 0.60 mm	1.3 mm
0.61 to 0.70 mm	1.4 mm

Refitting

21 Wipe clean the mating surfaces of the cylinder head and cylinder block/crankcase.
22 Check that the two locating dowels are in position then fit a new gasket to the cylinder block **(see illustration)**.
23 Ensure the crankshaft is locked in the TDC position and the camshaft is correctly positioned with the lobes of No 1 cylinder pointing upwards and the slot on the left-hand end of the camshaft parallel with the cylinder head surface (timing hole at the top).
24 With the aid of an assistant, carefully refit the cylinder head assembly to the block, aligning it with the locating dowels. As the head is fitted, pass the upper timing chain up through the cylinder head, holding it in position by passing a screwdriver through the upper chain and resting it on the head upper surface.
25 Apply a smear of oil to the threads and the underside of the heads of the new cylinder head bolts and carefully enter each bolt into its relevant hole (*do not drop them in*). Screw all bolts in, by hand only, until finger-tight.
26 Working progressively and in the sequence shown, tighten the cylinder head bolts to their Stage 1 torque setting, using a torque wrench and suitable socket **(see illustration)**.

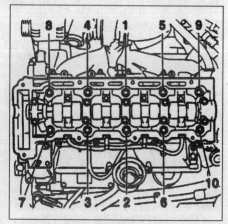

11.26 Cylinder head bolt tightening sequence

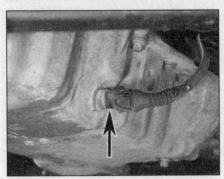

12.4 Disconnect the wiring connector from the oil temperature sensor (arrowed)

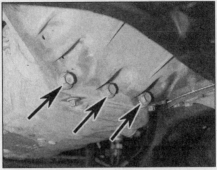

12.5 Slacken and remove the bolts securing the sump flange to the transmission housing (lower bolts arrowed)

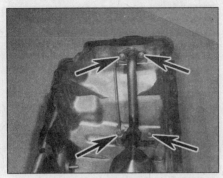

12.7 Oil pump pick-up/strainer retaining bolts (arrowed)

27 Once all bolts have been tightened to the Stage 1 torque, working again in the specified sequence, go around and tighten all bolts through the specified Stage 2 angle. It is recommended that an angle-measuring gauge is used to ensure accuracy. If a gauge is not available, use white paint to make alignment marks prior to tightening; the marks can then be used to check that the bolt has been rotated through the correct angle.
28 Go around again in the specified sequence and angle tighten the bolts through the specified Stage 3 angle.
29 Working again in the specified sequence, go around and tighten all bolts through the specified Stage 4 angle.
30 Go around again in the specified sequence and angle tighten the bolts through the specified Stage 5 angle.
31 Finally go around in the specified sequence and angle tighten the bolts through the specified Stage 6 angle.
32 Refit the bolts securing the right-hand end of the cylinder head to the block/timing cover and tighten them to the specified torque setting.
33 Pivot the alternator back into position and tighten its upper mounting bolt to the specified torque (Chapter 5A).
34 Reconnect the coolant hoses to the cylinder head and secure them in position with the retaining clips.
35 Refit/reconnect the inlet and exhaust manifolds and associated components as described in Chapter 4A.

36 Refit the camshaft sprocket to the camshaft as described in paragraphs 27 to 37 of Section 10.
37 Position a new sealing washer on each side of the injection pump fuel hose unions then refit both union bolts and tighten them to the specified torque (Chapter 4A).
38 On completion refill the cooling system as described in Chapter 3.

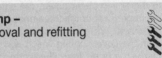

12 Sump –
removal and refitting

Removal

1 Disconnect the battery negative terminal.
Note: Before disconnecting the battery, refer to 'Disconnecting the battery' in the reference section at the rear of this manual.
2 Firmly apply the handbrake then jack up the front of the car and support it on axle stands. Where necessary, undo the retaining clips/screws and remove the engine undertray.
3 Drain the engine oil as described in Chapter 1, then fit a new sealing washer and refit the drain plug, tightening it to the specified torque.
4 Disconnect the wiring connector(s) from the oil temperature sensor and (where fitted) the oil level sensor **(see illustration)**.

5 Slacken and remove the bolts securing the sump flange to the transmission housing **(see illustration)**.
6 Progressively slacken and remove the bolts securing the sump to the base of the cylinder block/oil pump. Break the sump joint by striking the sump with the palm of the hand, then lower the sump away from the engine and withdraw it. Remove the gasket and discard it.
7 While the sump is removed, take the opportunity to check the oil pump pick-up/strainer for signs of clogging or splitting. If necessary, unbolt the pick-up/strainer and remove it from the sump along with its sealing ring **(see illustration)**. The strainer can then be cleaned easily in solvent or renewed.

Refitting

8 Remove all traces of dirt and oil from the mating surfaces of the sump and cylinder block and (where removed) the pick-up/strainer.
9 Where necessary, position a new sealing ring on the oil pump pick-up/strainer flange and fit the strainer to the sump, tightening its retaining bolts to the specified torque.
10 Apply a smear of suitable sealant (available from your Vauxhall dealer) to the areas of the cylinder block mating surface around the oil pump housing and rear main bearing cap joints **(see illustrations)**.
11 Fit a new gasket to the sump then offer up the sump to the cylinder block and loosely refit all the retaining bolts **(see illustration)**.

12.10a Apply a smear of sealant to the areas of the cylinder block/timing chain cover joints . . .

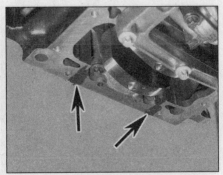

12.10b . . . and the rear main bearing cap/cylinder block joints

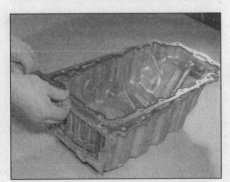

12.11 Fit a new gasket to the sump and manoeuvre it up into position

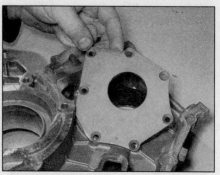

13.2 Remove the oil pump cover from the rear of the timing chain cover . . .

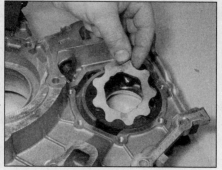

13.4a . . . then lift out the pump inner . . .

13.4b . . . and outer rotors

12 Working out from the centre in a diagonal sequence, progressively tighten the bolts securing the sump to the cylinder block/oil pump to their specified torque setting.
13 Tighten the bolts securing the sump flange to the transmission housing to their specified torque settings.
14 Reconnect the oil temperature/level sensor wiring connector(s) (as applicable). Where necessary refit the engine undertray.
15 Lower the vehicle to the ground then fill the engine with fresh oil (see Chapter 1).

13 Oil pump – removal, inspection and refitting

Removal

1 The oil pump assembly is built into the timing chain cover. Removal and refitting is as described in Section 7. **Note:** *The oil pump safety valve can be removed with the timing chain cover in position on the engine and the pressure relief valve can be removed once the sump has been removed (see below).*

Inspection

2 Undo the retaining screws and lift off the pump cover from the inside of the timing chain cover **(see illustration)**.
3 Using a suitable marker pen, mark the surface of both the pump inner and outer

rotors; the marks can then be used to ensure the rotors are refitted the correct way around.
4 Lift out the inner and outer rotors from the cover **(see illustrations)**.
5 Unscrew the oil pressure relief valve bolt from the base of the timing chain cover and withdraw the spring, spring sleeve and plunger, noting which way around the plunger is fitted. Remove the sealing ring from the valve bolt **(see illustrations)**.
6 Unscrew the safety valve bolt from the rear of the timing chain cover, the safety valve is the uppermost of the three bolts on the rear of the cover. Withdraw the spring and plunger from the cover, noting which way around the plunger is fitted **(see illustrations)**. Remove the sealing ring from the valve bolt.

7 Clean the components, and carefully examine the rotors, pump body and valve plungers for any signs of scoring or wear. Renew any component which shows signs of wear or damage; if the rotors or pump housing are marked then the complete pump assembly should be renewed.
8 If the pump is satisfactory, reassemble the components in the reverse order of removal, noting the following.
a) *Ensure both rotors and the valve plungers are fitted the correct way around.*
b) *Fit new sealing rings to the pressure relief valve and safety valve bolts and tighten both bolts to their specified torque settings.*
c) *Refit the pump cover tightening the cover*

13.5a Unscrew the oil pressure relief valve bolt and sealing washer . . .

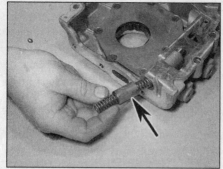

13.5b . . . and withdraw the spring, spring sleeve (arrowed) . . .

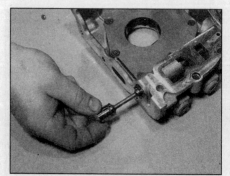

13.5c . . . and plunger from the timing chain cover

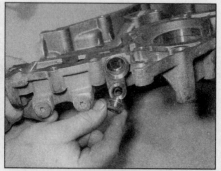

13.6a Unscrew the safety valve bolt and washer . . .

13.6b . . . then remove the spring and valve plunger from the timing chain cover

13.8 On refitting tighten the pump cover screw to the specified torque

15.2 Lever the right-hand crankshaft oil seal out from the timing chain cover

15.4 Press/tap the new seal squarely into position until it is flush with the cover

screws to the specified torque **(see illustration)**.

d) *On completion prime the oil pump by filling it with clean engine oil whilst rotating the inner rotor.*

Refitting

9 Refit the timing chain cover as described in Section 7.

14 Oil cooler – removal and refitting

Removal

1 The oil cooler is mounted on the front, left-hand end of cylinder block. The cooler is bolted onto the front of the oil filter housing. To improve access, firmly apply the handbrake then jack up the front of the car and support it on axle stands. Where necessary, undo the retaining clips/screws and remove the engine undertray.

2 To minimise coolant loss, clamp the coolant hoses on either side of the oil cooler then release the retaining clips and detach both hoses. Be prepared for some coolant loss and mop up any spilt coolant.

3 Wipe clean the area around the oil cooler then undo the retaining bolts and remove the cooler and sealing rings from the oil filter housing.

Refitting

4 Refitting is the reverse of removal, using new sealing rings. Check and top up the coolant as described in Chapter 3.

15 Crankshaft oil seals – renewal

Right-hand (timing chain end) oil seal

1 Remove the crankshaft pulley as described in Section 6.
2 Using a large flat-bladed screwdriver, carefully lever the seal out from the timing chain cover **(see illustration)**.
3 Clean the seal housing and polish off any burrs or raised edges which may have caused the seal to fail in the first place.
4 Lubricate the lips of the new seal with clean engine oil and press/tap it squarely into position until it is flush with the cover **(see illustration)**. If necessary, a suitable tubular drift, such as a socket, which bears only on the hard outer edge of the seal can be used to tap the seal into position.
5 Wash off any traces of oil, then refit the crankshaft pulley as described in Section 6.

Left-hand (flywheel/driveplate end) oil seal

6 Remove the flywheel as described in Section 16.

7 Carefully punch or drill two small holes opposite each other in the oil seal. Screw a self-tapping screw into each and pull on the screws with pliers to extract the seal **(see illustration)**.
8 Clean the seal housing and polish off any burrs or raised edges which may have caused the seal to fail in the first place.
9 Lubricate the lips of the new seal with clean engine oil and ease it into position on the end of the crankshaft. Press the seal squarely into position until it is flush with the bearing cap. If necessary, a suitable tubular drift, such as a socket, which bears only on the hard outer edge of the seal can be used to tap the seal into position. Take great care not to damage the seal lips during fitting and ensure that the seal lips face inwards **(see illustration)**.
10 Refit the flywheel as described in Section 16.

16 Flywheel – removal, inspection and refitting

Note: *New flywheel retaining bolts will be required on refitting.*

Removal

1 Remove the transmission as described in Chapter 7 then remove the clutch assembly as described in Chapter 6.
2 Prevent the flywheel from turning by locking the ring gear teeth **(see illustration)**.

15.7 Removing the crankshaft left-hand oil seal

15.9 Carefully ease the new seal over the end of the crankshaft and tap/press it squarely into position

16.2 Lock the flywheel ring gear . . .

Alternatively, bolt a strap between the flywheel and the cylinder block/crankcase. Make alignment marks between the flywheel and crankshaft using paint or a suitable marker pen.

3 Slacken and remove the retaining bolts and remove the flywheel **(see illustration)**. Do not drop it, as it is very heavy.

Inspection

4 Examine the flywheel for wear or chipping of the ring gear teeth. Renewal of the ring gear is possible but is not a task for the home mechanic; renewal requires the new ring gear to be heated (up to 180° to 230°C) to allow it to be fitted.

5 Examine the flywheel for scoring of the clutch face. If the clutch face is scored, the flywheel may be surface-ground, but renewal is preferable.

6 If there is any doubt about the condition of the flywheel, seek the advice of a Vauxhall dealer or engine reconditioning specialist. They will be able to advise if it is possible to recondition it or whether renewal is necessary.

16.3 . . . then unscrew the retaining bolts and remove the flywheel

Refitting

7 Clean the mating surfaces of the flywheel and crankshaft.

8 Offer up the flywheel and fit the new retaining bolts. If the original is being refitted align the marks made prior to removal.

9 Lock the flywheel using the method employed on dismantling then, working in a diagonal sequence, evenly and progressively tighten the retaining bolts to the specified Stage 1 torque setting.

10 Once all bolts have been tightened to the Stage 1 torque, go around and tighten all bolts through the specified Stage 2 angle. It is recommended that an angle-measuring gauge is used during the final stages of the tightening, to ensure accuracy. If a gauge is not available, use white paint to make alignment marks prior to tightening; the marks can then be used to check that the bolt has been rotated through the correct angle.

11 Finally go around again and angle tighten the bolts through the specified Stage 3 angle.

12 Refit the clutch as described in Chapter 6 then remove the locking tool and refit the transmission as described in Chapter 7.

17 Engine/transmission mountings – inspection and renewal

Refer to Chapter 2B, Section 20.

Chapter 2 Part D:
Engine removal and overhaul procedures

Contents

Degrees of difficulty

Easy, suitable for novice with little experience	Fairly easy, suitable for beginner with some experience	Fairly difficult, suitable for competent DIY mechanic	Difficult, suitable for experienced DIY mechanic	Very difficult, suitable for expert DIY or professional

Specifications

Note: *Where specifications are given as N/A, no information was available at the time of writing. Refer to your Vauxhall dealer for the latest information available.*

1.7 litre SOHC engine

Cylinder head

Maximum gasket face distortion	0.1 mm
Cylinder head height:	
Standard	106.10 mm
Service limit	105.75 mm
Valve seat width:	
Standard	1.3 mm
Service limit	2.0 mm

Valves and guides

	Inlet	Exhaust
Valve stem diameter:		
Standard:		
Inlet	7.970 to 7.985 mm	
Exhaust	7.955 to 7.970 mm	
0.75 mm Oversize:		
Inlet	8.045 to 8.060 mm	
Exhaust	8.030 to 8.045 mm	
1.50 mm Oversize:		
Inlet	8.120 to 8.135 mm	
Exhaust	8.105 to 8.120 mm	
Valve guide bore diameter:		
Standard	8.000 to 8.017 mm	
0.075 mm Oversize	8.075 to 8.092 mm	
0.150 mm Oversize	8.150 to 8.167 mm	
Stem-to-guide clearance:	**Inlet**	**Exhaust**
Standard	0.015 mm	0.030 mm
Service limit	0.047 mm	0.062 mm
Valve length	123.22 to 123.27 mm	123.22 to 123.27 mm
Valve head diameter	36.0 mm	32.0 mm

1.7 litre SOHC engine (continued)

Gudgeon pins
Diameter	26 mm
Length	69 mm
Gudgeon pin-to-piston clearance	0.007 to 0.011 mm
Gudgeon pin-to-connecting rod clearance	0.014 to 0.025 mm

Cylinder block
Cylinder bore diameter:
Standard size index 8	82.475 to 82.485 mm
Standard size index 99	82.485 to 82.495 mm
Standard size index 00	82.495 to 82.505 mm
Standard size index 01	82.505 to 82.515 mm
Standard size index 02	82.525 to 82.525 mm
Oversize index 7 + 0.5	82.965 to 82.975 mm
Maximum cylinder bore ovality	0.015 mm
Maximum cylinder bore taper	0.015 mm

Pistons and rings
Piston diameter:
Standard size:
Index 8	82.445 to 82.455 mm
Index 99	82.455 to 82.465 mm
Index 00	82.465 to 82.475 mm
Index 01	82.475 to 82.485 mm
Index 02	82.485 to 82.495 mm
Oversize index 7 + 0.5	82.935 to 82.945 mm
Piston-to-bore clearance	0.02 to 0.04 mm
Piston projection	0.65 to 0.95 mm

Piston ring end gaps (fitted in bore):
Top compression ring	0.20 to 0.40 mm
Second compression ring	0.20 to 0.40 mm
Oil control ring	0.25 to 0.50 mm

Piston ring-to-groove clearance:
Top compression ring	0.12 to 0.18 mm
Second compression ring	0.12 to 0.15 mm
Oil control ring	0.025 to 0.15 mm

Piston ring thickness:
Top and second compression ring	2.0 mm
Oil control ring	3.0 mm

Connecting rod
Big-end side clearance	0.20 to 0.40 mm
Maximum permissible weight difference between connecting rods	4 grams

Crankshaft
Endfloat	0.06 to 0.30 mm

Main bearing journal diameter:
Standard size	57.974 to 57.995 mm
Undersize (0.25 mm)	57.732 to 57.738 mm
Undersize (0.50 mm)	57.482 to 57.495 mm

Big-end bearing journal (crankpin) diameter:
Standard size	48.970 to 48.988 mm
Undersize (0.25 mm)	48.720 to 48.738 mm
Undersize (0.50 mm)	48.470 to 48.488 mm
Journal out-of round	N/A
Journal taper	N/A
Crankshaft run-out	Less than 0.06 mm
Main bearing running clearance	0.030 to 0.080 mm
Big-end bearing (crankpin) running clearance	0.025 to 0.100 mm

Torque wrench settings
Refer to Chapter 2A Specifications

1.7 litre DOHC engine

Cylinder head
Maximum gasket face distortion	0.1 mm
Cylinder head height	94.95 to 95.05 mm
Valve seat width	1.5 to 1.7 mm
Valve head depth below gasket face	N/A
Valve seat angle	90°

Valves and guides

Valve stem diameter:
  Inlet .... 6.00 mm
  Exhaust .... 6.00 mm
Valve guide bore diameter .... 7.000 to 7.015 mm
Valve guide length .... 41.75 to 42.25 mm

Stem-to-guide clearance:	Inlet	Exhaust
Standard	0.019 mm	0.0215 mm
Service limit	N/A	N/A
Valve length	98.45 mm	98.10 mm
Valve head diameter	27.5 mm	26.5 mm
Valve seat angle at valve head	89°	89°

Gudgeon pins

Diameter .... 27 mm
Length . .64 mm
Gudgeon pin-to-piston clearance .... 0.002 to 0.012 mm
Gudgeon pin-to-connecting rod clearance .... 0.002 to 0.015 mm

Cylinder block

Cylinder bore diameter:
  Size group A .... 79.000 to 79.009 mm
  Size group B .... 79.010 to 79.019 mm
  Size group C .... 79.020 to 79.029 mm
Maximum cylinder bore ovality .... 0.015 mm
Maximum cylinder bore taper .... 0.015 mm
Main bearing bore diameter (bearing shells removed):
  Size group 1 .... 55.992 to 56.000 mm
  Size group 2 .... 55.984 to 55.992 mm
  Size group 3 .... 55.976 to 55.984 mm

Pistons and rings

Piston diameter:
  Size group A .... 78.93 to 78.939 mm
  Size group B .... 78.94 to 78.949 mm
  Size group C .... 78.95 to 78.959 mm
Piston-to-bore clearance .... 0.061 to 0.08 mm
Piston projection .... 0.63 to 0.83 mm
Piston ring end gaps (fitted in bore):
  Top compression ring .... 0.25 to 0.35 mm
  Second compression ring .... 0.20 to 0.30 mm
  Oil control ring .... 0.20 to 0.40 mm
Piston ring-to-groove clearance:
  Top compression ring .... 0.09 to 0.15 mm
  Second compression ring .... 0.04 to 0.15 mm
  Oil control ring .... 0.02 to 0.15 mm
Piston ring thickness:
  Top compression ring .... 2.0 mm
  Second compression ring .... 1.5 mm
  Oil control ring .... 3.0 mm

Connecting rod

Big-end side clearance .... 0.25 to 0.58 mm
Maximum permissible weight difference between connecting rods ... 4 grams

Crankshaft

Endfloat .... 0.03 to 0.15 mm
Main bearing journal diameter:
  1st size group (single cut-out) .... 51.928 to 51.938 mm
  2nd size group (double cut-out) .... 51.918 to 51.928 mm
Big-end bearing journal (crankpin) diameter .... N/A
Journal out-of round .... N/A
Journal taper .... N/A
Crankshaft run-out .... 0.040 to 0.082 mm
Main bearing running clearance .... 0.030 to 0.058 mm
Big-end bearing (crankpin) running clearance .... 0.025 to 0.058 mm

Torque wrench settings

Refer to Chapter 2B Specifications

2.0 litre engine

Cylinder head

Maximum gasket face distortion	N/A
Cylinder head height	140 mm
Valve seat width	1.4 to 1.8 mm

Gudgeon pins

Diameter	29 mm
Length	68 mm

Valves and guides

	Inlet	Exhaust
Valve guide height in cylinder head	11.20 to 11.50 mm	
Valve stem diameter*:	**Inlet**	**Exhaust**
Standard (K)	5.955 to 5.970 mm	5.945 to 5.960 mm
1st oversize (0.075 mm – K1)	6.030 to 6.045 mm	6.020 to 6.035 mm
2nd oversize (0.150 mm – K2)	6.105 to 6.120 mm	6.095 to 6.110 mm
Valve stem run-out	Less than 0.03 mm	
Valve guide bore diameter*:		
Standard (K)	6.000 to 6.012 mm	
1st oversize (0.075 mm – K1)	6.075 to 6.090 mm	
2nd oversize (0.150 mm – K2)	6.150 to 6.165 mm	
Stem-to-guide clearance	N/A	
Valve length:		
Inlet	97.1 to 97.2 mm	
Exhaust	96.9 to 97.0 mm	
Valve head diameter:		
Inlet	28.9 to 29.1 mm	
Exhaust	25.9 to 26.1 mm	

Identification marking in brackets

Cylinder block

Maximum gasket face distortion	N/A
Cylinder bore diameter:	
Standard:	
Size group 8	83.975 to 83.985 mm
Size group 99	83.985 to 83.995 mm
Size group 00	83.995 to 84.005 mm
Size group 01	84.005 to 84.015 mm
Size group 02	84.015 to 84.025 mm
Oversize (0.5 mm)	84.465 to 84.475
Maximum cylinder bore ovality	N/A
Maximum cylinder bore taper	N/A

Pistons and rings

	X20DTL/Y20DTL	Y20DTH
Piston diameter:		
Standard:		
Size group 8	83.905 to 83.915 mm	83.885 to 83.895 mm
Size group 99	83.915 to 83.925 mm	83.895 to 83.905 mm
Size group 00	83.925 to 83.935 mm	83.905 to 83.915 mm
Size group 01	83.935 to 83.945 mm	83.915 to 83.925 mm
Size group 02	83.945 to 83.955 mm	83.925 to 83.935 mm
Oversize (0.5 mm)	84.395 to 84.405 mm	84.375 to 84.385 mm
Piston-to-bore clearance	0.06 to 0.08 mm	0.08 to 0.10 mm
Piston ring end gaps (fitted in bore):		
Top and second compression rings	0.20 to 0.45 mm	0.25 to 0.50 mm
Oil control ring	0.25 to 0.50 mm	0.25 to 0.50 mm
Piston ring-to-groove clearance:		
Top compression ring	0.11 to 0.13 mm	0.08 to 0.12 mm
Second compression ring	0.05 to 0.09 mm	0.05 to 0.09 mm
Oil control ring	0.03 to 0.07 mm	0.03 to 0.07 mm
Piston ring thickness:		
Top compression ring:		
X20DTL/Y20DTL engine	2.00 mm	
Y20DTH engine	2.50 mm	
Second compression ring	1.75 mm	
Oil control ring	3.00 mm	

Connecting rod

Big-end side clearance	0.07 to 0.28 mm

Crankshaft

Endfloat	0.05 to 0.15 mm
Main bearing journal diameter:	
Standard:	
1st size group (green)	67.966 to 67.974 mm
2nd size group (brown)	67.974 to 67.982 mm
1st (0.25 mm) undersize	67.716 to 67.732 mm
2nd (0.50 mm) undersize	67.466 to 67.482 mm
Big-end bearing journal (crankpin) diameter:	
Standard	48.971 to 48.990 mm
1st (0.25 mm) undersize	48.721 to 48.740 mm
2nd (0.50 mm) undersize	48.471 to 48.490 mm
Journal out-of round	0.03
Journal taper	N/A
Crankshaft run-out	Less than 0.03 mm
Main bearing running clearance	0.016 to 0.069 mm
Big-end bearing (crankpin) running clearance	0.022 to 0.061 mm

Torque wrench settings

Refer to Chapter 2C Specifications

1 General information

1 Included in this Part of Chapter 2 are details of removing the engine/transmission from the car and general overhaul procedures for the cylinder head, cylinder block and all other engine internal components.

2 The information given ranges from advice concerning preparation for an overhaul and the purchase of replacement parts, to detailed step-by-step procedures covering removal, inspection, renovation and refitting of engine internal components.

3 After Section 5, all instructions are based on the assumption that the engine has been removed from the car. For information concerning in-car engine repair, as well as the removal and refitting of those external components necessary for full overhaul, refer to the relevant in-car repair procedure section (Chapter 2A to 2C) of this Chapter and to Section 5. Ignore any preliminary dismantling operations described in the relevant in-car repair sections that are no longer relevant once the engine has been removed from the car.

4 Apart from torque wrench settings, which are given at the beginning of the relevant in-car repair procedure Chapter 2A to 2C, all specifications relating to engine overhaul are at the beginning of this Part of Chapter 2.

2 Engine overhaul – general information

1 It is not always easy to determine when, or if, an engine should be completely overhauled, as a number of factors must be considered.

2 High mileage is not necessarily an indication that an overhaul is needed, while low mileage does not preclude the need for an overhaul. Frequency of servicing is probably the most important consideration. An engine which has had regular and frequent oil and filter changes, as well as other required maintenance, should give many thousands of miles of reliable service. Conversely, a neglected engine may require an overhaul very early in its life.

3 Excessive oil consumption is an indication that piston rings, valve seals and/or valve guides are in need of attention. Make sure that oil leaks are not responsible before deciding that the rings and/or guides are worn. Perform a compression test, as described in the relevant Part A to C of this Chapter, to determine the likely cause of the problem.

4 Check the oil pressure with a gauge fitted in place of the oil pressure switch, and compare it with that specified. If it is extremely low, the main and big-end bearings, and/or the oil pump, are probably worn out.

5 Loss of power, rough running, knocking or metallic engine noises, excessive valve gear noise, and high fuel consumption may also point to the need for an overhaul, especially if they are all present at the same time. If a complete service does not remedy the situation, major mechanical work is the only solution.

6 An engine overhaul involves restoring all internal parts to the specification of a new engine. During an overhaul, the pistons and the piston rings are renewed. New main and big-end bearings are generally fitted; if necessary, the crankshaft may be renewed, to restore the journals. The valves are also serviced as well, since they are usually in less-than-perfect condition at this point. While the engine is being overhauled, other components, such as the starter and alternator, can be overhauled as well. The end result should be an as-new engine that will give many trouble-free miles. **Note:** *Critical cooling system components such as the hoses, thermostat and water pump should be renewed when an engine is overhauled. The radiator should be checked carefully, to ensure that it is not clogged or leaking. Also, it is a good idea to renew the oil pump whenever the engine is overhauled.*

7 Before beginning the engine overhaul, read through the entire procedure, to familiarise yourself with the scope and requirements of the job. Overhauling an engine is not difficult if you follow carefully all of the instructions, have the necessary tools and equipment, and pay close attention to all specifications. It can, however, be time-consuming; plan on the car being off the road for a minimum of two weeks, especially if parts must be taken to an engineering works for repair or reconditioning. Check on the availability of parts and make sure that any necessary special tools and equipment are obtained in advance. Most work can be done with typical hand tools, although a number of precision measuring tools are required for inspecting parts to determine if they must be renewed. Often the engineering works will handle the inspection of parts and offer advice concerning reconditioning and renewal. **Note:** *Always wait until the engine has been completely dismantled, and until all components (especially the cylinder block and the crankshaft) have been inspected, before deciding what service and repair operations must be performed by an engineering works. The condition of these components will be the major factor to consider when determining whether to overhaul the original engine, or to buy a reconditioned unit. Do not, therefore, purchase parts or have overhaul work done on other components until they have been thoroughly inspected.* As a general rule, time is the primary cost of an overhaul, so it does not pay to fit worn or sub-standard parts.

8 As a final note, to ensure maximum life and minimum trouble from a reconditioned engine, everything must be assembled with care, in a spotlessly-clean environment.

3 Engine removal – methods and precautions

1 If you have decided that the engine must be removed for overhaul or major repair work, several preliminary steps should be taken.
2 Locating a suitable place to work is extremely important. Adequate work space, along with storage space for the car, will be needed. If a workshop or garage is not available, at the very least, a flat, level, clean work surface is required.
3 Cleaning the engine compartment and engine/transmission before beginning the removal procedure will help keep tools clean and organised.
4 An engine hoist or A-frame will also be necessary. Make sure the equipment is rated in excess of the combined weight of the engine and transmission. Safety is of primary importance, considering the potential hazards involved in lifting the engine/transmission out of the car.
5 If this is the first time you have removed an engine, an assistant should ideally be available. Advice and aid from someone more experienced would also be helpful. There are many instances when one person cannot simultaneously perform all of the operations required when lifting the engine out of the vehicle.
6 Plan the operation ahead of time. Before starting work, arrange for the hire of or obtain all of the tools and equipment you will need. Some of the equipment necessary to perform engine/transmission removal and installation safely and with relative ease (in addition to an engine hoist) is as follows: a heavy duty trolley jack, complete sets of spanners and sockets as described in the back of this manual, wooden blocks, and plenty of rags and cleaning solvent for mopping-up spilled oil, coolant and fuel. If the hoist must be hired, make sure that you arrange for it in advance, and perform all of the operations possible without it beforehand. This will save you money and time.
7 Plan for the car to be out of use for quite a while. An engineering works will be required to perform some of the work which the do-it-yourselfer cannot accomplish without special equipment. These places often have a busy schedule, so it would be a good idea to consult them before removing the engine, in order to accurately estimate the amount of time required to rebuild or repair components that may need work.
8 Always be extremely careful when removing and refitting the engine/transmission. Serious injury can result from careless actions. Plan ahead and take your time, and a job of this nature, although major, can be accomplished successfully.

4 Engine and transmission unit – removal, separation and refitting

Removal

Note: *The engine can be removed from the car only as a complete unit with the transmission; the two are then separated for overhaul. The engine/transmission unit is lowered out of position, and withdrawn from under the vehicle. Bearing this in mind, ensure the vehicle is raised sufficiently so that there is enough clearance between the front of the vehicle and the floor to allow the engine/transmission assembly to be slid out once it has been lowered out of position.*
1 Park the vehicle on firm, level ground then remove the bonnet as described in Chapter 11. Turn the steering wheel to the straight-ahead position, remove the ignition key, and engage the steering lock.
2 Unclip the heater plug control unit from the left-hand side of the battery tray (1.7 litre engines only). Remove the battery and mounting tray as described in Chapter 5A.
Note: *Before disconnecting the battery, refer to 'Disconnecting the battery' in the reference section at the rear of this manual.*
3 Chock the rear wheels, then firmly apply the handbrake. Slacken both the front roadwheel retaining bolts, then jack up the front of the vehicle. Securely support it on axle stands, bearing in mind the note at the start of this Section. Remove the front roadwheels. Where fitted, undo the retaining screws/clips and remove the engine undertray
4 If the engine is to be dismantled, working as described in Chapter 1, first drain the engine oil and remove the oil filter.
5 Referring to Chapter 4A, carry out the following procedures.
  a) *Remove the air cleaner housing and trunking complete associated components.*
  b) *Remove the exhaust front/intermediate pipe.*
  c) *On 1.7 litre DOHC engines, release the retaining clips and disconnect the fuel return and supply hoses from the injection pump. On all other engines disconnect the fuel pump supply pipe at the fuel filter, and the fuel return pipe* **(see illustration).**
  d) *Disconnect the brake servo hose from the vacuum pump, noting the hose's routing and release the retaining clips.*
  e) *Undo the retaining clips and remove the air charge pipe from the turbo-to-intercooler, and the intercooler-to-inlet manifold charge pipe. Disconnect the vacuum pipe from the vacuum pump and the EGR solenoid valve, and lay to one side.*
6 On 1.7 litre SOHC engines, pull out the clips securing the oil cooler hoses to the pipes between the engine block and radiator, and pull the hoses from the pipes. Refit the clips to the hose unions.
7 Referring to Chapter 3, carry out the following procedures.
  a) *Drain the coolant.*
  b) *Release the retaining clips and disconnect the upper and lower coolant hoses from the radiator. Disconnect any coolant hoses connected to the engine unit.*
  c) *At the engine compartment bulkhead, disconnect the heater coolant hoses by depressing the clip, pulling forward the collar, and pulling the hose from the connection. Note that the hose with the black collar is fitted to the top connection.*
  d) *Secure the radiator/air conditioning condenser in place by inserting suitable bolts or rods through the holes in the radiator mounting brackets* **(see illustration).**
8 Disconnect the following wiring plugs:
  a) *The large engine loom multiplug in front of the engine compartment relay box. Twist the collar and pull the plug apart* **(see illustration).**

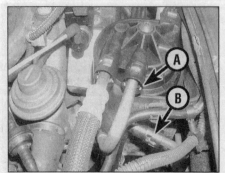

4.5 Disconnect the fuel supply pipe (A) and return pipe (B)

4.7 Support the radiator with a bolt through each mounting bracket

4.8a Disconnect the multiplug

4.8b Battery clamp loom connections

4.8c Slide the green relay, relay socket, fuse and fuse holder from the relay box

4.8d Rear wiring trough bolts (arrowed)

b) Unscrew the bolts and disconnect the loom connection to the battery positive clamp, and the two loom connections to the negative clamp **(see illustration)**.

c) On engines, open the engine compartment relay box (left-hand rear) and slide the green relay/socket and the green fuse and holder up and out of the relay box **(see illustration)**.

d) On 1.7 litre DOHC engines, lift the locking lever and disconnect the rear most connector from the engine ECU mounted above the inlet manifold.

e) Release the loom from any retaining clips and fold the loom(s) over the engine.

f) On 1.7 litre SOHC engines, disconnect the following items:
EGR solenoid valve
Coolant temperature sensor
Injection pump ECM (pull out the lock element)
Heater plugs
Crankshaft position sensor
Oil temperature sensor
Reversing light switch

g) Then undo the three bolts securing the wiring trough to the rear of the camshaft cover and position the trough/loom away from the engine **(see illustration)**. Release the loom at the front of the block from its retaining clips and position it clear of the engine.

9 Carry out the following procedures.

a) Drain the transmission oil (see Chapter 7)

or be prepared for oil spillage as the engine/transmission unit is removed.

b) Working underneath the vehicle, undo the clamp bolt and disconnect the shift rod from the guide tube **(see illustration)**. On models equipped with the F23 transmission, disconnect the shift cables from the shift linkage (see Chapter 7).

c) Clamp the flexible hose next to the connection, and using a screwdriver, release the clutch pressure hose connector-retaining clip from the connector at the clutch bellhousing, and withdraw the pressure hose with the connector from the bellhousing (refer to Chapter 6) **(see illustration)**. With the connector released, gently squeeze the retaining clip together and refit it to the exact same position in the connector.

10 Manoeuvre the engine hoist into position, and attach it to the lifting brackets bolted onto the engine. Raise the hoist until it is supporting the weight of the engine **(see illustration)**.

11 Refer to Chapter 8 and remove both driveshafts.

12 With the engine securely supported, remove the front suspension subframe assembly as described in Chapter 10.

13 Make a final check that any components which would prevent the removal of the engine/transmission from the car have been removed or disconnected.

14 Mark the relative positions of the left and

right-hand engine/transmission mounting brackets to the cylinder block bracket/ transmission adapter plate. Slacken and remove the three bolts securing the right-hand engine mounting bracket to the cylinder block bracket, and the three bolts securing the mounting to the body. Slacken and remove the three bolts securing the left-hand transmission mounting to transmission adapter plate. On models with air conditioning, disconnect the wiring plug, unbolt the compressor, and tie it to the bonnet slam panel using a cable tie or similar **(see illustration)**. If necessary undo the refrigerant hose retaining clip beside the right-hand engine mounting. **Do not** open the refrigerant circuit.

15 If available, a low trolley should be placed

4.9a Slacken the shift linkage clamp bolt – F17/18 transmissions

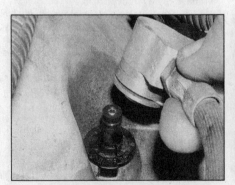

4.9b Remove the retaining clip and disconnect the clutch hose

4.10 Attach the lifting hoist to the lifting brackets bolted to the engine

4.14 Tie the compressor to the slam panel

under the engine/transmission assembly, to facilitate its easy removal from under the vehicle. Lower the engine/transmission assembly, making sure that nothing is trapped, taking great care not to damage the radiator/cooling fan assembly. Enlist the help of an assistant during this procedure, as it may be necessary to tilt the assembly slightly to clear the body panels. Great care must be taken to ensure that no components are trapped and damaged during the removal procedure.

16 Detach the hoist and withdraw the engine/transmission unit from under the vehicle.

Separation

17 With the engine/transmission assembly removed, support the assembly on suitable blocks of wood, on a workbench (or failing that, on a clean area of the workshop floor).

18 On models with a pressed steel sump, undo the retaining bolts and remove the flywheel lower cover plate from the transmission.

19 With reference to Chapter 5A, remove the starter motor.

20 Ensure that both engine and transmission are adequately supported, then slacken and remove the remaining bolts securing the transmission housing to the engine. Note the correct fitted positions of each bolt (and the relevant brackets) as they are removed, to use as a reference on refitting.

21 Carefully withdraw the transmission from the engine, ensuring that the weight of the transmission is not allowed to hang on the input shaft while it is engaged with the clutch friction disc.

22 If they are loose, remove the locating dowels from the engine or transmission, and keep them in a safe place.

Refitting

23 If the engine and transmission have been separated, perform the operations described below in paragraphs 24 to 27. If not, proceed as described from paragraph 28 onwards.

24 Ensure the locating dowels are correctly positioned then carefully offer the transmission to the engine, until the locating dowels are engaged. Ensure that the weight of the transmission is not allowed to hang on the input shaft as it is engaged with the clutch friction disc.

25 Refit the transmission housing-to-engine bolts, ensuring that all the necessary brackets are correctly positioned, and tighten them to the specified torque setting.

26 Refit the starter motor and tighten its mounting bolts to the specified torque (see Chapter 5A).

27 On models with a pressed steel sump, refit the flywheel lower cover plate to the transmission, and tighten its retaining bolts securely.

28 Slide the engine/transmission unit into position and reconnect the hoist and lifting tackle to the engine lifting brackets.

29 With the aid of an assistant, carefully lift the assembly into position in the engine compartment, manipulating the hoist and lifting tackle as necessary, taking great care not to trap any components.

30 Align the engine with the right-hand side of the engine compartment then refit the engine mounting and bracket. Tighten the bolts by hand only at this stage. Align the transmission with the left-hand engine mounting, and refit the three bolts securing the mounting bracket to the adapter plate on the transmission. On models equipped with air conditioning, manoeuvre the compressor into place. Refit and tighten the compressor retaining bolts to the specified torque.

31 Renew the driveshaft oil seals (see Chapter 7) then carefully refit the driveshafts (see Chapter 8).

32 Refit the front suspension subframe as described in Chapter 10.

33 With the subframe assembly correctly installed, align the previously made marks and tighten the right and left-hand engine/transmission mounting bolts to the specified torque.

34 The remainder of the refitting procedure is a direct reversal of the removal sequence, noting the following points:

a) *Ensure that all wiring is correctly routed and retained by all the relevant retaining clips and that all connectors are correctly and securely reconnected.*

b) *Ensure that all disturbed hoses are correctly reconnected, and securely retained by their retaining clips. Engage the heater hoses over the raised ridges on the heater pipes at the engine compartment bulkhead, and then push the locking collars to the rear. Note that the hose with the black collar should be fitted to the upper heater connection* **(see illustration)**.

c) *Fit a new sealing ring to the clutch hose end fitting on the transmission unit and reconnect the end fitting, ensuring it is securely retained by the clip. On completion, bleed the hydraulic system as described in Chapter 6.*

d) *Refit the gearchange shift rod to the shift guide tube and adjust as described in Chapter 7.*

4.34 The hose with the black collar is fitted to the upper heater connection

e) *Refill the transmission with correct quantity and type of oil, as described in Chapter 7. If the oil was not drained, top-up the level as described in Chapter 7.*

f) *Refill the engine with oil as described in Chapter 1 and also refill the cooling system (Chapter 3).*

5 Engine overhaul – dismantling sequence

1 It is much easier to dismantle and work on the engine if it is mounted on a portable engine stand. These stands can often be hired from a tool hire shop. Before the engine is mounted on a stand, the flywheel should be removed, so that the stand bolts can be tightened into the end of the cylinder block.

2 If a stand is not available, it is possible to dismantle the engine with it blocked up on a sturdy workbench, or on the floor. Be extra-careful not to tip or drop the engine when working without a stand.

3 If you are going to obtain a reconditioned engine, all the external components must be removed first, to be transferred to the replacement engine (just as they will if you are doing a complete engine overhaul yourself). These components include the following:

a) *Inlet and exhaust manifolds (Chapter 4A).*

b) *Alternator/air conditioning compressor bracket(s) (as applicable).*

c) *Water pump (Chapter 3).*

d) *Fuel system components (Chapter 4A).*

e) *Wiring harness and all electrical switches and sensors.*

f) *Oil filter (Chapter 1).*

g) *Flywheel (relevant Part of this Chapter).*

Note: *When removing the external components from the engine, pay close attention to details that may be helpful or important during refitting. Note the fitted position of gaskets, seals, spacers, pins, washers, bolts, and other small items.*

4 If you are obtaining a 'short' engine (which consists of the engine cylinder block, crankshaft, pistons and connecting rods all assembled), then the cylinder head, sump, oil pump, and timing belt/chains (as applicable) will have to be removed also.

5 If you are planning a complete overhaul, the engine can be dismantled, and the internal components removed, in the order given below, referring to the relevant Part of this Chapter unless otherwise stated.

a) *Inlet and exhaust manifolds (Chapter 4A).*

b) *Timing belt, sprockets and tensioner – all models except 2.0 litre engine.*

c) *Cylinder head.*

d) *Flywheel.*

e) *Sump.*

f) *Oil pump.*

g) *Timing chains and sprockets – 2.0 litre engine.*

h) *Piston/connecting rod assemblies.*

i) *Crankshaft.*

6.4a Using a valve spring compressor . . .

6.4b . . . compress the valve spring until the collets can be removed from the valve

6.4c Remove the compressor then lift off the spring retainer . . .

6 Before beginning the dismantling and overhaul procedures, make sure that you have all of the correct tools necessary. Refer to the *Tools and working facilities* Section of this manual for further information.

6 Cylinder head – dismantling

Note: *New and reconditioned cylinder heads are available from the manufacturer, and from engine overhaul specialists. Be aware that some specialist tools are required for the dismantling and inspection procedures, and new components may not be readily available. It may therefore be more practical and economical for the home mechanic to purchase a reconditioned head, rather than dismantle, inspect and recondition the original head.*

1 On 1.7 litre SOHC engines, referring to Part A of this Chapter, remove the cylinder head from the engine then lift the camshaft followers, thrust pads and hydraulic tappets out from the cylinder head.
2 On 1.7 litre DOHC engines, referring to Part B of this Chapter, remove the cylinder head from the engine and unscrew the heater plugs (Chapter 5B).
3 On 2.0 litre engines, working as described in Part C of this Chapter, remove the

camshaft, followers and hydraulic tappets from the cylinder head. Unscrew the heater plugs (Chapter 5B) then remove the cylinder head from the engine.
4 On all models, using a valve spring compressor, compress each valve spring in turn until the split collets can be removed. Release the compressor, and lift off the spring retainer and spring. Using a pair of pliers, carefully extract the valve stem seal from the top of the guide then slide off the spring seat **(see illustrations)**.
5 If, when the valve spring compressor is screwed down, the spring retainer refuses to free and expose the split collets, gently tap the top of the tool, directly over the retainer, with a light hammer. This will free the retainer.
6 Withdraw the valve through the combustion chamber. It is essential that each valve is stored together with its collets, retainer, spring, and spring seat. The valves should also be kept in their correct sequence, unless they are so badly worn that they are to be renewed.

7 Cylinder head and valves – cleaning and inspection

1 Thorough cleaning of the cylinder head and valve components, followed by a detailed

inspection, will enable you to decide how much valve service work must be carried out during the engine overhaul. **Note:** *If the engine has been severely overheated, it is best to assume that the cylinder head is warped – check carefully for signs of this.*

Cleaning

2 Scrape away all traces of old gasket material from the cylinder head.
3 Scrape away the carbon from the combustion chambers and ports, then wash the cylinder head thoroughly with paraffin or a suitable solvent.
4 Scrape off any heavy carbon deposits that may have formed on the valves, then use a power-operated wire brush to remove deposits from the valve heads and stems.

Inspection

Note: *Be sure to perform all the following inspection procedures before concluding that the services of a machine shop or engine overhaul specialist are required. Make a list of all items that require attention.*

Cylinder head

5 Inspect the head very carefully for cracks, evidence of coolant leakage, and other damage. If cracks are found, a new cylinder head should be obtained.
6 Use a straight-edge and feeler gauge blade to check that the cylinder head surface is not

6.4d . . . and remove the valve spring

6.4e Pull the seal off the top of the valve guide . . .

6.4f . . . then remove the spring seat

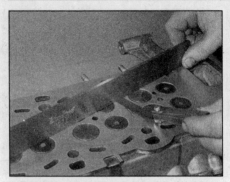

7.6 Using a straight-edge and feeler gauge to check cylinder head surface distortion

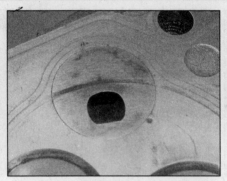

7.11 Small cracks in the swirl chamber can be ignored

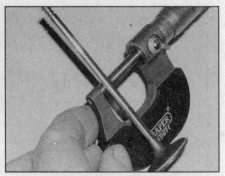

7.13 Measure the valve stem diameter using a micrometer

distorted (see illustration). If it is, it may be possible to resurface it, provided that the cylinder head is not reduced to less than the minimum specified height.

7 Examine the valve seats in each of the combustion chambers. If they are severely pitted, cracked or burned, then they will need to be renewed (this is only possible on 1.7 litre SOHC engines) or re-cut by an engine overhaul specialist. If they are only slightly pitted, this can be removed by grinding-in the valve heads and seats with fine valve-grinding compound, as described below.

8 If the valve guides are worn (indicated by a side-to-side motion of the valve, and accompanied by excessive blue smoke in the exhaust when running) new guides must be fitted. Measure the diameter of the existing valve stems (see below) and the bore of the guides, then calculate the clearance and compare the result with the specified value. If the clearance is not within the specified limits, renew the valves and/or guides as necessary.

9 The renewal of valve guides is best carried out by an engine overhaul specialist. If the work is to be carried out at home, however, use a stepped, double-diameter drift to drive out the worn guide towards the combustion chamber. On fitting the new guide, place it first in a deep-freeze for one hour, then drive it into its cylinder head bore from the camshaft side until it projects the specified amount above the cylinder head surface (where no measurement is given seek the advice of a Vauxhall dealer).

10 If the valve seats are to be re-cut this must be done only after the guides have been renewed.

11 On 1.7 litre SOHC engines, inspect the swirl chambers for burning or damage such as cracking. Small cracks in the chambers are acceptable; renewal of the chambers will only be required if chamber tracts are badly burned and disfigured, or if they are no longer a tight fit in the cylinder head. If there is any doubt as to the swirl chamber condition, seek the advice of a Vauxhall dealer or a suitable repairer who specialises in diesel engines. Swirl chamber renewal should be entrusted to a specialist (see illustration).

Valves

12 Examine the head of each valve for pitting, burning, cracks and general wear, and check the valve stem for scoring and wear ridges. Rotate the valve, and check for any obvious indication that it is bent. Look for pitting and excessive wear on the tip of each valve stem. Renew any valve that shows any such signs of wear or damage.

13 If the valve appears satisfactory at this stage, measure the valve stem diameter at several points using a micrometer (see illustration). Any significant difference in the readings obtained indicates wear of the valve stem. Should any of these conditions be apparent, the valve(s) must be renewed.

14 If the valves are in satisfactory condition, they should be ground (lapped) into their respective seats, to ensure a smooth gas-tight seal. If the seat is only lightly pitted, or if it has

been re-cut, fine grinding compound only should be used to produce the required finish. Coarse valve-grinding compound should not be used unless a seat is badly burned or deeply pitted; if this is the case, the cylinder head and valves should be inspected by an expert to decide whether seat re-cutting, or even the renewal of the valve or seat insert, is required.

15 Valve grinding is carried out as follows. Place the cylinder head upside-down on a bench.

16 Smear a trace of the appropriate grade of valve-grinding compound on the seat face, and press a suction grinding tool onto the valve head. With a semi-rotary action, grind the valve head to its seat, lifting the valve occasionally to redistribute the grinding compound (see illustration). A light spring placed under the valve head will greatly ease this operation.

17 If coarse grinding compound is being used, work only until a dull, matt even surface is produced on both the valve seat and the valve, then wipe off the used compound and repeat the process with fine compound. When a smooth unbroken ring of light grey matt finish is produced on both the valve and seat, the grinding operation is complete. Do not grind in the valves any further than absolutely necessary, or the seat will be prematurely sunk into the cylinder head.

18 When all the valves have been ground-in, carefully wash off all traces of grinding compound using paraffin or a suitable solvent before reassembly of the cylinder head.

Valve components

19 Examine the valve springs for signs of damage and discoloration; if possible; also compare the existing spring free length with new components.

20 Stand each spring on a flat surface, and check it for squareness. If any of the springs are damaged, distorted or have lost their tension, obtain a complete new set of springs.

8 Cylinder head – reassembly

1 Lubricate the stems of the valves, and insert them into their original locations (see illustration). If new valves are being fitted,

7.16 Grinding-in a valve

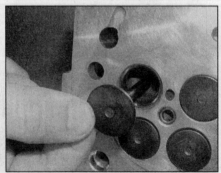

8.1 Insert the valves into their original locations

insert them into the locations to which they have been ground.

2 Working on the first valve, refit the spring seat. Dip the new valve stem seal in fresh engine oil, then carefully locate it over the valve and onto the guide. Take care not to damage the seal as it is passed over the valve stem. Use a suitable socket or metal tube to press the seal firmly onto the guide **(see illustrations)**.

3 Locate the spring on the seat and fit the spring retaining collar **(see illustration)**.

4 Compress the valve spring, and locate the split collets in the recess in the valve stem **(see illustration)**. Release the compressor, then repeat the procedure on the remaining valves.

5 With all the valves installed, support the cylinder head on two blocks of wood, one at each end positioned so as to not obstruct the valves. Using a hammer and interposed block of wood, tap the end of each valve stem to settle the components.

6 On 1.7 litre SOHC engines, working as described in Part A, refit the cylinder head.

7 On 1.7 litre DOHC engines, working as described in Part B, refit the cylinder head.

8 On 2.0 litre engines, working as described in Part C, refit the cylinder head.

8.2a Fit the spring seat . . .

8.2b . . . and the valve stem oil seal

8.3 Refit the spring and retaining collar

8.4 Compress the spring and locate the split collets in the recess in the valve stem

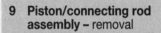

9 Piston/connecting rod assembly – removal

Note: *New connecting rod big-end cap bolts/nuts will be needed on refitting*

1 Referring to Part A, B or C of this Chapter where applicable, remove the cylinder head and sump and then unbolt the pick-up strainer from the base of the oil pump/cylinder block. Where fitted, unbolt and remove the baffle plate from the base of the cylinder block **(see illustration)**.

2 On all models, if there is a pronounced wear ridge at the top of any bore, it may be necessary to remove it with a scraper or ridge reamer, to avoid piston damage during removal. Such a ridge indicates excessive wear of the cylinder bore.

3 Prior to removal, using feeler blades,

measuring the connecting rod big-end side clearance of each rod **(see illustration)**. If any rod exceeds the specified clearance, it must be renewed.

4 Using paint or similar, mark each connecting rod and its bearing cap with its respective cylinder number on the flat machined surface provided; if the engine has been dismantled before, note carefully any identifying marks made previously **(see illustration)**. Note that No 1 cylinder is at the timing belt/chain (as applicable) end of the engine.

5 Turn the crankshaft to bring pistons 1 and 4 to BDC (bottom dead centre).

6 Unscrew the nuts or bolts from No 1 piston big-end bearing cap. Take off the cap and recover the bottom half bearing shell. If the

bearing shells are to be re-used, tape the cap and the shell together.

Caution: On some engines, the connecting rod/bearing cap mating surfaces are not machined flat; the big-end bearing caps are 'cracked' off from the rod during production and left untouched to ensure the cap and rod mate perfectly. Where this type of connecting rod is fitted, great care must be taken to ensure the mating surfaces of the cap and rod are not marked or damaged in anyway. Any damage to the mating surfaces will adversely affect the strength of the connecting rod and could lead to premature failure.

7 Using a hammer handle, push the piston up through the bore, and remove it from the top

9.1 Where fitted, unbolt the baffle plate from the base of the cylinder block

9.3 Checking connecting rod big-end side clearance

9.4 Prior to removal make identification markings on the connecting rods and bearing caps (circled)

10.3 Remove the main bearing bridge

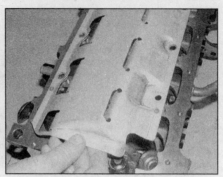

10.9 Remove the oil baffle plate

of the cylinder block. Recover the bearing shell, and tape it to the connecting rod for safe-keeping.

8 Loosely refit the big-end cap to the connecting rod, and secure with the nuts/bolts – this will help to keep the components in their correct order.

9 Remove No 4 piston assembly in the same way.

10 Turn the crankshaft through 180° to bring pistons 2 and 3 to BDC (bottom dead centre), and remove them in the same way.

10 Crankshaft – removal

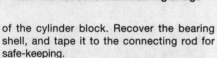

Note: *If the crankshaft endfloat is to be checked, this must be done when the crankshaft is still installed in the cylinder block (see Section 13).*

1.7 litre SOHC engine

Note: *New main bearing cap bolts will be required on refitting.*

1 Working as described in Part A of this Chapter, remove the flywheel, main sump casting, oil pump, and oil pick-up pipe.

2 Remove the connecting rod bearing caps as described in Section 9.

3 Unscrew the 15 retaining bolts and remove the main bearing bridge **(see illustration)**.

4 Using paint or similar number the main bearing caps 1 to 5 starting at the timing belt

end of the crankshaft. Note that the lug cast into the bearing caps points towards the flywheel end of the engine.

5 Unbolt the main bearing cap bolts and remove the bearing caps.

6 Carefully lift the crankshaft from the block.

1.7 litre DOHC engine

7 Working as described in Part B of this Chapter, remove the flywheel, main sump casting, oil pump cover and oil pick-up pipe.

8 Unbolt the crankshaft rear oil seal housing and remove it from the cylinder block. If the housing locating dowels are a loose fit, remove them and store them with the housing for safe-keeping.

9 Undo the retaining bolts, and remove the oil baffle plate from the cylinder block **(see illustration)**.

10 Remove the connecting rod bearing caps as described in Section 9.

11 Unscrew the main bearing cap bolts and remove the bearing caps. Note that the caps should are numbered 1 to 5, Number 1 cap being at the timing belt end, and the arrow on each cap should point towards the timing belt end of the engine.

12 Carefully remove the crankshaft, and recover the thrustwasher halves from the sides of Number 2 main bearing.

2.0 litre engine

Note: *New main bearing cap bolts will be required on refitting.*

13 Working as described in Part C of this

Chapter, remove the crankshaft timing chain sprocket and the flywheel.

14 Evenly and progressively slacken and remove the retaining bolts then remove the main bearing bridge casting from the base of the bearing caps, noting which way around it is fitted.

15 Remove the connecting rod bearing caps as described in Section 9.

16 On this engine, it will be necessary to make identification markings on each main bearing cap as only caps Number 1 and 2 are marked by the manufacturer **(see illustration)**. Number the caps 1 to 5 from the timing chain end of the engine, marking each cap to indicate its correct fitted direction to avoid confusion on refitting.

17 Unbolt the main bearing cap bolts and remove the bearing caps.

18 Carefully lift the crankshaft from the cylinder block.

11 Cylinder block – cleaning and inspection

Cleaning

1 Remove all external components and electrical switches/sensors from the block. For complete cleaning, the core plugs should ideally be removed. Drill a small hole in the plugs, then insert a self-tapping screw into the hole. Pull out the plugs by pulling on the screw with a pair of grips, or by using a slide hammer.

2 Remove the piston oil spray nozzles from inside the cylinder block. On 1.7 litre engines the nozzles are a push-fit in the block and the use of a special Vauxhall tool is required for removal. On 2.0 litre models they are retained by bolts **(see illustration)**.

3 Scrape all traces of gasket from the cylinder block, and from the main bearing bridge (where fitted), taking care not to damage the gasket/sealing surfaces.

4 Remove all oil gallery plugs (where fitted). The plugs are usually very tight – they may have to be drilled out, and the holes re-tapped. Use new plugs when the engine is reassembled.

5 If any of the castings are extremely dirty, all should be steam-cleaned.

6 After the castings are returned, clean all oil holes and oil galleries one more time. Flush all internal passages with warm water until the water runs clear. Dry thoroughly, and apply a light film of oil to all mating surfaces, to prevent rusting. Also oil the cylinder bores. If you have access to compressed air, use it to speed up the drying process, and to blow out all the oil holes and galleries.

 Warning: Wear eye protection when using compressed air.

7 If the castings are not very dirty, you can do an adequate cleaning job with hot (as hot as

10.16 On 2.0 litre engines only number 1 and 2 main bearing caps are marked by the manufacturer (arrowed)

11.2 On 2.0 litre engines unscrew the retaining bolts and remove the piston oil spray nozzles from the cylinder block

you can stand), soapy water and a stiff brush. Take plenty of time, and do a thorough job. Regardless of the cleaning method used, be sure to clean all oil holes and galleries very thoroughly, and to dry all components well. Protect the cylinder bores as described above, to prevent rusting.

8 All threaded holes must be clean, to ensure accurate torque wrench readings during reassembly. To clean the threads, run the correct-size tap into each of the holes to remove rust, corrosion, thread sealant or sludge, and to restore damaged threads. If possible, use compressed air to clear the holes of debris produced by this operation. A good alternative is to inject aerosol-applied water-dispersant lubricant into each hole, using the long spout usually supplied.

 Warning: Wear eye protection when cleaning out these holes in this way.

9 Apply suitable sealant to the new oil gallery plugs, and insert them into the holes in the block. Tighten them securely.

10 Refit the piston oil spray nozzles to the cylinder block. On 1.7 litre engines press the nozzles securely into position ensuring that each one is positioned exactly at a right-angle to the crankshaft axis. On 2.0 litre models refit the nozzles to the block and tighten the retaining bolts to the specified torque **(see illustration)**.

11 If the engine is not going to be reassembled right away, cover it with a large plastic bag to keep it clean; protect all mating surfaces and the cylinder bores as described above, to prevent rusting.

Inspection

12 Visually check the castings for cracks and corrosion. Look for stripped threads in the threaded holes. If there has been any history of internal water leakage, it may be worthwhile having an engine overhaul specialist check the cylinder block/crankcase with special equipment. If defects are found, have them repaired if possible, or renew the assembly.

13 Check the bore of each cylinder for scuffing and scoring.

14 Measure the diameter of each cylinder bore at the top (just below the wear ridge), centre and bottom of the bore, both parallel to the crankshaft axis and at right angles to it, so that a total of six measurements are taken. Note that there are various size groups of standard bore diameter to allow for manufacturing tolerances; the size group markings are stamped on the cylinder block.

15 Compare the results with the Specifications at the beginning of this Chapter; if any measurement exceeds the service limit specified, the cylinder block must be rebored if possible, or renewed and new piston assemblies fitted.

16 If the cylinder bores are badly scuffed or scored, or if they are excessively worn, out-of-round or tapered, or if the piston-to-bore

clearance is excessive (see Section 12), the cylinder block must be rebored (if possible) or renewed and new pistons fitted. Oversize (0.5 mm) pistons are available for all engines except the 1.7 litre DOHC engine.

17 If the bores are in reasonably good condition and not worn to the specified limits, then the piston rings should be renewed. If this is the case, the bores should be honed to allow the new rings to bed in correctly and provide the best possible seal. The conventional type of hone has spring-loaded stones, and is used with a power drill. You will also need some paraffin (or honing oil) and rags. The hone should be moved up and down the bore to produce a crosshatch pattern, and plenty of honing oil should be used. Ideally, the crosshatch lines should intersect at approximately a 60° angle. Do not take off more material than is necessary to produce the required finish. If new pistons are being fitted, the piston manufacturers may specify a finish with a different angle, so their instructions should be followed. Do not withdraw the hone from the bore while it is still being turned – stop it first. After honing a bore, wipe out all traces of the honing oil. If equipment of this type is not available, or if you are not sure whether you are competent to undertake the task yourself, an engine overhaul specialist will carry out the work at moderate cost.

12 Piston/connecting rod assembly – inspection

1 Before the inspection process can begin, the piston/connecting rod assemblies must be cleaned, and the original piston rings removed from the pistons.

2 Carefully expand the old rings over the top of the pistons. The use of two or three old feeler blades will be helpful in preventing the rings dropping into empty grooves **(see illustration)**. Be careful not to scratch the piston with the ends of the ring. The rings are brittle, and will snap if they are spread too far. They're also very sharp – protect your hands and fingers. Note that the third (oil control) ring consists of a spacer and two side rails.

Always remove the rings from the top of the piston. Keep each set of rings with its piston if the old rings are to be re-used.

3 Scrape away all traces of carbon from the top of the piston. A hand-held wire brush (or a piece of fine emery cloth) can be used, once the majority of the deposits have been scraped away. The piston identification markings should now be visible.

4 Remove the carbon from the ring grooves in the piston, using an old ring. Break the ring in half to do this (be careful not to cut your fingers – piston rings are sharp). Be careful to remove only the carbon deposits – do not remove any metal, and do not nick or scratch the sides of the ring grooves.

5 Once the deposits have been removed, clean the piston/connecting rod assembly with paraffin or a suitable solvent, and dry thoroughly. Make sure that the oil return holes in the ring grooves are clear.

6 If the cylinder bores are not damaged or worn excessively, and if the cylinder block does not need to be rebored (see Section 11), check the pistons as follows.

7 Carefully inspect each piston for cracks around the skirt, around the gudgeon pin holes, and at the piston ring 'lands' (between the ring grooves).

8 Look for scoring and scuffing on the piston skirt, holes in the piston crown, and burned areas at the edge of the crown. If the skirt is scored or scuffed, the engine may have been suffering from overheating, and/or abnormal combustion which caused excessively high operating temperatures. The cooling and lubrication systems should be checked thoroughly. Scorch marks on the sides of the pistons show that blow-by has occurred. A hole in the piston crown, or burned areas at the edge of the piston crown, indicates that abnormal combustion (knocking or detonation) has been occurring. If any of the above problems exist, the causes must be investigated and corrected, or the damage will occur again. The causes may include incorrect injection pump timing, or a faulty injector.

9 Corrosion of the piston, in the form of pitting, indicates that coolant has been leaking into the combustion chamber and/or the crankcase. Again, the cause must be

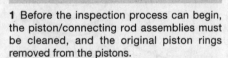

11.10 Oil spray nozzles – 1.7 litre engines

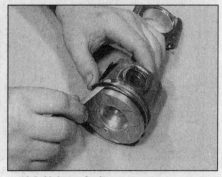

12.2 Using a feeler gauge to remove a piston ring

12.15 Prise out the piston circlip

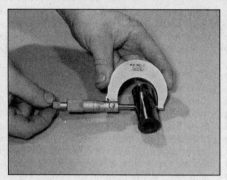

12.16 Measuring a gudgeon pin diameter with a micrometer

12.19 On 1.7 litre SOHC engines the cast lug on the connecting rod (A) points towards the flywheel, whilst the arrow on the piston crown (B) points towards the timing end of the engine

corrected, or the problem may persist in the rebuilt engine.

10 Measure the piston diameter at right-angles to the gudgeon pin axis; compare the results with the Specifications at the beginning of this Chapter. Note that there are various size groups of standard piston diameter to allow for manufacturing tolerances; the size group markings are stamped on the piston crown.

11 To measure the piston-to-bore clearance, either measure the bore (see Section 11) and piston skirt as described and subtract the skirt diameter from the bore measurement, or insert each piston into its original bore, then select a feeler gauge blade and slip it into the bore along with the piston. The piston must be aligned exactly in its normal attitude, and the feeler gauge blade must be between the piston and bore, on one of the thrust faces, just up from the bottom of the bore. Divide the measured clearance by two, to provide the clearance when the piston is central in the bore. If the clearance is excessive, a new piston will be required. If the piston binds at the lower end of the bore and is loose towards the top, the bore is tapered. If tight spots are encountered as the piston/feeler gauge blade is rotated in the bore, the bore is out-of-round.

12 Repeat this procedure for the remaining pistons and cylinder bores. Any piston which is worn beyond the specified limits must be renewed.

13 Examine each connecting rod carefully for

signs of damage, such as cracks around the big-end and small-end bearings. Check that the rod is not bent or distorted. Damage is highly unlikely, unless the engine has been seized or badly overheated. Detailed checking of the connecting rod assembly can only be carried out by a Vauxhall dealer or engine repair specialist with the necessary equipment.

14 The gudgeon pins are of the floating type, secured in position by two circlips. The pistons and connecting rods can be separated as follows.

15 Using a small flat-bladed screwdriver, prise out the circlips, and push out the gudgeon pin **(see illustration)**. Hand pressure should be sufficient to remove the pin. Identify

the piston and rod to ensure correct reassembly. Discard the circlips – new ones *must* be used on refitting.

16 Examine the gudgeon pin and connecting rod small-end bearing for signs of wear or damage **(see illustration)**. Wear will require the renewal of both the pin and connecting rod, except on 1.7 litre DOHC engines where a replacement small-end bush may be available – check with a Vauxhall dealer.

17 The connecting rods themselves should not be in need of renewal, unless seizure or some other major mechanical failure has occurred. Check the alignment of the connecting rods visually, and if the rods are not straight, take them to an engine overhaul specialist for a more detailed check.

18 Examine all components, and obtain any new parts from your Vauxhall dealer. If new pistons are purchased, they will be supplied complete with gudgeon pins and circlips. Circlips can also be purchased individually.

19 On 1.7 litre SOHC engines, assemble the piston and connecting rod so that the lug cast into the side of the rod, next to the bearing surface, faces towards the flywheel end of the engine, whilst the arrow on the piston crown points towards the timing belt end of the engine **(see illustration)**.

20 On 1.7 litre DOHC engines, assemble the piston and connecting rod so that the mark (dot) on the piston crown is on the same side as the raised mark which is cast onto the side of the connecting rod **(see illustration)**.

21 On 2.0 litre engines, assemble the piston and connecting rod so that the arrow on the piston crown is pointing away from the assembly mark which is cast onto one side of the connecting rod, on the top of the big-end bore **(see illustration)**.

22 Apply a smear of clean engine oil to the gudgeon pin. Slide it into the piston and through the connecting rod small-end. Check that the piston pivots freely on the rod, then secure the gudgeon pin in position with two new circlips, ensuring that each circlip is correctly located in its groove in the piston. Make sure that both circlips are positioned so that their end gaps are at the top.

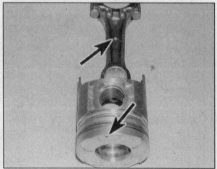

12.20 On 1.7 litre DOHC engines, the mark on the connecting rod must be on the same side as the mark on the piston crown

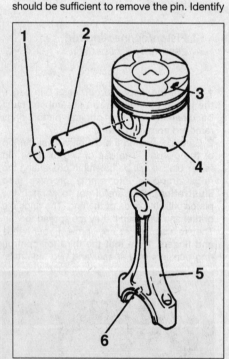

12.21 Piston/connecting rod assembly components – 2.0 litre engines

1 Circlip
2 Gudgeon pin
3 Arrow on piston crown
4 Piston
5 Connecting rod
6 Connecting rod assembly mark

13.2 Check the crankshaft endfloat using a dial gauge . . .

13.3 . . . or a feeler gauge

13.10 Use a micrometer to measure the crankshaft bearing journals

13 Crankshaft – inspection

Checking crankshaft endfloat

1 If the crankshaft endfloat is to be checked, this must be done when the crankshaft is still installed in the cylinder block, but is free to move.
2 Check the endfloat using a dial gauge in contact with the end of the crankshaft. Push the crankshaft fully one way, and then zero the gauge. Push the crankshaft fully the other way, and check the endfloat **(see illustration)**. The result can be compared with the specified amount, and will give an indication as to whether a new thrustwasher main bearing shell (1.7 litre DOHC engine) or thrustwashers (all other engines) are required.
3 If a dial gauge is not available, feeler gauges can be used. First push the crankshaft fully towards the flywheel end of the engine, then use feeler gauges to measure the gap between the web of the crankpin and the side of thrustwasher **(see illustration)**. On 1.7 litre DOHC engines thrustwashers are fitted to the sides of Number 2 main bearing upper shell and on all other engines the thrustwashers are fitted to Number 3 main bearing.

Inspection

4 Clean the crankshaft using paraffin or a suitable solvent, and dry it, preferably with compressed air if available. Be sure to clean the oil holes with a pipe cleaner or similar probe, to ensure that they are not obstructed.

 Warning: Wear eye protection when using compressed air.

5 Check the main and big-end bearing journals for uneven wear, scoring, pitting and cracking.
6 Big-end bearing wear is accompanied by distinct metallic knocking when the engine is running (particularly noticeable when the engine is pulling from low speed) and some loss of oil pressure.
7 Main bearing wear is accompanied by severe engine vibration and rumble – getting progressively worse as engine speed increases – and again by loss of oil pressure.

8 Check the bearing journal for roughness by running a finger lightly over the bearing surface. Any roughness (which will be accompanied by obvious bearing wear) indicates that the crankshaft requires regrinding (where possible) or renewal.
9 Check for burrs around the crankshaft oil holes (the holes are usually chamfered, so burrs should not be a problem unless regrinding has been carried out carelessly). Remove any burrs with a fine file or scraper, and thoroughly clean the oil holes as described previously.
10 Using a micrometer, measure the diameter of the main and big-end bearing journals, and compare the results with the Specifications **(see illustration)**. By measuring the diameter at a number of points around each journal's circumference, you will be able to determine whether or not the journal is out-of-round. Take the measurement at each end of the journal, near the webs, to determine if the journal is tapered. Compare the results obtained with those given in the Specifications.
11 Check the oil seal contact surfaces at each end of the crankshaft for wear and damage. If the seal has worn a deep groove in the surface of the crankshaft, consult an engine overhaul specialist; repair may be possible, but otherwise a new crankshaft will be required.
12 Set the crankshaft up in V-blocks, and position a dial gauge on the top of the crankshaft Number 1 main bearing journal. Zero the dial gauge, then slowly rotate the crankshaft through two complete revolutions, noting the journal run-out. Repeat the procedure on the remaining four main bearing journals, so that a run-out measurement is

available for all main bearing journals. If the run-out of any journal exceeds the service limit given in the Specifications, the crankshaft must be renewed.
13 Undersize (0.25 mm and 0.50 mm) big-end and main bearing shells are produced by Vauxhall for all engines except the 1.7 litre DOHC engine. If the crankshaft journals have not already been reground, it may be possible to have the crankshaft reconditioned, and to fit undersize shells. On 1.7 litre DOHC engines, if the crankshaft has worn beyond the specified limits, it will have to be renewed.

14 Main and big-end bearings – inspection

1 Even though the main and big-end bearings should be renewed during the engine overhaul, the old bearings should be retained for close examination, as they may reveal valuable information about the condition of the engine **(see illustration)**.
2 Bearing failure can occur due to lack of lubrication, the presence of dirt or other foreign particles, overloading the engine, or corrosion **(see illustration)**. Regardless of the

14.1 Typical main bearing shell identification markings

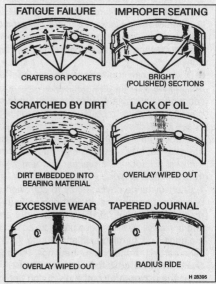

14.2 Typical bearing failures

cause of bearing failure, the cause must be corrected (where applicable) before the engine is reassembled, to prevent it from happening again.

3 When examining the bearing shells, remove them from the cylinder block, the main bearing caps, the connecting rods and the connecting rod big-end bearing caps. Lay them out on a clean surface in the same general position as their location in the engine. This will enable you to match any bearing problems with the corresponding crankshaft journal.

4 Dirt and other foreign matter gets into the engine in a variety of ways. It may be left in the engine during assembly, or it may pass through filters or the crankcase ventilation system. It may get into the oil, and from there into the bearings. Metal chips from machining operations and normal engine wear are often present. Abrasives are sometimes left in engine components after reconditioning, especially when parts are not thoroughly cleaned using the proper cleaning methods. Whatever the source, these foreign objects often end up embedded in the soft bearing material, and are easily recognised. Large particles will not embed in the bearing, and will score or gouge the bearing and journal. The best prevention for this cause of bearing failure is to clean all parts thoroughly, and keep everything spotlessly-clean during engine assembly. Frequent and regular engine oil and filter changes are also recommended.

5 Lack of lubrication (or lubrication breakdown) has a number of interrelated causes. Excessive heat (which thins the oil), overloading (which squeezes the oil from the bearing face) and oil leakage (from excessive bearing clearances, worn oil pump or high engine speeds) all contribute to lubrication breakdown. Blocked oil passages, which usually are the result of misaligned oil holes in a bearing shell, will also oil-starve a bearing, and destroy it. When lack of lubrication is the cause of bearing failure, the bearing material is wiped or extruded from the steel backing of the bearing. Temperatures may increase to the point where the steel backing turns blue from overheating.

6 Driving habits can have a definite effect on bearing life. Full-throttle, low-speed operation (labouring the engine) puts very high loads on bearings, tending to squeeze out the oil film. These loads cause the bearings to flex, which produces fine cracks in the bearing face (fatigue failure). Eventually, the bearing material will loosen in pieces, and tear away from the steel backing.

7 Short-distance driving leads to corrosion of bearings, because insufficient engine heat is produced to drive off the condensed water and corrosive gases. These products collect in the engine oil, forming acid and sludge. As the oil is carried to the engine bearings, the acid attacks and corrodes the bearing material.

8 Incorrect bearing installation during engine assembly will lead to bearing failure as well.

Tight-fitting bearings leave insufficient bearing running clearance, and will result in oil starvation. Dirt or foreign particles trapped behind a bearing shell result in high spots on the bearing, which lead to failure.

9 As mentioned at the beginning of this Section, the bearing shells should be renewed as a matter of course during engine overhaul; to do otherwise is false economy.

15 Engine overhaul – reassembly sequence

1 Before reassembly begins, ensure that all new parts have been obtained, and that all necessary tools are available. Read through the entire procedure to familiarise yourself with the work involved, and to ensure that all items necessary for reassembly of the engine are at hand. In addition to all normal tools and materials, thread-locking compound will be needed. A good quality tube of liquid sealant will also be required for the joint faces that are fitted without gaskets.

2 In order to save time and avoid problems, engine reassembly can be carried out in the following order:

  a) Crankshaft.
  b) Piston/connecting rod assemblies.
  c) Timing chains and sprockets – 2.0 litre engine.
  d) Oil pump.
  e) Sump (including baffle plate).
  f) Flywheel.
  g) Cylinder head.
  h) Water pump
  i) Timing belt tensioner and sprockets, and belts – all models except 2.0 litre engine.
  j) Inlet and exhaust manifolds (Chapter 4A).
  k) Engine external components.

3 At this stage, all engine components should be absolutely clean and dry, with all faults repaired. The components should be laid out (or in individual containers) on a completely clean work surface.

16 Piston rings – refitting

1 Before fitting new piston rings, the ring end gaps must be checked as follows.

2 Lay out the piston/connecting rod assemblies and the new piston ring sets, so that the ring sets will be matched with the same piston and cylinder during the end gap measurement and subsequent engine reassembly.

3 Insert the top ring into the first cylinder, and push it down the bore using the top of the piston. This will ensure that the ring remains square with the cylinder walls. Push the ring down into the bore until it is positioned 15 to 20 mm down from the top edge of the bore, then withdraw the piston.

4 Measure the end gap using feeler gauges,

16.4 Measuring a piston ring end gap using a feeler gauge

and compare the measurements with the figures given in the Specifications (see illustration).

5 If the gap is too small (unlikely if genuine Vauxhall parts are used), it must be enlarged, or the ring ends may contact each other during engine operation, causing serious damage. Ideally, new piston rings providing the correct end gap should be fitted. As a last resort, the end gap can be increased by filing the ring ends very carefully with a fine file. Mount the file in a vice with soft jaws, slip the ring over the file with the ends contacting the file face, and slowly move the ring to remove material from the ends. Take care, as piston rings are sharp, and are easily broken.

6 With new piston rings, it is unlikely that the end gap will be too large. If the gaps are too large, check that you have the correct rings for your engine and for the particular cylinder bore size.

7 Repeat the checking procedure for each ring in the first cylinder, and then for the rings in the remaining cylinders. Remember to keep rings, pistons and cylinders matched up.

8 Once the ring end gaps have been checked and if necessary corrected, the rings can be fitted to the pistons.

9 Fit the piston rings using the same technique as for removal. Fit the bottom (oil control) expander spring first then install the bevelled oil control ring, noting that the expander and oil control ring can be installed either way up (see illustrations).

10 On 1.7 litre DOHC engines, the second

16.9a Fit the expander ring . . .

16.9b ... followed by the oil control ring

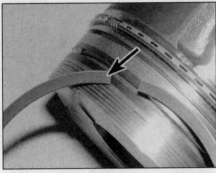

16.10 Fit the compression rings with any identification marks uppermost (arrowed)

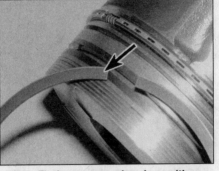

16.11 Sectional view of piston rings

and top rings are different and can be identified by the marks on the ring top surface; the top ring is marked T whilst the second ring is marked T2. Fit the second and top compression rings ensuring that each ring is fitted the correct way up with its identification mark uppermost **(see illustration)**. **Note:** *Always follow any instructions supplied with the new piston ring sets – different manufacturers may specify different procedures. Do not mix up the top and second compression rings.*

11 On all other engines, the second and top compression rings are different and can be identified by their cross-sections; the top ring is rectangular (Y20DTH: 'Keystone' cross-section) whilst the second ring is tapered. Fit the second and top compression rings ensuring that each ring is fitted the correct way up with its identification (TOP) mark uppermost **(see illustration)**. **Note:** *Always follow any instructions supplied with the new piston ring sets – different manufacturers may specify different procedures. Do not mix up the top and second compression rings. On some engines the top ring will not have an identification marking and can be fitted either way up.*

12 With the piston rings correctly installed, check that each ring is free to rotate easily in its groove. Check the ring-to-groove clearance of each ring using feeler gauges and check that the clearance is within the specified range then position the ring end gaps as shown **(see illustrations)**.

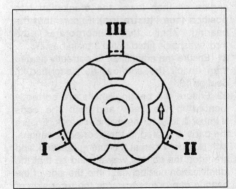

16.12a Piston ring end gap positions – 1.7 DOHC and 2.0 litre engines

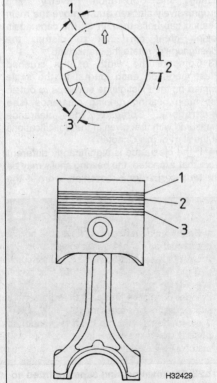

16.12b Piston ring end gap positions – 1.7 litre SOHC engine

---

17 Crankshaft – refitting and main bearing clearance check

Note: *It is recommended that new main bearing shells are fitted regardless of the condition of the original ones.*

Selection of bearing shells

1.7 litre DOHC engine

1 The main bearing running clearance is controlled in production by selecting one of four grades of bearing shell. The grades are identified by a colour-coding marked on the edge of each shell which indicates the shell's thickness. In order, from the thinnest to the thickest, the shell grades are: Green, Brown, Black and Blue. Bearing shells are produced in standard size only, no undersize shells are available from Vauxhall.

2 If the bearing shells are to be renewed, first check and record the identification marking stamped on the crankshaft adjacent to each main bearing journal. The marking is in the form of either a single or double notch on the crankshaft web. Number 1 (timing belt end of the engine) bearing code is situated to the right of the journal, whereas all other codes are on the left-hand side of the relevant journal.

3 Secondly, check and record the main bearing bore size code identification markings which are stamped on the right-hand, rear end of the cylinder block lower mating surface. The markings are in the form of numbers (1 to 3). The first marking indicates the size-group of Number 1 (timing belt end) main bearing bore and the last Number 5.

4 Match the relevant main bearing bore code with its crankshaft journal code, and select a new set of bearing shells using the following table. The crankshaft codes are listed down the left-hand side, and the main bearing bore codes along the top; the required bearing grade is indicated where the two columns intersect.

	1	2	3
Single notch	Black	Brown	Green
Double notch	Blue	Black	Brown

All other engines

5 On all engines except the 1.7 litre DOHC engine, although the original bearing shells fitted at the factory maybe of various grades, all replacement bearing shells sold are of the same grade. Vauxhall supply both standard size bearing shells and undersize shells for use when the crankshaft has been reground. The required size of shell required can be determined by measuring the crankshaft journals (see Section 13).

Main bearing clearance check

6 Clean the backs of the bearing shells and the bearing locations in both the cylinder block and the main bearing caps.

7 Press the bearing shells into their locations, ensuring that the tab on each shell engages in the notch in the cylinder block or main bearing

17.7 The tab on each bearing shell locates in the notch in the cylinder block

17.11 Place a length of Plastigauge on the crankshaft journal axis

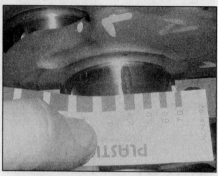

17.13 Compare the width of the crushed Plastigauge with the measurement scale

cap **(see illustration)**. If the original bearing shells are being used for the check, ensure they are refitted in their original locations. The clearance can be checked in either of two ways.

8 One method (which will be difficult to achieve without a range of internal micrometers or internal/external expanding calipers) is to refit the main bearing caps to the cylinder block, with bearing shells in place. With the cap retaining bolts correctly tightened (use the original bolts for the check, not the new ones), measure the internal diameter of each assembled pair of bearing shells. If the diameter of each corresponding crankshaft journal is measured and then subtracted from the bearing internal diameter, the result will be the main bearing running clearance.

9 The second (and more accurate) method is to use a product known as Plastigauge. This consists of a fine thread of perfectly-round plastic which is compressed between the bearing shell and the journal. When the shell is removed, the plastic is deformed and can be measured with a special card gauge supplied with the kit. The running clearance is determined from this gauge. Plastigauge is sometimes difficult to obtain but enquiries at one of the larger specialist quality motor factors should produce the name of a stockist in your area. The procedure for using Plastigauge is as follows.

10 With the main bearing upper shells in place, carefully lay the crankshaft in position.

Do not use any lubricant; the crankshaft journals and bearing shells must be perfectly clean and dry.

11 Cut several lengths of the appropriate size Plastigauge (they should be slightly shorter than the width of the main bearings) and place one length on each crankshaft journal axis **(see illustration)**.

12 With the main bearing lower shells in position, refit the main bearing caps, using the identification marks to ensure each one is correctly positioned. Refit the original retaining bolts and tighten them to the specified torque (1.7 litre DOHC engine) or to the specified Stage 1 torque and then through the Stage 2 and 3 angles (all other engines) Take care not to disturb the Plastigauge and **do not** rotate the crankshaft at any time during this operation. Evenly and progressively slacken and remove the main bearing cap bolts then lift off the caps again taking great care not to disturb the Plastigauge or rotate the crankshaft.

13 Compare the width of the crushed Plastigauge on each journal to the scale printed on the Plastigauge envelope to obtain the main bearing running clearance **(see illustration)**. Compare the clearance measured with that given in the Specifications at the start of this Chapter.

14 If the clearance is significantly different from that expected, the bearing shells may be the wrong size (or excessively worn if the

original shells are being re-used). Before deciding that the crankshaft is worn, make sure that no dirt or oil was trapped between the bearing shells and the caps or block when the clearance was measured. If the Plastigauge was wider at one end than at the other, the crankshaft journal may be tapered.

15 Before condemning the components concerned, seek the advice of your Vauxhall dealer or suitable engine repair specialist. They will also be able to inform as to the best course of action or whether renewal will be necessary.

16 Where necessary, obtain the correct size of bearing shell and repeat the running clearance checking procedure as described above.

17 On completion, carefully scrape away all traces of the Plastigauge material from the crankshaft and bearing shells using a fingernail or other object which is unlikely to score the bearing surfaces.

Final crankshaft refitting

1.7 litre SOHC engine

18 Carefully lift the crankshaft out of the cylinder block.

19 Place the bearing shells in their locations as described above in paragraphs 6 and 7 **(see illustration 17.7)**. If new shells are being fitted, ensure that all traces of the protective grease are cleaned off using paraffin. Wipe dry the shells and caps with a lint-free cloth.

20 Lubricate the upper shells with clean engine oil then lower the crankshaft into position **(see illustration)**. Ensure that the bearing shell that incorporates the thrustwasher is fitted to No 3 main bearing.

21 Ensure the crankshaft is correctly seated then check the endfloat as described in Section 13.

22 Ensure the bearing shells are correctly located in the caps and refit the caps Number 1 to 4 to the cylinder block. Ensure the caps are fitted in their correct locations, with Number 1 cap at the timing belt end, and are fitted the correct way around so that the identification number cast into the side of the bearing cap points towards the front side of the cylinder block **(see illustration)**.

23 Ensure the rear (Number 5) bearing cap is

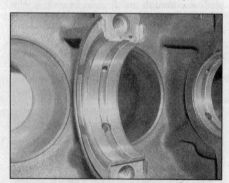

17.20 No 3 main bearing incorporates the thrustwasher

17.22 The main bearing caps are fitted so that the identification number cast into the side of the cap points towards the front of the cylinder block

17.23 Fill the groove on each side of the No 5 main bearing cap with sealant

17.26 Use an angle gauge to accurately tighten the main bearing caps to the Stage 2 and 3 settings

17.27 Inject more sealant between the No 5 main bearing cap and the cylinder block

clean and dry then fill the groove on each side of the cap with sealing compound (available from your Vauxhall dealer) **(see illustration)**. Fit the bearing cap to the engine, ensuring it is fitted the correct way around.

24 Apply a smear of clean engine to oil to the threads and underneath the heads of the new main bearing cap bolts. Fit the bolts, tightening them all by hand.

25 Working in a diagonal sequence from the centre outwards, tighten the main bearing cap bolts to the specified Stage 1 torque setting.

26 Once all bolts are tightened to the specified Stage 1 torque, go around again and tighten all bolts through the specified Stage 2 angle then go around once more and tighten all bolts through the specified Stage 3 angle. It is recommended that an angle-measuring gauge is used during the final stages of the tightening, to ensure accuracy **(see illustration)**. If a gauge is not available, use white paint to make alignment marks between the bolt head and cap prior to tightening; the marks can then be used to check that the bolt has been rotated through the correct angle.

27 Once all the bolts have been tightened, inject more sealant down the grooves in the rear main bearing cap until sealant is seen to be escaping through the joints. Once you are sure the cap grooves are full of sealant, wipe off all excess sealant using a clean cloth **(see illustration)**.

28 Check that the crankshaft is free to rotate

smoothly; if excessive force is required to turn the crankshaft, investigate the cause before proceeding further.

29 Refit/reconnect the piston connecting rod assemblies to the crankshaft as described in Section 18.

30 Position the main bearing bridge correctly and fit the new retaining bolts. Tighten the bolts to the Stage 1 torque setting, and then Stage 2 angle setting, working in a diagonal sequence from the centre outwards **(see illustration)**.

31 Referring to Part A, fit a new left-hand crankshaft oil seal, then refit the flywheel, oil pump, cylinder head, timing belt sprocket and a new timing belt.

1.7 litre DOHC engine

32 Carefully lift the crankshaft out of the cylinder block.

33 Place the bearing shells in their locations as described above in paragraphs 6 and 7. If new shells are being fitted, ensure that all traces of the protective grease are cleaned off using paraffin. Wipe dry the shells and caps with a lint-free cloth.

34 Using a little grease, stick the thrustwashers to each side of the Number 2 main bearing upper location; ensure that the oilway grooves on each thrustwasher face outwards **(see illustration)**.

35 Lubricate the upper shells with clean engine oil then lower the crankshaft into position **(see illustration)**.

36 Ensure the crankshaft is correctly seated then check the endfloat as described in Section 13.

37 Ensure the bearing shells are correctly located in the caps and refit the caps to the cylinder block **(see illustration)**. Ensure the caps are fitted in their correct locations, with Number 1 cap at the timing belt end, and are fitted the correct way around so that the arrows all point towards the timing belt end of the engine. Prior to refitting Number 1 cap, apply a smear of sealant to its mating surface.

38 Apply a smear of clean engine to oil to the threads and underneath the heads of the new main bearing cap bolts. Fit the bolts tightening them all by hand then working in a diagonal sequence from the centre outwards,

17.30 Tighten the main bearing bridge bolts to the specified torque

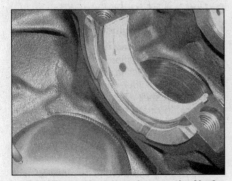

17.34 Fit the thrust washers to the No 2 main bearing with the oil grooves facing outwards

17.35 Lower the crankshaft into position

17.37 Fit the bearing caps with the arrows towards the timing belt end of the engine

17.38 Tighten the main bearing cap bolts to the specified torque

17.41 Apply sealant to the oil seal housing mating surface

17.42 Fit the input shaft guide into the end of the crankshaft

17.44a With the rear bearing cap in position, inject sealant down the groove . . .

17.44b . . . until it is seen to be forced out through the hole in the cap (arrowed)

17.45a Refit the main bearing bridge casting . . .

evenly and progressively tighten them to the specified torque setting **(see illustration)**.
39 Check that the crankshaft is free to rotate smoothly; if excessive force is required to turn the crankshaft, investigate the cause before proceeding further.
40 Ensure that the mating surfaces of the oil seal housing and cylinder block are clean and dry. Note the correct fitted depth of the oil seal then tap/lever the seal out of the housing.
41 Apply a smear of sealant to the oil seal housing mating surface, and make sure that the locating dowels are in position **(see illustration)**. Slide the housing over the end of the crankshaft, and into position on the cylinder block. Put a drop of locking compound on the threads, then tighten the

retaining bolts to the specified torque setting.
42 Fit the transmission input shaft guide into the end of the crankshaft **(see illustration)**.
43 Refit/reconnect the piston connecting rod assemblies to the crankshaft as described in Section 18. Referring to Part B of this Chapter fit a new crankshaft oil seal, then refit the flywheel, oil pump cover, cylinder head, timing belt sprockets and a new timing belt.

2.0 litre engine

44 Refit the crankshaft as described in paragraphs 18 to 29, using the marks made on removal to ensure the bearing caps are correctly positioned (see Section 10) **(see illustrations)**.
45 Ensure the bearing cap and main bearing bridge casting surfaces are clean and dry. Refit the casting to the engine, ensuring that the arrow on the casting is pointing towards the timing chain end of the engine, then refit

the retaining bolts and tighten them to the specified torque, working in a diagonal sequence from the centre outwards **(see illustrations)**.
46 Working as described Part C of this Chapter, fit a new left-hand oil crankshaft oil seal then refit the flywheel, timing chains, sprockets and cylinder head.

18 Piston/connecting rod assembly – refitting and big-end clearance check

Note: *It is recommended that new piston rings and big-end bearing shells are fitted regardless of the condition of the original ones.*

Selection of bearing shells

1.7 litre DOHC engine

1 The big-end bearing running clearance is controlled in production by selecting one of three grades of bearing shell. The grades are identified by a colour-coding marked on the edge of each shell which indicates the shell's thickness. In order, from the thinnest to the thickest, the shell grades are: Brown, Black and Blue. Bearing shells are produced in standard size only, no undersize shells are available from Vauxhall.
2 If the bearing shells are to be renewed, first check and record the identification marking stamped on the side face of each connecting rod **(see illustration)**. The markings are used

17.45b . . . ensuring its arrow is pointing towards the timing chain of the engine, and tighten its retaining bolts to the specified torque

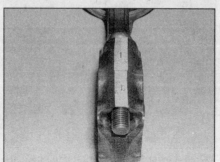

18.2 Connecting rod identification marks

to select the correct grade of bearing shell required as follows.

Connecting rod mark	Bearing shell grade required
I	Blue
II	Black
III	Brown

All other engines

3 On all engines except the 1.7 litre DOHC 16V, although the original bearing shells fitted at the factory maybe of various grades, all replacement bearing shells sold are of the same grade. Vauxhall supply both standard size bearing shells and undersize shells for use when the crankshaft has been reground. The required size of shell required can be determined by measuring the crankshaft journals (see Section 13).

Big-end bearing running clearance check

4 Clean the backs of the bearing shells and the bearing locations in both the connecting rod and bearing cap.
5 Press the bearing shells into their locations, ensuring that the tab on each shell engages in the notch in the connecting rod and cap (see illustration). If the original bearing shells are being used for the check, ensure they are refitted in their original locations. The clearance can be checked in either of two ways.
6 One method is to refit the big-end bearing cap to the connecting rod, with bearing shells in place. With the cap retaining bolts/nuts (use the original bolts for the check) correctly tightened, use an internal micrometer or vernier caliper to measure the internal diameter of each assembled pair of bearing shells. If the diameter of each corresponding crankshaft journal is measured and then subtracted from the bearing internal diameter, the result will be the big-end bearing running clearance.

7 The second method is to use Plastigauge as described in Section 17, paragraphs 9 to 17. Place a strand of Plastigauge on each (cleaned) crankpin journal and refit the (clean) piston/connecting rod assemblies, shells and big-end bearing caps. Tighten the bolts/nuts (as applicable) correctly taking care not to disturb the Plastigauge. Dismantle the assemblies without rotating the crankshaft and use the scale printed on the Plastigauge envelope to obtain the big-end bearing running clearance. On completion of the measurement, carefully scrape off all traces of Plastigauge from the journal and shells using a fingernail or other object which will not score the components.

Final piston/connecting rod assembly refitting

8 Ensure the bearing shells are correctly refitted as described above in paragraphs 4 and 5. If new shells are being fitted, ensure that all traces of the protective grease are cleaned off using paraffin. Wipe dry the shells and connecting rods with a lint-free cloth.
9 Lubricate the bores, the pistons and piston rings then lay out each piston/connecting rod assembly in its respective position.
10 Starting with assembly Number 1, make sure that the piston rings are still spaced as described in Section 16, then clamp them in position with a piston ring compressor.

1.7 litre SOHC engine

11 Insert the piston/connecting rod assembly into the top of cylinder No 1, ensuring that the arrow marking on the piston crown is pointing towards the timing belt end of the engine. Using a block of wood or hammer handle against the piston crown, tap the assembly into the cylinder until the piston crown is flush with the top of the cylinder (see illustration).
12 Taking care not to mark the cylinder bore, liberally lubricate the crankpin and both bearing shells, then pull the piston/connecting

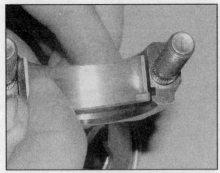

18.5 Ensure the tabs of the bearing shell engage with the notch

rod assembly down the bore and onto the crankpin and refit the big-end bearing cap using the markings to ensure it is fitted the correct way around (the lug on the bearing cap base should be facing the flywheel end of the engine), and screw in the new retaining bolts (see illustration).
13 Tighten both bearing cap bolts to the specified Stage 1 torque setting then tighten them through the specified Stage 2 angle, and finally through the specified Stage 3 angle. It is recommended that an angle-measuring gauge is used during the final stages of the tightening, to ensure accuracy. If a gauge is not available, use white paint to make alignment marks between the bolt head and cap prior to tightening; the marks can then be used to check that the bolt has been rotated through the correct angle.
14 Refit the remaining three piston and connecting rod assemblies in the same way.
15 Rotate the crankshaft, and check that it turns freely, with no signs of binding or tight spots.
16 Refit the main bearing bridge, oil pump, oil pump strainer, sump and the cylinder head as described in Part A of this Chapter.

18.11 Use a hammer handle to tap the piston into the cylinder until the crown of the piston is flush with the top of the cylinder

18.12 The lug on the bearing cap base should point towards the flywheel end of the engine (arrowed)

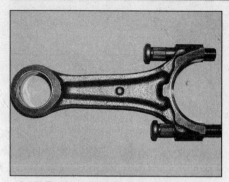

18.17 Replace the big-end bolts – 1.7 litre DOHC engines

18.18 Tap the piston assembly into the cylinder using a block of wood or a hammer handle

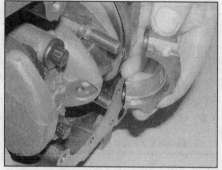

18.19 Lubricate the bearing surface and refit the bearing cap

1.7 litre DOHC engine

17 Prior to refitting, carefully tap the original bolts out from the connecting rod and install the new bolts (see illustration).

18 Insert the piston/connecting rod assembly into the top of cylinder No 1, ensuring that the mark (dot) on the piston crown is pointing towards the timing belt end of the engine. Using a block of wood or hammer handle against the piston crown, tap the assembly into the cylinder until the piston crown is flush with the top of the cylinder (see illustration).

19 Taking care not to mark the cylinder bore, liberally lubricate the crankpin and both bearing shells, then pull the piston/connecting rod assembly down the bore and onto the crankpin and refit the big-end bearing cap, using the markings to ensure it is fitted the correct way around (align the previously made marks), and fit the new retaining nuts (see illustration).

20 Tighten both bearing cap nuts to the specified Stage 1 torque setting then tighten them through the specified Stage 2 angle, and finally through the specified Stage 3 angle (see illustration). It is recommended that an angle-measuring gauge is used during the final stages of the tightening, to ensure accuracy. If a gauge is not available, use white paint to make alignment marks between the nut and cap prior to tightening; the marks can then be used to check that the bolt has been rotated through the correct angle.

21 Refit the remaining three piston and connecting rod assemblies in the same way.

22 Rotate the crankshaft, and check that it turns freely, with no signs of binding or tight spots.

23 Refit the baffle plate to the base of the cylinder block and tighten its retaining bolts to the specified torque.

24 Refit the oil pump strainer, sump and the cylinder head as described in Part B of this Chapter.

2.0 litre engine

25 Insert the piston/connecting rod assembly into the top of cylinder No 1, ensuring that the arrow marking on the piston crown is pointing towards the timing chain end of the engine.

Using a block of wood or hammer handle against the piston crown, tap the assembly into the cylinder until the piston crown is flush with the top of the cylinder (see illustration).

26 Taking care not to mark the cylinder bore, liberally lubricate the crankpin and both bearing shells, then pull the piston/connecting rod assembly down the bore and onto the crankpin and refit the big-end bearing cap using the markings to ensure it is fitted the correct way around (the lug on the bearing cap base should be facing the flywheel end of the engine), and screw in the new retaining bolts (see illustration).

18.20 Use and angle measuring gauge to accurately tighten the bearing cap bolts

18.26 Lubricate the bearing shell with clean engine oil and then refit the bearing cap to the connecting rod . . .

27 Tighten both bearing cap bolts to the specified Stage 1 torque setting then tighten them through the specified Stage 2 angle, and finally through the specified Stage 3 angle. It is recommended that an angle-measuring gauge is used during the final stages of the tightening, to ensure accuracy (see illustrations). If a gauge is not available, use white paint to make alignment marks between the bolt head and cap prior to tightening; the marks can then be used to check that the bolt has been rotated through the correct angle.

28 Refit the remaining three piston and connecting rod assemblies in the same way.

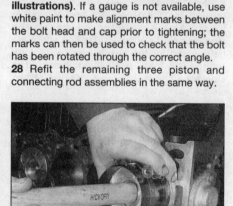

18.25 On 2.0 litre engines, tap the piston/connecting rod assembly onto the bore using the handle of a hammer

18.27a . . . making sure its lug (arrowed) is facing the flywheel end of the engine. Tighten the bearing cap bolts to the specified Stage 1 torque . . .

18.27b . . . and then through the specified Stages 2 and 3 angles

29 Rotate the crankshaft, and check that it turns freely, with no signs of binding or tight spots.
30 Refit the oil pump strainer, sump and the cylinder head as described in Part C of this Chapter.

19 Engine – initial start-up after overhaul

1 With the engine refitted in the vehicle, double-check the engine oil and coolant levels. Make a final check that everything has been reconnected, and that there are no tools or rags left in the engine compartment.
2 Switch on the ignition and immediately turn the engine on the starter (without allowing the glow plugs to heat up) until the oil pressure warning light goes out.
3 Start the engine as normal noting that this may take a little longer than usual, due to the fuel system components having been disturbed.
4 While the engine is idling, check for fuel, water and oil leaks. Don't be alarmed if there are some odd smells and smoke from parts getting hot and burning off oil deposits.
5 Assuming all is well, keep the engine idling until hot water is felt circulating through the top hose, then switch off the engine.
6 Allow the engine to cool then recheck the oil and coolant levels as described in *Weekly checks*, and top-up as necessary.
7 On 1.7 litre SOHC engines, the cylinder head bolts should be tightened further, using the angular tightening method described in Section 11 of Chapter 2A.
8 If new pistons, rings or crankshaft bearings have been fitted, the engine must be treated as new, and run-in for the first 500 miles (800 km). *Do not* operate the engine at full-throttle, or allow it to labour at low engine speeds in any gear. It is recommended that the oil and filter be changed at the end of this period.

Chapter 3
Cooling, heating and air conditioning systems

Contents

Degrees of difficulty

Easy, suitable for novice with little experience		Fairly easy, suitable for beginner with some experience		Fairly difficult, suitable for competent DIY mechanic	🔧	Difficult, suitable for experienced DIY mechanic	🔧	Very difficult, suitable for expert DIY or professional	🔧

Specifications

System type .... Pressurised, with front-mounted radiator, remote expansion tank, and electric cooling fan. Water pump driven by timing belt on 1.7 litre engine or by auxiliary drivebelt on 2.0 litre engine

Thermostat
Starts to open:
  1.7 litre DOHC engine .... 89°C
  Except 1.7 litre DOHC engine .... 92°C
Fully open:
  1.7 litre DOHC engine .... 92°C
  Except 1.7 litre DOHC engine .... 107°C

Air conditioning compressor
Lubricant capacity .... 150 cc
Lubricant type .... Vauxhall part number 90509933/1949873

Torque wrench settings

	Nm	lbf ft
Air conditioning compressor mounting	20	15
Air conditioning condenser to radiator	5	4
Air conditioning refrigerant line to receiver-dryer and condenser	20	15
Automatic transmission fluid cooler lines to radiator	30	22
Condensation drain to floor	5	4
Coolant temperature sensor:		
1.7 litre DOHC engines	23	17
1.7 litre SOHC engines	20	15
2.0 litre engines	10	7
Electric cooling fan assembly frame to radiator	5	4
Pressure pick-up to receiver-dryer	9	7
Radiator lower mounting bracket to subframe	15	11
Steering crossmember to bulkhead	25	18
Thermostat housing:		
1.7 litre DOHC engines	24	18
1.7 litre SOHC engines and 2.0 litre engines	8	6
Water pump:		
1.7 litre DOHC engines	24	18
1.7 litre SOHC engines	25	18
2.0 litre engines	20	15
Water pump pulley:		
1.7 litre engines	10	7
2.0 litre engines	20	15

1 Cooling system – general

General information

The cooling system is of pressurised type, comprising a pump driven by the timing belt (1.7 litre SOHC engines) or by the auxiliary drivebelt (1.7 litre DOHC and all 2.0 litre engines), a crossflow radiator, electric cooling fan, and thermostat. The system functions as follows: Cold coolant from the radiator passes through the bottom hose to the water pump, where it is pumped around the cylinder block, head passages and heater matrix. After cooling the cylinder bores, combustion surfaces and valve seats, the coolant reaches the underside of the thermostat, which is initially closed. After circulating through the heater, the coolant is returned to the water pump.

When the engine is cold, the coolant circulates only through the cylinder block, cylinder head and heater. When the coolant reaches a predetermined temperature, the thermostat opens and the coolant passes through to the radiator. As the coolant circulates through the radiator, it is cooled by the inrush of air when the car is in forward motion. Airflow is supplemented by the action of the electric cooling fan when necessary. Once the coolant has passed through the radiator, and has cooled, the cycle is repeated.

The electric cooling fan, mounted on the rear of the radiator, is controlled by a cooling module located behind the left-hand side of the front bumper. At a predetermined coolant temperature, the fan is actuated.

An expansion tank is fitted to the left-hand side of the engine compartment to accommodate expansion of the coolant when hot. The expansion tank is connected to the top of the radiator by a small bore hose.

Precautions

 Warning: Do not attempt to remove the expansion tank filler cap, or disturb any part of the cooling system, while the engine is hot; there is a high risk of scalding. If the cap must be removed before the engine and radiator have fully cooled (even though this is not recommended) the pressure in the cooling system must first be relieved. Cover the cap with a thick layer of cloth, to avoid scalding, and slowly unscrew the filler cap until a hissing sound can be heard. When the hissing has stopped, indicating that the pressure has reduced, slowly unscrew the filler cap until it can be removed; if more hissing sounds are heard, wait until they have stopped before unscrewing the cap completely. At all times, keep well away from the filler cap opening.

Warning: Do not allow antifreeze to come into contact with the skin, or with the painted surfaces of the vehicle. Rinse off spills immediately, with plenty of water.
Warning: If the engine is hot, the electric cooling fan may start rotating even if the engine is not running; be careful to keep hands, hair and loose clothing well clear when working in the engine compartment.
Warning: Refer to Section 11 for precautions to be observed when working on models equipped with air conditioning.

2 Cooling system – draining, flushing and refilling

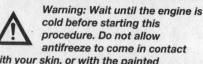

Warning: Wait until the engine is cold before starting this procedure. Do not allow antifreeze to come in contact with your skin, or with the painted surfaces of the vehicle. Rinse off spills immediately with plenty of water.

Draining

1 To drain the cooling system, first unscrew and remove the expansion tank filler cap **(see illustration)**. If the engine is not completely cold, place a thick cloth over the cap, and unscrew it slowly to release any pressure.
2 Where necessary, remove the undertray from under the radiator and engine.
3 Position a container beneath the right-hand side of the radiator and connect a short length of hose from the radiator drain tap to the container. Open the tap and allow the coolant to drain into the container **(see illustrations)**.
4 As no cylinder block drain plug is fitted, the engine cannot be drained completely. Care should therefore be taken when refilling the system to maintain antifreeze strength.
5 If the coolant has been drained for a reason other than renewal, then provided it is clean and less than two years old, it can be re-used. Vauxhall do not specify renewal intervals for the coolant installed in the system when the vehicle is new, so renewal is up to the discretion of the owner. We recommend renewing the coolant every two years.

Flushing

6 If coolant renewal has been neglected, or if the antifreeze mixture has become diluted, then in time, the cooling system may gradually lose efficiency, as the coolant passages become restricted due to rust, scale deposits, and other sediment. The cooling system efficiency can be restored by flushing the system clean.
7 The radiator should be flushed independently of the engine, to avoid unnecessary contamination.
8 To flush the radiator, disconnect the top and bottom hoses from the radiator, then insert a garden hose into the radiator top inlet. Direct a flow of clean water through the radiator and continue flushing until clean water emerges from the radiator bottom outlet. If after a reasonable period, the water still does not run clear, the radiator can be flushed with a flushing solution, available at all good motorist outlets. It is important that the cleaning agent manufacturer's instructions are followed carefully. If the contamination is particularly bad, remove the radiator then insert the hose in the bottom outlet, and flush the radiator in reverse ('reverse-flushing').
9 To flush the engine, remove the thermostat as described in Section 5 and disconnect the bottom hose from the radiator.
10 Insert a hose in the cylinder head and direct a flow of clean water through the engine until clean water emerges from the bottom hose.

2.1 Removing the expansion tank filler cap

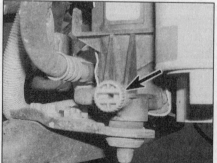

2.3a The drain tap is located on the right-hand side of the radiator

2.3b Connect a hose to the drain tap to drain the cooling system

11 On completion of flushing, refit the thermostat, referring to Section 5 and reconnect the hoses.

Refilling

12 Before attempting to fill the cooling system, make sure that all hoses and clips are in good condition, and that the clips are tight. An antifreeze solution must be used all year round, to prevent corrosion of the alloy engine components.

13 Unscrew and remove the expansion tank cap, and fill the system slowly until the level reaches the KALT (or COLD) mark on the tank. During refilling, occasionally assist the purging of air locks by squeezing the radiator top and bottom hoses several times. If the coolant is being renewed, begin by pouring in a couple of litres of water, followed by the correct quantity of antifreeze, then top-up with more water.

14 Refit and tighten the expansion tank cap.

15 Start the engine and run it until it reaches normal operating temperature, then stop the engine and allow it to cool.

16 Check for leaks, particularly around disturbed components. Check the coolant level in the expansion tank, and top-up if necessary. Note that the system must be cold before an accurate level is indicated in the expansion tank. If the expansion tank cap is removed while the engine is still warm, cover the cap with a thick cloth and unscrew the cap slowly to gradually relieve the system pressure (a hissing sound will normally be heard). Wait until any pressure remaining in the system is released, then continue to turn the cap until it can be removed.

17 Refit the cap, then where necessary, refit the undertray beneath the radiator and engine.

3 Cooling system hoses – disconnection and renewal

Note: *Refer to the warnings given in Section 1 of this Chapter before proceeding. Do not attempt to disconnect any hose while the system is still hot.*

1 If the checks described in Chapter 1 reveal a faulty hose, it must be renewed as follows.

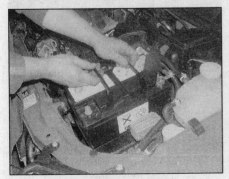
4.2a Removing the battery . . .

The hose clips fitted as original equipment are particularly difficult to remove with grips or pliers, however, a home-made tool can easily be fabricated out of a worm-drive clip. Cut the clip with reference to the photograph and bend over one end to hook around the square end of the original clip. Drill a hole in the other end to fit over the protruding end of the original clip. Fit the home-made tool to the original clip and tighten to expand the clip.

2 First drain the cooling system (see Section 2). If the coolant is not due for renewal, it may be re-used if it is collected in a clean container.

3 Before disconnecting a hose, first note its routing in the engine compartment, and its fitted position. Loosen the clips then move the clips along the hose, clear of the relevant inlet/outlet union **(see Haynes Hint)**. Carefully ease the hose free.

4 Note that the radiator inlet and outlet unions are fragile; do not use excessive force when attempting to remove the hoses. If a hose proves to be difficult to remove, try to release it by rotating the hose ends before attempting to free it.

HAYNES HINT *If all else fails, cut the coolant hose with a sharp knife, then slit it so that it can be peeled off in two pieces. Although this may prove expensive if the hose is otherwise undamaged, it is preferable to buying a new radiator.*

5 When fitting a hose, first slide the clips onto the hose, then work the hose into position. If the hose is stiff, use a little soapy water (washing-up liquid is ideal) as a lubricant, or soften the hose by soaking it in hot water.

4.2b . . . and mounting bracket

6 Slide each clip along the hose until it passes over the flared end of the relevant inlet/outlet union, before tightening the clips securely.

7 Refill the cooling system with reference to Section 2.

8 Check thoroughly for leaks as soon as possible after disturbing any part of the cooling system.

4 Radiator – removal, inspection and refitting

Removal

1 Apply the handbrake, then jack up the front of the vehicle and support it on axle stands (see *Jacking and vehicle support*). Remove the undertray from under the engine compartment.

2 On models with the DOHC engines, remove the battery and mounting bracket with reference to Chapter 5A **(see illustrations)**. Also unbolt the wiring harness from the mounting.

3 Remove the front bumper as described in Chapter 11.

4 On models with the Y20DTH engine, remove the impact absorber from behind the front bumper and also remove the intercooler complete as described in Chapter 4A.

5 Remove the engine top cover, then on 1.7 litre engine models, remove the electric fan assembly from the rear of the radiator as described in Section 6.

6 Remove the air cleaner assembly, inlet ducting and airflow meter as described in Chapter 4A.

7 On models with air conditioning, disconnect the wiring from the air conditioning compressor, receiver-dryer, auxiliary cooling fan and cooling module control unit. Remove the earth cable from the body, and position the wiring harness to one side.

4.9a Disconnecting the top hose

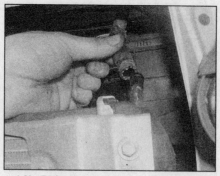

4.9b Disconnecting the air purge hose

4.11a Unscrew the mounting bolts . . .

8 Drain the cooling system as described in Section 2.

9 Disconnect the upper and lower hoses from the radiator. Also disconnect the purge hose **(see illustrations)**.

10 Insert two lengths of welding rod or two screwdrivers through the radiator side mountings from inside the engine compartment in order to support the radiator while the bottom mounting brackets are removed.

11 Unbolt the bottom mounting brackets from the subframe and slide the brackets with rubbers from the extensions on the bottom of the radiator **(see illustrations)**.

12 On models with air conditioning, unscrew the bolts securing the air conditioning

condenser to the front of the radiator, then tie the condenser to the front crossmember with plastic ties or wire **(see illustrations)**. **Do not disconnect the refrigerant pipes**. Also unbolt the intercooler mounting bracket.

13 Support the radiator, then remove the rods or screwdrivers from the side mountings, then lower the radiator out of its mountings and withdraw from under the vehicle **(see illustration)**.

14 Where necessary, remove the electric fan and intercooler from the radiator and transfer to the new unit.

Inspection

15 If the radiator has been removed due to suspected blockage, reverse flush it with reference to Section 2. Clean dirt and debris from the radiator fins, using an air line (in which case, wear eye protection) or a soft brush.

Caution: Be careful, as the fins are easily damaged, and are sharp.

16 If necessary, a radiator specialist can perform a 'flow test' on the radiator, to establish whether an internal blockage exists.

17 In an emergency, minor leaks from the radiator can be cured by using a suitable radiator sealant (in accordance with its manufacturer's instructions).

18 A leaking radiator must be referred to a specialist for permanent repair. Do not attempt to weld or solder a leaking radiator, as damage may result.

19 Inspect the radiator mounting rubbers, and renew them if necessary.

Refitting

20 Refitting is a reversal of removal, bearing in mind the following points.

a) *Ensure that the lower mounting rubbers are correctly located in the bottom mounting brackets.*

b) *Ensure that all hoses are correctly reconnected, and their retaining clips securely tightened.*

c) *On completion, refill the cooling system as described in Section 2.*

5 Thermostat –
removal, testing and refitting

1.7 litre engine

Removal

1 Remove the battery and mounting with reference to Chapter 5A.

2 Apply the handbrake, then jack up the front of the vehicle and support it on axle stands (see *Jacking and vehicle support*). Remove the undertray from the bottom of the engine compartment.

3 Drain the cooling system as described in Section 2.

4 Loosen the clip and disconnect the top

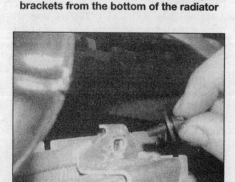

4.11b . . . and remove the mounting brackets from the bottom of the radiator

4.12a Unscrew the bolts securing the air conditioning condenser to the front of the radiator . . .

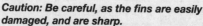

4.12b . . . and tie it to the front crossmember with plastic ties

4.14 Lowering the radiator from its mountings

5.5 Removing the thermostat cover – DOHC engine

5.6 Removing the thermostat – DOHC engine

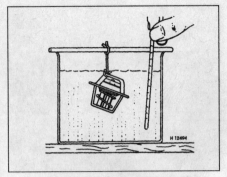

5.7 Testing the thermostat opening temperature

hose from the thermostat cover located on the right-hand end of the cylinder head on SOHC engines and on the left-hand end of the cylinder head on DOHC engines.

5 Unscrew the bolts and remove the thermostat cover from the housing **(see illustration)**.

6 Lift the thermostat from its housing and recover the sealing ring **(see illustration)**.

Testing

7 A rough test of the thermostat's operation may be made by suspending it with a piece of string in a container full of water. Heat the water to bring it to the boil – the thermostat must open by the time the water boils. If not, renew it **(see illustration)**.

8 The opening temperature is usually marked on the thermostat. If a thermometer is available, the precise opening temperature of the thermostat may be determined, and compared with the value marked on the thermostat.

9 A thermostat which fails to close as the water cools must also be renewed.

Refitting

10 Thoroughly clean the mating faces of the thermostat cover and housing.

11 Locate the thermostat together with a new sealing ring in the housing, then refit the cover and tighten the bolts to the specified torque.

12 Reconnect the top hose and tighten the clip.

13 Refit the battery and mounting with reference to Chapter 5A.

14 Refill and bleed the cooling system as described in Section 2.

15 Refit the undertray to the bottom of the engine compartment.

2.0 litre engine

Removal

16 Remove the air cleaner assembly, inlet ducting and airflow meter as described in Chapter 4A.

17 Apply the handbrake, then jack up the front of the vehicle and support it on axle stands (see *Jacking and vehicle support*). Remove the undertray from the bottom of the engine compartment.

18 Drain the cooling system as described in Section 2.

19 Where necessary, disconnect the wiring from the temperature sensor located on the thermostat housing.

20 Loosen the clips and disconnect the top, bottom and purge hoses from the thermostat housing located on the right-hand end of the cylinder head. Unscrew the bolts and remove the housing which includes the integral thermostat. Recover the gasket **(see illustrations)**.

Testing

21 Refer to paragraphs 7 to 9 inclusive. If the thermostat is renewed, unscrew the

temperature sensor and transfer it to the new housing.

Refitting

22 Thoroughly clean the mating faces of the thermostat housing and cylinder head.

23 Refit the housing together with a new gasket and tighten the mounting bolts to the specified torque.

24 Reconnect the hoses and tighten the clips, the reconnect wiring as applicable.

25 Refit the undertray, and lower the vehicle to the ground.

26 Refit the air cleaner assembly, inlet ducting and airflow meter with reference to Chapter 4A.

27 Refill and bleed the cooling system as described in Section 2.

5.20a Release the clip . . .

5.20b . . . and disconnect the top hose from the thermostat housing cover

5.20c Unscrew the mounting bolts . . .

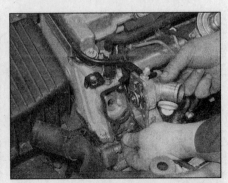

5.20d . . . then remove the thermostat and cover together with the gasket – 2.0 litre engine

6.1 The cooling module control unit is located on the left-hand side of the front valance

6.4a With the battery terminals disconnected, unscrew the mounting clamp bolt . . .

6.4b . . . remove the insulation . . .

6 Electric cooling fan –
testing, removal and refitting

⚠️ **Warning: If the engine is hot, the cooling fan may start up at any time. Take extra precautions when working in the vicinity of the fan.**

Testing

1 The cooling fan is supplied with current via a fuse, the ignition switch, and a relay (see Chapter 12). The circuit is activated by the cooling module control unit, using an engine coolant temperature sensor. The cooling module control unit is located on the left-hand side of the front valance, behind the front bumper **(see illustration)**. Some models are also equipped with an auxiliary cooling fan.

2 To test the electric fan, run the engine until normal operating temperature is reached, then allow it to idle. The fan should cut in within a few minutes, or at least before the temperature gauge indicates overheating. If it does not, check that battery voltage is available at the feed wire to the fan motor, and at the relay (refer to Chapter 12). No voltage indicates a blown fuse, a faulty ignition switch, or a faulty relay or wiring.

3 If the switch, wiring and relay are in good working order, the fault must be in the motor itself.

1.7 litre engine

Removal

4 Remove the battery and support bracket as described in Chapter 5A **(see illustrations)**.

5 Remove the front bumper as described in Chapter 11.

6 Loosen the clips and disconnect the air inlet duct from the intercooler and air inlet plenum intermediate pipe **(see illustration)**.

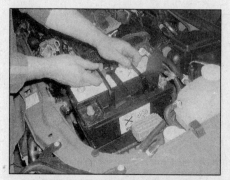

6.4c . . . and lift out the battery, . . .

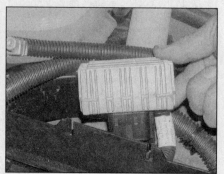

6.4d . . . then detach the module . . .

6.4e . . . unscrew the mounting bolts . . .

6.4f . . . release the wiring harness . . .

6.4g . . . and remove the battery support bracket

6.6 Disconnecting the air inlet duct from the air inlet plenum intermediate pipe

6.13a Unscrew the mounting bolt . . .

6.13b . . . and carefully lift the electric cooling fan upwards from the radiator

6.15a Unscrew the bolts . . .

6.15b . . . and remove the fan

7 Loosen the clip and disconnect the remaining air inlet duct from the intercooler. Tie the duct to one side.

8 Apply the handbrake, then jack up the front of the vehicle and support it on axle stands (see *Jacking and vehicle support*).

9 Remove the undertray from under the engine compartment.

10 On models with air conditioning, disconnect the wiring at the connector located near the horns on the right-hand side of the valance. Also disconnect the pressure sensor wiring at the same location.

11 Detach the multipin connector from the cooling control module on the left-hand side of the valance. Also remove the earth wire from the body.

12 Where applicable, detach the connector for the auxiliary fan located on the lower, front of the radiator.

13 Unscrew the mounting bolt and carefully lift the electric cooling fan upwards from the radiator. Withdraw the fan from the engine compartment (**see illustrations**).

14 On models with an auxiliary electric fan, remove the resonator from the crossmember, then disconnect the wiring and lower the auxiliary cooling fan assembly. Withdraw from under the vehicle.

15 With the assembly on the bench, unclip the protective grille (where fitted), then undo the screws and remove the fan (**see illustrations**).

16 Undo the screw and detach the

wiring plug and series resistor (**see illustrations**).

17 Unscrew the mounting bolts and remove the fan motor (**see illustration**).

Refitting

18 Refitting is a reversal of removal.

2.0 litre engine

Removal

19 Remove the radiator together with the electric fan assembly as described in Section 4.

20 Unclip and remove the fan shroud from the radiator.

21 Disconnect the fan motor wiring at the plug.

22 Unscrew the mounting bolts and remove the fan together with the fan motor.

23 Unbolt and remove the fan.

24 On models with an auxiliary electric fan, remove the front bumper as described in Chapter 11, then disconnect the wiring and unbolt the connector. Unscrew the mounting nuts and lower the assembly from the radiator, then unclip the grille and remove the resistor.

Refitting

25 Refitting is a reversal of removal. Refit the radiator and refill the cooling system with reference to Section 4.

7	Cooling system electrical switches and sensors – testing, removal and refitting

Coolant temperature sensor

Testing

1 Testing of the coolant temperature sensor circuit is best entrusted to a Vauxhall dealer, who will have the necessary specialist diagnostic equipment.

Removal – 1.7 litre engines

2 On the DOHC engine, the coolant temperature sensor is located on the thermostat housing on the left-hand end of

6.16a Remove the series resistor . . .

6.16b . . . and disconnect the wiring . . .

6.17 . . . then unbolt the motor

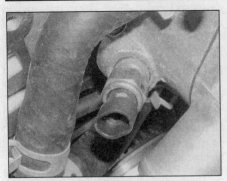

**7.2 Coolant temperature sensor –
1.7 litre DOHC engines**

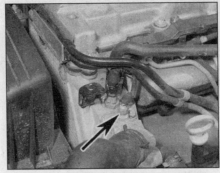

**7.7 Coolant temperature sensor –
2.0 litre engines**

the cylinder head **(see illustration)**. On the SOHC engine, the coolant temperature sensor is located on the thermostat housing on the right-hand front of the cylinder head (the housing is bolted to the right-hand end of the cylinder head).

3 Apply the handbrake then jack up the front of the vehicle and support it on axle stands (see *Jacking and vehicle support*). Remove the undertray from under the engine compartment, then position a suitable container beneath the sensor position to catch the spilled coolant.

4 With the engine cold, unscrew the cap from the coolant expansion tank then refit and tighten it. This will reduce the loss of coolant when the sensor is removed. Have a suitable plug available to insert in the sensor hole.

5 Remove the engine top cover.

6 Disconnect the wiring from the temperature sensor, then unscrew and remove it from the thermostat housing. Either insert the new sensor or fit the plug to prevent loss of coolant.

Removal – 2.0 litre engines

7 On all 2.0 litre engines, the coolant temperature sensor is located on top of the thermostat housing, at the right-hand end of the cylinder head **(see illustration)**.

8 Apply the handbrake then jack up the front of the vehicle and support it on axle stands (see *Jacking and vehicle support*). Remove the undertray from under the engine compartment, then position a suitable

container beneath the sensor position to catch the spilled coolant.

9 With the engine cold, unscrew the cap from the coolant expansion tank then refit and tighten it. This will reduce the loss of coolant when the sensor is removed. Have a suitable plug available to insert in the sensor hole.

10 Remove the engine top cover.

11 Disconnect the wiring from the temperature sensor, then unscrew and remove it from the thermostat housing and recover the sealing ring. Either insert the new sensor or fit the plug to prevent loss of coolant.

Refitting

12 Refitting is a reversal of removal, but renew the sealing ring or apply sealant to the threads of the sensor as applicable. Tighten the sensor to the specified torque and top-up the cooling system with reference to Section 2.

Coolant level warning sensor

Removal

13 The sensor is located in the bottom of the expansion tank. With the engine cold, unscrew the expansion tank filler cap to dissipate any remaining pressure.

14 Unclip or unbolt the tank from its mounting bracket, then pour the coolant into a suitable container.

15 Disconnect the wiring, then remove the switch from the tank.

Refitting

16 Refitting is a reversal of removal.

Coolant control module

Removal

17 Disconnect the battery negative (earth) lead and position it away from the terminal.

18 Remove the front bumper as described in Chapter 11.

19 The coolant control module is located on the left-hand side of the front valance. Pull out the locking sliders and unhook the two wiring plugs from the coolant control module **(see illustrations)**.

20 Unscrew the mounting bolts and remove the module from the front valance.

Refitting

21 Refitting is a reversal of removal.

| 8 | Water pump – removal and refitting |

1.7 litre DOHC engine

Removal

1 Apply the handbrake, then jack up the front of the vehicle and support it on axle stands (see *Jacking and vehicle support*). Remove the undertray from under the engine compartment.

2 Disconnect the battery negative (earth) lead (see Chapter 5A).

3 Remove the engine top cover, then drain the cooling system as described in Section 2.

4 Remove the air cleaner assembly together with the airflow meter and inlet air ducting with reference to Chapter 4A.

5 Remove the auxiliary drivebelt as described in Chapter 1.

> **HAYNES HINT** *Before removing the drivebelt, loosen the water pump pulley retaining bolts.*

6 Hold the pump pulley stationary (if necessary using an old auxiliary drivebelt or an oil filter strap wrench), then unscrew and remove the bolts and remove the pulley from the drive flange on the coolant pump **(see illustration)**.

7.19a The coolant control module is located on the left-hand side of the front valance

7.19b Disconnecting the wiring plugs from the coolant control module

8.6 Removing the water pump pulley – 1.7 litre DOHC engines

7 Unscrew and remove the water pump mounting bolts **(see illustration)**.

8 Withdraw the water pump from the cylinder block, noting that it may be necessary to tap the pump lightly with a soft-faced mallet to free it from the cylinder block.

9 Recover the gasket and discard it; a new one must be used on refitting **(see illustration)**.

10 Note that it is not possible to overhaul the pump. If it is faulty, the unit must be renewed complete.

Refitting

11 Ensure that the pump and cylinder block mating surfaces are clean and dry.

12 Refit the water pump to the cylinder block together with a new gasket.

13 Insert the mounting bolts and tighten progressively to the specified torque.

14 Refit the pulley and tighten the bolts to the specified torque while holding the pulley stationary using the method used on removal.

15 Refit and tension the auxiliary drivebelt as described in Chapter 1.

16 Refit the air cleaner, inlet air ducting and airflow meter with reference to Chapter 4A.

17 Reconnect the battery negative lead (see Chapter 5A).

18 Refill and bleed the cooling system with reference to Section 2, then refit the engine top cover.

19 Refit the undertray and lower the vehicle to the ground.

1.7 litre SOHC engine

Removal

20 Apply the handbrake, then jack up the front of the vehicle and support it on axle stands (see *Jacking and vehicle support*). Remove the undertray from under the engine compartment.

21 Disconnect the battery negative (earth) lead (see Chapter 5A).

22 Remove the engine top cover, then drain the cooling system as described in Section 2.

23 Remove the timing belt and tensioner/roller as described in Chapter 2A. This work includes supporting the engine

8.7 Water pump and mounting bolts – 1.7 litre DOHC engines

and removing the right-hand engine mounting and mounting block from the cylinder block.

24 Unscrew and remove the three water pump mounting bolts, then withdraw the pump from the cylinder block, noting that it may be necessary to tap it lightly with a soft-faced mallet to free it.

25 Recover the O-ring seal and discard it; a new one must be used on refitting.

26 Note that it is not possible to overhaul the pump. If it is faulty, the unit must be renewed complete.

Refitting

27 Ensure that the pump and cylinder block mating surfaces are clean and dry, then smear some white silicone grease on the surfaces of the pump which contact the cylinder block. Locate a new O-ring seal on the water pump.

28 Locate the water pump on the cylinder block then insert the mounting bolts and tighten them progressively to the specified torque.

29 Refit the tensioner/roller, timing belt and engine mounting/block with reference to Chapter 2A.

30 Reconnect the battery negative (earth) lead (see Chapter 5A).

31 Refill and bleed the cooling system with reference to Section 2, then refit the engine top cover.

32 Refit the undertray and lower the vehicle to the ground.

8.9 Water pump gasket – 1.7 litre DOHC engines

2.0 litre engines

Removal

33 Apply the handbrake, then jack up the front of the vehicle and support it on axle stands (see *Jacking and vehicle support*). Remove the undertray from under the engine compartment.

34 Disconnect the battery negative (earth) lead (see Chapter 5A).

35 Remove the engine top cover, then drain the cooling system as described in Section 2.

36 Remove the air cleaner assembly together with the airflow meter and inlet air ducting with reference to Chapter 4A.

37 Remove the auxiliary drivebelt as described in Chapter 1.

 HAYNES HiNT *Before removing the drivebelt, loosen the water pump pulley retaining bolts.*

38 The engine must now be lifted from the right-hand mounting and moved as far as possible to the left to provide room to remove the water pump. Support the weight of the engine using either a trolley jack and block of wood beneath the engine, or alternatively connect a hoist to the right-hand side of the engine. Whichever method is used, make sure the equipment is adequate for the job and can be used safely. Remove the engine mounting from the engine and body with reference to Chapter 2C.

39 Hold the pump pulley stationary (if necessary using an old auxiliary drivebelt or an oil filter strap wrench), then unscrew and remove the bolts and remove the pulley from the drive flange on the coolant pump.

40 Unscrew and remove the three water pump mounting bolts **(see illustration)**.

41 Withdraw the water pump from the timing chain cover, noting that it may be necessary to tap the pump lightly with a soft-faced mallet to free it **(see illustration)**.

42 Recover the pump sealing ring, and

8.40 Unscrew the mounting bolts . . .

8.41 . . . withdraw the water pump from the timing chain cover . . .

8.42 . . . and recover the sealing ring – 2.0 litre engines

discard it; a new one must be used on refitting **(see illustration)**.

43 Note that it is not possible to overhaul the pump. If it is faulty, the unit must be renewed complete.

Refitting

44 Ensure that the pump and timing cover mating surfaces are clean and dry, and apply a smear of silicone grease to the pump mating surfaces.

45 Fit a new sealing ring to the pump, and install the pump in the timing chain cover.

46 Insert the mounting bolts and tighten to the specified torque.

47 Refit the pulley and tighten the securing bolts to the specified torque.

48 Refit the engine mounting with reference to Chapter 2C and remove the trolley jack or hoist.

49 Refit the auxiliary drivebelt with reference to Chapter 1.

50 Refit the air cleaner assembly together with the airflow meter and inlet air ducting with reference to Chapter 4A.

51 Reconnect the battery negative (earth) lead (see Chapter 5A).

52 Refill and bleed the cooling system with reference to Section 2, then refit the engine top cover.

53 Refit the undertray and lower the vehicle to the ground.

9 Heating and ventilation system – general information

The heater/ventilation system consists of a four-speed blower motor (housed behind the facia), face-level vents in the centre and at each end of the facia, and air ducts to the front and rear footwells. Zafira models additionally have central vents at the rear of the centre console.

The heater controls are located in the centre of the facia, and the controls operate flap valves to deflect and mix the air flowing through the various parts of the heater/ventilation system. The flap valves are contained in the air distribution housing, which acts as a central distribution unit, passing air to the various ducts and vents.

Cold air enters the system through the grille at the rear of the engine compartment.

The air (boosted by the blower fan when required) then flows through the various ducts, according to the settings of the controls. Stale air is expelled through ducts at the rear corners of the vehicle. If warm air is required, the cold air is passed through the heater matrix, which is heated by the engine coolant.

A recirculation switch enables the outside air supply to be closed off, while the air inside the vehicle is recirculated. This can be useful to prevent unpleasant odours entering from outside the vehicle, but should only be used briefly, as the recirculated air inside the vehicle will soon deteriorate.

10 Heater/ventilation system components – removal and refitting

Air vents (Astra models)

Removal

1 To remove an air vent grille from the centre of the facia, insert a small screwdriver on each side and carefully lever it out. Removal of the air vent housing involves first removing the facia surround panel as described in Chapter 11, then removing the hazard warning switch and carefully prising out the vent housing.

2 To remove the vent from the driver's side of the facia, it will be necessary to remove the lighting switch assembly first (see Chapter 12, Section 4), then turn the vent down past its stop position and undo the two upper and single lower retaining screws, using a screwdriver through the grille. The screws will drop inside the housing, but take care not to allow them to enter the rear vent tubing. Disconnect the wiring and remove the vent.

3 To remove the vent from the passenger's side of the facia, first open the glovebox, then turn the vent past its stop position and undo the two upper and single lower retaining screws, using a screwdriver through the grille. Withdraw the vent assembly from the facia.

Refitting

4 Refitting of the centre air vent grille is a reversal of removal. To refit the side vents, first use a screwdriver to lever out the side clip, then turn the grille down so that the upper mounting holes are visible – this will enable the upper screws to be inserted without dropping them into the vent housing.

Air vents (Zafira models)

5 To remove the passenger's side vent, first remove the glovebox as described in Chapter 11. Pull out the upper grille from the air vent. Undo the upper and lower screws and remove the vent.

6 To remove the air vent from the rear of the centre console, first remove the cover beneath the handbrake lever, then release the lever gaiter. Insert the hand through the aperture in the console and push out the vent.

7 The centre vent is part of the surround.

Blower motor resistor

Removal

8 Remove the glovebox with reference to Chapter 11.

9 Remove the lower trim panel from under the passenger side of the facia panel, then where applicable disconnect the fastener and withdraw the heater air duct.

10 Unclip the cover and remove the pollen filter. Note that there are two types of cover, one requiring sealant to seal it to the housing. Alternatively, remove the blower motor as described later in this Section.

11 Carefully push the resistor upwards, disconnect the wiring, and withdraw it from the housing **(see illustrations)**.

Refitting

12 Refitting is a reversal of removal, but apply sealant to the pollen filter cover where applicable.

Delphi heater blower motor

Removal

13 Remove the glovebox with reference to Chapter 11.

14 Remove the lower trim panel from under the passenger side of the facia panel, then

10.11a Push the resistor upwards . . .

10.11b . . . and withdraw it from the housing

10.14 Disconnecting the heater air duct

10.15a Disconnect the recirculating flap
servo motor linkage . . .

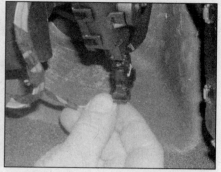

10.15b . . . and disconnect the servo wiring

disconnect the fastener and withdraw the heater air duct from the side of the heater housing (see illustration).
15 Temporarily switch on the ignition then set the heater controls to the 'air recirculating' position. Switch off the ignition, then disconnect the recirculating flap servo motor linkage and the servo wiring. Undo the screws and remove the servo motor (see illustrations).
16 Disconnect the blower motor wiring, then unscrew the three bolts and release the clips. Withdraw the motor from its housing (see illustrations).

Refitting

17 Refitting is a reversal of removal.

Behr heater blower motor

Removal

18 Temporarily switch on the ignition then set the heater controls to the 'air recirculating' position.
19 Switch off the ignition, then disconnect the recirculating flap servo motor linkage and the servo wiring. Undo the screws and remove the servo motor. **Note:** *New servo motors are supplied set to the 'recirculating' position.*
20 Undo the five bolts and release the single clip, and withdraw the motor from its housing. Note that sealant is used in the housing groove – thoroughly clean out the groove.

Refitting

21 Refitting is a reversal of removal, but apply new sealant to the housing groove. Make sure that the servo motor master gear aligns with the master gear on the flap.

Delphi heater control panel (Astra models)

Removal

22 Remove the ashtray, then unclip and remove the storage compartment.
23 Remove the radio/cassette and the mounting box as described in Chapter 12. Also, where applicable, remove the navigation system unit.
24 Carefully prise the surround from the facia.
25 Unclip the controls and press out the vents from the surround. Remove the multi-info display unit with reference to Chapter 12.
26 Set the temperature control knob vertical, then disconnect the control cable after noting its fitted position.
27 Disconnect the wiring from the controls.
28 Disconnect the remaining control cables after noting their fitted position, then remove the control panel from the surround.

Refitting

29 Refitting is a reversal of removal, however, first make sure that the bulbs are correctly fitted. Note that the mixed air cable is correctly adjusted if the control knob does not spring back from either the maximum cold or hot positions.

10.15c Servo motor removed –
Astra models

Behr heater control panel (Astra models)

Removal

30 Remove the glovebox as described in Chapter 11.
31 Remove the trim panel from under each side of the facia.
32 On LHD models, remove the air duct from the passenger's side. Also remove the instrument panel as described in Chapter 12.
33 Disconnect the control cables from the upper and lower air distribution flaps.
34 Release the cables from the support clips.
35 Remove the ashtray, then unclip and remove the storage compartment.
36 Remove the radio/cassette and the mounting box as described in Chapter 12.

10.16a Disconnect the wiring . . .

10.16b . . . then undo the bolts . . .

10.16c . . . and withdraw the motor from its housing

10.44a Undo the lower screws . . .

10.44b . . . and unhook the upper part of the heater control panel

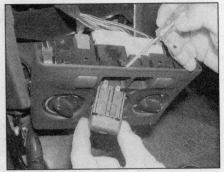

10.45a Remove the switches . . .

Also, where applicable, remove the navigation system unit.

37 Carefully prise the surround from the facia.

38 Disconnect the wiring from the control panel.

39 Note the location of the control cables, then disconnect them from the control panel.

Refitting

40 Refitting is a reversal of removal, however, first make sure that the bulbs are correctly fitted.

Heater control panel (Zafira models)

Removal

41 Remove the glovebox as described in Chapter 11.

10.45b . . . then disconnect the wiring

42 Remove the trim panel from under each side of the facia.

43 Remove the front ashtray.

44 Undo the lower screws and unhook the upper part of the control panel. Withdraw the panel from the facia (see illustrations).

45 Using a screwdriver, carefully prise out the hazard warning switch, traction control switch (where fitted), and seat heating switch (where fitted). Disconnect the wiring from the control panel (see illustrations).

46 Unclip the heating and air conditioning controls from the rear of the control panel, and withdraw the panel (see illustration).

47 Note the location of the control cables, then disconnect them (see illustration).

Refitting

48 Refitting is a reversal of removal.

Heater main housing

Note: *On models with air conditioning it is necessary to drain the refrigerant. This work **must** be carried out by qualified personnel.*

Removal

49 On models with air conditioning, have the refrigerant drained from the system by a qualified air conditioning engineer.

50 Remove the centre console and facia panel as described in Chapter 11.

51 Remove the rear footwell air duct from the heater main housing, then place cloth rags on the floor to absorb any spilt coolant from the heater matrix.

52 Remove the passenger airbag as described in Chapter 12.

53 With both front doors open, unscrew the Torx bolts and remove the steering crossmember from the bulkhead.

54 On models with air conditioning, remove the condensation drain from the floor. To do this, apply the handbrake then jack up the front of the vehicle and support it on axle stands (see *Jacking and vehicle support*). Where necessary, remove the undertray from the bottom of the engine compartment. Remove the rear engine mounting (see the relevant part of Chapter 2), then unscrew the two bolts and remove the condensation drain. **Note:** *Access is possible without having to remove the rear engine mounting, however the work is much easier with the mounting removed.*

55 Drain the cooling system as described in Section 2.

56 Remove the plastic insert from the windscreen scuttle, then unbolt and remove the lower cover panel.

57 Working in the engine compartment, disconnect the hoses from the heater matrix stubs. Identify each hose for position to ensure correct refitting. **Note:** *The original hoses have quick-release fittings.*

58 On models with air conditioning, remove the coolant line lock bolt connection on the expansion valve.

59 Unbolt the air distribution housings from the top of the bulkhead.

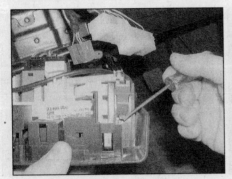

10.46a Release the clips . . .

10.46b . . . and withdraw the controls from the control panel

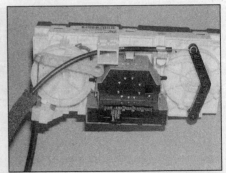

10.47 Cable connections on the rear of the heater control panel – Zafira models

10.61 Control cable on the side of the heater housing

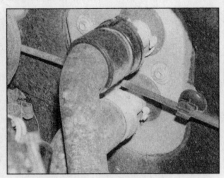

10.65 Hose connections to the heater matrix stubs in the engine compartment

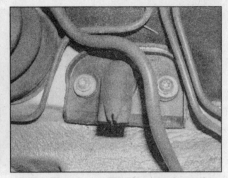

10.67a The air conditioning condensation drain is located at the rear of the engine compartment

60 On models with air conditioning, disconnect the wiring from the coolant cut-off valve.

61 Inside the vehicle, disconnect the wiring for the recirculation flap servo motor and the blower motor. Also disconnect the control cables from the heater housing **(see illustration)**.

62 With the help of an assistant, withdraw the heater main housing from the bulkhead and remove it from inside the vehicle.

Refitting

63 Refitting is a reversal of removal, but refill the cooling system as described in Section 2. On models with air conditioning, have the system charged by the air conditioning engineer. When refitting the steering crossmember, make sure that the upper guides are located first before tightening the bolts.

Heater matrix

Removal

64 Drain the cooling system as described in Section 2.

65 Working in the engine compartment, disconnect the hoses from the heater matrix stubs **(see illustration)**. Identify each hose for position to ensure correct refitting. **Note:** *The original hoses have quick-release fittings.*

66 At this stage, if an airline is available, it is

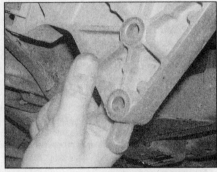

10.67b Removing the rear engine mounting

possible to blow the remaining coolant from the matrix to prevent it spilling onto the interior carpet when the matrix is removed. Connect a drain tube to one of the matrix stubs with its free end in a suitable container, then blow through the other stub. If an airline is not available, plug the ends of the stubs.

67 On models with air conditioning, remove the condensation drain from the floor. To do this, apply the handbrake then jack up the front of the vehicle and support it on axle stands (see *Jacking and vehicle support*). Where necessary, remove the undertray from the bottom of the engine compartment.

68 Remove the rear engine mounting (see the relevant part of Chapter 2), then unscrew the

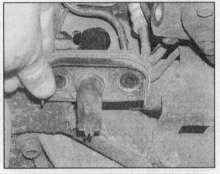

10.67c Removing the air conditioning condensation drain

two bolts and remove the condensation drain **(see illustrations). Note:** *Access is possible without having to remove the rear engine mounting, although the work is much easier with the mounting removed.*

68 Remove the centre console as described in Chapter 11, then pull the rear footwell air distribution housing forwards and remove **(see illustration)**. On Zafira models, unbolt the stays before removing the rear footwell air housing.

70 Release the 9 clips securing the cover to the heater main housing, and lower the cover **(see illustrations)**. Note on certain models, there are also two retaining bolts.

71 On models with air conditioning,

10.67d Air conditioning condensation drain removed

10.69 Removing the rear footwell air distribution housing

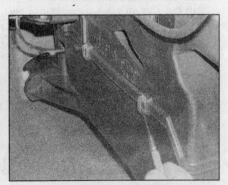

10.70a Release the clips . . .

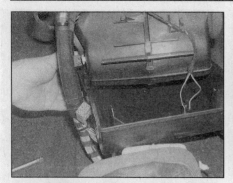

10.70b . . . and lower the cover

disconnect the wiring from the coolant cut-off valve **(see illustration)**.
72 Pull out the clips and disconnect the coolant pipes (non-air conditioned models) or cut-off valves (air conditioned models) from the matrix. Withdraw the matrix from the housing **(see illustrations)**.
73 Recover the O-rings and discard them – new ones must be used on refitting. Check the quick-release fittings and if necessary renew the O-ring seals.

Refitting

74 Refitting is a reversal of removal, but apply a little silicone grease to the new O-rings before fitting them. On Zafira models, support the connection pipes against the bulkhead with a suitable tool (eg, hammer handle), in order to ensure the matrix stubs engage correctly. On completion refill the cooling system as described in Section 2. Make sure that the quick-release hose fittings are correctly engaged by checking that the green lock ring is released.

10.72a Cut-off valve connection to the heater matrix – air conditioned models

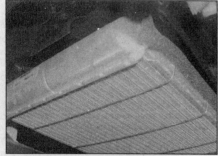

10.72b Removing the heater matrix

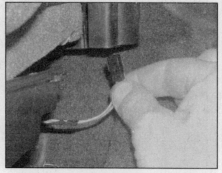

10.71 On models with air conditioning, disconnect the wiring from the coolant cut-off valve

Heater switch

Removal

75 Remove the heater control panel as described earlier in this Section.
76 Position the temperature control knob vertical to the warm-air setting. Position the air distributor control knob to the head-space setting.
77 Carefully pull off the heater blower speed control knob.
78 Using a screwdriver, release the clips on the rear of the control panel, then remove the switch.

Refitting

79 Refitting is a reversal of removal.

11 Air conditioning system – general information and precautions

General information

Air conditioning is fitted as standard on certain models, and optional on other models **(see illustrations)**. It enables the temperature of incoming air to be lowered, and also dehumidifies the air, which makes for rapid demisting and increased comfort.

The cooling side of the system works in the same way as a domestic refrigerator. Refrigerant gas is drawn into a belt-driven compressor, and passes into a condenser mounted in front of the radiator, where it loses heat and becomes liquid. The liquid passes through an expansion valve to an evaporator, where it changes from liquid under high pressure to gas under low pressure. This change is accompanied by a drop in temperature, which cools the evaporator. The refrigerant returns to the compressor, and the cycle begins again.

Air blown through the evaporator passes to the heater assembly, where it is mixed with hot air blown through the heater matrix, to achieve the desired temperature in the passenger compartment.

The heating side of the system works in the same way as on models without air conditioning (see Section 9).

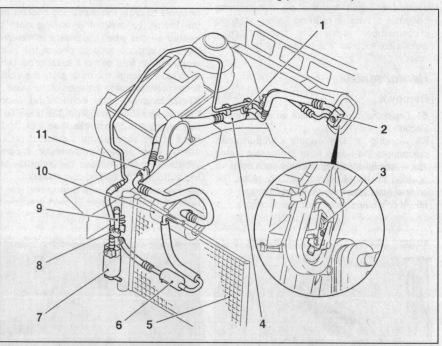

11.1a Air conditioning components – Zafira models

Note: The evaporator is located in the heater housing	2 Lock bolt connection 3 Expansion valve 4 Pulsation damper 5 Condenser	8 Pressure sensor 9 High pressure service connection
1 Low-pressure service connection	6 Pulsation damper 7 Receiver-dryer	10 Compressor 11 Refrigerant line bolted connection

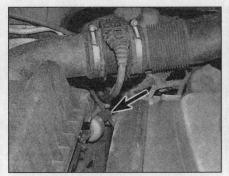

11.1b Low-pressure service connection

11.1c High-pressure service connection

Many car accessory shops sell one-shot air conditioning recharge aerosols. These generally contain refrigerant, compressor oil, leak sealer and system conditioner. Some also have a dye to help pinpoint leaks.

⚠️ *Warning: These products must only be used as directed by the manufacturer, and do not remove the need for regular maintenance.*

The operation of the system is controlled electronically. Any problems with the system should be referred to a Vauxhall dealer or an air conditioning specialist (see Tool Tip).

Precautions

It is necessary to observe special precautions whenever dealing with any part of the system, its associated components, and any items which necessitate disconnection of the system.

⚠️ *Warning: The refrigeration circuit contains a liquid refrigerant (R134a). This refrigerant is potentially dangerous, and should only be handled by qualified persons. If it is splashed onto the skin, it can cause frostbite. It is not itself poisonous, but in the presence of a naked flame it forms a poisonous gas; inhalation of the vapour through a lighted cigarette could prove fatal. Gaseous refrigerant is heavier than air and can therefore become concentrated in certain working conditions (for instance in a pit). Uncontrolled discharging of the refrigerant is dangerous, and potentially damaging to the environment. It is therefore dangerous to disconnect any part of the system without specialised knowledge and equipment. If for any reason the system must be disconnected, entrust this task to an authorised dealer or an air conditioning specialist. The system should be sealed by the specialist until just before recharging. It is recommended that the receiver-dryer is renewed whenever the refrigerant lines are depressurised, and it should be kept sealed until just before fitting it – it should be the*

last item fitted before recharging the system. All O-rings should be renewed, and they must be coated with genuine Vauxhall lubricant (part number 90001810/1949870) before fitting. Any spilt compressor lubricant must be replaced with genuine Vauxhall lubricant (part number 90509933/1949873). Caution: Do not operate the air conditioning system if it is known to be short of refrigerant, as this may damage the compressor.

12 Air conditioning system components – removal and refitting

⚠️ *Warning: Read the precautions given in Section 11, and have the system discharged by a Vauxhall dealer or an air conditioning specialist. Do not carry out the following work unless the system has been discharged.*

Compressor

Removal

1 Have the air conditioning system discharged by a qualified engineer.
2 Apply the handbrake, then jack up the front of the vehicle and support it on axle stands (see *Jacking and vehicle support*). Remove the undertray from the bottom of the engine compartment.
3 Remove the auxiliary drivebelt as described in Chapter 1.
4 Unscrew the bolt and detach the combined line adapter from the compressor. Recover

the seal. Tape over the apertures in the compressor and adapter to prevent entry of dust and dirt.
5 Disconnect the wiring plug.
6 Unscrew the mounting bolts and remove the compressor downwards from the mounting bracket (see illustrations). Withdraw it from under the engine compartment.

Refitting

7 Refitting is a reversal of removal but tighten the bolts to the specified torque and tension the auxiliary drivebelt with reference to Chapter 1. On completion, have the refrigerant engineer charge the system and fit new O-rings to the line connections. If a new compressor is being fitted, make sure that the oil level is topped-up before fitting it. Note that a new compressor must be run-in as follows:
a) Open all vents on the facia, then run the engine at idle speed for 5 seconds.
b) Switch the blower to its maximum speed.
c) Switch on the air conditioning system for at least 2 minutes with the engine speed less than 1500 rpm.

Evaporator (Astra models)

Removal

8 Have the air conditioning system discharged by a qualified refrigerant engineer.
9 At the rear of the engine compartment, unbolt the refrigerant line lock-bolt connection for the thermostatically-controlled expansion valve, then insert a bolt and remove the expansion valve. Also remove the seal. Plug or seal the open apertures. **Note:** *Two guide rods must be inserted when refitting the valve, and Vauxhall technicians use a special tool (KM-6012) to press the connection onto the valve without damaging the pipes.*
10 Remove the glovebox and facia lower trim panels as described in Chapter 11.

12.6a Air conditioning compressor

12.6b Air conditioning compressor rear mounting

12.12 Removing the pollen filter

12.13 On some models it is necessary to cut the evaporator cover free

12.17 Air conditioning evaporator refrigerant line lock-bolt located at the rear of the engine compartment

11 Remove the heater blower motor as described in Section 10.
12 Remove the pollen filter (see Chapter 1), then disconnect the wiring for the defroster sensor **(see illustration)**.
13 Undo the screws and remove the cover for the evaporator. Note if the cover has any sealant; if necessary obtain new sealant. **Note:** *On some models, it may be necessary to cut free the cover using a knife on the inner groove **(see illustration)**.*
14 Note its fitted location, then remove the defroster sensor. Carefully pull the evaporator from the heater housing.

Refitting

15 Refitting is a reversal of removal, but have the refrigerant engineer charge the system and fit new O-rings to the line connections. To ensure the pipes are not damaged, have the engineer refit the expansion valve as well. Where the evaporator cover was cut free, it will be necessary to obtain a sealing kit from a Vauxhall dealer.

Evaporator (Zafira models)

Note: *Some models also have a rear evaporator located behind the rear quarter trim panel.*

Removal

16 Have the air conditioning system discharged by a qualified refrigerant engineer.
17 At the rear of the engine compartment, unbolt the refrigerant line lock-bolt connection for the thermostatically-controlled expansion valve **(see illustration)**, then insert a bolt and

remove the expansion valve. Also remove the clamp and seal, noting that the outer seal must be renewed on refitting. Plug or seal the open apertures. **Note:** *Two guide rods must be inserted when refitting the valve.*
18 Remove the pollen filter (see Chapter 1), then disconnect the wiring for the defroster sensor.
19 Unbolt the cover for the pollen filter and evaporator, and remove the filter **(see illustrations)**.
20 Note its fitted location, then remove the defroster sensor. Carefully pull the evaporator from the heater housing.

Refitting

21 Refitting is a reversal of removal, but have the refrigerant engineer charge the system and fit new O-rings to the line connections.

Condenser

Removal

22 Have the air conditioning system discharged by a qualified refrigerant engineer.
23 With the bonnet open, reach down behind the front bumper and disconnect the wiring plug for the auxiliary cooling fan. Unscrew the upper mounting bolts and remove the auxiliary cooling fan.
24 Unscrew the bolts and disconnect the refrigerant lines from the condenser and receiver-dryer. Also disconnect the wiring from the system pressure sensor.
25 Unscrew the mounting bolts for the receiver-dryer.
26 Unscrew the upper mounting bolts securing the condenser to the radiator, then

lift it from the lower mounting clips and withdraw it together with the receiver-dryer.
27 If necessary, detach the receiver-dryer from the condenser.

Refitting

28 Refitting is a reversal of removal. On completion, have the refrigerant engineer charge the system and fit new O-rings to the line connections.

Receiver-dryer

Removal

29 Have the air conditioning system discharged by a qualified refrigerant engineer.
30 On models with an auxiliary electric fan, remove the fan assembly from the front of the condenser as described later in this Section.
31 On models without an auxiliary electric fan, remove the front bumper as described in Chapter 11.
32 Unscrew the bolt and disconnect the compressor refrigerant line from the receiver-dryer.
33 Unscrew the receiver-dryer cap from the condenser.
34 Withdraw the receiver-dryer upwards, then disconnect the wiring plug and remove the air conditioning pressure sensor pick-up.
35 Remove the receiver-dryer.

Refitting

36 Refitting is a reversal of removal. On completion, have the refrigerant engineer charge the system and fit new O-rings to the line connections.

Auxiliary fan and motor

Removal

37 Remove the front bumper as described in Chapter 11.
38 Disconnect the wiring plug for the auxiliary cooling fan.
39 Unscrew the upper mounting bolts from the crossmember and remove the auxiliary cooling fan assembly downwards.
40 To remove the motor, unclip the plastic grille, then unbolt the wiring plug connector and series resistor. Unscrew the three bolts and remove the fan from the motor, then unbolt the motor from the housing.

Refitting

41 Refitting is a reversal of removal.

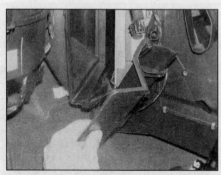

12.19a Removing the cover for the pollen filter and evaporator

12.19b Removing the pollen filter from the heater housing

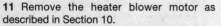

Chapter 4 Part A:
Fuel and exhaust systems

Contents

Degrees of difficulty

Easy, suitable for novice with little experience		Fairly easy, suitable for beginner with some experience		Fairly difficult, suitable for competent DIY mechanic	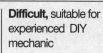	Difficult, suitable for experienced DIY mechanic		Very difficult, suitable for expert DIY or professional	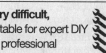

Specifications

General

System type:

1.7 litre SOHC models . . . .
EDC MSA 15M indirect injection system incorporating an electronically controlled VP29 distributor fuel injection pump. Low pressure turbocharger and intercooler fitted to all models

1.7 litre DOHC models . . . .
ECD V5 direct injection system incorporating an electronically-controlled Nippon Denso V5 distributor fuel injection pump with integral transfer pump. Two stage injectors with pilot and post injection. Turbocharger and intercooler fitted to all models

2.0 litre models . . . .
EDC 15M direct injection system incorporating an electronically-controlled VP 44 fuel injection pump. Turbocharger fitted to all models and intercooler fitted to high-pressure turbo models

Adjustment data

Idle speed:

1.7 litre SOHC models . . . .   780 to 900 rpm – controlled by ECU
1.7 litre DOHC models . . . .   825 to 875 rpm – controlled by ECU
2.0 litre models . . . .   750 to 850 rpm – controlled by ECU

Maximum speed:

1.7 litre SOHC models . . . .   5400 to 5500 rpm – controlled by ECU
1.7 litre DOHC models . . . .   5100 to 5300 rpm – controlled by ECU
2.0 litre models . . . .   4900 to 5100 rpm – controlled by ECU

Injection pump

Direction of rotation . . . .   Clockwise, viewed from sprocket end

Pump timing (static):

1.7 litre SOHC models . . . .   Preset – controlled by ECU
1.7 litre DOHC models . . . .   0.28 to 0.33 mm pump piston travel @ TDC
2.0 litre models . . . .   Preset – controlled by ECU

Injectors

Opening pressure:

1.7 litre SOHC models . . . .   130 to 143 bar
1.7 litre DOHC models . . . .   175 bar (1st stage) to 335 bar (2nd stage)
2.0 litre models:
   Low-pressure turbo models . . . .   180 to 365 bar
   High-pressure turbo models . . . .   220 to 380 bar

Torque wrench settings	Nm	lbf ft
1.7 litre SOHC models		
Accelerator pedal to bulkhead	6	4
Charge pressure sensor	8	6
Coolant temperature sensor	20	15
Crankshaft sensor	8	6
Exhaust manifold nuts*	22	16
Exhaust manifold support bolts	25	18
Exhaust pipe-to-manifold bolts	20	15
Fuel injector	70	52
Fuel pipe union nuts	25	18
Injection pump:		
Pump to support bracket (timing cover side)	25	18
Pump to bracket	25	18
Pump pulley to pump	25	18
Inlet manifold nuts*	22	16
Inlet manifold bolts	22	16
Intercooler to radiator	5	4
Turbocharger to exhaust manifold	30	22
Turbocharger heat shield bolts	8	6
Turbocharger oil supply pipe to cylinder block	20	15
Turbocharger oil supply pipe to turbo	30	22
Turbocharger oil return pipe to sump	45	33
Turbocharger oil return pipe to turbo	8	6
1.7 litre DOHC models		
Accelerator pedal to bulkhead	12	9
Atmospheric pressure sensor	10	7
Charge air pipe bracket to camshaft housing	24	18
Charge pressure regulator solenoid	5	4
Charge pressure sensor	10	7
Coolant temperature sensor	22	16
Crankshaft sensor	10	7
Engine control unit	6	4
Engine control unit bracket to camshaft housing	10	7
Exhaust gas recirculation pipe bracket to camshaft housing	8	6
Exhaust gas recirculation pipe to exhaust manifold	28	21
Exhaust front pipe-to-turbocharger nuts	65	48
Exhaust manifold:		
Retaining nuts and bolts*	24	18
Support bracket bolts	51	38
Fuel injector return pipe unions	15	11
Fuel injectors	22	16
Fuel pipe union nuts	25	18
Heat shield	12	9
Inlet manifold nuts and bolts*	24	18
Injection pump:		
Pump to pump bracket	18	13
Pump to cylinder block	20	15
Pump bracket to cylinder block	54	40
Timing belt sprocket nut	69	51
Injection pump control unit	10	7
Injection pump control unit bracket to cylinder block	48	35
Oil pressure switch	20	15
Turbocharger:		
Exhaust flange nuts	27	20
Oil feed pipe unions	10	7
Turbocharger-to-manifold nuts	27	20
2.0 litre models		
Accelerator pedal to bulkhead	12	9
Auxiliary drivebelt tensioner assembly bolts:		
Pulley backplate pivot bolt	42	31
Strut mounting bolts	23	17
Charge pressure sensor bolt	8	6
Camshaft sprocket bolt*:		
Stage 1	90	66
Stage 2	Angle-tighten a further 60°	
Stage 3	Angle-tighten a further 30°	

Coolant temperature sensor	18	13
Crankshaft sensor bolt	8	6
Exhaust front pipe:		
Pipe-to-intermediate pipe bolts	12	9
Pipe-to-turbocharger nuts	20	15
Exhaust manifold:		
Retaining nuts*	22	16
Support bracket bolts	25	18
Fuel pipe union nuts	25	18
Injection pump:		
Front mounting bolts	25	18
Fuel pipe union bolts	15	11
Rear mounting bracket bolts	20	15
Sprocket cover bolts	6	4
Sprocket retaining bolts	20	15
Inlet manifold:		
Lower section-to-cylinder head nuts*	22	16
Upper section-to-lower section bolts	8	6
Timing chain:		
Tensioner cap (upper and lower)	60	44
Upper chain guide bolts	8	6
Turbocharger:		
Exhaust flange bolts	30	22
Oil feed pipe:		
Pipe-to-cylinder block union nut	20	15
Pipe-to-turbo charger union bolt	20	15
Oil return pipe:		
Pipe-to-cylinder block union nut	25	18
Pipe-to-turbocharger bolts	8	6
Turbocharger-to-manifold bolts	30	22

*Do not re-use

1 General information and precautions

General information

1.7 litre SOHC models

1 The fuel system consists of a rear-mounted fuel tank, a fuel filter with integral water separator and fuel heater, a fuel injection pump, injectors and associated components.

2 Fuel is drawn from the fuel tank by the fuel injection pump. Before reaching the pump, the fuel passes through a fuel filter, where foreign matter and water are removed. Excess fuel lubricates the moving components of the pump, and is then returned to the tank.

3 The fuel injection pump is driven at half-crankshaft speed by the timing belt. The high pressure required to inject the fuel into the compressed air in the swirl chamber is achieved by a radial piston pump.

4 The injection pump is electronically-controlled to meet the latest emission standards. The system consists of the engine electronic control unit, injection pump electronic control unit (integral with the injection pump) and the following sensors:

a) *Accelerator pedal position sensor – informs the ECUs of the accelerator pedal position.*

b) *Coolant temperature sensor – informs the ECUs of the engine temperature.*

c) *Hot film mass airflow meter – informs the ECUs of the mass and temperature of the air passing through the intake duct.*

d) *Crankshaft sensor – informs the ECUs of the engine speed and crankshaft position.*

e) *Charge pressure sensor – informs the ECUs of the pressure in the inlet manifold.*

f) *Injection pump sensors and regulators (integral with the injection pump) – used be the ECUs to determine and control injection timing and quantity.*

g) *Clutch switch – used by the ECUs for cruise control functions.*

h) *Air conditioning system compressor switch – informs the ECUs when the air conditioning system is switched on.*

5 All the above information is analysed by the ECUs and, based on this, the ECUs determine the appropriate injection requirements for the engine. The engine ECU controls the injection pump timing, via the pump control unit, to provide the best setting for cranking, starting (with either a hot or cold engine), warm-up, idle, cruising, and acceleration.

6 Basic injection timing is determined when the pump is fitted. When the engine is running, it is varied automatically to suit the prevailing engine speed by a mechanism which turns the cam plate or ring – controlled by the ECU.

7 The engine ECU also controls the exhaust gas recirculation (EGR) system (see Chapter 4B) and the pre-heating system (see Chapter 5B).

8 The four fuel injectors produce a spray of fuel indirectly into the cylinders via the swirl chambers. The injectors are calibrated to open and close at critical pressures to provide efficient and even combustion. Each injector needle is lubricated by fuel, which accumulates in the spring chamber and is channelled to the injection pump return hose by leak-off pipes.

9 A low-pressure turbocharger is fitted to increase engine efficiency by raising the pressure in the inlet manifold above atmospheric pressure. Instead of the air simply being sucked into the cylinders, it is forced in. Additional fuel is supplied by the injection pump in proportion to the increased air intake. Mounted between the exhaust manifold and front exhaust pipe, and driven by exhaust gases, the turbocharger takes its air supply from the filter housing and passes air under pressure to the inlet manifold via an intercooler (air cooler) which is mounted on the left-hand side of the radiator.

10 A dedicated oil supply pipe that runs from the cylinder block provides lubrication for the turbocharger. Oil is returned to the sump. The turbocharger has an integral wastegate valve and vacuum actuator diaphragm, which is used to control the charge pressure applied to the inlet manifold. The internal components of a turbocharger rotate at very high speed and are very sensitive to contamination. A great deal of damage can be caused by small particles of dirt, particularly if they strike the delicate turbine blades. To prevent the ingress of dirt during maintenance, thoroughly clean the area around all connections before disturbing them. Always stored dismantled components in a sealed container to prevent contamination. Cover the turbocharger air inlet ducts to prevent the ingress of debris and only use lint-free cloths when cleaning.

11 Never run the engine with the turbocharger air inlet hose disconnected. Depression at the inlet can build up very suddenly if the engine speed is raised, thereby increasing the risk of foreign objects being sucked in and ejected at high speed.

12 If there is an abnormality in any of the readings obtained from any sensor, the ECU enters its back-up mode. In this event, the ECU ignores the abnormal sensor signal, and assumes a pre-programmed value, which will allow the engine to continue running (albeit at reduced efficiency). If the ECU enters this back-up mode, the warning light on the instrument panel will come on, and the relevant fault code will be stored in the ECU memory.

13 If the warning light comes on, the vehicle should be taken to a Vauxhall dealer at the earliest opportunity. A complete test of the injection system can then be carried out, using a special electronic diagnostic test unit, which is simply plugged into the system's diagnostic connector. The connector is located behind the centre console; unclip the trim panel situated just in front of the handbrake lever to gain access **(see illustration)**.

1.7 litre DOHC and 2.0 litre models

14 The fuel system consists of a rear-mounted fuel tank, a fuel filter with integral water separator and fuel heater, a fuel injection pump, injectors and associated components.

15 Fuel is drawn from the fuel tank by the fuel injection pump. Before reaching the pump, the fuel passes through a fuel filter, where foreign matter and water are removed. Excess fuel lubricates the moving components of the pump, and is then returned to the tank.

16 On 1.7 litre engines the fuel injection pump is driven at half-crankshaft speed by the timing belt. On 2.0 litre engines, the fuel injection pump is driven at half-crankshaft speed by the timing chain. The high pressure required to inject the fuel into the compressed air in the cylinder is achieved by a radial piston pump.

1.13 Unclip the trim panel in front of the handbrake lever to gain access to the diagnostic plug

17 The injection pump is electronically-controlled to meet the latest emission standards. The system consists of the engine electronic control unit, the injection electronic control unit, and the following sensors:

a) *Accelerator pedal position sensor – informs the ECUs of the accelerator pedal position.*

b) *Coolant temperature sensor – informs the ECUs of engine temperature.*

c) *Intake air temperature sensor – informs the ECUs of the temperature of the air passing through the intake duct.*

d) *Oil temperature sensor (2.0 litre engines) – informs ECUs of the temperature of the engine oil.*

e) *Hot film mass airflow meter – informs the ECUs of the amount of air passing through the intake duct.*

f) *Crankshaft sensor – informs the ECUs of engine speed and crankshaft position.*

g) *Charge pressure sensor – informs ECUs of the pressure in the inlet manifold.*

h) *ABS control unit – informs the ECUs of the vehicle speed.*

i) *Atmospheric pressure sensor – informs the ECUs of the atmospheric pressure.*

j) *Fuel temperature sensor – informs the ECUs of the fuel temperature.*

k) *Injection pump shaft sensor – used by the ECUs to determine the exact injection timing.*

l) *Oil pressure switch – used by the Engine ECU to control the instrument cluster oil warning lamp.*

m) *Clutch switch – used by the ECUs for cruise control functions.*

n) *Air conditioning system compressor switch (where fitted) – informs ECUs when the air conditioning system is switched on.*

18 All the above information is analysed by the ECUs and, based on this, the ECUs determine the appropriate injection requirements for the engine. The engine ECU controls the injection pump timing, via the pump control unit, to provide the best setting for cranking, starting (with either a hot or cold engine), warm-up, idle, cruising, and acceleration.

19 Basic injection timing is determined when the pump is fitted. When the engine is running, it is varied automatically to suit the prevailing engine speed by a mechanism which turns the cam plate or ring – controlled by the ECU.

20 The engine ECU also controls the exhaust gas recirculation (EGR) system (see Chapter 4B) and the pre-heating system (see Chapter 5B).

21 The four fuel injectors produce a spray of fuel directly into the cylinders. The injectors are calibrated to open and close at critical pressures to provide efficient and even combustion. Each injector needle is lubricated by fuel, which accumulates in the spring chamber and is channelled to the injection pump return hose by leak-off pipes.

22 On 2.0 litre engines, the inlet manifold is fitted with a butterfly valve arrangement to improve efficiency at low engine speeds. Each cylinder has two intake tracts in the manifold, one of which is fitted a valve; the operation of the valve is controlled by the ECU via a solenoid valve and vacuum diaphragm unit. At low engine speeds (below approximately 1500 rpm) the valves remain closed, meaning that air entering each cylinder is passing through only one of the two manifold tracts. At higher engine speeds, the ECU opens up each of the four valves allowing the air passing through the manifold to pass through both inlet tracts.

23 On 1.7 litre engines, the inlet manifold is a two-part assembly sealed by a metal gasket. The EGR (exhaust gas recirculation) valve and charge pressure sensor are mounted to the upper part of the manifold.

24 A turbocharger is fitted to increase engine efficiency by raising the pressure in the inlet manifold above atmospheric pressure. Instead of the air simply being sucked into the cylinders, it is forced in. Additional fuel is supplied by the injection pump in proportion to the increased air intake.

25 Energy for the operation of the turbocharger comes from the exhaust gas. The gas flows through a specially-shaped housing (the turbine housing) and in so doing, spins the turbine wheel. The turbine wheel is attached to a shaft, at the end of which is another vaned wheel known as the compressor wheel. The compressor wheel spins in its own housing, and compresses the inlet air on the way to the inlet manifold.

26 Between the turbocharger and the inlet manifold, the compressed air passes through an intercooler (except Y20DTL engine). This is an air-to-air heat exchanger is mounted next to the radiator, and supplied with cooling air from the front of the vehicle. The purpose of the intercooler is to remove some of the heat gained in being compressed from the inlet air. Because cooler air is denser, removal of this heat further increases engine efficiency.

27 Charge pressure (the pressure in the inlet manifold) is limited by a wastegate, which diverts the exhaust gas away from the turbine wheel in response to a pressure-sensitive actuator. A pressure-operated switch operates a warning light on the instrument panel in the event of excessive charge pressure developing.

28 The turbo shaft is pressure-lubricated by an oil feed pipe from the engine main oil so that the shaft 'floats' on a cushion of oil. A drain pipe returns the oil to the sump.

29 The charge pressure wastegate is controlled by the ECU via a solenoid valve.

30 If there is an abnormality in any of the readings obtained from any sensor, the ECU enters its back-up mode. In this event, the ECU ignores the abnormal sensor signal, and assumes a pre-programmed value which will allow the engine to continue running (albeit at reduced efficiency). If the ECU enters this back-up mode, the warning light on the instrument panel will come on, and the relevant fault code will be stored in the ECU memory.

31 If the warning light comes on, the vehicle should be taken to a Vauxhall dealer at the earliest opportunity. A complete test of the injection system can then be carried out, using a special electronic diagnostic test unit which is simply plugged into the system's diagnostic connector. The connector is located behind the centre console; unclip the trim panel situated just in front of the handbrake lever to gain access **(see illustration 1.13)**.

Precautions

 Warning: It is necessary to take certain precautions when working on the fuel system components, particularly the fuel injectors.
Before carrying out any operations on the fuel system, refer to the precautions given in 'Safety first!' at the beginning of this manual, and to any additional warning notes at the start of the relevant Sections.
Caution: Do not operate the engine if any of air intake ducts are disconnected or the filter element is removed. Any debris entering the engine will cause severe damage to the turbocharger.
Caution: To prevent damage to the turbocharger, do not race the engine immediately after start-up, especially if it is cold. Allow it to idle smoothly to give the oil a few seconds to circulate around the turbocharger bearings. Always allow the engine to return to idle speed before switching it off – do not blip the throttle and switch off, as this will leave the turbo spinning without lubrication.
Caution: Observe the recommended intervals for oil and filter changing, and use a reputable oil of the specified quality. Neglect of oil changing, or use of inferior oil, can cause carbon formation on the turbo shaft, leading to subsequent failure.

2 Air cleaner assembly and intake ducts – removal and refitting

Removal

1.7 litre models

1 Release the retaining clip and detach the intake duct from the rear of the air cleaner housing **(see illustrations)**.

2 Undo the Torx screw at the rear securing the air cleaner mounting to the body then free the housing from its air intake, and remove the assembly from the engine compartment. Note that the lower air cleaner housing incorporates a location lug which engages with a corresponding location bush mounted on the inner wing.

3 The remaining ducts linking the turbocharger, intercooler and inlet manifold

2.1a Air cleaner and ducting – 1.7 litre SOHC models

1 Air cleaner housing upper part
2 Air intake hose
3 Hot film mass airflow meter
4 Air intake hose
5 Turbocharger
6 Charge air pipe
7 Charge air hose
8 Intercooler
9 Air intake pipe
10 Connecting hose
11 Air cleaner housing lower part

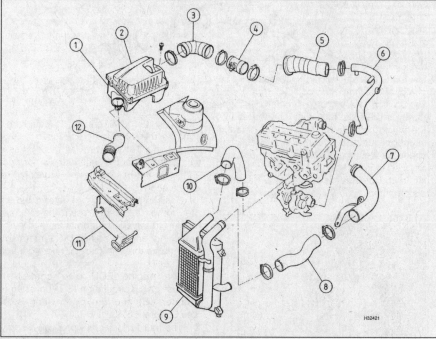

2.1b Air cleaner and ducting – 1.7 litre DOHC models

1 Air cleaner housing lower part
2 Air cleaner housing upper part
3 Air intake hose
4 Hot film mass airflow meter
5 Air intake hose
6 Air intake manifold
7 Charge air pipe
8 Charge air hose
9 Intercooler
10 Charge air hose
11 Air intake pipe
12 Connecting hose

2.3 Release the wiring plug and disconnect the hot film mass airflow meter

2.5 Disconnect the wiring connector from the airflow meter and (where fitted) the intake air temperature sensor (arrowed)

can be removed once their retaining clips and (where necessary) bolts have been slackened. Note that the inlet duct from the air cleaner housing to the air intake manifold connected to the turbocharger incorporates the hot film mass airflow meter. Release the wiring plug and disconnect the hot film mass airflow meter prior to removing the inlet duct **(see illustration)**.

2.0 litre models

4 On Zafira models, remove the engine compartment seal and water deflector cover from in front of the windscreen. Undo the retaining nuts and bolts, and remove the bulkhead cover plate to allow access to the air intake trunking.

5 On all models, disconnect the battery negative terminal then disconnect the wiring connector(s) from the hot film mass airflow meter and (where fitted) the intake air temperature sensor **(see illustration)**. **Note:** *Before disconnecting the battery, refer to 'Disconnecting the battery' in the reference section at the rear of this manual.*

6 Disconnect the breather hose from the intake duct then slacken the retaining clips and remove the duct assembly, complete with hot film mass airflow meter, from the engine compartment.

7 Unclip the air cleaner housing lid and remove the filter element, noting which way up it is fitted. Undo the retaining bolt and remove the housing from the engine compartment, freeing it from its intake.

8 On low-pressure turbo (X20DTL/Y20DTL engine) models, to remove the ducts linking the turbocharger and inlet manifold, first undo the retaining screws and remove the plastic cover from the top of the engine. Slacken the retaining clip securing the duct connecting the metal pipe to the manifold. Undo the bolts securing the pipe to the cylinder head cover, then slacken the retaining clamp and detach the pipe from the turbocharger. Remove the pipe and duct assembly from the top of the engine and recover the sealing ring which is fitted between the pipe and turbocharger **(see illustration)**.

9 On high-pressure turbo (Y20DTH engine) models, the ducts linking the intercooler to the manifold and turbocharger pipe can be removed once their retaining clips/bolts have been slackened. To remove the metal pipe, detach the duct then slacken the clamp securing it to the turbocharger. Undo the retaining bolt and remove the pipe from the engine, noting the sealing ring which is fitted

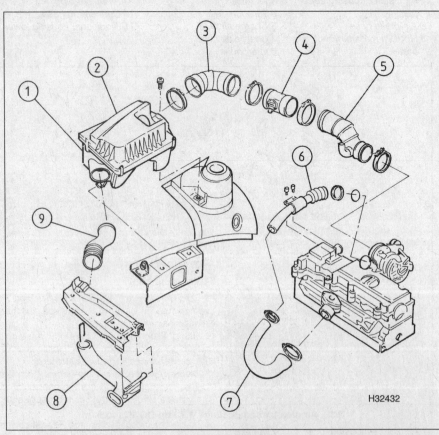

H32432

2.8 Air cleaner and ducting – 2.0 litre low-pressure models

1 Air cleaner housing lower part	4 Hot film mass airflow meter	7 Connecting hose
2 Air cleaner housing upper part	5 Air intake hose	8 Air intake pipe
3 Air intake hose	6 Charge air pipe	9 Connecting hose

between the pipe and turbocharger **(see illustration)**.

Refitting

10 Refitting is the reverse of removal, ensuring that all intake ducts are properly reconnected and their retaining clips securely tightened. On 2.0 litre models, renew the sealing ring if the metal pipe has been disconnected from the turbocharger.

3 Accelerator pedal – removal and refitting

1 From inside the vehicle, unscrew the fasteners and remove the lower trim panel from underneath the driver's side of the facia to gain access to the accelerator pedal (see Chapter 11, Section 44).
2 Unscrew the retaining nuts and remove the pedal assembly from the bulkhead **(see illustration)**.
3 Disconnect the wiring connector from the accelerator pedal position sensor by sliding out the locking element of the wiring plug.
4 At the time of writing, the pedal was only available as a complete assembly with the pedal position sensor. If the pedal is defective, the complete assembly will have to be renewed.
5 Refit the pedal assembly and tighten its retaining nuts to the specified torque setting.
6 Reconnect the wiring connector then refit the trim panel to the facia.

4 Fuel system – priming and bleeding

1 It is not necessary to manually prime and bleed the fuel system after any operation on the system components. Start the engine (this may take longer than usual, especially if the fuel system has been allowed to run dry – operate the starter in ten second bursts with 5 seconds rest in between each operation) and run it a fast idle speed for a minute or so to purge any trapped air from the fuel lines. After

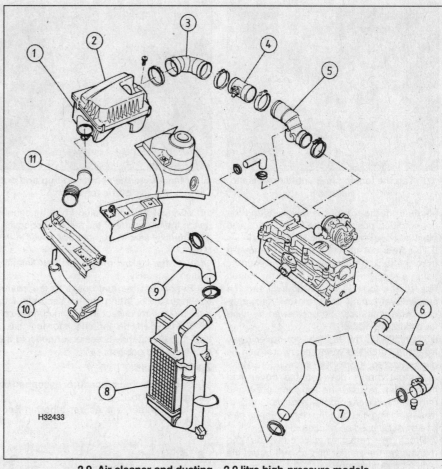

2.9 Air cleaner and ducting – 2.0 litre high-pressure models

1 Air cleaner housing lower part	4 Hot film mass airflow meter	8 Intercooler
2 Air cleaner housing upper part	5 Air intake hose	9 Charge air hose
3 Air intake hose	6 Charge air pipe	10 Air intake pipe
	7 Charge air hose	11 Connecting hose

this time the engine should idle smoothly at a constant speed.
2 If the engine idles roughly, then there is still some air trapped in the fuel system. Increase the engine speed again for another minute or so then recheck the idle speed. Repeat this procedure as necessary until the engine is idling smoothly.

5 Fuel gauge sender unit – removal and refitting

Removal

Astra models

1 Fold the rear seat cushion forwards and lift up the flap in the carpet to reveal the fuel sender maintenance cover.
2 Using a screwdriver, carefully prise the plastic access cover from the floor to expose the fuel sender cover **(see illustration)**.
3 Disconnect the wiring connector from the fuel sender cover, and tape the connector to the vehicle body, to prevent it disappearing behind the tank.
4 Mark the fuel hoses for identification purposes. The hoses are equipped with quick-release fittings to ease removal. To disconnect each hose, compress the clips located on each side of the fitting and ease the fitting off of its union. Disconnect both

3.2 Undo the three pedal assembly nuts

5.2 Prise the plastic access panel from the floor

5.5 Tap the locking ring anti-clockwise to release it

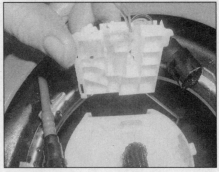

5.7 Manoeuvre the sender unit up and out of the tank

hoses from the top of the cover, noting the correct fitted position of the sealing rings and plug the hose ends to minimise fuel loss.

5 Unscrew the locking ring and remove it from the tank. This is best accomplished by using a screwdriver or punch on the raised ribs of the locking ring. Carefully tap the screwdriver/punch to turn the ring anti-clockwise until it can be unscrewed by hand **(see illustration)**.

6 Carefully lift the fuel sender cover away from tank until the wiring connector can be disconnected from its underside. Make alignment marks between the cover and hoses then release the retaining clips and remove the cover from the vehicle along with its sealing ring. Discard the sealing ring; a new one must be used on refitting.

7 Press the retaining clip outwards and manoeuvre the sender unit up and out of the tank **(see illustration)**.

Zafira models

8 Remove the fuel tank as described in Section 6.

9 Proceed as described in paragraphs 3 to 7 above.

Refitting

Astra models

10 Refit the sender unit to the tank, ensuring that it is correctly located.

11 Fit a new seal to the tank opening and reconnect the fuel return and supply hoses to the underside of the cover.

12 Connect the wiring plug from the sender unit to the underside of the fuel sender cover.

13 Carefully seat the sender unit cover to the tank.

14 Refit the locking ring to the fuel tank and tighten it securely.

15 Reconnect the fuel hoses to the cover, ensuring each fitting clicks securely into position, and reconnect the wiring connector.

16 Start the engine and check for fuel leaks. If all is well, refit the access cover and fold the seat back into position.

Zafira models

17 Carry out the procedure described in Paragraphs 10 to 15 above.

18 Refit the fuel tank as described in Section 6.

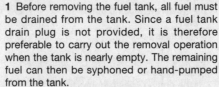

6 Fuel tank – removal and refitting

1 Before removing the fuel tank, all fuel must be drained from the tank. Since a fuel tank drain plug is not provided, it is therefore preferable to carry out the removal operation when the tank is nearly empty. The remaining fuel can then be syphoned or hand-pumped from the tank.

2 Remove the exhaust system and relevant heat shield(s) as described in Section 17.

3 Chock the front wheels, and slacken the handbrake cable adjusting nut, with reference to Chapter 9.

4 On rear drum brake models, disconnect the handbrake cable at the connector just forward of the brake drum. Models with disc rear brakes, press the rear caliper handbrake lever downwards, detach the handbrake inner cable from the lever, remove the retaining clip and remove the outer cable from the retaining bracket on the caliper. Refer to Chapter 9 if necessary.

5 Release the handbrake cable from the retaining clips and brackets, and position clear of the fuel tank.

6 On Astra models, disconnect the wiring connector from the fuel gauge sender unit as described in paragraphs 1 to 3 of Section 5. On Zafira models, working under the vehicle, disconnect the wiring plug for the fuel gauge sender unit **(see illustration)**.

7 Open the fuel filler flap and remove the rubber cover from around the filler neck aperture. Slacken and remove the retaining bolt which secures the filler neck to the body **(see illustration)**.

8 Remove the right-hand rear wheel then undo the retaining screws and nuts and remove the plastic wheelarch liner.

9 Make alignment marks between the small hoses and the top of the filler neck assembly then release the retaining clips and disconnect both hoses.

10 Slacken the retaining clips and disconnect the main hoses from the base of the filler neck. Unscrew the filler neck lower retaining bolt and manoeuvre the assembly out from underneath the vehicle.

11 Trace the fuel feed and return hoses from the tank to their unions in front of the tank. Make alignment marks between the hoses then release the retaining clips and disconnect both hoses. If the hoses are equipped with quick-release fittings, disconnect each hose by depressing the clips on each side of the fitting and easing the fitting from the pipe.

12 Place a trolley jack with an interposed block of wood beneath the tank, then raise the jack until it is supporting the weight of the tank.

13 Slacken and remove the retaining bolts and remove the retaining straps from underneath the fuel tank.

14 Slowly lower the fuel tank out of position, disconnecting any other relevant pipes as they become accessible (where necessary), and remove the tank from underneath the vehicle.

15 If the tank is contaminated with sediment or water, remove the fuel gauge sender unit (Section 5), and swill the tank out with clean fuel. The tank is injection-moulded from a synthetic material – if seriously damaged, it should be renewed. However, in certain cases, it may be possible to have small leaks or minor damage repaired. Seek the advice of a specialist before attempting to repair the fuel tank.

16 Refitting is the reverse of the removal procedure, noting the following points:

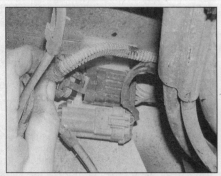

6.6 Disconnect the fuel gauge sender unit wiring plug – Zafira models

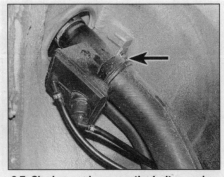

6.7 Slacken and remove the bolt securing the filler neck to the body (arrowed)

a) When lifting the tank back into position, take care to ensure that none of the hoses become trapped between the tank and vehicle body. Refit the retaining straps and tighten the bolts securely.

b) Ensure all pipes and hoses are correctly routed and all hoses unions are securely joined.

c) Adjust the handbrake as described in Chapter 9.

d) On completion, refill the tank with a small amount of fuel, and check for signs of leakage prior to taking the vehicle out on the road.

7 Maximum speed – checking and adjustment

Caution: The maximum speed is controlled by the ECU and cannot be adjusted by the home mechanic. The speed can be checked using a tachometer as described below, but if adjustment is needed it will have be necessary to take the vehicle to a Vauxhall dealer. They will have access to the necessary diagnostic equipment required to test and adjust the settings.

1 Run the engine to normal operating temperature.

2 Have an assistant fully depress the accelerator pedal, and check that the maximum engine speed is as given in the Specifications. Do not keep the engine at maximum speed for more than two or three seconds.

8 Injection system electrical components – removal and refitting

1.7 litre SOHC models

Hot film mass airflow meter

Note: The intake air temperature sensor is built into the airflow meter.

1 Ensure the ignition is switched off and disconnect the wiring plug from the hot film mass airflow meter (see illustration 2.3).

2 Release the retaining clips then free the airflow meter from the intake ducts and remove it from the engine compartment.

3 Refitting is the reverse of removal, ensuring the intake ducts are correctly seated and their retaining clips are securely tightened.

Accelerator pedal position sensor

4 At the time of writing, the pedal position sensor was only available as a complete assembly with the accelerator pedal. If the sensor is defective, the complete assembly will have to be renewed.

5 From inside the vehicle, unscrew the fasteners and remove the lower trim panel from underneath the driver's side of the facia to gain access to the accelerator pedal (see Chapter 11, Section 44).

6 Unscrew the retaining nuts and remove the pedal assembly from the bulkhead (see illustration 3.2).

7 Disconnect the wiring connector from the accelerator pedal position sensor by sliding out the locking element of the wiring plug.

8 Reconnect the wiring connector.

9 Refit the pedal assembly and tighten its retaining nuts to the specified torque setting, then refit the trim panel to the facia.

Crankshaft sensor

10 The crankshaft sensor is located at the base of the cylinder block front face. Disconnect the wiring plug, and note the cable routing.

11 Undo the retaining bolt and remove the sensor.

12 Refitting is a reversal of removal. Tighten the sensor retaining bolt to the specified torque.

Coolant temperature sensor

13 The coolant temperature sensor is located in the thermostat housing at the right-hand end of the cylinder head. Disconnect the sensor wiring plug (see illustration).

14 Drain the cooling system as described in Chapter 3, or be prepared for fluid spillage.

15 Unscrew the sensor from the thermostat housing.

16 Apply a little locking compound to the threads of the sensor, and refit the sensor to the housing. Tighten the sensor to the specified torque.

17 Reconnect the wiring plug to the sensor.

18 Top up the coolant system (see Chapter 3).

Charge pressure sensor

19 The charge pressure sensor is fitted to the right-hand end of the inlet manifold. Disconnect the wiring plug from the sensor (see illustration).

20 Undo the screw and remove the sensor from the manifold.

21 Refitting is a reversal of removal. Tighten the sensor retaining bolt to the specified torque.

Engine electronic control unit

Caution: Before removing an ECU, the control unit security code must be reset using specialist test equipment. Refer to your Vauxhall dealer.

22 The engine ECU is located behind the left-hand front inner wing protective panelling. Firmly apply the handbrake, jack up the front of the vehicle and support it on axle stands. Remove the front-left roadwheel.

23 Release the panelling retaining screws and clips. Remove the panelling from under the wheel arch.

24 Disconnect the two ECU wiring plugs and remove the unit from the retaining bracket (see illustration).

25 Refitting is a reversal of removal, noting that the ECU wiring plugs should be locked in place.

Injection electronic control unit (ECU)

26 The injection ECU is integral with the injection pump, and it is recommended that no attempt be made to separate the ECU from the pump.

Fuel temperature sensor

27 The fuel temperature sensor is integral with the fuel pump. It is recommended that no attempt be made to remove the sensor.

Injection pump shaft position sensor

28 The injection pump shaft position sensor is integral with the fuel pump. It is recommended that no attempt be made to remove the sensor.

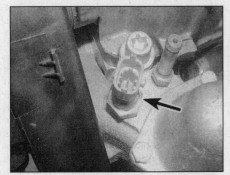
8.13 Disconnect the coolant temperature sensor (arrowed)

8.19 Charge pressure sensor

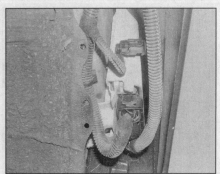
8.24 Disconnect the wiring plugs and remove the engine ECU

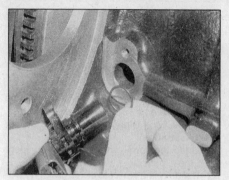

8.42 Crankshaft position sensor

8.45 Engine coolant temperature sensor

Injection commencement sensor

29 The injection commencement sensor is integral with the fuel pump. It is recommended that no attempt be made to remove the sensor.

Fuel cut-off solenoid

30 The fuel cut-off solenoid is integral with the fuel pump. It is recommended that no attempt be made to remove the sensor.

1.7 litre DOHC models

Hot film mass airflow meter

Note: The intake air temperature sensor is built into the airflow meter.

31 Ensure the ignition is switched off and disconnect the wiring plug from the hot film mass airflow meter (see illustration 2.3).
32 Release the retaining clips then free the airflow meter from the intake ducts and remove it from the engine compartment.
33 Refitting is the reverse of removal, ensuring the intake ducts are correctly seated and their retaining clips are securely tightened.

Accelerator pedal position sensor

34 At the time of writing, the pedal position sensor was only available as a complete assembly with the accelerator pedal. If the sensor is defective, the complete assembly will have to be renewed.
35 From inside the vehicle, unscrew the fasteners and remove the lower trim panel from underneath the driver's side of the facia

to gain access to the accelerator pedal (see Chapter 11, Section 44).
36 Unscrew the retaining nuts and remove the pedal assembly from the bulkhead (see illustration 3.2).
37 Disconnect the wiring connector from the accelerator pedal position sensor by sliding out the locking element of the wiring plug.
38 Reconnect the wiring connector.
39 Refit the pedal assembly and tighten its retaining nuts to the specified torque setting, then refit the trim panel to the facia.

Crankshaft sensor

40 Firmly apply the handbrake then jack up the front of the vehicle and support it on axle stands. Where necessary, undo the retaining bolts/clips and remove the undertray from beneath the engine/transmission unit.
41 The sensor is located on the rear of the cylinder block, underneath the starter motor. Working from under the vehicle, disconnect the wiring plug from the sensor.
42 Undo the retaining bolt and remove the sensor. Recover the sealing ring (see illustration).
43 Refitting is a reversal of removal. If necessary renew the sealing ring and tighten the sensor retaining bolt to the specified torque.

Coolant temperature sensor

44 With reference to Chapter 3, drain the coolant system, or be prepared for coolant spillage.

45 The coolant temperature sensor is located in the thermostat housing at the left-hand end of the cylinder head. Disconnect the wiring plug from the sensor (see illustration).
46 Unscrew the sensor from the thermostat housing. Mop up any spilled coolant.
47 Apply a little locking compound to the threads of the sensor, and refit the sensor to the housing. Tighten the sensor to the specified torque.
48 Reconnect the wiring plug to the sensor.
49 Top up the coolant system (see Chapter 3).

Charge pressure sensor

50 Remove the air cleaner ducting at the rear of the engine compartment (see Section 2).
51 With reference to Chapter 4B, remove the exhaust gas recirculation solenoid valve from the inlet manifold.
52 Disconnect the wiring plug from the sensor on the right-hand end of the inlet manifold.
53 Undo the retaining bolts and remove the sensor (see illustration).
54 Refitting is a reversal of removal. Tighten the sensor retaining bolts to the specified torque.

Oil pressure switch

55 The signal from the oil pressure switch is used by the injection control unit to determine whether or not to illuminate the oil pressure warning light.
56 To remove the oil pressure switch, remove the battery and battery tray as described in Chapter 5A. Note: Before disconnecting the battery, refer to 'Disconnecting the battery' in the reference section at the rear of this manual.
57 The oil pressure switch is located at the left-hand end of the cylinder block. Disconnect the wiring plug from the switch.
58 Unscrew the switch from the cylinder block. Be prepared for oil spillage (see illustration).
59 Apply some suitable silicone sealant (available from Vauxhall dealers) to the threads, and screw the switch into place. Tighten the switch to the specified torque.
60 Reconnect the wiring plug, and refit the battery tray, and battery.
61 Start the vehicle and check for oil leaks.

Engine electronic control unit (ECU)

Caution: Before removing an ECU, the control unit security code must be reset using specialist test equipment. Refer to your Vauxhall dealer.

62 The engine control unit is located on top of the engine above the exhaust gas recirculation valve.
63 Disconnect the battery negative lead. Note: Before disconnecting the battery, refer to 'Disconnecting the battery' in the reference section at the rear of this manual.
64 Disconnect the two wiring plugs from the

8.53 Undo the bolts and remove the charge pressure sensor

8.58 Oil pressure switch – 1.7 litre DOHC engine

8.64 Lift the metal levers to unplug the engine ECU

8.70 Unscrew the injection ECU retaining bolts

8.80 Slide the atmospheric pressure sensor from the bracket

ECU. The plugs are unlocked by lifting up the metal levers (see illustration).
65 Undo the retaining bolts/nuts, and remove the ECU.
66 Refitting is a reversal of removal. Tighten the ECU retaining bolts/nuts to the specified torque. The ECU wiring plugs are shaped such that each plug will only fit its correct socket. The plug from the left-hand side of the engine compartment connects to the rearmost socket. Take great care when refitting the plugs, as the terminals are very delicate and easily damaged.

Injection electronic control unit (ECU)

67 The injection ECU is located at the rear of the injection pump.
68 Firmly apply the handbrake then jack up the front of the vehicle and support it on axle stands. Where necessary, undo the retaining bolts/clips and remove the undertray from beneath the engine/transmission unit.

69 Working under the vehicle, disconnect the ECU wiring plug.
70 Undo the retaining bolts, and remove the ECU (see illustration).
71 Refitting is a reversal of removal.

Turbocharger wastegate control solenoid valve

72 Firmly apply the handbrake then jack up the front of the vehicle and support it on axle stands. Where necessary, undo the retaining bolts/clips and remove the undertray from beneath the engine/transmission unit.
73 Remove the injection ECU as described in paragraphs 67 to 70.
74 Disconnect the vacuum pipes, and wiring plug from the solenoid valve.
75 Undo the two retaining bolts and remove the solenoid valve.
76 Refitting is a reversal of removal. Tighten the solenoid valve retaining bolts securely. Note that the vacuum pipes are of two

different diameters. The smaller pipe is fitted to the outer connection.

Atmospheric pressure sensor

77 The atmospheric pressure sensor is located at the rear of the cylinder block, between the injection pump and the starter motor.
78 Firmly apply the handbrake then jack up the front of the vehicle and support it on axle stands. Where necessary, undo the retaining bolts/clips and remove the undertray from beneath the engine/transmission unit.
79 Disconnect the wiring plug from the pressure sensor.
80 Lift the sensor up and off the retaining bracket (see illustration).
81 Refitting is a reversal of removal.

Fuel temperature sensor

82 The fuel temperature sensor is fitted to the right-hand top of the injection pump (see illustration).
83 To remove the sensor, disconnect the wiring plug and unscrew the sensor from the top of the injection pump.
84 With a new seal fitted, screw the sensor into the injection pump and tighten the nut securely (see illustration).
85 Reconnect the wiring plug.

Injection pump shaft position sensor

86 The sensor is located on the side of the fuel injection pump (see illustration 8.82).
87 The sensor may not be available as a separate item. Check with a Vauxhall dealer prior to any attempt to remove the sensor.

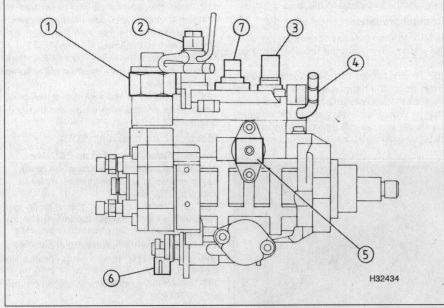

8.82 Fuel injection pump – 1.7 litre DOHC models

1 Spill valve
2 Fuel return line
3 Fuel temperature sensor
4 Fuel supply line
5 Programmable read-only memory
6 Timing control solenoid
7 Injection pump shaft position sensor

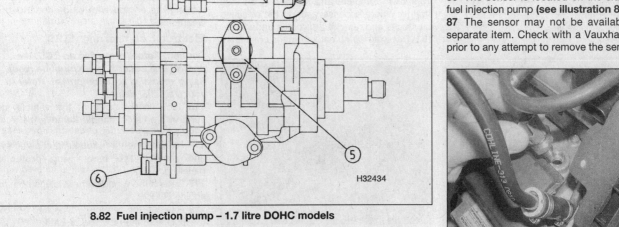

8.84 Screw the fuel temperature sensor into the injection pump

8.103 Disconnect the wiring connector . . .

Injection commencement sensor

88 The sensor is located on the underside of the fuel injection pump at the flywheel end.
89 The sensor may not be available as a separate item. Check with a Vauxhall dealer prior to any attempt to remove the sensor.

Fuel cut-off solenoid

90 The fuel cut-off solenoid is located on top of the fuel injection pump, at the flywheel end.
91 The solenoid may not be available as a separate item. Check with a Vauxhall dealer prior to any attempt to remove the sensor.

2.0 litre models

Hot film mass airflow meter

Note: *The air temperature sensor is built into the hot film mass airflow meter.*

92 Ensure the ignition is switched off then disconnect the wiring connector from the airflow meter (see illustration 2.3). On Zafira models, to improve access, remove the engine compartment seal and water deflector cover from in front of the windscreen. Undo the retaining nuts and bolts, and remove the bulkhead cover plate to allow access to the air intake trunking
93 Slacken the retaining clips then free the airflow meter from the intake ducts and remove it from the engine compartment.
94 Refitting is the reverse of removal, ensuring the intake ducts are correctly seated and their retaining clips are securely tightened.

8.108 Disconnect the wiring connector then undo the retaining bolt (arrowed) and remove the charge pressure sensor

8.104 . . . then undo the retaining screw and remove the crankshaft sensor from the front of the cylinder block (sealing ring arrowed)

Accelerator pedal position sensor

95 At the time of writing, the pedal position sensor was only available as a complete assembly with the accelerator pedal. If the sensor is defective, the complete assembly will have to be renewed.
96 From inside the vehicle, unscrew the fasteners and remove the lower trim panel from underneath the driver's side of the facia to gain access to the accelerator pedal (see Chapter 11, Section 44).
97 Unscrew the retaining nuts and remove the pedal assembly from the bulkhead (see illustration 3.2).
98 Disconnect the wiring connector from the accelerator pedal position sensor by sliding out the locking element of the wiring plug.
99 Reconnect the wiring connector.
100 Refit the pedal assembly and tighten its retaining nuts to the specified torque setting, then refit the trim panel to the facia.

Crankshaft sensor

101 Undo the retaining screws and remove the plastic cover from the top of the cylinder head.
102 To gain access to the sensor from below, firmly apply the handbrake then jack up the front of the vehicle and support it on axle stands. Where necessary, undo the retaining clips/bolts and remove the engine undertray.
103 Trace the wiring back from the crankshaft

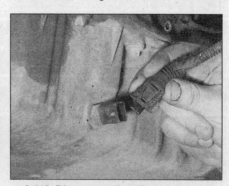

8.113 Disconnect the oil temperature sensor wiring connector

sensor to its wiring connector then free the connector from its bracket and disconnect it from the main harness (see illustration).
104 Wipe clean the area around the crankshaft sensor then slacken and remove the retaining bolt. Remove the sensor from the front of the cylinder block and recover the sealing ring (see illustration).
105 Refitting is the reverse of removal, using a new sealing ring. Tighten the sensor retaining bolt to the specified torque.

Coolant temperature sensor

106 The coolant temperature sensor is screwed into the front of the cylinder head, at the right-hand end. Refer to Chapter 3, Section 7, for removal and refitting details.

Charge pressure sensor

107 Undo the retaining screws and remove the plastic cover from the top of the cylinder head.
108 Slacken and remove the screws securing the wiring harness tray to the top of the inlet manifold and disconnect the wiring connector from the charge pressure sensor (see illustration).
109 Undo the retaining bolt and remove the sensor from the top of the inlet manifold, noting the sealing ring fitted to the sensor shaft.
110 Refitting is the reverse of removal, using a new sealing ring and tightening the retaining bolt to the specified torque.

Oil temperature sensor

111 Firmly apply the handbrake then jack up the front of the vehicle and support it on axle stands. Where necessary, undo the retaining clips/bolts and remove the engine undertray.
112 Drain the engine oil as described in Chapter 1. Once the oil has finished draining, fit a new sealing ring then refit the drain plug and tighten it to the specified torque.
113 Disconnect the wiring connector then unscrew the sensor from the front of the sump (see illustration).
114 On refitting is the reverse of removal, refilling the engine with oil as described in Chapter 1.

Electronic control unit (ECU)

Caution: Before removing an ECU, the control unit security code must be reset using specialist test equipment. Refer to your Vauxhall dealer.
115 Jack up the front of the vehicle and support it on axle stands. Remove the front-left roadwheel.
116 Release the three retaining clips/screws and remove the inner wing protective panelling.
117 Detach the wiring harness plugs from the engine ECU.
118 Release the retaining clips and remove the ECU from the retaining bracket.
119 Refitting is the reverse of removal, ensuring the wiring connectors are securely reconnected.

Injection pump control unit

120 The control unit is an integral part of the injection pump and should not be disturbed. **Never** attempt to separate the control unit and pump.

Inlet manifold switchover solenoid valve

121 Note that there are two valves, the EGR system valve and the manifold switchover valve; the manifold switchover valve is nearest the front of the vehicle **(see illustration)**.
122 Disconnect the wiring connector and vacuum hoses from the valve then undo the retaining screws and remove the valve from its mounting bracket.
123 Refitting is the reverse of removal.

Turbocharger wastegate solenoid valve

124 The solenoid valve is located in the right-hand rear corner of the engine compartment.
125 To gain access to the valve, remove the intake duct assembly (complete with hot film mass airflow meter) linking the air cleaner housing to the turbocharger (see Section 2).
126 Disconnect the wiring connector and vacuum hoses from the valve then undo the retaining screws and remove the valve from its mounting bracket.
127 Refitting is the reverse of removal.

9 Fuel injection pump – removal and refitting

Caution: Be careful not to allow dirt into the injection pump or injector pipes during this procedure.

1.7 litre SOHC models

1 Disconnect the battery negative lead. **Note:** *Before disconnecting the battery, refer to 'Disconnecting the battery' in the reference section at the rear of this manual.*
2 Remove the injection pump timing belt sprocket as described in Chapter 2A, Section 8.
3 Undo the union nuts and remove the injector fuel pipes, refer to Section 12 if necessary.

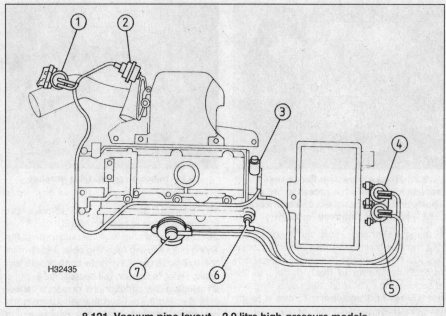

8.121 Vacuum pipe layout – 2.0 litre high-pressure models

1 Charge pressure control solenoid valve
2 Charge pressure control actuator
3 Vacuum pump
4 EGR (exhaust gas recirculation) valve
5 Inlet manifold switchover solenoid valve
6 Inlet manifold switchover valve
7 EGR (exhaust gas recirculation) valve

4 Slide the injection pump ECU wiring plug-locking element towards the front of the engine, and disconnect **(see illustration)**.
5 Remove all traces of dirt and make identification marks between the fuel feed and return pipes. Disconnect the injection pump fuel supply and return pipes. Recover the seal rings **(see illustration)**. Plug the hose ends to minimise fuel loss and prevent the entry of dirt.
6 Slacken and remove the retaining bolts securing the pump rear mounting bracket to the cylinder block bracket **(see illustration)**.
7 Slacken and remove the pump front mounting nuts and remove the pump assembly from the engine.
Caution: Never attempt to dismantle the pump assembly. If there is a problem, take the pump to a Vauxhall dealer/diesel injection specialist for testing/repair.

8 Manoeuvre the pump into position. Refit the front and rear retaining bolts and tighten them to the specified torques.
9 Reconnect the wiring plug to the injection ECU and secure the plug in place by pushing the locking element towards the left-hand end of the engine.
10 Reconnect the feed and return hoses to the injection pump, tightening the unions to the specified torque.
11 Ensure the unions are clean and dry then refit the injector pipes, tightening their union nuts to the specified torque.
12 Refit the injection pump sprocket, and finger-tighten the retaining nut at this stage. It must be possible to rotate the sprocket independently of the shaft.
13 With an open-ended spanner on the injection pump flange retaining nut, rotate the injection pump flange until the recess

9.4 Slide the connector locking element to the front and disconnect the injection pump ECU

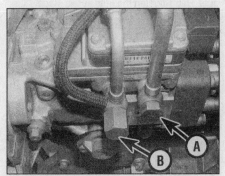
9.5 Disconnect the injection pump supply (A) and return (B) pipes. Recover the seal rings

9.6 Remove the injection pump rear mounting bolts

9.13 Rotate the pump flange until its recess aligns with the recess in the pump body and the locking pin can be inserted (sprocket removed for clarity)

9.21 Injection pump ECU bracket

9.23 Injection pump wiring plugs

in the sprocket aligns with the flange recess and the pump retaining bore. Insert Vauxhall tool KM 6011 into the flange and pump body to lock the pump in this position. In the absence of the Vauxhall tool, use a length of rod 9.5 mm in diameter and 75 mm in length **(see illustration)**.

14 Refit the timing belt as described in Chapter 2A.

15 The remainder of the procedure is a reversal of removal, noting the following points:

a) *Tighten all nuts and bolts to the correct torque where specified.*

b) *The engine may take longer to start than normal, due to the fuel system having to 'self-bleed'.*

c) *Ensure all wiring plugs are securely reconnected, the wiring looms routed as noted on removal, and secured using new cable ties where necessary.*

d) *After starting the engine, check all fuel unions for leaks, and rectify where necessary.*

1.7 litre DOHC models

16 Disconnect the battery negative lead. **Note:** *Before disconnecting the battery, refer to 'Disconnecting the battery' in the reference section at the rear of this manual.*

17 With reference to Section 8 of Chapter 2B, remove the injection pump sprocket.

18 Remove the inlet manifold as described in Section 15 of this Chapter.

19 Refer to Section 8, and remove the injection electronic control unit (ECU).

20 Disconnect the two vacuum pipes, the wiring plug, the two retaining bolts and remove the turbocharger wastegate control solenoid valve. Refer to Section 8 if necessary.

21 Unplug the atmospheric pressure sensor (see Section 8), remove the sensor from the mounting bracket. Undo the two retaining bolts and remove the bracket. Remove the injection pump ECU bracket **(see illustration)**.

22 Disconnect the fuel supply and return pipes from the pump.

23 Pull out the injection pump insulation, disconnect the various sensor wiring plugs from the injection pump, and release the wiring harness from the various retaining clips **(see illustration)**. Note the routing of the various wiring looms.

24 Undo the bolts and remove the injection pump mounting bracket from the left-hand end of the pump **(see illustration)**.

25 Remove the two retaining nuts, and manoeuvre the injection pump from the timing case. Recover the foam insulator from between the pump and cylinder block.

Caution: Never attempt to dismantle the pump assembly. If there is a problem, take the pump to a Vauxhall dealer/diesel injection specialist for testing/repair.

26 To refit the pump, hold the correct piece of foam insulator against the cylinder block, engage the pump shaft with the corresponding hole in the timing case, and fit the two retaining nuts. Hand-tighten the nuts at this stage.

27 Refit the pump mounting bracket to the cylinder block, and tighten the bolts to the specified torque. Fit the bolts securing the bracket to the pump, but only hand-tighten the bolts at this stage. Refit the foam insulation pieces around the pump **(see illustration)**. **Note:** *Reconnect the wiring plug to the PROM (Programmable read-only memory) on the side of the pump before fitting the rearmost foam insulation piece.*

28 With reference to Chapter 2B, Section 8, refit the injection pump sprocket.

29 Refit the timing belt (Chapter 2B, Section 7).

30 Carry out the *Injection timing – checking and adjustment* procedure described in Section 11.

31 The remainder of the procedure is a reversal of the removal procedure, bearing in mind the following points:

a) *Tighten all fixings to the correct torque setting where specified.*

b) *Ensure all wiring plugs are securely reconnected, the wiring looms routed as noted on removal, and secured using new cable ties where necessary* **(see illustration)**.

c) *The engine may take longer to start than normal, due to the fuel system having to 'self-bleed'.*

d) *Check all fuel connections for leaks.*

2.0 litre models

Note: *Since it is necessary to remove the upper timing chain and sprockets to remove*

9.24 Fuel injection pump mounting bracket bolts

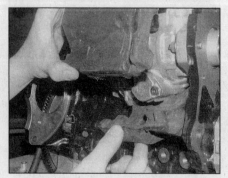

9.27 Refit the foam insulation pieces

9.31 Note the injection pump wiring loom/vacuum pump routing

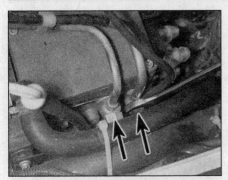

9.33 Undo the union bolts (arrowed) and disconnect the feed and return pipes from the pump

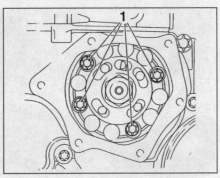

9.35 Slacken and remove the injection pump front mounting bolts (1) through the holes in the lower timing chain sprocket

10 Injection timing – checking methods

1.7 litre SOHC models

1 On these models the injection timing is determined by the ECU using the information supplied by the various sensors. Checking of the injection system can only be carried out using specialist diagnostic equipment (see Section 1).

1.7 litre DOHC models

2 Although on these models the injection timing is determined by the engine ECU, the basic injection timing has to be set when the pump is fitted. Checking of the injection system can only be carried out using specialist diagnostic equipment.

2.0 litre models

3 On these models the injection timing is determined by the ECU using the information supplied by the various sensors. Checking of the injection system can only be carried out using specialist diagnostic equipment (see Section 1).

the injection pump, several special Vauxhall service tools (or suitable alternatives) will be required on refitting to enable the valve timing to be accurately adjusted (see Section 4 of Chapter 2C). If access to suitable tools cannot be gained then it is recommended that this task is entrusted to a Vauxhall dealer or suitably-equipped garage. If the task is to be carried out without the tools then accurate alignment marks must be made between the sprockets, camshaft and injection pump flange prior to removal. It is also likely that the special socket (MKM-604-30) will also be needed to unscrew the pump front mounting bolts.

Note: *A new camshaft sprocket bolt and upper timing chain guide bolts will be required on refitting.*

32 Refer to Section 15, and remove the inlet manifold.

33 Remove all traces of dirt from around the injection pump fuel feed and return pipe unions. Slacken and remove the union bolts and sealing washers then disconnect both pipes and position them clear of the pump **(see illustration)**.

34 With reference to Chapter 2C, remove the upper timing chain and sprockets.

35 Working through the holes in the lower timing chain sprocket, slacken and remove the pump front mounting bolts **(see illustration)**.

36 Slacken and remove the retaining bolts and remove the pump rear mounting bracket.

Manoeuvre the pump out of position along with its sealing ring. Discard the sealing ring, a new one must be used on refitting **(see illustrations)**.

Caution: Never attempt to dismantle the pump assembly. If there is a problem, take the pump to a Vauxhall dealer/diesel injection specialist for testing/repair.

37 Prior to refitting, ensure the timing cut-out in the pump sprocket flange is correctly aligned with the locating hole in the pump body and check that the camshaft and crankshaft are still correctly positioned.

38 Ensure the mating surfaces are clean and dry and fit a new sealing ring to the pump flange.

39 Manoeuvre the pump into position, engaging the lower timing chain sprocket with the pump flange. Refit the pump front mounting bolts and tighten them to the specified torque setting.

40 Refit the mounting bracket to the rear of the injection pump and tighten its retaining bolts to the specified torque.

41 Refit the upper timing chain and sprockets as described in Chapter 2C.

42 Position a new sealing washer on each side of the injection pump feed and return pipe unions then refit the union bolts, tightening them to the specified torque.

43 Refit the inlet manifold as described in Section 15.

44 Reconnect the battery negative lead then start the engine.

11 Injection timing – checking and adjustment

Caution: Be careful not to allow dirt into the injection pump or injector pipes during this procedure.

Caution: Some of the injection pump settings and access plugs may be sealed by the manufacturers at the factory, using paint or locking wire and lead seals. Do not disturb the seals if the vehicle is still within the warranty period, otherwise the warranty will be invalidated. Also do not attempt the timing procedure unless accurate instrumentation is available.

1.7 litre SOHC models

1 On these models the injection timing is determined by the ECU using the information supplied by the various sensors. Checking and adjustment of the injection system can only be carried out using specialist diagnostic equipment (see Section 1).

1.7 litre DOHC models

2 If not already done so, remove the air cleaner housing and ducting (Section 2), and the upper timing belt cover (Chapter 2B, Section 6).

3 Undo the unions and remove the fuel injection delivery pipes. We found it necessary to remove the oil cooler housing retaining bolt (Chapter 2B, Section 17) and push the housing to the rear, to allow sufficient access to the rear of the pump. Be prepared for fluid spillage.

9.36a Slacken and remove the retaining bolts (arrowed – one hidden) and remove the rear mounting bracket . . .

9.36b . . . then remove the pump from the engine, noting the sealing ring

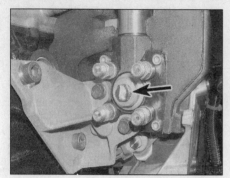

11.5 Remove the central bleed screw

11.6 Screw the adapter into the pump and mount the dial gauge

4 With reference to Chapter 2B, Section 3, position the crankshaft at approximately 45° before TDC for No 1 piston.

5 Remove the central bleed screw from the centre of the four fuel delivery unions at the left-hand end of the injection pump **(see illustration)**.

6 Screw the adapter into the rear of the pump and mount the dial gauge in the adapter **(see illustration)**. The special adapter and dial gauge (Vauxhall tool No KM-798) can be purchased from most good motor factors. Position the dial gauge so that its plunger is at the mid-point of its travel and securely tighten the adapter locknut.

7 Slowly rotate the crankshaft back and forth whilst observing the dial gauge, to determine when the injection pump piston is at the bottom of its travel (BDC). When the piston is correctly positioned, zero the dial gauge.

8 Rotate the crankshaft slowly in the correct direction until the crankshaft pulley mark is correctly aligned with the pointer (No 1 cylinder at TDC on its compression stroke).

9 The reading obtained on the dial gauge should be equal to the specified pump timing measurement given in the Specifications at the start of this Chapter. If adjustment is necessary, slacken the pump front mounting nuts and rear mounting bolts and slowly rotate the pump body until the point is found where the specified reading is obtained. If the reading is too large turn the pump towards the engine, and if the reading is too small turn the pump away from the engine. When the pump

is correctly positioned, tighten both its front and rear mounting nuts and bolts to the specified torque.

10 Rotate the crankshaft through one and three quarter rotations in the normal direction of rotation. Find the injection pump piston BDC as described in paragraph 7 and zero the dial gauge.

11 Rotate the crankshaft slowly in the correct direction of rotation until the crankshaft pulley mark is realigned with the pointer (bringing the engine back to TDC). Recheck the timing measurement.

12 If adjustment is necessary, slacken the pump sprocket bolts and repeat the operations in paragraphs 9 to 11.

13 When the pump timing is correctly set unscrew the adapter and remove the dial gauge.

14 Refit the central bleed screw.

15 Refit the fuel injection pipes, tightening the unions to the specified torque, and refit the oil cooler housing and retaining bolt (if removed).

16 Refit the upper timing belt cover, and air filter housing and ducting.

17 The fuel system should 'self-bleed' as the engine is cranked, although it may take longer than normal to restart. Check for fuel leaks from the disturbed pipes and unions.

2.0 litre models

18 On these models the injection timing is

determined by the ECU using the information supplied by the various sensors. Checking and adjustment of the injection system can only be carried out using specialist diagnostic equipment (see Section 1).

12 Fuel injectors – removal and refitting

> **Warning: Exercise extreme caution when working on the fuel injectors. Never expose the hands or any part of the body to injector spray, as the high working pressure can cause the fuel to penetrate the skin, with possibly fatal results. You are strongly advised to have any work which involves testing the injectors under pressure carried out by a dealer or fuel injection specialist.**
> **Caution: Be careful not to allow dirt into the injection pump, injectors or pipes during this procedure.**
> **Caution: Take care not to drop the injectors, or allow the needles at their tips to become damaged. The injectors are precision-made to fine limits, and must not be handled roughly. In particular, never mount them in a bench vice.**

1.7 litre SOHC models

1 Pull the leak-back pipes from the injectors **(see illustration)**.

2 Wipe clean the pipe unions then slacken the union nuts securing the injector pipes to the top of each injector and the four union nuts securing the pipes to the rear of the injection pump; as each pump union nut is slackened, retain the adapter with a suitable open-ended spanner to prevent it being unscrewed from the pump **(see illustration)**. With all the union nuts undone, remove the injector pipes from the engine unit and mop up any spilt fuel.

3 Clean around the base of the injector(s) to be removed then unscrew the injector(s) and remove them from the cylinder head.

Caution: Ensure you unscrew each injector holder from the cylinder head and remove the complete injector assembly rather than unscrewing the injector body from the holder. If the body is unscrewed from the holder, the small internal components of the injector will be disturbed and it will be necessary to take them to a specialist to have them reassembled and tested prior to refitting.

4 Remove the sealing ring cylinder head and discard; new ones must be used on refitting. **Do not** attempt to dismantle the injectors any further.

5 Testing of the injectors requires the use of special equipment. If any injector is thought to be faulty have it tested and, if necessary, reconditioned by a diesel engine specialist or Vauxhall dealer.

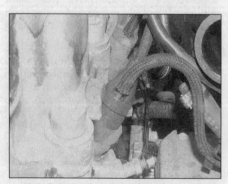

12.1 Pull the leak-back pipes from the injectors

12.2 Using two open-ended spanners, counter-hold the adaptor to prevent it from being unscrewed as the pipe union is unscrewed

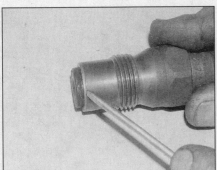

12.6 Fit new sealing washers to the injectors before refitting

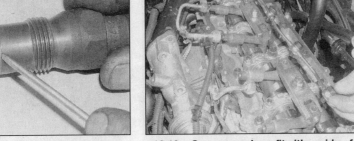

12.10a Copper washers fit either side of the fuel leak-back pipe unions on the injectors . . .

12.10b . . . and the union on the camshaft housing

6 Commence refitting by inserting the sealing rings into the cylinder head **(see illustration)**.
7 Carefully fit the injector(s) and tighten to the specified torque.
8 Refit the injector pipes to the injection pump and injectors, and tighten the union nuts to the specified torque.

1.7 litre DOHC models

9 Remove the camshaft cover as described in Chapter 2B.
10 Undo the five bolts and remove the inner fuel leak-back pipe **(see illustrations)**. Recover the copper washers.
11 Slacken and remove the retaining nuts, and remove the injector clamps **(see illustration)**.
12 Lift the injectors out of the cylinder head. Discard the rubber seals and copper washers, new seals/washers must be fitted prior to reassembly. **Do not** attempt to dismantle the injectors any further.
13 Testing of the injectors requires the use of special equipment. If any injector is thought to be faulty have it tested and, if necessary, reconditioned by a diesel engine specialist or Vauxhall dealer.
14 Commence reassembly by ensuring that the injector and cylinder head mating faces are clean, and fitting new copper sealing washers/rubber seals to each injector. Note

the correct orientation of the copper washers **(see illustration)**.
15 Carefully fit each injector into the cylinder head, and secure them in place by fitting the injector clamps. Tighten the clamps retaining nuts to the specified torque.
16 Refit the inner fuel leak-back pipe to the injectors and the camshaft housing. The larger diameter bolt secures the leak-back pipe to the camshaft housing. Note that new copper washers should be fitted to the top of each injector, and the underside of each bolt. Reconnect the pipe to the camshaft housing using new copper washers. Tighten the bolts to the specified torque.
17 Refit the camshaft cover as described in Chapter 2B.
18 Restart the engine and check for leaks.

2.0 litre models

Note: *If the injector nozzle is to be removed from the cylinder head, it is likely that the special Vauxhall puller (KM-928-B) and adapter (KM-931) will be needed. New injector crossover pipe bolts should be used on refitting.*
19 Remove the upper section of the inlet manifold as described in Section 15.
20 With reference to Chapter 2C, remove the camshaft and followers.
21 Disconnect the return pipe from the injector crossover pipe.

22 Unscrew the retaining bolt then carefully free the crossover pipe from the top of the injector nozzle and ease it from the cylinder head **(see illustration)**.
23 Remove the sealing rings from the crossover pipe and the top of the injector nozzle and discard, new ones must be used on refitting **(see illustration)**.
24 Fit the adapter and puller to the top of the injector nozzle and carefully pull the nozzle squarely out of the top of the cylinder head. Recover the sealing washer which is fitted to the base of the nozzle and discard it.
25 Fit a new sealing washer to the base of the injector nozzle then carefully ease the nozzle into position in the cylinder head,

12.11 The injector clamp washer fits dished with the side facing down

12.14 Note the rubber seal and copper washer

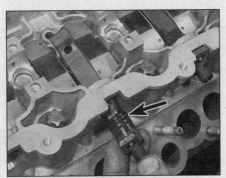

12.22 On 2.0 litre engines, remove the injector crossover pipe from the cylinder head (sealing ring arrowed) . . .

12.23 . . . then remove the sealing ring from the top of the injector nozzle

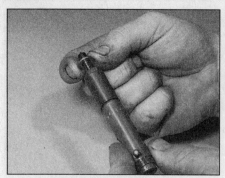

12.25a Fit a new sealing washer to the base of the nozzle . . .

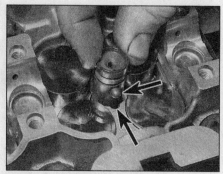

12.25b . . . then refit the nozzle to the cylinder head, aligning its locating pin with the head cut-out (arrowed)

12.27a Tighten the injector crossover pipe bolt as tight as possible by hand . . .

aligning its locating pin with the cylinder head cut-out (see illustrations).

26 Ensure the injector nozzle is pushed fully into the cylinder head then fit a new sealing ring to its upper end.

27 Fit a new sealing ring to the crossover pipe recess. Ease the crossover pipe into position in the cylinder head, seating it correctly on the top of the injector nozzle, fit the new retaining bolt. Tighten the retaining bolt as tight as possible by hand, then using a socket and extension bar, tighten it through a further complete rotation (360º) (see illustrations).

28 Connect the return pipe to the crossover pipe then refit the inlet manifold section as described in Section 15.

29 Refit the camshaft and followers as described in Chapter 2C.

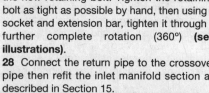

13 Turbocharger – removal and refitting

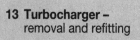

Removal

1 Remove the exhaust manifold and

12.27b . . . then tighten the bolt by one complete turn

turbocharger assembly as described in Section 16 and proceed as described under the relevant sub-heading.

1.7 litre SOHC models

2 With the assembly on the bench, undo the retaining nuts and remove the exhaust connection flange and gasket from the turbocharger (see illustration).

3 Unscrew the union nut and remove the oil feed pipe from the turbocharger (see illustration).

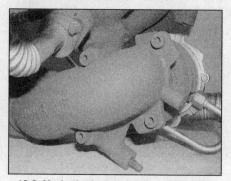

13.2 Undo the bolts and disconnect the exhaust connection flange from the turbocharger

4 Undo the retaining bolts and remove the oil return pipe union and gasket.

5 Slacken and remove the three mounting bolts then remove the turbocharger and gasket from the manifold (see illustration).

6 Do not attempt to dismantle the turbocharger any further. If the unit is thought to be faulty take it to a turbo specialist or Vauxhall dealer for testing and examination. They will be able to inform you if the unit can be overhauled or will need renewing.

13.3 Disconnect the oil feed pipe from the turbocharger

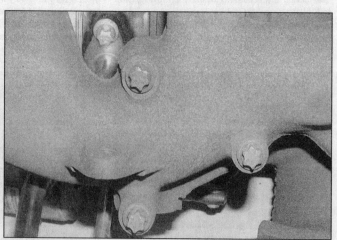

13.5 Remove the three Torx bolts and remove the turbocharger and gasket from the manifold

13.7 Exhaust flange connection nuts

13.8 Turbocharger oil feed pipe union

1.7 litre DOHC models

7 With the assembly on the bench, undo the retaining nuts and remove the exhaust connection flange and gasket from the turbocharger **(see illustration)**.

8 Undo the union nut and remove the oil feed pipe along with the sealing washers which are fitted on each side of the pipe union **(see illustration)**.

9 Unscrew the retaining bolts and remove the oil return pipe union and gasket **(see illustration)**.

10 Slacken and remove the four mounting nuts then remove the turbocharger and gasket from the manifold **(see illustration)**.

11 Do not attempt to dismantle the turbocharger any further. If the unit is thought to be faulty take it to a turbo specialist or Vauxhall dealer for testing and examination. They will be able to inform you if the unit can be overhauled or will need renewing.

2.0 litre models

12 With the assembly on the bench, undo the retaining bolts and remove the exhaust connection flange and gasket from the turbocharger.

13 Unscrew the union bolt and remove the oil feed pipe. Recover the sealing washers fitted on each side of the pipe union.

14 Undo the retaining bolts and remove the oil return pipe and gasket.

15 Slacken and remove the mounting bolts then remove the turbocharger and gasket from the manifold.

16 Do not attempt to dismantle the turbocharger any further. If the unit is thought to be faulty take it to a turbo specialist or Vauxhall dealer for testing and examination. They will be able to inform you if the unit can be overhauled or will need renewing.

Refitting

17 Refitting is the reverse of removal, using new gaskets/sealing washers, and tightening the fasteners to their specified torque settings (where given). Refit the manifold and turbocharger assembly as described in Section 16.

14 Intercooler –
removal and refitting

Removal

1 With reference to Chapter 11, remove the front bumper.

2 Unscrew the six retaining bolts and remove the front cross member (impact absorber).

3 Release the retaining clip and disconnect the turbocharger-to-intercooler pipe from the intercooler.

4 Undo the retaining clip and disconnect the inlet manifold charge air pipe from the intercooler. Lay the pipe to one side.

5 On 1.7 litre SOHC models, unscrew the retaining bolt and detach the oil cooler from the intercooler. Release the oil cooler pipes

fastening clips and pull the oil cooler away from the intercooler. There is no need to disconnect the oil pipes from the cooler.

6 Undo the retaining bolt, and lift the intercooler upwards and out of the bracket.

Refitting

7 Refitting is a reversal of removal.

15 Inlet manifold –
removal and refitting

1.7 litre SOHC models

Note: *New manifold retaining nuts will be required on refitting*

1 Disconnect the battery negative terminal.

Note: *Before disconnecting the battery, refer to 'Disconnecting the battery' in the reference section at the rear of this manual.*

2 With reference to Section 2 if necessary, remove the air cleaner housing and intake ducts, complete with the hot film mass airflow meter.

3 On right-hand drive models, remove the alternator as described in Chapter 5A.

4 Remove the exhaust manifold as described in Section 16.

5 Disconnect the wiring plug from the charge pressure sensor fitted to the inlet manifold **(see illustration 8.19)**.

6 Undo the retaining nuts and remove the inlet manifold and gasket from the cylinder head.

7 Ensure the manifold and cylinder mating surfaces are clean and dry and fit a new gasket over the manifold studs.

8 Refit the manifold and fit the retaining nuts. Working in a diagonal sequence, evenly and progressively tighten the manifold nuts to the specified torque setting.

9 Refit the wiring plug to the charge pressure sensor.

10 Ensure the mating surfaces are clean and dry then refit the exhaust manifold as described in Section 16.

11 On right-hand drive vehicles, refit the alternator as described in Chapter 5A.

12 Refit the air intake ducts and air cleaner housing, complete with the hot film mass airflow meter – refer to Section 2 if necessary.

13 Reconnect the battery.

1.7 litre DOHC models

Note: *New manifold retaining nuts will be required on refitting*

14 Disconnect the battery negative terminal.

Note: *Before disconnecting the battery, refer to 'Disconnecting the battery' in the reference section at the rear of this manual.*

15 Disconnect the two wiring plugs from the engine ECU. The plugs are unlocked by lifting up the metal levers **(see illustration 8.64)**.

16 Undo the retaining bolts/nuts, and remove the ECU.

17 Release the retaining clips and remove

13.9 Turbocharger oil return union

13.10 Undo the nuts and separate the turbocharger from the exhaust manifold

15.26a Remove the rear section of the manifold . . .

15.26b . . . and the front section

15.31a On 2.0 litre engines, slacken and remove the retaining bolts (arrowed) . . .

the intake air ducting from the hot film mass airflow meter-to-the turbocharger inlet pipe.

18 Remove the bolts securing the charge air pipe and bracket to the left-hand end of the camshaft housing, and EGR (exhaust gas recirculation) valve.

19 Unscrew the bolts securing the EGR pipe to the exhaust manifold, and the left-hand end of the camshaft housing. Undo the large union at the EGR valve, and remove the pipe.

20 Undo the unions and remove the fuel injection delivery pipes. We found it necessary to remove the oil cooler housing retaining bolt (Chapter 2B, Section 17) and push the housing to the rear, to allow sufficient access to the rear of the pump. Be prepared for fluid spillage. Due to the high injection pressures,

under no circumstances should the pipes be bent.

21 Disconnect the wiring plug and vacuum hoses from the EGR solenoid valve (refer to Chapter 4B if necessary)

22 Unplug the charge pressure sensor wiring plug.

23 Release the inlet manifold wiring loom from the various retaining clips. Note the routing of the loom.

24 Disconnect the fuel leak-back hose from the leak-back pipe on the top of the inlet manifold and the injection pump.

25 Undo the two retaining bolts and remove the EGR valve from the inlet manifold.

26 Unscrew the fastening nuts and bolts, and remove the inlet manifold rear section and, if necessary, front section **(see illustrations)**.

27 Clean the cylinder head and manifold(s) gasket faces, and fit a new gasket(s) in place.

28 The remainder of the refitting procedure is a reversal of removal, noting the following points:

   a) Tighten all nuts and bolts to the correct torque setting where specified.

   b) Tighten the injector pipe unions to the specified torque, and check them for leaks after starting the engine.

2.0 litre models

Note: New lower manifold section retaining nuts will be required on refitting.

29 Disconnect the battery negative terminal then undo the retaining screws and remove

the plastic cover from the top of the cylinder head. **Note:** Before disconnecting the battery, refer to 'Disconnecting the battery' in the reference section at the rear of this manual.

30 Referring to Section 2, on low-pressure turbo (X20DTL/Y20DTL engines) models remove the metal pipe and duct linking the inlet manifold to the turbocharger, and on high-pressure turbo (Y20DTH engine) models remove the duct linking the manifold to the intercooler.

31 Undo the retaining screws securing the wiring harness tray to the top of the inlet manifold. Disconnect the wiring connectors from the coolant sensors, the fuel injection pump (slide out the retaining clip to release the connector), the crankshaft sensor and the manifold charge pressure sensor then position the tray clear of the manifold **(see illustrations)**.

32 Disconnect the vacuum pipe from the exhaust gas recirculation (EGR) valve on the top of the manifold **(see illustration)**.

33 Wipe clean the pipe unions then slacken the union nuts securing the injector pipes to the injectors, and the four union nuts securing the pipes to the rear of the injection pump; as each pump union nut is slackened, retain the adapter with a suitable open-ended spanner to prevent it being unscrewed from the pump. With all the union nuts undone, remove the injector pipes from the engine unit and mop up any spilt fuel **(see illustrations)**. Seal the pipe end fittings to

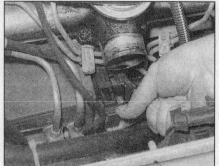

15.31b . . . then disconnect the various wiring connectors and position the wiring harness tray clear of the manifold

15.32 Disconnect the EGR valve vacuum pipe

15.33a Slacken the union nuts securing the injector pipes to the injectors . . .

15.33b . . . and injection pump . . .

15.33c . . . and remove them from the engine

15.34 Slacken and remove the retaining bolts and remove the upper section of the inlet manifold

15.35a Disconnect the vacuum pipe from the manifold switchover valve . . .

15.35b . . . then remove the bolt securing the crankshaft sensor wiring to the manifold lower section

minimise fuel loss and prevent the entry of dirt.

34 Evenly and progressively slacken and remove the retaining bolts then lift off the upper part of the manifold (see illustration). Recover the gasket and discard it.

35 To remove the lower section of the manifold, disconnect the vacuum pipe from the manifold switchover valve diaphragm unit, and unbolt the wiring connector bracket from the manifold. Evenly and progressively slacken and remove the retaining nuts then remove the manifold lower section and gasket from the cylinder head (see illustrations).

36 Ensure the all mating surfaces are clean and dry.

37 Fit a new gasket to the cylinder head then refit the lower manifold section (see illustration). Fit the new retaining nuts and, working in a diagonal sequence, evenly and progressively tighten them to the specified torque setting. Reconnect the switchover valve hose and refit the wiring bracket.

38 Fit a new gasket to the top of the manifold lower section then refit the upper section of the manifold, tightening its retaining bolts to the specified torque.

39 Refit the injector pipes, tightening the union nuts to the specified torque.

40 Refit the wiring harness tray to the top of the manifold, tightening its retaining bolts securely, and reconnect the wiring connectors. Reconnect the vacuum pipe to the EGR valve.

41 Refit the intake duct/pipe (see Section 2) then refit the plastic cover to the cylinder head.

42 Reconnect the battery.

16 Exhaust manifold – removal and refitting

1.7 litre SOHC models

Note: *New manifold retaining nuts will be required on refitting*

1 The exhaust manifold should be removed with the turbocharger. Firmly apply the handbrake then jack up the front of the vehicle so access can be gained both from above and below. Where fitted, unclip/unbolt the undertray and remove it from beneath the engine/transmission unit.

2 Remove the air cleaner housing and intake ducts complete with hot film mass airflow meter – refer to Section 2.

3 On right-hand drive vehicles remove the alternator as described in Chapter 5A.

4 Release the retaining clips, undo the retaining bracket bolts, and remove the air charge pipe from the intercooler to the turbocharger.

5 Slacken the retaining clips, undo the retaining bracket bolt, and remove the duct connecting the intake manifold to the intercooler.

6 Disconnect the wiring plug and vacuum hoses from the EGR (exhaust gas recirculation) valve on the left-hand end of the manifold. Note the fitted locations of the vacuum hoses (see illustration),

7 Undo the two retaining bolts and remove the EGR solenoid valve from the inlet manifold.

8 Unclip the fuel filter from the filter housing and lay to one side. Do not disconnect the fuel pipes.

9 Undo the three retaining screws and remove the turbocharger heat shield.

10 Slacken and remove the four retaining bolts and remove the corrugated metal EGR pipe from the inlet and exhaust

15.35c Unscrew the retaining nuts and remove the inlet manifold lower section from the engine

15.37 On refitting, use a new manifold gasket

16.6 Disconnect the EGR wiring plug and vacuum hose

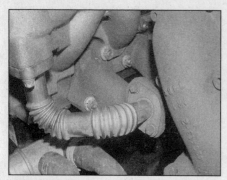

16.10 Slacken and remove the four retaining bolts, and remove the corrugated EGR pipe

16.13 Detach the turbocharger oil return pipe from the upper section of the sump

16.14 Detach the turbocharger oil feed pipe from the cylinder block

manifolds **(see illustration)**. Recover the two gaskets.

11 Undo the two fastening screws and one nut, and remove the starter motor heat shield.

12 Unscrew the retaining bolts and remove the front exhaust pipe.

13 Detach the turbocharger oil return pipe from the upper part of the oil sump. Recover the sealing washers from either side of the union **(see illustration)**. Be prepared for fluid spillage.

14 Undo the union bolt and detach the turbocharger oil feed pipe from the rear face of the cylinder block. Recover the sealing washers from either side of the union **(see illustration)**. Be prepared for fluid spillage.

15 Undo the two bolts and remove the exhaust manifold support bracket from the exhaust manifold to the cylinder block.

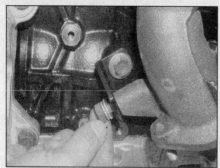

16.25 Unbolt the turbocharger from the cylinder block mounting bracket

16 Slacken the union nut and remove the turbocharger oil feed pipe from the turbocharger **(see illustration 13.8)**.

17 Working in a diagonal sequence, evenly and progressively slacken and remove the exhaust manifold retaining nuts. Manoeuvre the manifold assembly out of position and recover the gasket. If necessary, separate the turbocharger from the manifold as described in Section 13.

18 Refitting is the reverse of removal, noting the following points.

a) *Ensure all mating surfaces are clean and dry and renew all gaskets.*

b) *Tighten the manifold nuts and the support bracket bolts to their specified torque settings.*

c) *Securely reconnect the turbocharger oil and pipes/hoses.*

d) *Refit the intake ducts ensuring then are securely reconnected.*

1.7 litre DOHC models

Note: *New exhaust manifold nuts and bolts will be required on refitting.*

19 The exhaust manifold should be removed with the turbocharger. Firmly apply the handbrake then jack up the front of the vehicle so access can be gained both from above and below. Where necessary, unbolt the undertray and remove it from beneath the engine/transmission unit.

20 Release the air cleaner ducting retaining clips, and the air cleaner housing retaining bolt. Manoeuvre the housing out of the engine compartment.

21 On models equipped with air conditioning, disconnect the compressor wiring plug, remove the compressor mounting bolts, and move the compressor to one side. By unscrewing the air conditioning retaining bracket on the right-hand side inner wing, we were able to position the compressor behind the bonnet stay hinge, and secure it there using cable ties. **Do not** open the refrigerant hoses.

22 Undo the three bolts and remove the air conditioning compressor mounting bracket.

23 Release the retaining clips and remove the turbocharger-to-intercooler hose.

24 Undo the two retaining nuts and separate the front exhaust pipe from the manifold.

25 Unscrew the bolt securing the turbocharger to the cylinder block mounting bracket **(see illustration)**.

26 Slacken and remove the turbocharger oil feed pipe nut from the cylinder block. Recover the copper sealing washers and be prepared for oil spillage **(see illustration)**.

27 Release the retaining clips and disconnect the oil return hose from the turbocharger **(see illustration)**.

28 Disconnect the vacuum hose from the turbocharger wastegate actuator **(see illustration)**.

29 Undo the retaining bolts and remove the exhaust manifold and turbocharger heat shields.

30 Unscrew the bolts securing the oil dipstick guide tube bracket to the cylinder block, and the two bolts securing

16.26 Remove the oil feed pipe from the cylinder block

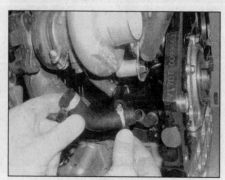

16.27 Disconnect the oil return hose

16.28 Wastegate actuator vacuum pipe

16.30 Remove the oil dipstick guide tube mounting bolt

16.38a Undo the retaining screws (arrowed) . . .

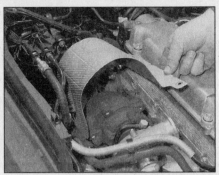

16.38b . . . and remove the heat shields from the manifold assembly

the guide tube to the sump (see illustration).

31 The EGR (exhaust gas recirculation) pipe is mounted at the left-hand end of the manifold. Undo the two retaining bolts, and recover the gasket.

32 Undo the exhaust manifold retaining nuts/bolts, unscrew and remove the two manifold studs, and remove the exhaust manifold.

33 If required, the manifold can now be separated from the turbocharger as described in Section 13.

34 Refitting is the reverse of removal, noting the following points.

a) Ensure all mating surfaces are clean and dry and renew all gaskets/sealing washers.

b) Tighten the manifold nuts and bolts and the support bracket bolts to their specified torque settings.

c) Securely reconnect the turbocharger oil and coolant pipes/hoses.

d) Refit the intake ducts ensuring then are securely reconnected.

e) On completion check and, if necessary,

top-up the oil and coolant levels as described in 'Weekly checks'.

2.0 litre models

Note: New manifold retaining nuts and exhaust front pipe nuts will be required on refitting.

35 Disconnect the battery negative terminal then undo the retaining screws and remove the plastic cover from the top of the cylinder head. Note: Before disconnecting the battery, refer to 'Disconnecting the battery' in the reference section at the rear of this manual. Jack up the front of the vehicle and support it on axle stands. Release the retaining clips/screws and remove the engine undertray (where fitted)

36 Referring to Section 2, remove the air cleaner housing duct assembly and remove the metal pipe linking the turbocharger to the manifold/intercooler duct (as applicable).

37 Disconnect the wiring plug from the top of the each glow plug.

38 Undo the retaining screws and remove the heat shields from the top of the manifold assembly (see illustrations).

39 Undo the nuts securing the exhaust system front pipe to the manifold and free the pipe from the manifold (see illustration).

40 Working underneath the vehicle, undo the retaining bolts and remove the heat shield from the rear of the starter motor.

41 Undo the retaining bolts and remove the wiring harness guide from the rear of the cylinder block.

42 Remove all traces of dirt from around the turbocharger oil feed and return pipe unions. Slacken the union nuts securing the pipes to the cylinder block and allow the oil to drain into a suitable container. Mop up any spilt oil.

43 Slacken and remove the retaining bolts and remove the manifold support bracket. Disconnect the vacuum hose from the turbocharger wastegate diaphragm (see illustration).

44 Working in a diagonal sequence, evenly and progressively slacken and remove the exhaust manifold retaining nuts. Manoeuvre the manifold assembly out of position and recover the gasket (see

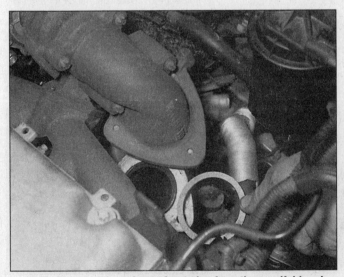

16.39 Separate the exhaust front pipe from the manifold and collect the gasket

16.43 Disconnect the vacuum hose from the turbocharger wastegate

illustrations). If necessary, separate the turbocharger from the manifold as described in Section 13.

45 Refitting is the reverse of removal, noting the following points.

a) *Ensure all mating surfaces are clean and dry and renew all gaskets.*

b) *Fit the new manifold nuts and tighten them evenly and progressively to the specified torque, working in a diagonal sequence. Also tighten the support bracket bolts to the specified torque.*

c) *Tighten the turbocharger oil pipe union nuts to the specified torque.*

d) *Ensure the intake duct and metal pipe are securely reconnected (see Section 2).*

e) *Fit the exhaust front pipe as described in Section 17.*

f) *On completion check and, if necessary, top-up the oil and coolant levels as described in 'Weekly checks'.*

g) *On start the engine for the first time, allow the engine to idle for a few minutes before increasing the engine speed; this will allow oil to be circulated around the turbocharger bearings.*

---

17 Exhaust system – general information, removal and refitting

General information

1 The exhaust system consists of three sections: the front pipe (which incorporates the catalytic converter), the intermediate pipe and the tailpipe. The front pipe is fitted with a flexible section to allow for movement in the exhaust system. The intermediate pipe to tailpipe joint is spring-loaded to allow for movement in the system.

2 The system is suspended throughout its entire length by rubber mountings.

Removal

3 Each exhaust section can be removed individually, or the complete system can be removed as a unit. Even if only one part of the system needs attention, in some cases it will be easier to remove the whole system and separate the sections on the bench.

16.44a Remove the manifold assembly from the engine . . .

4 To remove the system or part of the system, first jack up the front or rear of the car, and support it on axle stands. Alternatively, position the car over an inspection pit, or on car ramps. Where necessary, undo the retaining bolts and remove the undertray from beneath the engine/transmission unit.

Front pipe (incorporating the catalytic converter)

5 Undo the nuts securing the front pipe to the turbocharger. Slacken and remove the bolts securing the front pipe to the intermediate pipe.

6 Free the front pipe from the turbocharger, recovering the gasket, and intermediate pipe then remove it from underneath the vehicle **(see illustration)**.

Intermediate pipe

7 Slacken and remove the bolts securing the intermediate pipe to the front pipe and the bolts and springs securing it to the tailpipe.

8 Release the intermediate pipe from its mounting rubbers **(see illustration)**. Disengage the intermediate pipe from the front pipe and tailpipe and remove it from underneath the vehicle. Recover gasket which is fitted to the tailpipe joint.

Tailpipe

9 Slacken and remove the bolts and springs securing the tailpipe to the intermediate pipe joint **(see illustration)**.

10 Unhook the tailpipe from its mounting rubbers, and free it from the intermediate pipe. Recover the gasket from the joint.

16.44b . . . and remove the gasket

Complete system

11 Slacken and remove the nuts securing the front pipe flange joint to the turbocharger.

12 Free the system from its mounting rubbers and remove it from underneath the vehicle. Recover the gasket from the front pipe joint.

Heat shield(s)

13 The heat shields are secured to the underside of the body by various nuts and bolts. Each shield can be removed once the relevant exhaust section has been removed. If a shield is being removed to gain access to a component located behind it, it may prove sufficient in some cases to remove the retaining nuts and/or bolts, and simply lower the shield, without disturbing the exhaust system.

Refitting

14 Each section is refitted by reversing the removal sequence, noting the following points:

a) *Ensure that all traces of corrosion have been removed from the flanges, and renew all necessary gaskets. Where no gasket is fitted, apply a smear of exhaust system jointing paste to the joint to ensure a gas-tight seal.*

b) *Inspect the rubber mountings for signs of damage or deterioration, and renew as necessary.*

c) *Prior to tightening the exhaust system fasteners, ensure that all rubber mountings are correctly located, and that there is adequate clearance between the exhaust system and vehicle underbody.*

17.6 Free the front pipe from the turbocharger

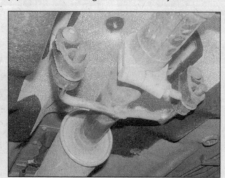
17.8 Release the pipe from the mounting rubbers

17.9 Slacken and remove the bolts and springs securing the intermediate pipe to the tailpipe

Chapter 4 Part B:
Emission control systems

Contents

Degrees of difficulty

Easy, suitable for novice with little experience	**Fairly easy,** suitable for beginner with some experience	**Fairly difficult,** suitable for competent DIY mechanic	**Difficult,** suitable for experienced DIY mechanic	**Very difficult,** suitable for expert DIY or professional

Specifications

Torque wrench settings	Nm	lbf ft
Exhaust gas recirculation (EGR) valve bolts	24	18
Exhaust gas recirculation (EGR) solenoid bolts:		
1.7 litre engines	8	6
2.0 litre engines	4	3
Exhaust gas recirculation (EGR) pipe to intake manifold:		
1.7 litre SOHC engines	8	6
Exhaust gas recirculation (EGR) pipe to camshaft housing/		
cylinder head	8	6
Exhaust gas recirculation (EGR) pipe to exhaust manifold:		
1.7 litre SOHC engines	8	6
1.7 litre DOHC engines	28	21

1 General information

1 All models are also designed to meet strict emission requirements. All models are fitted with a crankcase emission control system and a catalytic converter to keep exhaust emissions down to a minimum. All models are also fitted with an exhaust gas recirculation (EGR) system to further decrease exhaust emissions.

2 The emission control systems function as follows.

Crankcase emission control

3 To reduce the emission of unburned hydrocarbons from the crankcase into the atmosphere, the engine is sealed and the blow-by gases and oil vapour are drawn from inside the crankcase, through a wire mesh oil separator, into the inlet tract to be burned by the engine during normal combustion.

Exhaust emission control

4 To minimise the level of exhaust pollutants released into the atmosphere, a catalytic converter is fitted in the exhaust system.

5 The catalytic converter consists of a canister containing a fine mesh impregnated with a catalyst material, over which the hot exhaust gases pass. The catalyst speeds up the oxidation of harmful carbon monoxide, unburned hydrocarbons and soot, effectively reducing the quantity of harmful products released into the atmosphere via the exhaust gases.

Exhaust gas recirculation (EGR) system

6 This system is designed to recirculate small quantities of exhaust gas into the inlet tract, and therefore into the combustion process. This process reduces the level of unburnt hydrocarbons present in the exhaust gas before it reaches the catalytic converter. The system is controlled by the injection system ECU, using the information from its various sensors, via the EGR valve on the upper section of the inlet manifold. The EGR valve is vacuum-operated and is switched on and off by an electrical solenoid valve.

2 Emission control systems – testing and component renewal

Crankcase emission control

1 The components of this system require no attention other than to check that the hose(s) are clear and undamaged at regular intervals.

Exhaust emission control

Testing

2 The performance of the catalytic converter can be checked only by measuring the exhaust gases using a good-quality, carefully-calibrated exhaust gas analyser.

3 If the catalytic converter is thought to be faulty, before assuming the catalytic converter is faulty, it is worth checking the problem is not due to a faulty injector(s). Refer to your Vauxhall dealer for further information.

Catalytic converter renewal

4 The catalytic converter is an integral part of the exhaust system front pipe. Refer to Chapter 4A for removal and refitting details.

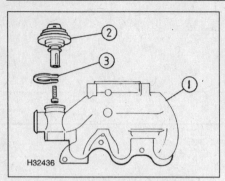

2.7 1.7 litre SOHC engine EGR valve

1 Inlet manifold
2 EGR valve
3 Retaining clip

2.12 Undo the large EGR valve union nut

2.13 EGR valve retaining bolts (arrowed)

Exhaust gas recirculation (EGR) system

Testing

5 Comprehensive testing of the system can only be carried out using specialist electronic equipment which is connected to the injection system diagnostic wiring connector (see Chapter 4A, Section 1). If the EGR or solenoid valves are thought to be faulty, they must be renewed.

Exhaust gas recirculation (EGR) valve – renewal

1.7 litre SOHC engines

6 Release the retaining clips and retaining bracket bolts, and remove the charge air pipe from the intercooler to the turbocharger.
7 Disconnect the vacuum hose from the EGR valve, pull out the retaining clip, and remove the EGR valve from the left-hand end of the inlet manifold (see illustration).
8 Refitting is a reversal of removal.

1.7 litre DOHC engines

9 Remove the engine ECU as described in Chapter 4A, Section 8. Undo the bolts and remove the ECU bracket from above the EGR valve.
10 Disconnect the vacuum pipe from the EGR valve.
11 Undo the bolts and disconnect the inlet pipe from the top of the EGR valve.
12 Using a large open-ended spanner, undo

the union securing the EGR pipe to the valve (see illustration).
13 Slacken and remove the nuts securing the EGR valve to the inlet manifold (see illustration). Note the fitted locations of the bracket(s) also retained by the nuts.
14 If the EGR valve is faulty, it must be renewed.
15 Refitting is a reversal of removal.

2.0 litre engines

16 If the EGR valve is to be renewed, it will be necessary to renew the complete upper section of the inlet manifold (see Chapter 4A). The valve assembly is not available separately and should not be removed from the manifold.

Exhaust gas recirculation (EGR) system solenoid valve – renewal

1.7 litre SOHC engines

17 Disconnect the wiring plug and the vacuum hoses from the EGR solenoid valve on the rear face of the inlet manifold. Note the fitted positions of the vacuum hoses (see illustration).
18 Undo the two retaining bolts and remove the solenoid valve.
19 Refitting is a reversal of removal.

1.7 litre DOHC engines

20 With reference to Chapter 4A, if necessary, remove the air cleaner housing and inlet ducting from the right-hand side of the engine compartment.
21 The EGR solenoid valve is located on the

right-hand side of the inlet manifold. Disconnect the vacuum hoses from the solenoid, noting that the hoses are two different diameters.
22 Disconnect the wiring plug from the solenoid.
23 Unscrew the two retaining bolts and remove the solenoid (see illustration).
24 Refitting is a reversal of removal.

2.0 litre engines

25 The valve is located in the front left-hand corner of the engine compartment. Note that there are two valves: the EGR system valve and the inlet manifold switchover valve; the EGR system valve is the rear-most valve and can be identified by its black wiring connector.
26 Disconnect the wiring connector and vacuum hoses from the valve then undo the retaining screws and remove the valve from its mounting bracket, noting their fitted locations.
27 Refitting is the reverse of removal.

3 Catalytic converter – general information and precautions

1 The catalytic converter is a reliable and simple device which needs no maintenance in itself, but there are some facts of which an owner should be aware if the converter is to function properly for its full service life.

a) DO NOT use fuel or engine oil additives – these may contain substances harmful to the catalytic converter.
b) DO NOT continue to use the car if the engine burns oil to the extent of leaving a visible trail of blue smoke.
c) Remember that the catalytic converter operates at very high temperatures. DO NOT, therefore, park the car in dry undergrowth, over long grass or piles of dead leaves after a long run.
c) Remember that the catalytic converter is FRAGILE – do not strike it with tools during servicing work.
d) The catalytic converter, used on a well-maintained and well-driven car, should last for between 50 000 and 100 000 miles – if the converter is no longer effective it must be renewed.

2.17 EGR solenoid valve

2.23 EGR solenoid valve retaining bolts (arrowed)

Chapter 5 Part A:
Starting and charging systems

Contents

Degrees of difficulty

Easy, suitable for novice with little experience		Fairly easy, suitable for beginner with some experience		Fairly difficult, suitable for competent DIY mechanic	⚒	Difficult, suitable for experienced DIY mechanic	⚒	Very difficult, suitable for expert DIY or professional	⚒

Specifications

System type .... 12-volt, negative earth

Battery
Charge condition:
  Poor .... 12.5 volts
  Normal .... 12.6 volts
  Good .... 12.7 volts

Torque wrench settings

	Nm	lbf ft
Alternator fixings:		
1.7 litre engines:		
Alternator-to-bracket bolts – M10	46	34
Alternator-to-bracket bolts – M8	25	18
Alternator bracket-to-cylinder block bolts	35	26
Alternator locking bolt to tension rail	35	26
2.0 litre engines:		
Alternator to bracket (coolant flange)	35	26
Alternator bracket to cylinder head	20	15
Alternator lower fixing bolt	35	26
Auxiliary drivebelt tensioner mounting bolt:		
1.7 litre SOHC engines	25	18
1.7 litre DOHC engines	50	37
2.0 litre engines:		
Pulley backplate pivot bolt	42	31
Strut mounting bolts	23	17
Auxiliary drivebelt idler pulley mounting bolt	38	28
Oil level sensor bolts	8	6
Oil pressure switch:		
1.7 litre SOHC engines	40	30
1.7 litre DOHC engines	20	15
2.0 litre engines	30	22
Starter motor bolts:		
1.7 litre SOHC engines, lower bolt	45	33
1.7 litre SOHC engines, upper bolt	60	44
1.7 litre DOHC engines	38	28
2.0 litre engine	45	33
Starter heat shield	6	4

1 General information and precautions

General information

1 The engine electrical system consists mainly of the charging and starting systems. Because of their engine-related functions, these components are covered separately from the body electrical devices such as the lights, instruments, etc (which are covered in Chapter 12). Refer to Part B for information on the pre-heating systems.

2 The electrical system is of the 12-volt negative earth type.

3 The battery is of the low maintenance or 'maintenance-free' (sealed for life) type and is charged by the alternator, which is belt-driven from the crankshaft pulley.

4 The starter motor is of the pre-engaged type incorporating an integral solenoid. On starting, the solenoid moves the drive pinion into engagement with the flywheel ring gear before the starter motor is energised. Once the engine has started, a one-way clutch prevents the motor armature being driven by the engine until the pinion disengages from the flywheel.

Precautions

5 Further details of the various systems are given in the relevant Sections of this Chapter. While some repair procedures are given, the usual course of action is to renew the component concerned. The owner whose interest extends beyond mere component renewal should obtain a copy of the *Automobile Electrical & Electronic Systems Manual*, available from the publishers of this manual.

6 It is necessary to take extra care when working on the electrical system to avoid damage to semi-conductor devices (diodes and transistors), and to avoid the risk of personal injury. In addition to the precautions given in *Safety first!* at the beginning of this manual, observe the following when working on the system:

7 *Always remove rings, watches, etc, before working on the electrical system.* Even with the battery disconnected, capacitive discharge could occur if a component's live terminal is earthed through a metal object. This could cause a shock or nasty burn.

8 *Do not reverse the battery connections.* Components such as the alternator, electronic control units, or any other components having semi-conductor circuitry could be irreparably damaged.

9 If the engine is being started using jump leads and a slave battery, connect the batteries *positive-to-positive* and *negative-to-negative* (see *Jump starting*). This also applies when connecting a battery charger.

10 Never disconnect the battery terminals, the alternator, any electrical wiring or any test instruments when the engine is running.

11 Do not allow the engine to turn the alternator when the alternator is not connected.

12 Never 'test' for alternator output by 'flashing' the output lead to earth.

13 Never use an ohmmeter of the type incorporating a hand-cranked generator for circuit or continuity testing.

14 Always ensure that the battery negative lead is disconnected when working on the electrical system.

15 Before using electric-arc welding equipment on the car, disconnect the battery, alternator and components such as the fuel injection/ignition electronic control unit to protect them from the risk of damage.

16 The radio/cassette unit fitted as standard equipment by Vauxhall is equipped with a built-in security code to deter thieves. If the power source to the unit is cut, the anti-theft system will activate. Even if the power source is immediately reconnected, the radio/cassette unit will not function until the correct security code has been entered. Therefore, if you do not know the correct security code for the radio/cassette unit, **do not** disconnect the battery negative terminal of the battery or remove the radio/cassette unit from the vehicle. Refer to *Disconnecting the Battery* in the reference section at the rear of this manual for further information.

2 Electrical fault finding – general information

Refer to Chapter 12.

3 Battery – testing and charging

Testing

Traditional-style and low maintenance battery

1 If the vehicle covers a small annual mileage, it is worthwhile checking the specific gravity of the electrolyte every three months to

3.5 Battery charge condition indicator – 'Delco' type battery

determine the state of charge of the battery. Use a hydrometer to make the check and compare the results with the following table. Note that the specific gravity readings assume an electrolyte temperature of 15°C (60°F); for every 10°C (18°F) below 15°C (60°F) subtract 0.007. For every 10°C (18°F) above 15°C (60°F) add 0.007.

	Ambient temperature above 25°C (77°F)	Ambient temperature below 25°C (77°F)
Fully-charged	1.210 to 1.230	1.270 to 1.290
70% charged	1.170 to 1.190	1.230 to 1.250
Discharged	1.050 to 1.070	1.110 to 1.130

2 If the battery condition is suspect, first check the specific gravity of electrolyte in each cell. A variation of 0.040 or more between any cells indicates loss of electrolyte or deterioration of the internal plates.

3 If the specific gravity variation is 0.040 or more, the battery should be renewed. If the cell variation is satisfactory but the battery is discharged, it should be charged as described later in this Section.

Maintenance-free battery

4 In cases where a 'sealed for life' maintenance-free battery is fitted, topping-up and testing of the electrolyte in each cell is not possible. The condition of the battery can therefore only be tested using a battery condition indicator or a voltmeter.

5 Certain models may be fitted with a 'Delco' type maintenance-free battery, with a built-in charge condition indicator. The indicator is located in the top of the battery casing, and indicates the condition of the battery from its colour **(see illustration)**. If the indicator shows green, then the battery is in a good state of charge. If the indicator turns darker, eventually to black, then the battery requires charging, as described later in this Section. If the indicator shows clear/yellow, then the electrolyte level in the battery is too low to allow further use, and the battery should be renewed. **Do not** attempt to charge, load or jump start a battery when the indicator shows clear/yellow.

All battery types

6 If testing the battery using a voltmeter, connect the voltmeter across the battery and compare the result with those given in the Specifications under 'charge condition'. The test is only accurate if the battery has not been subjected to any kind of charge for the previous six hours. If this is not the case, switch on the headlights for 30 seconds, then wait four to five minutes before testing the battery after switching off the headlights. All other electrical circuits must be switched off, so check that the doors and tailgate are fully shut when making the test.

7 If the voltage reading is less than 12.2 volts, then the battery is discharged, whilst a reading of 12.2 to 12.4 volts indicates a partially discharged condition.

8 If the battery is to be charged, remove it

from the vehicle (Section 4) and charge it as described later in this Section.

Charging

Traditional-style and low maintenance battery

Note: *The following is intended as a guide only. Always refer to the manufacturer's recommendations (often printed on a label attached to the battery) before charging a battery.*

9 Charge the battery at a rate of 3.5 to 4 amps and continue to charge the battery at this rate until no further rise in specific gravity is noted over a four hour period.

10 Alternatively, a trickle charger charging at the rate of 1.5 amps can safely be used overnight.

11 Specially rapid 'boost' charges which are claimed to restore the power of the battery in 1 to 2 hours are not recommended, as they can cause serious damage to the battery plates through overheating.

12 While charging the battery, note that the temperature of the electrolyte should never exceed 37.8°C (100°F).

Maintenance-free battery

Note: *The following is intended as a guide only. Always refer to the manufacturer's recommendations (often printed on a label attached to the battery) before charging a battery.*

13 This battery type takes considerably longer to fully recharge than the standard type, the time taken being dependent on the extent of discharge, but it will take anything up to three days.

14 A constant voltage type charger is required, to be set, when connected, to 13.9 to 14.9 volts with a charger current below 25 amps. Using this method, the battery should be usable within three hours, giving a voltage reading of 12.5 volts, but this is for a partially-discharged battery and, as mentioned, full charging can take considerably longer.

15 If the battery is to be charged from a fully-discharged state (condition reading less than 12.2 volts), have it recharged by your Vauxhall dealer or local automotive electrician, as the charge rate is higher and constant supervision during charging is necessary.

4 Battery – removal and refitting

Note: *Before disconnecting the battery, refer to 'Disconnecting the battery' in the reference section at the rear of this manual.*

Removal

1 The battery is located on the left-hand side of the engine compartment. On some models the battery will be housed in a protective casing.

2 Unclip the cover (where fitted) then slacken the clamp nut and disconnect the clamp from the battery negative (earth) terminal **(see illustration)**. **Note:** *The battery must be disconnected within 15 seconds of the ignition switch being turned off, otherwise the alarm system will activate.*

3 Lift the insulation cover and disconnect the positive terminal lead in the same way **(see illustration)**.

4 Unscrew the bolt and remove the battery retaining clamp and lift the battery out of the engine compartment **(see illustration)**.

5 If necessary, unbolt the mounting tray and remove it from the engine compartment, freeing all the relevant wiring from its retaining clips **(see illustration)**.

Refitting

6 Refitting is a reversal of removal, but smear petroleum jelly on the terminals when reconnecting the leads, and always reconnect the positive lead first, and the negative lead last.

5 Charging system – testing

Note: *Refer to the warnings given in 'Safety first!' and in Section 1 of this Chapter before starting work.*

1 If the ignition warning light fails to illuminate when the ignition is switched on, first check

4.2 Disconnect the battery negative terminal

4.4 Unscrew the bolt and remove the battery retaining clamp

the alternator wiring connections for security. If satisfactory, check that the warning light bulb has not blown, and that the bulbholder is secure in its location in the instrument panel. If the light still fails to illuminate, check the continuity of the warning light feed wire from the alternator to the bulbholder. If all is satisfactory, the alternator is at fault and should be renewed or taken to an auto-electrician for testing and repair.

2 If the ignition warning light illuminates when the engine is running, stop the engine and check that the drivebelt is correctly tensioned (see Chapter 1) and that the alternator connections are secure. If all is so far satisfactory, have the alternator checked by an auto-electrician for testing and repair.

3 If the alternator output is suspect even though the warning light functions correctly, the regulated voltage may be checked as follows.

4 Connect a voltmeter across the battery terminals and start the engine.

5 Increase the engine speed until the voltmeter reading remains steady; the reading should be approximately 12 to 13 volts, and no more than 14 volts.

6 Switch on as many electrical accessories (eg, the headlights, heated rear window and heater blower) as possible, and check that the alternator maintains the regulated voltage at around 13 to 14 volts.

7 If the regulated voltage is not as stated, the fault may be due to worn brushes, weak brush springs, a faulty voltage regulator, a faulty

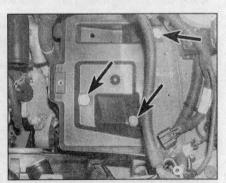

4.3 Disconnect the positive terminal

4.5 Undo the three bolts and remove the battery mounting tray (arrowed)

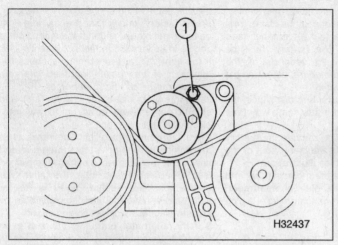

7.5 Turn the bolt head (1) clockwise to relieve the tension

7.13 Remove the auxiliary drivebelt idler pulley retaining bolt (arrowed)

diode, a severed phase winding or worn or damaged slip-rings. The alternator should be renewed or taken to an auto-electrician for testing and repair.

6 Alternator drivebelt – removal, refitting and tensioning

1 Refer to the procedure given for the auxiliary drivebelt(s) in Chapter 1.

7 Alternator drivebelt tensioner – removal and refitting

1.7 litre SOHC engines

Removal

1 Only models equipped with air conditioning are fitted with an alternator (or auxiliary) belt tensioner. On non-air conditioned models, the drivebelt is tensioned by the position of the alternator – see Chapter 1.
2 Firmly apply the handbrake then jack up the front of the vehicle and support it securely on axle stands. Remove the right-hand front roadwheel and undo the retaining

7.15 Align the tensioner with the support bracket

screws/clips and remove the undertray from beneath the engine/transmission unit.
3 With reference to Chapter 4A, remove the air cleaner housing, and air intake ducts complete with hot film mass airflow meter.
4 If the drivebelt is to be re-used, mark the direction of travel to ensure the belt is refitted the same way around.
5 Release the tension by turning the bolt head on the tensioner clockwise **(see illustration)**.
6 Lift the drivebelt from the pulleys.
7 Undo the retaining bolts and remove the tensioner assembly from the compressor support bracket. Further dismantling of the tensioner is not recommended.

Refitting

8 Align the tensioner assembly with the compressor support bracket. Fit and tighten the retaining bolts to the specified torque.
9 Hold the tensioner against the spring pressure and refit the drivebelt around the pulleys (refer to Chapter 1 if necessary).
10 Refit the engine undertray and the roadwheel. Lower the vehicle to the ground.

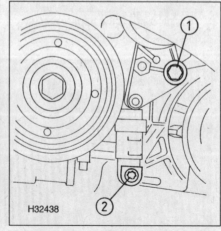

7.21 Undo the tensioner retaining bolt (1) and the tensioning strut mounting bolt (2)

1.7 litre DOHC engines

Removal

11 If the drive belt is to be re-used, mark the direction of travel to ensure the belt is refitted the same way around.
12 Hold the tensioner arm against the spring pressure, and lift the drivebelt from the pulleys. Refer to Chapter 1 if necessary.
13 Unscrew the auxiliary drivebelt idler pulley retaining bolt and remove the pulley **(see illustration)**.
14 Undo the central mounting bolt, and remove the tensioner assembly from the alternator support bracket. Further dismantling of the tensioner assembly is not recommended.

Refitting

15 Align the tensioner assembly with the alternator support bracket. Tighten the tensioner central mounting bolt to the specified torque **(see illustration)**.
16 Refit the auxiliary drivebelt idler pulley to the support bracket, and tighten the retaining bolt to the specified torque.
17 Hold the tensioner against the spring pressure, and refit the drivebelt around the pulleys (refer to Chapter 1 if necessary).
18 Refit the engine undertray and the roadwheel. Lower the vehicle to the ground.

2.0 litre engines

19 With reference to Chapter 4A if necessary, remove the air cleaner housing and intake ducting complete with hot film mass airflow meter.
20 Remove the auxiliary drivebelt as described in Chapter 1.
21 Unscrew the tensioner retaining bolt, and the lower tensioning strut mounting bolt **(see illustration)**.
22 Refit the tensioner and strut, tightening the retaining bolts to the specified torque.
23 Hold the tensioner against the spring pressure, and refit the drivebelt around the pulleys (refer to Chapter 1 if necessary).
24 Refit the air cleaner housing and intake ducting as described in Chapter 4A.

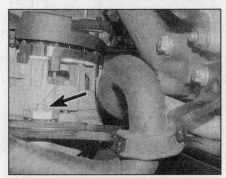

8.4 Undo the tension rail locking nut (arrowed) and remove it along with the adjusting nut

8.7 Lower alternator support bracket

8.11 Disconnect the wiring plug and unbolt the wiring connector (arrowed)

8 Alternator – removal and refitting

Removal

1 Firmly apply the handbrake then jack up the front of the vehicle and support it securely on axle stands undo the retaining bolts/clips and remove the undertray from beneath the engine/transmission unit. Disconnect the battery negative lead and proceed as described under the relevant sub-heading. **Note:** *Before disconnecting the battery, refer to 'Disconnecting the battery' in the reference section at the rear of this manual.*

1.7 litre SOHC engine

2 Remove the air cleaner housing and intake duct complete with hot film mass airflow meter (see Chapter 4A).
3 Release the auxiliary drivebelt as described in Chapter 1 and disengage it from the alternator pulley. Slacken and remove the mounting bolts and remove the support bracket from the alternator to the inlet manifold.
4 On models without air conditioning, undo the tension rail locking bolt and remove it along with the adjusting nut **(see illustration)**. Undo the retaining bolt and remove the tension rail from the cylinder head.
5 On models with air conditioning, unscrew

the retaining bolts and release the alternator top mounting.
6 Remove the rubber covers (where fitted) from the alternator terminals, then unscrew the retaining nuts and disconnect the wiring from the rear of the alternator.
7 Slacken and remove the lower alternator support bracket-to-cylinder block retaining bolts, and manoeuvre the alternator upwards and out of position **(see illustration)**. If required the alternator can be separated from the support bracket by unscrewing the nut and withdrawing the support-to-alternator bolt.

1.7 litre DOHC engine

8 Push the auxiliary drivebelt tensioner against the spring pressure, and disengage the belt from the pulleys (refer to Chapter 1 if necessary)
9 Undo the retaining screws/clips and remove the undertray from beneath the engine/transmission unit.
10 Unscrew the retaining bolts, disconnect the wiring plugs and remove the horn(s). Refer to Chapter 12 if necessary.
11 Disconnect the wiring plug and unbolt the electrical connection to the alternator **(see illustration)**.
12 Unscrew the oil feed pipe to the vacuum pump on the rear of the alternator, and unclip the oil return pipe. Be prepared for fluid spillage **(see illustration)**.
13 Detach the EGR solenoid and servo vacuum pipes from the vacuum pump.

14 Unscrew the upper and lower alternator mounting bolts, and manoeuvre the alternator, complete with vacuum pump, out through the aperture created by removing the horn(s) **(see illustrations)**.
15 Although it is possible to separate the alternator from the vacuum pump, at the time of writing no replacement parts were available. Consult your Vauxhall dealer prior to any repair attempt **(see illustration)**.

2.0 litre engine

16 With reference to Chapter 4A if necessary, remove the air cleaner housing and intake ducting complete with hot film mass airflow meter.
17 Push the auxiliary drivebelt tensioner against the spring pressure, and disengage

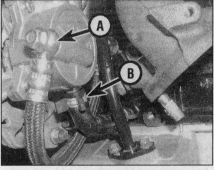

8.12 Vacuum pump oil feed pipe (A) and return pipe (B)

8.14a Alternator upper mounting bolt . . .

8.14b . . . and lower mounting bolt

8.15 Consult your Vauxhall dealer before dismantling the vacuum pump

8.18 Alternator wiring connections (arrowed) – viewed from underneath the vehicle

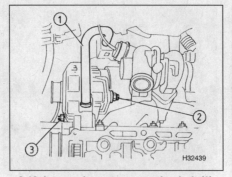

8.19 Lower alternator mounting bolt (3), upper mounting bolt (2), and coolant hose (1)

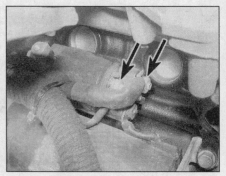

10.6 Disconnect the wiring from the starter solenoid (arrowed)

the belt from the pulleys (refer to Chapter 1 if necessary)

18 Unscrew the three bolts securing the rear wiring trough, and disconnect the wiring connections from the alternator **(see illustration)**.

19 Remove the starter motor and turbocharger heatshields, and slacken the lower alternator retaining bolt **(see illustration)**.

20 Disconnect the vacuum pipe and wiring plug, and remove the turbocharger wastegate solenoid valve as described in Chapter 4A, Section 8.

21 Unscrew the nut and remove the upper alternator retaining bolt **(see illustration 8.19)**.

22 Drain the cooling system as described in Chapter 1, or be prepared for coolant spillage. Disconnect the coolant flange from the right-hand end of the cylinder head.

23 Remove the lower retaining bolt, and remove the alternator upwards and out of the engine compartment.

Refitting

24 Refitting is the reverse of removal tightening all mounting bolts to their specified torque settings (where given). Ensure the drivebelt is correctly refitted and tensioned as described in Chapter 1.

9 Starting system – testing

Note: *Refer to the precautions given in 'Safety first!' and in Section 1 of this Chapter before starting work.*

1 If the starter motor fails to operate when the ignition key is turned to the appropriate position, the following possible causes may be to blame.
  a) *The battery is faulty.*
  b) *The electrical connections between the switch, solenoid, battery and starter motor are somewhere failing to pass the necessary current from the battery through the starter to earth.*

  c) *The solenoid is faulty.*
  d) *The starter motor is mechanically or electrically defective.*

2 To check the battery, switch on the headlights. If they dim after a few seconds, this indicates that the battery is discharged – recharge (see Section 3) or renew the battery. If the headlights glow brightly, operate the ignition switch and observe the lights. If they dim, then this indicates that current is reaching the starter motor, therefore the fault must lie in the starter motor. If the lights continue to glow brightly (and no clicking sound can be heard from the starter motor solenoid), this indicates that there is a fault in the circuit or solenoid – see following paragraphs. If the starter motor turns slowly when operated, but the battery is in good condition, then this indicates that either the starter motor is faulty, or there is considerable resistance somewhere in the circuit.

3 If a fault in the circuit is suspected, disconnect the battery leads (including the earth connection to the body), the starter /solenoid wiring and the engine/transmission earth strap. Thoroughly clean the connections, and reconnect the leads and wiring, then use a voltmeter or test lamp to check that full battery voltage is available at the battery positive lead connection to the solenoid, and that the earth is sound. Smear petroleum jelly around the battery terminals to prevent corrosion – corroded connections are amongst the most frequent causes of electrical system faults.

4 If the battery and all connections are in good condition, check the circuit by disconnecting the wire from the solenoid blade terminal. Connect a voltmeter or test lamp between the wire end and a good earth (such as the battery negative terminal), and check that the wire is live when the ignition switch is turned to the 'start' position. If it is, then the circuit is sound – if not the circuit wiring can be checked as described in Chapter 12.

5 The solenoid contacts can be checked by connecting a voltmeter or test lamp between the battery positive feed connection on the

starter side of the solenoid, and earth. When the ignition switch is turned to the 'start' position, there should be a reading or lighted bulb, as applicable. If there is no reading or lighted bulb, the solenoid is faulty and should be renewed.

6 If the circuit and solenoid are proved sound, the fault must lie in the starter motor. In this event, it may be possible to have the starter motor overhauled by a specialist, but check on the cost of spares before proceeding, as it may prove more economical to obtain a new or exchange motor.

10 Starter motor – removal and refitting

Removal

1 Disconnect the battery negative lead, then firmly apply the handbrake then jack up the front of the vehicle and support it on axle stands. Where necessary, undo the retaining bolts/clips and remove the undertray from beneath the engine/transmission unit. Proceed as described under the relevant sub-heading. **Note:** *Before disconnecting the battery, refer to 'Disconnecting the battery' in the reference section at the rear of this manual.*

1.7 litre SOHC engine

2 With reference to Chapter 4A, remove the air cleaner housing, and air intake ducts complete with hot film mass airflow meter.

3 With reference to Chapter 1, remove the auxiliary drivebelt.

4 On right-hand drive models, remove the alternator as described in Section 8.

5 Remove the exhaust manifold as described in Chapter 4A.

6 Disconnect the wiring connections from the starter motor solenoid **(see illustration)**.

7 Unscrew the upper starter motor mounting bolt from the transmission side.

8 Slacken and remove the lower retaining bolt from the engine side, then manoeuvre the

10.8 Unscrew the lower starter motor retaining bolt

10.10 Unscrew the bolts and remove the atmospheric pressure sensor bracket (arrowed)

10.11 Disconnect the starter solenoid wiring connections (arrowed)

starter motor upwards from above the engine **(see illustration)**.

1.7 litre DOHC engine

9 Detach the oil filter housing-to-cylinder block oil return hose from the rear of the engine. Be prepared for fluid spillage.
10 With reference to Chapter 4A, Section 8, remove the atmospheric pressure sensor. Undo the retaining bolts and remove the atmospheric pressure sensor bracket from the injection ECU bracket **(see illustration)**.
11 Slacken and remove the retaining nut and screw, and disconnect the wiring from the starter motor solenoid. Recover the washers under the nut **(see illustration)**.
12 Unscrew the retaining nut and disconnect the earth lead from the starter motor lower bolt.
13 Slacken and remove the retaining bolts, then manoeuvre the starter motor out from underneath the engine. Note the dissimilar lengths of the securing bolts – the lower bolt is the longer **(see illustration)**.

2.0 litre engine

14 Where fitted, release the retaining clips/screws and remove the engine undertray.
15 Undo the two bolts and remove the starter heat shield.
16 Unscrew the wiring trough retaining bolts at the back of the cylinder block **(see illustration)**.
17 Slacken and remove the retaining bolts and remove the exhaust manifold/starter motor support bracket **(see illustration 10.16)**.
18 Slacken and remove the two retaining nuts and disconnect the wiring from the starter motor solenoid **(see illustration 10.16)**. Recover the washers under the nuts.
19 Undo the three retaining bolts and remove the turbocharger heat shield.
20 Unscrew the starter motor retaining bolts. The lower bolt is removed from the right-hand side, whilst the upper bolt is removed from the transmission side **(see illustration 10.16)**. Remove the starter motor upwards and out of the engine compartment.

Refitting

21 Refitting is a reversal of removal tightening the retaining bolts to the specified

torque, where given. Ensure all wiring is correctly routed and its retaining nuts are securely tightened.

11 Starter motor – testing and overhaul

1 If the starter motor is thought to be suspect, it should be removed from the vehicle and taken to an auto-electrician for testing. Most auto-electricians will be able to supply and fit brushes at a reasonable cost. However, check on the cost of repairs before proceeding as it may prove more economical to obtain a new or exchange motor.

12 Ignition switch – removal and refitting

1 The ignition switch is integral with the steering column lock, and can be removed as described in Chapter 14, Section 4.

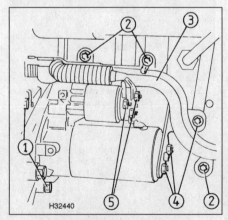

10.16 Starter motor fixings

1   Starter motor retaining bolts
2   Wiring trough retaining bolts
3   Wiring trough
4   Starter bracket and exhaust manifold
    support bolts
5   Starter wiring connections

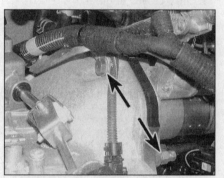

10.13 Slacken and remove the starter motor retaining bolts (arrowed)

13 Oil pressure warning light switch – removal and refitting

Removal

1.7 litre SOHC engines

1 The switch is screwed into the rear of the oil pump housing. Undo the retaining clips/bolts and remove the engine undertray.
2 Disconnect the wiring plug from the switch.
3 Unscrew the switch. Be prepared for oil spillage, and if the switch is to be left removed from the engine for any length of time, plug the switch aperture **(see illustration)**.

13.3 Oil pressure warning light switch – 1.7 litre SOHC engines

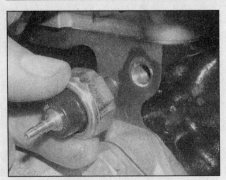

**13.5 Oil pressure warning light switch –
1.7 litre DOHC engines**

1.7 litre DOHC engines

4 The switch is screwed into the left-hand end of the cylinder block, below and slightly to the rear of the thermostat housing. To improve access to the switch, remove the battery and battery tray as described in Section 4.

5 Disconnect the wiring connector by pulling, then unscrew the switch. Be prepared for oil spillage, and if the switch is to be left removed from the engine for any length of time, plug the switch aperture **(see illustration)**.

2.0 litre engines

6 Where fitted, release the retaining clips/ screws and remove the engine undertray.

7 The switch is located on the rear of the cylinder block, above the right-hand driveshaft. Disconnect the wiring plug.

8 Unscrew the switch from the cylinder block.

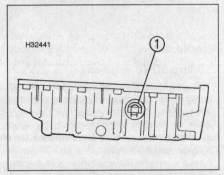

14.5 Secure the oil level sensor connector using the retaining ring (1)

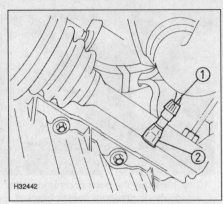

13.8 Oil pressure warning light switch (2) and wiring connector (1) – 2.0 litre engines

Be prepared for oil spillage, and if the switch is to be left removed from the engine for any length of time, plug the switch aperture **(see illustration)**.

Refitting

9 Apply a few drops of locking compound to the threads of the switch.

10 Refit the switch, tightening it to the specified torque, and reconnect the wiring connector.

11 1.7 litre SOHC engines: Refit the engine undertray.

12 1.7 litre DOHC engines: With reference to Section 4, refit the battery and tray.

13 2.0 litre engines: Refit the engine undertray.

14 Check and, if necessary, top up the engine oil as described in *Weekly checks*.

15.3 Unscrew the oil temperature sensor from the sump

14 Oil level sensor –
removal and refitting

Removal

1 The oil level sensor (where fitted) is located inside the sump which must first be removed (see Chapter 2C)

2 Prise off the retaining ring, and push the sensor connector back into the sump.

3 Undo the bolts and remove the sensor from the sump.

Refitting

4 Reattach the oil level sensor to the sump and tighten the retaining bolts to the specified torque.

5 With a new sealing ring fitted, engage the sensor connector in the hole in the sump. Secure the connector in place with the retaining ring **(see illustration)**.

6 Refit the sump as described in Chapter 2C.

15 Oil temperature sensor –
removal and refitting

Removal

1 Where fitted, release the retaining clips/screws and remove the engine undertray.

2 Undo the sump plug and drain the engine oil as described in Chapter 1.

3 The sensor (where fitted) is located at the front of the sump. Disconnect the wiring plug from the sensor.

4 Unscrew the sensor from the sump **(see illustration)**.

Refitting

5 With a new sealing ring fitted, apply a few drops of locking compound to the threads of the sensor, securely refit the sensor to the sump. Take care not to overtighten.

6 Reconnect the sensor wiring plug.

7 Refit the engine undertray.

8 On completion refill the engine with oil (see Chapter 1).

Chapter 5 Part B:
Pre-heating system

Contents

Degrees of difficulty

Easy, suitable for novice with little experience	**Fairly easy,** suitable for beginner with some experience	**Fairly difficult,** suitable for competent DIY mechanic 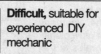	**Difficult,** suitable for experienced DIY mechanic	**Very difficult,** suitable for expert DIY or professional

Specifications

Pre-heating system

Glow plugs:
1.7 litre SOHC engines	Bosch 0 250 201 039
2.0 litre engines	Bosch 0 250 202 042

Torque wrench settings	**Nm**	**lbf ft**
Glow plugs:		
1.7 litre engines	20	15
2.0 litre engines	10	7

---

1 Pre-heating system – description and testing

Description

1 Each cylinder of the engine is fitted with a heater plug (commonly called a glow plug) screwed into it. The plugs are electrically-operated before and during start-up when the engine is cold. Electrical feed to the glow plugs is controlled via the pre-heating system control unit (1.7 litre and 2.0 litre Y20DTL engines) or the injection system ECU (2.0 litre except for Y20DTL engine).

2 A warning light in the instrument panel tells the driver that pre-heating is taking place. When the light goes out, the engine is ready to be started. The voltage supply to the glow plugs continues for several seconds after the light goes out. If no attempt is made to start, the timer then cuts off the supply, in order to avoid draining the battery and overheating the glow plugs.

3 The glow plugs also provide a 'post-heating' function, whereby the glow plugs remain switched on for a period after the engine has started. The length of time 'post-heating' takes place for is also determined by the control unit, and is anything up to 6 minutes, depending on engine temperature.

4 The fuel filter is also fitted with a heating element to prevent the fuel 'waxing' in extreme conditions and to improve combustion. The heating element is fitted between the filter and its housing and is controlled by the pre-heating system control unit via the temperature switch on the filter housing. The heating element is switched on if the temperature of the fuel passing through the filter is less than 5°C (41°F) and switches off when the fuel temperature reaches 16°C (61°F).

Testing

5 If the system malfunctions, testing is ultimately by substitution of known good units, but some preliminary checks may be made as follows.

6 Connect a voltmeter or 12-volt test lamp between the glow plug supply cable and earth (engine or vehicle metal). Make sure that the live connection is kept clear of the engine and bodywork.

7 Have an assistant switch on the ignition, and check that voltage is applied to the glow plugs. Note the time for which the warning light is lit, and the total time for which voltage is applied before the system cuts out. Switch off the ignition.

8 At an underbonnet temperature of 20°C (68°F), typical times noted should be approximately 3 seconds for warning light operation. Warning light time will increase with lower temperatures and decrease with higher temperatures.

9 If there is no supply at all, the control unit or associated wiring is at fault.

10 To locate a defective glow plug, slacken and remove the nuts and washers (where fitted) then disconnect the main supply lead(s) and the electrical supply rail from the plugs. On later models simply pull off the wiring connector from each plug

11 Use a continuity tester, or a 12-volt test lamp connected to the battery positive terminal, to check for continuity between each glow plug terminal and earth. The resistance of a glow plug in good condition is very low (less than 1 ohm), so if the test lamp does not light or the continuity tester shows a high resistance, the glow plug is certainly defective.

12 If an ammeter is available, the current draw of each glow plug can be checked. After an initial surge of 15 to 20 amps, each plug should draw 12 amps. Any plug which draws much more or less than this is probably defective.

13 As a final check, the glow plugs can be removed and inspected as described in the following Section.

2 Glow plugs – removal, inspection and refitting

Caution: If the pre-heating system has just been energised, or if the engine has been running, the glow plugs will be very hot.

Removal

Note: Before disconnecting the battery, refer to 'Disconnecting the battery' in the reference section at the rear of this manual.

1.7 litre SOHC engines

1 Disconnect the battery negative lead.

2 Slacken the nuts securing the electrical supply to the 2nd and 3rd cylinder glow plugs, and the nuts securing the supply rail s to the 1st and 4th cylinder glow plugs. Disengage the rails from the glow plugs.

3 Unscrew the glow plug(s) and remove from the cylinder head **(see illustration)**.

1.7 litre DOHC engines

4 Remove the engine ECU and mounting bracket, with reference to Chapter 4A, Section 8.

5 Disconnect the glow plugs by squeezing the connectors with thumb and forefinger, and pulling the connectors from the plugs.

6 Unscrew the glow plug(s) and remove them from the cylinder head **(see illustration)**.

2.0 litre engines

7 Disconnect the battery negative lead. On high-pressure turbo models (Y20DTH) release the retaining clips/screws and remove the charge air pipe from the turbocharger above the exhaust manifold.

8 On early models undo the retaining nuts and washers from the top of each glow plug then disconnect the wiring connectors and lift off the electrical connecting rails **(see illustrations)**. On later models simply disconnect the connector from the top of the each glow plug.

2.3 Unscrew the glow plug from the cylinder head – 1.7 litre SOHC engine

9 Unscrew the glow plug(s) and remove them from the cylinder head.

Inspection

10 Inspect each glow plug for physical damage. Burnt or eroded glow plug tips can be caused by a bad injector spray pattern. Have the injectors checked if this sort of damage is found.

11 If the glow plugs are in good physical condition, check them electrically using a 12-volt test lamp or continuity tester as described in the previous Section.

12 The glow plugs can be energised by applying 12 volts to them to verify that they heat up evenly and in the required time. Observe the following precautions.

a) Support the glow plug by clamping it carefully in a vice or self-locking pliers. Remember it will become red-hot.

b) Make sure that the power supply or test lead incorporates a fuse or overload trip to protect against damage from a short-circuit.

c) After testing, allow the glow plug to cool for several minutes before attempting to handle it.

13 A glow plug in good condition will start to glow red at the tip after drawing current for 5 seconds or so. Any plug which takes much longer to start glowing, or which starts glowing in the middle instead of at the tip, is defective.

Refitting

1.7 litre SOHC engines

14 Carefully refit the plug(s) and tighten to

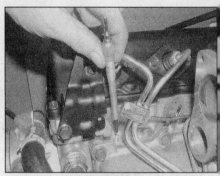

2.6 Remove the glow plug from the cylinder head – 1.7 litre DOHC engine

the specified torque. Do not overtighten, as this can damage the glow plug element.

15 Ease the electrical supply rails into position, ensuring each is correctly engaged with two of the four glow plugs, and securely tighten the 1st and 4th cylinder glow plug nuts.

16 Refit the electrical supply cables to the 2nd and 3rd cylinder glow plugs and securely tighten the glow plug nuts.

17 Reconnect the battery.

1.7 litre DOHC engines

18 Carefully refit the plug(s) and tighten to the specified torque. Do not overtighten, as this can damage the glow plug element.

19 Push the electrical connectors firmly onto the glow plug(s).

20 With reference to Chapter 4A, Section 8, refit the engine ECU, bracket and air cleaner trunking. Check the operation of the glow plugs.

2.0 litre engines

21 Carefully refit the plug(s) and tighten to the specified torque. Do not overtighten, as this can damage the glow plug element.

22 On early models, refit the supply rail(s) to the glow plugs, reconnect the wiring connector(s) then refit the washers and retaining nuts and tighten securely. On later models reconnect the connectors securely to the plugs.

23 Refit the metal pipe (where removed) to the turbocharger/duct then reconnect the battery and check the operation of the glow plugs.

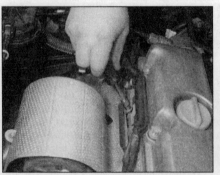

2.8a On 2.0 litre models, unscrew the retaining nut from each glow plug . . .

2.8b . . . then disconnect the wiring . . .

2.8c . . . and lift off the electrical connecting rails

3 Pre-heating system components – removal and refitting

Pre-heating system control unit

1.7 litre and 2.0 litre low-pressure turbo engines

1 The unit is located on the left-hand side of the engine compartment where it is mounted onto the left-hand side of the battery tray.
2 Disconnect the battery negative lead.
3 Slide the control unit up and off the battery tray.
4 Disconnect the wiring connector from the base of the unit. Remove the unit from the engine compartment **(see illustration)**.
5 Refitting is a reversal of removal.

2.0 litre high-pressure turbo engines

6 The operation of the pre-heating system is controlled by the injection system ECU and its sensors. Refer to Chapter 4A, Section 8, for further information.

Coolant temperature switch

7 The coolant temperature switch is screwed into the thermostat housing. Refer to Chapter 3, Section 7, for removal and refitting details.

Fuel filter heating element

8 Prior to attempting any repair procedure, check spares availability with your Vauxhall dealer. Remove the fuel filter as described in Chapter 1. If the filter is damaged on removal (which is likely), a new one should be used on refitting.
9 Disconnect the battery negative terminal then disconnect the wiring connector from the heating element.
10 Unscrew the centre bolt and remove the heating element from the filter housing. Recover the sealing ring and discard, a new one should be used on refitting.
11 Fit a new sealing ring the heating element recess then refit the element to the filter housing and securely tighten the centre bolt.
12 Reconnect the battery then fit the fuel filter as described in Chapter 1.

Fuel filter heating element temperature switch

13 Prior to attempting any repair procedure, check spares availability with your Vauxhall dealer. Disconnect the battery negative terminal then disconnect the wiring connector from the temperature switch which is screwed into the fuel filter housing.
14 Position a wad of rag beneath the filter

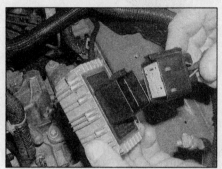

3.4 Disconnect the glow plug ECU

housing to catch any spilt fuel then unscrew the switch and remove it from the housing. Plug the housing aperture to prevent the entry of dirt and minimise fuel loss. Remove the sealing ring from the switch and renew them.
15 Fit new sealing rings to the switch recesses then refit the switch to the filter housing and tighten securely. Reconnect the wiring connector to the switch then reconnect the battery.

Relays and fuses

16 The fuel heating element relays and fuses are located in the box in the engine compartment. Refer to Chapter 12 for further details.

Chapter 6
Clutch

Contents

Degrees of difficulty

| Easy, suitable for novice with little experience | | Fairly easy, suitable for beginner with some experience | | Fairly difficult, suitable for competent DIY mechanic | | Difficult, suitable for experienced DIY mechanic | | Very difficult, suitable for expert DIY or professional | |

Specifications

Type .... Single dry plate with diaphragm spring, hydraulically-operated

Friction disc
Diameter:
1.7 litre SOHC engines	200 mm
1.7 litre DOHC engines	205 mm
2.0 litre engines	228 mm
New lining thickness	7.65 mm

Torque wrench settings	Nm	lbf ft
Hydraulic pipe union nut	14	10
Master cylinder retaining nuts*	20	15
Pedal mounting bracket nuts*	20	15
Pedal mounting bracket-to-steering crossmember bolts/nut	20	15
Pressure plate retaining bolts*	15	11
Release cylinder mounting bolts	5	4

*Use new bolts/nuts

1 General information

1 The clutch consists of a friction disc, a pressure plate assembly, and the hydraulic release cylinder (which incorporates the release bearing); all of these components are contained in the large cast-aluminium alloy bellhousing, sandwiched between the engine and the transmission **(see illustration)**.

2 The friction disc is fitted between the engine flywheel and the clutch pressure plate, and is allowed to slide on the transmission input shaft splines.

3 The pressure plate assembly is bolted to the engine flywheel. When the engine is running, drive is transmitted from the crankshaft, via the flywheel, to the friction disc (these components being clamped securely together by the pressure plate assembly) and from the friction disc to the transmission input shaft.

4 To interrupt the drive, the spring pressure must be relaxed. This is achieved using a hydraulic release mechanism which consists of the master cylinder, the release cylinder and the pipe/hose linking the two components. Depressing the pedal pushes on

the master cylinder pushrod which hydraulically forces the release cylinder piston against the pressure plate spring fingers. This causes the springs to deform and releases the clamping force on the friction disc.

5 The clutch is self-adjusting and requires no manual adjustment.

2 Clutch hydraulic system – bleeding

Warning: Hydraulic fluid is poisonous; wash off immediately and thoroughly in the case of skin contact, and seek immediate medical advice if any fluid is swallowed or gets into the eyes. Certain types of hydraulic fluid are flammable, and may ignite when allowed into contact with hot components; when servicing any hydraulic system, it is safest to assume that the fluid is flammable, and to take precautions against the risk of fire as though it is petrol that is being handled. Hydraulic fluid is also an effective paint stripper, and will attack plastics; if any is spilt, it should be washed off immediately, using copious quantities of fresh water.

Finally, it is hygroscopic (it absorbs moisture from the air) – old fluid may be contaminated and unfit for further use. When topping-up or renewing the fluid, always use the recommended type, and ensure that it comes from a freshly-opened sealed container.

1 The correct operation of any hydraulic system is only possible after removing all air from the components and circuit; this is achieved by bleeding the system.

2 During the bleeding procedure, add only clean, unused hydraulic fluid of the recommended type; never re-use fluid that has already been bled from the system. Ensure that sufficient fluid is available before starting work.

3 If there is any possibility of incorrect fluid being already in the system, the hydraulic circuit must be flushed completely with uncontaminated, correct fluid.

4 If hydraulic fluid has been lost from the system, or air has entered because of a leak, ensure that the fault is cured before continuing further.

5 The bleed screw is located in the hose end fitting which is situated on the top of the transmission housing. On some models access to the bleed screw is limited and it may be necessary to jack up the front of the vehicle and support it on axle stands so that the screw can be reached from below, or remove the battery and battery tray (see Chapter 5A) so that the screw can be reached from above.

6 Check that all pipes and hoses are secure, unions tight and the bleed screw is closed. Clean any dirt from around the bleed screw.

7 Unscrew the master cylinder fluid reservoir cap (the clutch shares the same fluid reservoir as the braking system), and top the master cylinder reservoir up to the upper (MAX) level line. Refit the cap loosely, and remember to maintain the fluid level at least above the lower (MIN) level line throughout the procedure, or there is a risk of further air entering the system.

8 There are a number of one-man, do-it-yourself bleeding kits currently available from motor accessory shops. It is recommended that one of these kits is used whenever possible, as they greatly simplify the bleeding operation, and reduce the risk of expelled air and fluid being drawn back into the system. If such a kit is not available, the basic (two-man) method must be used, which is described in detail below.

9 If a kit is to be used, prepare the vehicle as described previously, and follow the kit manufacturer's instructions, as the procedure may vary slightly according to the type being used; generally, they are as outlined below in the relevant sub-section.

Bleeding – basic (two-man) method

10 Collect a clean glass jar, a suitable length of plastic or rubber tubing which is a tight fit

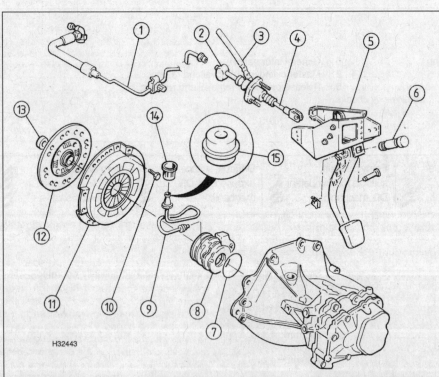

H32443

1.1 Clutch components

1 *Pressure line*	6 *Clutch control switch*	10 *Pressure plate bolt*
2 *Damper*	*(where fitted)*	11 *Pressure plate*
3 *Supply hose*	7 *O ring*	12 *Clutch (friction) disc*
4 *Master cylinder*	8 *Release cylinder*	13 *Guide*
5 *Clutch pedal assembly*	9 *Release cylinder pressure*	14 *Fastening sleeve*
	line	15 *Seal*

over the bleed screw, and a ring spanner to fit the screw. The help of an assistant will also be required.

11 Remove the dust cap from the bleed screw. Fit the spanner and tube to the screw, place the other end of the tube in the jar, and pour in sufficient fluid to cover the end of the tube.

12 Ensure that the fluid level is maintained at least above the lower level line in the reservoir throughout the procedure.

13 Have the assistant fully depress the clutch pedal several times to build up pressure, then maintain it on the final downstroke.

14 While pedal pressure is maintained, unscrew the bleed screw (approximately one turn) and allow the compressed fluid and air to flow into the jar. The assistant should maintain pedal pressure and should not release it until instructed to do so. When the flow stops, tighten the bleed screw again, have the assistant release the pedal slowly, and recheck the reservoir fluid level.

15 Repeat the steps given in paragraphs 13 and 14 until the fluid emerging from the bleed screw is free from air bubbles. If the master cylinder has been drained and refilled allow approximately five seconds between cycles for the master cylinder passages to refill.

16 When no more air bubbles appear, tighten the bleed screw securely, remove the tube and spanner, and refit the dust cap. Do not overtighten the bleed screw.

Bleeding – using a one-way valve kit

17 As their name implies, these kits consist of a length of tubing with a one-way valve fitted, to prevent expelled air and fluid being drawn back into the system; some kits include a translucent container, which can be positioned so that the air bubbles can be more easily seen flowing from the end of the tube.

18 The kit is connected to the bleed screw, which is then opened. The user returns to the driver's seat, depresses the clutch pedal with a smooth, steady stroke, and slowly releases it; this is repeated until the expelled fluid is clear of air bubbles.

19 Note that these kits simplify work so much that it is easy to forget the clutch fluid reservoir level; ensure that this is maintained at least above the lower level line at all times.

Bleeding – using a pressure-bleeding kit

20 These kits are usually operated by the reservoir of pressurised air contained in the spare tyre. However, note that it will probably be necessary to reduce the pressure to a lower level than normal; refer to the instructions supplied with the kit.

21 By connecting a pressurised, fluid-filled container to the clutch fluid reservoir, bleeding can be carried out simply by opening the bleed screw and allowing the fluid to flow out until no more air bubbles can be seen in the expelled fluid.

22 This method has the advantage that the large reservoir of fluid provides an additional safeguard against air being drawn into the system during bleeding.

All methods

23 When bleeding is complete, and correct pedal feel is restored, tighten the bleed screw securely and wash off any spilt fluid. Refit the dust cap to the bleed screw.

24 Check the hydraulic fluid level in the master cylinder reservoir, and top-up if necessary (see *Weekly Checks*).

25 Discard any hydraulic fluid that has been bled from the system; it will not be fit for re-use.

26 Check the operation of the clutch pedal. If the clutch is still not operating correctly, air must still be present in the system, and further bleeding is required. Failure to bleed satisfactorily after a reasonable repetition of the bleeding procedure may be due to worn master cylinder/release cylinder seals.

3 Master cylinder – removal and refitting

Note: *A new hydraulic pipe union sealing ring will be required on refitting.*

Removal

Right-hand drive models

1 Working in the engine compartment, remove all traces of dirt from the outside of the master cylinder and position some cloth beneath the cylinder to catch any spilt fluid.

2 Detach the fluid supply hose from the brake fluid reservoir. Plug the apertures to minimise fluid loss.

3 Slide out the retaining clip, and free the hydraulic pipe from the connector in the end of the master cylinder at the engine compartment bulkhead. Plug the pipe end and master cylinder port to minimise fluid loss and prevent the entry of dirt. Recover the sealing ring from the union and discard it; a new one must be used on refitting **(see illustration)**. Gently squeeze the two legs of

3.3 Slide out the retaining clip and free the hydraulic pipe from the connector

the retaining clip together, and re-insert the clip into the pipe end fitting.

4 From inside the vehicle, remove the driver's side footwell trim below the facia (see Chapter 11, Section 44), release the pedal return spring, slide off the retaining clip and remove the clevis pin securing the master cylinder pushrod to the pedal.

5 Still inside the vehicle, undo the two retaining nuts securing the master cylinder to the bulkhead/pedal bracket. Return to the engine compartment and manoeuvre the master cylinder from its position.

Left-hand drive models

6 To gain access to the master cylinder, unclip the relay box from the top of the ABS hydraulic modulator unit. Remove the relay holder bracket and position it clear.

7 Remove all traces of dirt from the outside of the master cylinder and position some cloth beneath the cylinder to catch any spilt fluid.

8 Detach the fluid supply hose from the brake fluid reservoir. Plug the apertures to minimise fluid loss.

9 Slide out the retaining clip and free the hydraulic pipe from the connector in the end of the master cylinder. Plug the pipe end and master cylinder port to minimise fluid loss and prevent the entry of dirt. Recover the sealing ring from the union and discard it; a new one must be used on refitting. Gently squeeze the two legs of the retaining clip together, and re-insert the clip into the pipe end fitting.

10 From inside the vehicle, remove the driver's side footwell trim below the facia (see Chapter 11, Section 44), detach the return spring from the pedal, slide off the retaining clip and remove the clevis pin securing the master cylinder pushrod to the pedal.

11 Still inside the vehicle, undo the two retaining nuts securing the master cylinder to the bulkhead/pedal bracket. Return to the engine compartment and manoeuvre the master cylinder from its position.

Refitting

Right-hand drive models

12 Ensure the cylinder and bulkhead mating surfaces are clean and dry and the gasket is in position.

13 Manoeuvre the master cylinder into position whilst ensuring that the pushrod clevis engages correctly with the pedal. Ensure the pushrod is correctly engaged then tighten the new master cylinder retaining nuts to the specified torque.

14 Apply a smear of multi-purpose grease to the clevis pin then align the clevis and pedal and insert the pin. Secure the clevis pin in position with the retaining clip, making sure it is correctly located in the pin groove. Reconnect the pedal return spring, and refit the lower trim panel.

15 Fit a new sealing ring to the hydraulic pipe union. Reconnect the pipe to the release cylinder, pushing the connectors together until a distinct 'click' can be heard.

16 Reconnect the fluid supply hose to the brake master cylinder reservoir.
17 Bleed the clutch hydraulic system as described in Section 2.

Left-hand drive models

18 Carry out the operations described in paragraphs 12 to 17.
19 Refit the relay holder bracket, and the relay box.

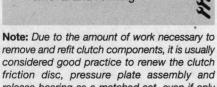

4 Release cylinder – removal and refitting

Note: *Due to the amount of work necessary to remove and refit clutch components, it is usually considered good practice to renew the clutch friction disc, pressure plate assembly and release bearing as a matched set, even if only one of these is actually worn enough to require renewal. It is also worth considering the renewal of the clutch components on a preventative basis if the engine and/or transmission have been removed for some other reason.*

Removal

Note: *Refer to the warning concerning the dangers of asbestos dust at the beginning of Section 6.*

Removal

1 Unless the complete engine/transmission unit is to be removed from the car and separated for major overhaul (see Chapter 2D), the clutch release cylinder can be reached by removing the transmission only, as described in Chapter 7.
2 Wipe clean the outside of the release cylinder then slacken the union nut and disconnect the hydraulic pipe **(see illustration)**. Wipe up any spilt fluid with a clean cloth.
3 Unscrew the three retaining bolts and slide the release cylinder from the transmission input shaft. Remove the sealing ring which is fitted between the cylinder and transmission housing and discard it; a new one must be used on refitting. Whilst the cylinder is removed, take care not to allow any debris to enter the transmission unit.

4 The release cylinder is a sealed unit and cannot be overhauled. If the cylinder seals have leaking or the release bearing is noisy or rough in operation, then the complete unit must be renewed.

Refitting

5 Ensure the release cylinder and transmission mating surfaces are clean and dry and fit the new sealing ring to the transmission recess.
6 Lubricate the release cylinder seal with a smear of transmission oil then carefully ease the cylinder along the input shaft and into position. Ensure the sealing ring is still correctly seated in its groove then refit the release cylinder retaining bolts and tighten them to the specified torque.
7 Reconnect the hydraulic pipe to the release cylinder, tightening its union nut to the specified torque.
8 Refit the transmission unit as described in Chapter 7.
9 Bleed the clutch hydraulic system as described in Section 2.

5 Clutch pedal – removal and refitting

Removal

1 From inside the passenger compartment, remove the driver's side footwell lower trim panel from under the facia (see Chapter 11, Section 44).
2 Detach the return spring from the clutch pedal. Slide off the retaining clip and remove the clevis pin securing the master cylinder pushrod to the clutch pedal **(see illustration)**.
3 Slacken and remove the two bolts (LHD) or nut (RHD) securing the pedal bracket to the steering crossmember.
4 On models with cruise control, disconnect the wiring connector from the clutch switch then remove the switch from the pedal bracket.
5 Slacken and remove the two nuts securing the pedal bracket to the master cylinder/bulkhead.

6 Push the master cylinder studs back until they no longer protrude into the footwell.
7 Carefully manoeuvre the pedal and mounting bracket assembly from the footwell.
8 Check the pedal mounting brackets for signs of damage or deformation (the brackets are designed to bend easily as a safety feature in the event of a collision) and check the pedal mounting bushes for signs of wear. If any components is worn or damage it should be renewed; the pedal and brackets can be separated once the bracket bolts have been unscrewed.

Refitting

9 If the pedal and bracket assembly has been dismantled, apply a smear of multi-purpose grease to the pedal pivot shaft and bushes prior to reassembly. Reassemble all components, making sure the pedal return spring is correctly engaged with the bracket, then securely tighten the bracket bolts. Check that the pedal pivots smoothly before refitting the assembly to the vehicle.
10 Manoeuvre the pedal and bracket assembly into position, engaging the pedal with the master cylinder pushrod, then loosely refit the bolts or nut securing the bracket to the steering crossmember.
11 Pull the master cylinder pushrod so that the mounting studs protrude once again into the footwell and through the corresponding holes in the pedal bracket. Fit the new retaining nuts and tighten them to the specified torque.
12 From inside the vehicle, apply a smear of multi-purpose grease to the clevis pin then align the pushrod with the clutch pedal hole and insert the pin. Secure the pin in position with the retaining clip, making sure it is correctly located in the groove.
13 Tighten the bolts or nut securing the pedal bracket to the steering crossmember to the specified torque setting.
14 Hook the return spring into position behind the clutch pedal **(see illustration 5.2)**.
15 On models with cruise control, ensure the switch plunger is fully depressed then refit the switch to the bracket and connect the wiring connector. Fully depress the clutch pedal and extend the switch plunger then release the pedal to set the switch adjustment.
16 Refit the lower cover to the facia and check the operation of the clutch before using the vehicle on the road.

6 Clutch assembly – removal, inspection and refitting

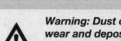

Warning: Dust created by clutch wear and deposited on the clutch components may contain asbestos, which is a health hazard. DO NOT blow it out with compressed air, or inhale any of it. DO NOT use petrol or petroleum-based

4.2 Clutch release cylinder hydraulic pipe union nut (A) and retaining bolts (B)

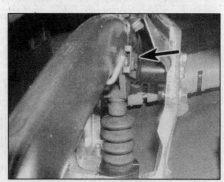

5.2 Slide of the retaining clip and remove the clevis pin (arrowed)

solvents to clean off the dust. Brake
system cleaner or methylated spirit should
be used to flush the dust into a suitable
receptacle. After the clutch components
are wiped clean with rags, dispose of the
contaminated rags and cleaner in a sealed,
marked container.

Note: *Although some friction materials may
no longer contain asbestos, it is safest to
assume that they do, and to take precautions
accordingly.*

Removal

1 Unless the complete engine/transmission
unit is to be removed from the car and
separated for major overhaul (see Chapter 2D),
the clutch can be reached by removing the
transmission as described in Chapter 7.
2 Before disturbing the clutch, use chalk or a
marker pen to mark the relationship of the
pressure plate assembly to the flywheel.
3 Working in a diagonal sequence, slacken
the pressure plate bolts by half a turn at a
time, until spring pressure is released and the
bolts can be unscrewed by hand.
4 Remove the pressure plate assembly and
collect the friction disc, noting which way
round the disc is fitted.

Inspection

Note: *Due to the amount of work necessary to
remove and refit clutch components, it is
usually considered good practice to renew the
clutch friction disc, pressure plate assembly
and release bearing as a matched set, even if
only one of these is actually worn enough to
require renewal. It is also worth considering
the renewal of the clutch components on a
preventative basis if the engine and/or
transmission have been removed for some
other reason.*

**6.14 The friction disc may be marked to
show which way round the disc is to be
fitted**

5 Remove the clutch assembly.
6 When cleaning clutch components, read
first the warning at the beginning of this
Section; remove dust using a clean, dry cloth,
and working in a well-ventilated atmosphere.
7 Check the friction disc facings for signs of
wear, damage or oil contamination. If the
friction material is cracked, burnt, scored or
damaged, or if it is contaminated with oil or
grease (shown by shiny black patches), the
friction disc must be renewed.
8 If the friction material is still serviceable,
check that the centre boss splines are
unworn, that the torsion springs are in good
condition and securely fastened, and that all
the rivets are tight. If any wear or damage is
found, the friction disc must be renewed.
9 If the friction material is fouled with oil, this
must be due to an oil leak from the crankshaft
oil seal, from the sump-to-cylinder block joint,
or from the release cylinder assembly (either
the main seal or the sealing ring). Renew the
crankshaft oil seal or repair the sump joint as
described in the relevant part of Chapter 2,
before installing the new friction disc. The
clutch release cylinder is covered in Section 4.
10 Check the pressure plate assembly for
obvious signs of wear or damage; shake it to
check for loose rivets, or worn or damaged
fulcrum rings, and check that the drive straps
securing the pressure plate to the cover do
not show signs of overheating (such as a deep
yellow or blue discoloration). If the diaphragm
spring is worn or damaged, or if its pressure is
in any way suspect, the pressure plate
assembly should be renewed.
11 Examine the machined bearing surfaces
of the pressure plate and of the flywheel; they
should be clean, completely flat, and free from
scratches or scoring. If either is discoloured
from excessive heat, or shows signs of

**6.17 Centralise the friction disc using a
clutch aligning tool or similar**

cracks, it should be renewed – although minor
damage of this nature can sometimes be
polished away using emery paper.
12 Check that the release cylinder bearing
rotates smoothly and easily, with no sign of
noise or roughness. Also check that the
surface itself is smooth and unworn, with no
signs of cracks, pitting or scoring. If there is
any doubt about its condition, the
clutch release cylinder should be renewed (it
is not possible to renew the bearing
separately).

Refitting

13 On reassembly, ensure that the bearing
surfaces of the flywheel and pressure
plate are completely clean, smooth, and
free from oil or grease. Use solvent to
remove any protective grease from new
components.
14 Fit the friction disc so that its spring hub
assembly faces away from the flywheel; there
may also be a marking showing which way
round the plate is to be refitted. For example:
'Flywheel side' or 'Getriebeseite', meaning
'Gearbox side' **(see illustration)**.
15 Refit the pressure plate assembly,
aligning the marks made on dismantling (if the
original pressure plate is re-used). Fit new
pressure plate bolts, but tighten them only
finger-tight so that the friction disc can still be
moved.
16 The friction disc must now be centralised
so that, when the transmission is refitted, its
input shaft will pass through the splines at the
centre of the friction disc.
17 Centralisation can be achieved by passing
a screwdriver or other long bar through the
friction disc and into the hole in the
crankshaft; the friction disc can then be
moved around until it is centred on the
crankshaft hole. Alternatively, a clutch-
aligning tool can be used to eliminate the
guesswork; these can be obtained from most
accessory shops. A home-made aligning tool
can be fabricated from a length of metal rod
or wooden dowel which fits closely inside
the crankshaft hole, and has insulating
tape wound around it to match the diameter
of the friction disc splined hole **(see
illustration)**.
18 When the friction disc is centralised,
tighten the pressure plate bolts evenly and in
a diagonal sequence to the specified torque
setting.
19 Refit the transmission as described in
Chapter 7.

Chapter 7
Manual transmission

Contents

Degrees of difficulty

Easy, suitable for novice with little experience	Fairly easy, suitable for beginner with some experience	Fairly difficult, suitable for competent DIY mechanic 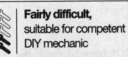	Difficult, suitable for experienced DIY mechanic	Very difficult, suitable for expert DIY or professional

Specifications

General

Type .... Manual, five forward speeds and reverse. Synchromesh on all forward speeds

Identification code*:
1.7 litre engines F17
2.0 litre engines .... F18 or F23

*The transmission identification code is cast onto the top of the transmission housing, next to the selector mechanism cover (F17 and F18), or engraved onto the rear of the differential housing (F23).

Lubrication
Oil type .... See Lubricants and fluids
Oil capacity .... See Chapter 1

Torque wrench settings

	Nm	lbf ft
Clutch housing to transmission casing	28	21
Differential lower cover plate bolts:		
F18 transmission unit	40	30
All other transmission units:		
Models with an alloy cover plate	18	13
Models with a steel cover plate	30	22
Drain plug to transmission – F23 unit	35	26
Engine-to-transmission unit bolts	60	44
Flywheel cover plate	8	6
Gearchange mechanism:		
Selector rod clamp bolt:		
Stage 1	12	9
Stage 2	Angle-tighten a further 180°	
Lever mounting bolts	10	7
Level plug:		
F17/18 units:		
Stage 1	4	3
Stage 2	Angle-tighten a further 45 to 180°	
F23 unit	35	26
Oil filler plug – F23 unit	35	26
Oil sump-to-transmission unit bolts	40	30
Reversing light switch	20	15
Roadwheel bolts	110	81
Shift assembly-to-transmission – F23 unit	25	18
Shift Bowden cable bracket to transmission – F23 unit	20	15
Speed sensor bolt	5	4

1 General information

1 The transmission is contained in a cast-aluminium alloy casing bolted to the engine's left-hand end, and consists of the gearbox and final drive differential – often called a transaxle.

2 Drive is transmitted from the crankshaft via the clutch to the input shaft, which has a splined extension to accept the clutch friction disc, and rotates in sealed ball-bearings. From the input shaft, drive is transmitted to the output shaft, which rotates in a roller bearing at its right-hand end, and a sealed ball-bearing at its left-hand end. From the output shaft, the drive is transmitted to the differential crownwheel, which rotates with the differential case and planetary gears, thus driving the sun gears and driveshafts. The rotation of the planetary gears on their shaft allows the inner roadwheel to rotate at a slower speed than the outer roadwheel when the car is cornering.

3 The input and output shafts are arranged side-by-side, parallel to the crankshaft and driveshafts, so that their gear pinion teeth are in constant mesh. In the neutral position, the output shaft gear pinions rotate freely, so that drive cannot be transmitted to the crownwheel.

4 Gear selection is via a floor-mounted lever and selector linkage/cable mechanism. The selector linkage/cable causes the appropriate selector fork to move its respective synchro-sleeve along the shaft, to lock the gear pinion to the synchro-hub. Since the synchro-hubs are splined to the output shaft, this locks the pinion to the shaft, so that drive can be transmitted. To ensure that gearchanging can be made quickly and quietly, a synchro-mesh system is fitted to all forward gears, consisting of baulk rings and spring-loaded fingers, as well as the gear pinions and synchro-hubs. The synchro-mesh cones are formed on the mating faces of the baulk rings and gear pinions.

2 Transmission oil – draining and refilling

Note: *F17 and F18 transmissions: A new differential lower cover plate gasket will be required for this operation.*

1 This operation is much more efficient if the car is first taken on a journey of sufficient length to warm the engine/transmission up to normal operating temperature.

Caution: If the procedure is to be carried out on a hot transmission unit, take care not to burn yourself on the hot exhaust or the transmission/engine unit.

2.5 To drain the transmission oil undo the bolts and remove the cover plate

2 Park the car on level ground, switch off the ignition and apply the handbrake firmly. Jack up the front of the car and support it securely on axle stands. Where necessary, undo the retaining bolts/clip and remove the engine undertray.

F17 and F18 transmissions

3 Since the transmission oil is not renewed as part of the manufacturer's maintenance schedule, no drain plug is fitted to the transmission. If for any reason the transmission needs to be drained, the only way of doing so is to remove the differential lower cover plate.

4 Wipe clean the area around the differential cover plate and position a suitable container underneath the cover.

5 Evenly and progressively slacken and remove the retaining bolts then withdraw the cover plate and allow the transmission oil to drain in to the container. Remove the gasket and discard it; a new one should be used on refitting **(see illustration)**.

6 Allow the oil to drain completely into the container. If the oil is hot, take precautions against scalding. Remove all traces of dirt and oil from the cover and transmission mating surfaces and wipe clean the inside of the cover plate.

7 Once the oil has finished draining, ensure the mating surfaces are clean and dry then refit the cover plate to the transmission unit, complete with a new gasket. Refit the retaining bolts and evenly and progressively tighten them to the specified torque setting. Lower the vehicle to the ground.

8 The transmission is refilled via the reversing light switch aperture until oil begins to trickle out of the level plug aperture. Wipe clean the area around the reversing light switch and level plug, and remove the switch and plug as described in Section 9. Refill the transmission with the specified type and amount of oil given in the Specifications, using the procedure described in Section 9. On completion, refit the reversing light switch and level plug and tighten both to the specified torque **(see illustration)**.

9 Take the vehicle on a short journey so that the new oil is distributed fully around the transmission components.

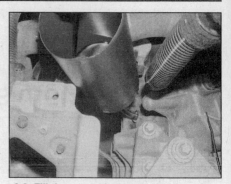

2.8 Fill the transmission via the reversing light switch aperture

10 On your return, park the vehicle on level ground and check the transmission oil level again as described in Section 9.

F23 transmissions

11 As with the F17 and F18 transmissions, the transmission oil is not renewed as part of the manufacturer's maintenance schedule and no drain plug is fitted to the transmission. On the F23 transmission, the only way to drain the transmission completely is by extensive dismantling.

12 Refer to Section 9 for oil level checking and topping up procedures.

3 Gearchange mechanism – adjustment

F17 and F18 transmissions

Note: *A 5 mm drill or punch will be required to carry out this procedure.*

1 Adjustment of the gearchange mechanism is not a routine operation and should only be needed if the mechanism has been removed. If the gearchange action is stiff or imprecise, check that it is correctly adjusted as follows.

2 The mechanism is adjusted via the clamp bolt which secures the selector rod to the transmission linkage (see Section 4). The bolt is located at the rear of the engine/transmission unit, just in front of the engine compartment bulkhead and, on most models, access to the bolt can be gained from above. If the bolt can not be reached from above, firmly apply the handbrake then jack up the front of the vehicle and support it securely on axle stands. Limited access can then be gained from underneath the vehicle.

3 Slacken the gearchange selector rod clamp bolt which is situated at the front of the rod. Do not remove the bolt completely.

4 From inside the vehicle, unclip the gear lever gaiter from the console and fold it back. Lock the gear lever in position by inserting a 5 mm drill or punch through the clamp on the

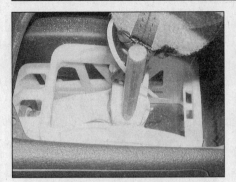

3.4 Insert a 5 mm drill or punch through the clamp and into the locating hole

3.5 Lock the selector mechanism by pressing in the spring-loaded locking pin

3.6 Tighten the selector rod clamp bolt to the specified torque

left-hand side of the lever base and into its locating hole **(see illustration)**.

5 With the selector mechanism in the neutral position, turn the selector shaft against the spring pressure, and lock the transmission selector mechanism in position by pressing in the spring-loaded locking pin on the selector mechanism cover, which is located on the top of the transmission unit **(see illustration)**.

6 With both the lever and transmission locked in position, tighten the selector rod clamp bolt to the specified torque Stage 1 setting then tighten it through the specified Stage 2 angle **(see illustration)**.

7 Remove the locking rod from the gear lever and check the operation of the gearchange mechanism; the transmission locking pin will automatically release when the lever is moved into the reverse position.

8 Ensure the transmission locking pin has released then (where necessary) lower the vehicle to the ground.

F23 transmission

9 With reference to Chapter 11, remove the centre console cover and gear lever gaiter.

10 Using a small screwdriver, release both gearshift cable clamping pieces **(see illustration)**.

11 Working in the engine compartment, set the gearchange selector to 'neutral' position.

12 Position the gear lever in the 'neutral' position, and lock it there by pushing in the clamp **(see illustration)**.

13 Lock both cable clamping pieces by pushing down **(see illustration)**.

14 Pull out the clamp locking the gear lever, and refit the gear lever gaiter and centre console cover. Check the gear selector mechanism for correct operation.

4 Gearchange mechanism – removal and refitting

Removal – F17 and F18 transmissions

1 The gearchange mechanism consists of the gear lever, the selector rod and the linkage assembly on the transmission. The lever and selector rod and the linkage assembly can be removed separately.

Gear lever and selector rod

2 Firmly apply the handbrake then jack up the front of the vehicle and support it on axle stands. Where necessary, undo the retaining bolts and remove the undercover from beneath the engine/transmission unit.

3 Using paint or a suitable marker pen, make alignment marks between the selector rod and the clamp on the front end of the rod. Loosen the clamp bolt by a couple of turns but do not remove it completely. Move the gear lever into the 4th gear position then free the selector rod from the clamp and slide off the rubber gaiter.

4 Remove the centre console as described in Chapter 11.

5 Undo the retaining screws and remove the switch panel from around the gear lever, disconnecting the wiring connectors as they become accessible.

6 Slacken and remove the four nuts securing the gear lever to the floor then manoeuvre the lever and selector rod assembly out of position.

7 To dismantle the lever and rod assembly, carefully release the retaining clip from the base of the lever then separate the rod and lever and remove them from the housing. Examine all components for signs of wear or damage, paying particular attention to the selector rod and lever locating pivot bushes, and renew as necessary.

Transmission linkage assembly

Note: *A new linkage-to-transmission lever pivot pin should be used on refitting.*

8 Separate the selector rod from its clamp as described in paragraph 3. The bolt is located at the rear of the engine/transmission unit, just in front of the engine compartment bulkhead and on most models access to the bolt can be gained from above. If the bolt can not be reached from above, firmly apply the handbrake then jack up the front of the vehicle and support it securely on axle stands. Limited access can then be gained from underneath the vehicle.

9 Depress the detent mechanism and remove the pivot pin connecting the linkage to the

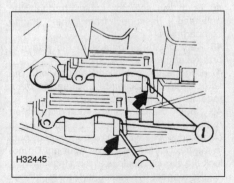

3.10 Use a small screwdriver to release the cable clamping pieces (1)

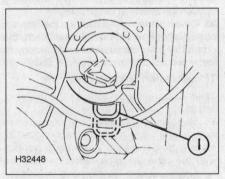

3.12 Lock the gear lever in 'neutral' by pushing in the clamp (1)

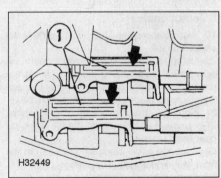

3.13 Lock the cable clamping pieces (1) by pushing down

4.9 Remove the linkage pivot pin

4.11 Examine the linkage assembly for signs of wear and renew worn components as necessary

4.35 Secure the linkage assembly in position with the retaining clips

selector lever on the top of the transmission unit **(see illustration)**. Discard the pivot pin, a new one should be used on refitting.

10 Slide off the retaining clips securing the linkage bracket to its mountings then manoeuvre the assembly upwards and out of position. If necessary, the mounting brackets can then be unbolted and removed.

11 Examine the linkage assembly closely for signs of wear or damage, renewing worn components as necessary **(see illustration)**.

Removal – F23 transmission

12 The gearchange mechanism consists of the gear lever, selector cables, and linkage assembly on the transmission.

Gear lever

13 With reference to Chapter 11, remove the centre console.

14 Using a small screwdriver, open the selector cables clamping pieces as far as the notch. Opening them any further may damage the clamping pieces **(see illustration 3.10)**.

15 Note the fitted locations of the cables, then prise the ends of the cables from the gear lever assembly.

16 Prise the cable clamping pieces from the front of the gearchange assembly.

17 Undo the four retaining bolts and lift the gear lever assembly from the floor.

18 If required, the cable end fittings attached to the gear lever can be prised from their position. No further dismantling of the assembly is recommended.

Selector cables

19 With reference to Chapter 11, remove the centre console.

20 Using a small screwdriver, open the selector cables clamping pieces as far as the notch. Opening them any further may damage the clamping pieces **(see illustration 3.10)**.

21 Note the fitted locations of the cables, then prise the ends of the cables from the gear lever assembly.

22 Prise the cable clamping pieces from the front of the gearchange assembly.

23 Remove the air distribution duct.

24 Remove the battery and battery tray as described in Chapter 5A. **Note:** *Before*

disconnecting the battery, refer to 'Disconnecting the battery' in the reference section at the rear of this manual.

25 Note the fitted locations of the cables, then prise the ends of the cables from the selector linkage assembly above/behind the transmission.

26 Release the outer cables from the linkage assembly bracket.

27 Pull the cables through the bulkhead passage and into the engine compartment.

Refitting – F17 and F18 transmissions

Gear lever and selector rod

28 If necessary, reassemble the lever and rod, making sure the lever base is correctly located in the housing pivot, and secure them in position with the retaining clip.

29 Lubricate all pivot points and bearing surfaces with silicone grease then manoeuvre the assembly into position. Refit the housing retaining bolts and tighten them to the specified torque setting.

30 Refit the switch panel, making sure its wiring is correctly routed, then refit the centre console as described in Chapter 11.

31 From underneath the vehicle, slide the rubber gaiter onto the end of the selector rod and locate it securely in the bulkhead.

32 Engage the selector rod end with its linkage clamp. Align the marks made prior to removal and tighten the clamp bolt to the specified Stage 1 torque then tighten it through the specified Stage 2 angle.

33 Check the gearchange mechanism operation before lowering the vehicle to the ground. If the mechanism seems notchy or imprecise, adjust it as described in Section 3.

Transmission linkage assembly

34 Prior to refitting, lubricate the balljoints and pivot points with silicone grease.

35 Manoeuvre the assembly into position and locate the linkage bracket on its mountings. Secure the assembly in position with the retaining clips, ensuring they are correctly located in the mounting bracket pin grooves **(see illustration)**.

36 Align the linkage with the transmission

selector lever and insert the new pivot pin. Ensure the pin is securely retained by its detent mechanism **(see illustration 4.9)**.

37 Engage the selector rod end with its linkage clamp. Align the marks made prior to removal and tighten the clamp bolt to the specified stage 1 torque then tighten it through the specified stage 2 angle.

38 Check the gearchange mechanism operation before lowering the vehicle to the ground. If the mechanism seems notchy or imprecise, adjust it as described in Section 3.

Refitting – F23 transmission

Gear lever

39 If previously removed, attached the cable end fittings to the base of the lever using a pair of pliers.

40 Position the gear lever assembly on the floor, insert the securing bolts and tighten to the specified torque.

41 Refit the cable clamping pieces into the front of the gear lever housing. Do not lock the clamping pieces at this stage.

42 Reconnect the ends of the cables to the cable end fittings attached to the base of the gear lever.

43 Carry out the *Gearchange mechanism adjustment* procedure, as described in the previous Section.

44 Refit the centre console.

Selector cables

45 Push the selector cables through the bulkhead passage from the engine compartment.

46 Refit the outer cables to the retaining bracket at the transmission end.

47 Engage the cable end fittings with the selector linkage assembly, squeezing them together with pliers if necessary.

48 Check the cables are routed as noted during removal, and refit the outer cable clamping pieces with corresponding cut-outs in the front of the gear lever housing. Do not lock the clamping pieces at this stage.

49 Reconnect the cables to the end fittings attached to the base of the gear lever.

50 Carry out the *Gearchange mechanism*

adjustment procedure, as described in the previous Section.
51 Refit the air distribution duct and centre console.

5 Oil seals – renewal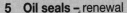

Driveshaft oil seals

1 Chock the rear wheels, apply the handbrake, then jack up the front of the car and support it on axle stands. Remove the appropriate front roadwheel.
2 Drain the transmission oil as described in Section 2 or be prepared for oil loss as the seal is changed.
3 Remove the driveshaft as described in Chapter 8.
4 Carefully prise it out of position using a large flat-bladed screwdriver **(see illustration)**.
5 Remove all traces of dirt from the area around the oil seal aperture, then apply a smear of grease to the outer lip of the new oil seal. Ensure the seal is correctly positioned, with its sealing lip and spring facing inwards, and tap it squarely into position, using a suitable tubular drift (such as a socket) which bears only on the hard outer edge of the seal **(see illustration)**. Ensure the seal is fitted flush with the seal housing.
6 Refit the driveshaft as described in Chapter 8.
7 If the transmission was drained, refill the transmission with the specified type and amount of oil, as described in Section 2. If the oil was not drained top-up the transmission oil level and check as described in Section 9.

Input shaft oil seal

8 The input shaft oil seal is an integral part of the clutch release cylinder; if the seal is leaking the complete release cylinder assembly must be renewed. Before condemning the release cylinder, check that the leak is not coming from the sealing ring which is fitted between the cylinder and the transmission housing; the sealing ring can be renewed once the release cylinder assembly

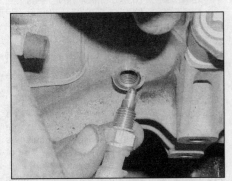
6.6 Remove the reversing light switch along with the sealing washer

5.4 Prising out a driveshaft oil seal

has been removed. Refer to Chapter 6 for removal and refitting details.

Selector rod oil seal

9 Renewal of the selector rod oil seal requires the selector mechanism cover to be unbolted from the transmission and dismantled. This task is considered to be beyond the scope of the DIY mechanic, and should therefore be entrusted to a Vauxhall dealer or specialist.

6 Reversing light switch – testing, removal and refitting

Testing
F17 and F18 transmissions

1 The reversing light circuit is controlled by a plunger-type switch that is screwed into the top of the transmission, towards the front of the housing. If a fault develops in the circuit, first ensure that the circuit fuse has not blown.
2 To test the switch, disconnect the wiring connector. Use a multimeter (set to the resistance function) or a battery-and-bulb test circuit to check that there is continuity between the switch terminals only when reverse gear is selected. If this is not the case, and there are no obvious breaks or other damage to the wires, the switch is faulty, and must be renewed.

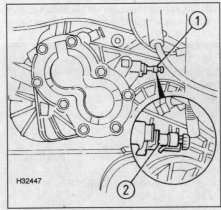
6.8 Disconnect the wiring connector (1) and unscrew the reversing light switch (2)

5.5 Fitting a new driveshaft oil seal using a socket as a tubular drift

F23 transmission

3 The reversing light circuit is controlled by a plunger-type switch that is screwed into the rear of the transmission. If a fault develops in the circuit, first check that the circuit fuse has not blown.
4 To test the switch, disconnect the wiring connector. Use a multimeter (set to the resistance function) or a battery-and-bulb test circuit to check that there is continuity between the switch terminals only when the reverse gear is selected. If this is not the case, and there are no obvious breaks or other damage to the wires, the switch is faulty, and must be renewed.

Removal
F17 and F18 transmissions

5 To improve access to the switch, remove the battery and mounting tray (see Chapter 5A).
6 Disconnect the wiring connector, then unscrew the switch and remove it from the transmission casing along with its sealing washer **(see illustration)**.
F23 transmission
7 Apply the handbrake firmly. Jack up the front of the car and support it securely on axle stands. Where necessary, undo the retaining bolts/clip and remove the undertray from beneath the engine/transmission unit.
8 Disconnect the wiring connector, then unscrew the switch and remove it from the transmission casing along with its sealing washer **(see illustration)**.

Refitting
F17 and F18 transmissions

9 Fit a new sealing washer to the switch, then screw it back into position in the top of the transmission housing and tighten it to the specified torque. Reconnect the wiring connector, then refit the battery (where removed) and test the operation of the circuit.
F23 transmission
10 Fit a new sealing washer to the switch, then screw it back into position in the rear of the transmission housing and tighten it to the specified torque. Reconnect the wiring connector, then refit the engine undertray and lower the vehicle to the ground.

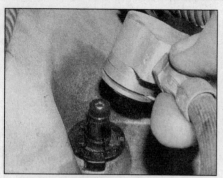

7.5a Disconnect the clutch hydraulic pipe . . .

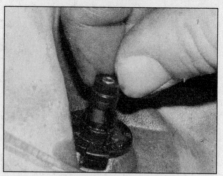

7.5b . . . and discard the seal. A new one must be fitted

7 Transmission – removal and refitting

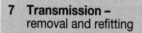

Removal

1 Chock the rear wheels, then firmly apply the handbrake. Jack up the front of the vehicle, and securely support it on axle stands. Remove both front roadwheels then, where necessary, undo the retaining clips/screws and remove the engine undertray. Remove the air cleaner housing and intake trunking (see Chapter 4A)

2 Drain the transmission oil as described in Section 2 or be prepared for oil loss as the transmission is removed.

3 Remove the battery and mounting tray, and the starter motor (see Chapter 5A).

4 Disconnect the wiring connector from the reversing light switch and free the wiring from the transmission unit and retaining brackets.

5 Minimise clutch fluid loss by clamping the flexible hose next to the connection on the transmission housing. Prise out the retaining clip securing the clutch hydraulic pipe/hose end fitting to the top of the transmission bellhousing and detach the end fitting from the transmission. Gently squeeze the two legs of the retaining clip together and re-insert the retaining clip back into position in the end fitting. Discard the sealing ring from the pipe end; a new sealing ring must be used on refitting **(see illustrations)**. Plug/cover both

the union and pipe ends to minimise fluid loss and prevent the entry of dirt into the hydraulic system. **Note:** *Whilst the hose/pipe is disconnected, do not depress the clutch pedal.*

6 Remove the front exhaust downpipe, catalytic converter and centre silencer, as described in Chapter 4A.

7 On models fitted with F17 or F18 transmissions detach the gearchange mechanism linkage assembly from the top of the transmission unit as described in Section 4. On models equipped with F23 transmissions, prise the ends of the gearchange cables from the linkage on the top of the transmission, and undo the bolt and lay aside the outer cable retaining bracket.

8 Referring to Chapter 8, remove both driveshafts. If the transmission has not been drained be prepared for fluid loss.

9 Remove the front subframe assembly as described in Chapter 10, ensuring that the engine unit is securely supported by connecting a hoist to the engine assembly. If available, the type of support bar which locates in the engine compartment side channels is to be preferred.

10 Place a jack with a block of wood beneath the transmission, and raise the jack to take the weight of the transmission.

11 Unscrew the retaining bolts, and remove the front engine mounting bracket from the transmission bellhousing.

12 Slacken and remove the six bolts securing the left-hand mounting block to the mounting

bracket on the transmission casing, and remove the bracket **(see illustration)**. Using the hoist or support bar, lower the transmission end of the assembly approximately 5 cm. Ensure that the various coolant hoses and wiring harnesses are not stretched.

13 On models where a pressed steel sump is fitted to the engine, unbolt the flywheel cover plate and remove it from the base of the transmission unit.

14 Slacken and remove the upper and lower bolts securing the transmission housing to the engine. Note the correct fitted positions of each bolt, and the necessary brackets, as they are removed to use as a reference on refitting. Make a final check that all components have been disconnected, and are positioned clear of the transmission so that they will not hinder the removal procedure **(see illustration)**.

15 With the bolts removed, move the trolley jack and transmission, to free it from its locating dowels. Once the transmission is free, lower the jack and manoeuvre the unit out from under the car. Remove the locating dowels from the transmission or engine if they are loose, and keep them in a safe place.

Refitting

16 The transmission is refitted by a reversal of the removal procedure, bearing in mind the following points.

a) *Ensure the locating dowels are correctly positioned prior to installation.*

b) *Tighten all nuts and bolts to the specified torque (where given).*

c) *Renew the driveshaft oil seals (see Section 5) before refitting the driveshafts.*

d) *Refit the front subframe assembly as described in Chapter 10.*

e) *Fit a new sealing ring to the transmission clutch hydraulic pipe before clipping the hose/pipe end fitting into position. Ensure the end fitting is securely retained by its clip then bleed the hydraulic system as described in Chapter 6.*

f) *If the transmission was drained, refill the transmission with the specified type and amount of oil, as described in Section 2. If the oil was not drained, top-up the transmission oil and check the level as described in Section 9.*

g) *On completion, adjust the gearchange mechanism/cables as described in Section 3.*

8 Transmission overhaul – general information

1 Overhauling a manual transmission unit is a difficult and involved job for the DIY home mechanic. In addition to dismantling and reassembling many small parts, clearances must be precisely measured and, if necessary, changed by selecting shims and

7.12 Undo the six bolts securing the mounting block/bracket to the transmission

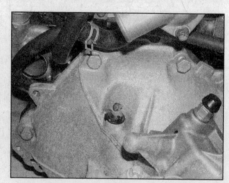

7.14 Undo the transmission housing-to-engine bolts

9.2a F17/18 transmission oil level hole

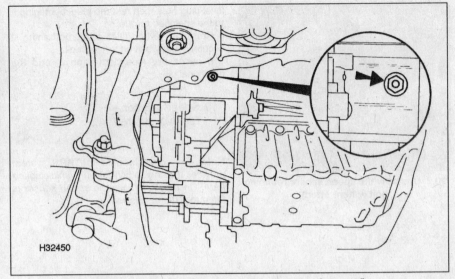

H32450

9.2b F23 transmission oil level checking plug (arrowed)

spacers. Internal transmission components are also often difficult to obtain, and in many instances, extremely expensive. Because of this, if the transmission develops a fault or becomes noisy, the best course of action is to have the unit overhauled by a specialist repairer, or to obtain an exchange reconditioned unit.

2 Nevertheless, it is not impossible for the more experienced mechanic to overhaul the transmission, provided the special tools are available, and the job is done in a deliberate step-by-step manner, so that nothing is overlooked.

3 The tools necessary for an overhaul include internal and external circlip pliers, bearing pullers, a slide hammer, a set of pin punches, a dial test indicator, and possibly a hydraulic press. In addition, a large, sturdy workbench and a vice will be required.

4 During dismantling of the transmission, make careful notes of how each component is fitted, to make reassembly easier and more accurate.

5 Before dismantling the transmission, it will help if you have some idea what area is malfunctioning. Certain problems can be closely related to specific areas in the transmission, which can make component examination and replacement easier. Refer to the *Fault finding* Section of this manual for more information.

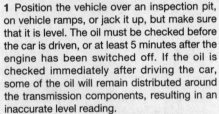

9 Transmission oil level check

1 Position the vehicle over an inspection pit, on vehicle ramps, or jack it up, but make sure that it is level. The oil must be checked before the car is driven, or at least 5 minutes after the engine has been switched off. If the oil is checked immediately after driving the car, some of the oil will remain distributed around the transmission components, resulting in an inaccurate level reading.

2 Wipe clean the area around the level plug. The level plug is located behind the driveshaft inner joint on the left-hand side of the transmission (F17 and F18 transmissions), or the rear of the differential housing (F23

transmissions) **(see illustrations)**. Unscrew the plug and clean it.

3 The oil level should reach the lower edge of the level plug hole. **Note:** *For some models fitted with the F23 transmission, the transmission is overfilled as part of a modification. These transmissions have a yellow mark on the oil filler plug. On these vehicles, after filling up to the bottom of the level plug, fit and tighten the plug and add a further 0.5 litres of oil to the transmission.*

4 If topping-up is necessary, unscrew the reversing light switch (F17 and F18 transmissions) or filler plug (F23 transmissions) and add the specified type of oil through the hole until oil begins to trickle out from the level plug hole **(see illustrations)**.

5 Allow the excess oil to drain out from the

9.4a Top up F17/18 transmissions through the reversing light switch aperture

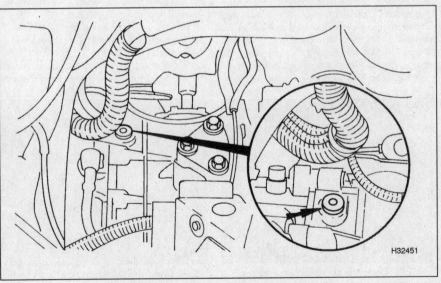

H32451

9.4b F23 transmission oil filler plug (arrowed)

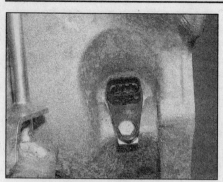

10.2 Unscrew the speed sensor retaining bolt (where fitted)

level plug hole then refit the plug, tightening it to the specified torque.

6 Refit the switch/filler plug, tightening it securely, and wash off any spilt oil.

7 If necessary (see paragraph 3) add the additional oil.

10 Speed sensor –
removal and refitting

Note: *On some models the ABS system provides the engine ECU(s) with vehicle speed data. On these vehicles no speed sensor is fitted to the transmission.*

Removal

1 The sensor is located at the top of the transmission casing. Working in the engine compartment, reach down and disconnect the wiring plug from the top of the sensor.

2 Unscrew the retaining bolt and remove the sensor from the casing **(see illustration)**.

Refitting

3 With a new sealing ring fitted, insert the sensor into the transmission casing aperture. Ensure that the gear teeth engage correctly.

4 Tighten the retaining bolt to the specified torque and reconnect the wiring plug.

Chapter 8
Driveshafts

Contents

Degrees of difficulty

| Easy, suitable for novice with little experience | Fairly easy, suitable for beginner with some experience | Fairly difficult, suitable for competent DIY mechanic | Difficult, suitable for experienced DIY mechanic | Very difficult, suitable for expert DIY or professional |

Specifications

Type .... Unequal-length open shafts, with constant velocity joint at each end; from model year 2000, the inner joints are of tripod type. All models have a vibration damper fitted to the right-hand driveshaft

Driveshaft vibration damper
Dimension from outer joint .... 310.0 mm

Driveshaft joint grease specification .... Special Grease (Vauxhall P/N 90094176)

Torque wrench settings	Nm	lbf ft
Front anti-roll bar to suspension strut	65	48
Front hub nut (refer to text):		
Stage 1	120	89
Stage 2	Loosen nut fully	
Stage 3	20	15
Stage 4	Angle-tighten by a further 80° (plus to next split pin hole as necessary)	
Front suspension lower balljoint clamp bolt	100	74
Roadwheels	110	81
Track rod end balljoint to knuckle	60	44
Vibration damper	10	8

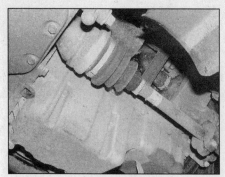

2.1 The right-hand driveshaft viewed from under the vehicle

2.2 Use a cold chisel to tap off the hub nut cap

2.3 Removing the split pin from the castellated hub nut

1 Description – general

Drive is transmitted from the differential to the front wheels by means of two, unequal-length driveshafts.

Each driveshaft is fitted with an inner and outer constant velocity (CV) joint. As from model year 2000, the inner joints are of tripod type. Each outer joint is splined to engage with the wheel hub, and is retained by a large nut. The inner joint is also splined to engage with the differential sunwheel and is held in place by an internal circlip. A vibration damper is attached to the right-hand driveshaft.

2 Driveshaft – removal and refitting

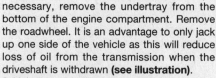

Note: *A new front hub nut and inner joint circlip will be required on refitting. The driveshaft outer joint splines may be a tight fit in the hub and it is possible that a puller/extractor will be required to draw the hub assembly off the driveshaft during removal.*

Removal

1 Apply the handbrake, then jack up the front of the vehicle and support it on axle stands (see *Jacking and vehicle support*). Where necessary, remove the undertray from the bottom of the engine compartment. Remove the roadwheel. It is an advantage to only jack up one side of the vehicle as this will reduce loss of oil from the transmission when the driveshaft is withdrawn **(see illustration)**.
2 Using a cold chisel or screwdriver, tap off the hub nut cap **(see illustration)**.
3 Extract the split pin from the castellated hub nut on the end of the driveshaft **(see illustration)**.
4 The hub nut must now be loosened. The nut is extremely tight, and an extension bar will be required to loosen it. To prevent the driveshaft from turning, insert two roadwheel bolts, and insert a metal bar between them to counterhold the hub. Remove the hub nut and washer from the driveshaft **(see illustration)**.
5 Unscrew the nut securing the track rod end to the steering arm on the hub carrier, then use a balljoint separator tool to remove the track rod end.
6 Unbolt the hydraulic brake hose support bracket from the front suspension strut, and release the hose from it.
7 Unscrew and remove the nut securing the anti-roll bar link to the strut, while holding the joint stub on the flats provided with a further spanner **(see illustration)**. Release the link from the strut and move it to one side.
8 Unscrew and remove the clamp bolt securing the front lower suspension arm to the hub carrier. Note that the bolt head faces the front of the vehicle **(see illustration)**.
9 Using a chisel or screwdriver as a wedge, expand the balljoint clamp at the bottom of the hub carrier **(see illustration)**.
10 Using a lever, push down on the suspension lower arm to free the balljoint from the hub carrier **(see illustration)**, then move

2.4 Removing the front hub nut and washer

2.7 Anti-roll bar link attachment to the front strut

2.8 Removing the clamp bolt securing the front lower suspension arm to the hub carrier

2.9 Using a cold chisel to expand the balljoint clamp at the bottom of the hub carrier

2.10 Push down the suspension lower arm to free the balljoint from the hub carrier

2.11a Use a soft-faced hammer to drive the driveshaft from the hub splines . . .

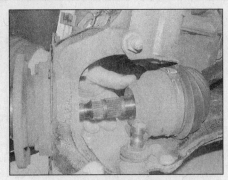

2.11b . . . then pull the hub carrier outwards

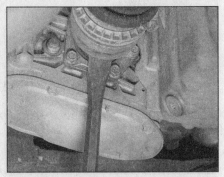

2.14 Carefully lever between the driveshaft and differential housing to release the driveshaft

the hub carrier to one side and release the arm taking care not to damage the balljoint rubber boot.

11 The hub must now be freed from the end of the driveshaft. It should be possible to pull the hub off the driveshaft, but if the end of the driveshaft is tight in the hub, temporarily refit the hub nut to protect the driveshaft threads, then tap the end of the driveshaft with a soft-faced hammer while pulling outwards on the hub carrier **(see illustrations)**. Alternatively, use a suitable puller to press the driveshaft through the hub.

12 With the driveshaft detached from the hub carrier, tie the suspension strut to one side and support the driveshaft on an axle stand.

13 Where fitted, remove the undertray from the bottom of the engine compartment. Position a suitable container beneath the transmission to accept any spilt oil.

14 A lever will now be required to release the inner end of the driveshaft from the differential. Carefully lever between the driveshaft and differential housing to release the driveshaft circlip **(see illustration)**.

15 Withdraw the driveshaft from the transmission, ensuring that the constant velocity joints are not placed under excessive strain, and remove the driveshaft from

beneath the vehicle. Whilst the driveshaft is removed, plug or tape over the differential aperture to prevent dirt entry.

Caution: Do not allow the vehicle to rest on its wheels with one or both driveshafts removed, as damage to the wheel bearings(s) may result. If the vehicle must be moved on its wheels, clamp the wheel bearings using spacers and a long threaded rod to take the place of the driveshaft.

16 All models have a vibration damper fitted to the right-hand driveshaft. If the damper is transferred to a new driveshaft, measure its fitted position before removing and locate it in the same position on the new driveshaft **(see illustration)**. The correct dimension from the outer gaiter is given in the Specifications.

Refitting

17 Before refitting the driveshaft, examine the oil seal in the transmission housing and renew it if necessary as described in Chapter 7 **(see illustration)**.

18 Remove the circlip from the end of the driveshaft inner joint splines and discard it. Fit a new circlip, making sure it is correctly located in the groove.

19 Thoroughly clean the driveshaft splines,

and the apertures in the transmission and hub assembly. Apply a thin film of grease to the oil seal lips, and to the driveshaft splines and shoulders. Check that all gaiter clips are securely fastened.

20 Offer up the driveshaft, and engage the inner joint splines with those of the differential sun gear, taking care not to damage the oil seal. Push the joint fully into position, then check that the circlip is correctly located and securely holds the joint in position. If necessary, use a soft-faced mallet or drift to drive the driveshaft inner joint fully into position.

21 Align the outer constant velocity joint splines with those of the hub, and slide the joint back into position in the hub.

22 Using the lever push down on the lower suspension arm, then relocate the balljoint and release the arm. Make sure that the balljoint stub is fully entered in the hub carrier.

23 Insert the clamp bolt with its head facing the front of the vehicle, and tighten it to the specified torque.

24 Refit the anti-roll bar link to the strut, and tighten the nut to the specified torque while holding the joint stub on the flats provided with a further spanner.

25 Locate the support bracket on the brake

2.16 Vibration damper fitted to the right-hand driveshaft

2.17 Examine the oil seal in the transmission before refitting the driveshaft

2.29a Insert the new split pin ...

2.29b ... and bend the legs to secure

hose, then refit the bracket to the strut and tighten the bolt.

26 Refit the track rod end to the steering arm on the hub carrier and tighten the nut to the specified torque.

27 Refit the washer to the end of the driveshaft, then screw on a new nut and tighten moderately at this stage.

28 Refit the undertray (where fitted), then refit the roadwheel and lower the vehicle to the ground. Tighten the wheel bolts to the specified torque.

29 Tighten the hub nut in the stages given in the Specifications, and fit a new split pin. Bend the outer leg of the split pin over the end of the driveshaft, then cut the inner leg as necessary and bend it inwards **(see illustrations)**.

3.4a Driveshaft joint retaining circlip

30 Tap the hub nut cap into position then refit the wheel trim.

31 Check and if necessary top-up the oil level in the transmission as described in Chapter 7.

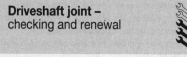

3 Driveshaft joint – checking and renewal

Checking

1 Road test the vehicle, and listen for a metallic clicking noise from the front as the vehicle is driven slowly in a circle on full-lock. If evident, this indicates wear in the outer constant velocity joint which must be renewed.

2 To check for wear on the inner joint, apply the handbrake then jack up the front of the vehicle and support it on axle stands (see *Jacking and vehicle support*). Where necessary, remove the undertray from the bottom of the engine compartment. Attempt to move the inner end of the driveshaft up and down, then hold the joint with one hand and attempt to rotate the driveshaft with the other. If excessive wear is evident, the joint must be renewed.

Renewal

Note: *It is not possible to renew the tripod*

type inner joint on later models, as it is integral with the driveshaft.

3 With the driveshaft removed, as described in Section 2, release the securing clips and slide back the rubber gaiter from the worn joint.

4 Using a screwdriver or circlip pliers, expand the circlip that secures the joint to the driveshaft **(see illustrations)**.

5 Using a soft-faced mallet, tap the joint from the driveshaft.

6 Ensure that a new circlip is fitted to the new joint, then tap the new joint onto the driveshaft until the circlip engages in its groove.

7 Pack the joint with the specified type of grease **(see illustration)**.

8 Refit the rubber gaiter to the new joint, referring to Section 4.

9 Refit the driveshaft to the vehicle, as described in Section 2.

4 Driveshaft joint gaiter – renewal

Note: *Where a tripod type inner joint is fitted, access to the inner gaiter is gained by first removing the outer gaiter.*

1 With the driveshaft removed as described in Section 2, remove the relevant joint as described in Section 3. Note that if both gaiters on a driveshaft are to be renewed it is only necessary to remove one joint, however on the right-hand driveshaft it will also be necessary to remove the vibration damper after noting its location.

2 Remove the gaiter from the driveshaft – if necessary, cut the gaiter free **(see illustration)**.

3 Clean the old grease from the joint, then re-pack the joint with the specified type of fresh grease. If excessively worn or damaged, the driveshaft joint should be renewed as described in Section 3.

4 Slide the new gaiter and new inner securing clip onto the driveshaft so that the smaller diameter opening is located in

3.4b Expanding the driveshaft joint retaining circlip

3.7 Packing the joint with grease

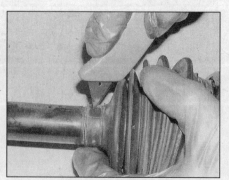

4.2 Cutting the gaiter free

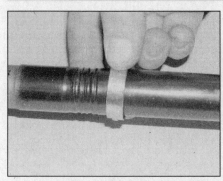

4.4a Locate the new inner securing clip on the driveshaft . . .

4.4b . . . followed by the new gaiter

4.5 Pack the joint with the specified type of grease

the groove in the driveshaft **(see illustrations)**.

5 Pack the joint with the specified type of grease **(see illustration)**.

6 Refit the joint, using a new inner securing circlip. Tap the joint onto the driveshaft until the circlip engages in its groove.

7 Slide the gaiter onto the joint, then release any excess air by lifting the gaiter from the joint with a screwdriver.

8 Secure the gaiter using new clips. To fit a loop-type clip, locate it over the gaiter then squeeze the raised loop using pincers – note that Vauxhall technicians use a special tool to do this, however careful use of pincers or a similar tool will be sufficient **(see illustrations)**. To fit a lug-and-slot type clip, wrap it around the gaiter and while pulling on

the clip as tight as possible, engage the lug on the end of the clip with one of the slots. Use a screwdriver if necessary to push the clip as tight as possible before engaging the lug and slot. Finally tighten the clip by compressing the raised square portion of the clip with pliers, taking care not to cut the gaiter.

9 Refit the driveshaft to the vehicle, as described in Section 2.

4.8a Fitting the outer securing clip

4.8b . . . and tightening using a pair of pincers

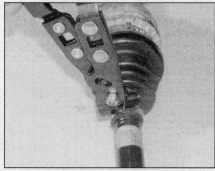

4.8c Tightening the outer securing clip using the special tool

Chapter 9
Braking system

Contents

Degrees of difficulty

Easy, suitable for novice with little experience	Fairly easy, suitable for beginner with some experience	Fairly difficult, suitable for competent DIY mechanic	Difficult, suitable for experienced DIY mechanic	Very difficult, suitable for expert DIY or professional

Specifications

System type
All models .... Front discs, and rear drums (1.7 litre engine models) or rear discs (2.0 litre engine models) with vacuum servo assistance, dual hydraulic circuit split diagonally, ABS is available as an option. Cable-operated handbrake on rear wheels

Front discs
Type	Ventilated
Diameter:	
1.7 litre engine	256 mm
2.0 litre engine	280 mm
Maximum disc run-out	0.11 mm
Minimum pad friction material thickness	2.0 mm
Minimum disc thickness after machining:	
Hub carrier with integrated caliper bracket	21 mm
Hub carrier without integrated caliper bracket	22 mm

Rear discs
Type	Solid
Diameter:	
Models without ABS	240 mm
Models with ABS	264 mm
Maximum disc run-out	0.13 mm
Minimum pad friction material thickness	2.0 mm
Minimum disc thickness after machining	8.0 mm

Rear drums
Internal diameter . . . . 230 mm
Maximum internal diameter . . . . 231 mm
Minimum shoe friction material thickness . . . . 1.0 mm

ABS system
Type . . . . ABS 5.3

Brake fluid type/specification
All models . . . . See *Lubricants and fluids*

Torque wrench settings

	Nm	lbf ft
ABS control unit to hydraulic modulator body:		
Stage 1	6	4
Stage 2	7	5
Brake disc securing screw	4	3
Brake fluid line unions	16	12
Brake hydraulic line to wheel cylinder	16	12
Brake pedal bracket side mounting nuts	20	15
Brake pedal bracket to vacuum servo	20	15
Caliper bleed screw:		
Front	9	7
Rear (M8)	7	5
Rear (M10)	10	7
Flexible brake hose to caliper	40	30
Front caliper guide bolts	28	21
Front caliper mounting bracket to hub carrier	95	70
Handbrake lever mounting	10	7
Hydraulic line branch bracket (LHD models without ABS)	20	15
Hydraulic line relay carrier bracket (LHD models without ABS)	20	15
Hydraulic lines union nuts	16	12
Hydraulic modulator (ABS)	8	6
Master cylinder	25	18
Rear brake drum	4	3
Rear brake proportioning valve	20	15
Rear caliper damping weight (where fitted)	11	8
Rear caliper mounting bolt	25	18
Rear caliper mounting bracket to trailing arm	100	74
Rear wheel cylinder	9	7
Rear wheel cylinder bleed screw	6	4
Roadwheel bolts	110	81
Wheel speed sensor	8	6
Vacuum pump to cylinder head:		
1.7 litre engine	28	21
2.0 litre engine	8	6

1 General information

The braking system is of servo-assisted, dual-circuit hydraulic type split diagonally. The arrangement of the hydraulic system is such that each circuit operates one front and one rear brake from a tandem master cylinder. Under normal circumstances, both circuits operate in unison. However, in the event of hydraulic failure in one circuit, full braking force will still be available at two wheels.

All models are fitted with front disc brakes, with rear drum brakes on 1.7 litre engine models and rear disc brakes on 2.0 litre models. The front disc brakes (and rear disc brakes where applicable) are actuated by single-piston sliding type calipers, which ensure that equal pressure is applied to each disc pad.

The rear drum brakes incorporate leading and trailing shoes, which are actuated by twin-piston wheel cylinders. A self-adjust mechanism is incorporated, to automatically compensate for brake shoe wear. As the brake shoe linings wear, the footbrake operation automatically operates the adjuster mechanism, which effectively lengthens the shoe strut and repositions the brake shoes, to reduce the lining-to-drum clearance.

Zafira models not fitted with ABS are equipped with a rear brake proportioning valve. The valve senses the load in the rear of the vehicle, and controls the effort transferred to the rear brakes. With a heavy load, more effort can be applied to the rear brakes before skidding occurs.

ABS (Anti-lock Braking System) is available as an option on all models. When the ignition is switched on, an ABS symbol illuminates in the instrument panel for a short time while the system performs a self-test. The system comprises an electronic control unit, roadwheel sensors, hydraulic modulator, and the necessary valves and relays. The purpose of the system is to stop wheel(s) locking during heavy brake applications. This is achieved by automatic release of the brake on the locked wheel, followed by re-application of the brake. This procedure is carried out several times a second by the hydraulic modulator. The modulator is controlled by the electronic control unit, which itself receives signals from the wheel sensors, which monitor the locked or unlocked state of the wheels. The ABS unit is fitted between the brake master cylinder and the brakes. If the ABS symbol in the instrument panel stays lit, or if it comes on whilst driving, there is a fault in the system and the vehicle must be taken to a Vauxhall dealer for assessment using specialist diagnostic equipment.

The handbrake is cable-operated on the rear brakes by a lever mounted between the front seats.

Warning: When servicing any part of the system, work carefully and methodically; also observe scrupulous cleanliness when overhauling any part of the hydraulic system. Always renew components (in axle sets, where applicable) if in doubt about their condition, and use only genuine Vauxhall replacement parts, or at least those of known good quality. Note the warnings given in 'Safety first!' and at relevant points in this Chapter concerning the dangers of asbestos dust and hydraulic fluid.

2 Hydraulic system – bleeding

Warning: Hydraulic fluid is poisonous; wash off immediately and thoroughly in the case of skin contact, and seek immediate medical advice if any fluid is swallowed or gets into the eyes. Certain types of hydraulic fluid are inflammable, and may ignite when allowed into contact with hot components; when servicing any hydraulic system, it is safest to assume that the fluid is inflammable, and to take precautions against the risk of fire as though it is petrol that is being handled. Hydraulic fluid is also an effective paint stripper, and will attack plastics; if any is spilt, it should be washed off immediately, using copious quantities of fresh water. Finally, it is hygroscopic (it absorbs moisture from the air) – old fluid may be contaminated and unfit for further use. When topping-up or renewing the fluid, always use the recommended type, and ensure that it comes from a freshly-opened sealed container.

General

1 The correct operation of any hydraulic system is only possible after removing all air from the components and circuit; this is achieved by bleeding the system.

2 During the bleeding procedure, add only clean, unused hydraulic fluid of the recommended type; never re-use fluid that has already been bled from the system. Ensure that sufficient fluid is available before starting work.

3 If there is any possibility of incorrect fluid being already in the system, the brake components and circuit must be flushed completely with uncontaminated, correct fluid, and new seals should be fitted to the various components.

4 If hydraulic fluid has been lost from the system, or air has entered because of a leak, ensure that the fault is cured before proceeding further.

5 Park the vehicle over an inspection pit or on car ramps. Alternatively, apply the handbrake then jack up the front and rear of the vehicle and support it on axle stands (see *Jacking and vehicle support*). Where necessary, remove the splash guard from the bottom of the engine

compartment. For improved access with the vehicle jacked up, remove the roadwheels.

6 Check that all pipes and hoses are secure, unions tight and bleed screws closed. Clean any dirt from around the bleed screws.

7 Unscrew the master cylinder reservoir cap, and top-up the master cylinder reservoir to the MAX level line; refit the cap loosely, and remember to maintain the fluid level at least above the MIN level line throughout the procedure, otherwise there is a risk of further air entering the system.

8 There are a number of one-man, do-it-yourself brake bleeding kits currently available from motor accessory shops. It is recommended that one of these kits is used whenever possible, as they greatly simplify the bleeding operation, and also reduce the risk of expelled air and fluid being drawn back into the system. If such a kit is not available, the basic (two-man) method must be used, which is described in detail below.

9 If a kit is to be used, prepare the vehicle as described previously and follow the kit manufacturer's instructions, as the procedure may vary slightly according to the type being used; generally, they are as outlined below in the relevant sub-section.

10 Whichever method is used, the same sequence must be followed (paragraphs 11 and 12) to ensure the removal of all air from the system.

Bleeding sequence

11 If the system has been only partially disconnected, and suitable precautions were taken to minimise fluid loss, it should be necessary only to bleed that part of the system (ie, the primary or secondary circuit).

12 If the complete system is to be bled, then it should be done working in the following sequence:

Right-hand drive models
a) *Left-hand rear brake.*
b) *Right-hand rear brake.*
c) *Left-hand front brake.*
d) *Right-hand front brake.*

Left-hand drive models
a) *Right-hand rear brake.*
b) *Left-hand rear brake.*
c) *Right-hand front brake.*
d) *Left-hand front brake.*

Bleeding – basic (two-man) method

13 Collect together a clean glass jar, a suitable length of plastic or rubber tubing which is a tight fit over the bleed screw, and a ring spanner to fit the screw. The help of an assistant will also be required.

14 Remove the dust cap from the first bleed screw in the sequence **(see illustration)**. Fit the spanner and tube to the screw, place the other end of the tube in the jar, and pour in sufficient fluid to cover the end of the tube.

15 Ensure that the master cylinder reservoir fluid level is maintained at least above the MIN level line throughout the procedure.

16 Unscrew the first bleed screw approximately half a turn, then have the assistant fully depress and release the brake pedal slowly several times. On the final stroke, have the assistant hold the pedal firmly to the floor, then tighten the bleed screw. If only a small amount or fluid flows from the bleed screw, have the assistant depress the pedal vigorously for several strokes in order to force any trapped air along the hydraulic lines.

17 Have the assistant release the pedal slowly, then top-up the reservoir fluid level as necessary.

18 Repeat the steps given in paragraphs 16 and 17 until the fluid emerging from the bleed screw is free from air bubbles.

19 When no more air bubbles appear, securely tighten the bleed screw, remove the tube and spanner, and refit the dust cap. Do not overtighten the bleed screw.

20 Repeat the procedure on the remaining screws in the sequence, until all air is removed from the system and the brake pedal feels firm again.

Bleeding – using a one-way valve kit

21 As the name implies, these kits consist of a length of tubing with a one-way valve fitted, to prevent expelled air and fluid being drawn back into the system; some kits include a translucent container, which can be positioned so that the air bubbles can be more easily seen flowing from the end of the tube.

22 The kit is connected to the bleed screw, which is then opened **(see illustration)**. The

2.14 Dust cap on a bleed screw (arrowed)

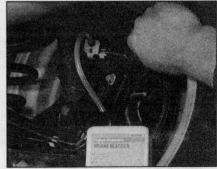

2.22 Using a one-way valve kit to bleed the rear brake

3.2 The front brake flexible hoses are supported in rubber grommets and retained with spring clips on the front suspension struts

user returns to the driver's seat, depresses the brake pedal with a smooth, steady stroke, and slowly releases it; this is repeated until the expelled fluid is clear of air bubbles.

23 Note that these kits simplify work so much that it is easy to forget the master cylinder reservoir fluid level; ensure that this is maintained at least above the MIN level line at all times.

Bleeding – using a pressure-bleeding kit

24 These kits are usually operated by a reservoir of pressurised air contained in the spare tyre. However, note that it will probably be necessary to reduce the pressure to a lower level than normal; refer to the instructions supplied with the kit.

25 By connecting a pressurised, fluid-filled container to the master cylinder reservoir, bleeding can be carried out simply by opening each screw in turn (in the specified sequence), and allowing the fluid to flow out until no more air bubbles can be seen in the expelled fluid.

26 This method has the advantage that the large reservoir of fluid provides an additional safeguard against air being drawn into the system during bleeding.

27 Pressure-bleeding is particularly effective when bleeding 'difficult' systems, or when bleeding the complete system at the time of routine fluid renewal.

All methods

28 When bleeding is complete, and firm pedal feel is restored, wash off any spilt fluid, securely tighten the bleed screws, and refit the dust caps.

29 Check the hydraulic fluid level in the master cylinder reservoir, and top-up if necessary (see *Weekly checks*).

30 Discard any hydraulic fluid that has been bled from the system; it will not be fit for re-use.

31 Check the feel of the brake pedal. If it feels at all spongy, air must still be present in the system, and further bleeding is required.

Failure to bleed satisfactorily after a reasonable repetition of the bleeding procedure may be due to worn master cylinder seals.

3 Hydraulic pipes and hoses – renewal

Note: *Before starting work, refer to the note at the beginning of Section 2 concerning the dangers of hydraulic fluid.*

1 If any pipe or hose is to be renewed, minimise fluid loss by first removing the master cylinder reservoir cap, then tightening it down onto a piece of polythene to obtain an airtight seal. Alternatively, hose clamps can be fitted to flexible hoses to isolate sections of the circuit; metal brake pipe unions can be plugged (if care is taken not to allow dirt into the system) or capped immediately they are disconnected. Place a wad of rag under any union that is to be disconnected, to catch any spilt fluid.

2 If a flexible hose is to be disconnected, unscrew the brake pipe union nut before removing the spring clip which secures the hose to its mounting bracket. Where applicable, unscrew the banjo union bolt securing the hose to the caliper and recover the copper washers. When removing the front flexible hose, pull out the spring clip and pull the rubber grommet from the bracket on the front suspension strut **(see illustration)**.

3 To unscrew union nuts, it is preferable to obtain a brake pipe spanner of the correct size; these are available from most motor accessory shops. Failing this, a close-fitting open-ended spanner will be required, though if the nuts are tight or corroded, their flats may be rounded-off if the spanner slips. In such a case, a self-locking wrench is often the only way to unscrew a stubborn union, but it follows that the pipe and the damaged nuts must be renewed on reassembly. Always clean a union and surrounding area before disconnecting it. If disconnecting a component with more than one union, make a careful note of the connections before disturbing any of them.

4 If a brake pipe is to be renewed, it can be obtained, cut to length and with the union nuts and end flares in place, from Vauxhall dealers. All that is then necessary is to bend it to shape, following the line of the original, before fitting it to the car. Alternatively, most motor accessory shops can make up brake pipes from kits, but this requires very careful measurement of the original, to ensure that the replacement is of the correct length. The safest answer is usually to take the original to the shop as a pattern.

5 On refitting, securely tighten the union nuts but do not overtighten.

6 When refitting hoses to the calipers, always use new copper washers and tighten the banjo union bolts to the specified torque. Make sure that the hoses are positioned so that they will not touch surrounding bodywork or the roadwheels.

7 Ensure that the pipes and hoses are correctly routed, with no kinks, and that they are secured in the clips or brackets provided. After fitting, remove the polythene from the reservoir, and bleed the hydraulic system as described in Section 2. Wash off any spilt fluid, and check carefully for fluid leaks.

4 Front brake pads – renewal

> ⚠ **Warning: Renew BOTH sets of front brake pads at the same time – NEVER renew the pads on only one wheel, as uneven braking may result. Note that the dust created by wear of the pads may contain asbestos, which is a health hazard. Never blow it out with compressed air, and do not inhale any of it. Use brake cleaner or methylated spirit to clean brake components.**

1 Apply the handbrake, then jack up the front of the vehicle and support it on axle stands (see *Jacking and vehicle support*). Remove both front roadwheels.

2 Where applicable, use a screwdriver lever out the brake pad warning sensor and unclip it from the retainer **(see illustrations)**.

4.2a Removing the front brake pad warning sensor . . .

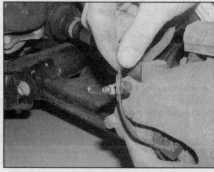

4.2b . . . and unclipping the wire from the retainer

4.3a Removing the retaining spring from the front caliper – Zafira model

4.3b Removing the retaining spring from the front caliper – Astra model

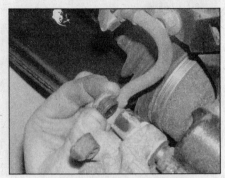

4.4 Remove the dust caps . . .

3 Prise the retaining spring from the outer edge of the caliper, noting its correct fitted position **(see illustrations)**.

4 Remove the dust caps from the inner ends of the guide bolts **(see illustration)**.

5 Unscrew the guide bolts from the caliper, and lift the caliper and pads away from the mounting bracket or hub carrier (as applicable) **(see illustrations)**. Tie the caliper to the suspension strut using a suitable piece of wire. Do not allow the caliper to hang unsupported on the flexible brake hose.

6 Remove the outer pad, then remove the inner pad, noting that it is retained by a spring clip attached to the pad backing plate **(see illustrations)**.

7 Brush the dirt and dust from the caliper and piston, but take care not to inhale it. Scrape any rust from the edge of the brake disc.

8 Measure the thickness of the friction lining on each brake pad **(see illustration)**. If either pad is worn at any point to the specified minimum thickness or less, all four pads must be renewed. The pads should also be renewed if any are contaminated with oil or grease, since there is no satisfactory way of degreasing friction material, once contaminated. If any of the brake pads are worn unevenly, or contaminate with oil or grease, trace and rectify the cause before reassembly.

9 If the brake pads are still serviceable, carefully clean them using a clean, fine wire brush or similar, paying particular attention to the sides and back of the metal backing. Clean out the grooves in the friction material, and pick out any large embedded particles of dirt or debris. Carefully clean the pad locations in the caliper body/mounting bracket.

10 Prior to fitting the pads, check that the guide bolts are a snug fit in the caliper

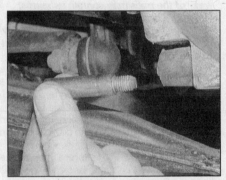

4.5a . . . then unscrew the guide bolts . . .

4.5b . . . and lift the caliper away from the mounting bracket – Zafira model

4.5c Removing the caliper from the hub carrier – Astra model

4.6a Removing the outer pad from the mounting bracket . . .

4.6b . . . and the inner pad from the caliper

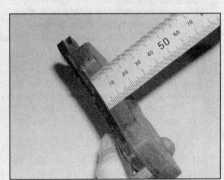

4.8 Using a rule to measure the thickness of the front brake pad lining

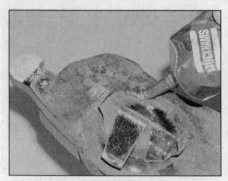

4.10 Apply a little copper grease to the contact areas of the pad backing plates

4.11a Using a clamp tool to force the piston into the front brake caliper

4.11b Clamping tool used to retract the caliper pistons

bushes. Apply a little copper brake grease to the areas on the pad backing plates which contact the caliper and piston (see illustration). Inspect the dust seal around the piston for damage, and the piston for evidence of fluid leaks, corrosion or damage. If attention to any of these components is necessary, refer to Section 9.

11 If new brake pads are to be fitted, the caliper piston must be pushed back into the cylinder to make room for them. Vauxhall technicians use a special tool, and a similar tool may be obtained from a car accessory shop (see illustrations). Alternatively, a G-clamp or similar tool may be used, or suitable pieces of wood may be used as levers. Provided that the master cylinder reservoir has not been overfilled with hydraulic fluid, there should be no spillage, but keep a watch on the fluid level while retracting the piston. If the fluid level rises above the MAX level line at any time, the surplus should be syphoned off or ejected via a plastic tube connected to the bleed screw.

There have been some instances of damage being caused to the master cylinder seals when pushing the piston back into the caliper, and we therefore recommend that a hose clamp is fitted to the brake hose leading to the caliper and hydraulic fluid drained through the bleed nipple. Using this method will also remove any deteriorated hydraulic fluid which may have accumulated near the caliper.

12 Fit the inner pad to the caliper, ensuring that its clip is correctly located in the caliper piston. Note: *The pads are 'handed' for each side – make sure that the arrow on the backing plate points in the direction of rotation of the brake disc when the vehicle is travelling forwards.*

13 Fit the outer pad to the caliper mounting bracket, ensuring that its friction material is facing the brake disc. Note that the outer pad has an acoustic pad wear warning spring attached to it (see illustration).

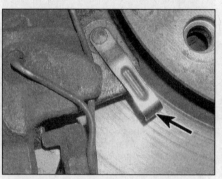

4.13 The outer pad has an acoustic pad wear warning spring attached to it

14 Slide the caliper and inner pad into position over the outer pad, and locate it in the mounting bracket.

15 Insert the caliper guide bolts, and tighten them to the specified torque setting (see illustration).

16 Refit the guide bolt dust caps.

17 Refit the retaining spring to the caliper it its previously-noted position. One of two types of spring are fitted – one is attached to the caliper and the other is attached to clips on the outer disc pad. With the latter, attach the spring to the pad first, then swivel it over the lugs on the caliper.

18 Refit the brake pad warning sensor.

19 Depress the brake pedal repeatedly, until normal pedal pressure is restored.

20 Repeat the above procedure on the remaining front brake caliper.

21 Refit the roadwheels, then lower the vehicle to the ground and tighten the roadwheel bolts to the specified torque setting.

22 Check the hydraulic fluid level as described in *Weekly checks*.

5 Rear brake pads – renewal

Warning: Renew BOTH sets of rear brake pads at the same time – NEVER renew the pads on only one wheel, as uneven braking

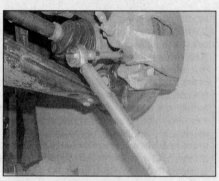

4.15 Tightening the caliper guide bolts with a torque wrench

may result. Note that the dust created by wear of the pads may contain asbestos, which is a health hazard. Never blow it out with compressed air, and do not inhale any of it. Use brake cleaner or methylated spirit to clean brake components.

1 Chock the front wheels, then jack up the rear of the vehicle and support it on axle stands (see *Jacking and vehicle support*). Remove both rear roadwheels.

2 Fully release the handbrake lever, then back off the adjustment nut to provide slack in the handbrake cable.

3 Using a screwdriver, press down the handbrake lever on the back of the rear caliper, then disconnect the inner cable. Disconnect the cable from the support bracket by first removing the retaining clip (see illustrations).

5.3a Disconnecting the handbrake inner cable from the lever on the rear caliper

5.3b Remove the retaining clip and disconnect the handbrake cable from the support bracket

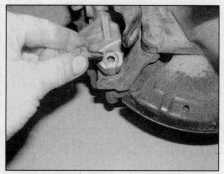

5.4a Unscrew the rear brake caliper lower mounting bolt . . .

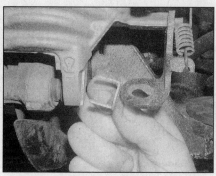

5.4b . . . and recover the special clip

4 Unscrew and remove the brake caliper lower mounting bolt, noting that the guide pin is held stationary by the special clip. Recover the special clip **(see illustrations)**.

5 Swivel the caliper upwards around the upper guide pin and withdraw the brake pads from their location in the mounting bracket **(see illustrations)**.

6 Brush the dirt and dust from the caliper and piston, but take care not to inhale it. Scrape any rust from the edge of the brake disc.

7 Measure the thickness of the friction lining on each brake pad **(see illustration)**. If either pad is worn at any point to the specified minimum thickness or less, all four pads must be renewed. The pads should also be renewed if any are contaminated with oil or grease; there is no satisfactory way of

degreasing friction material, once contaminated. If any of the brake pads are worn unevenly, or contaminated with oil or grease, trace and rectify the cause before reassembly.

8 If the brake pads are still serviceable, clean them using a clean, fine wire brush or similar, paying particular attention to the sides and back of the metal backing. Clean the pad locations in the caliper body/mounting bracket.

9 Apply a little copper brake grease to the areas on the pad backing plates which contact the caliper and piston. Inspect the dust seal around the piston for damage, and the piston for evidence of fluid leaks, corrosion or damage. If attention to any of these components is necessary, refer to Section 10.

10 If new brake pads are to be fitted, the caliper piston must be pushed back into the cylinder to make room for them. First, however note the alignment marks on the piston and caliper – the piston cut-out must be aligned with the raised nib on the caliper. Vauxhall technicians use a special tool which engages the cut-outs in the piston, and a similar tool may be obtained from a car accessory shop **(see illustrations)**. Alternatively, a G-clamp or similar tool may be used, but note that the piston must be turned as it is being forced into its bore. Provided that the master cylinder reservoir has not been overfilled with hydraulic fluid, there should be no spillage, but keep a careful watch on the fluid level while retracting the piston. If the fluid level rises above the MAX level line at any time, the surplus should be syphoned off or ejected via a plastic tube connected to the bleed screw.

> **HAYNES HiNT** *There have been some instances of damage being caused to the master cylinder seals when pushing the piston back into the caliper, and we therefore recommend that a hose clamp is fitted to the brake hose leading to the caliper and hydraulic fluid drained through the bleed nipple. Using this method will also remove any deteriorated hydraulic fluid which may have accumulated near the caliper.*

5.5a Removing the outer brake pad . . .

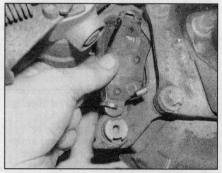

5.5b . . . and inner brake pad from the rear caliper mounting bracket

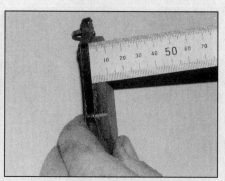

5.7 Using a rule to measure the thickness of the brake pad friction lining

5.10a The cut-out in the piston must be aligned with the raised nib on the caliper

5.10b Using the special tool to force the piston into the caliper

5.12 The audio wear sensor is located on the inner brake pad

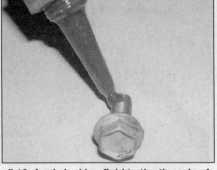

5.13 Apply locking fluid to the threads of the caliper mounting bolt before refitting it

6.3 Checking the wear of the rear brake shoe friction material

11 Turn the piston as necessary to align the mark with the nib on the caliper.

12 Swivel the caliper upwards, then locate the new pads in the mounting bracket, making sure that the friction material faces the disc, and the audio wear sensor is on the inner pad **(see illustration)**.

13 Swivel the caliper down and make sure that the pads are correctly seated. Use a wire brush to clean the threads of the caliper lower mounting bolt, then apply a little locking fluid to the threads and insert the bolt **(see illustration)**. Tighten the bolt to the specified torque while holding the guide pin with a further spanner.

14 Refit the handbrake cable to the support bracket and secure with the retaining clip.

15 Press down the handbrake lever and reconnect the end of the cable to it.

16 Depress the brake pedal several times to restore normal pedal feel.

17 Repeat the above procedure on the remaining rear brake caliper.

18 Adjust the handbrake cable as described in Section 18.

19 Refit the roadwheels, then lower the vehicle to the ground and tighten the roadwheel bolts to the specified torque.

20 Check the brake hydraulic fluid level as described in *Weekly checks*.

6 Rear brake shoes – renewal

⚠️ *Warning: Brake shoes must be renewed on both rear wheels at the same time – never renew the shoes on only one wheel, as uneven braking may result. Also, the dust created by wear of the shoes may contain asbestos, which is a health hazard. Never blow it out with compressed air, and do not inhale any of it. An approved filtering mask should be worn when working on the brakes. DO NOT use petrol or petroleum-based solvents to clean brake parts; use brake cleaner or methylated spirit only.*

1 Remove the rear brake drum as described in Section 8.

2 Taking precautions to avoid inhalation of dust, remove the brake dust from the brake drum, shoes and backplate.

3 Measure the thickness of the friction material of each brake shoe at several points; if either shoe is worn at any point to the specified minimum thickness or less, **all four** shoes must be renewed as a set **(see illustration)**. The shoes should also be renewed if any are contaminated with oil or grease, since there is no satisfactory way of degreasing the friction material.

4 If any of the brake shoes are worn excessively, or contaminated with oil or grease, trace and rectify the cause before reassembly.

5 Note the location and orientation of all components before dismantling, as an aid to reassembly **(see illustration)**.

6 Using a pair of pliers, carefully unhook the upper shoe return spring, and remove it from the brake shoes **(see illustration)**.

7 Prise the adjusting lever retaining spring out of the front shoe, and remove the retaining spring, lever and return spring from the brake shoe, noting each component's correct fitted position **(see illustration)**.

8 Prise the upper ends of the brake shoes apart, and withdraw the adjuster strut from between the shoes.

9 Using a pair of pliers, remove the front shoe retainer spring cup by depressing and turning it through 90°. With the cup removed, lift off the spring and withdraw the retainer pin **(see illustrations)**.

6.5 Prior to disturbing the shoes, note the correct fitted locations of all components, paying particular attention to the adjuster strut components

6.6 Unhook the upper return spring, and remove it from the brake shoes

6.7 Remove the retaining spring, followed by the lever and return spring (arrowed)

6.9a Using pliers, remove the spring cup . . .

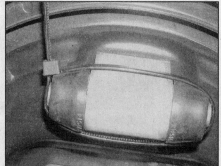

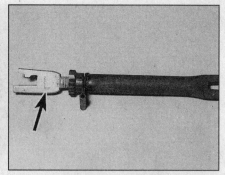

6.9b . . . then lift off the spring and retainer pin

6.12 Plastic cable tie retaining the wheel cylinder pistons

6.13 The left-hand adjuster strut assembly is marked L (arrowed)

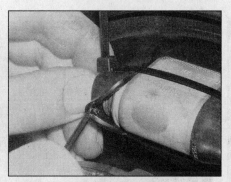

6.16 It may be necessary to transfer the adjusting lever pivot pin and clip (arrowed) from the original shoes to the new ones

6.17 Checking the wheel cylinder for hydraulic fluid leaks

6.18 Apply a smear of anti-seize compound to the shoe contact surfaces of the backplate

10 Detach the front shoe from the lower return spring, and remove both the shoe and return spring.

11 Remove the rear shoe retainer spring cup, spring and retainer pin as described in paragraph 9, then remove the shoe, detaching it from the handbrake cable.

12 **Do not** depress the brake pedal with the shoes removed. As a precaution, fit a strong elastic band or plastic cable tie around the wheel cylinder pistons to retain them **(see illustration)**.

13 If both brake assemblies are dismantled at the same time, take care not to mix them up. Note that the left-hand and right-hand adjuster components are marked as such; the threaded rod is marked L or R, and the other 'handed' components are colour-coded black for the left-hand side, and silver for the right-

hand side **(see illustration)**.

14 Dismantle and clean the adjuster strut. Apply a smear of silicone-based grease to the adjuster threads.

15 Examine the return springs. If they are distorted, or if they have seen extensive service, renewal is advisable. Weak springs may cause the brakes to bind.

16 If a new handbrake operating lever was not supplied with the new shoes (where applicable), transfer the lever from the old shoes. The lever may be secured with a pin and circlip, or by a rivet, which will have to be drilled out. It may also be necessary to transfer the adjusting lever pivot pin and clip from the original front shoe to the new shoe **(see illustration)**.

17 Peel back the rubber protective caps, and check the wheel cylinder for fluid leaks or

other damage **(see illustration)**. Ensure that both cylinder pistons are free to move easily. Refer to Section 11, if necessary, for information on wheel cylinder overhaul.

18 Prior to installation, clean the backplate thoroughly. Apply a thin smear of high-temperature copper-based brake grease or anti-seize compound to the shoe contact surfaces on the backplate and wheel cylinder pistons **(see illustration)**. Do not allow the grease to foul the friction lining material.

19 Ensure that the handbrake cable is correctly retained by the clip on the lower brake shoe pivot point, then engage the rear shoe with the cable. Locate the shoe on the backplate **(see illustration)**.

20 Install the rear shoe retainer pin and spring, and secure it in position with the spring cup **(see illustrations)**.

6.19 Engage the rear brake shoe with the handbrake cable, and locate the shoe on the backplate

6.20a Fit the rear shoe retainer pin . . .

6.20b . . . and spring . . .

6.20c ... then secure with the spring cup

6.21a Fit the lower return spring ...

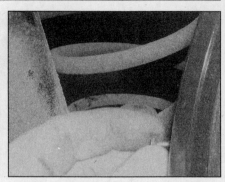

6.21b ... then secure the front shoe by fitting the shoe retainer pin ...

6.21c ... followed by the spring and spring cup

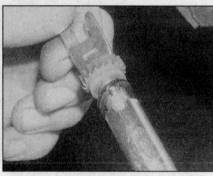

6.22 Screw in the adjuster strut to its shortest length

21 Hook the lower return spring onto the rear shoe, then engage the front shoe with the return spring. Locate the front shoe on the backplate, and secure it in position with its retainer pin, spring and spring cup (**see illustrations**).

22 Screw the adjuster strut wheel fully onto the forked end of the adjuster, so that the adjuster strut is set to its shortest possible length. Back the wheel off a half a turn, and check that it is free to rotate easily (**see illustration**).

23 Manoeuvre the adjuster strut assembly into position between the brake shoes. Make sure that both ends of the strut are correctly engaged with the shoes, noting that the forked end of the strut must be positioned so that its longer, straight fork is to the rear of the shoe (**see illustration**).

24 Engage the adjusting lever plate with the front shoe and strut ratchet, and locate the plate on its pivot pin. Check that the plate is correctly located, and secure in position with the retaining spring, making sure the spring ends are securely located in the retaining pin and shoe (**see illustrations**).

25 Remove the rubber band or plastic cable tie from the wheel cylinder. Make sure that both shoes are correctly positioned on the wheel cylinder pistons, then fit the upper return spring (**see illustrations**).

6.23 Fit the adjuster strut between the brake shoes, making sure that the longer fork is located to the rear of the shoe

6.24a Fit the adjusting lever plate ...

6.24b ... and secure with the retaining spring

6.25a Hook the rear end of the upper return spring in the trailing shoe ...

6.25b ... then pull the front end of the spring onto the leading shoe

6.26 Fitting the adjusting lever tension spring

7.2 Tighten the roadwheel bolts onto spacers before checking the brake disc for wear

7.3 Checking the brake disc thickness with a micrometer

26 Fit the tension spring to the adjusting lever plate and leading shoe **(see illustration)**.

27 Ensure that the handbrake operating lever stop peg is correctly positioned against the edge of the shoe web, then refit the brake drum as described in Section 8.

28 Repeat the operation on the remaining brake.

29 Once both sets of rear shoes have been renewed, with the handbrake fully released, adjust the lining-to-drum clearance by repeatedly depressing the brake pedal at least 20 to 25 times. Whilst depressing the pedal, have an assistant listen to the rear drums, to check that the adjuster strut is functioning correctly; if so, a clicking sound will be emitted by the strut as the pedal is depressed.

30 Check and, if necessary, adjust the handbrake as described in Section 18.

31 On completion, check the hydraulic fluid level as described in *Weekly checks.*
Caution: New shoes will not give full braking efficiency until they have bedded-in. Be prepared for this, and avoid hard braking as far as possible for the first hundred miles or so after shoe renewal.

7 Front/rear brake disc – inspection, removal and refitting

⚠️ *Warning: Before starting work, refer to the warning at the beginning of Section 4 concerning the dangers of asbestos dust. If either disc requires renewal, both should be renewed at the same time together with new pads, to ensure even and consistent braking.*

Inspection

1 Remove the wheel trim, then loosen the roadwheel bolts. If checking a front disc, apply the handbrake, and if checking a rear disc, chock the front wheels, then jack up the relevant end of the vehicle and support on axle stands (see *Jacking and vehicle support*). Remove the roadwheel.

2 Check that the brake disc securing screw is tight, then fit spacers approximately 10.0 mm thick to the roadwheel bolts, and tighten them into the hub **(see illustration)**.

3 Rotate the brake disc, and examine it for deep scoring or grooving. Light scoring is normal, but if excessive, the disc should be removed and either renewed or machined (within the specified limits) by an engineering

works. Check the thickness of the disc using a micrometer. The minimum thickness is stamped on the outer face of the rear disc **(see illustration)**.

4 Using a dial gauge, or a flat metal block and feeler blades, check that the disc run-out does not exceed the figure given in the Specifications **(see illustration)**. Measure the run-out 10.0 mm (0.4 in) in from the outer edge of the disc.

5 If the rear disc run-out is excessive, check the rear wheel bearing adjustment, as described in Chapter 10.

6 If the front disc run-out is excessive, remove the disc as described later, and check that the disc-to-hub surfaces are perfectly clean. Refit the disc and check the run-out again.

7 If the run-out is still excessive, the disc should be renewed.

8 To remove a disc, proceed as follows.

Front disc

Removal

9 Remove the roadwheel bolts and spacers used when checking the disc.

10 Unbolt and remove the front brake caliper complete with disc pads and mounting bracket and tie it to one side **(see illustrations)**. On models with ABS and all 2.0 litre models, remove the mounting bracket

7.4 Using a dial gauge to check the brake disc for run-out

7.10a Unscrew the mounting bolts . . .

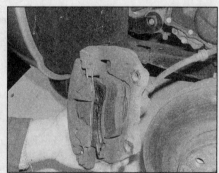

7.10b . . . and remove the front brake caliper complete with disc pads and mounting bracket

7.11a Remove the securing screw . . .

7.11b . . . and remove the front brake disc

7.17a Remove the securing screw . . .

7.17b . . . and remove the rear brake disc

with reference to Section 9, and also release the flexible brake hose from the support on the strut.

11 Remove the securing screw and withdraw the disc from the hub **(see illustrations)**.

Refitting

12 Refitting is a reversal of removal, but make sure that the mating faces of the disc and hub are perfectly clean, and apply a little locking fluid to the threads of the securing screw.

13 Refit the disc pads with reference to Section 4.

Rear disc

Removal

14 Remove the roadwheel bolts and spacers used when checking the disc.

15 Remove the rear brake pads, as described in Section 5, then slide the caliper from its upper swivel bearing. Move the caliper to one side, and suspend it using wire or string to avoid straining the pipe.

16 Unbolt the caliper mounting bracket from the trailing arm.

17 Undo the securing screw and withdraw the disc from the hub **(see illustrations)**.

Refitting

18 Refitting is a reversal of removal, but make sure that the mating faces of the disc and hub are perfectly clean, and apply a little locking fluid to the threads of the securing screw. Refit the caliper mounting bracket and tighten the mounting bolts to the specified

torque. Clean the caliper upper pin, then apply silicone grease to it. Slide the caliper into its upper swivel bearing and refit the brake pads as described in Section 5.

---

8   Rear brake drum – removal, inspection and refitting

⚠️ **Warning: Before starting work, refer to the warning at the beginning of Section 6 concerning the dangers of asbestos dust.**

Removal

1 Remove the relevant wheel trim, then loosen the rear roadwheel bolts and chock the front wheels. Jack up the rear of the vehicle, and support on axle stands (see *Jacking and*

8.3a Undo the screw . . .

vehicle support) positioned under the body sidemembers. Remove the roadwheel.

2 Fully release the handbrake.

3 Extract the drum securing screw and remove the drum **(see illustrations)**. If the drum is tight, remove the plug from the inspection hole in the brake backplate, and push the handbrake operating lever away from the brake shoe to allow the shoes to move away from the drums. If necessary, slacken the handbrake cable adjuster on the lever inside the vehicle.

Inspection

4 Brush the dirt and dust from the drum, taking care not to inhale it.

5 Examine the internal friction surface of the drum. If deeply scored, or so worn that the drum has become ridged to the width of the shoes, then both drums must be renewed.

6 Regrinding of the friction surface may be possible provided the maximum diameter given in the Specifications is not exceeded, but note that both rear drums should be reground to the identical diameter. The manufacturers recommend fitting oversize brake shoes after regrinding the drums – refer to your Vauxhall dealer.

Refitting

7 Before refitting the drum, make sure that the handbrake operating lever is returned to its normal position on the brake shoe.

8 Refit the brake drum and tighten the securing screw. If necessary, back off the adjuster wheel on the strut until the drum will pass over the shoes.

9 Adjust the brakes by operating the footbrake a number of times. A clicking noise will be heard at the drum as the automatic adjuster operates. When the clicking stops, adjustment is complete.

10 Refit the roadwheel and lower the vehicle to the ground.

---

9   Front brake caliper – removal, overhaul and refitting

⚠️ **Warning: Before starting work, refer to the note at the beginning of Section 2**

8.3b . . . and remove the brake drum

9.5 Type of hub carrier incorporating an integral caliper mounting bracket

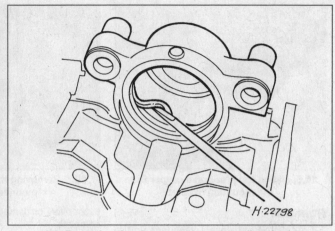

9.8 Removing the piston seal from the caliper body

concerning the dangers of hydraulic fluid, and to the warning at the beginning of Section 4 concerning the dangers of asbestos dust.

Removal

1 Apply the handbrake, then jack up the front of the vehicle and support it on axle stands (see Jacking and vehicle support). Remove the roadwheel.
2 Minimise fluid loss by first removing the master cylinder reservoir cap, then tightening it down onto a piece of polythene to obtain an airtight seal. Alternatively, use a brake hose clamp, a G-clamp or a similar tool to clamp the flexible hose leading to the brake caliper.
3 Clean the area around the caliper brake hose union. Unscrew and remove the union bolt, and recover the sealing washer from each side of the hose union. Discard the washers; new ones must be used on refitting. Plug the hose end and caliper hole, to minimise fluid loss and prevent the ingress of dirt into the hydraulic system.
4 Remove the brake pads as described in Section 4, then remove the caliper from the vehicle.
5 If necessary on 1.7 litre models with ABS and all 2.0 litre models, unbolt the caliper mounting bracket from the hub carrier. On all other models, the bracket is incorporated in the hub carrier casting (see illustration).

Overhaul

Note: It is not possible to overhaul the front brake caliper fitted to 1.7 litre models nor 2.0 litre models without ABS – if unserviceable, the caliper must be renewed complete. The following procedure refers to 2.0 litre models with ABS.
6 With the caliper on the bench, wipe it clean with a cloth rag.
7 Withdraw the partially-ejected piston from the caliper body, and remove the dust seal. The piston can be withdrawn by hand, or if necessary pushed out by applying compressed air to the brake hose union hole.

Only low pressure should be required, such as is generated by a foot pump, and as a precaution a block of wood should be positioned to prevent any damage to the piston. Note: The piston is manufactured of plastic on models where the caliper mounting bracket is integrated in the hub carrier.
8 Using a small screwdriver, carefully remove the piston seal from the caliper, taking care not to mark the bore (see illustration).
9 Carefully press the guide bushes out of the caliper body.
10 Thoroughly clean all components, using only methylated spirit or clean hydraulic fluid. Never use mineral-based solvents such as petrol or paraffin, which will attack the rubber components of the hydraulic system. Dry the components using compressed air or a clean, lint-free cloth. If available, use compressed air to blow clear the fluid passages.

 Warning: Wear eye protection when using compressed air.

11 Check all components, and renew any that are worn or damaged. If the piston and/or cylinder bore are scratched excessively, renew the complete caliper body. Similarly check the condition of the guide bushes and bolts; both bushes and bolts should be undamaged and (when cleaned) a reasonably tight sliding fit. If there is any doubt about the condition of any component, renew it.
12 If the caliper is fit for further use, obtain the necessary components from your Vauxhall dealer. Renew the caliper seals and dust covers as a matter of course, as these should never be re-used.
13 On reassembly, first ensure that all components are absolutely clean and dry.
14 Dip the piston and the new piston seal in clean hydraulic fluid, and smear clean fluid on the cylinder bore surface.
15 Locate the new seal in the cylinder bore groove, using only the fingers to manipulate it into position.
16 Fit the new dust seal to the piston, then

insert the piston into the cylinder bore using a twisting motion to ensure it enters the seal correctly. Make sure the piston enters squarely into the bore. Locate the dust seal in the body groove, and push the piston fully into the caliper bore.
17 Insert the guide bushes into position in the caliper body.

Refitting

18 On 1.7 litre models with ABS and all 2.0 litre models, locate the caliper mounting bracket on the hub carrier, then insert and tighten the bolts (with locking fluid applied to their threads) to the specified torque.
19 Refit the brake pads as described in Section 4, together with the caliper which at this stage will not have the hose attached.
20 Position a new copper sealing washer on each side of the hose union, and connect the brake hose to the caliper. Ensure that the hose is correctly positioned against the caliper body lug, then insert the union bolt and tighten it to the specified torque.
21 Remove the brake hose clamp or the polythene, where fitted, and bleed the hydraulic system as described in Section 2. Note that, providing the precautions described were taken to minimise brake fluid loss, it should only be necessary to bleed the relevant front brake circuit.
22 Refit the roadwheel, then lower the vehicle to the ground and tighten the roadwheel bolts to the specified torque.

10 Rear brake caliper – removal, overhaul and refitting

 Warning: Before starting work, refer to the note at the beginning of Section 2 concerning the dangers of hydraulic fluid, and to the warning at the beginning of Section 4 concerning the dangers of asbestos dust.

10.6 Sliding the rear brake caliper from the mounting bracket

10.7 Removing the rear brake caliper mounting bracket

Removal

1 Chock the front wheels, then jack up the rear of the vehicle and support it on axle stands (see *Jacking and vehicle support*). Remove the rear roadwheels.

2 Fully release the handbrake lever, then unscrew the adjustment nut to provide slack in the handbrake cable.

3 Using a screwdriver, press down the handbrake lever on the back of the rear caliper, then disconnect the inner cable. Disconnect the outer cable from the support bracket by first removing the retaining clip.

4 Minimise fluid loss by first removing the master cylinder reservoir cap, then tightening it down onto a piece of polythene to obtain an airtight seal. Alternatively, use a brake hose clamp, a G-clamp or a similar tool to clamp the flexible hose leading to the brake caliper.

5 Clean the area around the caliper brake hose union. Unscrew and remove the union bolt, and recover the sealing washer from each side of the hose union. Discard the washers; new ones must be used on refitting. Plug the hose end and caliper hole, to minimise fluid loss and prevent the ingress of dirt into the hydraulic system.

6 Remove the brake pads as described in Section 5, then slide the caliper from its upper swivel bearing **(see illustration)**.

7 If necessary, unbolt the caliper mounting bracket from the trailing arm **(see illustration)**.

Overhaul

8 It is **not** possible to overhaul the rear brake caliper. If the caliper is worn excessively or damaged, it must be renewed complete.

9 Remove the caliper lower guide pin from the mounting bracket and wipe it clean. Check the pin for excessive wear and renew it if necessary. Smear some silicone grease on the guide pin inner and outer surfaces, then refit it.

10 Where the caliper incorporates a damping weight/absorber, disconnect the spring and unbolt the handbrake cable bracket. Transfer the parts to the new caliper, and tighten the bolt to the specified torque. The bolt threads should have locking fluid applied to them.

Refitting

11 Where removed, refit the caliper mounting bracket to the trailing arm. Apply locking fluid to the threads of the mounting bolts, then insert them and tighten to the specified torque **(see illustrations)**.

12 Clean the caliper upper swivel pin, then apply silicone grease to it. Slide the caliper into its upper guide bearing and refit the brake pads as described in Section 5.

13 Position a new copper sealing washer on each side of the hose union, and connect the brake hose to the caliper. Ensure that the hose is correctly positioned, then insert the union bolt and tighten it to the specified torque.

14 Remove the brake hose clamp or the polythene, where fitted, and bleed the hydraulic system as described in Section 2. Note that, providing the precautions described were taken to minimise brake fluid loss, it should only be necessary to bleed the relevant rear brake circuit.

15 Refit the handbrake cable to the support bracket and secure with the retaining clip.

16 Press down the handbrake lever and reconnect the end of the cable to it.

17 Depress the brake pedal several times to ensure the brake pads are set to their normal position.

18 Adjust the handbrake cable as described in Section 18, then refit the lever gaiter.

19 Refit the roadwheels, then lower the vehicle to the ground and tighten the roadwheel bolts to the specified torque.

20 Check the brake hydraulic fluid level as described in *Weekly checks*.

21 Refit the roadwheel, then lower the vehicle to the ground and tighten the roadwheel bolts to the specified torque.

11 Rear wheel cylinder – removal, overhaul and refitting

Warning: Before starting work, refer to the note at the beginning of Section 2 concerning the dangers of hydraulic fluid, and to the warning at the beginning of Section 4 concerning the dangers of asbestos dust.
Note: *Check that an overhaul kit of rubbers is available.*

Removal

1 Remove the brake drum (see Section 8).

2 Minimise fluid loss by first removing the master cylinder reservoir cap, and then tightening it down onto a piece of polythene, to obtain an airtight seal. Alternatively, use a brake hose clamp, a G-clamp or a similar tool to clamp the flexible hose at the nearest convenient point to the wheel cylinder.

3 Carefully unhook the brake shoe upper return spring, and remove it from both brake shoes. Pull the upper ends of the shoes away from the wheel cylinder to disengage them from the pistons.

4 Wipe away all traces of dirt around the brake pipe union nut at the rear of the wheel cylinder, and unscrew the nut. Carefully ease the pipe out of the wheel cylinder, and plug or tape over its end to prevent dirt entry. Wipe off any spilt fluid immediately.

5 Unscrew the retaining bolt from the rear of the backplate, and remove the wheel cylinder, taking care not to allow surplus hydraulic fluid to contaminate the brake shoe linings.

Overhaul

6 Brush the dirt and dust from the wheel cylinder, but take care not to inhale it.

10.11a Apply locking fluid to the threads . . .

10.11b . . . before inserting and tightening the rear caliper mounting bracket bolts

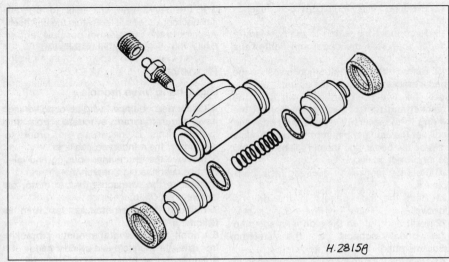

11.7 Exploded view of the rear brake wheel cylinder

12.2 Brake master cylinder and fluid reservoir – Zafira model

7 Pull the rubber dust seals from the ends of the cylinder body **(see illustration)**.

8 The pistons will normally be ejected by the pressure of the coil spring, but if they are not, tap the end of the cylinder body on a piece of wood, or apply low air pressure (eg, from a foot pump) to the hydraulic fluid union hole to eject the pistons from their bores.

9 Inspect the surfaces of the pistons and their bores in the cylinder body for scoring, or evidence of metal-to-metal contact. If evident, renew the complete wheel cylinder assembly.

10 If the pistons and bores are in good condition, discard the seals and obtain a repair kit, which will contain all the necessary renewable items.

11 Lubricate the piston seals with clean brake fluid, and insert them into the cylinder bores, with the spring between them, using finger pressure only.

12 Dip the pistons in clean brake fluid, and insert them into the cylinder bores.

13 Fit the dust seals, and check that the pistons can move freely in their bores.

Refitting

14 Ensure that the backplate and wheel cylinder mating surfaces are clean, then spread the brake shoes and manoeuvre the wheel cylinder into position.

15 Insert the brake pipe, and screw in the union nut two or three turns to ensure that the thread has started.

16 Insert the wheel cylinder retaining bolt, and tighten to the specified torque setting. Now tighten the brake pipe union nut to the specified torque.

17 Remove the clamp from the flexible brake hose, or the polythene from the master cylinder reservoir (as applicable).

18 Ensure that the brake shoes are correctly located in the cylinder pistons, then refit the brake shoe upper return spring.

19 Refit the brake drum as described in Section 8.

20 Bleed the brake hydraulic system as described in Section 2. Providing suitable precautions were taken to minimise loss of fluid, it should only be necessary to bleed the relevant rear brake.

21 Adjust the handbrake cable as described in Section 18; then refit the lever gaiter.

12 Master cylinder – removal, overhaul and refitting

> **Warning: Before starting work, refer to the note at the beginning of Section 2 concerning the dangers of hydraulic fluid, and to the warning at the beginning of Section 4 concerning the dangers of asbestos dust.**

Removal

1 Dissipate the vacuum present in the brake servo unit by repeatedly depressing the brake pedal. On Zafira models, remove the windscreen plastic deflector from the rear of the engine compartment.

2 Remove the master cylinder reservoir cap and syphon the hydraulic fluid from the reservoir **(see illustration)**. Alternatively, open any convenient bleed screw in the system, and pump the brake pedal to expel the fluid through a plastic tube connected to the bleed screw (see Section 2).

> **Warning: Do not syphon the fluid by mouth, as it is poisonous; use a syringe or an old poultry baster.**

3 Disconnect the wiring connector from the brake fluid level sender unit, and unclip the wiring from the top of the reservoir.

4 Place cloth rags beneath the master cylinder, then unscrew the union nuts and disconnect the hydraulic fluid lines. Carefully pull back the lines so that they are just clear of

the master cylinder. Identify the lines to ensure correct refitting.

5 Disconnect the clutch hydraulic fluid line from the reservoir. Plug the end of the line.

6 Unscrew the mounting nuts and withdraw the master cylinder from the front of the vacuum servo. Recover the seal. Take care not to spill fluid on the vehicle paintwork.

7 Using a screwdriver, carefully lever out the reservoir retaining shackle, then prise the reservoir from the top of the master cylinder. Prise the two seals from the master cylinder apertures.

Overhaul

8 At the time of writing, master cylinder overhaul is not possible as no spares are available.

9 The only parts available individually are the fluid reservoir, its mounting seals, the filler cap and the master cylinder mounting seal.

10 If the master cylinder is worn excessively, it must be renewed.

Refitting

11 Ensure that the mating surfaces are clean and dry then fit the new seal to the rear of the master cylinder.

12 Fit the master cylinder to the servo unit, ensuring that the servo unit pushrod enters the master cylinder piston centrally. Fit the retaining nuts and tighten them to the specified torque setting.

13 Refit the brake lines and tighten the union nuts securely.

14 Smear a little brake fluid on the rubber seals and locate them in the top of the master cylinder, then press the fluid reservoir firmly into the seals.

15 Reconnect the clutch hydraulic pipe and tighten the clip.

16 Reconnect the wiring connector to the brake fluid level sender unit, and fit the wiring in the clips on top of the reservoir.

17 Top-up the reservoir with fresh hydraulic fluid to the MAX mark (see *Weekly checks*).

18 Bleed the brake hydraulic system as described in Section 2 and the clutch as described in Chapter 6 then refit the filler cap. Thoroughly check the operation of the braking system before using the vehicle on the road.

13 Brake pedal – removal and refitting

Removal

1 Disconnect the battery negative (earth) lead and position it away from the terminal.
2 Remove the instrument panel as described in Chapter 12.
3 Unbolt the side nuts securing the pedal support to the steering crossmember.
4 Undo the screws and remove the side panels from the driver's footwell.
5 Turn the fasteners and remove the facia lower panels for access to the stop-light switch. Remove the footwell air duct, then disconnect the wiring from the switch. Turn the switch to remove it from the pedal support bracket.
6 Unscrew the nuts and remove the accelerator pedal from the floor. Disconnect the wiring.
7 Disconnect the wiring loom from the fusebox carrier.
8 Unhook and remove the brake pedal return spring.
9 Use a screwdriver to prise the retaining plate and remove the pin attaching the vacuum servo pushrod to the pedal. Recover the washer.
10 Unscrew the nuts securing the vacuum servo to the pedal bracket, and withdraw the bracket together with the pedal from inside the vehicle. There is little working room to do this, however, first release the bracket from the steering crossmember studs, then tilt it upwards and turn it as necessary to remove it. Take care not to damage the wiring loom and surrounding components. On left-hand drive models it may be necessary to remove the steering column intermediate shaft with reference to Chapter 10.
11 Note the fitted position of the pedal, then unscrew the nuts and push out the pivot shaft. Recover the pedal, bushes and return spring.
12 Inspect the pedal for signs of wear or damage, paying particular attention to the pivot bushes, and renew worn components as necessary.

Refitting

13 Apply some multi-purpose grease to the bearing surfaces of the pedal, pivot shaft and bushes. Fit the pedal and components to the bracket then refit the nuts and tighten securely.
14 Carefully locate the pedal and bracket on the bulkhead and onto the vacuum servo studs. Refit the nuts and tighten to the specified torque. Where necessary on left-hand drive models, refit the steering column intermediate shaft with reference to Chapter 10.
15 Refit the vacuum servo pushrod onto the brake pedal, then insert the pin and washer and retain with the plate.
16 Refit the brake pedal return spring.

17 Reconnect the wiring loom to the fusebox carrier.
18 Reconnect the wiring to the accelerator pedal, then refit the pedal and tighten the nuts.
19 Before refitting the stop-light switch to the pedal bracket, first push the actuator pin fully into the switch. Insert the switch in the bracket and turn to secure. Reconnect the wiring to the switch. Depress the pedal and pull out the actuator pin from the switch. Now release the pedal, and the pin will be adjusted to its correct position.
20 Refit the footwell air duct and facia lower panels.
21 Refit the side panels to the driver's footwell.
22 Refit and tighten the side nuts securing the pedal support to the steering crossmember.
23 Refit the instrument panel as described in Chapter 12.
24 Reconnect the battery negative (earth) lead.
25 Check the operation of the brake pedal and stop-light switch before using the vehicle on the road.

14 Vacuum servo unit – testing, removal and refitting

Testing

1 To test the operation of the servo unit, with the engine off, depress the footbrake several times to exhaust the vacuum. Now start the engine, keeping the pedal firmly depressed. As the engine starts, there should be a noticeable 'give' in the brake pedal as the vacuum builds up. Allow the engine to run for at least two minutes, then switch it off. The brake pedal should now feel normal, but further applications should result in the pedal feeling firmer, the pedal stroke decreasing with each application.
2 If the servo does not operate as described, first inspect the servo unit check valve as described in Section 15. Also check the operation of the vacuum pump as described in Section 17.

3 If the servo unit still fails to operate satisfactorily, the fault lies within the unit itself. Repairs to the unit are not possible, and, if faulty, the servo unit must be renewed.

Removal

Right-hand drive models

4 On models equipped with air conditioning, have the refrigerant evacuated from the system. This is necessary in order to disconnect the refrigerant lines later.
5 Remove the air cleaner housing and inlet duct as described in Chapter 4A.
6 Remove the windscreen wiper motor as described in Chapter 12.
7 Remove the alternator as described in Chapter 5A.
8 Unbolt the alternator mounting bracket from the inlet manifold and cylinder head.
9 Remove the brake master cylinder as described in Section 12.
10 On 2.0 litre models remove the airflow meter, then disconnect the wiring and hoses and remove the load pressure control solenoid valve.
11 Disconnect the vacuum line from the vacuum servo unit, or alternatively remove the non-return valve from the unit.
12 On models with air conditioning, unscrew the refrigerant line lock bolt (located on the bulkhead behind the inlet manifold), then remove the expansion valve and inner sealing frame. **Note:** *If necessary, have this work carried out by a specialist refrigeration engineer, noting that if the system will be left open for a long period, it must be sealed until recharged.*
13 Remove the side panels from the driver's footwell, then disconnect the pedal return spring.
14 Use a screwdriver to prise the retaining plate and remove the pin attaching the vacuum servo pushrod to the pedal. Recover the washer.
15 Unscrew and remove the upper left and lower right nuts securing the pedal bracket to the vacuum servo unit **(see illustrations)**.
16 Working in the engine compartment, withdraw the vacuum servo unit from the bulkhead, taking care not to damage the hydraulic brake lines or surrounding components. Recover the gasket.

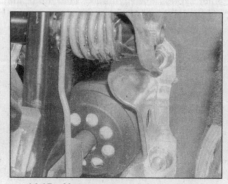

14.15a Vacuum servo left-hand side mounting nuts . . .

14.15b . . . and right-hand side mounting nuts viewed from the driver's footwell

Left-hand drive models with ABS

17 Remove the hydraulic modulator with reference to Section 24.

18 Remove the brake master cylinder as described in Section 12.

19 Unbolt the hydraulic modulator mounting bracket.

20 Disconnect the vacuum line from the vacuum servo unit, or alternatively remove the non-return valve from the unit.

21 Remove the side panels from the driver's footwell, then disconnect the pedal return spring.

22 Use a screwdriver to prise the retaining plate and remove the pin attaching the vacuum servo pushrod to the pedal. Recover the washer.

23 Unscrew and remove the upper left and lower right nuts securing the pedal bracket to the vacuum servo unit.

24 Working in the engine compartment, withdraw the vacuum servo unit from the bulkhead, taking care not to damage the hydraulic brake lines or surrounding components. Recover the gasket.

Left-hand drive models without ABS

25 Remove the brake master cylinder as described in Section 12.

26 Disconnect the vacuum line from the vacuum servo unit, or alternatively remove the non-return valve from the unit.

27 Detach the relay carrier from its mounting bracket, and position to one side, then disconnect the wiring multiplugs from the bracket.

28 Unscrew the union nuts and remove the hydraulic brake lines from between the master cylinder and the branch.

29 Place cloth rags beneath the branch bracket, then unbolt it.

30 Remove the side panels from the driver's footwell, then disconnect the pedal return spring.

31 Use a screwdriver to prise the retaining plate and remove the pin attaching the vacuum servo pushrod to the pedal. Recover the washer.

32 Unscrew and remove the upper left and lower right nuts securing the pedal bracket to the vacuum servo unit.

33 Working in the engine compartment, withdraw the vacuum servo unit from the bulkhead, taking care not to damage the hydraulic brake lines or surrounding components. Recover the gasket.

Refitting

34 Refitting is a reversal of removal, using a new gasket between the vacuum servo unit and bulkhead, and tightening all nuts and bolts to the specified torque where given. On completion, bleed the brake hydraulic system as described in Section 2. Start the engine and check for air leaks at the vacuum hose-to-servo unit connection.

15 Vacuum servo unit check valve and hose – removal, testing and refitting

Removal

1 Using a screwdriver, carefully ease the vacuum hose end adapter from the front of the servo unit.

2 At the inlet manifold end of the hose, depress the quick-release fitting and disconnect the hose. Withdraw the complete hose from the engine.

3 The hose sections can be renewed separate to the check valve and adapters. Cut the hose with a sharp knife and disconnect it from the relevant part. Cut the new hose to the same length and press it firmly onto the part. Note that the check valve must be fitted so that the arrow points towards the inlet manifold.

Testing

4 Examine the check valve, hoses and adapters for signs of damage, and renew if necessary. The check valve may be tested by blowing through it in both directions. Air should flow through the valve in one direction only – when blown through from the servo unit end. Renew the parts and hoses as necessary.

Refitting

5 Refitting is a reversal of removal but make sure that the arrow on the non-return check valve points towards the inlet manifold.

6 On completion, start the engine and check the hose for air leaks. Check the vacuum servo operation as described in Section 14.

16 Servo unit vacuum pump – removal and refitting

Removal

1 On the 1.7 litre engine the vacuum pump is attached to the rear of the alternator, however on the 2.0 litre engine it is bolted directly to the left-hand end of the cylinder head **(see illustrations)**. Access to the pump on the 1.7 litre engine can be improved by removal of the exhaust pipe heatshield adjacent to it, or alternatively, the alternator may be removed as described in Chapter 5A.

2 On the 1.7 litre engine, apply the handbrake then jack up the front of the vehicle and support it on axle stands (see *Jacking and vehicle support*); also remove the undertray from under the engine compartment.

3 On the 2.0 litre engine, loosen the clips and remove the air inlet duct and hose leading from the turbocharger to the intercooler – this is necessary for access to the servo unit vacuum pump. Disconnect the small vacuum hose from the bottom of the vacuum pump. Unscrew the bolts from the two engine lifting eyes on the left-hand end of the cylinder head. Release the fuel lines from the brackets, then position the wiring conduit and bracket downwards from the vacuum pump.

4 Disconnect the servo vacuum pipe from the pump by counterholding the large union nut and unscrewing the small one – on some later models a quick-release connector may be fitted **(see illustration)**.

16.1 The vacuum pump is on the left-hand end of the cylinder head – 2.0 litre engines

16.4 Unscrew the union nut (arrowed) and disconnect the pipe from the vacuum pump – 2.0 litre engines

16.7 Renew the O-ring in the alternator casing – 1.7 litre engines

18.3 Handbrake cable adjustment nut on the front of the handbrake lever

19.5 Handbrake lever and mounting bolts

5 On the 1.7 litre engine, unscrew the union nut and disconnect the oil feed line from the pump. Release the clip and disconnect the oil return line. Allow any oil to drain into a suitable container and plug or cap all lines.

6 Unscrew the mounting bolts, taking note of any cable clips/supports fitted beneath them, and withdraw the pump from the alternator drive spline (1.7 litre engine) or cylinder head (2.0 litre engine).

7 Remove the O-ring from the alternator (1.7 litre engine) or groove in the pump (2.0 litre engine). Discard the O-ring and obtain a new one. On 1.7 litre engines, if necessary, mark the inner plate in relation to the pump casing, then remove the plate and gasket **(see illustration)**.

Refitting

8 Refitting is a reversal of removal, noting the following points.
  a) *On the 1.7 litre engine, before fitting the pump pour approximately 5 cc of clean engine oil into the oil feed aperture.*
  b) *Clean the mating faces of the pump and alternator or cylinder head (as applicable) and fit a new O-ring.*
  c) *On the 1.7 litre engine, with the pump fitted to the alternator ensure that the alternator pulley can be turned easily by hand.*

17 Servo unit vacuum pump – testing and overhaul

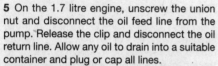

Note: *A vacuum gauge will be required for this check.*

Testing

1 The operation of the braking system vacuum pump can be checked using a vacuum gauge.

2 Disconnect the vacuum pipe from the pump, and connect the gauge to the pump union using a suitable length of hose.

3 Start the engine and allow it to idle, then measure the vacuum created by the pump. As a guide, after one minute, a minimum of approximately 500 mm Hg should be

recorded. If the vacuum registered is significantly less than this, it is likely that the pump is faulty. However, seek the advice of a Vauxhall dealer before condemning the pump.

Overhaul

4 Overhaul of the vacuum pump is not possible, since no components are available separately for it. If faulty, the complete pump assembly must be renewed.

18 Handbrake – adjustment

1 Adjust the handbrake at the specified intervals, and also after renewing or dismantling the rear brake shoes, or renewing the drum/disc.

2 Chock the front wheels, then jack up the rear of the vehicle and support on axle stands (see *Jacking and vehicle support*).

3 Prise out the console central cover then unclip the gaiter from the centre console and lift it up for access to the adjustment nut on the front of the handbrake lever **(see illustration)**.

4 Fully release the handbrake lever, then back off the adjustment nut to provide some slack in the cable.

5 Depress the brake pedal a minimum of 5 times. On drum brake models, have an assistant listen for the automatic self-adjustment mechanism to operate on the rear brakes – operate the brake pedal until this stops.

6 Fully apply and release the handbrake lever a minimum of 5 times.

7 Apply the handbrake lever to the 3rd notch, then tighten the adjustment nut until the rear wheels are binding, but it is still just possible to turn them. Each rear wheel brake should have identical resistance – if not, check for seized cables.

8 Fully apply the handbrake lever and check that both rear wheels are locked. Fully release the lever and check that both wheels turn freely.

9 Refit the gaiter to the centre console, and refit the console central cover.

10 Apply the handbrake, then lower the vehicle to the ground.

19 Handbrake lever – removal and refitting

Removal

1 Prise out the central cover from the console, then unclip and remove the handbrake lever gaiter.

2 Completely unscrew the handbrake adjustment nut from the front of the lever.

3 Remove the centre console as described in Chapter 11.

4 Remove the 'handbrake-on' warning switch from the lever as described in Section 22.

5 Unscrew and remove the lever mounting nuts **(see illustration)**.

6 Prise out the plastic clips from the mounting plate, then withdraw the lever and remove from inside the vehicle.

7 Withdraw the mounting plate from the front of the cable, and recover the gasket.

Refitting

8 Refitting is a reversal of removal, but adjust the handbrake as described in Section 18.

20 Handbrake cables – removal and refitting

Removal

1 On rear drum brake models, the handbrake cable consists of four sections, a short front (primary) section which connects the lever to the compensator plate, the main cable (secondary) section which links the compensator plate to the rear brakes, and two short rear cables which connect each main cable to the rear brake shoes. On rear disc models, the secondary cable sections connect directly to the rear brake calipers, and there are no short rear sections. Each section can be removed individually as follows.

20.17 Removing the exhaust heat shield from the underbody

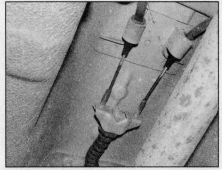
20.18 Handbrake cable compensator plate

20.19a Handbrake cable support on the rear suspension trailing arm

Primary (front) cable

2 Firmly chock the front wheels, then jack up the rear of the vehicle and support it on axle stands (see *Jacking and vehicle support*). Fully release the handbrake lever.

3 Inside the vehicle, remove the centre console as described in Chapter 11.

4 Unscrew and remove the adjustment nut from the front of the handbrake lever.

5 Release the cable from the guide on the mounting plate where necessary.

6 Working beneath the vehicle, disconnect the oxygen sensor wiring.

7 Remove the exhaust front pipe and intermediate section with reference to Chapter 4A. Also disconnect the rubber mountings for the central exhaust silencer on the underbody.

8 Unscrew the nuts and remove the exhaust heatshield from the underbody.

9 Detach the front cable from the compensator plate by twisting it through 90°.

10 Release the grommet from the lever mounting plate, and withdraw the front cable from inside the vehicle. Remove the grommet from the cable.

Secondary (main) cable

Note: *The secondary cables are supplied as one part, together with the compensator plate.*

11 Firmly chock the front wheels, then jack up the rear of the vehicle and support it on axle stands (see *Jacking and vehicle support*). Remove both rear roadwheels, then fully release the handbrake lever.

12 Prise out the console central cover then unclip the gaiter from the centre console and lift it up for access to the adjustment nut on the front of the handbrake lever.

13 Back off the adjustment nut to provide some slack in the cable.

14 Working on each side in turn, on rear drum models unclip the rear of each main cable from the connector to the short rear cables. On rear disc models, use a screwdriver to push down the lever on the calipers in order to disconnect the inner cables, the pull out the clips and disconnect the outer cables from the support bracket.

15 Working beneath the vehicle, disconnect the oxygen sensor wiring.

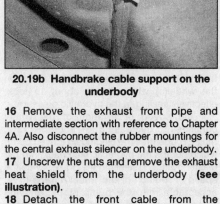
20.19b Handbrake cable support on the underbody

16 Remove the exhaust front pipe and intermediate section with reference to Chapter 4A. Also disconnect the rubber mountings for the central exhaust silencer on the underbody.

17 Unscrew the nuts and remove the exhaust heat shield from the underbody (see illustration).

18 Detach the front cable from the compensator plate by twisting it through 90° (see illustration).

19 Release the main cable sections from the supports on the rear axle and fuel tank, and withdraw from under the vehicle (see illustrations).

Rear cable (drum brake)

20 Firmly chock the front wheels, then jack up the rear of the vehicle and support it on axle stands (see *Jacking and vehicle support*).

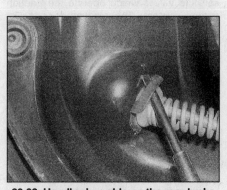
20.22 Handbrake cable on the rear brake backplate

20.19c Handbrake cable support on the rear torsion beam mounting bracket

Remove the relevant rear roadwheel, then fully release the handbrake lever.

21 Remove the rear brake shoes as described in Section 6.

22 Pull out the cable retaining clip from the backplate, and release the cable forwards (see illustration).

23 Disconnect the rear cable from the main cable at the connector (see illustration).

Refitting

24 Refitting is a reversal of the removal procedure, but adjust the handbrake as described in Section 18. Where applicable, make sure that the fitting on the rear of the front cable locates correctly in the compensator plate. Also make sure that the protective sleeve on the front cable is firmly located over the bead next to the compensator plate.

20.23 Rear cable-to-main cable connector

21 Stop-light switch – removal, refitting and adjustment

Removal

1 The stop-light switch is located on the pedal bracket in the driver's footwell.
2 To remove the switch, first remove the lower facia trim panel (see Chapter 11, Section 44), then disconnect the heating duct for access to the switch.
3 Disconnect the wiring plug from the top of the switch, then twist the switch and remove it from the pedal bracket **(see illustrations)**.

Refitting and adjustment

4 Before refitting the switch, push the actuation pin fully in.
5 Refit the switch to the pedal bracket and twist fully to secure.
6 Depress the brake pedal then pull the actuation pin fully out of the switch so that it contacts the pedal. Now release the pedal to set the pin.
7 Refit the heating duct and the lower facia trim panel. Check the operation of the stop-light.

22 Handbrake 'on' warning light switch – removal and refitting

Removal

1 Remove the centre console as described in Chapter 11.
2 Disconnect the wiring from the warning switch located on the front of the handbrake lever **(see illustration)**.
3 Unscrew the bolt and remove the switch from the handbrake lever bracket.

Refitting

4 Refitting is a reversal of removal.

23 Anti-lock Braking and Traction Control systems – general information

ABS is available on all models. Traction control is available as an option on 2.0 litre engine models.

The ABS system comprises a hydraulic modulator and electronic control unit together with four roadwheel sensors. The hydraulic modulator contains the electronic control unit (ECU), the hydraulic solenoid valves (one set for each brake) and the electrically-driven pump. The purpose of the system is to prevent the wheel(s) locking during heavy braking. This is achieved by automatic release of the brake on the relevant wheel, followed by re-application of the brake.

The solenoid valves are controlled by the

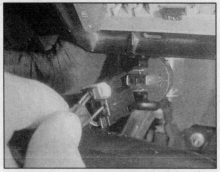
21.3a Disconnect the wiring . . .

22.2 Handbrake 'on' warning light switch

ECU, which itself receives signals from the four wheel sensors which monitor the speed of rotation of each wheel. By comparing these signals, the ECU can determine the speed at which the vehicle is travelling. It can then use this speed to determine when a wheel is decelerating at an abnormal rate, compared to the speed of the vehicle, and therefore predicts when a wheel is about to lock. During normal operation, the system functions in the same way as a non-ABS braking system.

If the ECU senses that a wheel is about to lock, it operates the relevant solenoid valve(s) in the hydraulic unit, which then isolates from the master cylinder the relevant brake(s) on the wheel(s) which is/are about to lock, effectively sealing-in the hydraulic pressure.

If the speed of rotation of the wheel continues to decrease at an abnormal rate, the ECU operates the electrically-driven pump which pumps the hydraulic fluid back into the master cylinder, releasing the brake. Once the speed of rotation of the wheel returns to an acceptable rate, the pump stops, and the solenoid valves switch again, allowing the hydraulic master cylinder pressure to return to the caliper/wheel cylinder (as applicable), which then re-applies the brake. This cycle can be carried out many times a second.

The action of the solenoid valves and return pump creates pulses in the hydraulic circuit. When the ABS system is functioning, these pulses can be felt through the brake pedal.

On models with traction control, the ABS hydraulic unit incorporates an additional set of solenoid valves which operate the traction control system. The system operates at

21.3b . . . then twist the switch and remove it from the pedal bracket

speeds up to approximately 30 mph (60 km/h) using the signals supplied by the wheel sensors. If the ECU senses that a driving wheel is about to lose traction, it prevents this by momentarily applying the relevant front brake.

The operation of the ABS and the traction control system is entirely dependent on electrical signals. To prevent the system responding to any inaccurate signals, a built-in safety circuit monitors all signals received by the ECU. If an inaccurate signal or low battery voltage is detected, the system is automatically shut down, and the warning light on the instrument panel is illuminated, to inform the driver that the system is not operational. Normal braking is still available, however.

If a fault develops in the ABS/traction control system, the vehicle must be taken to a Vauxhall dealer for fault diagnosis and repair.

24 Anti-lock Braking and Traction Control system components – removal and refitting

Hydraulic modulator and electronic control unit

Removal

1 Remove the battery as described in Chapter 5A.
2 Disconnect the two wiring multiplugs from the relay carrier bracket.
3 Remove the relay carrier cover, then detach the relay box from the bracket and position to one side.
4 Disconnect the wiring looms from the carrier bracket.
5 Unscrew the three nuts and remove the relay carrier bracket.
6 Remove the holder from the brake fluid hydraulic pipes.
7 Unscrew and remove the filler cap from the brake fluid reservoir, then draw out all of the hydraulic fluid using a poultry baster or old battery hydrometer.
8 Identify the hydraulic pipes for location then unscrew the union nuts and disconnect them from the modulator. Ideally, a special split ring

spanner should be used to unscrew the nuts as they may be tight. Be prepared for some loss of fluid by placing cloth rags beneath the lines. On LHD models, it will also be necessary to disconnect the hydraulic pipes from the master cylinder which is located on the left-hand side of the engine compartment. Plug or tape over the apertures in the modulator to prevent entry of dust and dirt.

9 Disconnect the special wiring multiplug from the top of the hydraulic modulator by lifting the clip and unhooking the multiplug **(see illustration)**.

10 Unscrew the mounting nuts/bolts and withdraw the modulator and ABS control unit from the bracket. Remove from the engine compartment taking care not to spill any hydraulic fluid on the vehicle's paintwork. *Caution: Keep the modulator upright while it is removed from the vehicle, so that no fluid is allowed to leak out.*

Refitting

11 Refitting is a reversal of removal, but finally bleed the hydraulic system as described in Section 2.

Wheel sensor

Renewal

12 Both the front and rear wheel sensors are integral with their hubs. If the sensor is faulty, the wheel hub must be renewed complete as described in Chapter 10.

Traction Control switch

Removal

13 Carefully prise the switch from the facia panel, using a small screwdriver. Use card or cloth to prevent damage to the facia.

Refitting

14 Refitting is a reversal of removal.

ABS Control Unit

Removal

15 Remove the hydraulic modulator and electronic control unit as previously described in this Section.

16 Disconnect the wiring then unscrew the mounting bolts and carefully remove the ABS control unit from the hydraulic body taking care not to damage the coil carrier.

17 Recover the seal from between the coil carrier and control unit.

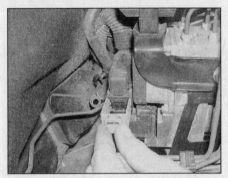

24.9 Lift the clip to disconnect the wiring multiplug from the top of the hydraulic modulator

Refitting

18 Insert the new seal, then carefully position the ABS control unit on the hydraulic modulator and tighten the (new) bolts to the specified torque in the stages given. **Do not** tilt the control unit when positioning it on the modulator. If the bolts become difficult to move during the tightening procedure, the unit is faulty and must be renewed complete. **Note:** *If a spring plate was positioned between the control unit and modulator on removal, leave this out when reassembling the unit.*

19 The remaining procedure is a reversal of the removal procedure.

---

25 Brake proportioning valve – removal and refitting

Removal

1 Chock the front roadwheels, then jack up the rear of the vehicle and support on axle stands (see *Jacking and vehicle support*).

2 Minimise fluid loss by first removing the master cylinder reservoir cap, then tightening it down onto a piece of polythene to obtain an airtight seal.

3 Unscrew the bolt and remove the bearing for the tension spring from the underbody bracket **(see illustration)**.

4 Note the fitted position of the clamp on the spring, then unscrew the clamp bolt and remove the stop. Remove the spring from the lever on the valve.

25.3 Brake proportioning valve viewed from under the rear of the vehicle

5 Clean the area around the hydraulic union nuts on the brake proportioning valve, then unscrew them and disconnect the hydraulic lines.

6 Unscrew the mounting bolts and remove the proportioning valve from the underbody bracket. Take care not to damage the brake pipes.

7 Note that three different valves are fitted, and it is important to fit the correct type.

Refitting and adjustment

8 Refitting is a reversal of removal, but tighten the bolts to the specified torque and bleed the brake hydraulic system as described in Section 2. Finally, adjust the proportioning valve as follows.

9 The vehicle should be empty with a maximum of half a tank of fuel, and with the correct tyre pressures. On models with ride height control, a minimum pressure of 0.8 bar should be in the system. The rear wheels of the vehicle must be on the ground so that the weight of the vehicle is on the rear suspension. Alternatively, the rear wheels can be lowered onto car ramps.

10 Have an assistant fully depress the brake pedal and quickly release it. The lever on the proportioning valve should move indicating that the unit is working correctly. If the lever does not move, renew the valve.

11 With the adjustment stop free of the valve lever, push the lever fully forwards onto the stop, then release it. Now locate the stop on the spring so that all free play is removed and tighten the clamp bolt in this position.

12 Lower the vehicle to the ground.

Chapter 10
Suspension and steering

Contents

Degrees of difficulty

Easy, suitable for novice with little experience	Fairly easy, suitable for beginner with some experience	Fairly difficult, suitable for competent DIY mechanic	Difficult, suitable for experienced DIY mechanic	Very difficult, suitable for expert DIY or professional

Specifications

General

Front suspension type . . . . Independent, with MacPherson struts, gas-filled shock absorbers and anti-roll bar

Rear suspension type . . . . Semi-independent torsion beam, with trailing arms, coil springs and telescopic shock absorbers. Level control system optional on Estate models

Steering type . . . . Rack-and-pinion. Power steering standard on all models

Front wheel alignment

Models up to and including 1999:
  Toe-in . . . . +0°00' ± 10'
  Toe-out on turns (inner wheel turned in 20°) . . . . 1°20' ± 45'
Models from model year 2000:
  Toe in . . . . +0°00' ± 20'
  Toe-out on turns (inner wheel turned in 20°):
    Astra . . . . 1°20' ± 45'
    Zafira . . . . 1°09' ± 45'

Steering

Ratio	17 : 1
Electro-hydraulic power steering fluid:	
Type	Vauxhall part number 90 544 116
Fluid capacity:	
TRW type (round shape)	0.7 litre
Delphi/Saginaw type (angular shape)	1.1 litre

Rear wheel bearings

Bearing lateral run-out	0.05 mm max
Bearing radial run-out	0.04 mm max
Bearing tilt	0.1 mm max

Torque wrench settings

	Nm	lbf ft
Front suspension		
Anti-roll bar link:		
To strut	65	48
To anti-roll bar	65	48
Anti-roll bar to subframe	20	15
Front engine mounting through-bolt	55	41
Lower arm to subframe:		
Stage 1	90	66
Stage 2	Angle-tighten 75°	
Stage 3	Angle-tighten 15°	
Lower balljoint to hub carrier clamp bolt	100	74
Lower balljoint to lower arm	35	26
Hub carrier to strut:		
Stage 1	50	37
Stage 2	90	66
Stage 3	Angle-tighten 45°	
Stage 4	Angle-tighten 15°	
Hub nut:		
Stage 1	120	89
Stage 2	Loosen nut fully (until it can be turned by hand)	
Stage 3	20	15
Stage 4	Angle-tighten by a further 80° (plus to next split pin hole as necessary)	
Rear engine mounting bracket to transmission	80	59
Strut upper mounting	55	41
Subframe mounting bolts:		
Stage 1	90	66
Stage 2	Angle-tighten 45°	
Stage 3	Angle-tighten 15°	
Wheel bearing hub to carrier:		
Stage 1	90	66
Stage 2	Angle-tighten 30°	
Stage 3	Angle-tighten 15°	
Rear suspension		
Brake hydraulic line union nuts	16	12
Hub bracket to trailing arm:		
Stage 1	50	37
Stage 2	Angle-tighten 30°	
Stage 3	Angle-tighten 15°	
Shock absorber:		
To body	90	66
To trailing arm	110	81
Torsion beam front mounting bracket:		
Centre bolt:		
Stage 1	90	66
Stage 2	Angle-tighten 60°	
Stage 3	Angle-tighten 15°	
Bracket-to-underbody bolts:		
Stage 1	90	66
Stage 2	Angle-tighten 30°	
Stage 3	Angle-tighten 15°	

Torque wrench settings

Steering

	Nm	lbf ft
Airbag unit to steering wheel	8	6
Electro-hydraulic pump to steering gear and subframe	22	16
Heat shield to steering gear	4	3
Hydraulic pressure and return line union nuts	27	20
Pressure and retune line bracket to steering gear	4	3
Rear engine mounting bracket to subframe (LHD models)	55	41
Steering column to bulkhead crossmember	22	16
Steering column intermediate shaft to steering gear pinion	22	16
Steering gear to subframe:		
Stage 1	45	33
Stage 2	Angle-tighten 45°	
Stage 3	Angle-tighten 15°	
Steering wheel	22	16
Track rod end locking nut	60	44
Track rod end to steering arm on hub carrier	60	44
Track rod to steering rack	90	66

Roadwheels

	Nm	lbf ft
All models	110	81

1 General information and precautions

General information

The front suspension is of independent type, with a subframe, MacPherson struts, lower arms, and an anti-roll bar. The struts, which incorporate coil springs and integral gas-filled shock absorbers, are attached at their upper ends to the reinforced strut mountings on the body shell. The lower end of each strut is bolted to the top of a cast hub carrier, which carries the hub, and the brake disc and caliper. The hubs run within non-adjustable bearings in the hub carriers. The lower end of each hub carrier is attached, via a balljoint, to a pressed-steel lower arm assembly. The balljoints are bolted to the lower arms and attached to the hub carriers by a clamp bolt. Each lower arm is attached at its inboard end to the subframe with flexible rubber bushes, and controls both lateral and fore-and-aft movement of the front wheels. An anti-roll bar is fitted to all models. The anti-roll bar is mounted on the subframe, and is connected to the suspension struts by vertical drop links.

The rear suspension is of semi-independent type, consisting of a torsion beam and trailing arms, with double-conical coil springs and telescopic shock absorbers. The front ends of the trailing arms are attached to the vehicle underbody by horizontal bushes, and the rear ends are located by the shock absorbers, which are bolted to the underbody at their upper ends. The coil springs are mounted independently of the shock absorbers, and act directly between the trailing arms and the underbody. Each rear wheel bearing, hub and stub axle assembly is manufactured as a sealed unit, and cannot be dismantled.

A manual rear suspension level control system is available on Estate models. The system operates using compressed air-filled shock absorbers. The rear suspension level is adjusted by altering the air pressure in the shock absorbers, through a valve located in the luggage compartment.

The steering is of conventional rack-and-pinion type, incorporating a collapsible safety column. The column is joined to the steering gear by an intermediate shaft incorporating two universal joints. The upper section of the column includes an outer slip coupling into which the steering lock engages. With the steering lock engaged, the coupling allows the column to turn at torques above 200 Nm only, so making it impossible to break the steering lock shear pin. However, at this torque it is not possible to control the vehicle. The steering gear is mounted on the front suspension subframe. The steering gear track rods are attached to the steering arms on the hub carriers by track rod ends.

All models are fitted with power-assisted steering. The electro-hydraulic power steering pump is located directly on the steering gear and is non-serviceable. The pump incorporates a hydraulic fluid reservoir.

Precautions

An airbag is fitted to the steering wheel. To ensure it operates correctly in the event of an accident, and to avoid the risk of personal injury from it being accidentally triggered, the following precautions must be observed. Also refer to Chapter 12 for more information:

a) Before carrying out any operations on the airbag system, disconnect the battery negative terminal, and wait at least 1 minute to ensure that the system capacitor has been discharged.

b) Note that the airbag must not be subjected to temperatures in excess of 90°C (194°F). When the airbag is removed, ensure that it is stored with the pad facing upwards.

c) Do not allow any solvents or cleaning agents to contact the airbag assembly. The unit must be cleaned using only a damp cloth.

d) The airbag and control unit are both sensitive to impact. If either is dropped from a height of more than 50 cm (20 in), they must be renewed.

e) Disconnect the airbag control unit wiring plug prior to using arc-welding equipment on the vehicle.

f) On vehicles fitted with a passenger airbag, do not fit accessories in the airbag zone. Items like telephones, cassette storage boxes, additional mirrors, etc, can be ripped off and cause serious injury if the airbag inflates.

2 Front hub carrier – removal and refitting

Note: It is recommended that all mounting nuts and bolts are renewed. A balljoint separator tool will be required for this operation.
Caution: The front wheel camber setting is controlled by the bolts securing the hub carrier to the front suspension strut. Before removing the bolts, mark the hub carrier in relation to the strut accurately. On completion, the camber setting must be checked and adjusted by a suitably-equipped garage.

Removal

1 Apply the handbrake, then jack up the front of the vehicle and support it on axle stands (see Jacking and vehicle support). Remove the relevant front wheel.

2 Unscrew the nut securing the track rod end to the steering arm on the hub carrier. Using a balljoint separator, separate the track rod end from the steering arm.

3 Remove the front wheel hub complete as described in Section 3.
4 Mark the position of the front hub carrier on the front suspension strut (see **Caution** at beginning of the Section), then unscrew and remove the two nuts and bolts, noting that their heads face the front of the vehicle. Remove the carrier from the strut. Discard the nuts and bolts and obtain new ones.

Refitting

5 Locate the hub carrier on the strut and fit the new bolts. Position the carrier as previously noted, then tighten the bolts to the specified torque and angle in the specified stages.
6 Refit the front wheel hub with reference to Section 3.
7 Refit the track rod end to the steering arm on the hub carrier and tighten the nut to the specified torque.
8 Refit the front wheel and lower the vehicle to the ground.
9 Check and if necessary adjust the steering toe-in setting at the earliest opportunity.

3 Front wheel hub and bearings – checking and renewal

Checking

1 To check the front wheel bearings for wear, apply the handbrake then jack up the front of the vehicle and support it on axle stands (see *Jacking and vehicle support*). Spin the wheel by hand and check for a noisy or rough bearing. Grip the wheel and rock it to check for excessive play in the bearing, however, be careful not to confuse wear in the suspension or steering joints with wear in the bearing.

Renewal

2 With the front of the vehicle supported on axle stands, remove the relevant front wheel.
3 Remove the brake disc as described in Chapter 9. This procedure involves removing the brake caliper and tying it to one side, leaving the hydraulic hose attached; pull out the spring clip and disconnect the flexible hose from the support bracket **(see illustration)**.
4 Carefully tap the protective cap from the centre of the hub, then extract the split pin and unscrew the driveshaft retaining nut while holding the hub stationary with a bar positioned between two wheel bolts temporarily refitted to the hub. **Note:** *The nut is tightened to a high torque.* Remove the nut and spacer.
5 Extract the split pin where necessary, then unscrew the nut securing the track rod end to the steering arm on the hub carrier. Using a balljoint separator, separate the track rod end from the steering arm. Also unscrew the nut and disconnect the anti-roll bar link from the strut.

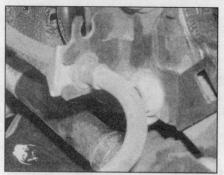

3.3 Brake flexible hose support bracket on the hub carrier

6 Unscrew and remove the clamp bolt securing the front suspension lower arm balljoint to the hub carrier, noting which way round it is fitted. It is recommended that the clamp bolt and nut are renewed.
7 Using a chisel or screwdriver as a wedge, expand the balljoint clamp at the bottom of the hub carrier.
8 Using a lever, push down on the suspension lower arm to free the balljoint from the hub carrier, then move the hub carrier to one side and release the arm taking care not to damage the balljoint rubber boot **(see illustration)**.
9 On models with ABS, disconnect the wiring from the front wheel sensor at the connector **(see illustration)**.
10 Pull the hub carrier out while pressing the driveshaft through the hub. If it is tight use a suitable puller to push the driveshaft from the hub.
11 Mark the hub, hub carrier and backplate in relation to each other.
12 From the rear of the hub carrier, unscrew and remove the three hub mounting bolts **(see illustration)**. Discard the bolts as new ones must be fitted.
13 Withdraw the hub from the hub carrier, and recover the backplate. Take care not to damage the ABS sensor wiring where fitted.
14 It is not possible to obtain the drive flange or bearings separate to the hub housing. If the bearings are worn excessively, the complete hub assembly must be renewed.
15 Clean the hub and hub carrier, then locate

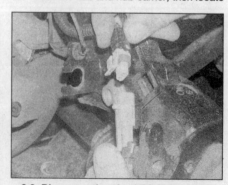

3.9 Disconnecting the ABS front wheel sensor wiring

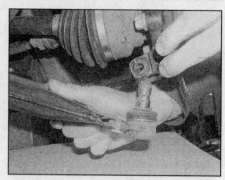

3.8 Separating the suspension lower arm balljoint from the hub carrier

the backplate on the carrier and insert the hub with the previously-made marks and bolt holes aligned. Apply locking fluid to the threads of the new mounting bolts then insert them and tighten to the specified torque and angle in the stages given in the Specifications.
16 Pull out the hub carrier then insert the driveshaft into the hub. Fit the spacer and new nut, and tighten the nut moderately to draw the driveshaft into the hub. Leave final tightening of the nut until later (see paragraph 20).
17 On models with ABS, reconnect the wiring for the front wheel sensor at the connector.
18 Push down on the suspension lower arm and locate the balljoint stub in the bottom of the hub carrier. Remove the wedge from the balljoint clamp and insert the new bolt. Tighten the nut to the specified torque.
19 Refit the track rod end to the steering arm, then refit the new nut and tighten to the specified torque. Where necessary, fit a new split pin. Also refit the anti-roll bar link to the strut and tighten the nut.
20 With the hub held stationary, tighten the hub nut to the specified torque and angle in the stages given in the Specifications, and fit a new split pin. Bend the outer leg of the split pin over the end of the driveshaft, then cut the inner leg as necessary and bend it inwards.
21 Tap the protective cap into position in the centre of the hub.
22 Refit the brake disc and caliper with reference to Chapter 9.
23 Refit the front wheel and lower the vehicle to the ground.

3.12 The front hub carrier mounting bolts, showing the ABS sensor wiring

4.3 Battery positive terminal and cable

4.8 Supporting the engine/transmission with a hoist

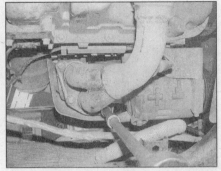

4.15 Unbolting the exhaust front pipe from the exhaust manifold

4 Front subframe – removal and refitting

Note: *Vauxhall technicians use special jigs to ensure that the engine/transmission is correctly aligned. Without the use of these tools it is important to note the position of the engine/transmission accurately before removal.*

Removal

1 Turn the steering to the straight-ahead position, then remove the ignition key and allow the steering lock to engage.
2 In the driver's footwell, unscrew the bolt securing the bottom of the steering column intermediate shaft to the steering gear pinion. Pull the shaft from the pinion and position to one side.
3 Remove the battery and battery tray as described in Chapter 5A **(see illustration)**.
4 On Zafira models only, at the rear of the engine compartment remove the rubber weatherseal and plastic access cover. Also unscrew the nuts and remove the main cover from the bulkhead.
5 Secure the radiator to the front panel using two bolts inserted through the side mountings. This is necessary as the radiator bottom mounting rubbers are located in the subframe.
6 Detach the cover from the fusebox on the left-hand side of the engine compartment, and

remove the fuse for the electric power steering system. Release the clips and detach the fuse carrier from the retainer, then slide out the power steering pump fuseholder and wire.
7 Unscrew the nut and remove the earth lead for the steering wiring harness from the body. Note the cable routing then feed the wiring harness down through the engine compartment and onto the steering gear.
8 Connect a hoist to the engine/transmission assembly and support its weight **(see illustration)**. If available, the type of support bar which locates in the engine compartment side channels is to be preferred, as this will ensure correct repositioning during refitting. Connect the hoist chains to the two eyes located at the left-hand end of the cylinder head, and also connect another chain to the eye located on the rear right-hand end of the cylinder head.
9 Apply the handbrake, then jack up the front of the vehicle and support it on axle stands (see *Jacking and vehicle support*). Where necessary, remove the undertray from the bottom of the engine compartment, and also remove the heat shield from the steering gear. Remove both front wheels.
10 Remove the front bumper as described in Chapter 11.
11 Remove the lower panelling from the right-hand wheel housing.
12 Working on each side in turn, unscrew the nuts and disconnect the anti-roll bar links from the front suspension struts.
13 Disconnect the steering track rod ends

from the steering arms on the hub carriers with reference to Section 24.
14 Unscrew the clamp bolts and lever the lower balljoints from the bottom of each hub carrier.
15 Remove the exhaust front pipe **(see illustration)**, catalytic converter and centre silencer as described in Chapter 4A.
16 Note the position of the gearchange mechanism located above the engine rear mounting, then disconnect it from the support bracket on the subframe (refer to Chapter 7 if necessary).
17 Unbolt the rear mounting from the transmission **(see illustration)**.
18 At the front of the engine, unscrew and remove the centre bolt from the front mounting.
19 On models with air conditioning, unclip the resonator from the front right-hand side of the subframe.
20 Support the subframe with a length of wood on a trolley jack. Ideally, a purpose-made cradle should be used. Enlist the help of an assistant.
21 Accurately mark the position of the subframe and mounting bolts to ensure correct refitting. Note that Vauxhall technicians use a special jig with guide pins located through the alignment holes in the subframe and underbody.
22 Unscrew and remove the subframe mounting bolts, noting the position of each bolt as they are of different lengths **(see illustrations)**. There are two bolts at the front,

4.17 The engine rear mounting

4.22a Unscrew the subframe front mounting bolts . . .

4.22b . . . side mounting bolts . . .

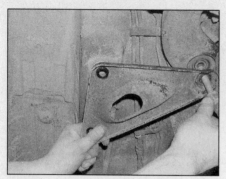

4.22c . . . and rear support bracket bolts

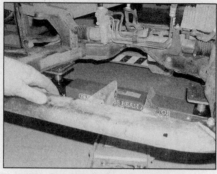

4.23a Lowering the front suspension subframe from the vehicle underbody

4.23b Steering gear showing rubber grommet in the floor

4.23c Guide the steering gear pinion through the rubber grommet when lowering the subframe

4.23d Front suspension subframe removed from the vehicle

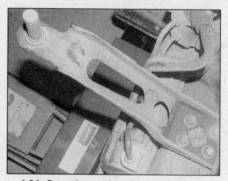

4.24 Gearchange bracket on the front subframe

two bolts located above the lower suspension arms, and six bolts located on the triangular rear support brackets.

23 With the help of an assistant, lower the subframe taking care not to damage the wiring harness for the power-assisted steering. As it is being lowered, guide the steering gear pinion through the rubber grommet in the floor **(see illustrations)**.

24 Remove the steering gear, front suspension lower arms and anti-roll bar with reference to Sections 21, 7 and 6. If necessary, the subframe mounting rubbers may be renewed, however, they must be renewed in pairs only (ie, left and right together). Use a metal tube, a long threaded bar, and two nuts and washers to force out

the rubbers. If necessary, unbolt and remove the gearchange bracket **(see illustration)**.

Refitting

25 Refitting is a reversal of removal, but tighten all nuts and bolts to the specified torque where necessary in the stages given. Make sure that the previously-made marks are correctly aligned, and make sure that the holes in the subframe and underbody are correctly aligned before fully tightening the mounting bolts. Make sure that the rubber grommet is correctly located on the steering gear and in the underbody – if the grommet has become displaced, have an assistant hold the upper half inside the vehicle while you press up the lower half from underneath until the two sections snap together **(see illustrations)**.

5 Front suspension strut – removal, overhaul and refitting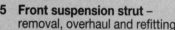

Note: *Both front suspension struts should be renewed at the same time in order to maintain good steering and suspension characteristics. It is recommended that all mounting nuts and bolts are renewed.*

Removal

1 Apply the handbrake, then jack up the front of the vehicle and support it on axle stands (see *Jacking and vehicle support*). Remove the front wheel.

2 Unscrew the nut and disconnect the anti-roll bar link from the strut **(see illustration)**.

4.25a Steering gear location for the rubber grommet

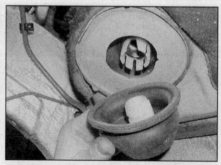

4.25b Fit the lower half of the rubber grommet while an assistant holds the upper half inside the vehicle

5.2 Removing the nut securing the anti-roll bar link to the strut

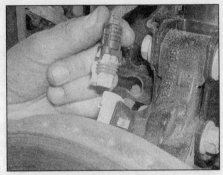

5.4 Disconnecting the wiring for the front wheel ABS sensor

5.5 Mark the position of the strut on the hub carrier to maintain the camber setting

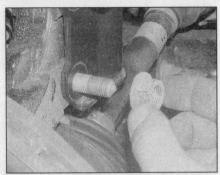

5.6a Unscrew the nuts . . .

Use a spanner on the special flats to hold the link while the nut is being loosened.
3 Pull out the clip and disconnect the

brake hose from the bracket on the strut.
4 Unclip the brake pad wiring harness from

the strut. On models with ABS, disconnect the wheel sensor wiring **(see illustration)**.
5 Mark the position of the strut on the hub carrier to ensure the camber setting is maintained **(see illustration)**.
6 Unscrew and remove the two bolts securing the hub carrier to the strut noting which way round they are fitted. With the two bolts removed, pull the hub carrier away from the strut and support on an axle stand **(see illustrations)**.
7 Support the strut beneath the front wing. In the engine compartment remove the cap then unscrew the strut upper mounting nut while counterholding the piston rod with a further spanner. Recover the upper mounting from the suspension tower **(see illustrations)**. On Zafira models it will be necessary to remove the plastic water deflectors from in front of the windscreen for access to the nut.
8 Lower the strut and withdraw from under the front wing **(see illustration)**.

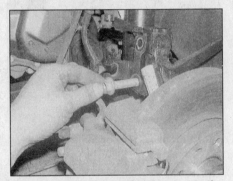

5.6b . . . and bolts securing the strut to the hub carrier

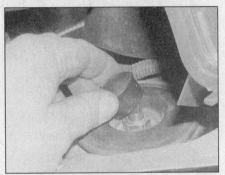

5.7a Remove the cap . . .

Overhaul

Note: *A spring compressor tool will be required for this operation.*
9 With the suspension strut resting on a bench, or clamped in a vice, fit a spring compressor tool, and compress the coil spring to relieve the pressure on the spring seats. Ensure that the compressor tool is securely located on the spring, in accordance with the tool manufacturer's instructions **(see illustration)**.
10 Counterhold the strut piston rod with a spanner, and unscrew the piston rod nut **(see illustrations)**.

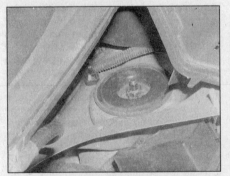

5.7b . . . for access to the front suspension strut upper mounting nut

5.7c Recover the upper mounting from the suspension tower

5.8 Lowering the strut from under the front wing

5.9 Fitting a spring compressor tool to the front suspension strut coil spring

5.10a Hold the strut piston rod with a spanner when loosening the nut . . .

5.10b . . . then remove the nut . . .

5.11a . . . the upper damping ring and support bearing . . .

5.11b . . . the upper spring seat . . .

11 Remove the upper damping ring with support bearing, upper spring seat, and (where fitted) the buffer **(see illustrations)**.

12 Remove the coil spring from the strut **(see illustration)**.

13 With the strut assembly now completely dismantled **(see illustration)**, examine all the components for wear, damage or deformation, and check the support bearing for smoothness of operation. Renew any of the components as necessary.

14 Examine the strut for signs of fluid leakage. Check the strut piston for signs of pitting along its entire length, and check the strut body for signs of damage. While holding it in an upright position, test the operation of the strut by moving the piston through a full stroke, and then through short strokes of 50 to 100 mm. In both cases, the resistance felt should be smooth and continuous. If the resistance is jerky or uneven or if there is any visible sign of wear or damage to the strut, renewal is necessary.

15 If any doubt exists as to the condition of the coil spring, carefully remove the spring compressors and check the spring for distortion and signs of cracking. Renew the spring if it is damaged or distorted, or if there is any doubt as to its condition.

16 Inspect all other components for damage or deterioration, and renew any that are suspect.

17 With the spring compressed with the compressor tool, locate the spring on the strut making sure that it is correctly seated with its lower end against the stop.

18 Refit the buffer, upper spring seat, and upper damping ring.

19 Refit the piston rod nut and tighten it securely while counterholding the piston rod with a spanner.

20 Slowly slacken the spring compressor tool to relieve the tension in the spring. Check that the ends of the spring locate correctly against the stops on the spring seats. If necessary, turn the spring and the upper seat so that the components locate correctly before the compressor tool is removed. Remove the compressor tool when the spring is fully seated.

5.12 . . . and the coil spring

Refitting

21 Refitting is a reversal of removal, bearing in mind the following points.
  a) Renew the two bolts securing the hub carrier to the strut, also the piston rod upper nuts.
  b) Tighten all nuts and bolts to the specified torque, where given.
  c) On completion have the front wheel alignment setting checked by a suitably-equipped garage.

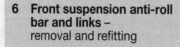

6 Front suspension anti-roll bar and links –
removal and refitting

Note: It is recommended that all mounting nuts and bolts are renewed.

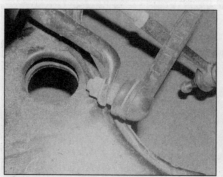

6.2 Side link connection to the anti-roll bar

5.13 Front suspension strut completely dismantled

Removal

1 Remove the front subframe as described in Section 4.

2 Identify the links side-for-side to ensure correct refitting, then unscrew the nuts and remove the links from the anti-roll bar **(see illustration)**. Use a spanner on the special flats to hold the links while the nuts are being loosened.

3 Unbolt the clamps securing the anti-roll bar to the subframe **(see illustration)**. **Note:** If the bolts are rusted in position, they can be cut off and drilled out and new inserts fitted. Consult a Vauxhall dealer for more information.

4 Lift the anti-roll bar from the subframe.

5 Note the position of the rubber bushes, then prise them from the anti-roll bar.

6 Examine the anti-roll bar, links, and rubber

6.3 One of the clamps securing the anti-roll bar to the front suspension subframe

7.4 Front suspension lower arm inner mounting located on the subframe

bushes for wear and damage and renew them if necessary.

Refitting

7 Refitting is a reversal of removal, but note the following points.
a) *The slits of the rubber bushes must face forwards when fitted to the anti-roll bar.*
b) *Renew all nuts and bolts and tighten them to the specified torque, where given.*
c) *Refit the front subframe with reference to Section 4.*

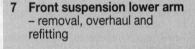

7 Front suspension lower arm – removal, overhaul and refitting

Note: *The lower arm inner pivot bolts must be renewed when refitting.*

Removal

1 Apply the handbrake, then jack up the front of the vehicle and support it on axle stands (see *Jacking and vehicle support*). Remove the front wheel.
2 Unscrew and remove the clamp bolt securing the front suspension lower arm balljoint to the bottom of the hub carrier, noting which way round it is fitted.
3 Using a suitable lever, push down the lower arm and separate it from the hub carrier. When releasing the lower arm, take care not to damage the balljoint rubber boot on the bottom of the hub carrier; if necessary protect it with a piece of card or plastic. **Note:** *If the*

8.2 Front suspension lower balljoint showing rivets securing it to the lower arm

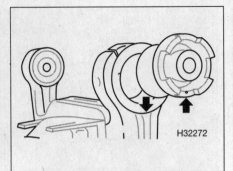

7.6 Alignment of the recess in the bush with the seam in the lower arm

balljoint stub is tight in the hub carrier, use a screwdriver or cold chisel as a wedge to force the clamp apart.
4 Note that the lower arm inner retaining bolt heads are facing the front of the vehicle. Unscrew and remove the bolts and withdraw the lower arm from the subframe **(see illustration)**. It will be necessary to slightly press the arms to release the rubber mountings.

Overhaul

5 The lower balljoint may be renewed as described in Section 8. The rubber bushes are a tight fit in the arm and must be pressed out. If a press is not available, the bushes can be drawn out using a long bolt, nut, washers and a socket or length of metal tubing.
6 Prior to fitting the new bushes, coat them with silicone grease or soapy water. Press both bushes fully into the lower arm, however, when fitting the rear bush, make sure that one of the recesses in the bush is aligned with the seam in the lower arm **(see illustration)**. Where applicable, refit the air duct.

Refitting

7 Locate the lower arm on the subframe and fit the retaining bolts from the front of the vehicle. Hand tighten the bolts at this stage.
8 Locate the lower balljoint stub fully in the bottom of the hub carrier, then refit the clamp bolt and tighten to the specified torque. Make sure the bolt head is facing the front.
9 Refit the front wheel and lower the vehicle to the ground.

9.2 Disconnecting the ABS wiring from the inside of the rear hub

10 With the weight of the vehicle on the suspension, tighten the lower arm inner pivot bolts to the specified torque and in the stages given.
11 Have the front wheel alignment settings checked by a suitably-equipped garage.

8 Front suspension lower balljoint – renewal

Note: *The original balljoint is riveted to the lower arm, but service replacements are bolted in position.*
1 Remove the front suspension lower arm as described in Section 7. **Note:** *If the fitted balljoint is a service replacement, it is not necessary to completely remove the arm but only to disconnect the balljoint from the bottom of the hub carrier then unbolt the old balljoint.*
2 Mount the lower arm in a vice, then drill the heads from the three rivets that secure the balljoint to the lower arm, using a 12.0 mm diameter drill **(see illustration)**.
3 If necessary, tap the rivets from the lower arm, then remove the balljoint.
4 Clean any rust from the rivet holes, and apply rust inhibitor.
5 The new balljoint must be fitted using three special bolts, spring washers and nuts, available from a Vauxhall parts centre.
6 Ensure that the balljoint is fitted the correct way up, noting that the securing nuts are positioned on the underside of the lower arm. Tighten the nuts to the specified torque.
7 Refit the front suspension lower arm as described in Section 7.

9 Rear hub and bracket – removal and refitting

Note: *New nuts will be required when refitting the rear hub bracket to the trailing arm.*

Removal

1 Remove the rear brake drum or disc as applicable as described in Chapter 9.
2 On models with ABS, disconnect the wiring for the wheel speed sensor located on the inside of the rear hub **(see illustration)**.
3 On rear drum models, support the rear brake backplate and shoes on an axle stand. On rear disc models, attach the brake caliper carrier plate to the rear coil spring with a plastic cable tie to prevent straining the hydraulic brake line.
4 Support the rear hub and unscrew the mounting nuts on the inside of the trailing arm. Withdraw the hub and bracket from the rear trailing arm. Note that the locating studs are spaced so that the hub bracket will only fit in one position. On rear disc models, remove the backplate.

11.4 Rear shock absorber lower mounting bolt on the trailing arm

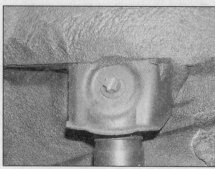

11.5 Rear shock absorber upper mounting bolt on the underbody bracket

clamping the lower mounting eye in a vice, then fully extending and compressing the shock absorber several times. Any evidence of jerky movement or lack of resistance indicates the need for renewal.

7 Examine the mounting rubbers in the shock absorber for excessive wear.

8 If the shock absorber or its mounting rubbers are worn excessively, renew the complete shock absorber.

Refitting

9 Refitting is a reversal of removal, but tighten the mounting bolts to the specified torque. On models with rear suspension level control, pre-charge the system with 0.8 bar pressure, then if necessary adjust the pressure according to the load being carried.

Refitting

5 Locate the backplate or caliper carrier plate on the trailing arm and align the mounting bolt holes.

6 Locate the hub and bracket on the trailing arm and fit new nuts to secure. Tighten the nuts to the specified torque and angles in the stages given.

7 Reconnect the wiring for the wheel speed sensor on models with ABS.

8 Refit the rear brake drum or disc as applicable as described in Chapter 9. Check and adjust the handbrake as described in Chapter 9.

7 Remove the indicator and refit the brake drums or brake disc with reference to Chapter 9.

8 Refit the rear wheels and lower the vehicle to the ground.

11 Rear shock absorber – removal, inspection and refitting

Note: *Always renew shock absorbers in pairs to maintain good road handling.*

Removal

1 Chock the front roadwheels, then jack up the rear of the vehicle and support on axle stands positioned on the rear jacking points (see *Jacking and vehicle support*). Remove the rear roadwheels.

2 On Estate models with a rear suspension level control system, remove the cover for the right-hand rear light cluster in the rear luggage compartment, and vent the air pressure from the system Schrader valve. At the shock absorber, release the clip and detach the pressure line.

3 Using a trolley jack, slightly raise the trailing arm on the relevant side.

4 Unscrew and remove the shock absorber lower mounting bolt from the trailing arm **(see illustration)**.

5 Support the shock absorber, then unscrew and remove the upper mounting bolt and withdraw the shock absorber from the underbody bracket **(see illustration)**.

Inspection

6 The shock absorber can be tested by

12 Rear suspension coil spring – removal and refitting

Note: *Due to the design of the rear suspension, it is important to note that only one coil spring should be removed at a time. Note that the rear springs should be renewed in pairs.*

Removal

1 Chock the front roadwheels, then jack up the rear of the vehicle and support on axle stands positioned on the rear jacking points (see *Jacking and vehicle support*). Remove the rear roadwheels.

2 On Estate models with a rear suspension level control system, remove the cover for the right-hand rear light cluster in the rear luggage compartment, and vent the air pressure from the system Schrader valve.

3 Using a trolley jack, slightly raise the trailing arm on the relevant side.

4 Unscrew and remove the shock absorber lower mounting bolt from the trailing arm **(see illustration)**.

5 Carefully lower the trailing arm as far as possible without straining the brake flexible hoses leading to the rear brakes.

6 Remove the coil spring and spring seats from the underbody and trailing arm, and withdraw from under the vehicle. Note that the upper spring seat incorporates a damper buffer **(see illustrations)**.

10 Rear wheel bearings – checking and renewal

1 Chock the front wheels, then jack up the rear of the vehicle and support on axle stands (see *Jacking and vehicle support*). Remove the rear wheels.

2 Remove the brake drums or brake disc (as applicable) as described in Chapter 9.

3 A dial test indicator (DTI) or datum bar and feeler blades will be required to measure the amount of radial and lateral run-out in the bearing. Zero the indicator on the outer edge of the hub flange. Alternatively, position the datum bar against the surface and use a feeler blade to measure the clearance.

4 To measure lateral run-out, locate the probe on the surface of the hub which contacts the drum or disc. To measure radial run-out, locate the probe on the outer perimeter of the hub so that it is pointing towards the centre of the hub.

5 Slowly turn the hub and note the maximum amount of run-out. If the run-out exceeds the amounts given in the Specifications, renew the hub bearing and bracket as described in Section 9.

6 Finally, check the amount of tilt in the bearing. To do this, use two wheel bolts to attach a metal bar to the outer face of the hub, then attempt to tilt the hub by pressing the bar in and out. The indicator probe must also be located on the outer face of the hub. If the tilt exceeds the maximum amount given in the Specifications, renew the hub bearing and bracket.

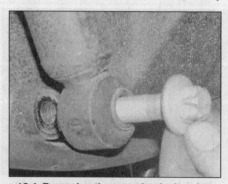

12.4 Removing the rear shock absorber lower mounting bolt

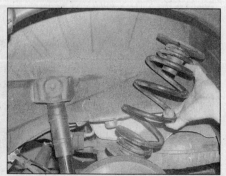

12.6a Remove the rear coil spring together with the spring seats . . .

12.6b ... then remove the upper spring seat ...

12.6c ... and lower spring seat

Refitting

7 Refitting is a reversal of removal, but note the following points.

  a) *Ensure that the spring locates correctly on the upper and lower seats, as well as on the trailing arm and underbody.*

  b) *Tighten the shock absorber lower mounting bolt to the specified torque.*

  c) *If both springs are being renewed, repeat the procedure on the remaining side of the vehicle.*

  d) *On models with rear suspension level control, pre-charge the system with 0.8 bar pressure, then if necessary adjust the pressure according to the load being carried.*

13 Rear suspension torsion beam and trailing arms – removal and refitting

Removal

1 Chock the front roadwheels, then jack up the rear of the vehicle and support on axle stands positioned on the rear jacking points (see *Jacking and vehicle support*). Remove the rear roadwheels.

2 On Estate models with a rear suspension level control system, remove the access cover for the right-hand rear light cluster in the rear luggage compartment, and vent the air pressure from the system Schrader valve.

3 Fully release the handbrake lever, then unclip the gaiter and pull it up the lever. Fully unscrew the adjustment nut on the front of the handbrake primary cable.

4 On rear disc brake models, working on each side in turn, use a screwdriver to press down the lever on the caliper, then disconnect the cable from the lever **(see illustration)**. Remove the clips and disconnect the outer cables from the support brackets on the trailing arms. Also release the handbrake cables from the supports on the torsion beam.

5 On rear drum brake models, disconnect the short rear cables at the connectors located each side just in front of the drums.

6 On models with ABS, disconnect the rear wheel sensor wiring from the rear hubs, and unclip the wiring from the torsion beam.

7 On models with a rear brake load proportioning valve, unbolt the retainer from the underbody bracket and disconnect the tension spring.

8 Remove the filler cap from the brake hydraulic fluid reservoir in the engine compartment, then tighten the cap down onto a piece of polythene sheeting. This will help prevent the fluid from draining from the system when the rear brake flexible hoses are disconnected.

9 Unscrew the union nuts and disconnect the rear brake hydraulic lines from the flexible hoses at the support brackets on the trailing arms on each side. Recover the retaining plates. Be prepared for some loss of brake fluid, and plug or tape over the ends of the lines and hoses to prevent entry of dust and dirt.

10 Support the weight of the torsion beam and trailing arms using two trolley jacks. Alternatively, one trolley jack and a length of wood may be used, but the help of an assistant will be required.

11 Unscrew the lower mounting bolts and detach both shock absorbers from the torsion beam.

12 Carefully lower the torsion beam until it is possible to remove the coil springs and spring seats. Note that the upper spring seats incorporate buffers.

13 Make sure that the torsion beam is supported, then unscrew and remove the front mounting bracket bolts from the underbody **(see illustration)**.

14 Lower the torsion beam to the ground and remove it from under the vehicle.

15 The brake components can be removed from the trailing arms, referring to the relevant Sections of Chapter 9. The hub units can be removed with reference to Section 9.

16 If necessary, the front mounting bushes can be renewed as described in Section 14.

Refitting

17 Refit any components that were removed from the torsion beam, referring to the relevant Sections of this Chapter and Chapter 9, as applicable.

18 Check the condition of the threads in the front mounting bracket captive nuts on the underbody. If necessary, use a tap to clean out the threads.

19 Support the torsion beam on the trolley jack, and position the assembly under the rear of the vehicle.

20 Raise the jack, and fit the mounting bracket bolts. Do not fully tighten the bolts at this stage.

21 Position the jack so that the distance between the coil spring contact surfaces on the trailing arms and underbody is 168.0 ± 10.0 mm on Saloon and Hatchback models, and 198.0 ± 10.0 mm on other models. With the torsion beam in this position, loosen then tighten the front mounting bracket centre bolts on each side to the specified torque.

22 Fully tighten the front mounting bracket-to-underbody bolts to the specified torque in the stages given.

23 Locate the upper and lower seats on the coil springs, then refit the springs on the torsion beam.

24 Raise the torsion beam until the shock absorber lower mounting bolts can be inserted. Tighten the bolts to the specified torque.

25 Refit the brake hydraulic lines and flexible hoses together with the retaining plates and tighten the union nuts to the specified torque.

26 On models with a rear brake load proportioning valve, refit the retainer and spring and tighten the bolt to the torque given in Chapter 9.

27 On models with ABS, clip the wiring to the torsion beam and reconnect it to the rear wheel sensors.

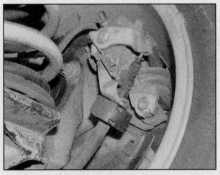

13.4 Handbrake cable connection to the rear disc caliper

13.13 Rear suspension torsion beam front mounting bracket

28 On rear drum models, reconnect the short rear cables at the connectors.

29 On rear disc models, reconnect the handbrake cables to the caliper levers and fit the cables in the supports.

30 Bleed the complete brake hydraulic system, as described in Chapter 9.

31 Adjust the handbrake cable as described in Chapter 9, then refit the handbrake lever gaiter.

32 On Estate models with a rear suspension level control system, pressurise the system to 0.8 bars then if necessary adjust the pressure according to the load being carried. Refit the access cover for the right-hand rear light cluster.

33 Refit the roadwheels and lower the vehicle to the ground.

14 Rear suspension torsion beam mounting bushes – renewal

Note: Trailing arm bushes should always be renewed in pairs – ie, on both sides of the vehicle.

Removal

1 Remove the torsion beam and trailing arms as described in Section 13.

2 Before removing the bushes, use a cold chisel to tap the spacers from the inner faces of the trailing arms.

3 A special Vauxhall tool is available for removal and refitting of the bushes, but an alternative can be improvised using a long bolt, nut, washers, and a length of metal tubing or a socket. Note the fitted position of the bushes, then draw them out from the arms.

Refitting

4 Lubricate the new bushes with silicone grease or soapy water, then draw them into position in the trailing arms.

5 Refit the torsion beam and trailing arms as described in Section 13.

15 Rear suspension level control system – general

1 Where fitted on Estate models, the rear suspension level control system is adjusted by altering the air pressure in the rear shock absorbers, through a valve located on the right-hand side of the luggage compartment.

2 For safety reasons, the level control system must not be fully pressurised when the vehicle is being driven in an unladen condition.

3 To adjust the system, continue as follows.

4 With the vehicle unladen, use a tyre pressure gauge on the air valve to check that the system pressure is 0.8 bar. Adjust if necessary. The system pressure must never be allowed to fall below 0.8 bar.

5 With the vehicle standing on a level surface, measure the distance from the bottom of the rear bumper to the ground. Subtract 40.0 mm from the distance measured, and note the new value.

6 Load the vehicle, and if necessary increase the pressure in the system until the noted value for the bumper height is reached. Do not exceed a pressure of 5.0 bars.

7 After unloading the vehicle, depressurise the system to the minimum pressure of 0.8 bar.

16 Rear suspension level air valve and lines – removal and refitting

Removal

1 With the tailgate open, turn the two fasteners through 90° and swivel open the cover for access to the right-hand rear light cluster. Remove the cap then release the pressure from the level system by depressing the centre core of the Schrader valve.

2 Unscrew the mounting nut and detach the air valve from the mounting bracket, then squeeze together the lugs and disconnect the air line.

3 Twist the retaining clip and disconnect the air valve line from the right-hand pressure line on the underbody.

4 Twist the retaining clips and disconnect the right and left-hand pressure lines from the tee-piece. Release the pressure lines from the underbody clips and remove.

Refitting

5 Refitting is a reversal of removal, but on completion, pressurise the system and check for air leaks.

17 Steering wheel – removal and refitting

⚠️ *Warning: Before removing the steering wheel, observe the safety precautions for airbags given in Chapter 12 and in Section 1 of this Chapter.*

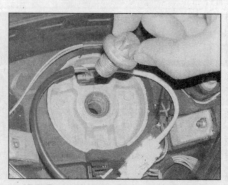

17.5 Removing the Torx retaining bolt securing the steering wheel to the column

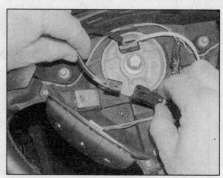

17.4 Disconnect the wiring for the radio control switches

Removal

1 Disconnect the battery negative (earth) lead (see Chapter 5A).

Caution: Wait at least one minute before proceeding. This is necessary to allow the airbag condenser to fully discharge.

2 Set the front wheels in the straight-ahead position, then lock the column in position after removing the ignition key.

3 Remove the airbag/horn-push from the steering wheel as described in Chapter 12. Position the airbag in a safe place where it cannot be tampered with, making sure that the padded side is facing upwards.

4 Where fitted, disconnect the wiring from the radio control switches **(see illustration)**.

5 Unscrew the Torx retaining bolt securing the steering wheel to the column **(see illustration)**.

6 Make alignment marks between the steering wheel and steering column shaft.

7 Grip the steering wheel with both hands and carefully rock it from side-to-side to release it from the splines on the steering column. As it is being removed, guide the wiring for the contact unit (and radio control if fitted) through the hole **(see illustration)**.

8 With the steering wheel removed, do not disturb the contact unit. If necessary hold it in its central position with tape.

Refitting

9 Check that the contact unit is positioned with the arrows aligned with each other. If it has been disturbed, return it to its central

17.7 Guide the wiring through the hole when removing the steering wheel

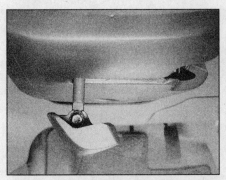

18.3 Removing the knob from the column adjuster lever

18.4a Prise out the covers . . .

18.4b . . . then undo the screws . . .

18.4c . . . and remove the upper steering column shroud

18.5a Undo the upper screws . . .

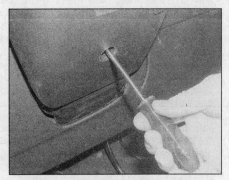

18.5b . . . and one lower screw . . .

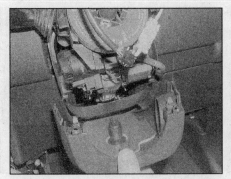

18.5c . . . and remove the lower steering column shroud

18.10 Removing the ignition switch

position by depressing the detent and rotating it fully anti-clockwise then clockwise to determine the central position – instructions are given on the unit.

10 Position the steering wheel over the column splines and guide the wiring for the contact unit (and radio control if fitted) through the hole.

11 Ensure that the indicator switch stalk is in its central (OFF) position, then locate the steering wheel on the column splines, aligning the marks made prior to removal. When locating the steering wheel on the splines, make sure that the contact unit is correctly engaged with both the steering column and indicator switch.

12 Fit the retaining bolt and tighten to the specified torque while holding the steering wheel stationary.

13 Reconnect the wiring for the radio control switches where fitted.

14 Refit the airbag/horn-push and reconnect the wiring. Insert the two screws and tighten to the specified torque.

15 Release the steering lock, then reconnect the battery negative lead.

18 Steering column – removal and refitting

Removal

1 Remove the steering wheel as described in Section 17.

2 Adjust the steering column to its maximum reach and lowest position, and lock it in this position.

3 Undo the screw and remove the knob from the column adjuster lever **(see illustration)**.

4 Prise out the covers, then undo the two screws and remove the upper steering column shroud **(see illustrations)**.

5 Undo the two upper and one lower screw and remove the lower steering column shroud **(see illustrations)**.

6 Using a screwdriver, carefully lever the wiring plug from the top of the airbag contact unit.

7 Release the clips and withdraw the contact unit from the steering column. **Note:** *All later units have a locking device which holds it in its central position.* **Do not** *release this device with the contact unit removed.*

8 Release and remove the indicator and wiper switches from the housing on the column with reference to Chapter 12, Section 4.

9 Remove the ignition key and prise out the circular trim for the immobiliser/transponder.

10 With the ignition key inserted and positioned in the 'Accessories' position, insert a screwdriver in the hole in the ignition switch and depress the locking tab, then carefully pull the switch from the steering lock housing **(see illustration)**.

11 Where fitted, remove the immobiliser/

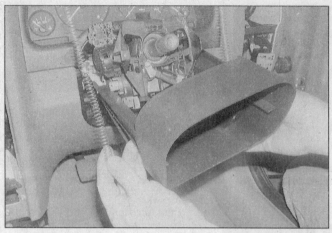

18.12 Removing the column cover and tension springs

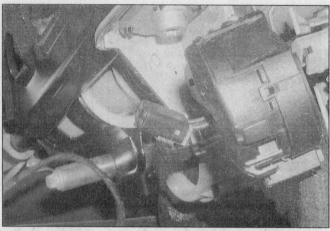

18.16 Steering column upper mounting bolt (left-hand side)

transponder unit from the steering column as follows. On models with an immobiliser/transponder **without** catch lugs, disconnect the wiring, then unclip the unit from the ignition lock housing. Remove the ignition lock cylinder as described in Chapter 12, Section 4. On models with an immobiliser/transponder **with** catch lugs, remove the ignition lock cylinder as described in Chapter 12, Section 4, then unclip the unit from the ignition lock housing. Where necessary, remove the protective cap, then disconnect the wiring.

12 Carefully remove the column cover and tension springs **(see illustration)**.

13 Unclip the wiring loom channel from the steering column, then, on the driver's side, remove the footwell panels and air vent duct.

14 Mark the steering column intermediate shaft upper joint in relation to the steering column to aid refitting, then unscrew the remove the clamp bolt. Push the joint from the splines on the bottom of the steering column, noting that the intermediate shaft is telescopic.

15 On models with ESP (Electronic Stabilisation system), disconnect the wiring from the steering angle sensor, then use a screwdriver to depress the tab and release the sensor from the adapter. Move the sensor down slightly.

16 Support the steering column, then unscrew the steering column lower clamp and upper mounting bolts **(see illustration)**. Where applicable, release the lower mounting catch, taking care not to bend the catch. On models with ESP, pull the column upwards slightly and release the sensor from the bottom of the column. Note the location of any shims located behind the lower mounting clamp upper mounting bracket.

17 Withdraw the column from the bulkhead bracket and remove from inside the vehicle.

Refitting

18 Before refitting the steering column, loosely fit the lower mounting clamp and screw on the bolt several threads; do not fit

the upper mounting bolts at this stage. Carefully locate the steering column through the lower mounting clamp, making sure that the wiring is not damaged. On models with ESP, locate the steering angle sensor on the bottom of the column making sure that the retaining tab is correctly engaged.

19 On models manufactured from 2000, refit the upper mounting bolts and tighten them to the specified torque.

20 On models manufactured up to and including 1999 where shims were fitted, insert them between the lower mounting bracket and crossmember, then insert the lower clamp and upper mounting bolts and tighten to the specified torque.

21 On models manufactured up to and including 1999 where no shims were fitted, obtain 4 shims (each 1.0 mm thick) from a Vauxhall dealer, and fit them as a 4.0 mm thick pack between the lower mounting bracket and crossmember. Tighten the clamp bolt to the specified torque, then grip the lower end of the inner column and attempt to push it upwards (ie, towards the steering wheel position). The grey guide sleeve on the lower mounting should not move. If it does, remove one of the shims and make the check again. If necessary, repeat the procedure until the guide sleeve is held firmly, then insert the upper mounting bolts and tighten to the specified torque. Where applicable, make sure that the detent is positioned in front of the lower bearing sleeve.

22 On models with ESP, reconnect the wiring to the steering angle sensor.

23 Engage the intermediate shaft with the splines on the bottom of the column, making sure that the previously-made marks are correctly aligned with each other. Note that if the shaft and column are not aligned correctly, it will be impossible to insert the clamp bolt. Insert the clamp bolt and tighten securely.

24 Refit the air vent duct and footwell panels, and clip the wiring loom channel to the steering column.

25 Refit the immobiliser/transponder unit to the steering column using a reversal of the

removal procedure. On models with an immobiliser/transponder **without** catch lugs, refit the ignition lock cylinder as described in Chapter 12, then clip the unit onto the ignition lock housing. On models with an immobiliser/transponder **with** catch lugs, clip the unit onto the ignition lock housing, then refit the ignition lock cylinder as described in Chapter 12. Where necessary, reconnect the wiring then refit the protective cap.

26 Refit the column cover and tension springs.

27 With the ignition key inserted in the 'Accessories' position, refit the ignition switch to the steering lock housing, making sure that the clip engages correctly.

28 Remove the ignition key then refit the circular trim for the immobiliser/transponder.

29 Refit the indicator and wiper switches to the housing on the column with reference to Chapter 12.

30 Refit the airbag contact unit to the steering column making sure that the guide pins enter their holes correctly and the retaining clips are engaged correctly. **Note:** *It is important that the retaining clips are fully engaged. If they are damaged in any way, the complete contact unit must be renewed.*

31 Carefully refit the wiring plug to the top of the contact unit.

32 Refit the lower steering column shroud followed by the upper shroud, and secure with the retaining screws.

33 Refit the knob to the column adjuster lever and tighten the screw.

34 Refit the steering wheel with reference to Section 17.

19 Steering column intermediate shaft – removal and refitting

Removal

1 Set the front wheels in the straight-ahead position. Remove the ignition key and allow the steering lock to engage.

19.3a Intermediate shaft joint connection to the steering gear pinion

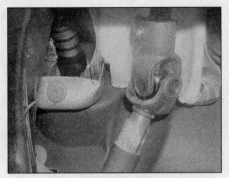

19.3b Intermediate shaft joint connection to the steering column

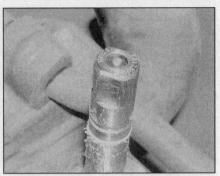

19.4 View of the pinion (steering gear removed from the vehicle)

2 Remove the footwell panels and air vent duct from the driver's footwell.

3 Mark the steering column intermediate shaft upper and lower joints in relation to the steering column and steering gear pinion as an aid to refitting, then unscrew both clamp bolts (see illustrations).

4 Compress the telescopic intermediate shaft and slide the joints from the column and pinion (see illustration). Withdraw the intermediate shaft from inside the vehicle.

Inspection

5 Inspect the intermediate shaft universal joints for excessive wear or damage. If either joint is worn or damaged, the complete shaft assembly must be renewed.

Refitting

6 Check that the front wheels and steering wheel are still in the straight-ahead position, and that the steering wheel is still locked.

7 Slide the intermediate shaft lower joint onto the steering gear pinion, aligning the previously-made marks. Note that it will not be possible to insert the clamp bolt if the splines are not correctly aligned. Apply a little locking fluid to the threads of the clamp bolt, then insert it and tighten to the specified torque.

8 Slide the upper end of the intermediate shaft onto the column splines, aligning the previously-made marks. Insert the clamp bolt and tighten securely.

9 Refit the air vent duct and footwell panels to the driver's footwell.

20 Steering gear rubber gaiters – renewal

1 Remove the relevant track rod end as described in Section 24.

2 Remove the inner and outer securing clips (see illustration), then slide the gaiter off the end of the track rod.

3 Thoroughly clean the track rod, then slide the new gaiter into position. Note that a groove is provided in the track rod for the outer end of the gaiter to locate in.

4 Fit the gaiter securing clips, using new clips if necessary, making sure that the gaiter is not twisted.

5 Refit the track rod end as described in Section 24.

6 Have the front wheel toe-setting checked and adjusted at the earliest opportunity.

21 Steering gear – removal and refitting

Removal

1 Set the front wheels in the straight-ahead position. Remove the ignition key and allow the steering lock to engage.

2 Remove the front subframe as described in Section 4.

3 On LHD models, unbolt the rear engine mounting bracket from the subframe.

4 Where fitted, unbolt the support bracket for the pressure and return lines from the subframe.

5 Position a suitable container beneath the steering gear fluid unions to catch spilt hydraulic fluid.

6 Unscrew the union nuts and disconnect the fluid pressure and return lines from the steering gear (see illustration).

7 Note the routing of the wiring loom then disconnect it from the electric hydraulic pump and remove it from the subframe.

8 Unscrew the mounting nuts and withdraw the electric hydraulic pump together with the fluid reservoir and pressure/return lines from the subframe and steering gear. Note that either a round (TRW) or angular (Delphi/Saginaw) hydraulic fluid reservoir is fitted.

9 Unscrew the mounting bolts and remove the steering gear from the subframe (see illustration). If necessary, remove the anti-roll bar first with reference to Section 6. The manufacturers recommend that the mounting bolts are renewed whenever removed.

10 If necessary, remove the track rod ends and track rods with reference to Sections 24 and 25. **Note:** *New steering gears are available from Vauxhall either with or without the track rods fitted.* Also remove the rubber grommets from the pinion.

Refitting

11 Refit the track rods and track rod ends

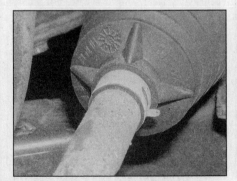

20.2 Outer clip for the steering gear rubber gaiter

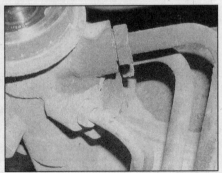

21.6 Hydraulic fluid lines on the steering gear

21.9 A steering gear mounting bolt

22.5a Power steering electro-hydraulic pump

22.5b Mounting nuts for the hydraulic pump

with reference to Sections 24 and 25. Also refit the rubber grommets to the pinion.

12 Clean any dirt from the steering gear and subframe, then locate the steering gear in position. Insert the mounting bolts and tighten to the specified torque.

13 Where removed, refit the anti-roll bar with reference to Section 6.

14 Refit the electro-hydraulic pump together with the fluid reservoir and pressure/return lines to the subframe and steering gear, and tighten the mounting nuts to the specified torque.

15 Reconnect the wiring loom to the electric hydraulic pump and attach it to the subframe.

16 Fit new rubber sealing rings to the pressure and return lines, then refit the lines to the steering gear and tighten the union nuts to the specified torque.

17 Where fitted, refit the support bracket for the pressure and return lines to the subframe and tighten the mounting bolts to the specified torque.

18 On LHD models, refit the rear engine mounting bracket to the subframe and tighten to the specified torque.

19 Refit the front subframe as described in Section 4.

20 Bleed the power steering hydraulic system as described in Section 23.

21 Have the front wheel toe-setting checked and adjusted at the earliest opportunity.

22 Electro-hydraulic power steering pump – removal and refitting

Removal

1 Remove the front subframe as described in Section 4.

2 Position a suitable container beneath the power steering pump fluid unions to catch spilt hydraulic fluid.

3 Disconnect the pressure and return lines from the power steering pump. Use a spanner to unscrew the pressure line union nut. If necessary, cut free the return line clip and replace it with a screw-type clip.

4 Note the routing of the wiring loom then disconnect it at the connector and body

earthing point. **Note:** *The wiring loom is supplied together with the pump and cannot be separated.*

5 Unscrew the mounting nuts and withdraw the electric hydraulic pump together with the bracket, wiring and fluid reservoir from the subframe and steering gear **(see illustrations)**. Note that either a round (TRW) or angular (Delphi/Saginaw) hydraulic fluid reservoir is fitted. Also note that the wiring connector is 2-pin before model year 2000, but 3-pin thereafter, and an adapter is available from Vauxhall in the event of a new pump being fitted to a pre-2000 model.

6 Unscrew the mounting nuts and remove the electro-hydraulic pump and mounting bushes from the bracket. Check the rubber mounting bushes for wear and damage and renew them if necessary.

Refitting

7 Refit the pump and bushes to the bracket and tighten the mounting nuts.

8 Refit the electro-hydraulic pump and bracket on the subframe and steering gear and tighten the mounting nuts to the specified torque.

9 Reconnect the wiring loom and attach the cable to the earthing point. Make sure that the loom is routed as noted during removal.

10 Fit a new rubber sealing ring to the pressure line, then reconnect the pressure and return lines to the power steering pump. Tighten the pressure line union nut securely, and fit a new clip to the return line.

23.3a Power steering fluid reservoir – Zafira model

11 Unscrew the cap from the fluid reservoir and remove the filter. Clean the filter and refit it, then fill the reservoir with the specified fluid and tighten the cap. Fluid level marks are provided on the reservoir, but note that on the TRW system the fluid level marks are on the dipstick integral with the cap, whereas on the Delphi/Saginaw system the level dipstick is attached to the bottom of the filter. **Note:** *Do not re-use drained hydraulic fluid.*

12 Refit the front subframe as described in Section 4.

13 Bleed the power steering hydraulic system as described in Section 23.

23 Power steering hydraulic system – bleeding

Note: *The system must be bled at room temperature – do not bleed the system immediately after using the vehicle on the road.*

1 Check and top-up the power steering fluid level in the reservoir to the MAX mark as described in *Weekly checks*. If the system regularly requires more fluid, check the hoses for leaks.

TRW system

Note: *Fluid level mark on reservoir and dipstick integral with cap.*

2 Start the engine, then slowly turn the steering wheel fully from left-to-right three times with the engine still running.

3 Switch off the engine and check the level of the fluid. If necessary, top up the level to the MAX mark **(see illustrations)**.

4 Start the engine and turn the steering wheel from left-to-right several times while checking for excessive noise. Repeat the bleeding procedure if the power steering operation is noisy, as this indicates there is still some air in the system.

Delphi/Saginaw system

Note: *Fluid level mark on dipstick attached to filter.*

5 Start the engine, then slowly turn the steering wheel fully from left-to-right twice with the engine still running.

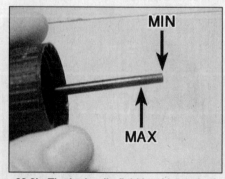

23.3b The hydraulic fluid level is marked on the cap integral dipstick on the TRW system

24.2 Hold the track rod stationary while loosening the track rod end securing locknut

6 Switch off the engine and check the level of the fluid. If necessary, top up the level to the MAX mark.
7 Start the engine and turn the steering wheel from left-to-right several times while checking for excessive noise. Repeat the bleeding procedure if the power steering operation is noisy, as this indicates there is still some air in the system.

24 Track rod end – removal and refitting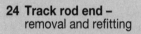

Note: *A balljoint separator tool will be required for this operation.*

Removal

1 Apply the handbrake, then jack up the front of the vehicle, and support securely on axle stands (see *Jacking and vehicle support*). Remove the relevant roadwheel.
2 Loosen the track rod end securing locknut on the track rod a quarter turn, while holding the track rod stationary with a second spanner on the flats provided **(see illustration)**. If necessary, use a wire brush to remove rust from the nut and threads and lubricate the threads with penetrating oil before unscrewing the nut. As an additional check, measure the visible amount of threads on the track rod using vernier calipers. This will ensure the track rod end is refitted in the same position.

24.4a Using a balljoint separator tool . . .

24.3 Unscrewing the balljoint nut securing the track rod end to the steering arm on the hub carrier

3 Where necessary, extract the split pin, then unscrew and remove the balljoint nut securing the track rod end to the steering arm on the hub carrier **(see illustration)**.
4 Disconnect the track rod end balljoint from the steering arm on the hub carrier using a balljoint separator tool, taking care not to damage the balljoint boot **(see illustrations)**.
5 Unscrew the track rod end from the track rod, counting the number of turns necessary to remove it and taking care not to disturb the locknut. **Note:** *The track rod ends are handed side-for-side. The right-hand track rod end is marked with an R and has a right-hand thread, whereas the left-hand one is marked with an L and has a left-hand thread.*

Refitting

6 Screw the track rod end onto the track rod the number of turns noted during removal. Check that the visible amount of threads on the track rod is as previously noted.
7 Insert the track rod end balljoint in the steering arm on the hub carrier, then fit the nut and tighten to the specified torque. If the balljoint stud turns as the nut is being tightened, press down on the track rod end to force the stud into the arm. Where necessary, fit a new split pin.
8 Tighten the track rod end securing locknut on the track rod while holding the track rod stationary with a second spanner on the flats provided. If possible, tighten the nut to the specified torque using a special crow's-foot adapter for the torque wrench.

24.4b . . . to disconnect the track rod end balljoint from the steering arm

9 Refit the roadwheel, then lower the vehicle to the ground, and tighten the wheelbolts.
10 Have the front wheel alignment checked and adjusted at the earliest opportunity.

25 Track rod – removal and refitting

Removal

1 Remove the track rod end from the relevant track rod as described in Section 24. Note, however, that on RHD models it is necessary to remove both track rod ends and bellows when removing the left-hand track rod. Conversely, on LHD models it is necessary to remove both track rod ends and bellows when removing the right-hand track rod.
2 Where necessary, remove the wheelarch liner or trim from under the wheel arch by removing the fasteners.
3 Release the clips and slide the rubber bellows from the steering gear and track rod. Remove the bellows from both sides where necessary (see paragraph 1). Where metal clips are fitted, either prise them free with a screwdriver, or carefully cut them off with a hacksaw.
4 Turn the steering on full lock so that the rack protrudes from the steering gear on the relevant side. Mark the inner joint housing and rack in relation to each other to indicate how tight it is (see paragraph 6).
5 Hold the rack stationary with a spanner on the flats provided, then unscrew and remove the track rod inner joint housing. Use either a large adjustable spanner or grips.

Refitting

6 Clean the threads and apply a little locking fluid to them, then screw the track rod inner joint housing into the rack and tighten to the specified torque. Because of its size and design, using a torque wrench may be difficult, in which case the joint housing should be tightened until the previously-made marks are aligned with each other.
7 Refit the bellows making sure that the inner end is pushed fully onto the steering gear and the outer end is seated in the groove on the track rod. Use new clips if necessary.
8 Where necessary, refit the wheelarch liner or trim.
9 Refit the track rod end(s) as described in Section 24.
10 Have the front wheel alignment checked and adjusted at the earliest opportunity.

26 Wheel alignment and steering angles – general information

Front wheel alignment

1 Accurate front wheel alignment is essential to good steering and for even tyre wear.

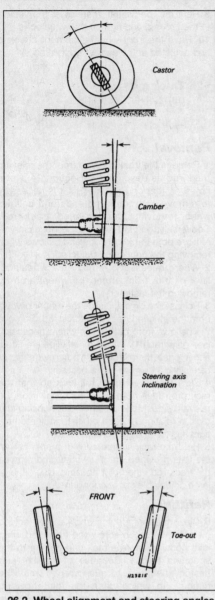

26.2 Wheel alignment and steering angles

Before considering the steering angles, check that the tyres are correctly inflated, that the front wheels are not buckled, the hub bearings are not worn and that the steering linkage is in good order without slackness or wear at the joints. The fuel tank must be half full and each front seat must be loaded with 70 kg.

2 Wheel alignment consists of four factors **(see illustration)**:

Camber, is the angle at which the roadwheels are set from the vertical when viewed from the front or rear of the vehicle. Positive camber is the angle (in degrees) that the wheels are tilted outwards at the top from the vertical. Negative camber is the angle that the wheels are tilted inwards at the top from the vertical. The camber angle is set during production and cannot be adjusted.

Castor, is the angle between the steering axis and a vertical line when viewed from each side of the vehicle. Positive castor is indicated when the steering axis is inclined towards the rear of the vehicle at its upper end. This angle is not adjustable.

Steering axis inclination (kingpin inclination), is the angle, when viewed from the front or rear of the vehicle, between the vertical and an imaginary line drawn between the upper and lower front suspension strut mountings. This angle is not adjustable.

Toe, is the amount by which the distance between the front inside edges of the roadwheel rim differs from that between the rear inside edges. If the distance between the front edges is less than that at the rear, the wheels are said to toe-in. If the distance between the front inside edges is greater than that at the rear, the wheels toe-out.

3 Owing to the need for precision gauges to measure the small angles of the steering and suspension settings, it is preferable that checking of camber and castor is left to a service station having the necessary equipment. Castor is set during production of the vehicle, and any deviation from the specified angle will be due to accident damage or gross wear in the suspension mountings.

4 To check the front wheel alignment, first make sure that the lengths of both track rods are equal when the steering is in the straight-ahead position. The track rod lengths can be adjusted if necessary by releasing the locknuts from the track rod ends and rotating the track rods. If necessary, self-locking grips can be used to rotate the track rods.

5 Obtain a tracking gauge. These are available in various forms from accessory stores, or one can be fabricated from a length of steel tubing suitably cranked to clear the sump and transmission, and having a setscrew and locknut at one end.

6 With the gauge, measure the distances between the two wheel inner rims (at hub height) at the rear of the wheel. Push the vehicle forward to rotate the wheel through 180° (half a turn) and measure the distance between the wheel inner rims, again at hub height, at the front of the wheel. This last measurement should differ from the first by the appropriate toe-in which is given in the Specifications. The vehicle must be on level ground.

7 If the toe-in is found to be incorrect, release the track rod end locknuts and turn both track rods equally. Only turn them a quarter-of-a-turn at a time before re-checking the alignment. If necessary use self-locking grips to turn the track rods. It is important not to allow the track rods to become unequal in length during adjustment, otherwise the alignment of the steering wheel will become incorrect and tyre scrubbing will occur on turns.

8 On completion tighten the locknuts without disturbing the setting. Check that the balljoints are at the centre of their arcs of travel.

Rear wheel alignment

9 The rear wheel toe and camber are set during production and are not adjustable.

Chapter 11
Bodywork and fittings

Contents

Degrees of difficulty

Easy, suitable for novice with little experience	Fairly easy, suitable for beginner with some experience	Fairly difficult, suitable for competent DIY mechanic	Difficult, suitable for experienced DIY mechanic	Very difficult, suitable for expert DIY or professional

Specifications

Torque wrench settings	Nm	lbf ft
Bonnet striker	22	16
Front seat	20	15
Front seat backrest to cushion	35	26
Front seat belt	20	15
Rear seat belt lock to floor	35	26
Seat belt height adjuster securing bolts	20	15
Seat belt reel to B-pillar	35	26
Seat belt reel to C-pillar	35	26
Seat belt reel to rear seat backrest	35	26
Seat belt tensioner to front seat	35	26
Seat belt to front seat	20	15
Seat belt to height adjuster	35	26

1 Bodywork information – general

The bodyshell and floorpan are manufactured from pressed-steel, and together make up the vehicle's structure. The Astra is available in 4-door Saloon, 3- and 5-door Hatchback and 5-door Estate. The Zafira is the 7-seater MPV version of the Astra. There is also a Cabriolet model (not covered in this Manual).

Various areas of the structure are strengthened to provide for suspension, steering and engine mounting points, and load distribution. One notable feature is the use of tubular reinforcing bars in the doors, to provide the occupants with additional protection in the event of a side impact.

Extensive corrosion protection is applied to all new vehicles. Various anti-corrosion preparations are used, including galvanising, zinc phosphatisation, and underseal. Protective wax is injected into the box sections and other hollow cavities.

Extensive use is made of plastic for peripheral components, such as the radiator grille, bumpers and wheel trims, and for much of the interior trim.

Interior fittings are to a high standard on all models, and a wide range of optional equipment is available throughout the range.

2 Maintenance of bodywork and underframe – general

Cleaning the vehicle's exterior

The general condition of a vehicle's bodywork is the one thing that significantly affects its value. Maintenance is easy but needs to be regular. Neglect, particularly after minor damage, can lead quickly to further deterioration and costly repair bills. It is important also to keep watch on those parts of the vehicle not immediately visible, for instance the underbody, inside all the wheelarches and the lower part of the engine compartment.

The basic maintenance routine for the bodywork is washing preferably with a lot of water, from a hose. This will remove all the loose solids that may have stuck to the vehicle. It is important to flush these off in such a way as to prevent grit from scratching the finish. The wheelarches and underbody need washing in the same way to remove any accumulated mud, which will retain moisture and tend to encourage rust, particularly in Winter, when it is essential that any salt (from that put down on the roads) is washed off. Paradoxically enough, the best time to clean the underbody and wheelarches is in wet weather, when the mud is thoroughly wet and

soft. In very wet weather, the underbody is usually cleaned automatically of large accumulations; this is therefore a good time for inspection.

If the vehicle is very dirty, especially underneath or in the engine compartment, it is tempting to use one of the pressure-washers or steam-cleaners available on garage forecourts, while these are quick and effective, especially for the removal of the accumulation of oily grime which sometimes is allowed to become thick in certain areas, their usage does have some disadvantages. If caked-on dirt is simply blasted off the paintwork, its finish soon becomes scratched and dull, and the pressure can allow water to penetrate door and window seals and the lock mechanisms; if the full force of such a jet is directed at the vehicle's underbody, the wax-based protective coating can easily be damaged, and water (with whatever cleaning solvent is used) could be forced into crevices or components that it would not normally reach. Similarly, if such equipment is used to clean the engine compartment, water can be forced into the components of the fuel and electrical systems, and the protective coating can be removed that is applied to many small components during manufacture; this may therefore actually promote corrosion (especially inside electrical connectors) and initiate engine problems or other electrical faults. Also, if the jet is pointed directly at any of the oil seals, water can be forced past the seal lips and into the engine or transmission. Great care is required, therefore, if such equipment is used and, in general, regular cleaning by such methods should be avoided.

A much better solution in the long term is just to flush away as much loose dirt as possible using a hose alone, even if this leaves the engine compartment looking 'dirty'. If an oil leak has developed, or if any other accumulation of oil or grease is to be removed, there are one or two excellent grease solvents available that can be brush-applied. The dirt can then be simply hosed off. Take care to replace the wax-based protective coat, if this was affected by the solvent.

Normal washing of the vehicle's bodywork is best carried out using cold or warm water, with a proprietary vehicle shampoo, tar spots can be removed by using white spirit, followed by soapy water to remove all traces of spirit. Try to keep water out of the bonnet air inlets, and check afterwards that the heater air inlet box drain tube is clear, so that any water has drained out of the box.

After washing the paintwork, wipe off with a chamois leather to give an unspotted clear finish. A coat of clear protective wax polish will give added protection against chemical pollutants in the air. If the paintwork sheen has dulled or oxidised, use a cleaner/polisher combination to restore the brilliance of the shine. This requires a little effort, but such dulling is usually caused because regular

washing has been neglected. Care needs to be taken with metallic paintwork, as special non-abrasive cleaner/polisher is required to avoid damage to the finish.

Any polished metals should be treated in the same way as paintwork.

Windscreens and windows can be kept clear of the smeary film that often appears with proprietary glass cleaner. Never use any form of wax or other body or chromium polish on glass.

Exterior paintwork and body panels check

Once the vehicle has been washed, and all tar spots and other surface blemishes have been cleaned off, check carefully all paintwork, looking closely for chips or scratches; check with particular care vulnerable areas such as the front (bonnet and spoiler) and around the wheelarches. Any damage to the paintwork must be rectified as soon as possible, to comply with the terms of the manufacturer's cosmetic and anti-corrosion warranties; check with a Vauxhall dealer for details.

If a chip or (light) scratch is found that is recent and still free from rust, it can be touched-up using the appropriate touch-up pencil; these can be obtained from Vauxhall dealers. Any more serious damage, or rusted stone chips, can be repaired as described in Section 4, but if damage or corrosion is so severe that a panel must be renewed, seek professional advice as soon as possible.

Always check that the door and ventilator opening drain holes and pipes are completely clear, so that water can drain out.

Underbody sealer check

The wax-based underbody protective coating should be inspected annually, preferably just before Winter. Wash the underbody down as thoroughly but gently as possible (see the above concerning steam cleaners, etc) and have any damage to the coating repaired. If any of the body panels are disturbed for repair or renewed, do not forget to replace the coating and to inject wax into door panels, sills, box sections, etc, to maintain the level of protection provided by the vehicle manufacturer.

3 Maintenance of upholstery and carpets – general

Mats and carpets should be brushed or vacuum-cleaned regularly, to keep them free of grit. If they are badly stained, remove them from the vehicle for scrubbing or sponging, and make quite sure they are dry before refitting. Seats and interior trim panels can be kept clean by wiping with a damp cloth. If they do become stained (which can be more apparent on light-coloured upholstery), use a little liquid detergent and a soft nail brush to scour the grime out of the grain of the material. Do not forget to keep the headlining clean in the same way as the upholstery. When using liquid cleaners inside the vehicle, do not over-wet the surfaces being cleaned. Excessive damp could get into the seams and padded interior, causing stains, offensive odours or even rot. If the inside of the vehicle gets wet accidentally, it is worthwhile taking some trouble to dry it out properly, particularly where carpets are involved. *Do not leave oil or electric heaters inside the vehicle for this purpose.*

4 Minor body damage repair – general

Repairs of minor scratches in bodywork

If the scratch is very superficial, and does not penetrate to the metal of the bodywork, repair is very simple. Lightly rub the area of the scratch with a paintwork renovator, or a very fine cutting paste, to remove loose paint from the scratch, and to clear the surrounding bodywork of wax polish. Rinse the area with clean water.

Apply touch-up paint to the scratch using a fine paint brush; continue to apply fine layers of paint until the surface of the paint in the scratch is level with the surrounding paintwork. Allow the new paint at least two weeks to harden, then blend it into the surrounding paintwork by rubbing the scratch area with a paintwork renovator or a very fine cutting paste. Finally, apply wax polish.

Where the scratch has penetrated right through to the metal of the bodywork, causing the metal to rust, a different repair technique is required. Remove any loose rust from the bottom of the scratch with a penknife, then apply rust-inhibiting paint to prevent the formation of rust in the future. Using a rubber or nylon applicator, fill the scratch with bodystopper paste. If required, this paste can be mixed with cellulose thinners to provide a very thin paste that is ideal for filling narrow scratches. Before the stopper-paste in the scratch hardens, wrap a piece of smooth cotton rag around the top of a finger. Dip the finger in cellulose thinners, and quickly sweep it across the surface of the stopper-paste in the scratch; this will ensure that the surface of the stopper-paste is slightly hollowed. The scratch can now be painted over as described earlier in this Section.

Repairs of dents in bodywork

When deep denting of the vehicle's bodywork has taken place, the first task is to pull the dent out, until the affected bodywork almost attains its original shape. There is little point in trying to restore the original shape completely, as the metal in the damaged area will have stretched on impact, and cannot be reshaped fully to its original contour. It is better to bring the level of the dent up to a point that is about 3 mm below the level of the surrounding bodywork. In cases where the dent is very shallow anyway, it is not worth trying to pull it out at all. If the underside of the dent is accessible, it can be hammered out gently from behind, using a mallet with a wooden or plastic head. Whilst doing this, hold a block of wood firmly against the outside of the panel, to absorb the impact from the hammer blows and thus prevent a large area of the bodywork from being 'belled-out'.

Should the dent be in a section of the bodywork that has a double skin, or some other factor making it inaccessible from behind, a different technique is called for. Drill several small holes through the metal inside the area – particularly in the deeper section. Then screw long self-tapping screws into the holes, just sufficiently for them to gain a good purchase in the metal. Now the dent can be pulled out by pulling on the protruding heads of the screws with a pair of pliers.

The next stage of the repair is the removal of the paint from the damaged area, and from an inch or so of the surrounding 'sound' bodywork. This is accomplished most easily by using a wire brush or abrasive pad on a power drill, although it can be done just as effectively by hand, using sheets of abrasive paper. To complete the preparation for filling, score the surface of the bare metal with a screwdriver or the tang of a file, or alternatively, drill small holes in the affected area. This will provide a good 'key' for the filler paste.

To complete the repair, see the Section on filling and respraying.

Repairs of rust holes or gashes in bodywork

Remove all paint from the affected area, and from an inch or so of the surrounding 'sound' bodywork, using an abrasive pad or a wire brush on a power drill. If these are not available, a few sheets of abrasive paper will do the job most effectively. With the paint removed, you will be able to judge the severity of the corrosion, and therefore decide whether to renew the whole panel (if this is possible) or to repair the affected area. New body panels are not as expensive as most people think, and it is often quicker and more satisfactory to fit a new panel than to attempt to repair large areas of corrosion.

Remove all fittings from the affected area, except those which will act as a guide to the original shape of the damaged bodywork (e.g. headlight shells, etc.). Then, using tin snips or a hacksaw blade, remove all loose metal and any other metal badly affected by corrosion. Hammer the edges of the hole inwards, to create a slight depression for the filler paste.

Wire-brush the affected area to remove the powdery rust from the surface of the remaining metal. Paint the affected area with rust-inhibiting paint, if the back of the rusted area is accessible, treat this also.

Before filling can take place, it will be necessary to block the hole in some way. This can be achieved with aluminium or plastic mesh, or aluminium tape.

Aluminium or plastic mesh, or glass-fibre matting, is probably the best material to use for a large hole. Cut a piece to the approximate size and shape of the hole to be filled, then position it in the hole so that its edges are below the level of the surrounding bodywork. It can be retained in position by several blobs of filler paste around its periphery.

Aluminium tape should be used for small or very narrow holes. Pull a piece off the roll, trim it to the approximate size and shape required, then pull off the backing paper (if used) and stick the tape over the hole. It can be overlapped if the thickness of one piece is insufficient. Burnish down the edges of the tape with the handle of a screwdriver or similar, to ensure that the tape is securely attached to the metal underneath.

Bodywork repairs – filling and respraying

Before using this Section, see the Sections on dent, deep scratch, rust holes and gash repairs.

Many types of bodyfiller are available, but generally speaking, those proprietary kits that contain a tin of filler paste and a tube of resin hardener are best for this type of repair. A wide, flexible plastic or nylon applicator will be found invaluable for imparting a smooth and well-contoured finish to the surface of the filler.

Mix up a little filler on a clean piece of card or board – measure the hardener carefully (follow the maker's instructions on the pack), otherwise the filler will set too rapidly or too slowly. Using the applicator, apply the filler paste to the prepared area; draw the applicator across the surface of the filler to achieve the correct contour and to level the surface. When a contour that follows the original is achieved, stop working the paste. If you carry on too long, the paste will become sticky and begin to 'pick-up' on the applicator. Continue to add thin layers of filler paste at 20-minute intervals, until the level of the filler is just proud of the surrounding bodywork.

Once the filler has hardened, the excess can be removed using a metal plane or file. From then on, progressively-finer grades of abrasive paper should be used, starting with a 40-grade production paper, and finishing with a 400-grade wet-and-dry paper. Always wrap the abrasive paper around a flat rubber, cork, or wooden block – otherwise the surface of the filler will not be completely flat. During the smoothing of the filler surface, the wet-and-dry paper should be periodically rinsed in water. This will ensure that a very smooth finish is imparted to the filler at the final stage.

At this stage, the 'dent' should be surrounded by a ring of bare metal, which in turn should be encircled by the finely 'feathered' edge of the good paintwork. Rinse the repair area with clean water, until all of the dust produced by the rubbing-down operation has gone.

Spray the whole area with a light coat of primer – this will show up any imperfections in the surface of the filler. Repair these imperfections with fresh filler paste or bodystopper, and again smooth the surface with abrasive paper. If bodystopper is used, it can be mixed with cellulose thinners, to form a thin paste that is ideal for filling small holes.

Repeat this spray-and-repair procedure until you are satisfied that the surface of the filler, and the feathered edge of the paintwork, are perfect. Clean the repair area with clean water, and allow to dry fully.

The repair area is now ready for final spraying. Paint spraying must be carried out in a warm, dry, windless and dust-free atmosphere. This condition can be created artificially if you have access to a large indoor working area, but if you are forced to work in the open, you will have to pick your day very carefully. If you are working indoors, dousing the floor in the work area with water will help to settle the dust that would otherwise be in the atmosphere. If the repair area is confined to one body panel, mask off the surrounding panels; this will help to minimise the effects of a slight mis-match in paint colours. Bodywork fittings (e.g. chrome strips, door handles, etc.), will also need to be masked off. Use genuine masking tape, and several thicknesses of newspaper, for the masking operations.

Before starting to spray, agitate the aerosol can thoroughly, then spray a test area (an old tin, or similar) until the technique is mastered. Cover the repair area with a thick coat of primer; the thickness should be built up using several thin layers of paint, rather than one thick one. Using 400-grade wet-and-dry paper, rub down the surface of the primer until it is smooth. While doing this, the work area should be thoroughly doused with water, and the wet-and-dry paper periodically rinsed

in water. Allow to dry before spraying on more paint.

Spray on the top coat, again building up the thickness by using several thin layers of paint. Start spraying at one edge of the repair area, and then, using a side-to-side motion, work until the whole repair area and about 2 inches of the surrounding original paintwork is covered. Remove all masking material 10 to 15 minutes after spraying on the final coat of paint.

Allow the new paint at least two weeks to harden, then, using a paintwork renovator, or a very fine cutting paste, blend the edges of the paint into the existing paintwork. Finally, apply wax polish.

Plastic components

With the use of more and more plastic body components by the vehicle manufacturers (e.g. bumpers. spoilers, and in some cases major body panels), rectification of more serious damage to such items has become a matter of either entrusting repair work to a specialist in this field, or renewing complete components. Repair of such damage by the DIY owner is not feasible, owing to the cost of the equipment and materials required for effecting such repairs. The basic technique involves making a groove along the line of the crack in the plastic, using a rotary burr in a power drill. The damaged part is then welded back together, using a hot-air gun to heat up and fuse a plastic filler rod into the groove. Any excess plastic is then removed, and the area rubbed down to a smooth finish. It is important that a filler rod of the correct plastic is used, as body components can be made of a variety of different types (e.g. polycarbonate, ABS, polypropylene).

Damage of a less serious nature (abrasions, minor cracks, etc.), can be repaired by the DIY owner using a two-part epoxy filler repair material. Once mixed in equal proportions, this is used in similar fashion to the bodywork filler used on metal panels. The filler is usually cured in twenty to thirty minutes, ready for sanding and painting.

If the owner is renewing a complete component himself, or if he has repaired it with epoxy filler, he will be left with the

problem of finding a paint for finishing which is compatible with the type of plastic used. At one time, the use of a universal paint was not possible, owing to the complex range of plastics encountered in body component applications. Standard paints, generally speaking, will not bond to plastic or rubber satisfactorily. However, it is now possible to obtain a plastic body parts finishing kit that consists of a pre-primer treatment, a primer and coloured top coat. Full instructions are normally supplied with a kit, but basically, the method of use is to first apply the pre-primer to the component concerned, and allow it to dry for up to 30 minutes. Then the primer is applied, and left to dry for about an hour before finally applying the special-coloured top coat. The result is a correctly coloured component, where the paint will flex with the plastic or rubber, a property that standard paint does not normally possess.

5 Major body damage repair – general

Where serious damage has occurred, or large areas need renewal due to neglect, it means that complete new panels will need welding-in; this is best left to professionals. If the damage is due to impact, it will also be necessary to check completely the alignment of the bodyshell; this can only be carried out accurately by a Vauxhall dealer using special jigs. If the body is left misaligned, it is primarily dangerous (as the car will not handle properly) and secondly, uneven stresses will be imposed on the steering, suspension and possibly transmission, causing abnormal wear or complete failure, particularly to items such as the tyres.

6 Front and rear bumpers – removal and refitting

Front bumper

Removal

1 Working under the front of the vehicle, remove the three plastic clips securing the front bumper to the undertray. To do this, depress the central pins.
2 On each side of the vehicle, unscrew the upper screws and remove the lower clips securing the wheelarch liners to the front bumper **(see illustration)**.
3 Have an assistant support the front bumper, then prise out the plastic covers and undo the three upper screws from the front body panel **(see illustration)**.
4 Carefully pull the sides of the front bumper out from the wing panels and withdraw it from the front of the vehicle. On models with front foglights or headlight washers, disconnect the wiring as it is being removed. Where

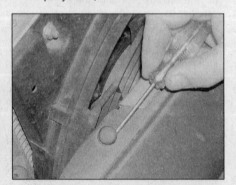

6.2 Removing the upper screws securing the front bumper to the wheelarch liners

6.3 Access to the front bumper upper screws is gained by removing the plastic covers

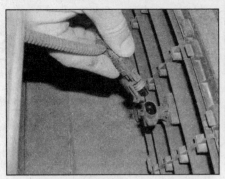

6.4a Disconnecting the wiring from the exterior temperature sensor on the front bumper

6.4b Removing the front bumper – Astra

6.5 Polystyrene packing for the front bumper

applicable, disconnect the wiring from the exterior temperature sensor **(see illustrations)**.

Refitting

5 Refitting is a reversal of removal. Check the condition of the bumper polystyrene packing on the front valance, and renew it if necessary **(see illustration)**.

Rear bumper

Removal

6 Open the rear tailgate.

7 Working under the rear of the vehicle, undo the screws securing the bottom of the rear bumper to the rear panel **(see illustration)**.

8 At the rear of each wheelarch, undo the two securing screws **(see illustration)**.

9 Have an assistant support the rear bumper, then undo the upper securing screws **(see illustration)**.

10 Carefully pull the sides of the rear bumper out from the guides on the wing panels and withdraw it from the rear of the vehicle **(see illustrations)**. On Zafira models fitted with a tow bar, access to the hitch is made by moving the sliders inwards and releasing the cover.

Refitting

11 Refitting is a reversal of removal.

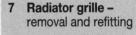

7 Radiator grille –
removal and refitting

Removal

1 Open the bonnet.

2 The radiator grille is secured to the bonnet by six screws. Undo the screws and withdraw the grille.

Refitting

3 Refitting is a reversal of removal, but clean the surface of the bonnet first.

6.7 Undo the rear bumper lower mounting screws . . .

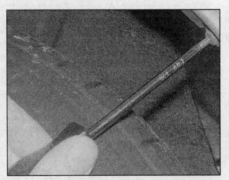

6.8 . . . the mounting screws located in the rear wheelarches . . .

6.9 . . . and the upper mounting screws . . .

6.10a . . . then remove the rear bumper – Zafira

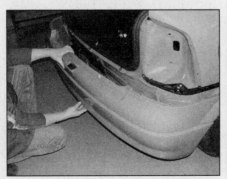

6.10b Removing the rear bumper – Astra

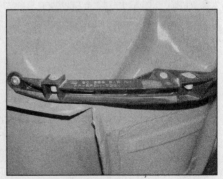

6.10c Rear bumper support guides – Astra

9.2 Bonnet-to-hinge mounting bolts

9.6 Bonnet striker

8 Windscreen cowl panel – removal and refitting

Removal

1 Open the bonnet.
2 Pull the weatherstrip from the firewall panel at the rear of the engine compartment.
3 Unclip and remove the water deflector panel located in front of the windscreen. Disconnect the tubing from the windscreen washer jets.
4 Remove the windscreen wiper arms, as described in Chapter 12.
5 Unscrew the two large nuts from the windscreen wiper arm spindles.
6 Note how the cowl panel engages with the weatherstrip at the base of the windscreen, then carefully release the ends of the cowl panel from the scuttle and withdraw from the vehicle.

Refitting

7 Refitting is a reversal of removal.

9 Bonnet – removal, refitting and adjustment

Removal

1 Open the bonnet and support it in the fully open position with the stay.
2 Mark the position of the mounting bolts on

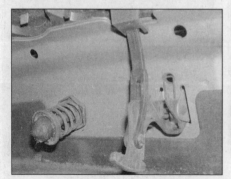

11.1 Bonnet lock safety hook

the hinges, to aid alignment on refitting **(see illustration)**.
3 With the help of an assistant, support the weight of the bonnet and lower the stay.
4 Unscrew the mounting bolts and lift the bonnet from the hinges. Rest it carefully on rags or cardboard, to avoid damaging the paint.
5 If necessary, remove the hinges as described in Section 10. If a new bonnet is to be fitted, transfer all the serviceable fixings to it with reference to Sections 7 and 11.

Refitting and adjustment

6 Refitting is a reversal of removal. Position the hinge bolts as previously noted and tighten them securely. Lower the bonnet slowly and check that the striker enters the centre of the lock. With the bonnet shut, check that the gap between it and the front wings is equal on both sides. Also check that the height of the bonnet matches the height of the front wings. Adjustment of the bonnet in its aperture is made on the bonnet-to-hinge bolts, and adjustment of the height is made at the hinge-to-body panel bolts and the bonnet striker **(see illustration)**. If necessary, adjust the front rubber buffers to obtain sufficient support.

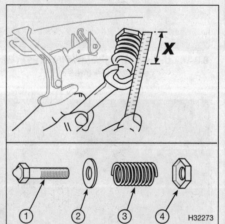

11.4 Bonnet lock striker adjustment

1 Striker   4 Locknut
2 Washer   X = 40 to 45 mm
3 Coil spring

10 Bonnet hinge – removal and refitting

Removal

1 Remove the bonnet, as described in Section 9.
2 Remove the windscreen cowl panel, as described in Section 8.
3 Mark the position of the hinges on the body panels, then unbolt them and remove the hinges.

Refitting

4 Refitting is a reversal of removal. Adjust the height of the bonnet as described in Section 9.

11 Bonnet lock components – removal and refitting

Bonnet lock safety hook

Removal

1 The bonnet lock hook is riveted to the bonnet, and removal involves drilling out the rivet **(see illustration)**.

Refitting

2 Refitting is a reversal of removal, using a new rivet.

Lock striker

Removal

3 To remove the lock striker from the bonnet, loosen the locknut, then unscrew the striker, and recover the washer and spring.

Refitting

4 Refitting is a reversal of removal, but adjust the striker dimension **(see illustration)** before tightening the locknut.

Locking spring

Removal

5 Disconnect the end of the bonnet release cable from the spring, then unhook the end of the spring from the slot in the front body panel, taking care not to damage the paint.

Refitting

6 Refitting is a reversal of removal.

12 Bonnet release cable – removal and refitting

Removal

1 Open the bonnet, and support it in the fully open position.
2 Unscrew the release cable clip from the front body cross-panel.

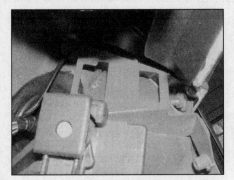

12.4a Removing the bonnet release lever from its mounting

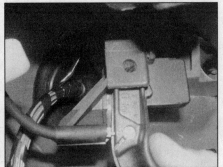

12.4b Bonnet release lever and cable

3 Disconnect the end of the release cable from the locking spring under the cross-panel.
4 Disconnect the release cable from the release lever in the driver's footwell. If necessary, remove the release lever from its mounting for access to the cable end **(see illustrations)**.
5 Pull the cable assembly through the grommet in the engine compartment bulkhead and into the engine compartment.
6 Note the routing of the cable, then release the cable from any remaining clips and cable-ties, and withdraw it from the engine compartment.

Refitting

7 Refitting is a reversal of removal, but ensure that the cable is correctly routed, and on completion, check the release mechanism for satisfactory operation.

13 Doors – removal, refitting and adjustment

Front door
Removal

1 To remove a door, open it fully and support it under its lower edge on blocks or axle stands covered with pads of rag.
2 Disconnect the wiring connector from the front edge of the door. To release the connector, pull out the locking clip, then twist the collar and pull the connector from the socket in the door **(see illustrations)**.

3 Unscrew the Torx bolt securing the door check arm pivot to the A-pillar **(see illustration)**.
4 Where applicable, remove the plastic covers from the hinge pins **(see illustration)**, then drive out the pins using a punch. Have an assistant support the door as the pins are driven out, then withdraw the door from the vehicle. If renewing a door, transfer all the serviceable fixings to the new door. **Note:** *On models without side airbags, the packing piece must be fitted inside the door.*

Refitting

5 Refitting is a reversal of removal.

Adjustment

6 The door hinges are welded onto the door frame and the body pillar, so that there is no provision for adjustment or alignment.
7 If the door can be moved up and down on its hinges due to wear in the hinge pins or their holes, it may be possible to drill out the holes and fit slightly oversized pins. Consult a Vauxhall dealer for further advice.
8 Door closure may be adjusted by altering the position of the lock striker on the body pillar, using an Allen key or a hexagon bit **(see illustration)**.

Rear door
Removal

9 Disconnect the wiring connector from the front edge of the door **(see illustration)**. To release the connector, twist the locking collar, then pull the connector from the socket in the door.

13.2a Pull out the locking clip . . .

13.2b . . . then twist the collar and pull the connector from the socket

13.3 The front door check arm pivot is attached to the A-pillar with a Torx bolt

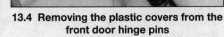

13.4 Removing the plastic covers from the front door hinge pins

13.8 Front door lock striker on the B-pillar

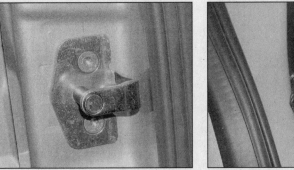

13.9 Disconnecting the wiring from the front edge of the rear door

13.10 Rear door check arm

13.11 Removing the plastic covers from the rear door hinge pins

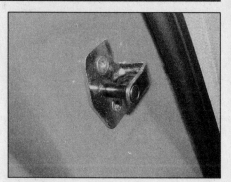

13.15 Rear door lock striker on the C-pillar

10 Unscrew the Torx bolt securing the door check arm pivot to the B-pillar **(see illustration)**.
11 Where applicable, remove the plastic covers from the hinge pins **(see illustration)**, then drive out the pins using a punch. Have an assistant support the door as the pins are driven out, then withdraw the door from the vehicle. If renewing a door, transfer all the serviceable fixings to the new door.

Refitting

12 Refitting is a reversal of removal.

Adjustment

13 The door hinges are welded onto the door frame and the body pillar, so that there is no provision for adjustment or alignment.
14 If the door can be moved up and down on its hinges due to wear in the hinge pins or their holes, it may be possible to drill out the

holes and fit slightly oversized pins. Consult a Vauxhall dealer for further advice.
15 Door closure may be adjusted by altering the position of the lock striker on the body pillar, using an Allen key or a hexagon bit **(see illustration)**.

---

14 Door interior handle – removal and refitting

Removal

1 Remove the door inner trim panel, as described in Section 44.
2 Release the spring clip and push out the interior handle from the inside of the trim panel.

Refitting

3 Refitting is a reversal of removal.

---

15 Door exterior handle – removal and refitting

Front door handle

Removal

1 Remove the door inner trim panel, and peel back the plastic insulating sheet for access to the handle, as described in Section 44. Also remove the window glass rear channel with reference to Section 19 **(see illustration)**.
2 Reach through the hole in the inner door panel, and disconnect the private lock and exterior handle operating rods. The rods are retained with plastic clips **(see illustration)**.
3 Unscrew the two nuts and withdraw the housing plate from inside the door **(see illustrations)**.
4 Carefully remove the exterior handle from the outside of the door **(see illustration)**.

Refitting

5 Refitting is a reversal of removal, but check the operation of the mechanism before refitting the door inner trim panel with reference to Section 44. If necessary, adjust the operating rod to eliminate play by turning the knurled plastic adjuster wheel.

15.1 Removing the window glass rear channel

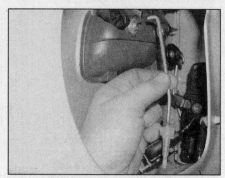

15.2 Disconnecting the operating rods from the exterior door handle

15.3a Unscrew the nuts . . .

15.3b . . . and remove the housing plate from inside the door

15.4 Removing the exterior handle from the front door

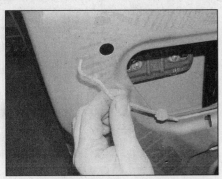

15.7a Disconnecting the rear door exterior handle operating rod

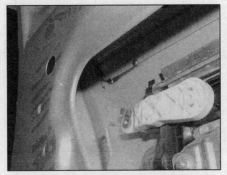

15.7b Rear door exterior handle viewed from inside the door

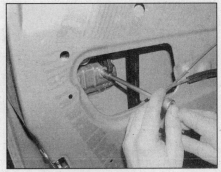

15.8a Unscrew the two nuts . . .

Rear door handle

Removal

6 Remove the door inner trim panel, and peel back the plastic insulating sheet for access to the handle, as described in Section 44.

7 Reach through the hole in the inner door panel, and disconnect the exterior handle operating rod **(see illustrations)**. The rod is retained with a plastic clip.

8 Unscrew the two nuts and withdraw the housing plate from inside the door **(see illustrations)**.

9 Carefully remove the exterior handle from the outside of the door **(see illustration)**.

Refitting

10 Refitting is a reversal of removal, but check the operation of the mechanism before refitting the door inner trim panel with reference to Section 44.

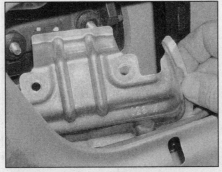

15.8b . . . and withdraw the housing plate from inside the door

15.9 Removing the rear door exterior handle

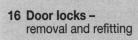

16 Door locks –
removal and refitting

Front

Removal

1 Remove the door inner trim panel, and peel back the plastic insulating sheet from the rear edge of the door, with reference to Section 44.

2 With the window closed, drill out the pop-rivets securing the rear window glass channel to the inner door panel, then withdraw the

channel through the aperture in the door. Working through the aperture in the door, disconnect the central locking wiring plug by pulling out the red button **(see illustration)**.

3 Reach through the aperture in the door and disconnect the exterior door handle and private lock cylinder operating rods from the lock. The rods are retained with plastic clips. Alternatively, the exterior door handle can be removed together with the door lock by referring to Section 15.

4 On the rear edge of the door, unscrew and remove the three screws securing the lock to the door panel **(see illustration)**.

5 Lower the lock and withdraw it from inside the door, at the same time, release the locking knob and guide it through the hole in the door panel **(see illustration)**.

6 Release the outer cable end fittings for the

inner door handle and locking knob, and disconnect the cables from the lock **(see illustrations)**.

16.2 Disconnecting the central locking wiring plug from the front door lock

16.4 Removing the front door lock retaining screws

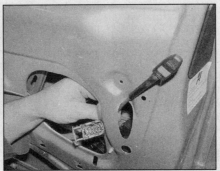

16.5 Removing the front door lock from the door

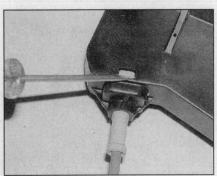

16.6a Release the clips . . .

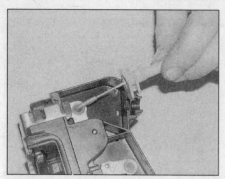

16.6b . . . and disconnect the cables from the lock

16.6c Front door lock with cables disconnected

16.11 Unscrewing the rear door lock retaining screws

Refitting

7 Refitting is a reversal of removal. Check the operation of the door lock by inserting a screwdriver in the lock mechanism to simulate the striker entry. Check that the door locks and unlocks correctly. If the lock operation is not satisfactory, note that the exterior handle operating rod can be adjusted by turning the knurled plastic adjuster wheel at the end of the rod.

Rear door

Removal

8 Fully lower the window, then remove the door inner trim panel and the plastic insulating sheet, as described in Section 44.
9 Undo the screws and release the locking knob outer cable from the door panel, then unhook the inner cable from the intermediate lever.
10 Disconnect the exterior handle operating rod by releasing the plastic clip.
11 On the rear edge of the door, unscrew and remove the three screws securing the lock to the door panel **(see illustration)**.
12 Reach through the aperture in the door and move the lock forwards until the wiring harness can be disconnected. Pull out the red

16.12 Disconnecting the wiring from the rear door lock

button to do this **(see illustration)**.
13 Release the locking cable from the clip, then withdraw the lock together with handle and locking knob cables from inside the door and at the same time release the locking knob **(see illustrations)**.
14 Release the outer cable end fittings for the inner door handle and locking knob, and disconnect the cables from the lock.

Refitting

15 Refitting is a reversal of removal. Check the operation of the door lock by inserting a screwdriver in the lock mechanism to simulate

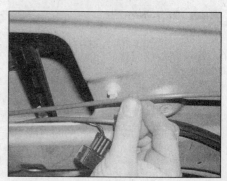

16.13a Release the locking cable from the clip . . .

the striker entry. Check that the door locks and unlocks correctly.

17 Front door lock cylinder –
removal and refitting

Removal

1 Remove the door exterior handle and housing plate, as described in Section 15.
2 Insert the key into the lock, then remove the

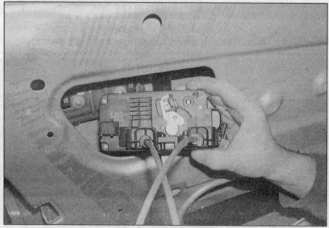

16.13b . . . then remove the lock from inside the rear door

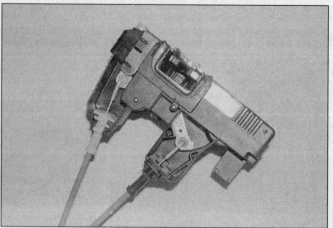

16.13c Rear door lock removed from the door

retaining ring from the inner end of the lock cylinder **(see illustration)**.

3 Note how it is fitted, then remove the carrier and arm from the inner end of the lock cylinder. Remove the torsion and pressure springs, noting how they are fitted.

4 Mark the lock cylinder housing and plate in relation to each other. Using a 2.5 mm diameter punch, drive out the retaining spring roll pin, taking care not to damage the hole.

5 Remove the lock cylinder, channel sleeve, balls and clutch. **Note:** *The lock cylinder and clutch must be renewed together.*

Refitting

6 Refitting is a reversal of removal, but use a centre punch to secure the bottom of the roll pin to the housing.

18 Lock striker – removal and refitting

Removal

1 The lock striker is screwed into the door pillar on the body.

2 Before removing the striker, mark its position, so that it can be refitted in exactly the same position.

3 To remove the striker, simply unscrew the securing screws using an Allen key or hexagon bit.

Refitting

4 Refitting is a reversal of removal, but if necessary, adjust the position of the striker to achieve satisfactory closing of the door.

19 Door window glass – removal and refitting

Front

Removal

1 Remove the door inner trim panel and the plastic insulating sheet, as described in Section 44. Make sure the window is fully raised.

2 On models with side airbags, make sure that the battery negative lead has been disconnected for at least 1 minute, then remove the sensor bracket and sensor. To do this, unbolt the bracket, then disconnect the wiring and remove the sensor. **Note:** *The sensors for each side of the vehicle are different – make sure the correct one is refitted.*

3 Drill out the pop-rivets securing the rear window glass channel to the inner door panel, then withdraw the channel through the aperture in the door **(see illustrations)**.

4 On models with electric front windows, temporarily reconnect the electric window switch to the wiring and reconnect the battery

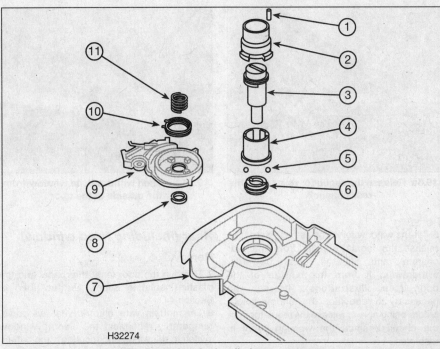

17.2 Front door lock cylinder components

1	Roll pin	5	Ball
2	Housing	6	Clutch
3	Lock cylinder	7	Housing plate
4	Sleeve	8	Retaining ring

9 *Carrier with lever (central locking version)*
10 *Torsion spring*
11 *Pressure spring*

19.3a Drill out the pop-rivets . . .

19.3b . . . and withdraw the rear window glass channel through the inner door aperture

19.4a The regulator-to-window channel bolts are visible through the access holes

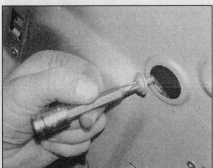

19.4b Unscrewing the front door regulator-to-window channel bolts

negative lead. On manual front windows, temporarily refit the regulator handle to the regulator. Position the window so that the

regulator-to-window channel bolts are visible through the access holes in the door, then unscrew and remove them **(see illustrations)**.

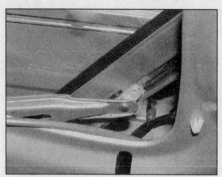

19.5a Release the regulator roller from the rear channel . . .

19.5b . . . then withdraw the window from the outside of the door

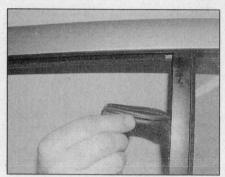

19.9a Pull the rubber weatherstrip away from the top of the window rear guide channel . . .

5 Tilt the window forwards as necessary then release the regulator roller from the rear channel and lift the glass upwards, withdrawing it from the outside of the door **(see illustrations)**. It may be necessary to reposition the window height before being able to release the regulator from the channel, since the working room is restricted.

Refitting

6 Refitting is a reversal of removal, but use new pop rivets to secure the window channel. The regulator-to-window channel bolts should first be hand-tightened, then the window raised and lowered before fully tightening the bolts.

Rear (including fixed window)
Removal

7 Remove the door inner trim panel and the plastic insulating sheet, as described in Section 44.

8 On models with electric rear windows, temporarily reconnect the electric window switch to the wiring and reconnect the battery negative lead. On manual rear windows, temporarily refit the regulator handle to the regulator. Fully lower the window.

9 Carefully pull the rubber weatherstrip away from the top of the window rear guide channel, then undo and remove the upper guide retaining screw. Unscrew and remove the guide lower retaining screws using a Torx

key through the holes in the inner door panel **(see illustrations)**.

10 Carefully ease the window guide channel away from the fixed window and withdraw it upwards from the door **(see illustration)**. The seal for the fixed window should remain in the channel.

11 Ease the fixed window glass forwards and withdraw it from the door **(see illustration)**.

12 Slightly tilt the window glass while releasing it from the regulator channel, and withdraw it upwards from the rear door **(see illustrations)**.

Note: *It may be necessary to partially remove the weatherstrip, and also reposition the window by turning the regulator handle.*

Refitting

13 Refitting is a reversal of removal.

19.9b . . . then unscrew the upper guide retaining screw . . .

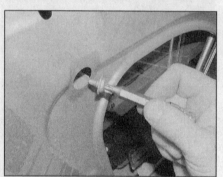

19.9c . . . and lower guide retaining screw . . .

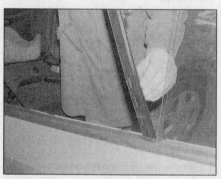

19.10 . . . and withdraw the window guide channel

19.11 Removing the fixed window glass from the rear door

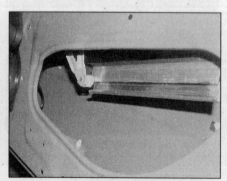

19.12a Release the window from the regulator channel . . .

19.12b . . . and remove the window glass from the rear door

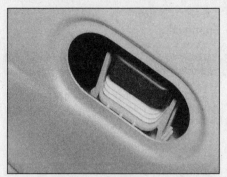

20.2a The wiring connector for the electric front window regulator is hooked onto the inner panel

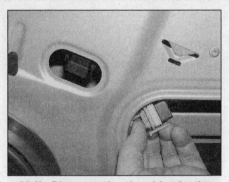

20.2b Disconnecting the wiring for the electric front window regulator

20 Window regulator –
removed and refitting

Front door
Removal

1 Remove the front door window glass as described in Section 19.

2 On models with electric front windows, make sure the battery negative lead is disconnected then reach inside the door and disconnect the wiring from the regulator. Unhook the connector from the door **(see illustrations)**.

3 Drill out the rivets securing the regulator to the door inner panel, and withdraw the regulator through the lower aperture. Note that the bottom of the regulator is located in a slot **(see illustrations)**.

Refitting

4 Refitting is a reversal of removal, but use new pop-rivets to secure the regulator **(see illustration)**. On models with electric windows programme the closed position of the glass in the control unit as follows. Sit in the driver's seat with all the doors closed. Switch on the ignition and slightly open the window. Close the window and hold the rocker switch depressed for a further 2 seconds.

Rear door
Removal

5 Remove the rear door window glass as described in Section 19.

6 On models with electric rear windows, make sure the battery negative lead is disconnected then reach inside the door and disconnect the wiring from the regulator.

7 Drill out the four rivets securing the regulator to the door inner panel, and withdraw the regulator through the upper aperture **(see illustration)**.

Refitting

8 Refitting is a reversal of removal, but use new pop-rivets to secure the regulator. On models with electric rear windows programme the closed position of the glass as described in paragraph 4.

21 Boot lid –
removal and refitting

Removal

1 Open the boot lid fully.

2 On models with central locking, disconnect the battery negative lead, then disconnect the wiring from the lock motor. If the original boot lid is to be refitted, first tie a length of string to the end of the wiring. Feed the wiring through

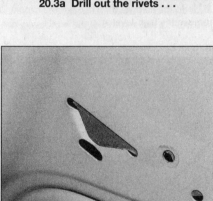

20.3a Drill out the rivets . . .

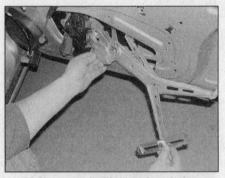

20.3b . . . and withdraw the window regulator from the door

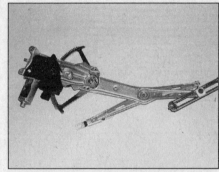

20.3c Window regulator removed from the front door

20.3d Note the bottom of the window regulator locates in a slot in the inner door panel

20.4 Securing the window regulator with new pop-rivets

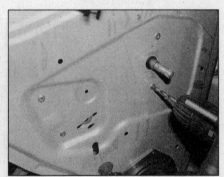

20.7 Drilling out the rivets securing the window regulator to the rear door inner panel

the boot lid, then untie the string, leaving it in position in the boot lid to assist refitting.

3 Mark the position of the hinges on the boot lid.

4 With the help of an assistant, support the weight of the boot lid, then unscrew the securing bolts from the hinges, and lift the boot lid from the vehicle.

Refitting

5 If a new boot lid is to be fitted, transfer all the serviceable fittings (rubber buffers, lock mechanism, etc) to it.

6 Refitting is a reversal of removal, but check that the boot lid closes correctly and is located centrally within the body aperture. If necessary, adjust the hinge bolts, rubber buffers and lock striker.

22 Boot lid hinge – removal and refitting

Removal

1 Remove the boot lid, as described in Section 21.

2 Remove the rear quarter trim panel, as described in Section 44.

3 Note the position of the hinge counterbalance spring in the bracket on the body, so that it can be refitted in its original position, then unhook the spring from the body. Use a lever to release the spring if necessary.

4 Unscrew the securing bolt, and remove the hinge from the body.

Refitting

5 Refitting is a reversal of removal.

23 Boot lid components – removal and refitting

Handle

Removal

1 Open the boot lid and remove the lock cylinder as described later in this Section.

2 Unscrew the two securing nuts, then withdraw the handle from outside the boot lid. Note that the securing nuts also secure the lock cylinder assembly to the boot lid.

Refitting

3 Refitting is a reversal of removal.

Lock

Removal

4 Proceed as described in paragraph 1.

5 Unscrew the two securing bolts, and withdraw the lock from the boot lid.

Refitting

6 Refitting is a reversal of removal, but if necessary, adjust the position of the lock striker on the body, to achieve satisfactory lock operation.

Lock cylinder

Removal

7 Open the boot lid fully.

8 Remove the four securing screws, and withdraw the lock cylinder assembly cover panel.

9 Unscrew the two securing nuts, and withdraw the lock cylinder assembly, unhooking the lock operating rod(s) as the assembly is withdrawn. Note that the securing nuts also secure the boot lid handle.

10 No spare parts are available for the lock cylinder assembly, and if faulty, the complete assembly must be renewed.

Refitting

11 Refitting is a reversal of removal.

Lock striker

Removal

12 The lock striker is screwed into the lower body panel.

13 Remove the securing screws, then unclip the rear boot trim panel to expose the lock striker securing bolt.

14 Before removing the striker, mark its position, so that it can be refitted in exactly the same position.

15 To remove the striker, simply unscrew the securing screw.

Refitting

16 Refitting is a reversal of removal, but if necessary, adjust the position of the striker to achieve satisfactory closing of the boot lid.

24 Tailgate – removal and refitting

Removal

1 With the tailgate open, prise out the plastic covers, undo the screws, and remove the lower and upper trim panels from the inside of the tailgate. Note that the lower panel has extensions which slot into the upper panels **(see illustrations)**.

2 Undo the screws, then release the clips and remove the high-level stop-light.

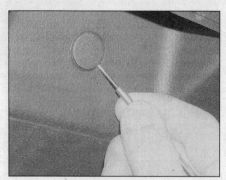
24.1a Prise out the plastic covers . . .

24.1b . . . then undo the screws . . .

24.1c . . . and remove the lower trim panel

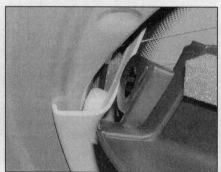
24.1d Note how the lower trim panel locates in the upper side trim panels

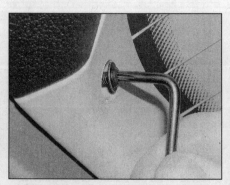
24.1e Removing the upper trim panel retaining screws

24.3 Release the rubber grommet and pull the wiring from the top of the tailgate

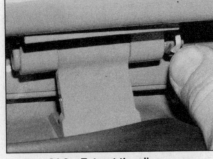

24.6a Extract the clips . . .

24.6b . . . then drive out the hinge pins

3 Inside the tailgate, disconnect the earth cable then tie a length of string to the wiring harness. Release the rubber grommet and pull the wiring from the top of the tailgate **(see illustration)**. Untie the string and leave it in position to aid refitting the wiring harness.

4 Using a screwdriver through the hole, depress the tabs of the washer jet and pull out the jet. Disconnect the washer tube and tie a length of string to it, then draw out the tube from the tailgate and untie the string.

5 Have an assistant support the tailgate, then use a screwdriver to prise out the spring clips from the support struts. Release the struts from the socket balls and lower them onto the body.

6 Extract the clips and carefully drive out the hinge pins, using a small drift **(see illustrations)**.

7 Lift the tailgate away from the body.

Refitting

8 If a new tailgate is to be fitted, transfer all serviceable components (rubber buffers, lock mechanism, etc) to it.

9 Refitting is a reversal of removal, but smear a little grease on the hinge pins before inserting them, and make sure that the tailgate closes correctly and that the gap between it and the surrounding bodywork is equal all the way around. If necessary, loosen the hinge bolts after removing the trim at the rear of the headlining and reposition the hinges as required. Check that the tailgate striker enters the lock centrally, and if necessary adjust the

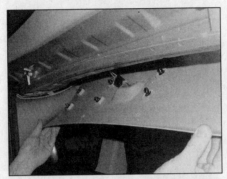

24.9a Removing the trim at the rear of the headlining

24.9b Tailgate support rubber buffer (adjustable)

position of the striker. When closed, the tailgate should be firmly supported by the rubber buffers – if necessary, adjust the buffers **(see illustrations)**.

25 Tailgate hinge – removal and refitting

Removal

1 Remove the tailgate as described in Section 24.

2 Carefully pull down the rubber weatherstrip from the upper edge of the tailgate aperture.

3 Remove the trim panels from the C-pillar on both sides of the rear luggage compartment as described in Section 44.

4 Remove the moulded trim panel from the rear of the headlining.

5 Mark the position of the hinges on the body to ensure correct refitting, then unbolt and remove them.

Refitting

6 Refitting is a reversal of removal, but align the hinges with the previously made marks on the body.

26 Tailgate components – removal and refitting

Support strut

Removal

1 Open the tailgate fully, and have an assistant support it.

2 Release the strut from its mounting balljoints by prising the spring clips out a little way, and pulling the strut off the balljoints **(see illustrations)**.

Refitting

3 Refitting is a reversal of removal.

Lock

Removal

4 With the tailgate open, remove the lower trim panel as described in Section 44.

5 Reach through the tailgate aperture and

26.2a Prise out the spring clip to release the strut from the balljoint

26.2b Tailgate strut lower balljoint and bracket on the body

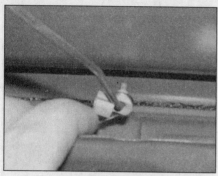

26.5 Disconnecting the operating rods

26.6a On Astra models, undo the screws . . .

26.6b . . . and withdraw the lock from the tailgate

26.6c On Zafira models, undo the screws . . .

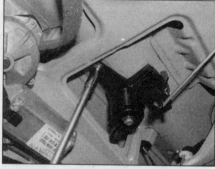

26.6d . . . and withdraw the lock from the tailgate

disconnect the private lock and lock operating rods by releasing the plastic clips **(see illustration)**.

6 Undo the securing screws and withdraw the lock **(see illustrations)**.

Refitting

7 Refitting is a reversal of removal, but if necessary, adjust the position of the lock striker on the body to achieve satisfactory lock operation.

Lock cylinder

Removal

8 With the tailgate open, remove the lower trim panel as described in Section 44.

9 Reach through the tailgate aperture and disconnect the operating rod by releasing the plastic clip **(see illustration)**.

10 Unscrew the mounting nuts and withdraw the lock cylinder from the tailgate **(see illustrations)**.

Refitting

11 Refitting is a reversal of removal.

Lock striker

Removal

12 The lock striker is screwed into the lower body panel **(see illustration)**.

13 Where applicable, extract the securing screws, and remove the luggage

26.9 Disconnect the operating rod . . .

26.10a . . . then unscrew the mounting nuts . . .

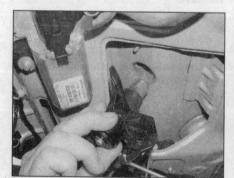

26.10b . . . and withdraw the lock cylinder from the tailgate – Zafira

26.10c Removing the lock cylinder from the tailgate – Astra Hatchback

26.12 Tailgate lock striker

compartment rear trim panel for access to the lock striker securing bolts.

14 Before removing the striker, mark its position, so that it can be refitted in exactly the same position.

15 Undo the screws and remove the striker.

Refitting

16 Refitting is a reversal of removal, but if necessary, adjust the position of the striker to achieve satisfactory closing of the tailgate.

Handle

Removal

17 Open the tailgate and remove the lower trim panel as described in Section 44.

18 Unscrew the two nuts and withdraw the handle from the tailgate.

Refitting

19 Refitting is a reversal of removal.

27 Central locking components – removal and refitting

Electronic control unit

Note: *If the electronic control unit is renewed, the new unit must be programmed by a Vauxhall dealer using specialist equipment. The unit also incorporates a crash sensor.*

Removal

1 The control unit is located behind the right-hand footwell side/sill trim panel.

2 Disconnect the battery negative lead as described in Chapter 5A.

3 Remove the footwell side/sill trim panel, as described in Section 44.

4 Disconnect the two wiring harness plugs.

5 Undo the two securing screws and lift the control unit from its location.

Refitting

6 Refitting is a reversal of removal.

Front and rear door servo units

Removal and refitting

7 The servo units are incorporated in the door locks and their removal and refitting is described in Section 16.

Tailgate/bootlid servo units

Removal

8 Remove the trim panel from the inside of the tailgate/bootlid.

9 On Saloon models remove the lock cylinder cover.

10 Release the plastic clip and disconnect the servo unit operating rod from the lock **(see illustration)**.

11 Disconnect the servo unit wiring **(see illustration)**.

12 Undo the screws and withdraw the servo unit from the tailgate/bootlid **(see illustrations)**.

Refitting

13 Refitting is a reversal of removal.

Fuel filler flap servo unit (Saloon/Hatchback models)

Removal

14 Remove the carpet from the rear luggage compartment.

15 Remove the rear quarter trim panel as described in Section 44.

16 Disconnect the wiring plug from the servo unit.

17 Open the fuel filler flap then undo the mounting screws and withdraw the servo unit from inside the vehicle.

Refitting

18 Refitting is a reversal of removal.

Fuel filler flap servo unit (Estate/Zafira models)

Removal

19 In the rear luggage compartment, turn the fasteners and open the access cover to the filler flap servo unit.

20 Disconnect the wiring plug from the servo unit.

21 Open the fuel filler flap then undo the mounting screws and withdraw the servo unit from inside the vehicle.

Refitting

22 Refitting is a reversal of removal.

28 Electric window components – removal and refitting

Switches

Removal

1 The switches are located in the driver's and passenger's doors.

2 Using a small screwdriver, carefully prise the switch from the door inner trim panel.

3 Disconnect the wiring and remove the switch.

Refitting

4 Refitting is a reversal of removal.

Window motors

Removal

5 Remove the door window regulator, as described in Section 20.

6 To remove the motor assembly from the regulator, unscrew the three securing screws.

Refitting

7 Refitting is a reversal of removal. On completion, programme the closed position of the windows as follows. Sit in the driver's seat with all the doors closed. Switch on the ignition and slightly open the window. Close the window and hold the rocker switch depressed for a further 2 seconds.

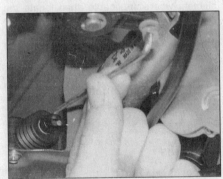
27.10 Disconnect the operating rod . . .

27.11 . . . then disconnect the wiring . . .

27.12a . . . and unbolt the servo unit

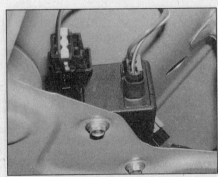
27.12b Central locking servo unit in the tailgate – Zafira model

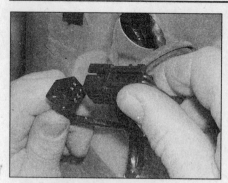

29.2 Disconnecting the wiring for the exterior door mirror

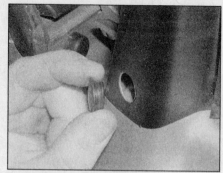

29.3 Prise out the rubber plugs for access to the exterior mirror retaining bolts

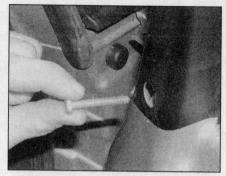

29.4a Unscrew the mounting bolts . . .

29 Exterior door mirror – removal and refitting

Removal

1 Remove the door inner trim panel as described in Section 44.

2 Disconnect the wiring for the exterior door mirror, and prise out the rubber grommet from the inner panel **(see illustration)**.

3 Prise out the rubber plugs as necessary for access to the mirror retaining bolts **(see illustration)**. To prevent the mirror mounting bolts dropping inside the inner trim panel, it is suggested that a cloth is put over the hole.

4 Support the mirror, then unscrew and remove the mounting bolts and withdraw the mirror from the outside of the door **(see illustrations)**.

Refitting

5 Refitting is a reversal of removal.

30 Exterior door mirror glass – removal and refitting

Removal

1 The mirror glass can be removed for renewal without removing the mirror. Using protective gloves, carefully push in the upper, inner (nearest the door) corner of the glass in order to release the lower, outer corner from the door mirror. If necessary, assist the removal of the glass by using a small screwdriver in the lower, outer corner of the glass. The upper internal clip may be released using a small screwdriver inserted through the hole in the mirror cover **(see illustration)**.

2 Where applicable, disconnect the two wires from the heating element while holding the riveted tags to avoid damage **(see illustration)**.

Refitting

3 Reconnect the wiring to the heating element where applicable, then locate the glass in the mirror making sure that the plastic retaining clips are correctly aligned with each other. Depress carefully until the retaining clips engage.

31 Electric mirror components – removal and refitting

Switches

Removal

1 The switches are located in the driver's and passenger's doors.

2 Using a small screwdriver, carefully prise the switch from the door inner trim panel.

3 Disconnect the wiring and remove the switch.

Refitting

4 Refitting is a reversal of removal.

Motor

Removal

5 Remove the exterior mirror as described in Section 29, and the mirror glass as described in Section 30.

6 Undo the three screws and remove the servo motor from the mirror body, then disconnect the wiring.

Refitting

7 Refitting is a reversal of removal, but ensure that the wiring is routed behind the motor, to avoid interfering with the adjustment mechanism.

32 Interior mirror – removal and refitting

Removal

1 Depress the plastic tabs and slide the

29.4b . . . and withdraw the exterior mirror from the outside of the door

30.1 Use a screwdriver to assist removing the glass from the exterior mirror

30.2 Disconnecting the wiring from the exterior mirror heating element

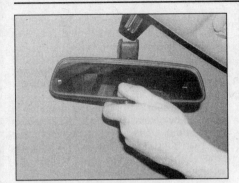

32.1 Removing the interior mirror from the mounting plate

interior mirror from the mounting plate (**see illustration**).

2 The mounting plate is fixed to the windscreen using a special adhesive, and should not normally be disturbed. Note that there is a risk of cracking the windscreen glass if an attempt is made to remove a securely bonded mounting plate.

Refitting

3 If necessary, the special adhesive required to fix the mounting plate to the windscreen can be obtained from a Vauxhall dealer or hardware store. The top of the mounting plate should be located 15.0 mm from the headlining, and the plate should be held in position with masking tape until the adhesive has cured.

4 Slide the interior mirror into the mounting plate until the plastic tabs engage.

33 Windscreen, rear window and quarter window glass – general

1 The windscreen, rear window, and quarter window glass is bonded in position, using a special adhesive.

2 Special tools, adhesives and expertise are required for successful removal and refitting of glass fixed by this method. Such work must therefore be entrusted to a Vauxhall dealer, a windscreen specialist, or other competent professional.

34 Sunroof glass panel – removal and refitting

Removal

1 Push the sunshade fully rearwards, and open the glass panel halfway.

2 Unscrew the four bolts from the front edge of the glass panel and remove the cover.

3 Unscrew the guide bolts at each side of the glass panel.

4 Carefully lift the glass panel from the roof aperture, taking care not to damage the vehicle paintwork. Check the weatherstrip for wear and damage and renew it if necessary.

Refitting

5 Refitting is a reversal of removal, but if necessary adjust the front height of the glass panel so that it is level with or a maximum of 1.0 mm below the roof panel. The rear height of the panel should be level with or a maximum of 1.0 mm above the roof panel.

35 Sunroof components – removal and refitting

Note: *The sunroof is a complex piece of equipment, consisting of a large number of components. It is strongly recommended that the sunroof mechanism is not disturbed unless necessary. If the sunroof mechanism is faulty, or requires overhaul, consult a Vauxhall dealer for advice. In an emergency the sunroof can be operated manually by removing the cover from the front interior light panel, and using a screwdriver to turn the motor (***see illustrations***).*

Wind deflector

Removal

1 Open the glass roof panel, then undo the bolts for the swing-out arm on both sides.

2 Disconnect the spring from the pin and lift out the wind deflector.

3 Press the swing-out spring from the guide by turning it.

Refitting

4 Refitting is a reversal of removal.

Electric drive

Removal

5 The electric drive unit is located on the roof above the headlining. Removal of the headlining involves removal of the front interior light, sun visors and handgrips and is a difficult job. It is recommended that a qualified upholsterer carries out this work.

6 With the headlining removed, disconnect the wiring plug from the drive unit (**see illustration**).

7 Unscrew the retaining screws and withdraw the electric drive unit from the roof panel.

Refitting

8 Before refitting the electric drive, set the switch in its basic position. To do this, the bore just inside the serrated centre drive must be located between the two outer extensions. The remaining refitting procedure is a reversal of removal.

Actuation cable

Adjustment

9 Remove the electric drive as described previously in this Section.

10 Loosen the front and rear guide screws, then align the front and rear guide pins with the marks on the guides.

11 Insert a 4.0 mm diameter drill bit or similar tool through the rear guide and bracket, then tighten the screws.

12 Refit the electric drive with reference to paragraph 8.

Actuation switch

Removal

13 Remove the front interior light as described in Chapter 12, Section 6.

14 Carefully unclip the actuation switch from the headlining and through the hole in the front interior light.

15 Disconnect the wiring and remove the switch.

Refitting

16 Refitting is a reversal of removal.

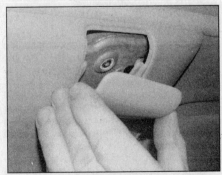

35.0a In an emergency, remove the cover . . .

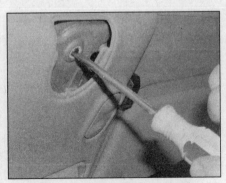

35.0b . . . and turn the motor with a screwdriver

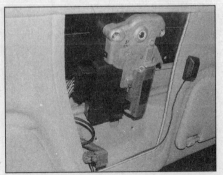

35.6 View of the sunroof electric drive unit with the front interior light panel removed

38.1 Undo the retaining screw . . .

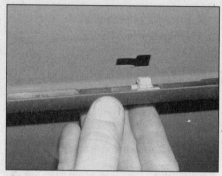

38.3 . . . and slide the strip from the slots in the door

Crank drive

Removal

17 Fully open the sunroof.

18 On the manually-operated roof, undo the screw and remove the crank handle from the splines.

19 On the electrically-operated roof, use a small screwdriver to carefully prise out the emergency cover on the rear of the front interior light housing.

20 Prise out the interior light lens and disconnect the wiring.

21 Undo the screws and lower the sun roof trim panel from the headlining.

22 Undo the two screws and lower the crank drive from the roof.

Refitting

23 Refitting is a reversal of removal, but first carry out the following adjustment. Turn the drive fully clockwise making sure that the locking pin does not engage. If the pin does engage, it will not be possible to turn the drive fully clockwise, in which case pull the pin outwards.

---

36 Wheelarch liners – general

1 The plastic wheelarch liners are secured by a combination of self-tapping screws and plastic bolts and plastic clips. Removal and refitting is self-evident, remembering the following points.

2 Some of the securing clips may be held in place using a central pin, which must be tapped out to release the clip.

3 The clips are easily broken during removal, and it is advisable to obtain a few spare clips for possible use when refitting.

4 Certain models may have additional underbody shields and undertrays fitted, which may be attached to the wheelarch liners.

---

37 Fuel filler flap –
removal and refitting

Removal

1 Open the flap for access to the two securing screws.

2 Remove the securing screws and withdraw the flap.

Refitting

3 Refitting is a reversal of removal.

---

38 Exterior body components –
removal and refitting

Door side strip

Removal

1 Remove the door inner trim panel as described in Section 44, then unscrew the side strip retaining screw using a screwdriver through the inner panel aperture **(see illustration)**.

2 The front door side protective trim strip is removed by carefully pulling it backwards. Slightly open the door before removing the strip.

3 The rear door side protective trim strip is removed by carefully pulling it forwards **(see illustration)**. Open the front door but leave the rear door closed before removing the strip.

Refitting

4 Refitting is a reversal of removal.

Rear quarter side strip

Removal

5 The side strip is held to the rear quarter panel by clips. Carefully release the strip from the clips.

Refitting

6 Check the condition of the clips and if necessary renew them.

7 Press the side strip onto the clips making sure that they are correctly engaged.

Roof trim strip

Removal

8 With the door open, release the upper rubber weatherstrip from the roof.

9 Undo the screws securing the trim strip to the roof above the door.

10 Release the strip from the rear clips and withdraw it to the rear.

Refitting

11 Refitting is a reversal of removal.

---

39 Front seats –
removal and refitting

 Warning: The seat belt tensioners fitted to the front seat assemblies may cause injury if triggered inadvertently. Before carrying out any work on the front seats, refer to the precautions for airbag systems given in Chapter 12.

Removal

1 Disconnect the battery negative lead and wait a minimum of 1 minute to allow the airbag system capacitor to discharge (refer to Chapter 12 if necessary).

2 Where necessary to provide additional working room, remove the oddments box from the sill panel by lifting out the padding and unscrewing the retaining screws **(see illustration)**.

3 Carefully unclip the plastic cover from the outside of the seat, then undo the screw and detach the seat belt from the front seat **(see illustrations)**.

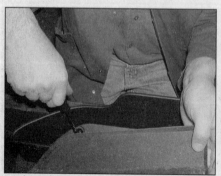

39.2 Removing the oddments box from the sill panel – Zafira models

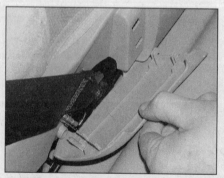

39.3a Unclip the cover from the outside of the front seat . . .

39.3b ... then undo the screw and detach the seat belt

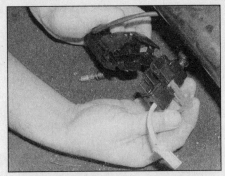

39.4 Disconnecting the seat wiring

39.5 Unscrewing the front seat front mounting bolts

39.6 Unscrewing the front seat rear mounting bolts

39.8a Unscrew the mounting bolts ...

39.8b ... and remove the seat base

4 Adjust the seat fully to the rear, then disconnect the wiring as applicable for the seat belt tensioner, side airbag, heating, and passenger detection as follows. Pull out the red locking pin and release the wiring plug from the seat base. Depress the tab and separate the wiring plug (see illustration).
5 Unscrew the front mounting bolts securing the seat to the base. The bolts are located on the front of each sliding channel (see illustration).
6 Adjust the seat fully to the front and unscrew the rear mounting bolts securing the seat to the base (see illustration).
7 With the help of an assistant, carefully lift the seat and remove it from inside the vehicle.
8 If necessary, unbolt the seat base from the floor (see illustrations).

Refitting

9 Refitting is a reversal of removal, but apply a little locking fluid to the threads of the bolts before inserting them, and tighten them to the specified torque.

40 Rear seats –
removal and refitting

Cushion
Removal

1 On the split-type rear seat, press in the spring-tensioned pins located at the front of the seat, and release the seat from the pivot brackets. Recover the pins and springs. Lift

the seat from the floor and remove from the vehicle.
2 On the non-split-type rear seat, first raise the rear of the cushion, then release the front hooks from the hinge brackets by pressing the cushion down directly over the brackets. Lift the seat from the floor and remove from the vehicle (see illustrations).

Refitting

3 Refitting is a reversal of removal, but make sure that the seat belt stalks are located on top of the cushion.

Backrest (Astra models)
Removal

4 Remove the rear seat cushion as previously described in this Section.

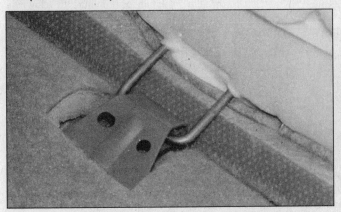

40.2a The non-split rear seat cushion is secured with metal loops ...

40.2b ... to hooks

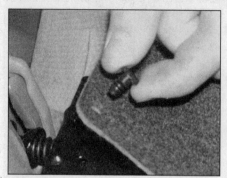

40.5a Prise out the plastic fasteners . . .

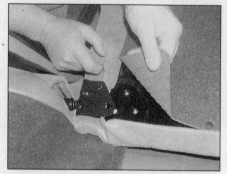

40.5b . . . and lift the felt flaps from the outer corners of the backrest

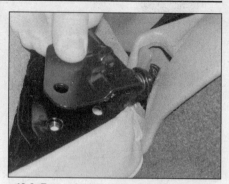

40.6 Removing the outer hinge brackets from the body slots

5 Fold the backrest forwards, then prise out the plastic fasteners and lift the felt flaps from the outer corners of the backrest **(see illustrations)**.
6 Using a Torx key, unscrew and remove the bolts securing the outer hinge brackets to the backrest, then remove the brackets from the body slots **(see illustration)**. If necessary, use a screwdriver to prise the spring-tensioned collars from the slots.
7 Unscrew the centre hinge bracket bolts, including the bolts securing the split seats together **(see illustrations)**.
8 Lift the front of the backrest and unscrew the front hinge bracket and seat belt stalk bolts **(see illustration)**.
9 Lift the backrest and withdraw from inside the vehicle **(see illustration)**.
10 If necessary, the armrest in the backrest

may be removed by carefully releasing each side from the housing **(see illustration)**.

Refitting

11 When refitting the backrest, it is easier to assemble the split sections and outer hinge brackets outside of the vehicle. First, fit the brackets to the outer lower corners of the backrest, and tighten the bolts.
12 Assemble the split sections together, then refit the bolts and tighten securely.
13 With the help of an assistant, locate the backrest inside the vehicle with the outer bracket hinge pins resting over the mounting slots in the floor. Press down the backrest ends so that the spring-tensioned collars engage with the cut-outs in the slots.
14 Refit the seat belt stalk and centre bracket bolts and tighten securely.

15 Secure the felt flaps with the plastic fasteners.
16 Refit the rear seat cushion as previously described in this Section.

Backrest (Zafira models)

Removal

17 Remove the floor covering from the rear luggage compartment.
18 Undo the screws and remove the seat belt lock bracket from the floor.
19 Undo the screws from the centre hinge bracket.
20 Release the rear catch and lift the rear seat backrest from inside the vehicle.

Refitting

21 Refitting is a reversal of removal.

---

41 Front seat belt tensioner – removal and refitting

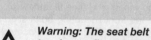

⚠️ **Warning: The seat belt tensioners fitted to the front seat assemblies may cause injury if triggered inadvertently. Before carrying out any work on the front seats, refer to the precautions for airbag systems given in Chapter 12.**

Removal

1 Disconnect the battery negative lead and wait a minimum of 1 minute to allow the

---

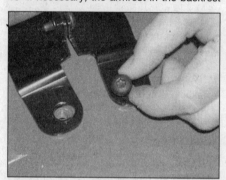

40.7a Unscrew the centre hinge bracket bolts . . .

40.7b . . . and the bolts securing the split seats together

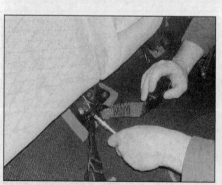

40.8 Unscrewing the front hinge bracket and seat belt stalk bolts

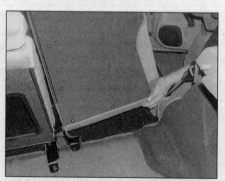

40.9 Removing the backrest from inside the vehicle

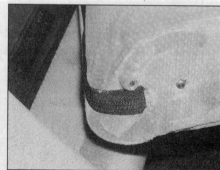

40.10 Removing the armrest from the rear seat backrest

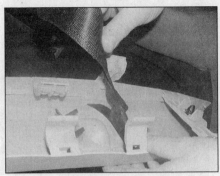

42.3a Feed the seat belt through the slot in the upper trim panel as it is being removed

42.3b Removing the lower trim panel from the B-pillar

42.4 Front seat belt upper anchor and height adjuster

airbag system capacitor to discharge (refer to Chapter 12 if necessary).

2 Remove the front seat as described in Section 39.

3 Release the seat belt tensioner wiring from the base of the seat.

4 Undo the single screw and remove the seat belt tensioner from the front seat.

Refitting

5 Refitting is a reversal of removal, but apply a little locking fluid to the threads before inserting the mounting screw. Tighten the screw to the specified torque.

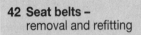

42 Seat belts –
removal and refitting

Front seat belt and reel

Removal

1 Remove the front seat as described in Section 39.

2 Unbolt and remove the belt lower guide rail from the bottom of the B-pillar. Slide the end of the seat belt from the rail.

3 Pull the rubber weatherstrip away from the B-pillar, then ease out the upper and lower trim panels. The panels are retained with clips, and a wide-bladed screwdriver will be

42.5 Unclipping the trim from the outside of the B-pillar

necessary to release them, but first make a careful note of how the panels clip into place as it is important they are refitted correctly. Feed the seat belt through the slot in the upper panel as it is being removed **(see illustrations)**.

4 Unscrew the bolt and remove the seat belt upper anchor from the height adjuster **(see illustration)**.

5 If necessary, unclip the outer trim, then undo the screws and remove the height adjuster from the B-pillar **(see illustration)**.

6 Release the belt, then if necessary undo the screw and remove the belt guide from the B-pillar **(see illustration)**.

7 Remove the sill inner trim panels for access to the bottom of the B-pillar **(see illustration)**.

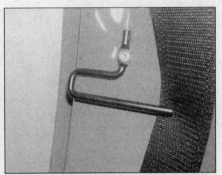

42.6 The belt guide on the B-pillar

8 On the outside of the B-pillar, prise out the plug for access to the reel mounting nut. A deep socket will be necessary to unscrew the nut as it is located at the end of a pin welded to the pillar. The pin is fitted to prevent loss of the nut, as otherwise it would fall inside the sill panel. Unscrew the nut, then withdraw the reel unit from inside and withdraw it together with the seat belt **(see illustrations)**.

9 The stalk is attached to the inner side of the seat and is removed by unscrewing the mounting bolt which also secures the tensioner.

Refitting

10 Refitting is a reversal of removal, but apply a little locking fluid to the threads of the

42.7 Removing the sill inner trim panels

42.8a View of the front seat belt reel from inside the vehicle

42.8b Prise out the plug . . .

42.8c . . . for access to the reel retaining nut which is located on a pin

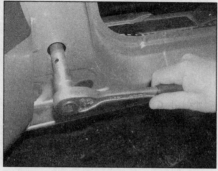

42.8d Unscrewing the front seat belt reel retaining nut

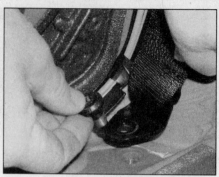

42.11 Unbolting the rear seat belt lower anchor from the body

42.12a Rear seat belt upper anchor and height adjuster – Zafira

42.12b Rear seat belt upper anchor – Astra

mounting bolts/nuts before inserting them and tightening them to the specified torque.

Rear seat belt and reel

Removal

11 Remove the rear quarter inner trim panel (Section 44). This procedure includes unbolting the seat belt lower anchor (**see illustration**).

12 Unscrew the bolt and remove the upper anchor. On Zafira models it is attached to the height adjuster (**see illustrations**).

13 On Zafira models, remove the trim and unscrew the bolt securing the seat belt to the lower side panel.

14 On Zafira models, unbolt the guide from the C-pillar and remove it from the seat belt.

15 Unscrew the bolt and remove the reel from the body (**see illustrations**).

16 On Zafira models, undo the screws and remove the height adjuster from the C-pillar.

17 The stalk can be unbolted after removing the rear seat cushion (**see illustration**).

Refitting

18 Refitting is a reversal of removal, but apply a little locking fluid to the threads of the mounting bolts/nuts before inserting them and tightening them to the specified torque (**see illustrations**).

42.15a Rear seat belt reel unit – Zafira

42.15b Rear seat belt reel unit – Astra

42.17 Removing the rear seat belt stalk – Zafira

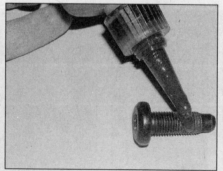

42.18a Apply locking fluid to the threads of the seat belt mounting bolts before fitting them . . .

42.18b . . . and tighten the bolts to the specified torque

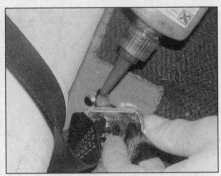

42.18c Refitting the central seat belt stalk

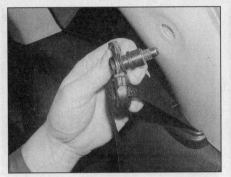

42.21a Removing the 3rd row seat belt upper anchor

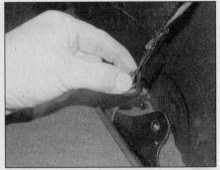

42.21b Removing the 3rd row seat belt lower anchor

3rd row rear seat belt and reel (Zafira)

Removal

19 Remove the floor covering from the rear luggage compartment.

20 Remove the upper trim panel from the side of the luggage compartment.

21 Prise off the cap and undo the screw securing the anchor to the C-pillar. Also remove the lower anchor (see illustrations).

22 Undo the screws and remove the belt guide from the C-pillar.

23 Remove the lower trim panel from the side of the luggage compartment.

24 Unscrew the mounting bolt and remove the seat belt reel unit from the side panel (see illustration).

25 The stalk can be removed after removing the centre trim (see illustration).

Refitting

26 Refitting is a reversal of removal, but apply a little locking fluid to the threads of the mounting bolt before inserting it and tightening it to the specified torque.

3rd row rear centre seat belt (Zafira)

Removal

27 Remove the rear seat cushion and backrest as described in Section 40.

28 Undo the screws and remove the cover for access to the centre seat belt stalks.

29 Undo the bolts and remove the stalks from the floor.

30 Disconnect the cable from the reel, then unbolt the reel from the backrest.

Refitting

31 Refitting is a reversal of removal, but tighten the mounting bolts to the specified torque.

43 Seat belt height adjuster – removal and refitting

Front

Removal

1 Remove the B-pillar upper trim panel, as described in Section 44.

2 Remove the two Torx type securing bolts, and withdraw the height adjuster assembly from the B-pillar.

Refitting

3 Refitting is a reversal of removal, but ensure that the height adjuster is fitted the correct way up. The top of the adjuster is marked with two arrows, which should point towards the vehicle roof.

Rear

General

4 The procedure is as described for the front seat belt height adjuster, but for access to the height adjuster, remove the rear quarter trim panel (see Section 44) instead of the B-pillar trim panel.

44 Inner trim panels – removal and refitting

⚠️ **Warning: Before carrying out any work in the vicinity of the front seats, refer to the precautions for airbag systems given in Chapter 12.**

Front door

Removal

1 Disconnect the battery negative lead and wait a minimum of 1 minute before proceeding. This will allow time for the airbag system capacitor to discharge.

2 On models with electrical exterior mirrors, carefully prise out the control switch from the trim panel and disconnect the wiring. Similarly, on models with electric front

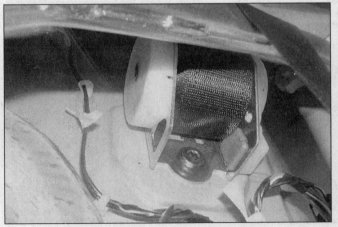

42.24 3rd row rear seat belt reel unit

42.25 Removing the 3rd row rear seat belt stalk

44.2a Ease the electric exterior mirror switch from the door interior trim panel . . .

44.2b . . . then disconnect the wiring plug

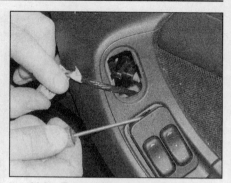

44.2c Ease out the electric window switch . . .

window winders, remove the window control switch **(see illustrations)**.

3 On models with manually-operated

windows, release the securing clip, and remove the window regulator handle. To release the securing clip, insert a length of

wire with a hooked end between the handle and the trim bezel on the door trim panel, and manipulate it to free the securing clip from the handle. Take care not to damage the door trim panel. Recover the trim bezel.

4 Pull off the knob rubber gaiter, then carefully prise the trim panel for the exterior door mirror from the inside of the door. Where the tweeter loudspeaker is located in the mirror trim panel, disconnect the wiring. Where the tweeter loudspeaker is located in the door inner trim panel, prise it out and disconnect the wiring **(see illustrations)**.

5 On Astra models, carefully prise the cover from the inner door handle **(see illustrations)**.

6 Undo the trim panel securing screws located on the lower edge of the panel. On some models one of the screws is located behind the grip, which can be removed by

44.2d . . . and disconnect the wiring plug

44.4a Pull off the rubber gaiter . . .

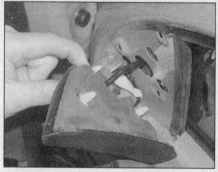

44.4b . . . then prise off the cover . . .

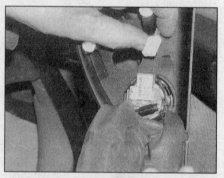

44.4c . . . and disconnect the wiring from the tweeter

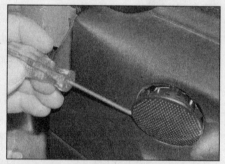

44.4d Where the tweeter loudspeaker is located in the door inner trim panel, prise it out . . .

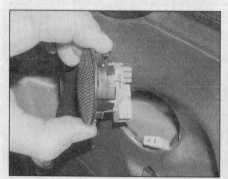

44.4e . . . and disconnect the wiring

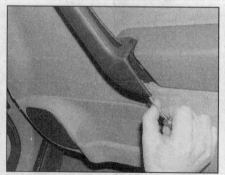

44.5a Use a screwdriver to carefully release the inner door handle cover . . .

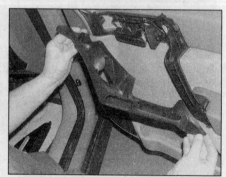

44.5b . . . then remove it from the panel

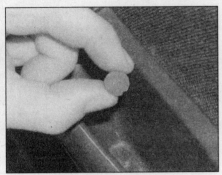

44.6a Remove the plug . . .

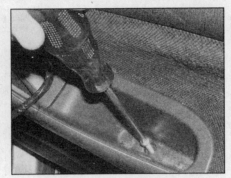

44.6b . . . undo the screw . . .

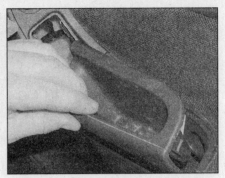

44.6c . . . and remove the grip from the door inner trim panel

44.6d Removing the door inner trim panel retaining screws

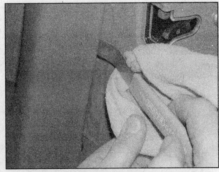

44.7a Releasing the inner trim panel retaining clips

44.7b Removing the trim panel from the door

prising out the plug and unscrewing the retaining screw (see illustrations).

7 The plastic clips securing the trim panel to the door must now be released. This can be done using a screwdriver, but it is preferable to use a forked tool, to minimise the possibility of damage to the trim panel and the clips. The clips are located around the outer edge of the trim panel and if necessary a piece of card or cloth may be used to protect the door paintwork (see illustrations).

8 With the clips released, disconnect the cable from the inner door handle located in the trim panel. Unhook the top of the panel and withdraw it from the vehicle (see illustrations).

9 The plastic insulating sheet can be peeled from the door. Peel the sheet back slowly to prevent damage to the sealant, and take care not to damage the sheet (see illustration).

Refitting

10 Refitting is a reversal of removal, but if necessary renew any broken plastic retaining clips. If the plastic insulating sheet has been removed from the door, make sure that it is refitted intact, and securely fixed to the door.

Rear door

Removal

11 Disconnect the battery negative lead and wait a minimum of 1 minute before proceeding. This will allow time for the airbag system capacitor to discharge.

12 On models with electric rear window winders, remove the window control switch by prising it out of the panel with a screwdriver and disconnecting the wiring. Note on certain models the switch is retained with screws.

13 On models with manually-operated windows, release the securing clip, and remove the window regulator handle. To release the securing clip, either use a special forked tool, or insert a length of wire with a hooked end between the handle and the trim bezel on the door trim panel, and manipulate it to free the securing clip from the handle.

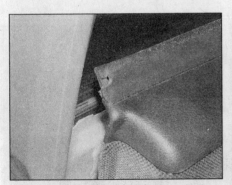

44.8a Unhook the top of the trim panel . . .

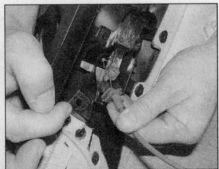

44.8b . . . and disconnect the cable from the inner door handle located in the trim panel

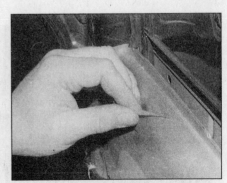

44.9 Peeling the plastic insulating sheet from the front door

44.13a Using a special forked tool to release the window regulator handle securing clip

44.13b Removing the window regulator handle and trim bezel

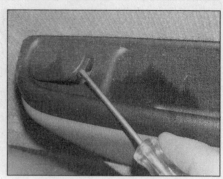

44.14a Prise out the cover . . .

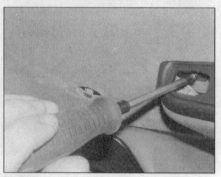

44.14b . . . then undo the front screw . . .

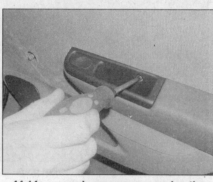

44.14c . . . and rear screw securing the pocket in the trim panel

Take care not to damage the door trim panel. Recover the trim bezel (see illustrations).

14 Where applicable, prise out the plastic cover, then undo the screws and remove the pocket from the trim panel (see illustrations).

15 Unclip and remove the ashtray, then, where necessary, unclip and remove the tweeter grille (see illustration).

16 Undo the trim panel securing screws located on the lower edge of the panel (see illustration).

17 The plastic clips securing the trim panel to the door must now be released. This can be done using a screwdriver, but it is preferable to use a forked tool, to minimise the possibility of damage to the trim panel and the clips. The clips are located around the outer edge of the trim panel.

18 With the clips released, disconnect the inner door handle cables and the tweeter wiring and withdraw the panel from the vehicle (see illustrations).

19 The plastic insulating sheet can be peeled from the door, but remove the operating cable and locking knob link. Peel the sheet back slowly to prevent damage to the sealant, and take care not to damage the sheet (see illustrations).

Refitting

20 Refitting is a reversal of removal, but if necessary renew any broken plastic retaining clips. If the plastic insulating sheet has been

44.15 Removing the tweeter grille

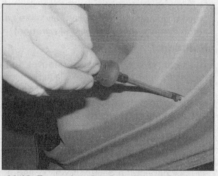

44.16 Removing the door inner trim panel securing screws

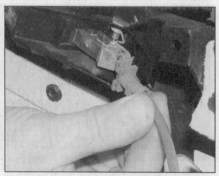

44.18a Release the rear door handle outer cable . . .

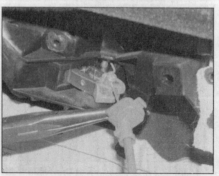

44.18b . . . and inner cable, then disconnect the wiring from the tweeter

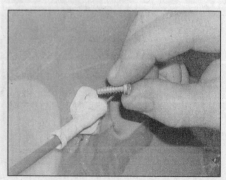

44.19a Undo the screws . . .

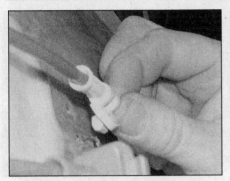

44.19b . . . and remove the operating cable . . .

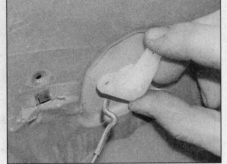

44.19c . . . and locking knob link . . .

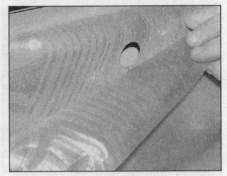

44.19d . . . then slowly peel the plastic insulating sheet from the door inner panel

removed from the door, make sure that it is refitted intact, and securely fixed to the door.

Tailgate

Removal

21 With the tailgate open, prise out the plastic covers, undo the screws, and remove the lower and upper trim panels from the inside of the tailgate. Note that the lower panel has extensions which slot into the upper panels.
22 Release the clips and remove the high-level stop-light.

Refitting

23 Refitting is a reversal of removal.

Rear quarter panel (Coupe models)

Removal

24 Remove the rear seat backrest as described in Section 40.
25 Using a wide-blade screwdriver, carefully prise the rear quarter panel from the body. Take care not to break the plastic clips.

Refitting

26 Refitting is a reversal of removal.

Rear quarter panel (Hatchback models)

Removal

27 With the tailgate and rear door open, prise the rubber weatherstrips from the body

aperture in the vicinity of the rear quarter panel and rear valance panel **(see illustration)**. Also remove the rear shelf.
28 Remove the rear door inner sill trim on the relevant side **(see illustration)**.
29 Remove the rear seat cushion (Section 40), then fold the rear seat backrest forwards.
30 Undo the screws and remove the plastic trim from the rear valance **(see illustration)**.
31 Prise out the plastic covers and undo the screws securing the upper rear quarter trim to the body **(see illustrations)**.
32 Unscrew the rear seat belt lower anchor bolt and remove the seat belt from the floor.
33 Unclip the upper rear quarter trim and feed the rear seat belt through the hole in the trim **(see illustrations)**.
34 Remove the rear seat backrest rubber

44.27 Removing the rubber weatherstrips from the body aperture

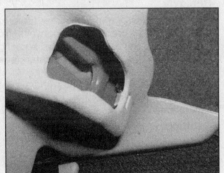

44.28 Rear door inner sill trim

44.30 Removing the plastic trim from the rear valance

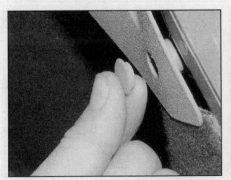

44.31a Prise out the plastic covers . . .

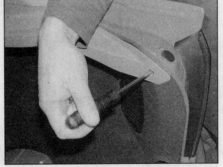

44.31b . . . and undo the screws securing the upper rear quarter trim

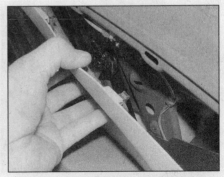

44.33a Unclip the upper rear quarter trim . . .

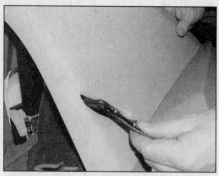

44.33b . . . and feed the rear seat belt through the hole in the trim

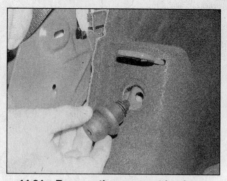

44.34a Remove the rear seat backrest rubber buffer . . .

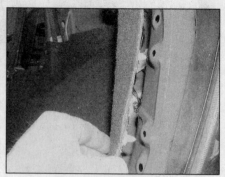

44.34b . . . release the clips . . .

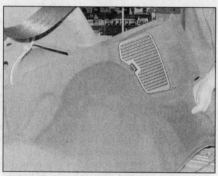

44.34c . . . and remove the lower rear quarter trim

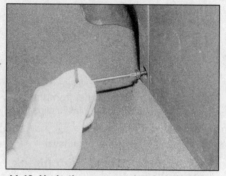

44.40 Undo the screws securing the lower trim panel to the side of the heater

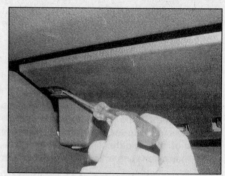

44.41a Undo the lower trim panel outer screws

buffer, then unclip and remove the lower rear quarter trim (see illustrations).

Refitting

35 Refitting is a reversal of removal. Use a block of wood and a mallet to tap the rubber weatherstrip fully onto the body flange.

C-pillar (Coupe models)

Removal

36 Remove the rear quarter panel as described above.
37 Undo the retaining screws.
38 Using a wide-blade screwdriver, carefully prise the panel from the body. Take care not to break the plastic clips.

Refitting

39 Refitting is a reversal of removal.

Facia lower trim panels

Removal

40 The facia lower trim panels are fitted to the driver's and passenger's footwells. To remove either, first undo the screws securing the panel to the side of the heater (see illustration).
41 Undo the outer screws and withdraw the lower trim panel from under the facia (see illustrations).

Refitting

42 Refitting is a reversal of removal.

Other inner trim panels

Removal and refitting

43 Most small trim panels are secured with

plastic clips which can easily be broken on removal. Always try to lever out the clips by inserting a forked tool directly beneath them, rather than levering out the panel.

45 Centre console – removal and refitting

Removal

1 Disconnect the battery negative lead with reference to Chapter 5A.
2 Prise out the central cover from under the handbrake lever (see illustration).
3 Prise the handbrake lever gaiter from the

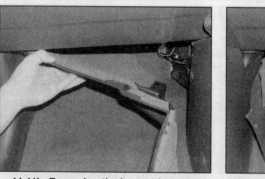

44.41b Removing the lower trim panel from the passenger's side footwell

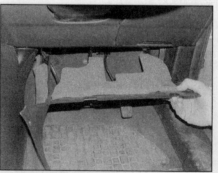

44.41c Removing the lower trim panel from the driver's side footwell

45.2 Removing the central cover from under the handbrake lever

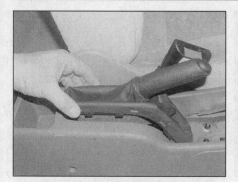

45.3 Removing the handbrake lever gaiter from the centre console

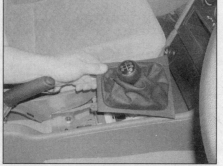

45.4 Removing the gear lever gaiter from the centre console

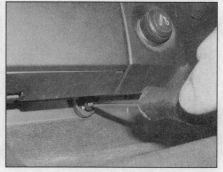

45.8a Undo the screw . . .

centre console. Make sure that the handbrake is applied **(see illustration)**.

4 Prise the gear lever gaiter from the centre console **(see illustration)**.

5 At the front of the console, carefully lever out the seat heating switch panel using a screwdriver.

6 On models with a TC switch, prise out the switch.

7 Unclip the panel then undo the screws and remove the ashtray from the front of the console.

8 Disconnect the wiring for the cigarette lighter **(see illustrations)**.

9 Prise out the covers where necessary then undo the mounting screws. There are two screws on each side of the console, one screw located beneath the handbrake lever, and one screw located at the front of the console **(see illustrations)**.

45.8b . . . remove the ashtray . . .

45.8c . . . and disconnect the wiring for the cigarette lighter – Zafira

45.8d Removing the ashtray . . .

45.8e . . . and disconnecting the wiring for the cigarette lighter

45.9a Undo the rear screws . . .

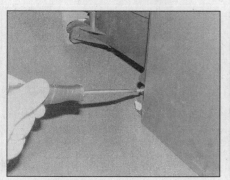

45.9b . . . front screws . . .

45.9c . . . central screw . . .

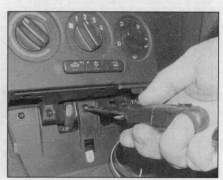

45.9d . . . and front screw

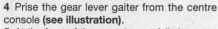

45.10 Removing the central console

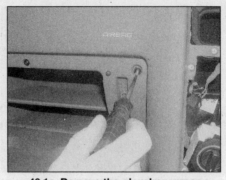

46.1a Remove the glovebox upper
mounting screws . . .

46.1b . . . and lower mounting screws . . .

10 Lift the central console from the floor and withdraw it through a door aperture **(see illustration)**.

Refitting

11 Refitting is a reversal of removal.

46 Glovebox –
removal and refitting

Removal

1 With the glovebox open, unscrew the three upper and three lower screws securing it to the facia panel **(see illustrations)**.
2 Pull out the glovebox a little way and

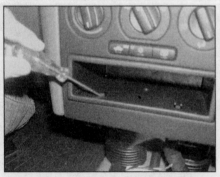

46.2 . . . then disconnect the wiring from
the illumination light

disconnect the wiring from the illumination light **(see illustration)**. On models with a CD changer or navigation control, disconnect the wiring/aerial from the respective unit.
3 Withdraw the glovebox from the facia and remove from inside the vehicle.
4 If necessary, remove the lid from the glovebox by driving out the hinge pins.
5 Where applicable, remove the CD changer or navigation control unit from the glovebox with reference to Chapter 12.

Refitting

6 Refitting is a reversal of removal. If a new glovebox is being fitted, transfer the self-adhesive cushions and interior light/CD changer/navigation control unit from the old unit.

47.3a Remove the mat . . .

47 Facia panel –
removal and refitting

⚠ **Warning: Working in the vicinity of airbags is potentially dangerous. Refer to the precautions for airbag systems given in Chapter 12.**

Astra models

Removal

1 Disconnect the battery negative lead and wait a minimum of 1 minute to allow the airbag system capacitor to discharge (refer to Chapter 12 if necessary).
2 Remove the centre console and ashtray, as described in Section 45.
3 Remove the storage compartment from the facia. To do this, remove the mat then use a screwdriver to release the upper and lower clips, and withdraw the compartment **(see illustrations)**.
4 Remove the radio and mounting box as described in Chapter 12. On models with a navigation system, remove the system unit with reference to Chapter 12.
5 Working through the apertures in the surround panel, release the clips securing the heater controls and separate the control panel **(see illustration)**.

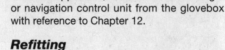

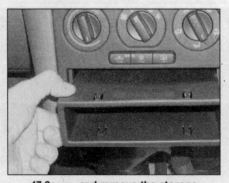

47.3c . . . and remove the storage
compartment

47.5 Releasing the heater controls from
the rear of the surround panel

47.3b . . . then release the clips with a
screwdriver . . .

47.6a Undo the lower screws . . .

47.6b . . . release the surround panel from the facia clips . . .

47.6c . . . slide the hazard switch wiring socket from the panel . . .

6 Undo the lower screws and carefully prise the surround panel from the facia, then reach up and disconnect the wiring from the multi-info display unit. Remove the hazard switch (Chapter 12, Section 4) then disconnect the wiring socket by sliding it down from the surround panel. If necessary, undo the screws and remove the multi-info display unit from the panel (see illustrations).

7 Remove the light switch located on the driver's side of the facia with reference to Chapter 12, Section 4, then undo the screws and remove the side vent and switch surround from the facia. The screws are accessed by pressing down the vent past its stop until the screws are visible through the grille. If the vent is tight, access the screws between the vent grille for removal, then release the side clips and turn the vent before refitting (see illustrations). Withdraw the vent from the facia and recover the screws.

8 Disconnect the wiring socket from the light switch surround and remove downwards (see illustrations).

9 Remove the glovebox as described in Section 46.

10 Press down the passenger vent past its stop, until the vent securing screws are visible through the grille. Undo the screws, then unscrew the lower mounting bolt and

47.6d . . . and disconnect the wiring from the multi-info display unit

47.7a Undo the lower screw . . .

47.7b . . . and upper screws, to remove the switch surround

47.7c Turning the vent past its stop . . .

47.7d . . . before refitting

47.8a Release the clip . . .

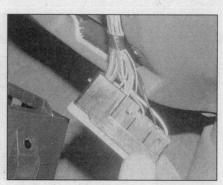

47.8b . . . and withdraw the socket from the surround

47.10a Undo the screws . . .

47.10b . . . and remove the passenger vent

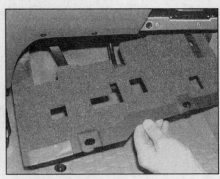

47.12 Removing the trim panel from under the facia on the driver's side

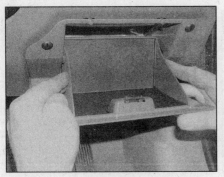

47.16a Remove the driver's side storage compartment . . .

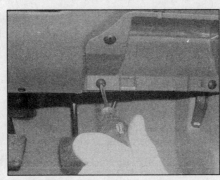

47.16b . . . then undo the screws . . .

withdraw the vent from the facia (see illustrations).

11 Reach through the glovebox location and disconnect the wiring from the passenger's airbag. Take care not to damage the wiring or terminals.

12 Remove the steering wheel as described in Chapter 10, then remove the trim panel from under the facia on the driver's side (see illustration).

13 Undo the screws and remove the upper and lower shrouds from the steering column.

14 Remove the indicator switch and wiper switch as described in Chapter 12, Section 4.

15 Remove the instrument panel as described in Chapter 12.

16 Remove driver's side storage compartment, then undo the four fasteners and remove the compartment (see illustrations).

17 For improved working room, remove both front seats as described in Section 39.

18 Carefully prise the inner trim panels from the sills, then undo the screws and release the footwell side trim panels (see illustrations).

19 Note the location of the wiring loom on the rear of the facia panel, then disconnect it (see illustration).

20 On the passenger's side of the facia, remove the trim from under the facia, then remove the fasteners and remove the footwell air duct (see illustrations).

47.16c . . . and remove the compartment from the facia

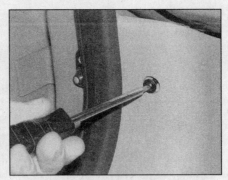

47.18a Undo the screws . . .

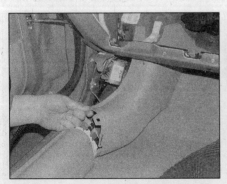

47.18b . . . and remove the footwell side trim panels

47.19 Disconnecting the wiring from the rear of the facia

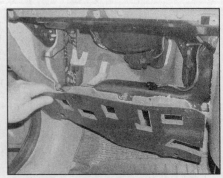

47.20a Remove the facia lower trim panel . . .

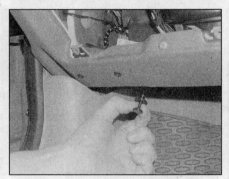

47.20b . . . then remove the fasteners . . .

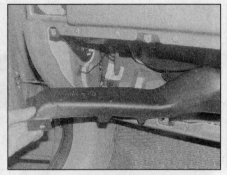

47.20c . . . and remove the footwell air duct

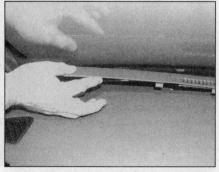

47.21 Removing the windscreen air duct panel

21 Unclip the windscreen air duct panel from the facia (see illustration).
22 At the front of the facia below the windscreen, undo and remove the three screws securing the facia to the bulkhead, then unscrew the remaining screws at the sides and on the bulkhead. The side screws are beneath plastic covers (see illustrations).
23 Check that all wiring has been disconnected from the facia components. Note the routing of the wiring to aid refitting.
24 With the help of an assistant, carefully ease the facia from the bulkhead and remove it from inside the vehicle. Take particular care not to damage the facia in the area around the steering column.

Refitting

25 Refitting is a reversal of removal, but make sure that the wiring is routed correctly and

connected to the various components as noted during removal. Refer to Chapter 3, Section 10, for information on refitting the side vents.

Zafira models

Removal

26 Disconnect the battery negative lead and wait a minimum of 1 minute to allow the airbag system capacitor to discharge (refer to Chapter 12 if necessary).
27 Remove the centre console and ashtray, as described in Section 45.
28 Remove the heater control panel as described in Chapter 3.
29 Remove the steering wheel as described in Chapter 10.
30 Remove the indicator and wiper switches as described in Chapter 12, Section 4.
31 Remove the ignition switch as described in Chapter 12, Section 4.

32 Remove the radio and mounting box as described in Chapter 12. On models with a navigation system, remove the system unit with reference to Chapter 12.
33 Using a small screwdriver, release the clip and remove the control knob from the light switch. Insert the screwdriver through the hole in the bottom of the knob (see illustration).
34 Insert two small screwdrivers in the holes located on the edge of the control knob aperture in order to release the clips, then withdraw the light switch from the facia (see illustration). Note that the wiring plug remains in the facia.
35 Unclip and remove the fusebox cover.
36 Unclip the upper air vent grille from the outer end of the facia, then unscrew the instrument panel surround securing screws (see illustrations). There are three screws located above the instrument panel, one screw in the upper outer corner, one screw

47.22a Front facia securing screws

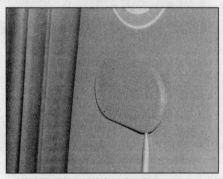

47.22b Prise off the plastic covers . . .

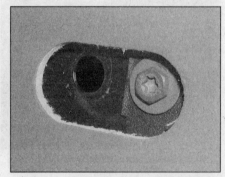

47.22c . . . for access to the side screws

47.33 Use a small screwdriver to release the control knob from the light switch

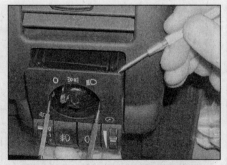

47.34 Using two small screwdrivers to release the clips when removing the light switch from the facia

47.36a Unclip and remove the upper air vent . . .

47.36b ... then undo the surround mounting screws

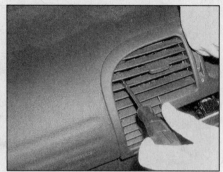

47.36c The inner screw is accessed through the air vent grille

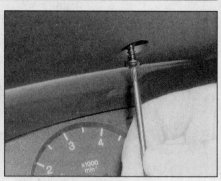

47.36d Unscrewing the surround upper retaining screws

47.37a Withdraw the surround ...

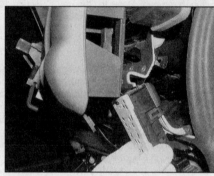

47.37b ... and disconnect the wiring

inside the grille of the upper inner corner, and four screws on the lower edge.

37 Withdraw the surround from the facia and disconnect the wiring **(see illustrations)**.

38 Remove the instrument panel with reference to Chapter 12. Also detach the wiring plug **(see illustration)**.

39 Unscrew the nut and screw securing the fusebox, then release the wiring plug from the retainer inside the instrument panel aperture, and release the plastic tie. Withdraw the fusebox and position it to one side **(see illustrations)**.

40 Using a wide-bladed screwdriver, carefully prise the windscreen trim panel from the front of the facia **(see illustrations)**.

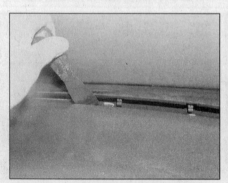

47.38 Releasing the wiring plug from the facia

47.39a Unscrew the nut and screw ...

47.39b ... and withdraw the fusebox from the facia

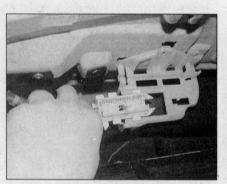

47.40a Prise out the windscreen trim panel ...

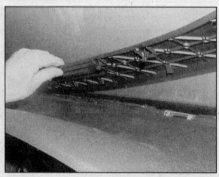

47.40b ... and remove it from the front of the facia

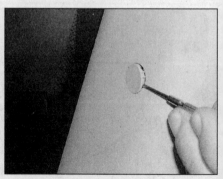

47.41a Prise out the plastic plugs ...

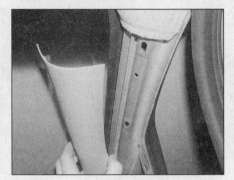

47.41b . . . and remove the vertical trim panels from the A-pillars . . .

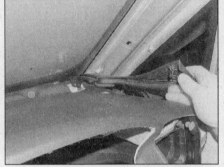

47.41c . . . then prise out and remove the facia outer panels

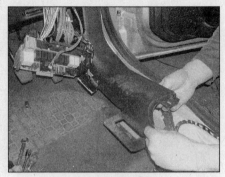

47.42 Removing the lower trim panels from the A-pillars

41 Prise out the plastic plugs, then undo the screws and remove the vertical trim panels from the A-pillars. Also remove the outer panels from each side of the facia (**see illustrations**).

42 Remove the front sill panels from each side, then remove the lower trim panels from the A-pillars (**see illustration**).

43 Remove the glovebox as described in Section 46.

44 Pull out the air vent from the passenger's side of the facia, then undo the screws and withdraw the air vent (**see illustrations**).

45 Remove the trim panels from under facia by releasing the fasteners, then remove the heater air ducts from both sides (**see illustration**).

46 Note the routing and location of the wiring plugs on the facia, then disconnect them.

47 Unscrew the facia mounting screws, noting that access to the end screws is gained by prising out the covers (**see illustrations**). Also pull out the rubber weatherstrip from the A-pillars on both sides in the area by the facia.

48 With the help of an assistant, carefully ease the facia from the bulkhead and remove it from inside the vehicle (**see illustration**). Take particular care not to damage the facia in the area around the steering column.

Refitting

49 Refitting is a reversal of removal, but make sure that the wiring is routed correctly and connected to the various components as noted during removal.

47.44a Pull out the passenger's side air vent . . .

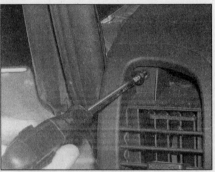

47.44b . . . then undo the screws . . .

47.44c . . . and withdraw the air vent

47.45 Removing the heater air ducts from under the facia

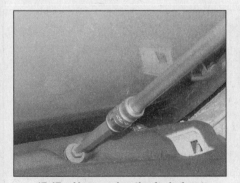

47.47a Unscrewing the facia front mounting screws

47.47b Prise out the side covers for access to the side mounting screws

47.48 Removing the facia from inside the vehicle

Chapter 12
Body electrical systems

Contents

Degrees of difficulty

Easy, suitable for novice with little experience	Fairly easy, suitable for beginner with some experience	Fairly difficult, suitable for competent DIY mechanic	Difficult, suitable for experienced DIY mechanic	Very difficult, suitable for expert DIY or professional

Specifications

System type	12-volt, negative earth
Fuses	See *Wiring diagrams*

Bulbs — Wattage

	Wattage
Headlights:	
Main beam	60
Dipped beam	55
Front sidelights	5
Front and rear indicators	21
Indicator side repeaters	5
Tail/stop-lights	21/4
Reversing lights	21
Rear foglights	21
Number plate light	10
Interior light and map-reading lights	10
Glovebox lighting	10
Cigar lighter illumination	0.5
Instrument panel warning lights:	
Headlight High Beam	1.1
Foglight	1.1
Instrument illumination	1.5
LCD illumination	1.5
Trailer turn signal	1.1
Charge warning light	3
Switch illumination	1.2

Note: *The electrical equipment fitted will vary according to the vehicle model and trim level. Refer to the vehicle's owner's handbook or check with the spares department of an authorised Vauxhall dealer for details of the bulbs used.*

Torque wrench settings

	Nm	lbf ft
Airbag:		
Airbag unit to steering wheel	8	6
Control unit	10	7
Passenger airbag brackets	22	16
Passenger airbag to bracket	5	4
Side airbag to seat backrest	5	4
Oil level sensor to sump	8	6
Radio aerial to roof	7	5
Tailgate wiper motor	9	6
Windscreen wiper motor linkage	14	10

1 General information and precautions

 Warning: Before carrying out any work on the electrical system, read through the precautions given in 'Safety first!' at the beginning of this manual, and in Chapter 5.

1 The electrical system is of 12-volt negative earth type. Power for the lights and all electrical accessories is supplied by a lead-acid type battery, which is charged by the alternator.

2 This Chapter covers repair and service procedures for the various electrical components not associated with the engine. Information on the battery, alternator and starter motor can be found in Chapter 5A.

3 It should be noted that, before working on any component in the electrical system, the battery negative terminal should first be disconnected, to prevent the possibility of electrical short-circuits and/or fires. On models fitted with an alarm system, the battery must be disconnected within 15 seconds of switching off the ignition, otherwise the alarm will be activated (the alarm has a temporary independent electrical supply).

4 At regular intervals, carefully check the routing of the wiring harness, ensuring that it is correctly secured by the clips or ties provided so that it cannot chafe against other components. If evidence is found of the harness having chafed against other components, repair the damage and ensure that the harness is secured or protected so that the problem cannot occur again.

Caution: If the radio/cassette player fitted to the vehicle is one with an anti-theft security code, refer to 'Disconnecting the battery' in the Reference Section of this manual before disconnecting the battery.

2 Electrical fault finding – general information

Note: *Refer to the precautions given in 'Safety first!' (at the beginning of this manual) and to Section 1 of this Chapter before starting work.*

The following tests relate to testing of the main electrical circuits, and should not be used to test delicate electronic circuits (such as anti-lock braking systems), particularly where an electronic control module is used.

General

1 A typical electrical circuit consists of an electrical component, any switches, relays, motors, fuses, fusible links or circuit breakers related to that component, and the wiring and connectors that link the component to both the battery and the chassis. To help to pinpoint a problem in an electrical circuit, wiring diagrams are included at the end of this chapter.

2 Before attempting to diagnose an electrical fault, first study the appropriate wiring diagram to obtain a complete understanding of the components included in the particular circuit concerned. The possible sources of a fault can be narrowed down by noting whether other components related to the circuit are operating properly. If several components or circuits fail at one time, the problem is likely to be related to a shared fuse or earth connection.

3 Electrical problems usually stem from simple causes, such as loose or corroded connections, a faulty earth connection, a blown fuse, a melted fusible link, or a faulty relay (refer to Section 3 for details of testing relays). Visually inspect the condition of all fuses, wires and connections in a problem circuit before testing the components. Use the wiring diagrams to determine which terminal connections will need to be checked, to pinpoint the trouble-spot.

4 The basic tools required for electrical fault-finding include the following:
 a) *a circuit tester or voltmeter (a 12-volt bulb with a set of test leads can also be used for certain tests).*
 b) *a self-powered test light (sometimes known as a continuity tester).*
 c) *an ohmmeter (to measure resistance).*
 d) *a battery.*
 e) *a set of test leads.*
 f) *a jumper wire, preferably with a circuit breaker or fuse incorporated, which can be used to bypass suspect wires or electrical components.*
Before attempting to locate a problem with test instruments, use the wiring diagram to determine where to make the connections.

5 To find the source of an intermittent wiring fault (usually due to a poor or dirty connection, or damaged wiring insulation), a 'wiggle' test can be performed on the wiring. This involves wiggling the wiring by hand, to see if the fault occurs as the wiring is moved. It should be possible to narrow down the source of the fault to a particular section of wiring. This method of testing can be used in conjunction with any of the tests described in the following sub-Sections.

6 Apart from problems due to poor connections, two basic types of fault can occur in an electrical circuit – open-circuit and short-circuit.

7 Open-circuit faults are caused by a break somewhere in the circuit, which prevents current from flowing. An open-circuit fault will prevent a component from working, but will not cause the relevant circuit fuse to blow.

8 Short-circuit faults are caused by a 'short' somewhere in the circuit, which allows the current flowing in the circuit to 'escape' along an alternative route, usually to earth. Short-circuit faults are normally caused by a breakdown in wiring insulation, which allows a feed wire to touch either another wire, or an earthed component such as the bodyshell. A short-circuit fault will normally cause the relevant circuit fuse to blow.

Finding an open-circuit

9 To check for an open-circuit, connect one lead of a circuit tester or voltmeter to either the negative battery terminal or a known good earth.

10 Connect the other lead to a connector in the circuit being tested, preferably nearest to the battery or fuse.

11 Switch on the circuit, remembering that some circuits are live only when the ignition switch is moved to a particular position.

12 If voltage is present (indicated either by the tester bulb lighting or a voltmeter reading, as applicable), this means that the section of the circuit between the relevant connector and the battery is problem-free.

13 Continue to check the remainder of the circuit in the same fashion.

14 When a point is reached at which no voltage is present, the problem must lie between that point and the previous test point with voltage. Most problems can be traced to a broken, corroded or loose connection.

Finding a short-circuit

15 To check for a short-circuit, first disconnect the load(s) from the circuit (loads are the components that draw current from a circuit, such as bulbs, motors, heating elements, etc).

16 Remove the relevant fuse from the circuit, and connect a circuit tester or voltmeter to the fuse connections.

17 Switch on the circuit, remembering that some circuits are live only when the ignition switch is moved to a particular position.

18 If voltage is present (indicated either by the tester bulb lighting or a voltmeter reading, as applicable), this means that there is a short-circuit.

19 If no voltage is present, but the fuse still blows with the load(s) connected, this indicates an internal fault in the load(s).

Finding an earth fault

20 The battery negative terminal is connected to 'earth' (the metal of the engine/transmission and the car body), and most systems are wired so that they only receive a positive feed. The current returning through the metal of the car body. This means that the component mounting and the body form part of that circuit. Loose or corroded mountings can therefore cause a range of electrical faults, ranging from total failure of a circuit, to a puzzling partial fault. In particular, lights may shine dimly (especially when another circuit sharing the same earth point is in operation). Motors (eg, wiper motors or the radiator cooling fan motor) may run slowly, and the operation of one circuit may have an affect on another. Note that on many vehicles, earth straps are used between certain components, such as the engine/transmission and the body, usually where there is no metal-to-metal contact between components, such as the flexible rubber mountings, etc.

21 To check whether a component is properly earthed, disconnect the battery, and connect one lead of an ohmmeter to a known good earth point. Connect the other lead to the wire or earth connection being tested. The

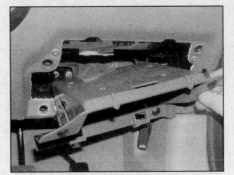

3.2a Remove the storage compartment and frame . . .

resistance reading should be zero; if not, check the connection as follows.

22 If an earth connection is thought to be faulty, dismantle the connection, and clean back to bare metal both the bodyshell and the wire terminal or the component earth connection mating surface. Be careful to remove all traces of dirt and corrosion, then use a knife to trim away any paint, so that a clean metal-to-metal joint is made. On reassembly, tighten the joint fasteners securely; if a wire terminal is being refitted, use serrated washers between the terminal and the bodyshell, to ensure a clean and secure connection. When the connection is remade, prevent the onset of corrosion in the future by applying a coat of petroleum jelly or silicone-based grease.

3 Fuses and relays – general information

Fuses

1 Fuses are designed to break a circuit when a predetermined current is reached, to protect the components and wiring which could be damaged by excessive current flow. Any excessive current flow will be due to a fault in the circuit, usually a short-circuit (see Section 2).

2 The main fuses and relays are located on

3.2b . . . then pull out the bottom of the fusebox

the driver's end of the facia. On Astra models they are behind the storage compartment, and access is gained by opening the compartment and pressing in the sides of the tray in order to remove it from the compartment housing, then undoing the screws and withdrawing the housing and pulling out the bottom of the fusebox (see illustrations). On Zafira models access is gained by pulling out the bottom of the cover, then lowering it from the facia. Additional engine-related fuses are located in the left-hand side of the engine compartment.

3 The circuits protected by the various fuses and relays are marked on the inside of the compartment housing on Astra models (see illustration), or on the inside of the cover on Zafira models.

4 A blown fuse can be recognised from its melted or broken wire.

5 To remove a fuse, first ensure that the relevant circuit is switched off. Then pull the relevant fuse from the panel using the tweezers supplied (see illustrations).

6 Before renewing a blown fuse, trace and rectify the cause, and always use a fuse of the correct rating. Never substitute a fuse of a higher rating, or make temporary repairs using wire or metal foil, as more serious damage or even fire could result.

7 Spare fuses are generally provided in the blank terminal positions in the fusebox.

8 Note that the fuses are colour-coded.

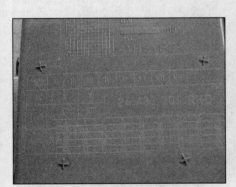

3.3 The fuse positions are marked on the back of the storage compartment

3.5a Removing a fuse from the fusebox located in the left-hand side of the engine compartment – Zafira

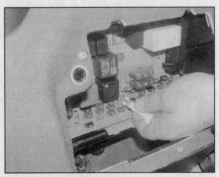

3.5b Removing a fuse from the fusebox – Astra

3.10 Engine-related relays located on the left-hand side of the engine compartment – Zafira

3.12 Removing a relay from the fusebox

Relays

9 A relay is an electrically-operated switch, which is used for the following reasons:

a) *A relay can switch a heavy current remotely from the circuit in which the control current is flowing, allowing the use of lighter-gauge wiring and control switch contacts.*

b) *A relay can receive more than one control input, unlike a mechanical switch.*

c) *A relay can have a timer function.*

10 The main relays are located on the main fusebox, although some engine-related relays are located in a box on the left-hand side of the engine compartment **(see illustration)**.

11 If a circuit or system controlled by a relay develops a fault, and the relay is suspect, operate the system. If the relay is functioning, it should be possible to hear it 'click' as it is energised. If this is the case, the fault lies with the components or wiring of the system. If the relay is not being energised, then either the relay is not receiving a main supply or a switching voltage, or the relay itself is faulty. Testing is by the substitution of a known good unit, but be careful – while some relays are identical in appearance and in operation,

others look similar but perform different functions.

12 To remove a relay, first ensure that the relevant circuit is switched off. The relay can then simply be pulled out from the socket, and pushed back into position **(see illustration)**.

13 Incorporated in the main fusebox is a multi-timer which combines the components and relays that were previously separate units. The timer slides into the side of the fusebox as a separate module.

---

4 Switches – removal and refitting

Ignition switch/steering column lock cylinder

Steering column lock cylinder

1 Remove the steering wheel as described in Chapter 10. Note that this procedure includes disconnecting the battery.

2 Undo the screws and remove the steering column shrouds and tilt lever knob.

3 Unclip the windscreen wiper switch from its position on the steering column. If necessary,

also remove the anti-theft immobiliser transceiver unit from the steering lock and disconnect the wiring.

4 Insert the ignition key and turn to position I.

5 Using a small screwdriver or pin punch, depress the locking pin through the hole in the top of the column, then withdraw the lock cylinder using the key.

6 To refit the lock cylinder, push the assembly into the lock housing, until the locking pin engages, then turn the ignition key to position 0 and withdraw the key. If the steering lock pin engages with the steering column as the cylinder is removed, it will not be possible to insert the cylinder so that the locking pin engages. In this case, use a screwdriver in the housing to press the steering lock pin down before inserting the lock cylinder.

Ignition switch

7 To remove the ignition switch, remove the lock cylinder as previously described in this Section, or insert the ignition key and turn it to position 0.

8 Insert a small screwdriver through the hole in the bottom of the switch and depress the internal lug, then use another screwdriver to lever off the wiring harness plug **(see illustration)**.

9 With the plug removed, unclip and remove the ignition switch.

10 Refitting is a reversal of removal.

Turn signal/wiper switch assembly

11 The turn signal and wiper switch assemblies are removed identically.

12 Remove the steering wheel as described in Chapter 10. Note that this procedure includes disconnecting the battery.

13 Undo the screws and remove the steering column shrouds and tilt lever knob.

14 Depress the clips and slide the turn signal/wiper switch from the steering column **(see illustration)**.

4.8 Use a screwdriver to depress the internal lug, and withdraw the ignition switch

4.14 Remove the wiper switch from the steering column . . .

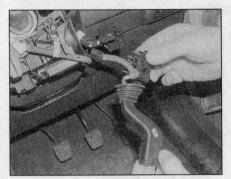

4.15 . . . and disconnect the wiring

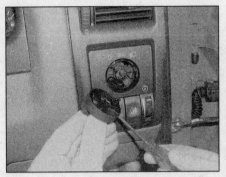

4.17 Removing the knob from the lighting switch

4.18 Insert two small screwdrivers as shown, and prise the switch from the facia

15 Disconnect the wiring and withdraw the switch (see illustration). Where applicable, also disconnect the wiring from the cruise control.

16 Refitting is a reversal of removal, but make sure that the switch clips engage correctly.

Lighting and foglight switch

17 Using a small screwdriver inserted through the hole in the bottom of the switch knob, carefully remove the knob from the switch (see illustration).

18 Insert two small screwdrivers on each side of the central hole to release the retaining lugs, then prise the switch from the socket in the facia (see illustration).

19 If necessary, the illumination bulb may be renewed, with reference to Section 6.

20 Refitting is a reversal of removal.

Hazard warning switch

21 Using a screwdriver, carefully prise the cover from the switch (see illustration).

22 Insert the screwdriver at the top and bottom of the switch, and carefully prise the switch from the facia/surround (see illustration).

23 Refitting is a reversal of removal.

Heater blower motor switch

24 Remove the heater control panel as described in Chapter 3.

25 Carefully pull off the knob from the blower motor switch.

26 Press the switch from the rear of the control panel, while releasing the clips located at the top, sides and bottom.

27 Refitting is a reversal of removal.

Stop-light switch and handbrake 'on' warning light switch

28 Refer to Chapter 9.

Courtesy light switch and rear luggage compartment switch

29 Undo the retaining screw and withdraw the switch (see illustration).

4.21 Prise off the cover . . .

30 Disconnect the wiring and tape it to the panel to prevent it dropping out of reach. Note when removing the tailgate switch it may be easier to remove the inner trim panels and disconnect the wiring from inside the tailgate (see illustration).

31 Make sure that the retaining screw makes good contact with the body and switch. If necessary clean the contact points.

32 Refitting is a reversal of removal.

Electric sunroof switch

33 Remove the front interior light as described in Section 6.

34 Undo the screws securing the switch panel to the headlining (see illustration).

35 Withdraw the panel from the headlining

4.22 . . . then remove the hazard switch from the facia/surround

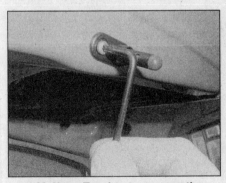

4.29 Use a Torx key to unscrew the courtesy light switch retaining screw

4.30 Wiring connected to the rear of the tailgate courtesy light switch – Zafira

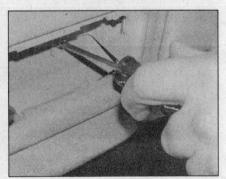

4.34 Remove the screws securing the switch panel to the headlining . . .

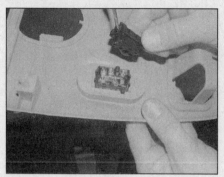

4.35 . . . disconnect the wiring from the switch . . .

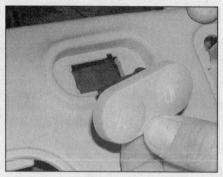

4.36 . . . and press the sunroof switch from the panel

5.2 Removing the headlight dipped beam bulbholder

and disconnect the wiring from the switch **(see illustration)**.

36 Press the switch from the panel **(see illustration)**.

37 Refitting is a reversal of removal.

Reversing light switch

38 Refer to Chapter 7.

5 Bulbs (exterior lights) – renewal

1 Whenever a bulb is renewed, note the following points.

a) *Remember that, if the light has just been in use, the bulb may be extremely hot.*
b) *Do not touch the bulb glass with the*

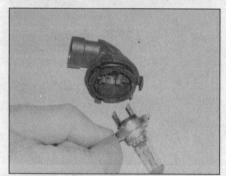

5.3 Removing the bulb from the dipped beam bulbholder

fingers, as this can result in early failure or a dull reflector. If the glass is accidentally touched, wipe it clean using methylated spirit.

c) *Always check the bulb contacts and holder, ensuring that there is clean metal-to-metal contact between the bulb and its live(s) and earth. Clean off any corrosion or dirt before fitting a new bulb.*

d) *Ensure that the new bulb is of the correct rating.*

⚠️ **Warning: Certain later models may be optionally equipped with a Xenon headlight system. All the bulbs in the headlight unit operate at very high voltages and there is a high risk of personal injury if any of the associated wiring is touched with the ignition switched on. For safety reasons it is recommended that bulb renewal on the Xenon system is entrusted to a Vauxhall dealer.**

Headlight dipped beam

2 With the bonnet open, twist anti-clockwise the brown bulbholder from the rear, outer end of the headlight **(see illustration)**. Note that the inner bulb is for the main beam.

3 Note the orientation of the bulb, then remove it from the bulbholder, using the fingers on the metal base **(see illustration)**. Note the location tang on the top of the base.

4 When handling the new bulb, use a tissue or clean cloth, to avoid touching the glass with the fingers; moisture and grease from the skin can cause blackening of the bulb.

5 Fit the new bulb using a reversal of the

removal procedure, using the fingers only to press the metal base into the bulbholder. Make sure that the bulb location tang is located in the top of the bulbholder.

Headlight main beam

6 With the bonnet open, twist anti-clockwise the black bulbholder from the rear, inner end of the headlight **(see illustration)**. Note that the outer bulb is for the dipped beam.

7 Release the clip and disconnect the wiring from the bulbholder. The bulb is integral with the bulbholder.

8 When handling the new bulb, use a tissue or clean cloth, to avoid touching the glass with the fingers; moisture and grease from the skin can cause blackening of the bulb.

9 Fit the new bulb using a reversal of the removal procedure. Twist the bulbholder fully clockwise into the rear of the headlight.

Sidelight

10 Open the bonnet. The front sidelight bulb is located under the rear of the headlight.

11 Twist the bulbholder anti-clockwise and withdraw it from the headlight **(see illustration)**.

12 Remove the bulb from the holder **(see illustration)**.

13 Fit the new bulb using a reversal of the removal procedure.

Front direction indicator

14 With the bonnet open, twist anti-clockwise the white bulbholder from the

5.6 Removing the headlight main beam bulbholder

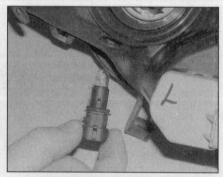

5.11 Removing the sidelight bulbholder from the headlight

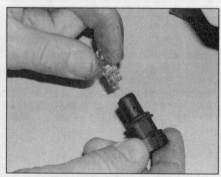

5.12 Removing the front sidelight bulb from the bulbholder

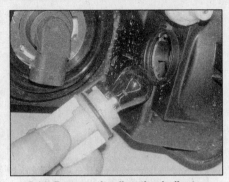

5.14 Remove the direction indicator bulbholder from the headlight . . .

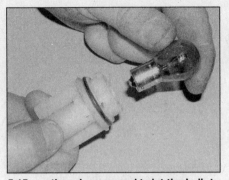

5.15 . . . then depress and twist the bulb to remove it

5.18 Twist the rear cover from the foglight . . .

direction indicator section of the headlight **(see illustration)**.
15 Depress and twist the bulb to remove it **(see illustration)**.
16 Refitting is a reversal of removal.

Front foglight

17 Remove the front bumper as described in Chapter 11.
18 Twist the cover from the rear of the foglight **(see illustration)**.
19 Disconnect the wiring at the connector **(see illustration)**.
20 Unhook the spring clips and remove the bulb from the foglight **(see illustrations)**. Note how the bulb is located in the reflector. The bulb is only available together with the fly-lead wire.
21 Refitting is a reversal of removal.

Front direction indicator side repeater

22 Carefully press the side repeater rearwards in order to release the front of the light from the front wing **(see illustrations)**.
23 Twist the bulbholder from the light **(see illustration)**.
24 Pull out the wedge-type bulb **(see illustration)**.
25 Fit the new bulb using a reversal of the removal procedure. Locate the front of the light in the front wing, then press in the rear until it clips in position.

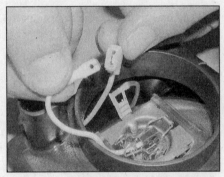

5.19 . . . disconnect the wiring at the connector . . .

5.20a . . . then unhook the spring clips . . .

5.20b . . . and remove the bulb

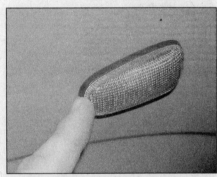

5.22a Carefully press the side repeater rearwards . . .

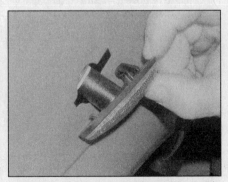

5.22b . . . to release the front of the light from the front wing

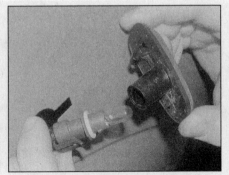

5.23 Twist the bulbholder from the light . . .

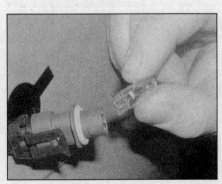

5.24 . . . then pull out the wedge-type bulb

5.26 Removing the access cover for the rear light cluster – Astra Hatchback

5.27 Disconnect the wiring . . .

5.28 . . . then unscrew the two knurled nuts . . .

Rear light cluster

Hatchback models

26 In the luggage compartment, release the clip and remove the access cover for the rear light cluster (see illustration).
27 Disconnect the wiring plug (see illustration).
28 Support the rear light cluster from the outside, then unscrew the two knurled nuts from inside (see illustration).
29 Withdraw the rear light cluster from the rear of the vehicle (see illustration).
30 Press in the retaining lugs and remove the bulbholder from the light (see illustration).
31 Depress and twist the relevant bulb to remove it (see illustration).
32 Refitting is a reversal of removal.

Estate models

33 In the luggage compartment, turn the fasteners and release the access cover from the side trim.
34 Support the rear light cluster from the outside, then unscrew the two knurled nuts from inside.
35 Withdraw the rear light cluster from the rear of the vehicle.
36 Press in the retaining lug and remove the bulbholder from the light.
37 Depress and twist the relevant bulb to remove it.
38 Refitting is a reversal of removal.

Zafira models

39 In the luggage compartment, remove the access cover from the side trim.
40 Support the rear light cluster from the outside, then unscrew the two knurled nuts from inside.
41 Withdraw the rear light cluster from the rear of the vehicle.

42 Release the retaining lug and remove the bulbholder from the light.
43 Depress and twist the relevant bulb to remove it (see illustration).
44 Refitting is a reversal of removal.

Rear number plate light

Hatchback and Saloon models

45 Open the tailgate or bootlid for improved access to the number plate light located on the top of the rear bumper.
46 Insert a screwdriver vertically into the hole in the light lens and press in to release the clip (see illustration).
47 Press down the right-hand end of the light and lift up the left-hand end to release it from the bumper.
48 Depress the clip and release the lens from the light (see illustration).

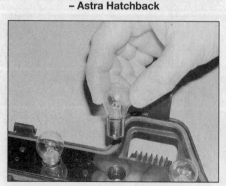

5.29 . . . and withdraw the rear light cluster – Astra Hatchback

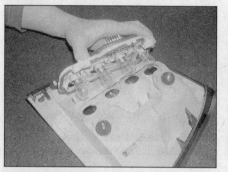

5.30 Remove the bulbholder . . .

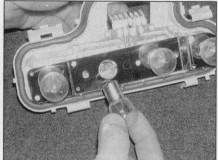

5.31 . . . then depress and twist the relevant bulb to remove it – Astra Hatchback

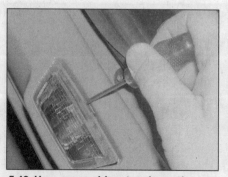

5.43 Removing a rear light cluster bulb – Zafira

5.46 Use a screwdriver to release the rear number plate light retaining clip

5.48 Releasing the lens from the rear number plate light

5.49 Depress and twist the bulb to remove it

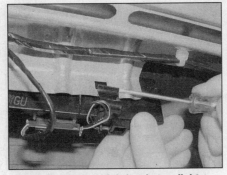

5.56a Unclip the high-level stop-light . . .

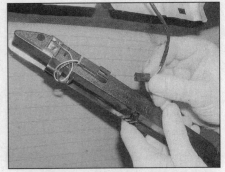

5.56b . . . and disconnect the wiring

49 Depress and twist the bulb to remove it from the bulbholder **(see illustration)**.
50 Refitting is a reversal of removal.

Estate and Zafira models

51 Open the tailgate and support at waist height for access to the number plate light located in the tailgate.
52 Undo the screws and withdraw the light unit.
53 Ease the festoon-type bulb from the spring contacts.
54 Refitting is a reversal of removal, but make sure that the spring contacts are tensioned sufficiently to hold the festoon-type bulb firmly.

High-level stop-light

Saloon and Hatchback models

55 With the tailgate open, prise out the plastic covers, undo the screws, and remove the lower and upper trim panels from the inside of the tailgate. Note that the lower panel has extensions which slot into the upper panels.
56 Undo the two screws then unclip and remove the high-level stop-light. Disconnect the wiring **(see illustrations)**.
57 The stop-light is a complete unit and it is not possible to remove individual bulbs.

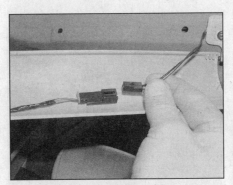

5.60 Disconnect the wiring . . .

58 Fit the new light using a reversal of the removal procedure.

Estate and Zafira models

59 With the tailgate open, prise out the plastic covers, undo the screws, and remove the lower and upper trim panels from the inside of the tailgate. Note that the lower panel has extensions which slot into the upper panels.
60 Disconnect the wiring from the high-level stop-light **(see illustration)**.
61 Undo the screws then unclip and remove the light **(see illustrations)**.

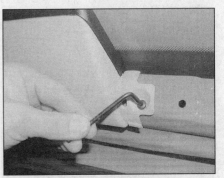

5.61a . . . then undo the screws . . .

62 The stop-light is a complete unit and it is not possible to remove individual bulbs.
63 Refitting is a reversal of removal.

6 Bulbs (interior lights) – renewal

1 Whenever a bulb is renewed, note the following points.
a) *Remember that, if the light has just been in use, the bulb may be extremely hot.*
b) *Do not touch the bulb glass with the*

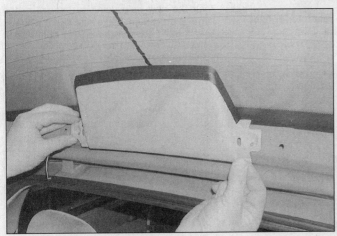

5.61b . . . unclip the high-level stop-light unit . . .

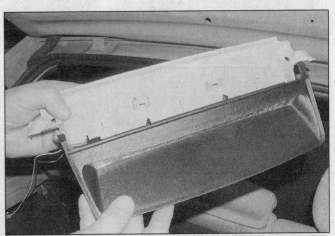

5.61c . . . and remove it from the tailgate

6.2a Prise out the interior light . . .

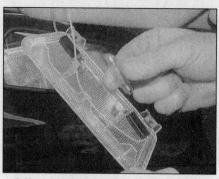

6.2b . . . then remove the festoon-type bulb – Astra

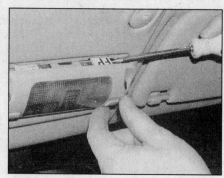

6.3a Prise out the front interior light . . .

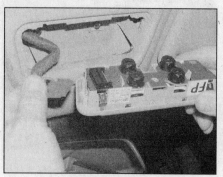

6.3b . . . disconnect the wiring . . .

6.3c . . . then twist free the bulbholder . . .

fingers, as this can result in early failure or a dull reflector.

c) Always check the bulb contacts and holder, ensuring that there is clean metal-to-metal contact between the bulb and its live(s) and earth. Clean off any corrosion or dirt before fitting a new bulb.

d) Ensure that the new bulb is of the correct rating.

Front interior light

2 On Astra models carefully prise the interior light from the headlining using a screwdriver, then remove the festoon-type bulb from the spring contacts **(see illustrations)**.

3 On Zafira models carefully prise the interior light from the headlining (or electric sunroof motor cover) using a screwdriver inserted beneath the front of the light. Disconnect the wiring then twist free the bulbholder and remove the wedge-type type bulb **(see illustrations)**.

4 Fit the new bulb using a reversal of the removal procedure.

Rear interior light

5 Carefully prise the interior light from the headlining **(see illustrations)**.

6 Remove the festoon-type bulb from the spring contacts **(see illustrations)**.

7 Fit the new bulb using a reversal of the removal procedure. Make sure that the bulb is held firmly between the spring contacts. If

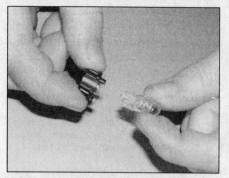

6.3d . . . and remove the wedge-type bulb – Zafira

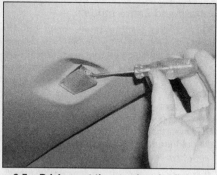

6.5a Prising out the rear interior light – Zafira

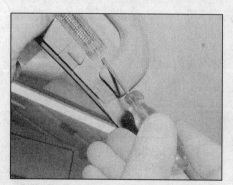

6.5b Prising out the rear interior light – Astra

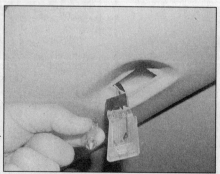

6.6a Removing the festoon-type bulb from the spring contacts – Zafira

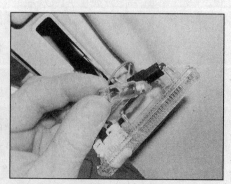

6.6b Removing the festoon-type bulb from the spring contacts – Astra

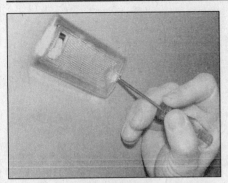

6.8 Prise out the luggage compartment interior light . . .

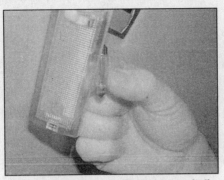

6.9 . . . and remove the festoon type bulb from the spring contacts

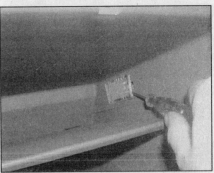

6.11 Prise the light from the glovebox . . .

necessary, pre-tension the contacts before fitting the bulb.

Luggage compartment interior light

8 Carefully prise the light from the side trim **(see illustration)**.
9 Remove the festoon-type bulb from the spring contacts **(see illustration)**.
10 Fit the new bulb using a reversal of the removal procedure. Make sure that the bulb is held firmly between the spring contacts. If necessary, pretension the contacts before fitting the bulb.

Glovebox light

11 With the glovebox open, carefully prise out the light unit **(see illustration)**.
12 Remove the festoon-type bulb from the spring contacts. To remove the light completely, disconnect the wiring **(see illustrations)**.
13 Fit the new bulb using a reversal of the removal procedure. Make sure that the bulb is held firmly between the spring contacts. If necessary, pre-tension the contacts before fitting the bulb.

Rear reading light

14 Carefully prise the light unit from the handle grip, using a screwdriver.
15 Remove the festoon-type bulb from the spring contacts.

16 Fit the new bulb using a reversal of the removal procedure. Make sure that the bulb is held firmly between the spring contacts. If necessary, pre-tension the contacts before fitting the bulb.

Cigarette lighter illumination

17 Unclip the panel located below the ashtray.
18 With the ashtray open, undo the screws and withdraw it from the centre console. Disconnect the wiring from the cigarette lighter.
19 Remove the heater coil, then use a screwdriver through the small hole to release the illumination light ring.
20 Remove the bulbholder and pull out the bulb **(see illustration 11.5)**.
21 Fit the new bulb using a reversal of the removal procedure.

Instrument panel illumination and warning light bulbs

22 Remove the instrument panel as described in Section 9.
23 To remove the bulbs, twist and turn the bulbholder and it remove from the instrument panel **(see illustration)**, then where possible remove the bulb from the bulbholder. Note that some bulbs cannot be removed from their bulbholders.

24 Fit the new bulb using a reversal of the removal procedure.

Light switch illumination

25 Remove the light switch as described in Section 4.
26 Using a screwdriver, twist the bulbholder from the rear of the switch **(see illustration)**.
27 Fit the new bulb using a reversal of the removal procedure.

Clock/multi-function display unit illumination

28 Remove the clock/display unit as described in Section 10.

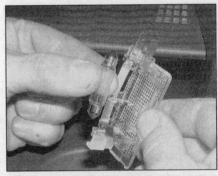

6.12a . . . then remove the festoon-type bulb from the spring contacts

6.12b Disconnecting the wiring from the glovebox light

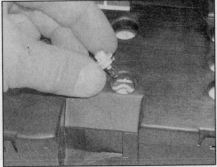

6.23 Removing a bulb from the instrument panel

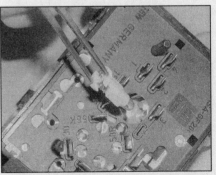

6.26 Removing the bulb from the rear of the light switch

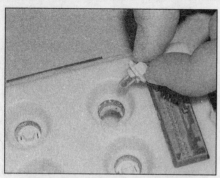

6.29a Removing a bulb from the clock/multi-function display unit – Zafira

6.29b Removing a bulb from the multi-function display unit – Astra

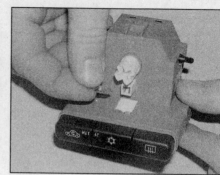

6.32 Removing a wedge-type bulb from the heater control panel

29 Twist the relevant bulbholder from the rear of the display unit **(see illustrations)**.

30 Fit the new bulb using a reversal of the removal procedure.

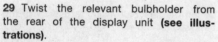

Heater control illumination

31 Remove the heater control assembly as described in Chapter 3.

32 Pull out the relevant wedge-type bulb from the assembly **(see illustration)**.

33 Fit the new bulb using a reversal of the removal procedure.

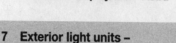

7	Exterior light units – removal and refitting

⚠️ *Warning: The Xenon headlight system (where fitted) operates at very high voltages. Do not touch the associated wiring when the headlights or ignition are switched on. If in doubt about the type of system fitted, consult a Vauxhall dealer.*

Headlight/front direction indicator

1 Remove the front bumper (see Chapter 11).

2 Unscrew and remove the two upper and one lower mounting bolts, then withdraw the headlight/front direction indicator light unit sufficiently to disconnect the wiring. Withdraw the unit from the vehicle, then undo the screws and remove the bumper trim from the bottom of the headlight **(see illustrations)**.

3 If necessary, the headlight range control servo may be removed by twisting it through 90° **(see illustration)**.

4 Refitting is a reversal of removal, but have the headlight beam alignment checked at the earliest opportunity.

Front foglight

5 Remove the front bumper (see Chapter 11).

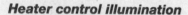

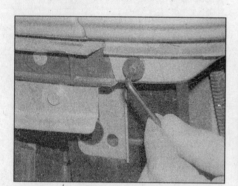

7.2a Unscrewing the headlight lower mounting bolt . . .

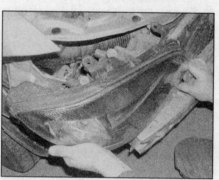

7.2b . . . withdraw the unit from the vehicle . . .

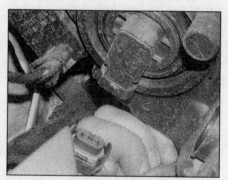

7.2c . . . and disconnect the wiring

7.2d Undo the screws . . .

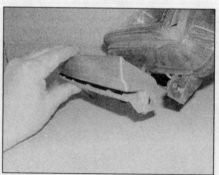

7.2e . . . and remove the bumper trim

7.3 Removing the headlight range control servo

7.6a Unscrew the mounting bolts . . .

7.6b . . . and remove the foglight from the front bumper

7.11 Remove the side trim cover for access to the rear light cluster

6 Unscrew the three mounting bolts and remove the foglight from the bumper, then disconnect the wiring **(see illustrations)**.

7 Refitting is a reversal of removal, but on completion have the beam alignment checked at the earliest opportunity.

Front direction indicator side repeater

8 Carefully press the side repeater light rearwards in order to release the front of the light from the front wing.

9 Remove the light and disconnect the wiring. If necessary remove the bulb with reference to Section 5.

10 Refitting is a reversal of removal. Locate the front of the light in the front wing, then press in the rear until the rear clip engages.

Rear light cluster

11 In the luggage compartment, remove the side trim cover for access to the rear light cluster **(see illustration)**.

12 Disconnect the wiring plug **(see illustration)**.

13 Support the rear light cluster from the outside, then unscrew the two knurled nuts from inside **(see illustration)**.

14 Withdraw the rear light cluster from the rear of the vehicle **(see illustration)**.

15 Press in the retaining lugs and remove the bulbholder from the light **(see illustration)**.

16 Refitting is a reversal of removal.

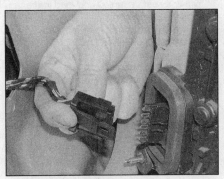

7.12 Disconnecting the wiring from the rear light cluster

Rear number plate light

Hatchback and Saloon models

17 Open the tailgate or bootlid for improved access to the number plate light located on the top of the rear bumper.

18 Insert a screwdriver vertically into the hole in the light lens and press to release the clip.

19 Press down the right-hand end of the light and lift up the left-hand end to release it from the bumper.

20 Disconnect the wiring **(see illustration)**. If necessary, remove the bulb with reference to Section 5.

21 Refitting is a reversal of removal.

Estate and Zafira models

22 Open the tailgate and support at waist

7.13 One of the plastic knurled nuts securing the rear light cluster to the body

height for access to the number plate light located in the tailgate.

23 Undo the screws and withdraw the light unit.

24 Disconnect the wiring. If necessary, remove the bulb with reference to Section 5.

25 Refitting is a reversal of removal.

High-level stop-light

26 The procedure is described in Section 5.

8 Headlight beam alignment – general information

1 Accurate adjustment of the headlight beam is only possible using optical beam-setting

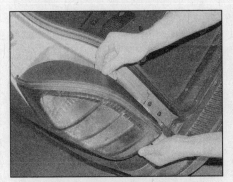

7.14 Withdrawing the rear light cluster from the rear of the vehicle

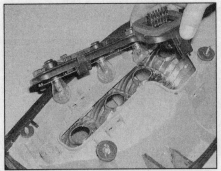

7.15 Removing the bulbholder from the rear light cluster

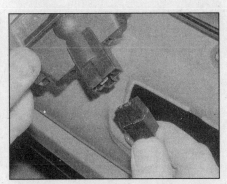

7.20 Disconnecting the wiring from the rear number plate light

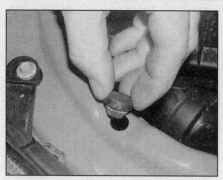

8.2a Remove the rubber grommet . . .

8.2b . . . for access to the vertical beam adjustment screw

8.2c The horizontal beam adjustment screw

equipment, and this work should therefore be carried out by a Vauxhall dealer or suitably-equipped workshop.

2 For reference, the headlights can be adjusted using the adjusters located on the front crossmember. The inner screw is for vertical adjustment and the outer one for horizontal adjustment. Remove the rubber grommet for access to the inner screw **(see illustrations)**.

3 All models have an electrically-operated headlight beam adjustment range system, controlled via a switch in the facia. The recommended settings are as follows.

Models without automatic level control

0 Front seat(s) occupied
1 All seats occupied
2 All seats occupied, and load in luggage compartment

3 Driver's seat occupied and load in the luggage compartment

Models with automatic level control

1 All seats occupied and full load in load compartment
0 All other load states

Note: *When adjusting the headlight aim, ensure that the switch is set to position 0.*

---

9 Instrument panel –
   removal and refitting

Removal

1 Remove the steering wheel as described in Chapter 10.
2 Undo the screws and remove the upper

steering column shroud. The screws are accessed by removing the plastic covers.
3 Undo the screw and remove the knob from the tilt steering lever.
4 Undo the screws and remove the lower steering column shroud.
5 On Astra models, prise out the covers, then undo the screws and remove the instrument panel surround from the facia **(see illustrations)**.
6 On Zafira models, remove the instrument panel surround as follows.

a) *Remove the lighting and foglight switch (Section 4 of this Chapter).*
b) *Remove the radio (Section 17 of this Chapter).*
c) *Carefully remove the outer vent from the facia.*
d) *Undo the retaining screws and remove the instrument panel surround panel, and disconnect the wiring as necessary. Note that the innermost screw is accessed through the grille of the inner vent.*

7 Undo the lower mounting screws on Astra models. Release the upper clip by moving the lever, then withdraw the instrument panel from the facia and disconnect the wiring **(see illustrations)**.

Refitting

8 Refitting is a reversal of removal. Check the operation of all the warning and illumination bulbs on completion.

9.5a Prise out the covers . . .

9.5b . . . then undo the screws . . .

9.5c . . . and remove the instrument panel surround

9.7a Undo the lower mounting screws . . .

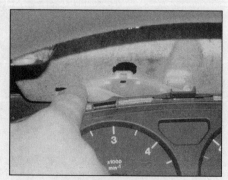

9.7b . . . then release the upper lever . . .

9.7c . . . and withdraw the instrument panel – Astra

9.7d Move the lever to release the instrument panel upper clips – Zafira

9.7e Instrument panel removed from the vehicle – Zafira

10 Multi-function display unit and components – removal and refitting

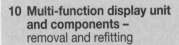

Note: *New multi-function display units must be programmed by a Vauxhall dealer after fitting. This is not necessary when removing and refitting an existing unit.*

Multi-function display unit

Astra models

1 Remove the front ashtray.
2 Unclip the storage compartment cover from the facia.
3 Remove the radio and mounting box as described in Section 17.
4 Where fitted, remove the navigation system unit.
5 Unclip the heater control panel from the rear of the surround panel.
6 Press the central air vents rearwards out of the surround panel.
7 Pull out the surround panel and disconnect the wiring from the multi-function display unit. Also slide the wiring plug from the rear of the hazard switch socket.
8 On the rear of the panel, undo the screws and remove the multi-function display unit **(see illustrations)**.
9 Refitting is a reversal of removal.

Zafira models

10 Remove the front ashtray.

11 Undo the two lower mounting screws, and unclip the heater/air conditioning control panel from the facia.
12 Unclip the hazard warning switch, TC switch, and seat heating switch from the control panel and disconnect the wiring.
13 Unclip the heater/air conditioning unit from the panel.
14 Remove the steering wheel as described in Chapter 10. Note that this procedure includes disconnecting the battery.
15 Undo the screws and remove the steering column shrouds and tilt lever knob.
16 Release the clips and slide the wiper and indicator switches from the steering column.
17 Remove the radio as described in Section 17.
18 Remove the lighting and foglight switch as described in Section 4.
19 Unclip the fusebox cover from the facia.
20 Using a screwdriver through the grille slots, undo the outer vent securing screw and remove the vent.
21 Undo the screws securing the instrument panel surround to the facia. There are three located directly above the instrument panel, one either side of the steering column, and one at each lower corner of the surround.
22 Withdraw the surround from the facia, and at the same time slide the lighting switch from its guide. Disconnect the wiring from the multi-function display unit **(see illustration)**, then release the remaining wiring from the rear of the surround.

23 Unclip the multi-function display unit from the surround.
24 Refitting is a reversal of removal.

Outside temperature sensor

25 With the bonnet open, reach down behind the front bumper and disconnect the wiring from the sensor located inside the front bumper.
26 Twist the sensor and unclip it from the front bumper **(see illustration)**.
27 Refitting is a reversal of removal.

Coolant temperature sensor

28 Refer to Chapter 3, Section 7.

Coolant residue sensor

29 The coolant residue sensor is located on the base of the coolant expansion tank. Refer

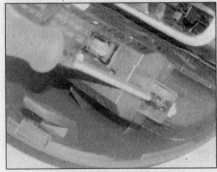

10.8a Undo the screws . . .

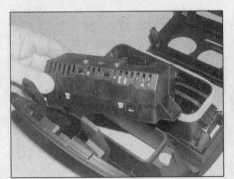

10.8b . . . and remove the multi-function display unit from the surround panel – Astra

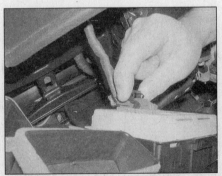

10.22 Disconnecting the wiring from the multi-function display unit – Zafira

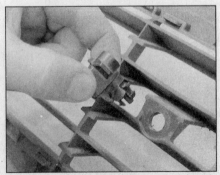

10.26 Removing the outside temperature sensor from the front bumper

11.2a Undo the screws . . .

11.2b . . . remove the ashtray and disconnect the wiring

11.3a Remove the heater coil . . .

to Chapter 3 and partially drain coolant from the system until the coolant level is below the sensor, then remove the expansion tank and disconnect the wiring from the sensor.

30 With the expansion tank inverted, use a screwdriver to release the sensor.

31 Refitting is a reversal of removal.

Windscreen washer fluid level sensor

32 The sensor is located beneath the left-hand end of the front bumper. First remove the bumper as described in Chapter 11.

33 Disconnect the wiring from the sensor located on the reservoir.

34 Carefully prise the sensor from the reservoir.

35 Refitting is a reversal of removal.

Engine oil level sensor

36 Remove the sump as described in the relevant part of Chapter 2.

37 Prise the retaining ring from the sump.

38 Press the sensor connection out of the sump.

39 Unbolt the sensor from the sump and remove the sealing ring.

40 Refitting is a reversal of removal, but use a new sealing ring and tighten the mounting bolts to the specified torque. Refit the sump with reference to the relevant part of Chapter 2.

11 Cigarette lighter – removal and refitting

Removal

1 Unclip the panel located below the ashtray.

2 With the ashtray open, undo the screws and withdraw it from the centre console. Disconnect the wiring from the cigarette lighter **(see illustrations)**.

3 Remove the heater coil, then remove the bulbholder and cover from the rear of the unit **(see illustrations)**.

4 Use a screwdriver to prise out the body, then remove the light ring **(see illustrations)**.

5 Pull the bulb from the bulbholder **(see illustration)**.

Refitting

6 Refitting is a reversal of removal.

12 Horn – removal and refitting

Removal

1 The horn or horns are located behind the right-hand end of the front bumper **(see**

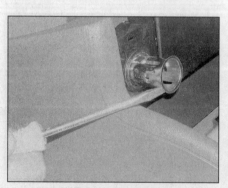

11.3b . . . then remove the bulbholder . . .

11.3c . . . and cover from the rear of the unit

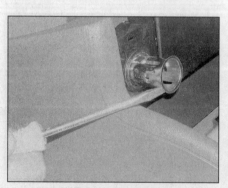

11.4a Prise out the body . . .

11.4b . . . then remove the light ring

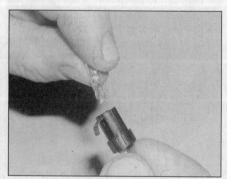

11.5 Removing the bulb from the bulbholder

12.1 The horns are located behind the right-hand end of the front bumper

illustration). If necessary for improved access, remove the front bumper as described in Chapter 11.

2 Disconnect the wiring from the horn(s).

3 Unscrew the nut(s) and remove the horn(s) from the mounting bracket. If necessary, unbolt the bracket from the body.

Refitting

4 Refitting is a reversal of removal.

13 Wiper arm – removal and refitting

Windscreen wiper arm

1 Operate the wiper motor, then switch it off so that the wiper arm returns to the at-rest position (see Haynes Hint).

2 Using a screwdriver prise the cover from the spindle end of the wiper arm (see illustration).

3 Unscrew the spindle nut and recover the small washer (see illustration).

4 Lift the blade off the glass, and pull the wiper arm off its spindle splines (see illustration). Note that the wiper arms may be very tight on the spindle splines – if necessary, lever the arm off the spindle, using a flat-bladed screwdriver (take care not to damage the scuttle cover panel).

5 If necessary, remove the blade from the arm with reference to *Weekly checks*.

6 If removed, refit the wiper blade to the arm at this stage. This will prevent any damage to the windscreen from the upper end of the arm.

7 Ensure that the wiper arm and spindle splines are clean and dry, then refit the arm to the spindle and align the blade with the previously noted rest position.

8 Refit the washer and spindle nut, and tighten it securely. Refit the cover.

Tailgate wiper arm

9 Operate the wiper motor, then switch it off so that the wiper arm returns to the at-rest position (see Haynes Hint).

10 Lift the cover from the base of the wiper arm and unscrew the retaining nut (see illustrations).

Stick a piece of masking tape on the windscreen, along the edge of the wiper blade, to use as an alignment aid on refitting.

11 Lift the blade off the glass, and pull the wiper arm off its spindle. If the arm is tight, use a suitable puller to release it from the spindle (see illustration).

12 If necessary, remove the blade from the arm with reference to *Weekly checks*.

13 If removed, refit the wiper blade to the arm at this stage. This will prevent any damage to the rear window from the upper end of the arm.

14 Ensure that the wiper arm and spindle splines are clean and dry, then refit the arm to the spindle and align the blade with the previously noted rest position.

13.2 Prise up the cover . . .

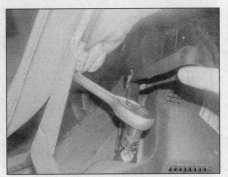

13.3 . . . unscrew the nut . . .

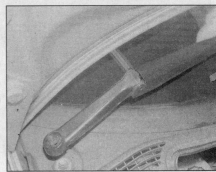

13.4 . . . and pull the wiper arm off its spindle splines

13.10a Lift the cover from the base of the wiper arm . . .

13.10b . . . then unscrew the retaining nut

13.11 Using a small puller to release the wiper arm from the spindle

14.2a Pull up the rubber weatherstrip . . .

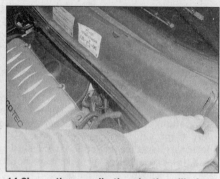

14.2b . . . then unclip the plastic grille from the water deflector – Zafira

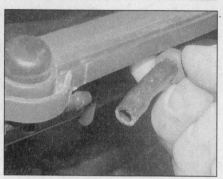

14.3 Disconnecting the tubing from the windscreen washer jets on the water deflector

14.4a Unscrew the nuts (Zafira only) . . .

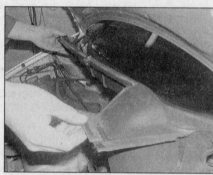

14.4b . . . and unclip the water deflector from the bulkhead

15 Refit the spindle nut, and tighten it securely. Close the cover on the base of the arm.

---

14 Windscreen wiper motor and linkage – removal and refitting

Removal

1 Remove both wiper arms as described in Section 13.

2 Pull the rubber weatherstrip from the rear of the engine compartment, then unclip the plastic grille from the water deflector at the front of the windscreen **(see illustrations)**.

3 Disconnect the tubing from the windscreen washer jets on the water deflector **(see illustration)**.

4 Unscrew the nuts and unclip the water deflector from the bulkhead **(see illustrations)**.

5 Disconnect the wiring from the windscreen wiper motor **(see illustration)**.

6 Unscrew the mounting bolts and withdraw the wiper motor and linkage **(see illustrations)**.

7 The motor can be removed from the linkage assembly by prising free the rod from the

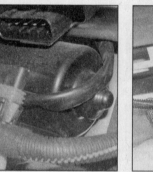

14.5 Disconnect the wiring . . .

14.6a . . . then unscrew the central mounting bolts . . .

14.6b . . . and outer mounting bolts . . .

14.6c . . . and withdraw the windscreen wiper motor and linkage

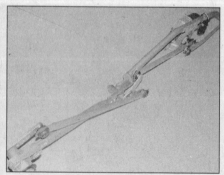

14.6d Windscreen wiper motor and linkage removed from the vehicle – Zafira

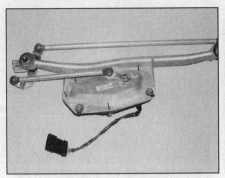

14.6e Windscreen wiper motor and linkage removed from the vehicle – Astra

14.7 Windscreen wiper motor crank and mounting bolts

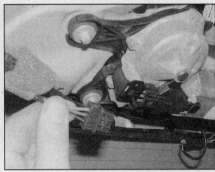

15.3 Disconnect the wiring . . .

crank and unbolting the motor **(see illustration)**. The remaining linkage rods can also be dismantled if necessary.
8 Clean the assembly and examine the spindles and joints for wear and damage. Renew the components as required.

Refitting

9 Refitting is a reversal of removal, but lubricate the joints with a little grease before assembling them. Refit the wiper arms with reference to Section 13.

15 Tailgate wiper motor – removal and refitting

Removal

1 Remove the wiper arm from the tailgate as described in Section 13, then remove the trim panelling from the inside of the tailgate with reference to Chapter 11, Section 44.
2 On Astra models only, remove the tailgate lock cylinder as described in Chapter 11, Section 26.
3 Disconnect the wiring at the plug **(see illustration)**.
4 Unscrew the mounting bolts and withdraw the wiper motor while sliding the spindle housing through the rubber grommet **(see illustrations)**.
5 If necessary remove the rubber grommet

from the tailgate. Examine the grommet for wear and damage and renew it if necessary **(see illustration)**.

Refitting

6 Refitting is a reversal of removal, but tighten the mounting bolts to the specified torque. Refit the wiper arm with reference to Section 13.

16 Windscreen/tailgate/headlight washer system components – removal and refitting

Washer fluid reservoir

1 Remove the front bumper as described in Chapter 11.
2 Remove the left-hand front wheel arch liner as described in Chapter 11.
3 Position a container beneath the washer fluid pump and reservoir to collect the fluid.
4 Disconnect the wiring from the pump and position to one side.
5 Disconnect the hose from the pump and allow the fluid to drain into the container.
6 On models with a multi-function display unit, disconnect the wiring from the level sensor on the fluid reservoir.
7 On models with a headlight washer system, disconnect the wiring and hose from the additional pump on the reservoir.
8 Disconnect the filler neck(s) from the reservoir.

9 Release the wiring from the clips on top of the reservoir.
10 Unscrew the mounting bolts and withdraw the reservoir from the front valance.
11 Refitting is a reversal of removal. Fill the reservoir with washer fluid with reference to *Weekly checks*.

Washer fluid pump

12 Remove the front bumper as described in Chapter 11.
13 Remove the left-hand front wheelarch liner as described in Chapter 11.
14 Position a suitable container beneath the washer fluid pump and reservoir to collect the fluid.
15 Disconnect the wiring from the top of the

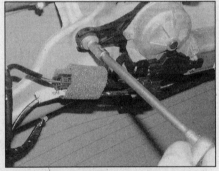

15.4a . . . then unscrew the mounting bolts . . .

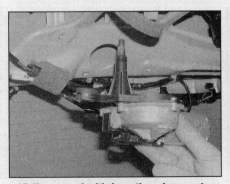

15.4b . . . and withdraw the wiper motor from the tailgate – Zafira

15.4c Removing the wiper motor from the tailgate – Astra

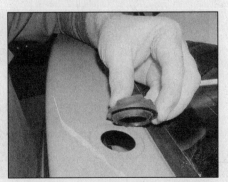

15.5 Check the rubber grommet in the tailgate before refitting the wiper motor

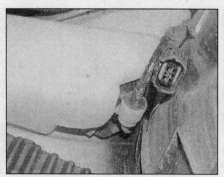

16.15 Washer fluid pump and wiring

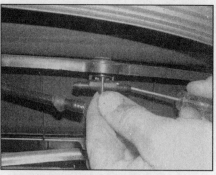

16.22 Prise out the windscreen washer nozzle with a screwdriver

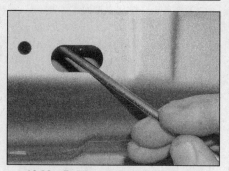

16.26a Release the nozzle from the tailgate using a screwdriver inserted through inner panel . . .

pump and position to one side **(see illustration)**.

16 Disconnect the hose from the pump and allow the fluid to drain into the container.

17 Pull the pump to the side and extract it from the reservoir.

18 If necessary, remove the grommet from the reservoir.

19 Refitting is a reversal of removal. Fill the reservoir with washer fluid with reference to *Weekly checks*.

Windscreen washer nozzle

20 Pull the rubber weatherstrip from the rear of the engine compartment, then unclip the plastic grille from the water deflector at the front of the windscreen.

21 Disconnect the tubing from the windscreen washer jets located on the water deflector.

22 Using a screwdriver, carefully release the plastic retaining tabs and remove the nozzle downwards from the water deflector **(see illustration)**.

23 Refitting is a reversal of removal.

Tailgate washer nozzle

24 On Hatchback models, carefully lever the nozzle out of the aerial base with a small screwdriver.

25 On Estate models, carefully insert a small screwdriver between the nozzle and the rubber seal. Depress the lugs and remove the nozzle from the tailgate.

26 On Zafira models, remove the top trim panel from inside the tailgate, then use a screwdriver to press the nozzle out of its location hole **(see illustrations)**.

27 Disconnect the nozzle from the hose.

28 Refitting is a reversal of removal.

Headlight washer nozzle

29 Remove the front bumper, as described in Chapter 11, and disconnect the washer tubing.

30 Pull out the clip and remove the nozzle from the front bumper.

31 If necessary, remove the adapter from the nozzle.

32 Refitting is a reversal of removal.

---

17 Radio/cassette/CD player/navigation units – removal and refitting

Note: *On models with a security-coded radio/cassette player, once the battery has been disconnected, the unit cannot be re-activated until the appropriate security code has been entered. Do not remove the unit unless the appropriate code is known. The following information applies to radio/cassette players having standard DIN fixings. Two DIN removal tools will be required for this operation.*

Radio/cassette player

1 Using an Allen key, undo the grub screws from the holes in each corner of the radio front face **(see illustration)**.

2 Insert the two DIN removal tools into the holes on each side of the radio until they are felt to engage with the retaining strips **(see illustration)**.

3 Carefully withdraw the radio/cassette player from the mounting box in the facia **(see illustrations)**.

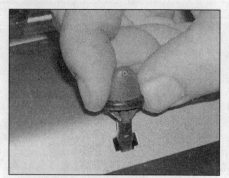

16.26b . . . then remove the tailgate washer nozzle – Zafira

17.1 Using an Allen key to unscrew the grub screws

17.2 Insert the two DIN removal tools . . .

17.3a . . . and carefully withdraw the radio/cassette player from the mounting box – Zafira

17.3b Removing the radio/cassette player – Astra

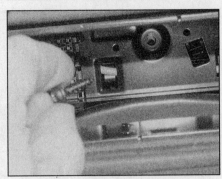

17.4a Unscrew the mounting screw . . .

17.4b . . . then release the side clips,
withdraw the mounting box . . .

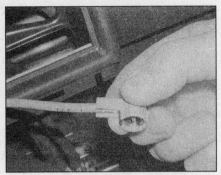

17.4c . . . and disconnect the aerial . . .

17.4d . . . and wiring plug – Zafira

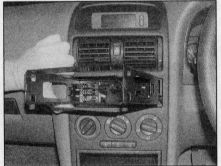

17.4e Removing the radio/cassette
mounting box – Astra

4 Undo the mounting screw then release the side clips and withdraw the box from the facia. Disconnect the wiring and aerial from the rear of the box (see illustrations).
5 Refitting is a reversal of removal, but make sure that the retaining clips are correctly engaged. On completion, enter the security code.

Navigation unit

Not NCDR 3000

6 The procedure is identical to that for the radio/cassette player described earlier.

NCDR 3000

7 Depress the release button and remove the control panel from the front of the unit.
8 Insert the two DIN removal tools into the holes on each side of the unit until they are felt to engage with the retaining strips.
9 Carefully withdraw the unit from the mounting box in the facia.
10 Undo the mounting screw then release the side clips and withdraw the box from the facia. Disconnect the wiring and aerial from the rear of the box.
11 Refitting is a reversal of removal.

CD player

12 Remove the glovebox as described in Chapter 11.
13 Unclip the CD player and mounting bracket from inside the glovebox and withdraw the wiring.
14 Undo the screws and remove the player from the mounting bracket.
15 Refitting is a reversal of removal.

Navigation control unit

16 Remove the glovebox as described in Chapter 11.
17 Unclip the navigation control unit and mounting bracket from inside the glovebox and withdraw the wiring.
18 Undo the screws and remove the navigation control unit from the mounting bracket.
19 Refitting is a reversal of removal.

18 Radio remote control switches – removal and refitting

Removal

1 Remove the driver's airbag from the steering wheel as described in Section 24.
2 Disconnect the two wiring plugs.
3 Undo the screws and remove the two remote control switches from the steering wheel.

Refitting

4 Refitting is a reversal of removal.

19 Loudspeakers – removal and refitting

Front door-mounted low frequency loudspeaker

1 Remove the front door inner trim panel, as described in Chapter 11, Section 44.
2 Undo the mounting screws and withdraw the loudspeaker from the door inner panel (see illustration).
3 Disconnect the wiring from the loudspeaker (see illustration).
4 Refitting is a reversal of removal.

Front door-mounted high frequency (tweeter) loudspeaker

5 On Astra models, carefully prise the exterior door mirror inner trim panel from the inside of the door, and remove the foam rubber insert.

19.2 Low frequency loudspeaker in the
front door

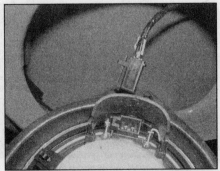

19.3 Disconnecting the wiring from the
low frequency loudspeaker

19.9 Removing the low frequency loudspeaker from the rear door

19.13 Removing the high frequency (tweeter) loudspeaker from the rear door

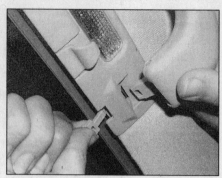

20.1 Remove the rear passenger grab handles by pulling out the plastic retainers

Disconnect the wiring, then carefully prise out the loudspeaker.

6 On Zafira models, it may be possible to remove the loudspeaker leaving the door inner trim panel *in situ*, however there may be only a short length of wire under the panel, making it difficult to disconnect and reconnect the wiring. Use a small screwdriver to carefully prise out the loudspeaker, then disconnect the wiring. If there is insufficient wiring, completely remove the inner trim panel as described in Chapter 11, Section 44.

7 Refitting is a reversal of removal.

Rear door-mounted low frequency loudspeaker

8 Remove the rear door inner trim panel, as described in Chapter 11, Section 44.

9 Undo the mounting screws and withdraw the loudspeaker from the door inner panel **(see illustration)**.

10 Disconnect the wiring from the loudspeaker.

11 Refitting is a reversal of removal.

Rear door-mounted high frequency (tweeter) loudspeaker

12 Remove the rear door inner trim panel, as described in Chapter 11, Section 44.

13 Release the retaining clips and remove the loudspeaker from the trim panel **(see illustration)**.

14 Refitting is a reversal of removal.

Rear quarter panel low frequency loudspeaker

15 Remove the inner trim panel from the rear quarter panel.

16 Undo the mounting screws, withdraw the loudspeaker, and disconnect the wiring.

17 Refitting is a reversal of removal.

20 Radio aerial – removal and refitting

Removal

1 On Hatchback models, open the tailgate then pull the rubber weatherstrip away from the headlining. Remove the rear quarter trim panels with reference to Chapter 11, Section 44, then remove both rear passenger grab handles by pulling out the plastic

retainers **(see illustration)**. The headlining is retained to the roof by Velcro – carefully pull down the rear of the headlining.

2 On Saloon models, remove the headlining.

3 On Estate and Zafira models, open the tailgate and remove the rubber weatherstrip in the vicinity of the headlining rear trim panel. Remove the interior light from the panel as described in Section 6, then release the clips using a wide-bladed screwdriver and withdraw the panel from the roof.

4 Disconnect the cable from the aerial. Where applicable, also disconnect the GPS cable, telephone cable, and power supply wiring.

5 Unscrew the nut and remove the aerial from the roof **(see illustration)**.

6 If the aerial cable between the aerial and

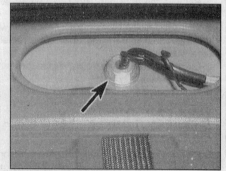

20.5 Aerial retaining nut on the roof

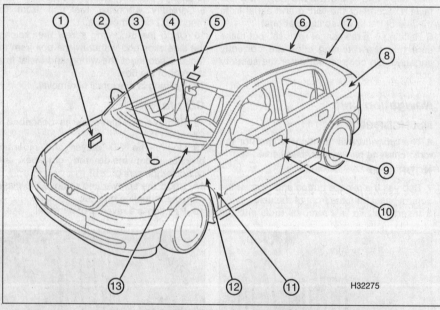

21.2 Anti-theft warning system

1 ATWS control unit including central door locking system (CDLS)
2 Bonnet contact
3 LED in hazard warning switch
4 Ignition lock
5 Ultrasonic sensor in interior lamp
6 ATWS rear screen heating – glass breakage detector

7 Luggage compartment lid/tailgate switch
8 Load/luggage compartment lamp
9 Driver's door lock cylinder
10 Rear left-hand door courtesy light switch
11 Front left-hand door courtesy light switch
12 Power sounder
13 ATWS Horn

radio/cassette is to be removed, it will be necessary to remove the centre console and side trim panels with reference to Chapter 11.

Refitting

7 Refitting is a reversal of removal, but tighten the nut to the specified torque.

21 Anti-theft alarm system and engine immobiliser – general information

1 All models have an engine immobiliser which effectively prevents the engine from being started except when using the original electronically-encoded ignition key. The system consists of the ignition key with integral transponder, and an electronic sensor mounted on the steering lock.

2 The anti-theft alarm system, where fitted, monitors the doors, bootlid or tailgate, bonnet, the passenger compartment, vehicle tilt, and the ignition system **(see illustration)**. Movement within the passenger compartment is monitored by an ultrasonic sensor located at the top of each B-pillar. Vehicle tilt is monitored so that the alarm is set off if the vehicle is raised (for example to remove the roadwheels). The anti-theft alarm system horn is located on the left-hand side of the bulkhead, and additionally a power-sounder horn is fitted beneath the liner at the rear of the left-hand wheelarch (LHD models) or right-hand wheelarch (RHD models). On Estate and Zafira models, a glass breakage detector is fitted to the luggage compartment rear side windows.

Removal

3 Before removing any component of the anti-theft or immobiliser systems, disconnect the battery as described in Chapter 5A.

Immobiliser/transponder unit

4 To remove the immobiliser/transponder unit, remove the steering wheel and column shrouds as described in Chapter 10, then proceed as follows. On models with an immobiliser/transponder **without** catch lugs, disconnect the wiring, then unclip the unit

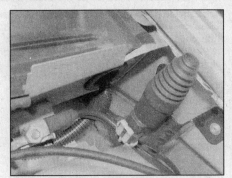

21.5 Anti-theft warning alarm system bonnet contact

from the ignition lock housing. On models with an immobiliser/transponder **with** catch lugs, remove the ignition lock cylinder as described in Section 4 of this Chapter, then unclip the unit from the ignition lock housing and disconnect the wiring. **Note:** *Note that if the immobiliser/transponder unit is renewed, it must be programmed by a Vauxhall dealer using specialist equipment.*

Bonnet contact

5 To remove the bonnet contact, undo the two mounting screws then lift the contact and disconnect the wiring **(see illustration)**.

System warning horn

6 To remove the system warning horn, remove the water deflector from the bulkhead, then unscrew the mounting nut and disconnect the wiring.

Power-sounder horn

7 To remove the power-sounder horn, first remove the relevant front wheelarch liner (Chapter 11), then disconnect the wiring and unbolt the horn together with its bracket from the inner wing panel.

Door contact

8 To remove a door contact (courtesy light) switch, refer to Section 4.

ATWS (anti-theft warning system)/central locking control unit

9 To remove the ATWS (anti-theft warning system)/central locking control unit, undo the

21.9 The ATWS (anti-theft warning system)/ Central locking control unit is located at the bottom of the right-hand A-pillar

single screw and remove the trim panel from the bottom of the right-hand A-pillar, then remove the footwell side trim panel. Disconnect the wiring, then unscrew the two mounting nuts and remove the control unit **(see illustration)**.

Central locking components

10 Refer to Chapter 11 for the removal and refitting of central locking components.

Remote control battery

11 To renew the remote control battery in the key fob, refer to Chapter 1 **(see illustrations)**.

Refitting

12 Refitting of the components is a reversal of the removal procedure. Any faults with the system should be referred to a Vauxhall dealer.

22 Speedometer sensor – general information

All models are fitted with an electronic speedometer sensor. This device measures the rotational speed of the transmission final drive or ABS wheel sensor (according to model) and converts the information into an electronic signal, which is then sent to the speedometer module in the instrument panel.

Refer to Chapter 7 for details of the removal and refitting procedure of the speed sensor.

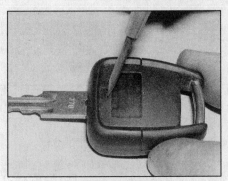

21.11a Use a small screwdriver to release the plastic catch . . .

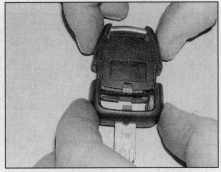

21.11b . . . then slide the fob directly from the key . . .

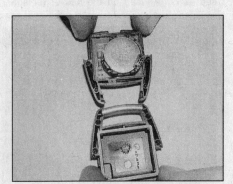

21.11c . . . for access to the battery

23 Airbag system – general information, precautions and system de-activation

General information

A driver's airbag, located on the steering wheel centre pad, is fitted as standard equipment on all models. A passenger's front airbag, front seat side airbags, and side curtain airbags (driver and passenger) may be fitted as an option. The passenger's airbag is located on the crossbar beneath the facia. The side airbags are located in the outer edge of the front seat backrests, and in the roof headlining.

The system is armed only when the ignition is switched on, however, a reserve power source maintains a power supply to the system in the event of a break in the main electrical supply. The system is activated by a 'g' sensor (deceleration sensor), incorporated in the electronic control unit. Note that the electronic control unit also controls the front seat belt tensioners. The airbags are inflated by gas generators, which force the bags out from their locations. The front airbags are only deployed in the event of a frontal impact at speeds in excess of 20 mph which occur within 30° each side of the vehicle centre line, and the side airbags are only deployed in the event of an impact on their respective sides. The front seat belt tensioners are deployed in the event of both front and rear impacts.

In the event of an accident which triggers the front airbags located in the steering wheel and facia, both the driver's and passenger's airbags must be renewed, however, the seat side airbags and seat belt tensioners can be deployed a maximum of three times before it is necessary to renew them. The airbag system control unit stores the number of deployments in its memory, and this can be read by Vauxhall technicians using specialist equipment.

On models fitted with a passenger airbag, the passenger seat incorporates a sensor mat. The passenger airbag is deactivated when the passenger seat is unoccupied. The system is also deactivated if a Vauxhall child seat is being used on the passenger seat, because transponders in the child seat are recognised by an antenna system in the passenger seat. The system can also detect if the child seat is fitted incorrectly (eg, the wrong way round), and a flashing warning light is illuminated in the front interior light.

In the event of a fault occurring in the airbag system, the warning light will illuminate on the instrument panel, and the system will need to be checked by a Vauxhall dealer.

Precautions

⚠️ **Warning: The following precautions must be observed when working on vehicles equipped with an airbag system, to prevent the possibility of personal injury.**

General precautions

The following precautions **must** be observed when carrying out work on a vehicle equipped with an airbag.

a) Do not disconnect the battery with the engine running.

b) Before carrying out any work in the vicinity of the airbag, removing of any of the airbag components, or welding any part of the vehicle, de-activate the system as described in the following sub-Section.

c) Do not attempt to test any of the airbag system circuits using test meters or any other test equipment.

d) If the airbag warning light comes on, or any fault in the system is suspected, consult a Vauxhall dealer without delay. **Do not** attempt to carry out fault diagnosis, or any dismantling of the components.

Precautions to be taken when handling an airbag

a) Transport the airbag by itself, bag upward.

b) Do not put your arms around the airbag.

c) Carry the airbag close to the body, bag outward.

d) Do not drop the airbag or expose it to impacts.

e) Do not attempt to dismantle the airbag unit.

f) Do not connect any form of electrical equipment to any part of the airbag circuit.

g) Do not allow any solvents or cleaning agents to contact the airbag assembly. The unit must be cleaned using only a damp cloth.

Precautions to be taken when storing an airbag unit

a) Store the unit in a cupboard with the airbag upward.

b) Do not expose the airbag to temperatures above 90° C.

c) Do not expose the airbag to flames.

d) Do not attempt to dispose of the airbag – consult a Vauxhall dealer.

e) Never refit an airbag which is known to be faulty or damaged.

De-activation of airbag system

The system must be de-activated as follows, before carrying out any work on the airbag components or surrounding area.

a) Switch off the ignition.

b) Remove the ignition key.

c) Switch off all electrical equipment.

d) Disconnect the battery negative lead (see Chapter 5A).

e) Insulate the battery negative terminal and the end of the battery negative lead to prevent any possibility of contact.

f) Wait for at least one minute before carrying out any further work. This will allow the system capacitor to discharge.

24 Airbag system components – removal and refitting

⚠️ **Warning: Refer to the precautions given in Section 23 before attempting to carry out work on the airbag components.**

Driver's airbag unit

1 The driver's airbag unit is an integral part of the steering wheel centre pad. First de-activate the airbag system as described in Section 23.

2 Set the front wheels in the straight-ahead position, then lock the column in position after removing the ignition key.

3 Unscrew and remove the two screws from the rear of the steering wheel and carefully lift the airbag/horn-push from the steering wheel **(see illustrations)**.

4 Disconnect the wiring and remove the airbag **(see illustration)**. Position the airbag in a safe place where it cannot be tampered

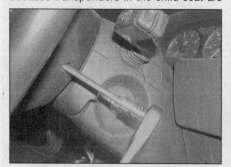

24.3a Remove the two screws . . .

24.3b . . . and carefully lift the airbag/horn-push from the steering wheel

24.4 Disconnecting the wiring from the airbag

24.8a Top view of the passenger's airbag (facia panel removed)

24.8b Bottom view of the passenger's airbag, showing mounting bolts

24.9 Passenger's airbag wiring

with, making sure that the padded side is facing upwards.

5 Refitting is a reversal of removal, but make sure that the wiring connector is securely reconnected and tighten the retaining screws to the specified torque.

Passenger's airbag unit

6 The passenger's airbag unit is located on the crossbar beneath the facia panel. First de-activate the airbag system as described in Section 23.

7 Remove the glovebox as described in Chapter 11.

8 Using a Torx key, unscrew the mounting bolts and remove the airbag unit from the bracket on the crossbar **(see illustrations)**.

9 Disconnect the wiring and remove the airbag unit from inside the vehicle **(see illustration)**. Note that the bottom of the unit is shaped to locate in the mounting bracket holes.

10 Refitting is a reversal of removal, but make sure that the wiring connector is securely reconnected and tighten the retaining screws to the specified torque.

Side airbag unit

 Warning: Removal and refitting of the side curtain airbags, located in the vehicle headlining should be entrusted to a Vauxhall dealer.

11 The side airbag is located in the front seat backrest. First de-activate the airbag system as described in Section 23.

12 Unclip and remove the upholstery from the back of the seat.

13 Disconnect the wiring from the airbag.

14 Unscrew the three securing nuts and remove the airbag from the seat backrest. **Note:** *The manufacturers recommend that the nuts are renewed whenever removed as the integral washers are self-locking.*

15 Refitting is a reversal of removal, but make sure that the wiring connector is securely reconnected and tighten the retaining nuts to the specified torque.

Airbag contact unit

16 Remove the driver's airbag unit as described earlier in this Section.

17 Remove the steering wheel as described in Chapter 10. Make sure that the front wheels are pointing straight-ahead, and that the steering is locked with the ignition key removed.

18 Remove the steering column shrouds with reference to Chapter 10, Section 18. Recover the ignition key position indicator.

19 Pull out the locking plate, then disconnect the wiring plug from the rear of the contact unit **(see illustration)**.

20 Release the four rear clips and remove the contact unit from the top of the column **(see illustration)**. **Note:** *Make sure that the contact unit halves remain in their central position with the arrows aligned at the bottom. The unit automatically locks in its central position, however, if necessary apply tape to the halves to hold them.*

21 Before refitting the contact unit, if the centre position has been lost or if a new unit is

being fitted, determine the centre position as follows. Depress the detent on top of the unit and carefully turn the centre part of the unit anti-clockwise until resistance is felt. Now turn it 2.5 turns clockwise and align the arrows on the centre part and outer edge.

22 If a new unit is fitted, first remove the transport clip.

23 Locate the contact unit on the top of the steering column making sure that the guide pins locate in the holes provided. Press the unit in until the clips engage. **Note:** *The clips must not be damaged in any way. If they are, the unit must be renewed.*

24 Reconnect the wiring and push in the locking plate.

25 Refit the ignition key position indicator, then refit the steering column shrouds and tighten the securing screws with reference to Chapter 10, Section 18.

26 Refit the steering wheel as described in Chapter 10.

27 Refit the driver's airbag unit as described earlier.

Electronic control unit

28 De-activate the airbag system as described in Section 23.

29 Remove the centre console as described in Chapter 11. On Zafira models, also remove the gear lever assembly with reference to Chapter 7, Section 4 (the electronic control unit is located beneath the assembly) **(see illustration)**.

30 Disconnect the wiring from the control unit

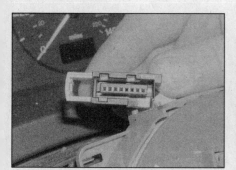

24.19 Disconnecting the wiring from the airbag contact unit

24.20 Removing the airbag contact unit from the top of the steering column

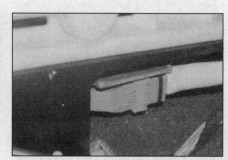

24.29 The airbag control unit is located beneath the gear lever assembly on Zafira models

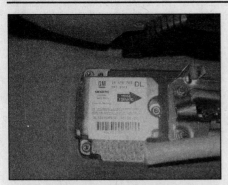

24.30 On Astra models the airbag control unit is located beneath the rear of the centre console

(see illustration), then unscrew the mounting nuts and remove the unit from inside the vehicle. Note that the arrow on top of the unit points towards the front of the vehicle, however the three mounting nuts are arranged so that it is impossible to fit it incorrectly.

31 Refitting is a reversal of removal but tighten the mounting nuts to the specified torque. **Note:** *Note that if the electronic control unit is renewed, it must be programmed by a Vauxhall dealer using specialist equipment.*

Side airbag sensor

32 The side airbag sensors are located inside the front doors. First, de-activate the airbag system as described in Section 23.

33 Remove the front door inner trim panel as described in Chapter 11, Section 44.

34 Pull back the water membrane for access to the sensor.

35 Disconnect the wiring, then unscrew the mounting bolts and remove the sensor.

36 Refitting is a reversal of removal but tighten the mounting bolts securely.

Front passenger seat sensor mat

37 It is recommended that a Vauxhall dealer carry out this work, as the upholstery has to be removed, and the position of the mat is critical.

VAUXHALL ASTRA 1998 to 2000   Diagram 1

Key to symbols

Bulb

Switch

Multiple contact
switch (ganged)

Fuse/fusible link

F24

Resistor

Variable resistor

Item no.

15

Pump/motor

M

Earth and location
(via lead)

E1

Gauge/meter

Diode

Light emitting diode
(LED)

Internal connection
(connecting wires)

Wire splice or soldered joint

Solenoid actuator

Plug and socket connector

Connections to other
circuits. Direction of
arrow denotes current
flow.

A   **Diagram 3, Arrow A**
High beam
warning light

Wire colour
(Red wire/white tracer)   Ro/Ws

Box shape denotes part
of a larger component.
Terminal identified by either standard
termination (bold *italic*) or by
connector number (plain text).

30   4

30   Terminal identification
(i.e. battery +ve)
4   Connector pin number

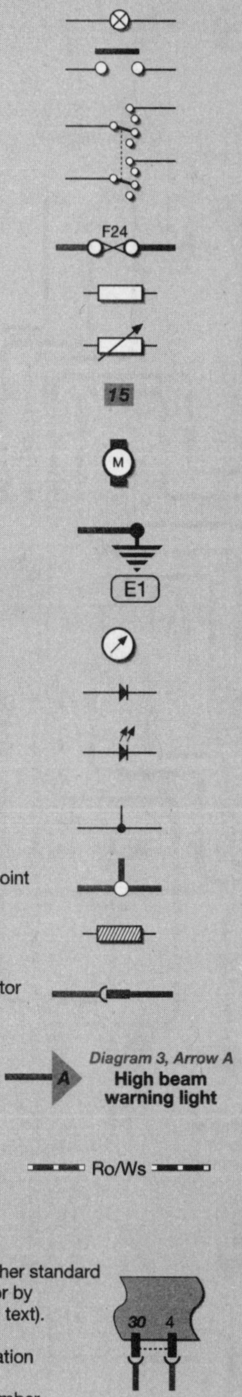

Earth locations

E1	Battery ground strap	E7	Engine (electronic)
E2	Engine ground strap	E8	Engine distribution
E3	Ignition coil earth	E9	Rear panel
E4	"A" pillar	E10	Tailgate
E5	Steering column	E11	Heater blower
E6	Transmission tunnel		

Key to circuits

Diagram 1	Information for wiring diagrams
Diagram 2	Starting, charging, airbag and typical radio/CD
Diagram 3	X17DTL & X20DTL engine management system
Diagram 4	X17DTL & X20DTL engine management system cont. and electric windows
Diagram 5	Y17DT engine management system
Diagram 6	Y17DT engine management system cont and engine cooling
Diagram 7	Y20DTH engine management system
Diagram 8	Y20DTH engine management system cont and ABS and speed sensor (non ABS models)
Diagram 9	Wash/wipe and auxiliary heating
Diagram 10	Front lights
Diagram 11	Fog, tail, reversing and direction indicator lights
Diagram 12	Number plate, interior lights, heated rear window, cigarette lighter, brake lights
Diagram 13	Multi-timer
Diagram 14	Glovebox light, horn, sunroof and central locking
Diagram 15	Power steering, exterior door mirrors, cruise control and heating
Diagram 16	Typical air con. and triple info display
Diagram 17	Multi info display
Diagram 18	Instrument display

Engine fuse box

Fuse	Rating				
F1	60A	F5	60A	F60	110A
F2	60A	F6	20A		
F3	60A	F7	80A		
F4	80A	F8	80A		

Main fuse box

Fuse	Rating	Circuit protected	Fuse	Rating	
F2	30A	Air conditioning	F23	10A	ABS and power steering
F3	40A	Heated rear window	F24	10A	LH dipped beam, headlight adjustment
F6	10A	RH dipped beam, headlight adjustment	F25	10A	LH parking, tail and number plate lights
F7	10A	RH parking, tail and number plate lights	F26	10A	LH main beam
F8	10A	RH main beam	F28	7.5A	Interior light
F9	30A	Headlamp wash	F29	10A	Hazard warning, interior light
F10	15A	Horn	F30	30A	Sunroof
F11	20A	Central locking	F33	20A	Trailer
F12	15A	Front fog lights	F34	20A	CD player, radio, information display and GPS
F13	7.5A	Information display			
F14	30A	Windscreen wipers	F35	10A	Engine cooling, air con.
F15	7.5A	Electric windows, sunroof and mirrors	F36	20A	Cigarette lighter
			F38	10A	Stop lights, info. display and cruise control
F16	10A	Rear fog lights			
F17	30A	Electric windows	F39	7.5A	Engine cooling and air con.
F18	7.5A	Number plate lights and headlight range adjustment	F40	7.5A	Engine cooling and air con.
			F41	10A	Heated mirrors
F20	30A	Electric windows	F50	40A	Engine cooling
F21	7.5A	Radio	F52	40A	Engine cooling
F22	15A	Hazard warning, info. display, indicators and trip computer			

MTS
H32207

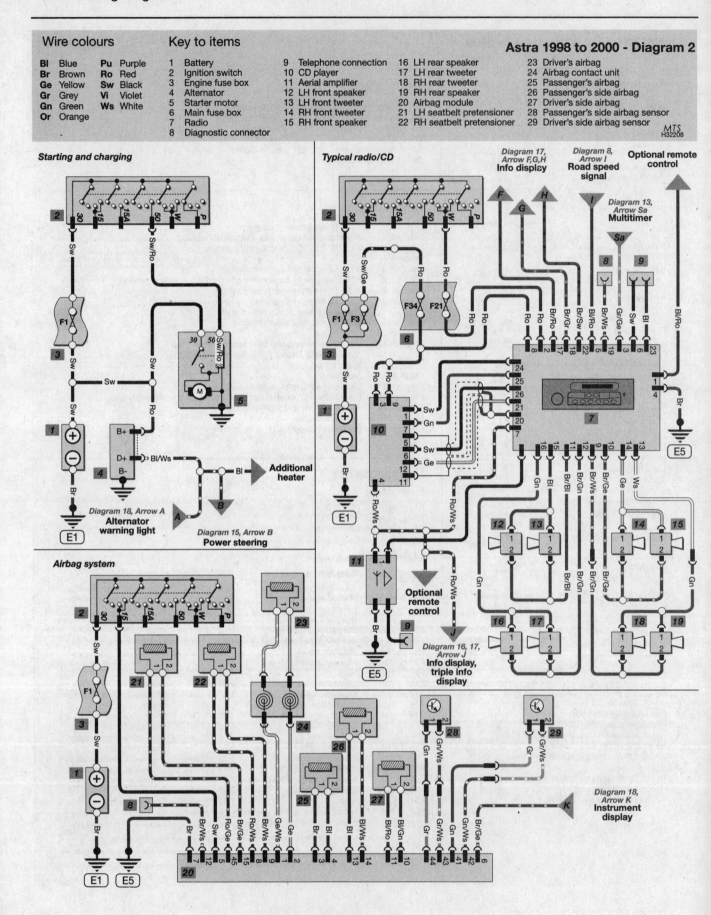

Wire colours

Bl	Blue	Pu	Purple
Br	Brown	Ro	Red
Ge	Yellow	Sw	Black
Gr	Grey	Vi	Violet
Gn	Green	Ws	White
Or	Orange		

Key to items

1 Battery
2 Ignition switch
3 Engine fuse box
4 Alternator
5 Starter motor
6 Main fuse box
7 Radio
8 Diagnostic connector

9   Telephone connection
10 CD player
11 Aerial amplifier
12 LH front speaker
13 LH front tweeter
14 RH front tweeter
15 RH front speaker

16 LH rear speaker
17 LH rear tweeter
18 RH rear tweeter
19 RH rear speaker
20 Airbag module
21 LH seatbelt pretensioner
22 RH seatbelt pretensioner

23 Driver's airbag
24 Airbag contact unit
25 Passenger's airbag
26 Passenger's side airbag
27 Driver's side airbag
28 Passenger's side airbag sensor
29 Driver's side airbag sensor

Astra 1998 to 2000 - Diagram 2

MTS
H32208

Starting and charging

Typical radio/CD

Diagram 17, Arrow F,G,H
Info display

Diagram 8, Arrow I
Road speed signal

Optional remote control

Diagram 13, Arrow Sa
Multitimer

Diagram 18, Arrow A
Alternator warning light

Diagram 15, Arrow B
Power steering

Additional heater

Airbag system

Optional remote control

Diagram 16, 17, Arrow J
Info display, triple info display

Diagram 18, Arrow K
Instrument display

Wire colours

Bl	Blue	**Pu**	Purple
Br	Brown	**Ro**	Red
Ge	Yellow	**Sw**	Black
Gr	Grey	**Vi**	Violet
Gn	Green	**Ws**	White
Or	Orange		

Key to items

1 Battery
2 Ignition switch
3 Engine fuse box
6 Main fuse box
30 Diesel control unit
31 Engine control unit relay
32 Filter pre-heating relay

33 Manifold crossover solenoid valve
34 Glow plug control unit
35 Glow plug
36 Filter heater
37 Exhaust gas recirculation solenoid valve

38 Boost pressure regulation solenoid valve
39 Air mass meter
40 Injection pump control unit
41 Boost pressure sensor
42 Engine oil temperature sensor

43 Coolant temperature sensor
44 Crankshaft sensor
45 Throttle potentiometer

Astra 1998 to 2000 - Diagram 3

Note: prefix 1/ = X59 multi plug
prefix 2/ = X60 multi plug

MTS
H32209

Engine management system X17DTL & X20DTL engine

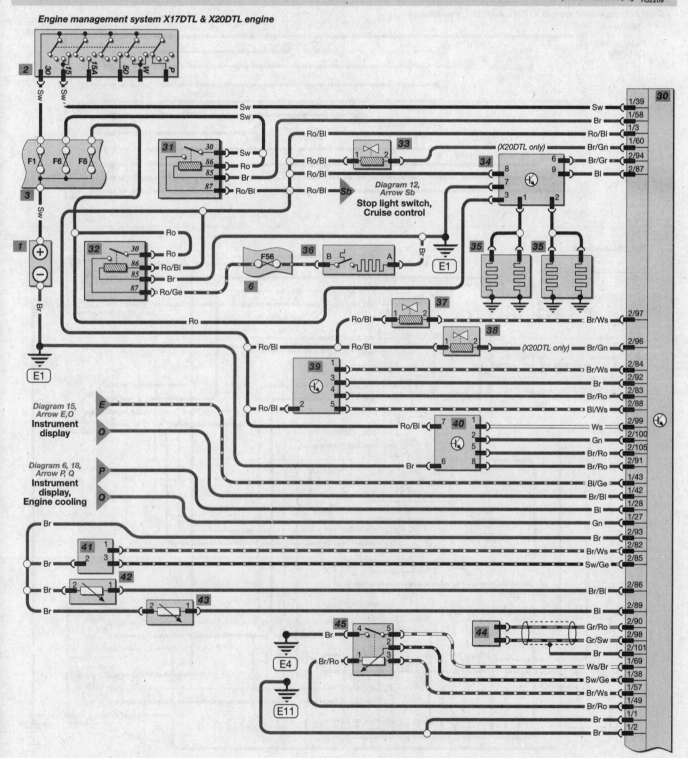

Wire colours

Bl	Blue	Pu	Purple
Br	Brown	Ro	Red
Ge	Yellow	Sw	Black
Gr	Grey	Vi	Violet
Gn	Green	Ws	White
Or	Orange		

Key to items

1 Battery
2 Ignition switch
3 Engine fuse box
6 Main fuse box
30 Diesel control unit
46 Drivers electric window switch unit
47 Passenger electric window switch

48 LH rear electric window switch
49 RH rear electric window switch
50 Drivers electric window motor
51 Passenger electric window motor
52 LH rear electric window motor
53 RH rear electric window motor

Astra 1998 to 2000 - Diagram 4

Note: prefix 1/ = X59 multi plug
prefix 2/ = X60 multi plug

MTS
H32210

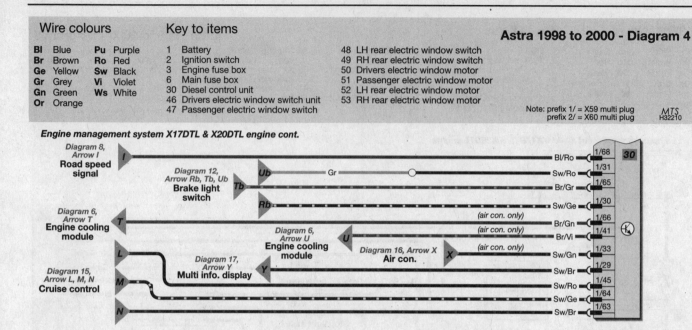

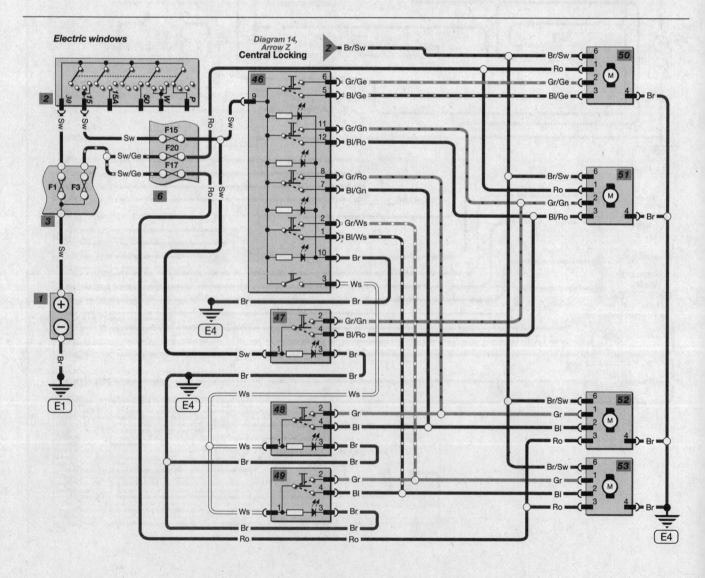

Wire colours

Bl Blue	**Pu** Purple
Br Brown	**Ro** Red
Ge Yellow	**Sw** Black
Gr Grey	**Vi** Violet
Gn Green	**Ws** White
Or Orange	

Key to items

1 Battery
2 Ignition switch
3 Engine fuse box
6 Main fuse box
30 Diesel control unit
31 Engine control unit relay
32 Filter pre-heating relay

34 Glow plug control unit
35 Glow plug
36 Filter heater
37 Exhaust gas recirculation
   solenoid valve
38 Boost pressure regulation
   solenoid valve

39 Air mass meter
40 Injection pump control unit
43 Coolant temperature sensor
44 Crankshaft sensor
45 Throttle potentiometer
54 Solenoid spill valve
55 Diesel pump

56 Spill valve relay
57 Injection start sensor
58 Injection pump position sensor
59 Fuel temperature sensor

Note: prefix 1/ = X73 multi plug
      prefix 2/ = X74 multi plug

MTS
H32211

Astra 1998 to 2000 - Diagram 5

Engine management system Y17DT engine

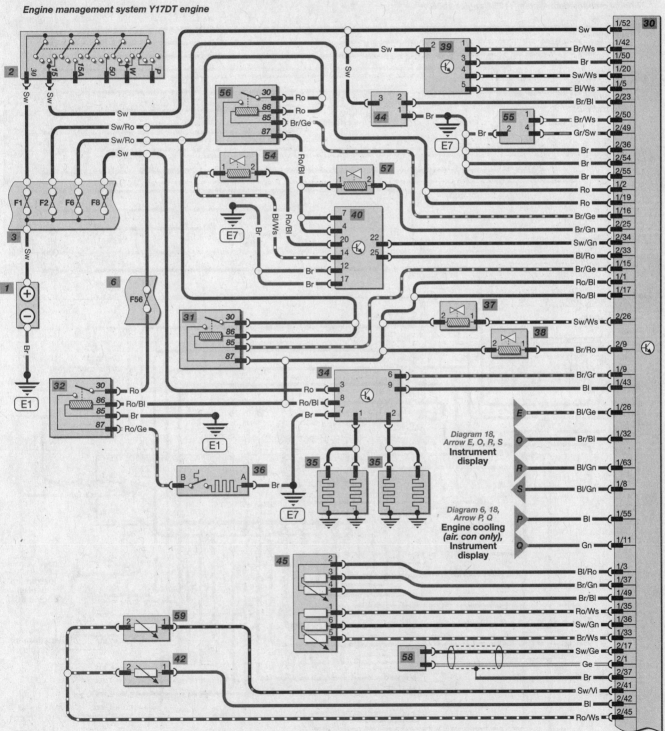

Wire colours

Bl	Blue	Pu	Purple
Br	Brown	Ro	Red
Ge	Yellow	Sw	Black
Gr	Grey	Vi	Violet
Gn	Green	Ws	White
Or	Orange		

Key to items

1 Battery
2 Ignition switch
3 Engine fuse box
6 Main fuse box
30 Diesel control unit
41 Boost pressure sensor
60 Athmospheric pressure sensor

61 Radiator blower motor
62 Radiator blower preresistor
63 Air con. compressor clutch
64 Air con. pressure sensor
65 Engine cooling control unit

Astra 1998 to 2000 - Diagram 6

Note: prefix 1/ = X73 multi plug
prefix 2/ = X74 multi plug
prefix 3/ = X63 multi plug
prefix 4/ = X64 multi plug

MTS
H32212

Engine management system Y17DT engine cont.

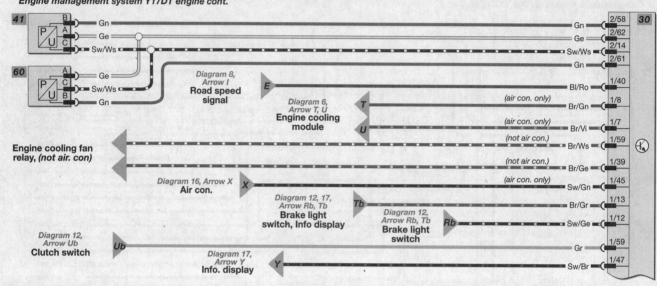

Engine cooling

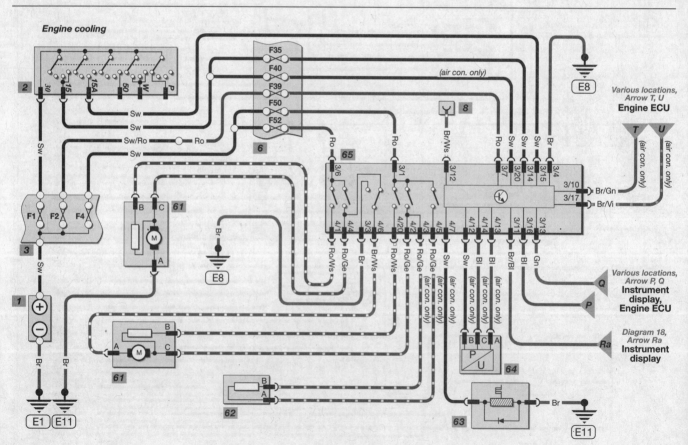

Wire colours

Bl	Blue	**Pu**	Purple
Br	Brown	**Ro**	Red
Ge	Yellow	**Sw**	Black
Gr	Grey	**Vi**	Violet
Gn	Green	**Ws**	White
Or	Orange		

Key to items

1   Battery
2   Ignition switch
3   Engine fuse box
6   Main fuse box
30 Diesel control unit
31 Engine control unit relay
32 Filter pre-heating relay

33 Manifold crossover
    solenoid valve
34 Glow plug control unit
35 Glow plug
36 Filter heater
37 Exhaust gas recirculation
    solenoid valve

38 Boost pressure regulation
    solenoid valve
39 Air mass meter
40 Injection pump control unit
41 Boost pressure sensor
42 Engine oil temperature
    sensor

43 Coolant temperature sensor
44 Crankshaft sensor
45 Throttle potentiometer

Astra 1998 to 2000 - Diagram 7

Note: prefix 1/ = X59 multi plug
prefix 2/ = X60 multi plug

MTS
H32213

Engine management system Y20DTH engine

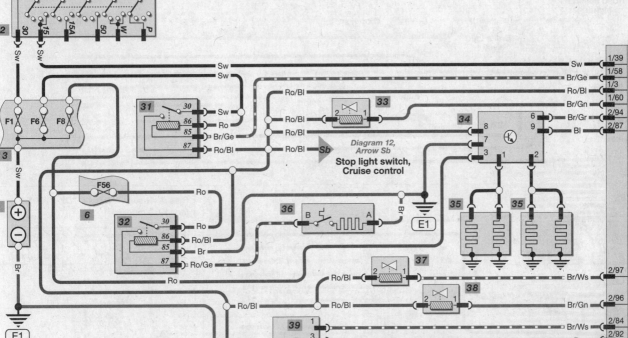
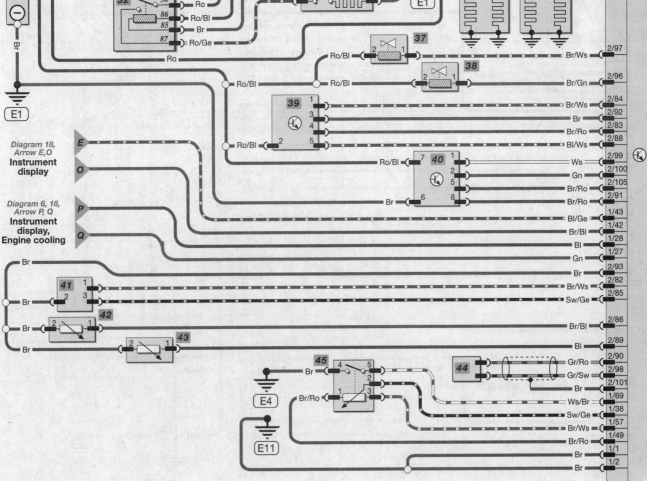

Wire colours

Bl	Blue	Pu	Purple
Br	Brown	Ro	Red
Ge	Yellow	Sw	Black
Gr	Grey	Vi	Violet
Gn	Green	Ws	White
Or	Orange		

Key to items

1 Battery
2 Ignition switch
3 Engine fuse box
6 Main fuse box
8 Diagnostic connector
30 Diesel control unit

66 ABS module
67 LH front wheel speed sensor
68 RH front wheel speed sensor
69 LH rear wheel speed sensor
70 RH rear wheel speed sensor
71 Vehicle speed sensor

72 Signal converter module

Astra 1998 to 2000 - Diagram 8

Note: prefix 1/ = X59 multi plug
prefix 2/ = X60 multi plug

MTS
H32214

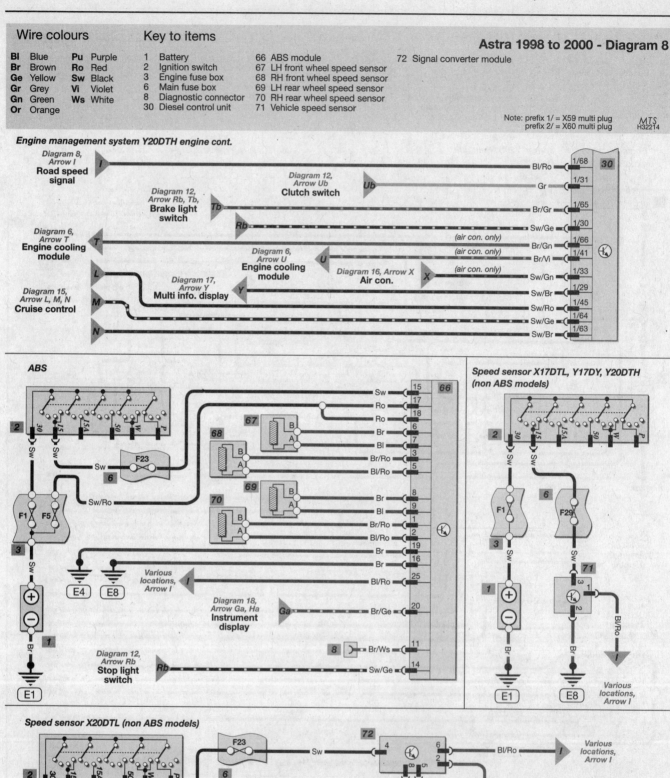

Engine management system Y20DTH engine cont.

Diagram 8, Arrow I **Road speed signal** — I — Bl/Ro — 1/68 — 30

Diagram 12, Arrow Ub **Clutch switch** — Ub — Gr — 1/31

Diagram 12, Arrow Rb, Tb, **Brake light switch** — Tb — Br/Gr — 1/65 / Rb — Sw/Ge — 1/30

Diagram 6, Arrow T **Engine cooling module** — T — (air con. only) — Br/Gn — 1/66

Diagram 6, Arrow U **Engine cooling module** — U — (air con. only) — Br/Vi — 1/41

Diagram 16, Arrow X **Air con.** — X — (air con. only) — Sw/Gn — 1/33

Diagram 17, Arrow Y **Multi info. display** — Y — Sw/Br — 1/29

Diagram 15, Arrow L, M, N **Cruise control** — L, M, N — Sw/Ro — 1/45 / Sw/Ge — 1/64 / Sw/Br — 1/63

ABS

		66
Sw	15	
Ro	17	
Ro	18	
Br	6	
Bl	7	
Br/Ro	3	
Bl/Ro	5	
Br	8	
Bl	9	
Br/Ro	1	
Bl/Ro	2	
Br	19	
Br	16	
Bl/Ro	25	
Br/Ge	20	
Br/Ws	11	
Sw/Ge	14	

67 (B/A)
68 (B/A)
69 (B/A)
70 (B/A)

F23 — 6
F1 F5
Sw / Sw/Ro
2 — 30 / 15 / 15A / 50 / W / P
3 — Sw
+ / − — 1 — Br — E1
E4 E8

Various locations, Arrow I — I

Diagram 18, Arrow Ga, Ha **Instrument display** — Ga

8 — Br/Ws

Diagram 12, Arrow Rb **Stop light switch** — Rb — Sw/Ge — 14

Speed sensor X17DTL, Y17DY, Y20DTH (non ABS models)

2 — 30 / 15 / 15A / 50 / W / P
F1 — 6 — F29
3 — Sw / Sw
+ / − — 1 / 71
Br / Br
E1 E8

3 / 2 / 1 — Bl/Ro — I

Various locations, Arrow I

Speed sensor X20DTL (non ABS models)

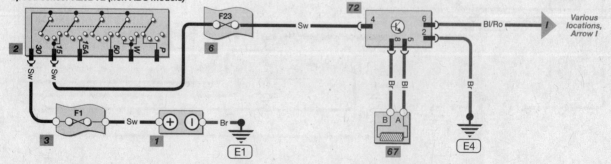

2 — 30 / 15 / 15A / 50 / W / P
Sw / Sw
F23 — 6 — Sw — 72
4 / 8 / 5 / 2 / 6

3 — F1 — Sw — + / I — Br — E1
Br / Bl — 67 (B/A)
Br — E4

Bl/Ro — I — *Various locations, Arrow I*

Wire colours

Bl	Blue	**Pu**	Purple
Br	Brown	**Pk**	Pink
Ge	Yellow	**Ro**	Red
Gr	Grey	**Sw**	Black
Gn	Green	**Vi**	Violet
Or	Orange	**Ws**	White

Key to items

1 Battery
2 Ignition switch
3 Engine fuse box
73 Headlight washer relay
74 Headlight washer pump
75 Wash/wipe switch
76 Windscreen washer pump
77 Windscreen wiper relay
78 Windscreen wiper motor
79 Rear wiper relay
80 Rear wiper motor
81 Auxiliary heater

Astra 1998 to 2000 - Diagram 9

MTS
H32215

Wash/Wipe

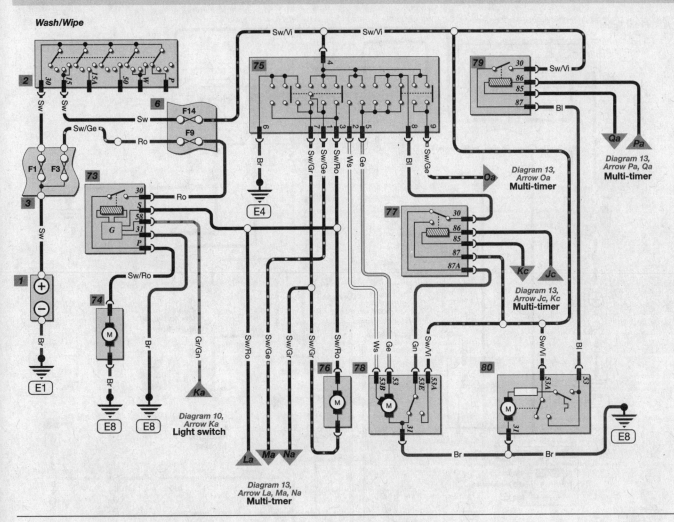

Auxiliary heating

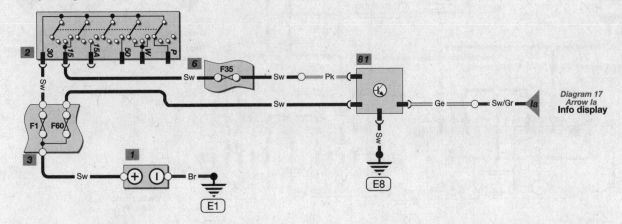

Wire colours

Bl	Blue	**Pu**	Purple
Br	Brown	**Ro**	Red
Ge	Yellow	**Sw**	Black
Gr	Grey	**Vi**	Violet
Gn	Green	**Ws**	White
Or	Orange		

Key to items

1 Battery
2 Ignition switch
3 Engine fuse box
6 Main fuse box
82 Main beam switch
83 Main beam relay
84 Light switch
85 LH headlight leveller
86 RH headlight leveller
87 LH front lights
  a) direction indicator
  b) main beam
  c) dipped beam
  d) side lights
  e) fog lights
88 RH front lights (as 87)
89 Trailer connection

Astra 1998 to 2000 - Diagram 10

MTS
H32216

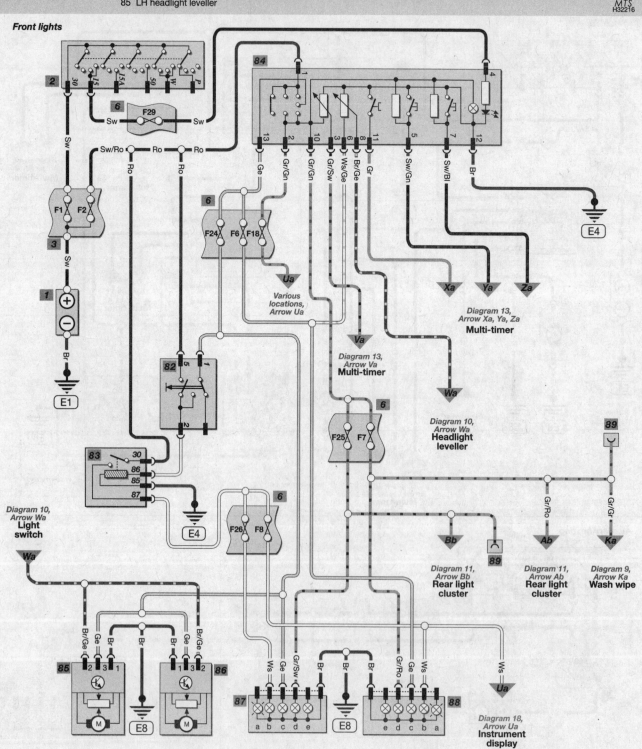

Wire colours

Bl	Blue	Pu	Purple
Br	Brown	Ro	Red
Ge	Yellow	Sw	Black
Gr	Grey	Vi	Violet
Gn	Green	Ws	White
Or	Orange		

Key to items

1 Battery
2 Ignition switch
3 Engine fuse box
6 Main fuse box
87 LH front light cluster
  a) direction indicator
  b) main beam
  c) dipped beam
  d) side lights
88 RH front light cluster (as 87)
89 Trailer connection
90 Front fog light relay
91 Rear fog light relay
92 LH rear light cluster
  a) direction indicator

  b) stop light
  c) tail light
  d) reversing light
  e) fog light
93 RH rear light cluster (as 92)
94 Trailer socket switch
95 Direction indicator relay
96 LH indicator side repeater

97 RH indicator side repeater
98 Reversing light switch
166 LH front foglight
167 RH front foglight

Astra 1998 to 2000 - Diagram 11

MTS
H32217

Fog lights, tail lights

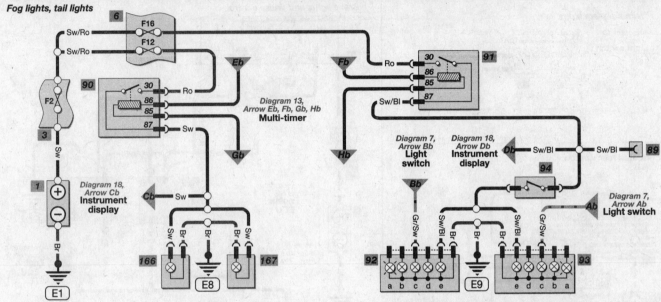

Direction indicators

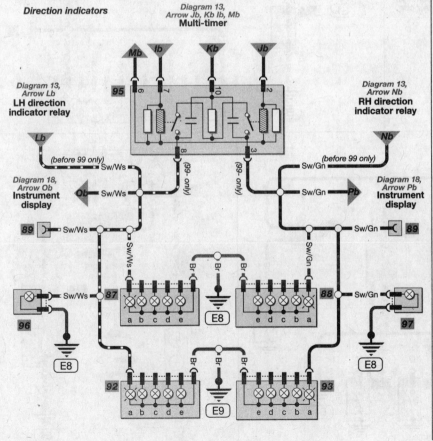

Reversing lights

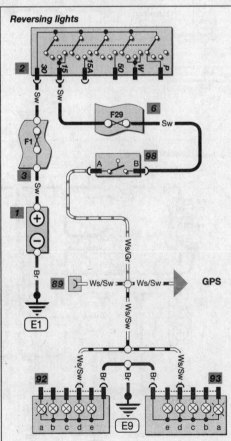

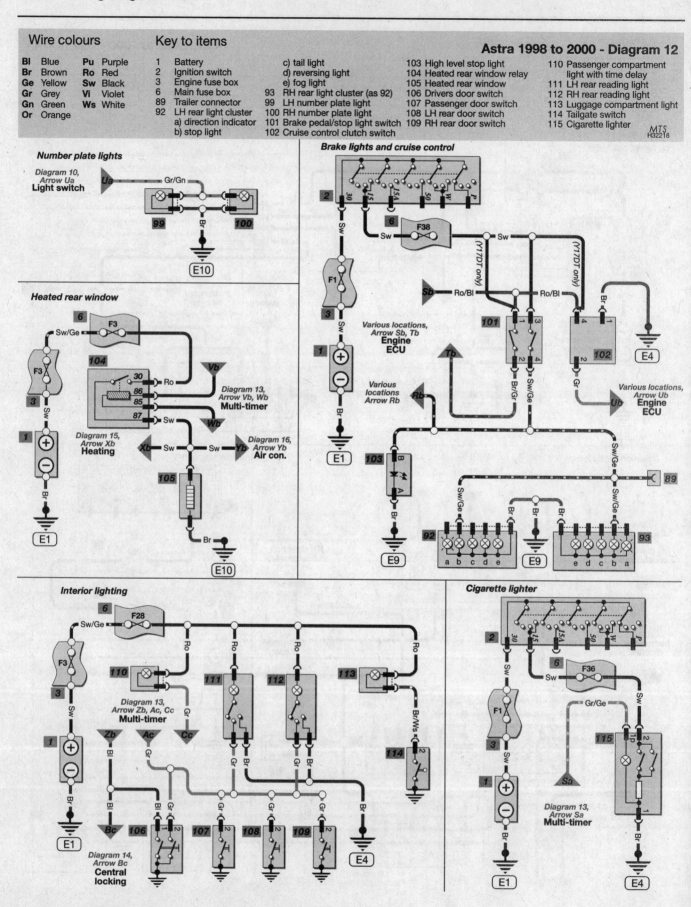

Wire colours

Bl	Blue	Pu	Purple
Br	Brown	Ro	Red
Ge	Yellow	Sw	Black
Gr	Grey	Vi	Violet
Gn	Green	Ws	White
Or	Orange		

Key to items

1 Battery
2 Ignition switch
3 Engine fuse box
6 Main fuse box
89 Trailer connector
92 LH rear light cluster
  a) direction indicator
  b) stop light

c) tail light
d) reversing light
e) fog light
93 RH rear light cluster (as 92)
99 LH number plate light
100 RH number plate light
101 Brake pedal/stop light switch
102 Cruise control clutch switch

103 High level stop light
104 Heated rear window relay
105 Heated rear window
106 Drivers door switch
107 Passenger door switch
108 LH rear door switch
109 RH rear door switch

110 Passenger compartment
    light with time delay
111 LH rear reading light
112 RH rear reading light
113 Luggage compartment light
114 Tailgate switch
115 Cigarette lighter

Astra 1998 to 2000 - Diagram 12

MTS
H32218

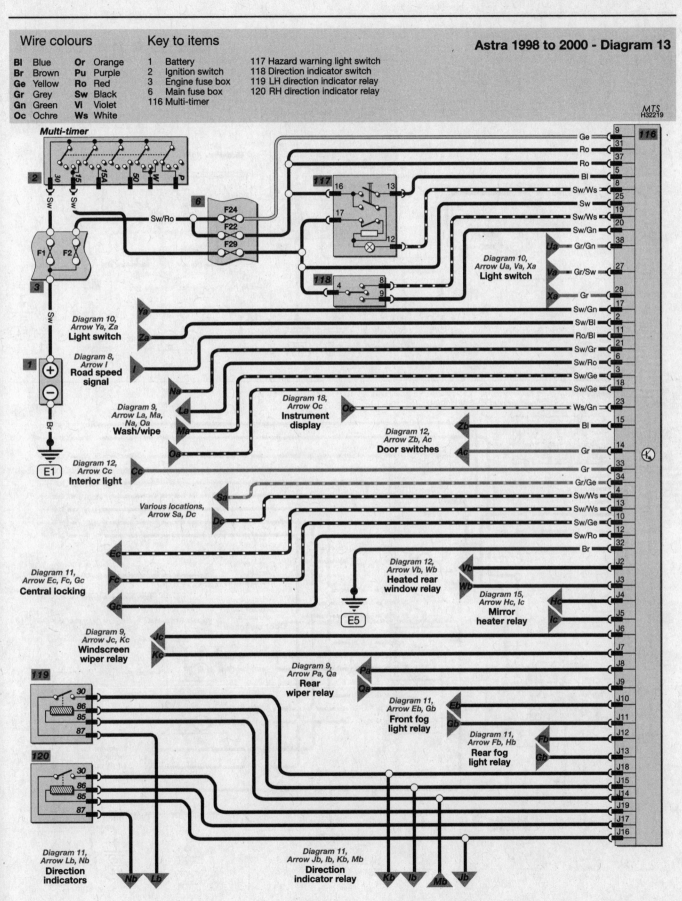

Wire colours

Bl	Blue	**Or**	Orange
Br	Brown	**Pu**	Purple
Ge	Yellow	**Ro**	Red
Gr	Grey	**Sw**	Black
Gn	Green	**Vi**	Violet
Oc	Ochre	**Ws**	White

Key to items

1 Battery
2 Ignition switch
3 Engine fuse box
6 Main fuse box
116 Multi-timer

117 Hazard warning light switch
118 Direction indicator switch
119 LH direction indicator relay
120 RH direction indicator relay

Astra 1998 to 2000 - Diagram 13

MTS
H32219

Wire colours

Bl	Blue	**Pu**	Purple
Br	Brown	**Ro**	Red
Ge	Yellow	**Sw**	Black
Gr	Grey	**Vi**	Violet
Gn	Green	**Ws**	White
Or	Orange		

Key to items

1 Battery
2 Ignition switch
3 Engine fuse box
6 Main fuse box
8 Diagnostic connector
24 Steering wheel clock spring
121 Horn switch
122 Horn relay
123 Horn
124 Glovebox light/switch
125 Central locking module
126 Drivers door lock motor
127 Passenger door lock motor
128 LH rear door lock motor

129 RH door lock motor
130 Tailgate lock motor
131 Filler flap lock motor
132 Sunroof motor
133 Sunroof switch

Astra 1998 to 2000 - Diagram 14

Note: prefix 1/ = X61 multi plug
prefix 2/ = X62 multi plug

MTS
H32220

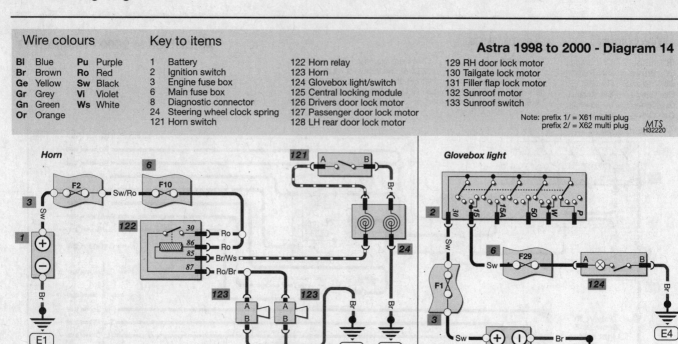

Horn

Glovebox light

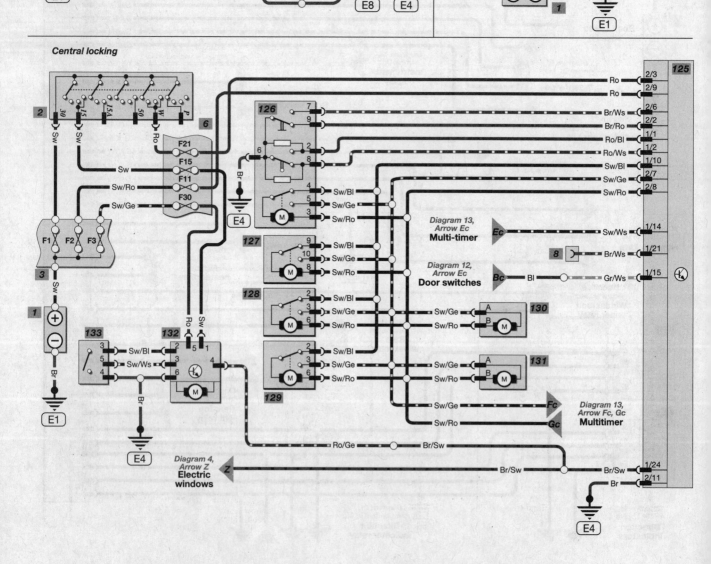

Central locking

Wire colours

Bl	Blue	**Pu**	Purple
Br	Brown	**Ro**	Red
Ge	Yellow	**Sw**	Black
Gr	Grey	**Vi**	Violet
Gn	Green	**Ws**	White
Or	Orange		

Key to items

1   Battery
2   Ignition switch
3   Engine fuse box
6   Main fuse box
8   Diagnostic connector
134 Power steering motor
135 Heated mirror relay
136 Electric mirror switch
137 Driver' exterior door mirror
138 Passenger exterior door mirror
139 Heater control module
140 Circulation flap motor
141 Heater blower motor resistor
142 Heater blower motor
143 Auxiliary heater switch
166 Cruise control switch

Astra 1998 to 2000 - Diagram 15

MTS
H32221

Power steering

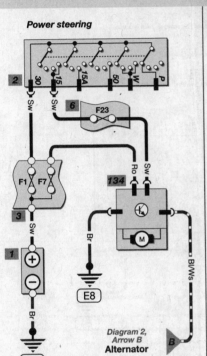

Exterior door mirrors

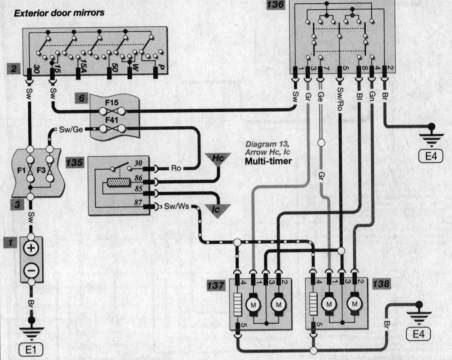

Cruise control

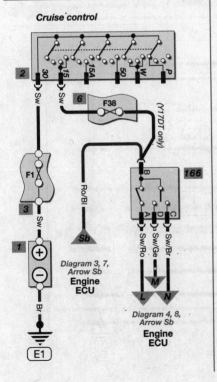

Heating

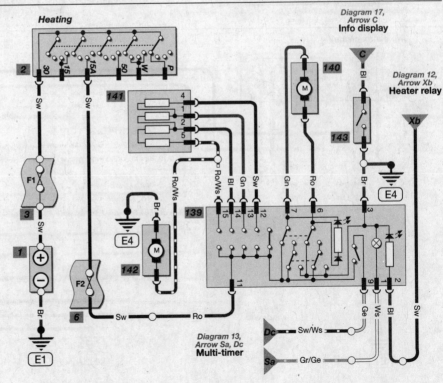

Wire colours

Bl	Blue	Pu	Purple
Br	Brown	Pk	Pink
Ge	Yellow	Ro	Red
Gr	Grey	Sw	Black
Gn	Green	Vi	Violet
Or	Orange	Ws	White

Key to items

1 Battery
2 Ignition switch
3 Engine fuse box
6 Main fuse box
8 Diagnostic connector
144 Auxiliary heater switch
145 Circulation flap motor
146 Heater blower motor resistor
147 Heater blower motor
148 Air conditioning module
149 Coolant actuator
150 Anti freeze protection switch
151 Triple info display
152 Outside temperature sensor

Astra 1998 to 2000 - Diagram 16

Note: prefix 1/ = X65 multi plug
prefix 2/ = X66 multi plug

Air conditioning

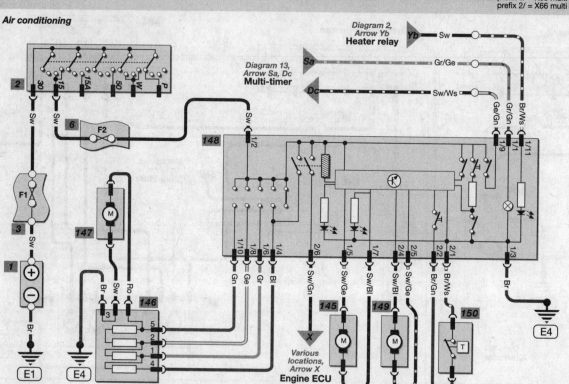

Triple info. display

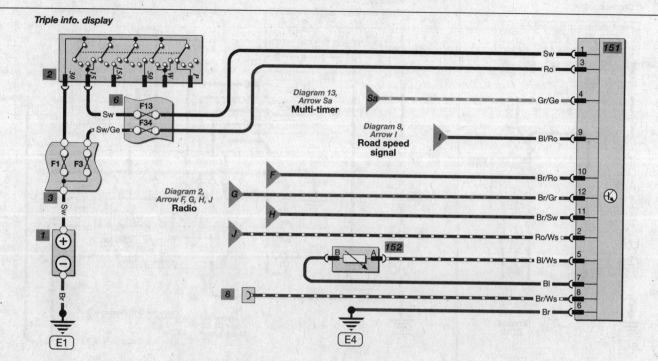

Wire colours

Bl	Blue	Pu	Purple
Br	Brown	Ro	Red
Ge	Yellow	Sw	Black
Gr	Grey	Vi	Violet
Gn	Green	Ws	White
Or	Orange		

Key to items

1 Battery
2 Ignition switch
3 Engine fuse box
6 Main fuse box
8 Diagnostic connector
153 Multi info display
154 LH front brake pad
    warning sensor
155 RH front brake pad
    warning sensor
156 Low washer fluid level switch
157 Low coolant level switch
158 Low oil level switch
159 Outside temperature sensor
160 Info display switch

Astra 1998 to 2000 – Diagram 17

MTS
H32223

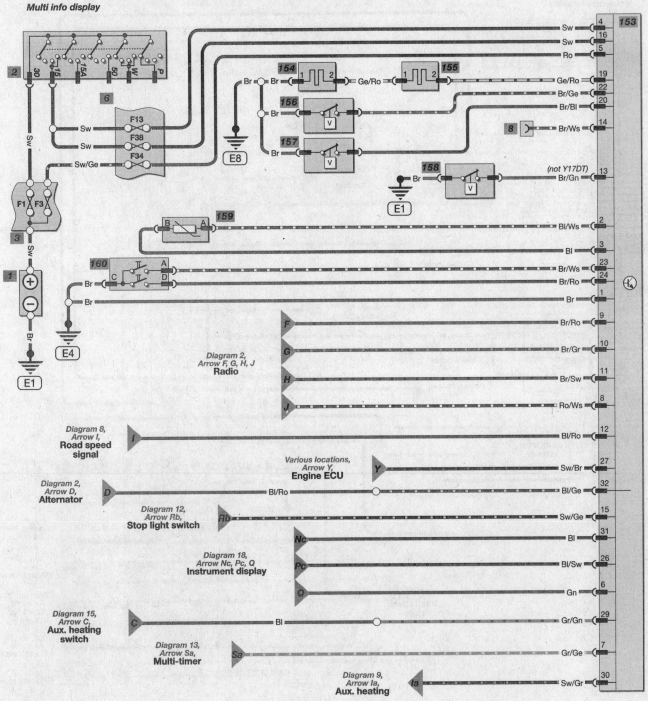

Multi info display

Wire colours

Bl	Blue	Pu	Purple
Br	Brown	Ro	Red
Ge	Yellow	Sw	Black
Gr	Grey	Vi	Violet
Gn	Green	Ws	White
Or	Orange		

Key to items

1 Battery
2 Ignition switch
3 Engine fuse box
6 Main fuse box
8 Diagnostic connector
161 Instrument panel
  a) alternator warning
  b) oil pressure warning
  c) airbag warning
  d) ABS warning

161 Instrument panel cont.
  e) pre-heating warning
  f) engine warning
  g) engine cooling light
  h) brake system warning
  i) trailer turning signal
  j) coolant temp. gauge
  k) fuel reserve warning
  l) fuel gauge
  m) tachometer

161 Instrument panel cont.
  n) speedometer
  o) coolant temp warning
  p) instrument illumination
  q) rear fog light warning
  r*) high beam warning
  r) high beam warning
    (tachometer only)
  s) front fog light warning
    (tachometer only)

161 Instrument panel cont.
  s*) front fog light warning
  t) LH indicator
  u) RH indicator
162 Oil pressure switch
163 Brake fluid switch
164 Parking brake switch
165 Fuel tank sender

Astra 1998 to 2000 - Diagram 18

MTS
H32224

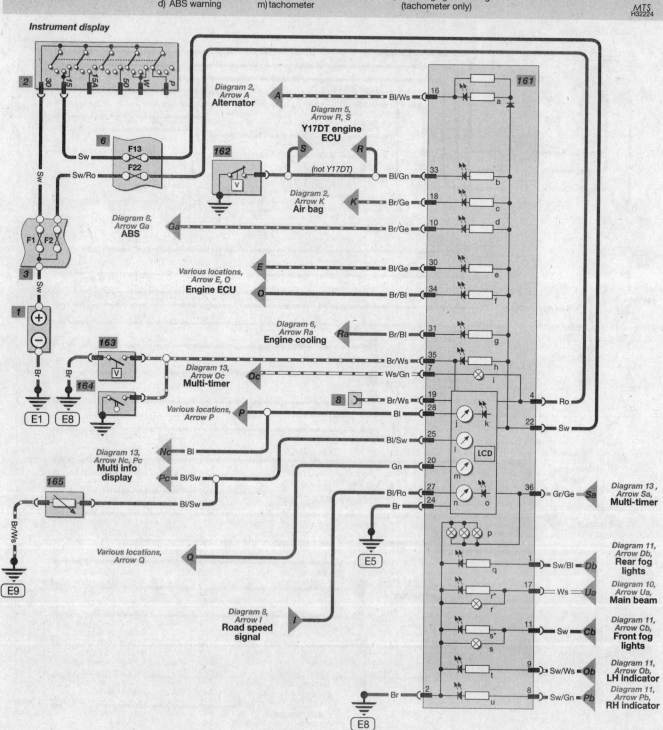

VAUXHALL ASTRA 2001 to 2004

Diagram 1

Key to symbols

Bulb	⊗
Switch	
Fuse/fusible link and current rating	F5 30A
Multiple contact switch (ganged)	
Resistor	
Variable resistor	
Connecting wires	
Item no.	2
Pump/motor	Ⓜ
Earth point and location	E12
Wire joint	
Solenoid actuator	
Diode	
Light emitting diode (LED)	
Wire colour (brown with black tracer)	Br/Bk
Plug and socket contact	
Screened cable	

Dashed outline denotes part of a larger item, containing in this case an electronic or solid state device.
Pin types:
2 - Unspecified connector, pin 2.
X53 1 - Connector 53, pin 1.

Earth points

E1	Battery earth	E8	Engine electric earth
E2	Main engine earth	E9	Blower motor
E3	Distributor	E10	LH rear panel
E4	Transmission tunnel	E11	RH side of rear window
E5	Steering column	E12	Tailgate
E6	'A' pillar	E13	Central locking earth
E7	Engine fan cowl		

Key to circuits

Diagram 1	Information for wiring diagrams
Diagram 2	Starting and charging, airbag and radio with CD player
Diagram 3	Electric windows and central locking
Diagram 4	Air conditioning and engine cooling
Diagram 5	Add-on heater Y17DT only, cigarette lighter, power steering, horns and ABS with traction control
Diagram 6	Multitimer, sunroof and heated seats
Diagram 7	Wash/wipe and multi info display
Diagram 8	Instrument panel, heated rear window, filter heater and electric mirrors
Diagram 9	Automatic rear view mirror, interior lights, side lights, headlight leveling, tail lights, licence plate lights and dipped beam headlights
Diagram 10	Main beam headlights, fog lights, reversing lights, brake lights, direction indicators and hazard lights

Fuse table

Engine fuse box

Fuses	Rating	Fuses	Rating
F1	60A	F5	60A
F2	60A	F6	20A
F3	60A	F7	80A
F4	80A	F8	80A

Engine bay fuse and relay box

Fuses	Rating	Circuit protected
F50	40A	Engine cooling
F52	40A	Engine cooling

Fuse box RH side of engine bay

Fuses	Rating	Circuit protected
F40	30A	Air conditioning
F41	1A	Air conditioning
F42	25A	Air conditioning

Main fuse box

Fuses	Rating	Circuit protected
F1	-	Not used
F2	30A	Air conditioning
F3	40A	Heated rear window
F4	-	Not used
F5	-	Not used
F6	10A	RH dipped beam, headlight adjustment
F7	10A	RH side light, RH tail light licence plate light
F8	10A	RH main beam
F9	30A	Headlight wash/wipe
F10	15A	Horn
F11	20A	Central locking
F12	15A	Front fog lights
F13	5A	Interior mirror
F14	30A	Central locking
F15	5A	Electric windows, sunroof, electric windows
F16	10A	Rear fog lights
F17	30A	Electric windows
F18	5A	Headlight adjustment
F19	30A	Radio
F20	30A	Electric windows
F21	5A	Central locking, radio, multitimer, telephone
F22	15A	Hazard lights, multitimer instrument panel, electronic climate control
F23	10A	ABS, power steering

Main fuse box

Fuses	Rating	Circuit protected
F24	10A	LH dipped beam, headlight adjustment
F25	10A	LH side light, LH tail light
F26	10A	LH main beam
F27	-	Not used
F28	5A	Interior lights
F29	10A	Direction indicators, hazard lights, reversing lights, multitimer, light switch
F30	20A	Sunroof
F31	20A	Rear wiper
F32	10A	Alarm
F33	20A	Trailer
F34	20A	Radio, information display
F35	10A	Engine cooling
F36	15A	Cigarette light
F37	20A	Heated seats
F38	10A	Brake lights, ABS, info display
F39	5A	Engine cooling
F40	5A	Engine cooling
F41	10A	Heated mirrors
F42	10A	Airbag, interior lights
F43	15A	RH xenon headlight
F44	15A	LH xenon headlight
F45	5A	Heated seats
F46	15A	Engine control unit, add-on heater
F47	20A	Add on heater
F48	-	Not used
F49	-	Not used

H32929

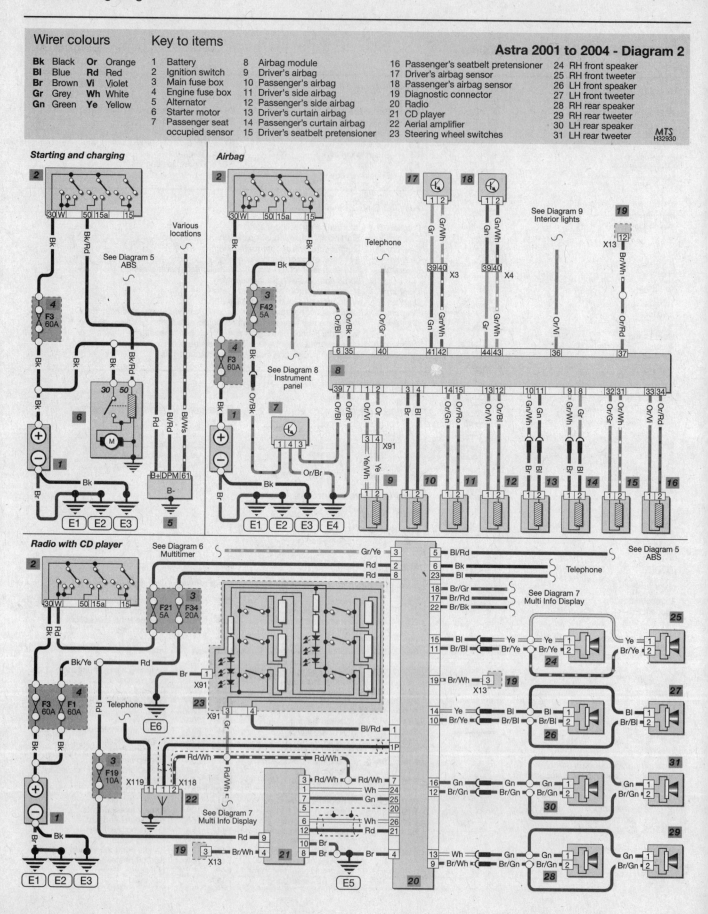

Wirer colours

Bk	Black	Or	Orange
Bl	Blue	Rd	Red
Br	Brown	Vi	Violet
Gr	Grey	Wh	White
Gn	Green	Ye	Yellow

Key to items

1 Battery
2 Ignition switch
3 Main fuse box
4 Engine fuse box
5 Alternator
6 Starter motor
7 Passenger seat occupied sensor
8 Airbag module
9 Driver's airbag
10 Passenger's airbag
11 Driver's side airbag
12 Passenger's side airbag
13 Driver's curtain airbag
14 Passenger's curtain airbag
15 Driver's seatbelt pretensioner
16 Passenger's seatbelt pretensioner
17 Driver's airbag sensor
18 Passenger's airbag sensor
19 Diagnostic connector
20 Radio
21 CD player
22 Aerial amplifier
23 Steering wheel switches
24 RH front speaker
25 RH front tweeter
26 LH front speaker
27 LH front tweeter
28 RH rear speaker
29 RH rear tweeter
30 LH rear speaker
31 LH rear tweeter

Astra 2001 to 2004 - Diagram 2

MTS H32930

Starting and charging

Airbag

Radio with CD player

Wirer colours

Bk	Black	**Or**	Orange
Bl	Blue	**Rd**	Red
Br	Brown	**Vi**	Violet
Gr	Grey	**Wh**	White
Gn	Green	**Ye**	Yellow

Key to items

1 Battery
2 Ignition switch
3 Main fuse box
4 Engine fuse box
19 Diagnostic connector
32 Driver's electric window switch
33 Passenger's electric window switch
34 LH rear electric window switch
35 RH rear electric window switch
36 Driver's window motor
37 Passengers's window motor
38 LH rear electric window motor
39 RH rear electric window motor
40 Central locking module
41 Driver's door switch
42 Filler flap lock motor
43 Tailgate lock motor
44 LH rear door lock motor
45 RH rear door lock motor
46 Passenger door lock motor
47 Driver's door lock motor
* Coupé only

Astra 2001 to 2004 - Diagram 3

MTS
H32931

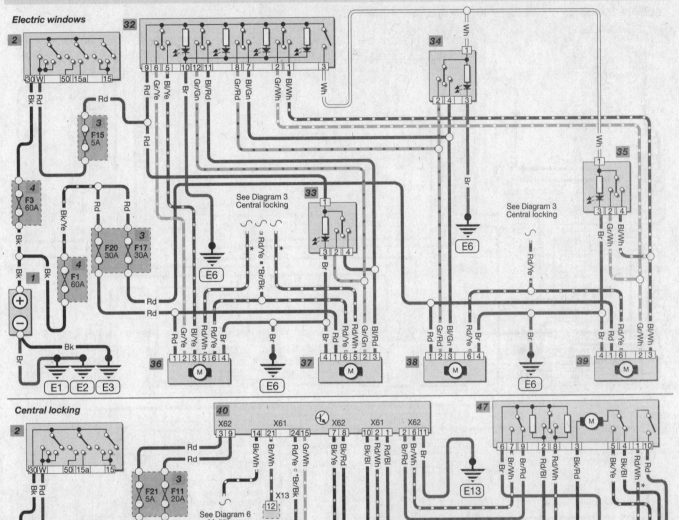

Electric windows

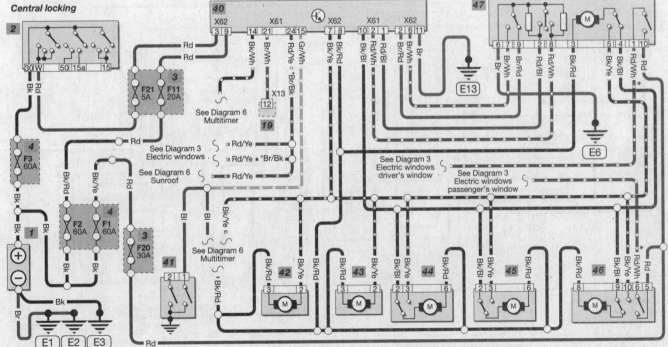

Central locking

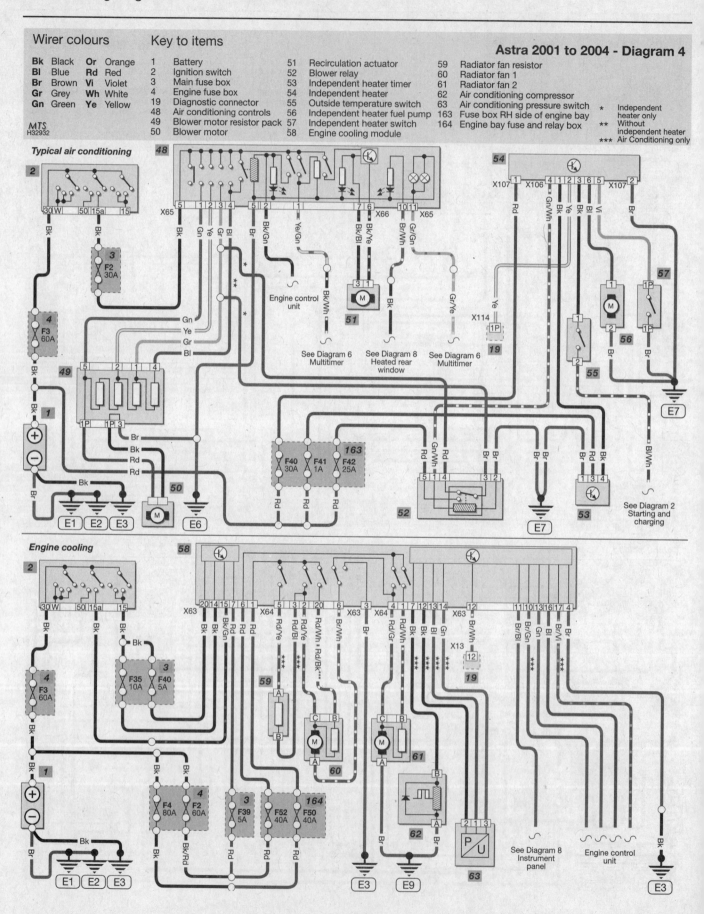

Wirer colours

Bk	Black	Or	Orange
Bl	Blue	Rd	Red
Br	Brown	Vi	Violet
Gr	Grey	Wh	White
Gn	Green	Ye	Yellow

MTS H32932

Key to items

1	Battery	51	Recirculation actuator	59	Radiator fan resistor
2	Ignition switch	52	Blower relay	60	Radiator fan 1
3	Main fuse box	53	Independent heater timer	61	Radiator fan 2
4	Engine fuse box	54	Independent heater	62	Air conditioning compressor
19	Diagnostic connector	55	Outside temperature switch	63	Air conditioning pressure switch
48	Air conditioning controls	56	Independent heater fuel pump	163	Fuse box RH side of engine bay
49	Blower motor resistor pack	57	Independent heater switch	164	Engine bay fuse and relay box
50	Blower motor	58	Engine cooling module		

Astra 2001 to 2004 - Diagram 4

* Independent heater only
** Without independent heater
*** Air Conditioning only

Typical air conditioning

Engine cooling

Wirer colours

Bk	Black	**Or**	Orange
Bl	Blue	**Rd**	Red
Br	Brown	**Vi**	Violet
Gr	Grey	**Wh**	White
Gn	Green	**Ye**	Yellow

Key to items

1 Battery
2 Ignition switch
3 Main fuse box
4 Engine fuse box
19 Diagnostic connector
23 Steering wheel switches
55 Outside temperature switch

64 Add-on heater
65 Fuel pump
66 Cigarette lighter
67 Power steering pump
68 ABS module
69 Brake light switch
70 RH rear wheel speed sensor

71 LH rear wheel speed sensor
72 RH front wheel speed sensor
73 LH front wheel speed sensor
74 Horn relay
75 Horn switch
76 Horns

Astra 2001 to 2004 - Diagram 5

MTS
H32933

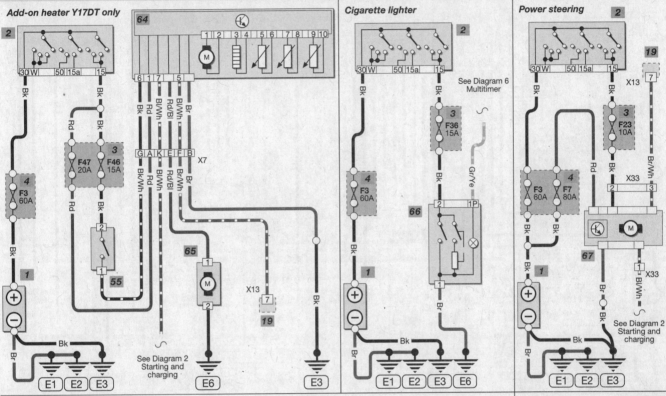

Add-on heater Y17DT only

Cigarette lighter

Power steering

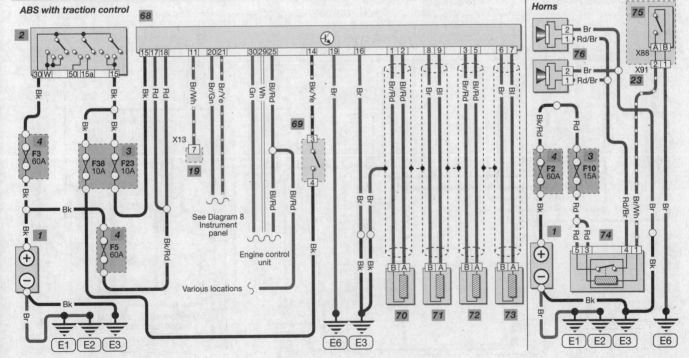

ABS with traction control

Horns

Wirer colours

Bk	Black	Or	Orange
Bl	Blue	Rd	Red
Br	Brown	Vi	Violet
Gr	Grey	Wh	White
Gn	Green	Ye	Yellow

Key to items

1 Battery
2 Ignition switch
3 Main fuse box
4 Engine fuse box
41 Driver's door switch
77 Multitimer
78 Passenger's door switch
79 RH rear door switch
80 LH rear door switch
81 LH seat heating switch
82 RH seat heating switch
83 LH seat heating
84 RH seat heating
85 Sunroof motor
86 Sunroof switch

Astra 2001 to 2004 - Diagram 6

MTS
H32934

Multitimer

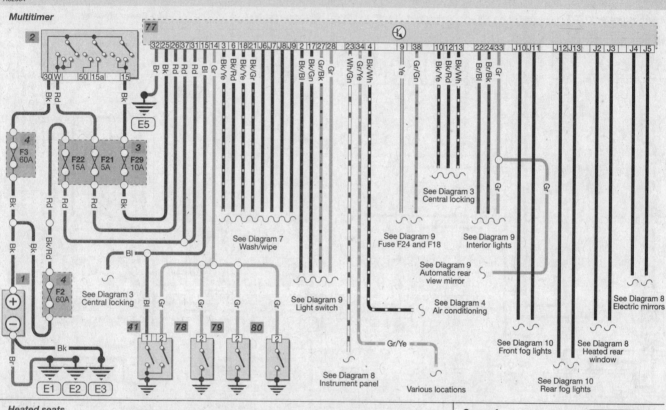

Heated seats

Sunroof

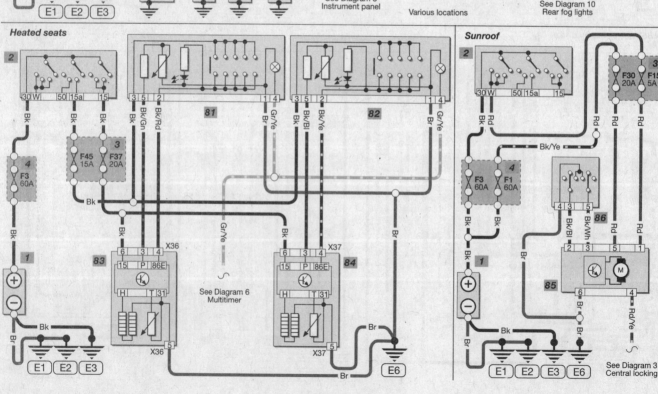

Wirer colours

Bk	Black	Or	Orange
Bl	Blue	Rd	Red
Br	Brown	Vi	Violet
Gr	Grey	Wh	White
Gn	Green	Ye	Yellow

MTS
H32935

Key to items

1	Battery	88	Engine oil level switch	95	Headlight washer pump	100	Rain sensor
2	Ignition switch	89	Maximum coolant level switch	96	Rear wiper relay	101	Washer pump
3	Main fuse box	90	Minimum coolant level switch	97	Rear wiper motor	102	Windscreen wiper motor
4	Engine fuse box	91	LH brake lining sensor	98	Windscreen wiper relay	103	Windscreen wiper relay
19	Diagnostic connector	92	RH brake lining sensor		(stage 1)	165	Outside temperature sensor
69	Brake light switch	93	Wash/wipe switch	99	Windscreen wiper relay		
87	Multi info display	94	Headlight washer pump relay		(stage 2)		

Astra 2001 to 2004 - Diagram 7

* Rain sensor only
** Without rain sensor
*** Y20DTH only

Wash/wipe

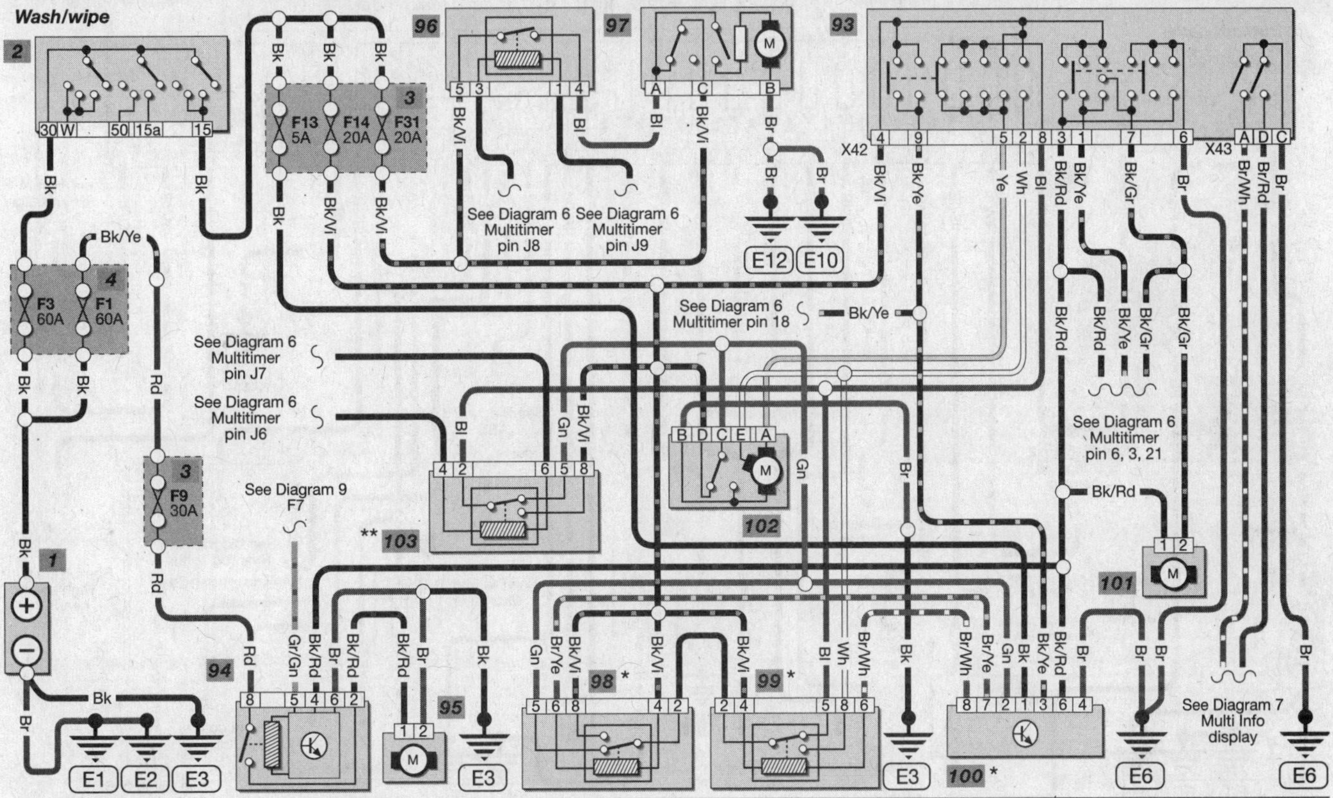

Multi Info display

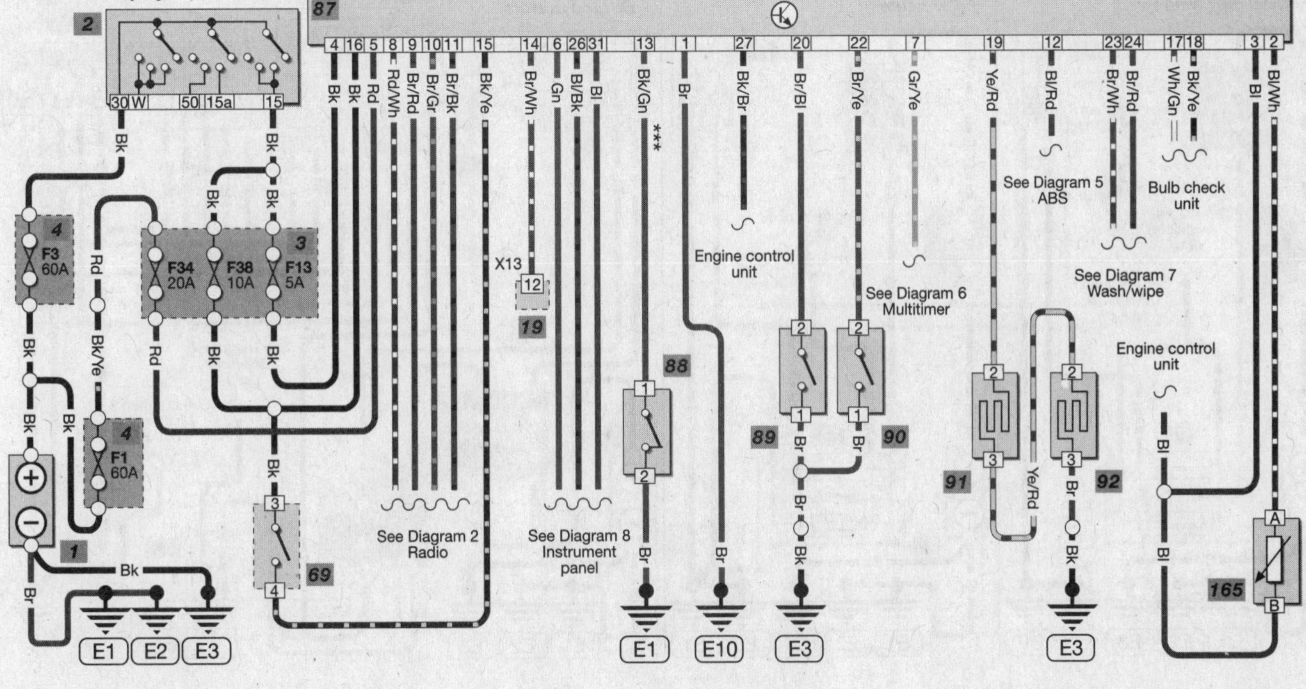

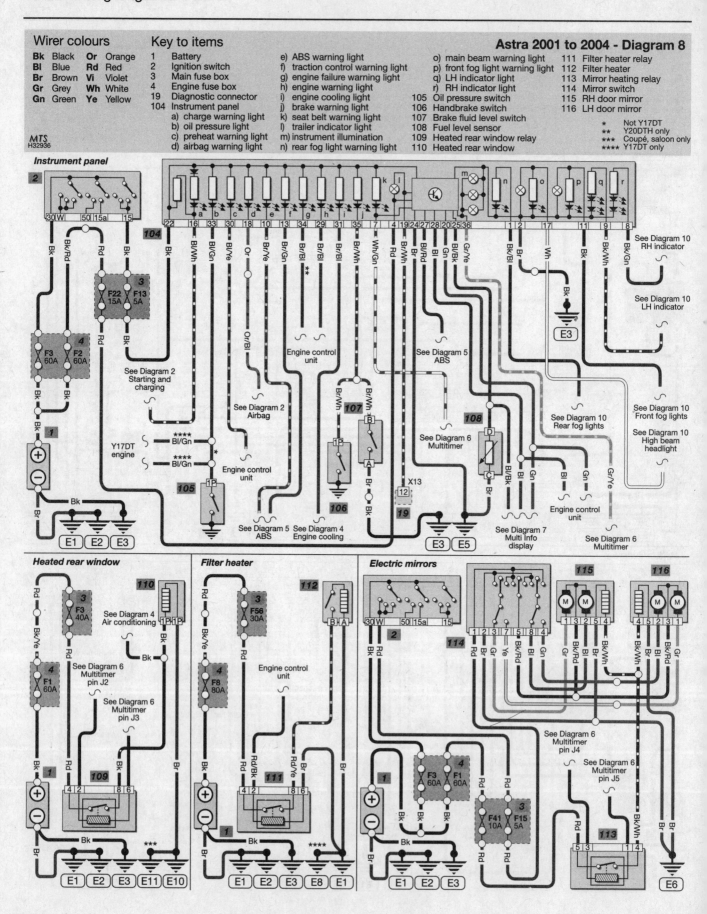

Wirer colours

Bk Black   Or Orange
Bl Blue   Rd Red
Br Brown   Vi Violet
Gr Grey   Wh White
Gn Green   Ye Yellow

MTS
H32936

Key to items

1   Battery
2   Ignition switch
3   Main fuse box
4   Engine fuse box
19   Diagnostic connector
104 Instrument panel
     a) charge warning light
     b) oil pressure light
     c) preheat warning light
     d) airbag warning light

e) ABS warning light
f) traction control warning light
g) engine failure warning light
h) engine warning light
i) engine cooling light
j) brake warning light
k) seat belt warning light
l) trailer indicator light
m) instrument illumination
n) rear fog light warning light

o)   main beam warning light
p)   front fog light warning light
q)   LH indicator light
r)   RH indicator light
105 Oil pressure switch
106 Handbrake switch
107 Brake fluid level switch
108 Fuel level sensor
109 Heated rear window relay
110 Heated rear window

Astra 2001 to 2004 - Diagram 8

111 Filter heater relay
112 Filter heater
113 Mirror heating relay
114 Mirror switch
115 RH door mirror
116 LH door mirror

*   Not Y17DT
**   Y20DTH only
***   Coupé, saloon only
****   Y17DT only

Wirer colours

Bk	Black	Or	Orange
Bl	Blue	Rd	Red
Br	Brown	Vi	Violet
Gr	Grey	Wh	White
Gn	Green	Ye	Yellow

MTS
H32937

Key to items

1 Battery
2 Ignition switch
3 Main fuse box
4 Engine fuse box
117 Light switch
  a) front fog lights
  b) rear fog lights
  c) interior illumination
  d) headlight leveling
  e) instrument dimming
  f) main light switch
118 LH dipped beam
119 RH dipped beam
120 LH side light
121 RH side light
122 LH headlight leveling motor
123 RH headlight leveling motor
124 Licence plate light
125 LH tail light
126 RH tail light
127 Interior light unit
128 Time delay relay
129 LH rear reading light
130 RH rear reading light
131 Glovebox light
132 Boot light
133 Boot light switch
134 Time delay light
135 LH sunvisor light
136 RH sunvisor light
137 Automatic rear
  view mirror

Astra 2001 to 2004 - Diagram 9

* Saloon only
** Hatchback only
*** Estate only
**** Alarm only
***** Not alarm

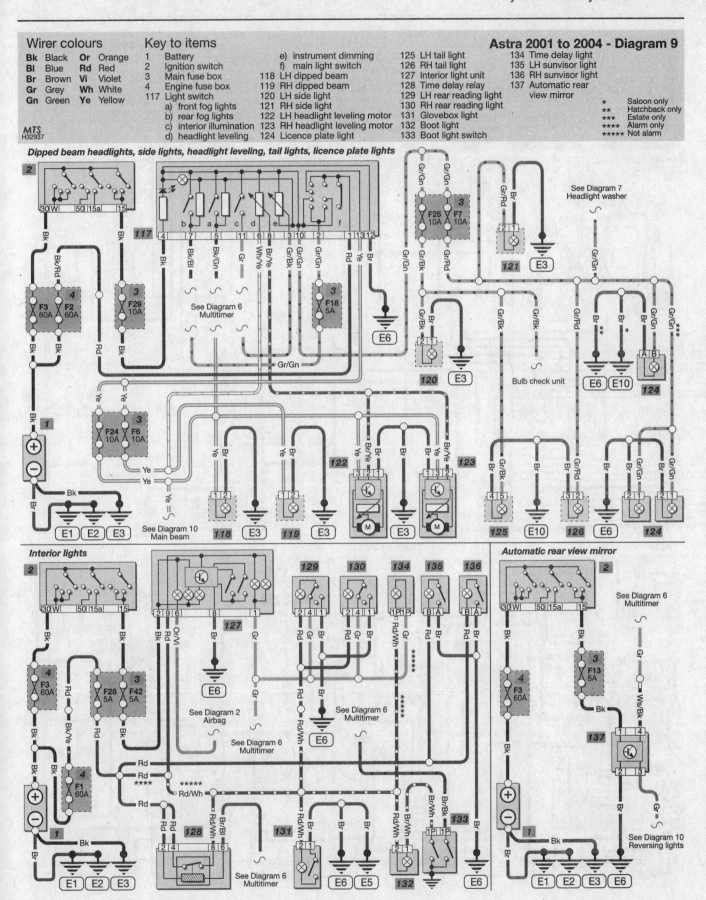

Dipped beam headlights, side lights, headlight leveling, tail lights, licence plate lights

Interior lights

Automatic rear view mirror

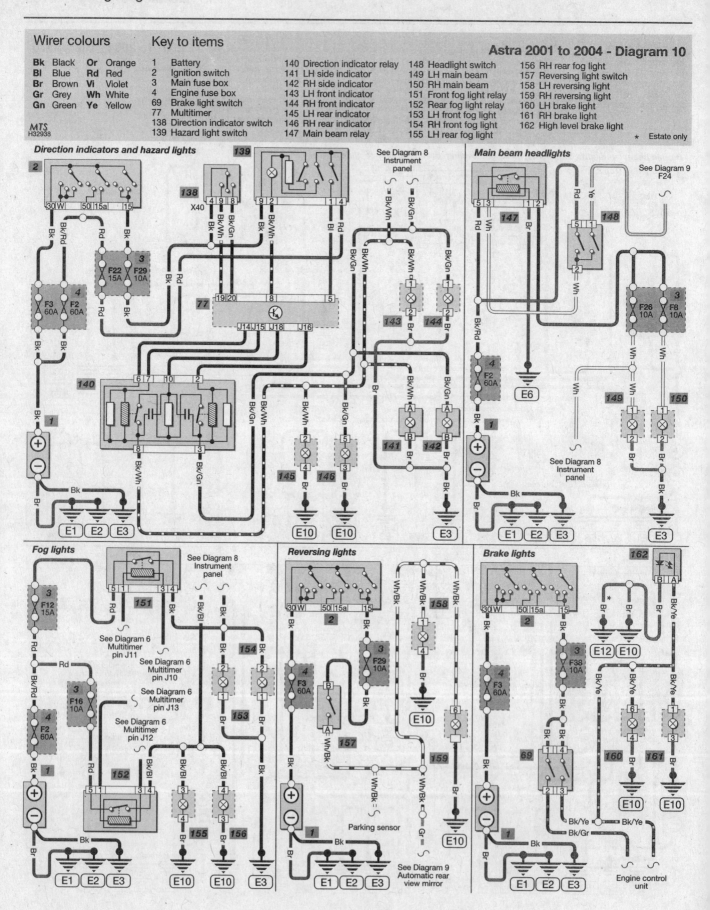

Wirer colours

Bk	Black	Or	Orange
Bl	Blue	Rd	Red
Br	Brown	Vi	Violet
Gr	Grey	Wh	White
Gn	Green	Ye	Yellow

MTS
H32938

Key to items

1 Battery
2 Ignition switch
3 Main fuse box
4 Engine fuse box
69 Brake light switch
77 Multitimer
138 Direction indicator switch
139 Hazard light switch

140 Direction indicator relay
141 LH side indicator
142 RH side indicator
143 LH front indicator
144 RH front indicator
145 LH rear indicator
146 RH rear indicator
147 Main beam relay

148 Headlight switch
149 LH main beam
150 RH main beam
151 Front fog light relay
152 Rear fog light relay
153 LH front fog light
154 RH front fog light
155 LH rear fog light

156 RH rear fog light
157 Reversing light switch
158 LH reversing light
159 RH reversing light
160 LH brake light
161 RH brake light
162 High level brake light

Astra 2001 to 2004 - Diagram 10

★ Estate only

Direction indicators and hazard lights

Main beam headlights

Fog lights

Reversing lights

Brake lights

VAUXHALL ZAFIRA 1998 to 2000

Diagram 1

Key to symbols

Bulb

Switch

Multiple contact switch (ganged)

Fuse/fusible link

F24

Resistor

Variable resistor

Item no.

15

Pump/motor

Earth and location (via lead)

E1

Gauge/meter

Diode

Light emitting diode (LED)

Internal connection (connecting wires)

Wire splice or soldered joint

Solenoid actuator

Plug and socket connector

Connections to other circuits. Direction of arrow denotes current flow.

Diagram 3, Arrow A
High beam warning light

Wire colour (Red wire/white tracer)

Ro/Ws

Box shape denotes part of a larger component. Terminal identified by either standard termination (bold *italic*) or by connector number (plain text).

30 Terminal identification (i.e. battery +ve)

4 Connector pin number

Earth locations

E1	Battery ground strap	E7	Engine (electronic)
E2	Engine ground strap	E8	Engine distribution
E3	Ignition coil earth	E9	Rear panel
E4	"A" pillar	E10	Tailgate
E5	Steering column	E11	Heater blower
E6	Transmission tunnel		

Key to circuits

Diagram 1	Information for wiring diagrams
Diagram 2	Starting, charging, airbag and typical radio/CD
Diagram 3	X20DTL engine management system
Diagram 4	X20DTL engine management system cont. and electric windows
Diagram 5	ABS and speed sensor (non ABS models), and engine cooling
Diagram 6	Wash/wipe and auxiliary heating
Diagram 7	Front lights
Diagram 8	Fog, tail, reversing and direction indicator lights
Diagram 9	Number plate, brake, interior lights, heated rear window and cigarette lighter
Diagram 10	Multi-timer
Diagram 11	Glovebox light, horn, sunroof and central locking
Diagram 12	Power steering, exterior door mirrors, cruise control and heating
Diagram 13	Typical air con. and triple info display
Diagram 14	Multi info display
Diagram 15	Instrument display

Engine fuse box

Fuse	Rating				
F1	60A	F5	60A	F60	110A
F2	60A	F6	20A		
F3	60A	F7	80A		
F4	80A	F8	80A		

Main fuse box

Fuse	Rating	Circuit protected	Fuse	Rating	Circuit protected
F2	30A	Air conditioning	F23	10A	ABS and power steering
F3	40A	Heated rear window	F24	10A	LH dipped beam, headlight adjustment
F6	10A	RH dipped beam, headlight adjustment	F25	10A	LH parking, tail and number plate lights
F7	10A	RH parking, tail and number plate lights	F26	10A	LH main beam
F8	10A	RH main beam	F28	7.5A	Interior light
F9	30A	Headlamp wash	F29	10A	Hazard warning, interior light
F10	15A	Horn	F30	30A	Sunroof
F11	20A	Central locking	F33	20A	Trailer
F12	15A	Front fog lights	F34	20A	CD player, radio, information display and GPS
F13	7.5A	Information display	F35	10A	Engine cooling, air con.
F14	30A	Windscreen wipers	F36	20A	Cigarette lighter
F15	7.5A	Electric windows, sunroof and mirrors	F38	10A	Stop lights, info. display and cruise control
F16	10A	Rear fog lights	F39	7.5A	Engine cooling and air con.
F17	30A	Electric windows	F40	7.5A	Engine cooling and air con.
F18	7.5A	Number plate lights and headlight range adjustment	F41	10A	Heated mirrors
F20	30A	Electric windows	F50	40A	Engine cooling
F21	7.5A	Radio	F52	40A	Engine cooling
F22	15A	Hazard warning, info. display, indicators and trip computer			

MTS
H32192

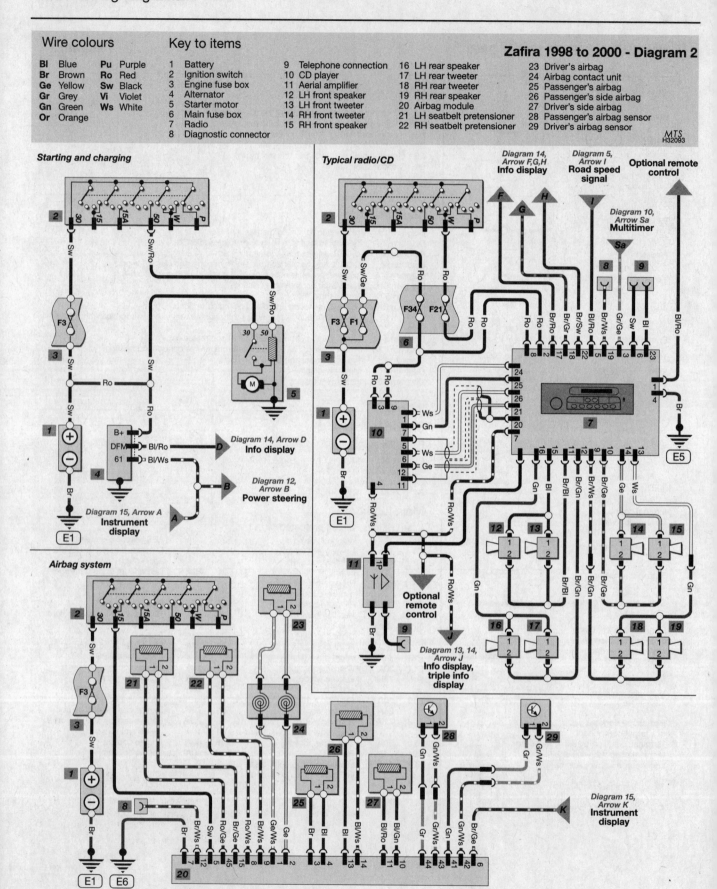

Wire colours

Bl	Blue
Br	Brown
Ge	Yellow
Gr	Grey
Gn	Green
Or	Orange
Pu	Purple
Ro	Red
Sw	Black
Vi	Violet
Ws	White

Key to items

1 Battery
2 Ignition switch
3 Engine fuse box
4 Alternator
5 Starter motor
6 Main fuse box
7 Radio
8 Diagnostic connector
9 Telephone connection
10 CD player
11 Aerial amplifier
12 LH front speaker
13 LH front tweeter
14 RH front tweeter
15 RH front speaker
16 LH rear speaker
17 LH rear tweeter
18 RH rear tweeter
19 RH rear speaker
20 Airbag module
21 LH seatbelt pretensioner
22 RH seatbelt pretensioner
23 Driver's airbag
24 Airbag contact unit
25 Passenger's airbag
26 Passenger's side airbag
27 Driver's side airbag
28 Passenger's airbag sensor
29 Driver's airbag sensor

Zafira 1998 to 2000 - Diagram 2

MTS H32093

Starting and charging

Typical radio/CD

Diagram 14, Arrow F,G,H
Info display

Diagram 5, Arrow I
Road speed signal

Optional remote control

Diagram 10, Arrow Sa
Multitimer

Diagram 14, Arrow D
Info display

Diagram 12, Arrow B
Power steering

Diagram 15, Arrow A
Instrument display

Optional remote control

Diagram 13, 14, Arrow J
Info display, triple info display

Airbag system

Diagram 15, Arrow K
Instrument display

Wire colours

Bl Blue   **Pu** Purple
Br Brown   **Ro** Red
Ge Yellow   **Sw** Black
Gr Grey   **Vi** Violet
Gn Green   **Ws** White
Or Orange

Key to items

1 Battery
2 Ignition switch
3 Engine fuse box
6 Main fuse box
30 Diesel control unit
31 Engine control unit relay
32 Filter pre-heating relay
33 Manifold crossover solenoid valve
34 Glow plug control unit
35 Glow plug
36 Filter heater
37 Exhaust gas recirculation solenoid valve
38 Boost pressure regulation solenoid valve
39 Air mass meter
40 Injection pump control unit
41 Boost pressure sensor
42 Engine oil temperature sensor
43 Coolant temperature sensor
44 Crankshaft sensor
45 Throttle potentiometer

Zafira 1998 to 2000 - Diagram 3

Note: prefix 1/ = X59 multi plug
prefix 2/ = X60 multi plug

MTS
H32094

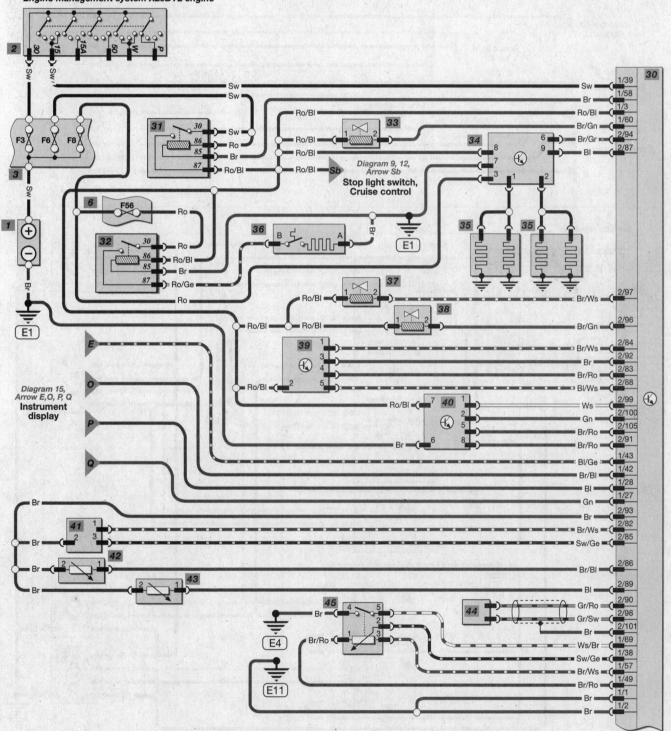

Engine management system X20DTL engine

Diagram 9, 12, Arrow Sb
Stop light switch, Cruise control

Diagram 15, Arrow E, O, P, Q
Instrument display

Wire colours

Bl	Blue	Pu	Purple
Br	Brown	Ro	Red
Ge	Yellow	Sw	Black
Gr	Grey	Vi	Violet
Gn	Green	Ws	White
Or	Orange		

Key to items

1 Battery
2 Ignition switch
3 Engine fuse box
6 Main fuse box
30 Diesel control unit
46 Drivers electric window switch unit
47 Passenger electric window switch

48 LH rear electric window switch
49 RH rear electric window switch
50 Drivers electric window motor
51 Passenger electric window motor
52 LH rear electric window motor
53 RH rear electric window motor

Zafira 1998 to 2000 - Diagram 4

Note: prefix 1/ = X59 multi plug
prefix 2/ = X60 multi plug

MTS
H32095

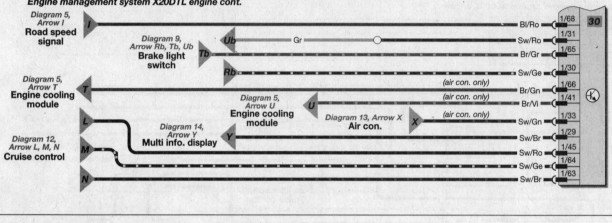

Engine management system X20DTL engine cont.

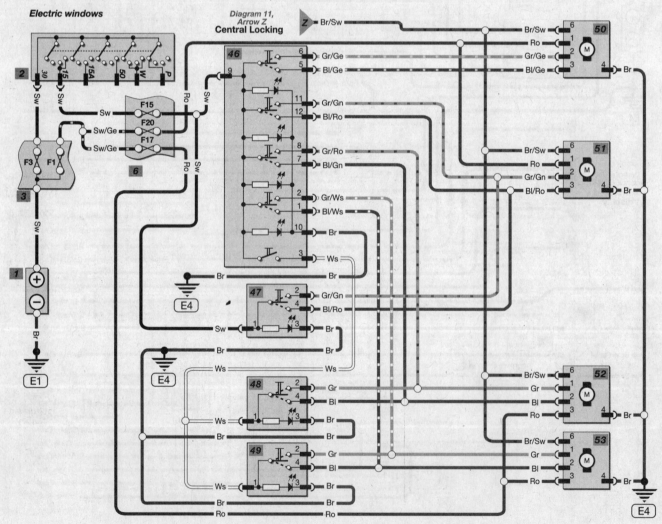

Electric windows

Wire colours

Bl	Blue	Pu	Purple
Br	Brown	Ro	Red
Ge	Yellow	Sw	Black
Gr	Grey	Vi	Violet
Gn	Green	Ws	White
Or	Orange		

Key to items

1 Battery
2 Ignition switch
3 Engine fuse box
8 Diagnostic connector
54 ABS module
55 LH front wheel speed sensor
56 RH front wheel speed sensor
57 LH rear wheel speed sensor
58 RH rear wheel speed sensor
59 Vehicle speed sensor
60 Engine cooling control unit
61 Radiator blower motor
62 Radiator blower preresistor
63 Air con. compressor clutch
64 Air con. pressure sensor

Zafira 1998 to 2000 - Diagram 5

Note: prefix 1/ = X63 multi plug
prefix 2/ = X64 multi plug

MTS
H32096

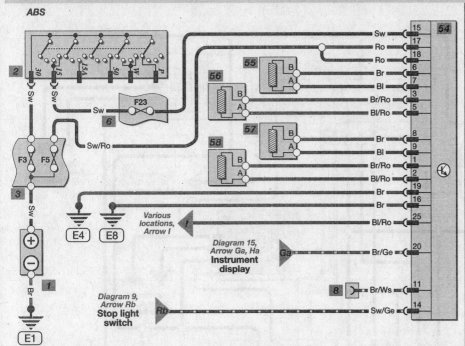
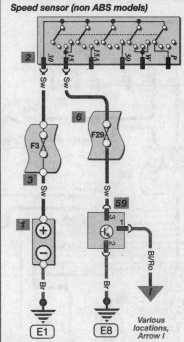

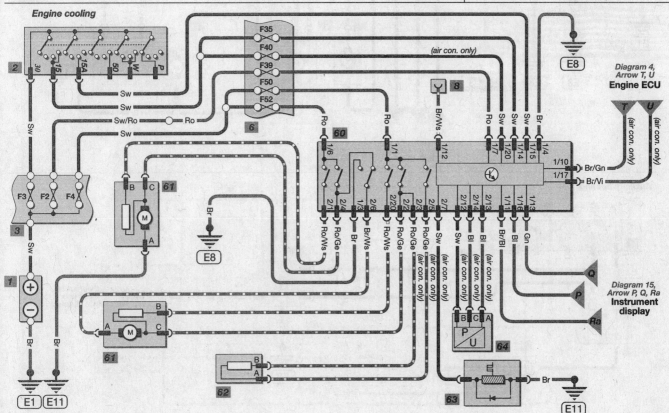

Wire colours

Bl	Blue	Pu	Purple
Br	Brown	Pk	Pink
Ge	Yellow	Ro	Red
Gr	Grey	Sw	Black
Gn	Green	Vi	Violet
Or	Orange	Ws	White

Key to items

1 Battery
2 Ignition switch
3 Engine fuse box
65 Headlight washer relay
66 Headlight washer pump
67 Wash/wipe switch

68 Windscreen washer pump
69 Windscreen wiper relay
70 Windscreen wiper motor
71 Rear wiper relay
72 Rear wiper motor
73 Auxiliary heater

Zafira 1998 to 2000 - Diagram 6

MTS
H32097

Wash/Wipe

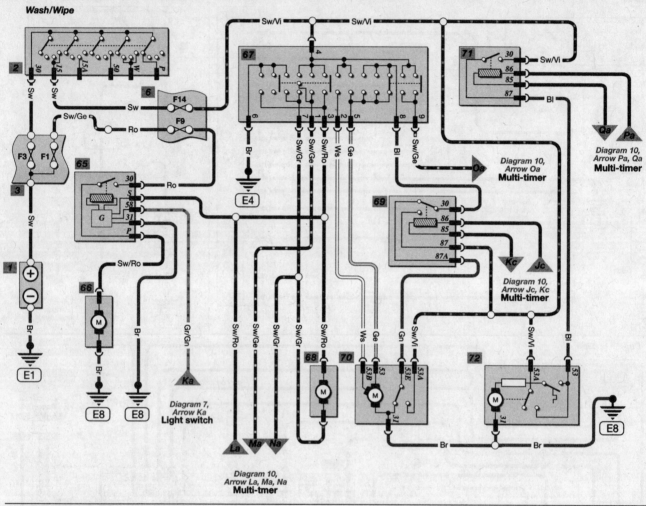

Auxiliary heating

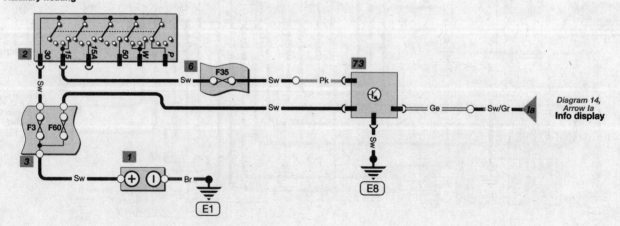

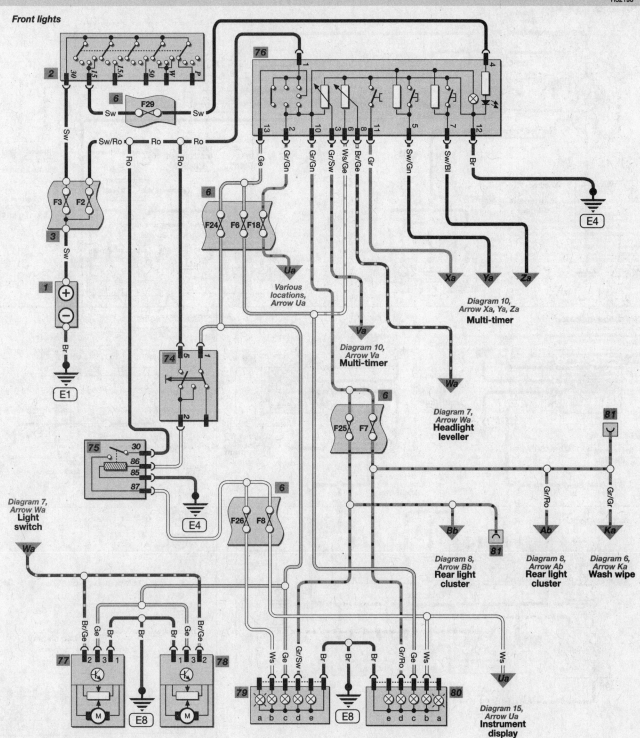

Wire colours

Bl Blue
Br Brown
Ge Yellow
Gr Grey
Gn Green
Or Orange

Pu Purple
Ro Red
Sw Black
Vi Violet
Ws White

Key to items

1 Battery
2 Ignition switch
3 Engine fuse box
6 Main fuse box
74 Main beam switch
75 Main beam relay
76 Light switch
77 LH headlight leveller

78 RH headlight leveller
79 LH front lights
   a) direction indicator
   b) main beam
   c) dipped beam
   d) side lights
   e) fog lights

80 RH front lights (as 79)
81 Trailer connection

Zafira 1998 to 2000 - Diagram 7

MTS
H32198

Front lights

Diagram 10,
Arrow Xa, Ya, Za
Multi-timer

Diagram 10,
Arrow Va
Multi-timer

Diagram 7,
Arrow Wa
Headlight leveller

Diagram 7,
Arrow Wa
Light switch

Various locations, Arrow Ua

Diagram 8,
Arrow Bb
Rear light cluster

Diagram 8,
Arrow Ab
Rear light cluster

Diagram 6,
Arrow Ka
Wash wipe

Diagram 15,
Arrow Ua
Instrument display

Wire colours

Bl	Blue	Pu	Purple
Br	Brown	Ro	Red
Ge	Yellow	Sw	Black
Gr	Grey	Vi	Violet
Gn	Green	Ws	White
Or	Orange		

Key to items

1 Battery
2 Ignition switch
3 Engine fuse box
6 Main fuse box
79 LH front light cluster
  a) direction indicator
  b) main beam
  c) dipped beam

d) side lights
80 RH front light cluster (as 79)
81 Trailer connection
82 Front fog light relay
83 Rear fog light relay
84 LH rear light cluster
  a) direction indicator
  b) stop light

c) tail light
d) reversing light
e) fog light
85 RH rear light cluster (as 84)
86 Trailer socket switch
87 LH direction indicator relay
88 RH direction indicator relay
89 LH indicator side repeater

90 RH indicator side repeater
91 Reversing light switch
157 LH front foglight
158 RH front foglight

Zafira 1998 to 2000 - Diagram 8

MTS
H32199

Fog lights, tail lights

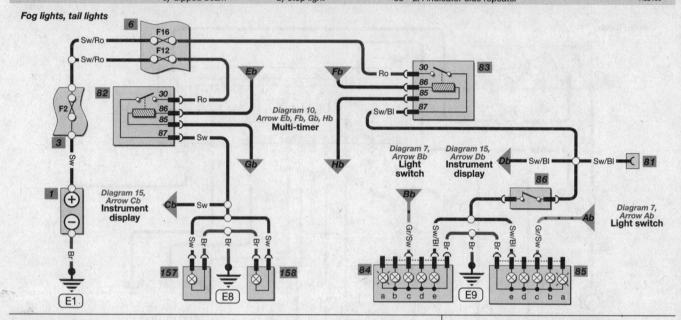

Direction indicators

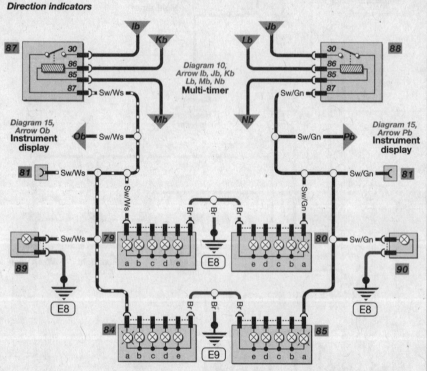

Reversing lights

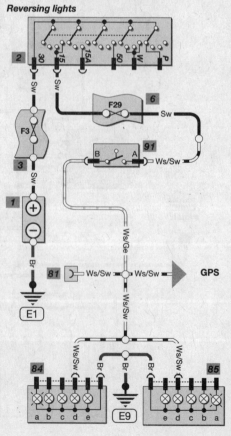

Wire colours

Bl	Blue	Pu	Purple
Br	Brown	Ro	Red
Ge	Yellow	Sw	Black
Gr	Grey	Vi	Violet
Gn	Green	Ws	White
Or	Orange		

Key to items

1 Battery
2 Ignition switch
3 Engine fuse box
6 Main fuse box
81 Trailer connector
79 LH rear light cluster
a) direction indicator
b) stop light
c) tail light
d) reversing light
e) fog light
80 RH rear light cluster (as 80)
92 LH number plate light
93 RH number plate light
94 Brake pedal/stop light switch
95 Cruise control clutch switch
96 High level stop light
97 Heated rear window relay
98 Heated rear window
99 Drivers door switch
100 Passenger door switch
101 LH rear door switch
102 RH rear door switch
103 Passenger compartment light with time delay
104 Rear reading light
105 Luggage compartment light
106 Tailgate switch
107 Cigarette lighter

Zafira 1998 to 2000 - Diagram 9

MTS
H32200

Number plate lights

Diagram 7, Arrow Ua
Light switch

Brake lights

Heated rear window

Diagram 4, Arrow Sb, Tb
Engine ECU

Various locations Arrow Rb

Diagram 10, Arrow Vb, Wb
Multi-timer

Diagram 12, Arrow Xb
Heating

Diagram 13, Arrow Yb
Air con.

Diagram 4, 12, Arrow Ub
Engine ECU, Cruise control

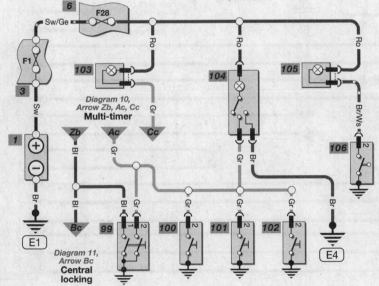

Interior lighting

Diagram 10, Arrow Zb, Ac, Cc
Multi-timer

Diagram 11, Arrow Bc
Central locking

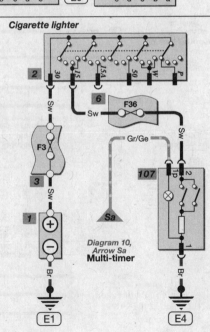

Cigarette lighter

Diagram 10, Arrow Sa
Multi-timer

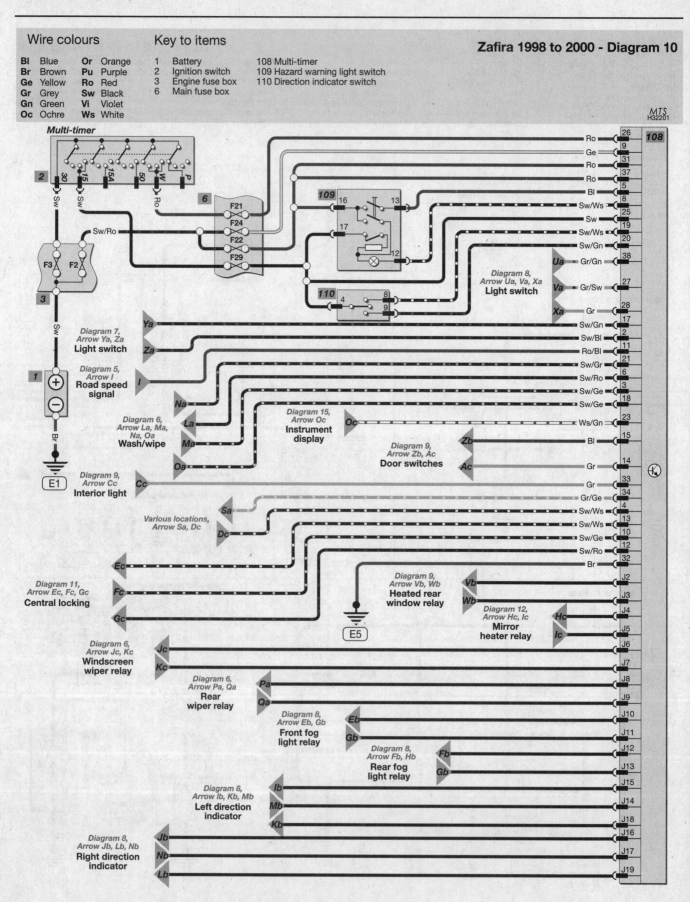

Wire colours

Bl	Blue	Or	Orange
Br	Brown	Pu	Purple
Ge	Yellow	Ro	Red
Gr	Grey	Sw	Black
Gn	Green	Vi	Violet
Oc	Ochre	Ws	White

Key to items

1 Battery
2 Ignition switch
3 Engine fuse box
6 Main fuse box

108 Multi-timer
109 Hazard warning light switch
110 Direction indicator switch

Zafira 1998 to 2000 - Diagram 10

MTS
H32201

Wire colours

Bl	Blue	**Pu**	Purple
Br	Brown	**Ro**	Red
Ge	Yellow	**Sw**	Black
Gr	Grey	**Vi**	Violet
Gn	Green	**Ws**	White
Or	Orange		

Key to items

1 Battery
2 Ignition switch
3 Engine fuse box
6 Main fuse box
8 Diagnostic connector
24 Steering wheel clock spring
111 Horn switch

112 Horn relay
113 Horn
114 Glovebox light/switch
115 Central locking module
116 Drivers door lock motor
117 Passenger door lock motor
118 LH rear door lock motor

119 RH door lock motor
120 Tailgate lock motor
121 Filler flap lock motor
122 Sunroof motor
123 Sunroof switch

Zafira 1998 to 2000 - Diagram 11

Note: prefix 1/ = X61 multi plug
prefix 2/ = X62 multi plug

MTS
H32202

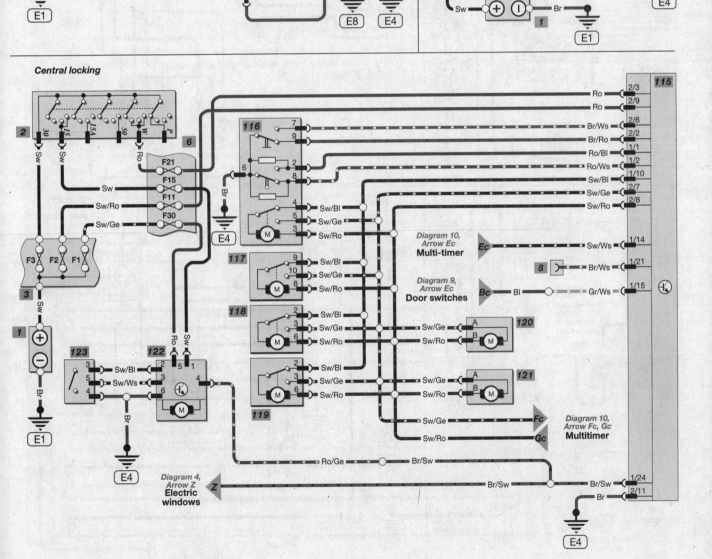

Wire colours

Bl	Blue	Pu	Purple
Br	Brown	Ro	Red
Ge	Yellow	Sw	Black
Gr	Grey	Vi	Violet
Gn	Green	Ws	White
Or	Orange		

Key to items

1 Battery
2 Ignition switch
3 Engine fuse box
6 Main fuse box
8 Diagnostic connector
124 Power steering motor
125 Heated mirror relay
126 Electric mirror switch
127 Driver' exterior door mirror
128 Passenger exterior door mirror
129 Cruise control switch
130 Cruise control module
131 Heater control module
132 Circulation flap motor
133 Heater blower motor resistor
134 Heater blower motor
135 Auxiliary heater switch

Zafira 1998 to 2000 - Diagram 12

MTS
H32203

Power steering

Exterior door mirrors

Diagram 10, Arrow Hc, Ic
Multi-timer

Diagram 2, Arrow B
Alternator

Cruise control

Diagram 4, Arrow Sb
Engine ECU

Diagram 4, Arrow L, M, N
Engine ECU

Diagram 5, Arrow I
Road speed signal

Diagram 9, Arrow Ub, Rb
Stop lights

Heating

Diagram 14, Arrow C
Info display

Diagram 10, Arrow Sa, Dc
Multi-timer

Diagram 9, Arrow Xb
Heater relay

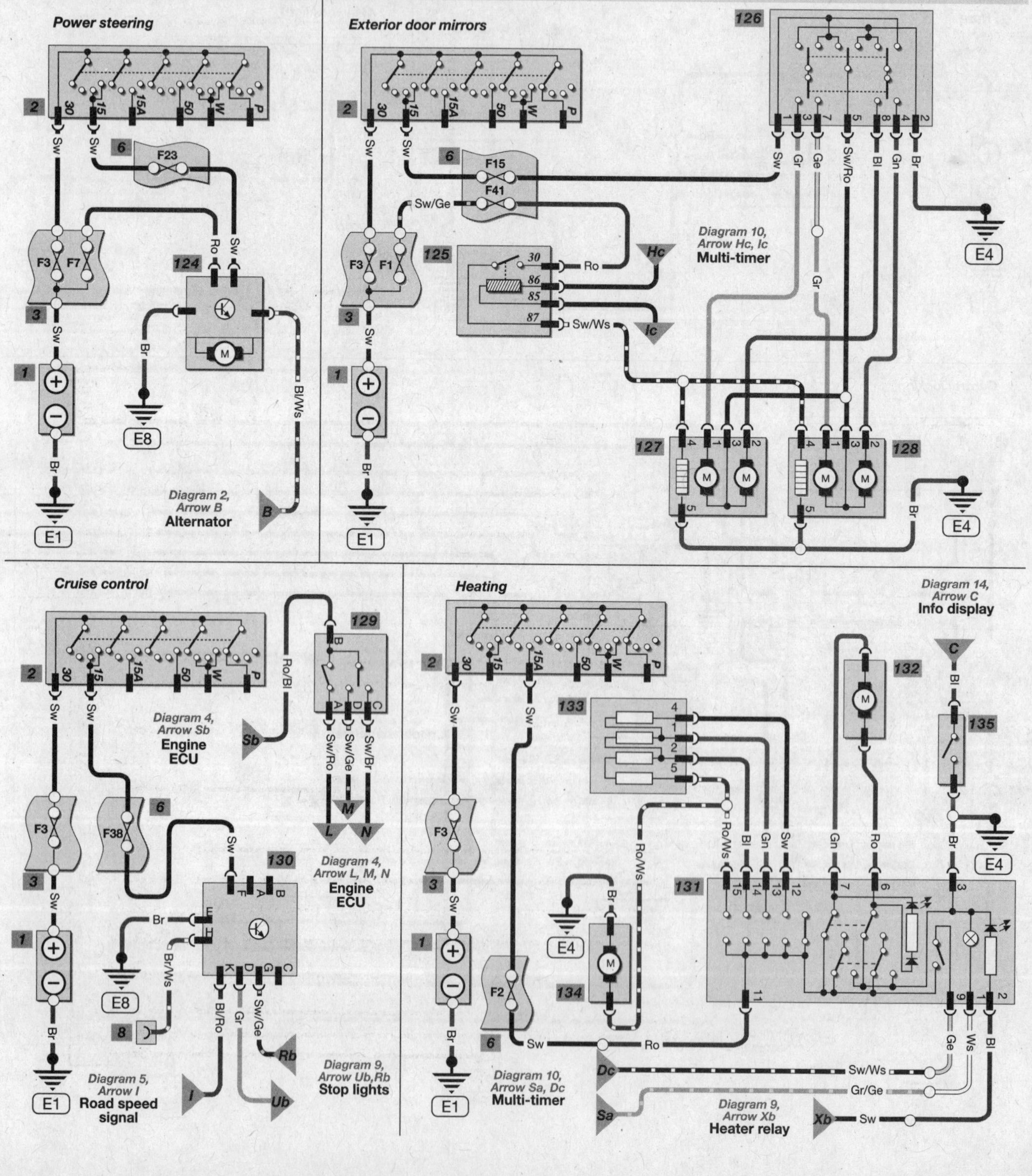

Wire colours

Bl	Blue	**Pu**	Purple
Br	Brown	**Pk**	Pink
Ge	Yellow	**Ro**	Red
Gr	Grey	**Sw**	Black
Gn	Green	**Vi**	Violet
Or	Orange	**Ws**	White

Key to items

1 Battery
2 Ignition switch
3 Engine fuse box
6 Main fuse box
8 Diagnostic connector
135 Auxiliary heater switch
136 Circulation flap motor
137 Heater blower motor resistor
138 Heater blower motor
139 Air conditioning module
140 Coolant actuator
141 Anti freeze protection switch
142 Triple info display
143 Outside temperature sensor

Zafira 1998 to 2000 - Diagram 13

MTS
H32204

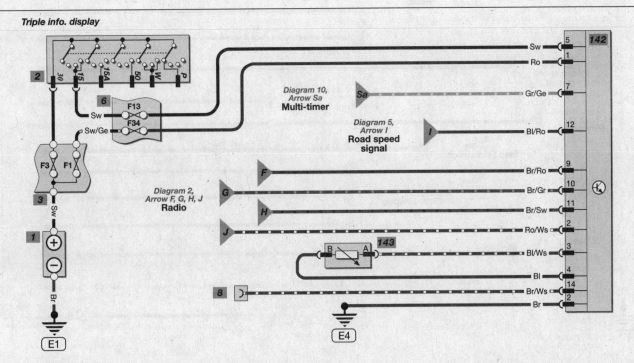

Wire colours

Bl	Blue	Pu	Purple
Br	Brown	Ro	Red
Ge	Yellow	Sw	Black
Gr	Grey	Vi	Violet
Gn	Green	Ws	White
Or	Orange		

Key to items

1 Battery
2 Ignition switch
3 Engine fuse box
6 Main fuse box
8 Diagnostic connector
144 Multi info display
145 LH front brake pad
     warning sensor
146 RH front brake pad
     warning sensor
147 Low washer fluid level switch
148 Low coolant level switch
149 Low oil level switch
150 Outside temperature sensor
151 Info display switch

Zafira 1998 to 2000 - Diagram 14

MTS
H32205

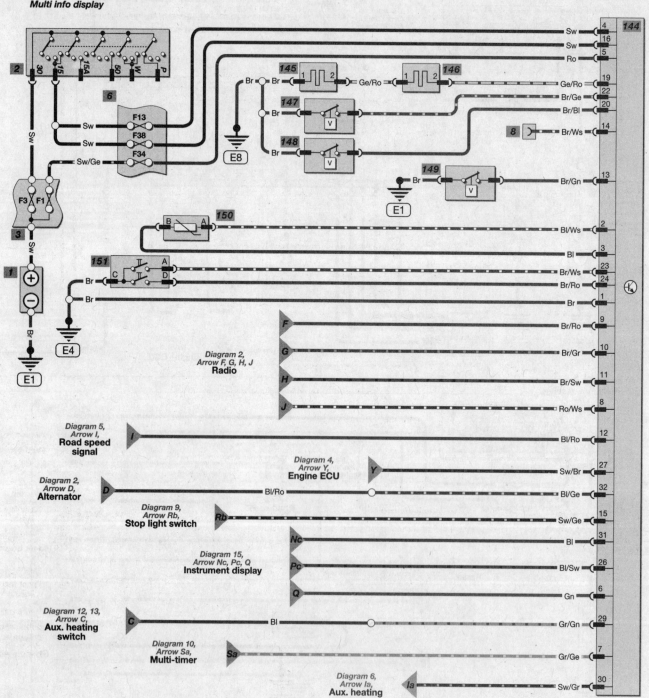

Multi info display

Wire colours

Bl	Blue	**Pu**	Purple
Br	Brown	**Ro**	Red
Ge	Yellow	**Sw**	Black
Gr	Grey	**Vi**	Violet
Gn	Green	**Ws**	White
Or	Orange		

Key to items

1 Battery
2 Ignition switch
3 Engine fuse box
6 Main fuse box
8 Diagnostic connector
152 Instrument panel
  a) alternator warning
  b) oil pressure warning
  c) airbag warning
  d) ABS warning

152 Instrument panel cont.
  e) pre-heating warning
  f) engine warning
  g) engine cooling light
  h) brake system warning
  i) trailer turning signal
  j) coolant temp. gauge
  k) fuel reserve warning
  l) fuel gauge
  m) tachometer

152 Instrument panel cont.
  n) speedometer
  o) coolant temp warning
  p) instrument illumination
  q) rear fog light warning
  r*) high beam warning
  r) high beam warning
    (tachometer only)
  s) front fog light warning
    (tachometer only)

152 Instrument panel cont.
  s*) front fog light warning
  t) LH indicator
  u) RH indicator
153 Oil pressure switch
154 Brake fluid switch
155 Parking brake switch
156 Fuel tank sender

Zafira 1998 to 2000 - Diagram 15

MTS
H32206

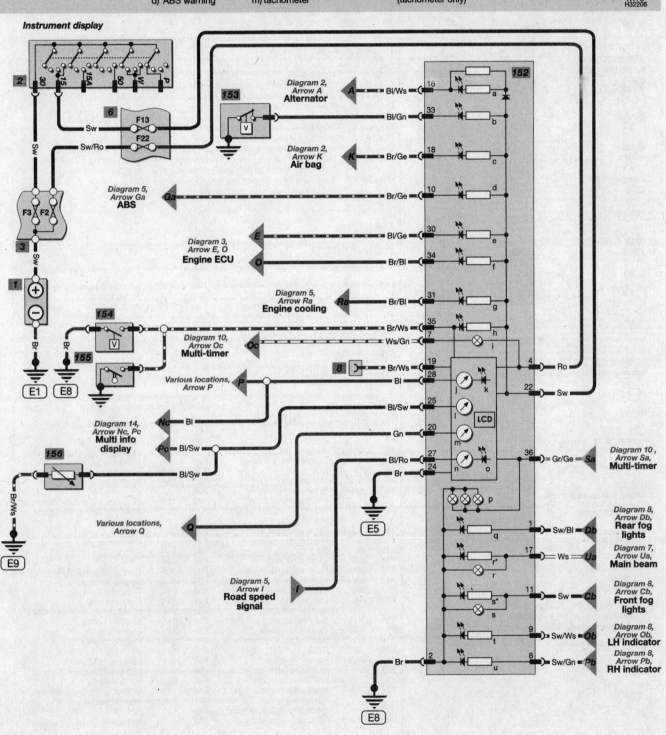

VAUXHALL ZAFIRA 2001 to 2004

Diagram 1

Key to symbols

Bulb	⊗
Switch	
Fuse/fusible link and current rating	F5 30A
Multiple contact switch (ganged)	
Resistor	
Variable resistor	
Connecting wires	
Item no.	2
Pump/motor	M
Earth point and location	E12
Wire joint	
Solenoid actuator	
Diode	
Light emitting diode (LED)	
Wire colour (brown with black tracer)	Br/Bk
Plug and socket contact	
Screened cable	

Dashed outline denotes part of a larger item, containing in this case an electronic or solid state device.
Pin types:
2 - Unspecified connector, pin 2.
X53 1 - Connector 53, pin 1.

Earth points

E1	Battery earth	E8	Engine electric earth
E2	Main engine earth	E9	Blower motor
E3	Distributor	E10	LH rear panel
E4	Transmission tunnel	E11	RH side of rear window
E5	Steering column	E12	Tailgate
E6	'A' pillar	E13	Central locking earth
E7	Engine fan cowl		

Key to circuits

Diagram 1	Information for wiring diagrams
Diagram 2	Starting and charging, airbag and radio with CD player
Diagram 3	Electric windows and central locking
Diagram 4	Air conditioning and engine cooling
Diagram 5	Power steering, heated seats, horns and ABS with traction control
Diagram 6	Multitimer, sunroof and cigarette lighter
Diagram 7	Wash/wipe and multi info display
Diagram 8	Instrument panel, heated rear window, filter heater and electric mirrors
Diagram 9	Automatic rear view mirror, interior lights, side lights, headlight leveling, tail lights, licence plate lights and dipped beam headlights
Diagram 10	Main beam headlights, fog lights, reversing lights, brake lights, direction indicators and hazard lights

Fuse table

Engine fuse box

Fuses	Rating	Fuses	Rating
F1	60A	F5	60A
F2	60A	F6	20A
F3	60A	F7	80A
F4	80A	F8	80A

Fuse box RH side of engine bay

Fuses	Rating	Circuit protected
F40	20A	Air conditioning
F41	1A	Air conditioning
F42	25A	Air conditioning

Engine bay fuse and relay box

Fuses	Rating	Circuit protected
F50	40A	Engine cooling
F52	40A	Engine cooling

Main fuse box

Fuses	Rating	Circuit protected	Fuses	Rating	Circuit protected
F1	-	Not used	F24	10A	LH dipped beam, headlight adjustment
F2	30A	Air conditioning	F25	10A	LH side light, LH tail light
F3	40A	Heated rear window	F26	10A	LH main beam
F4	-	Not used	F27	10A	Air conditioning
F5	-	Not used	F28	5A	Interior lights
F6	10A	RH dipped beam, headlight adjustment	F29	10A	Direction indicators, hazard lights, reversing lights, multitimer, light switch
F7	10A	RH side light, RH tail light licence plate light	F30	20A	Sunroof
F8	10A	RH main beam	F31	20A	Rear wiper
F9	30A	Headlight wash/wipe	F32	10A	Alarm
F10	15A	Horn	F33	20A	Trailer
F11	20A	Central locking	F34	10A	Radio, information display
F12	15A	Front fog lights	F35	10A	Engine cooling
F13	5A	Interior mirror	F36	15A	Cigarette light
F14	30A	Central locking	F37	20A	Heated seats
F15	5A	Electric windows, sunroof, electric windows	F38	10A	Brake lights, ABS, info display
F16	10A	Rear fog lights	F39	5A	Engine cooling
F17	30A	Electric windows	F40	5A	Engine cooling
F18	5A	Headlight adjustment	F41	10A	Heated mirrors
F19	30A	Radio	F42	10A	Airbag, interior lights
F20	30A	Electric windows	F43	15A	RH xenon headlight
F21	5A	Central locking, radio, multitimer, telephone	F44	15A	LH xenon headlight
F22	10A	Hazard lights, multitimer instrument panel, electronic climate control	F45	5A	Heated seats
			F46	15A	Engine control unit, add on heater
			F47	20A	Add on heater
			F48	-	Not used
F23	10A	ABS, power steering	F49	-	Not used

H32939

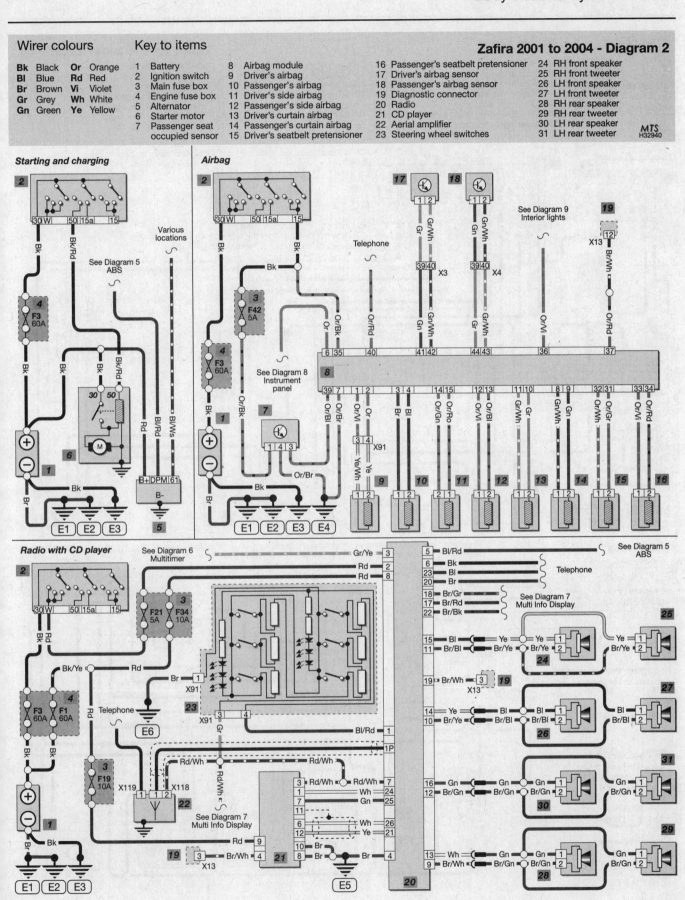

Wirer colours

Bk	Black	**Or**	Orange
Bl	Blue	**Rd**	Red
Br	Brown	**Vi**	Violet
Gr	Grey	**Wh**	White
Gn	Green	**Ye**	Yellow

Key to items

1 Battery
2 Ignition switch
3 Main fuse box
4 Engine fuse box
5 Alternator
6 Starter motor
7 Passenger seat occupied sensor
8 Airbag module
9 Driver's airbag
10 Passenger's airbag
11 Driver's side airbag
12 Passenger's side airbag
13 Driver's curtain airbag
14 Passenger's curtain airbag
15 Driver's seatbelt pretensioner
16 Passenger's seatbelt pretensioner
17 Driver's airbag sensor
18 Passenger's airbag sensor
19 Diagnostic connector
20 Radio
21 CD player
22 Aerial amplifier
23 Steering wheel switches
24 RH front speaker
25 RH front tweeter
26 LH front speaker
27 LH front tweeter
28 RH rear speaker
29 RH rear tweeter
30 LH rear speaker
31 LH rear tweeter

Zafira 2001 to 2004 - Diagram 2

MTS
H32940

Starting and charging

Airbag

Radio with CD player

Wirer colours

Bk	Black	Or	Orange
Bl	Blue	Rd	Red
Br	Brown	Vi	Violet
Gr	Grey	Wh	White
Gn	Green	Ye	Yellow

Key to items

1 Battery
2 Ignition switch
3 Main fuse box
4 Engine fuse box
19 Diagnostic connector
32 Driver's electric window switch
33 Passenger's electric window switch
34 LH rear electric window switch
35 RH rear electric window switch
36 Driver's window motor
37 Passengers's window motor
38 LH rear electric window motor
39 RH rear electric window motor
40 Central locking module
41 Driver's door switch
42 Filler flap lock motor
43 Tailgate lock motor
44 LH rear door lock motor
45 RH rear door lock motor
46 Passenger door lock motor
47 Driver's door lock motor

Zafira 2001 to 2004 - Diagram 3

MTS
H32941

Electric windows

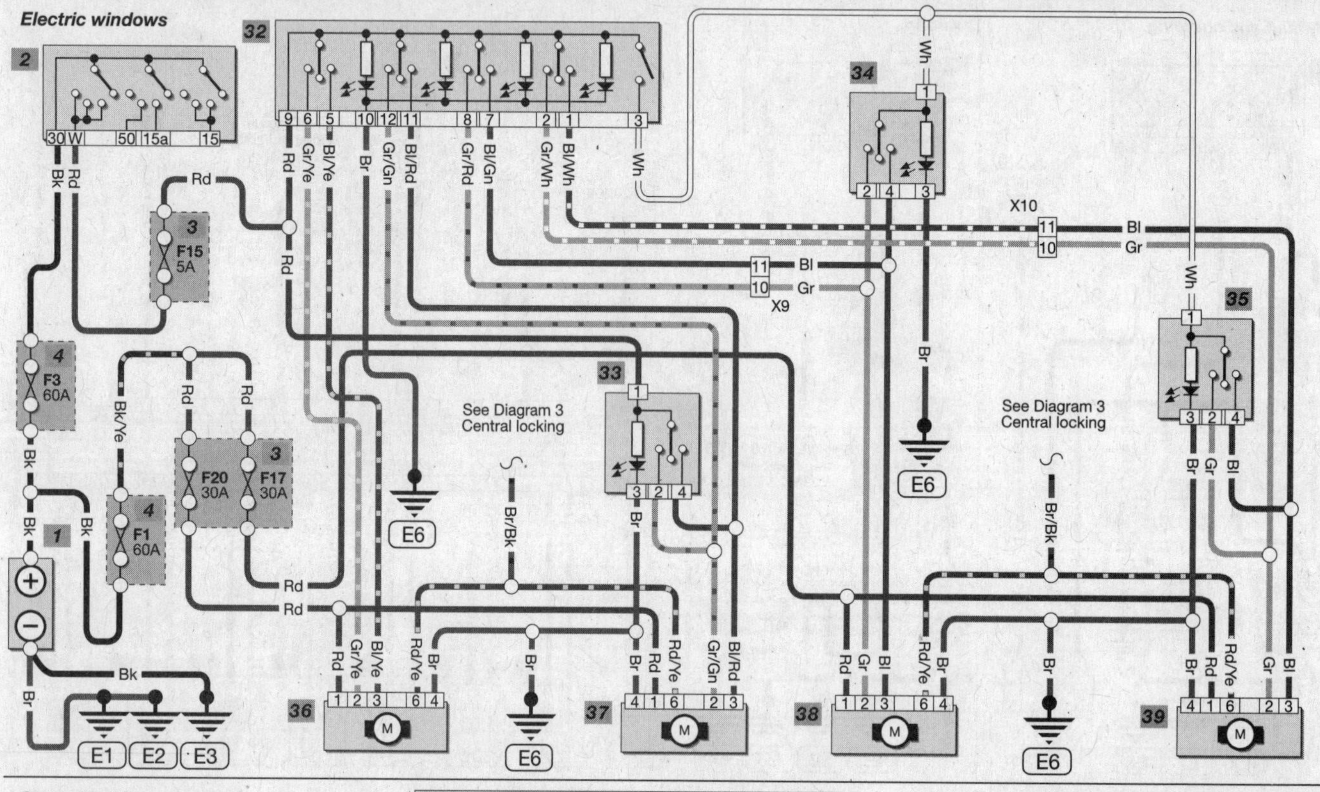

Central locking

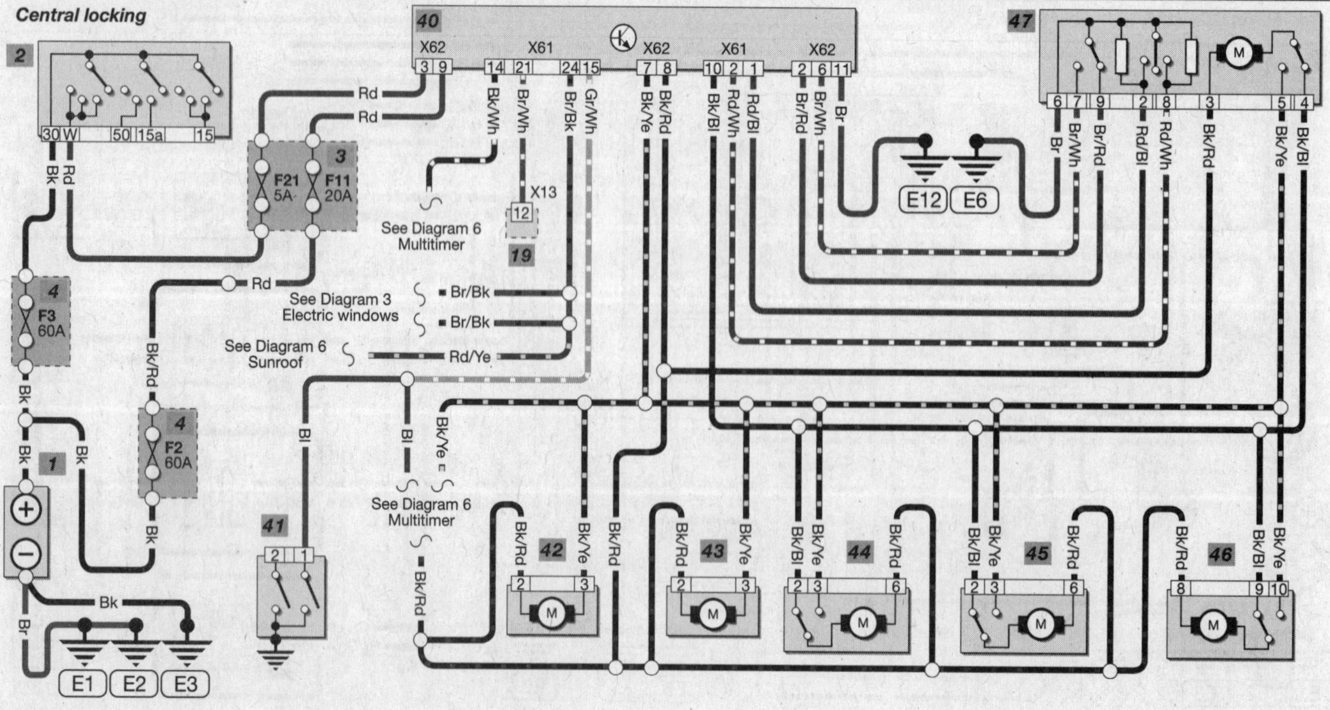

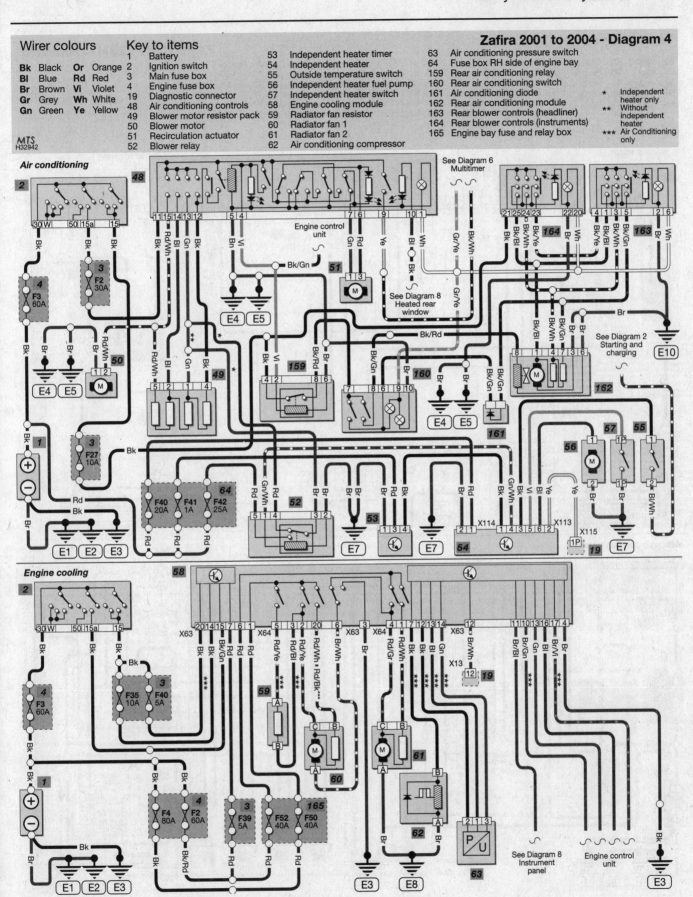

Zafira 2001 to 2004 - Diagram 4

Wirer colours

Bk	Black	Or	Orange
Bl	Blue	Rd	Red
Br	Brown	Vi	Violet
Gr	Grey	Wh	White
Gn	Green	Ye	Yellow

MTS H32942

Key to items
1 Battery
2 Ignition switch
3 Main fuse box
4 Engine fuse box
19 Diagnostic connector
48 Air conditioning controls
49 Blower motor resistor pack
50 Blower motor
51 Recirculation actuator
52 Blower relay
53 Independent heater timer
54 Independent heater
55 Outside temperature switch
56 Independent heater fuel pump
57 Independent heater switch
58 Engine cooling module
59 Radiator fan resistor
60 Radiator fan 1
61 Radiator fan 2
62 Air conditioning compressor
63 Air conditioning pressure switch
64 Fuse box RH side of engine bay
159 Rear air conditioning relay
160 Rear air conditioning switch
161 Air conditioning diode
162 Rear air conditioning module
163 Rear blower controls (headliner)
164 Rear blower controls (instruments)
165 Engine bay fuse and relay box

* Independent heater only
** Without independent heater
*** Air Conditioning only

Air conditioning

Engine cooling

Wirer colours

Bk Black   **Or** Orange
Bl Blue   **Rd** Red
Br Brown   **Vi** Violet
Gr Grey   **Wh** White
Gn Green   **Ye** Yellow

MTS
H32943

Key to items

1   Battery
2   Ignition switch
3   Main fuse box
4   Engine fuse box
19   Diagnostic connector
23   Steering wheel switches
65   Power steering pump
66   ABS module
67   Brake light switch
68   RH rear wheel speed sensor
69   LH rear wheel speed sensor
70   RH front wheel speed sensor
71   LH front wheel speed sensor
72   Horn relay
73   Horns
74   Horn switch
75   LH seat heating
76   RH seat heating
77   LH seat heating switch
78   RH seat heating switch

Zafira 2001 to 2004 - Diagram 5

Heated seats

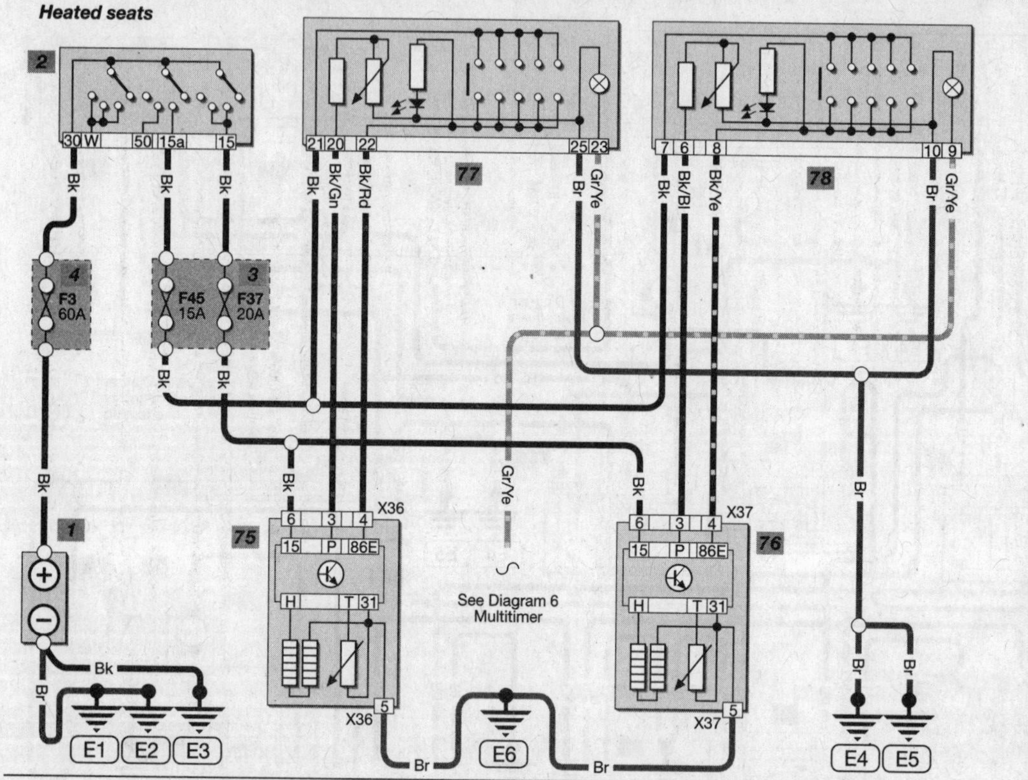

Power steering

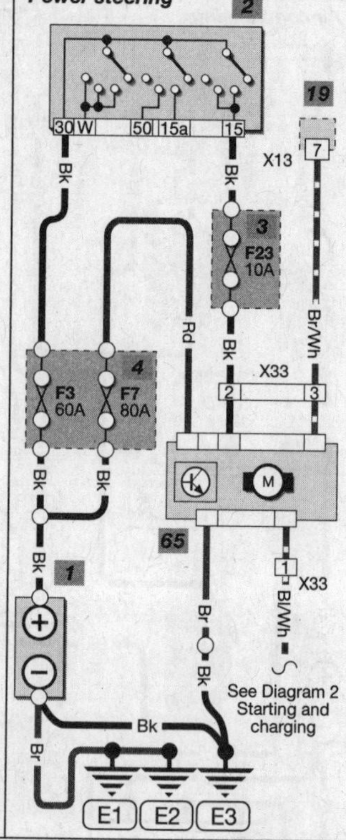

ABS with traction control

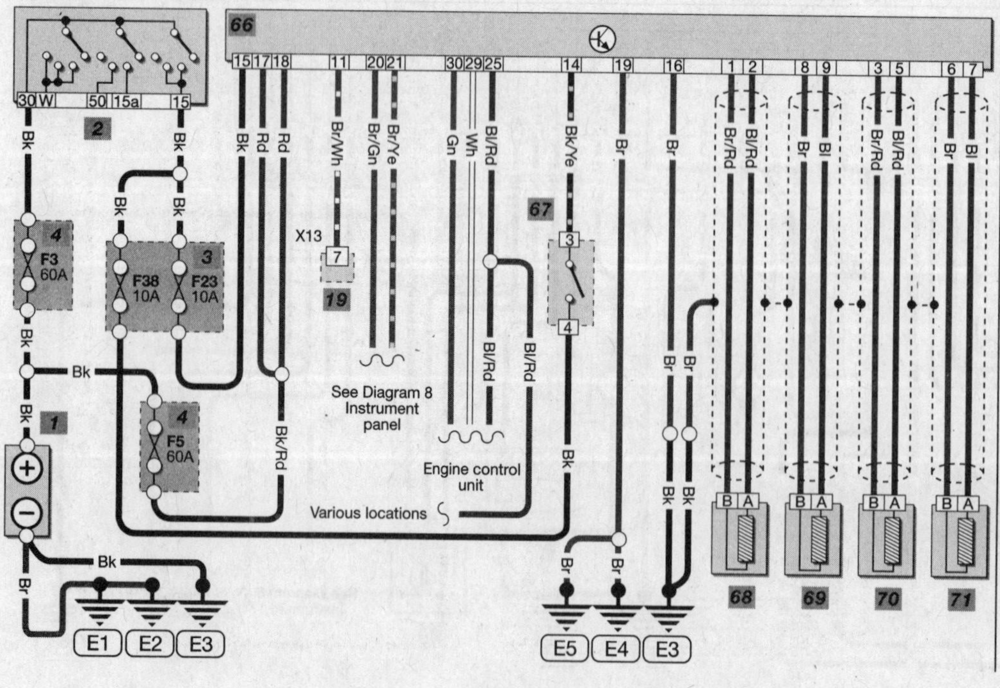

Horns

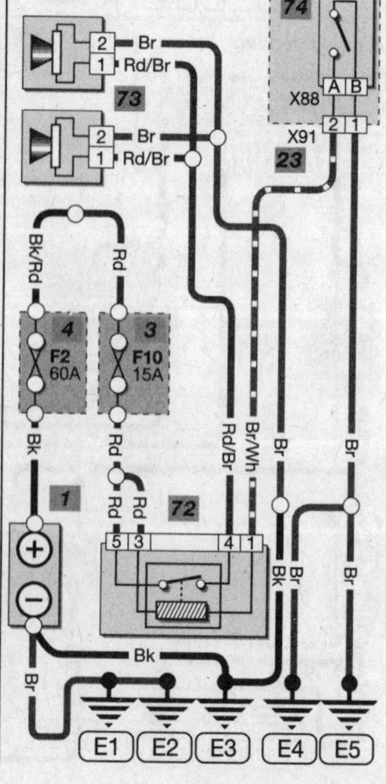

See Diagram 6 Multitimer

See Diagram 2 Starting and charging

See Diagram 8 Instrument panel

Engine control unit

Various locations

Wirer colours

Bk	Black	Or	Orange
Bl	Blue	Rd	Red
Br	Brown	Vi	Violet
Gr	Grey	Wh	White
Gn	Green	Ye	Yellow

Key to items

1   Battery
2   Ignition switch
3   Main fuse box
4   Engine fuse box
41 Driver's door switch
79 Multitimer
80 Passenger's door switch
81 RH rear door switch
82 LH rear door switch
83 Cigarette lighter
84 Front sunroof motor
85 Rear sunroof motor
86 Sunroof switch

Zafira 2001 to 2004 - Diagram 6

* Without rear sunroof

MTS
H32944

Multitimer

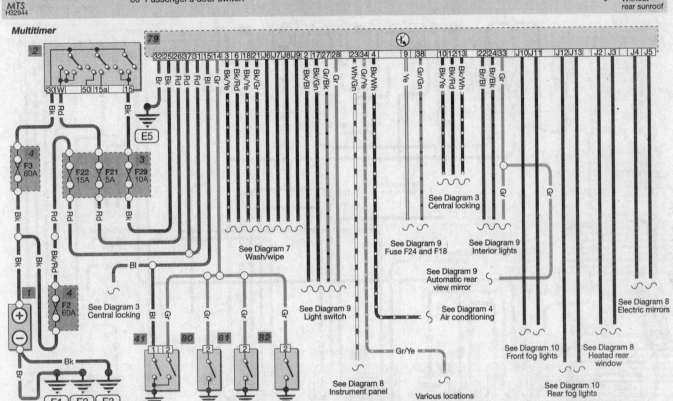

Cigarette lighter

Sunroof

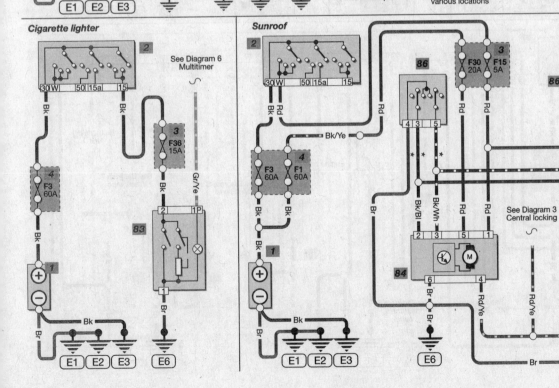

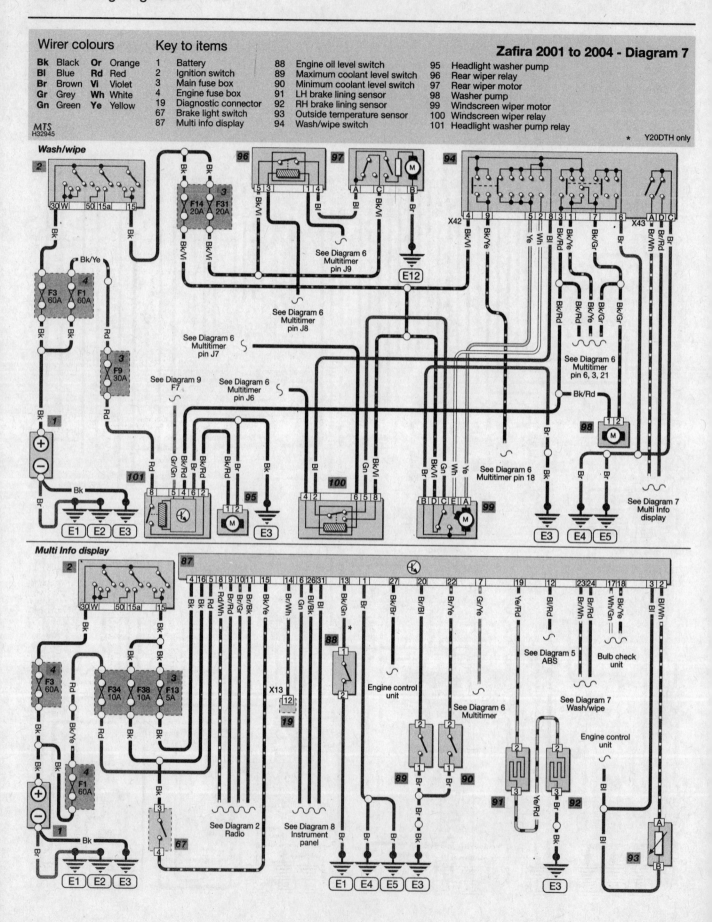

Wirer colours

Bk	Black	Or	Orange
Bl	Blue	Rd	Red
Br	Brown	Vi	Violet
Gr	Grey	Wh	White
Gn	Green	Ye	Yellow

Key to items

1 Battery
2 Ignition switch
3 Main fuse box
4 Engine fuse box
19 Diagnostic connector
67 Brake light switch
87 Multi info display

88 Engine oil level switch
89 Maximum coolant level switch
90 Minimum coolant level switch
91 LH brake lining sensor
92 RH brake lining sensor
93 Outside temperature sensor
94 Wash/wipe switch

95 Headlight washer pump
96 Rear wiper relay
97 Rear wiper motor
98 Washer pump
99 Windscreen wiper motor
100 Windscreen wiper relay
101 Headlight washer pump relay

Zafira 2001 to 2004 - Diagram 7

* Y20DTH only

MTS
H32945

Wirer colours

Bk	Black	**Or**	Orange
Bl	Blue	**Rd**	Red
Br	Brown	**Vi**	Violet
Gr	Grey	**Wh**	White
Gn	Green	**Ye**	Yellow

MTS
H32946

Key to items

1 Battery
2 Ignition switch
3 Main fuse box
4 Engine fuse box
19 Diagnostic connector
102 Filter heater relay
103 Filter heater
104 Instrument panel
  a) charge warning light
  b) oil pressure light

c) preheat warning light
d) airbag warning light
e) ABS warning light
f) traction control warning light
g) engine failure warning light
h) engine warning light
i) engine cooling warning light
j) brake warning light
k) seat belt warning light
l) trailer indicator light

m) instrument illumination
n) rear fog light warning light
o) main beam warning light
p) front fog light warning light
q) LH indicator light
r) RH indicator light
105 Oil pressure switch
106 Handbrake switch
107 Brake fluid level switch
108 Fuel level sensor

109 Heated rear window relay
110 Heated rear window
111 RH door mirror
112 LH door mirror
113 Mirror heating relay
114 Mirror switch

★ Y20DTH only

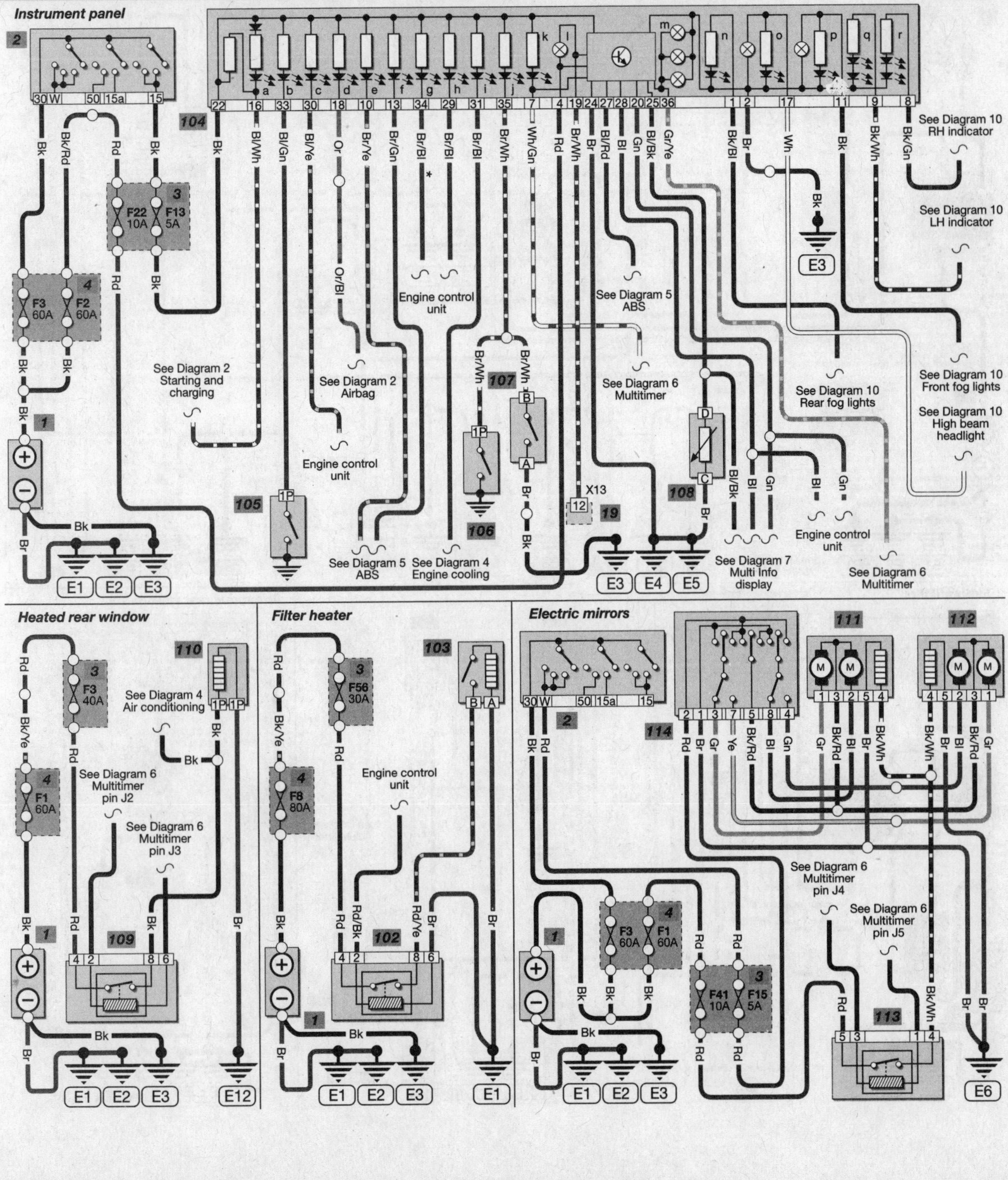

Zafira 2001 to 2004 - Diagram 8

Instrument panel

Heated rear window

Filter heater

Electric mirrors

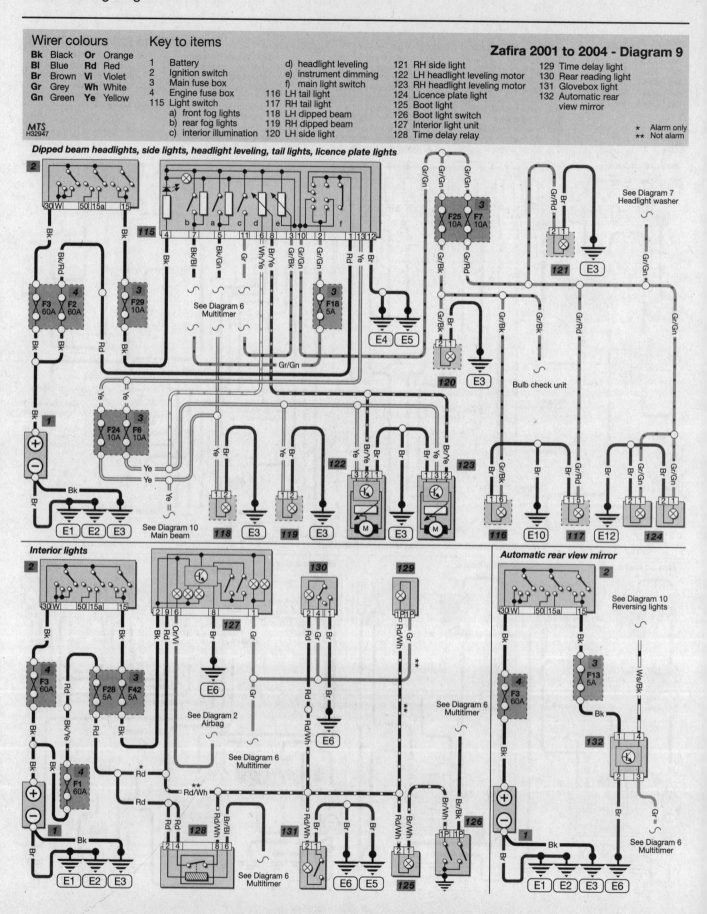

Wirer colours

Bk	Black	Or	Orange
Bl	Blue	Rd	Red
Br	Brown	Vi	Violet
Gr	Grey	Wh	White
Gn	Green	Ye	Yellow

MTS
H32947

Key to items

1 Battery
2 Ignition switch
3 Main fuse box
4 Engine fuse box
115 Light switch
   a) front fog lights
   b) rear fog lights
   c) interior illumination

d) headlight leveling
e) instrument dimming
f) main light switch
116 LH tail light
117 RH tail light
118 LH dipped beam
119 RH dipped beam
120 LH side light

121 RH side light
122 LH headlight leveling motor
123 RH headlight leveling motor
124 Licence plate light
125 Boot light
126 Boot light switch
127 Interior light unit
128 Time delay relay

129 Time delay light
130 Rear reading light
131 Glovebox light
132 Automatic rear
   view mirror

Zafira 2001 to 2004 - Diagram 9

* Alarm only
** Not alarm

Dipped beam headlights, side lights, headlight leveling, tail lights, licence plate lights

Interior lights

Automatic rear view mirror

Wirer colours

Bk	Black	Or	Orange
Bl	Blue	Rd	Red
Br	Brown	Vi	Violet
Gr	Grey	Wh	White
Gn	Green	Ye	Yellow

MTS
H32948

Key to items

1 Battery
2 Ignition switch
3 Main fuse box
4 Engine fuse box
67 Brake light switch
79 Multitimer
133 Direction indicator switch
134 Hazard light switch

135 LH indicator relay
136 RH indicator relay
137 LH side indicator
138 RH side indicator
139 LH front indicator
140 RH front indicator
141 LH rear indicator
142 RH rear indicator

143 Main beam relay
144 Headlight switch
145 LH main beam
146 RH main beam
147 Front fog light relay
148 Rear fog light relay
149 LH front fog light
150 RH front fog light

151 LH rear fog light
152 RH rear fog light
153 Reversing light switch
154 LH reversing light
155 RH reversing light
156 LH brake light
157 RH brake light
158 High level brake light

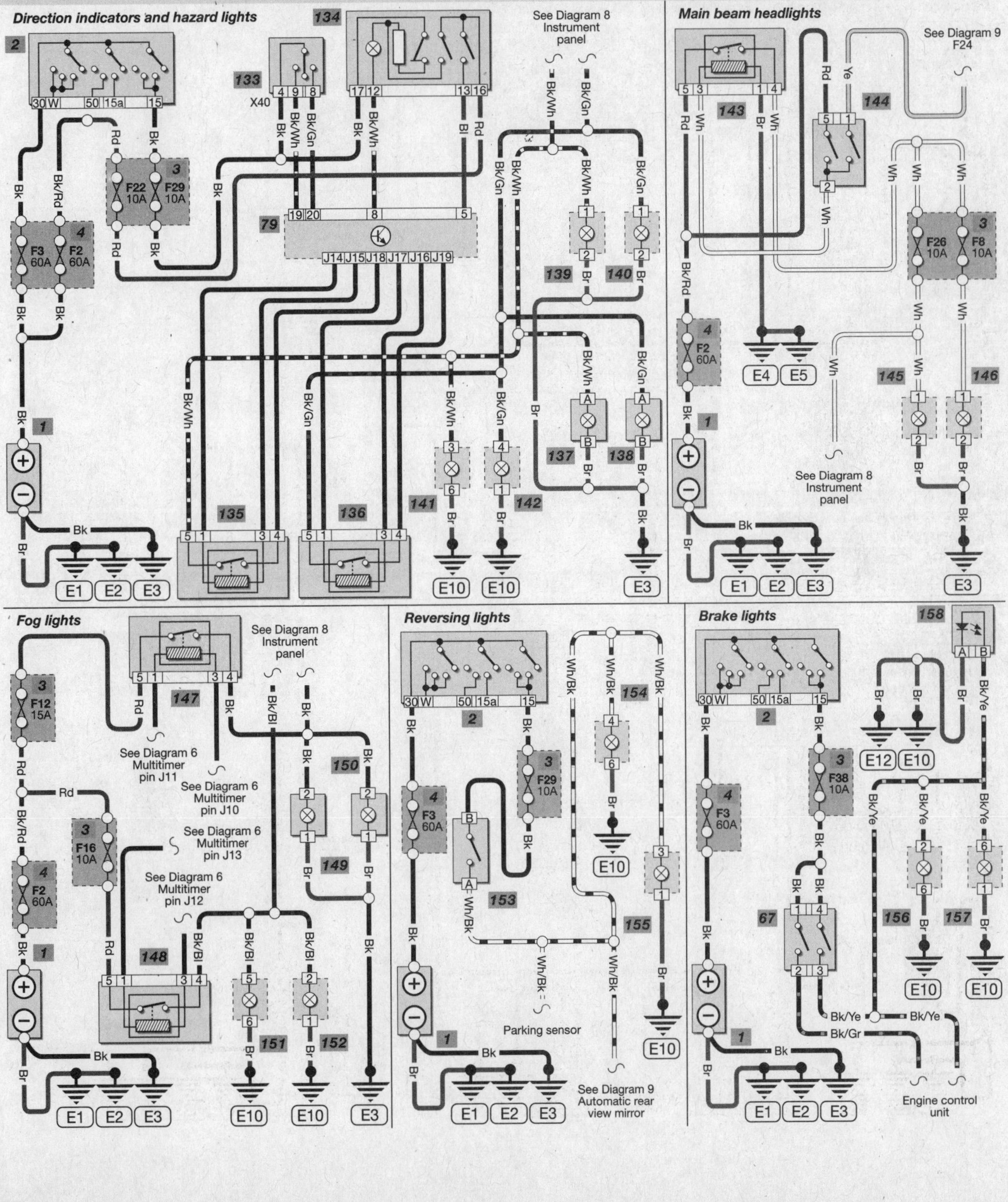

Zafira 2001 to 2004 - Diagram 10

Direction indicators and hazard lights

Main beam headlights

Fog lights

Reversing lights

Brake lights

Dimensions and weights

Note: *All figures are approximate, and vary according to model. Refer to manufacturer's data for exact figures.*

Dimensions

Overall length:
Astra Hatchback	4110 mm
Astra Estate	4288 mm
Zafira	4317 mm

Overall width:
Excluding wing mirrors	1709 mm
Including wing mirrors	1989 mm

Overall height (unladen):
Astra Hatchback	1425 mm
Astra Estate	1510 mm
Zafira	1634 mm

Wheelbase:
Astra Hatchback/Estate	2614 mm
Zafira	2694 mm

Track width:

Front:
Astra Hatchback/Estate	1464 mm
Zafira	1470 mm

Rear:
Astra Hatchback/Estate	1452 mm
Zafira	1487 mm

Weights

Kerb weight*:

1.7 litre engine models:
Hatchback	1215 kg
Estate	1255 kg

2.0 litre engine models:
Hatchback	1280 kg
Estate	1320 kg

For automatic transmission add 30 kg. For air conditioning add 30 kg.

Maximum roof rack load

Astra models	100 kg
Zafira models	75 kg

Turning circle

Astra Hatch/Estate	10.8 metres
Zafira	11.1 metres

Conversion factors

Length (distance)

Inches (in)	x 25.4	= Millimetres (mm)	x 0.0394	=	Inches (in)
Feet (ft)	x 0.305	= Metres (m)	x 3.281	=	Feet (ft)
Miles	x 1.609	= Kilometres (km)	x 0.621	=	Miles

Volume (capacity)

Cubic inches (cu in; in³)	x 16.387	= Cubic centimetres (cc; cm³)	x 0.061	=	Cubic inches (cu in; in³)
Imperial pints (Imp pt)	x 0.568	= Litres (l)	x 1.76	=	Imperial pints (Imp pt)
Imperial quarts (Imp qt)	x 1.137	= Litres (l)	x 0.88	=	Imperial quarts (Imp qt)
Imperial quarts (Imp qt)	x 1.201	= US quarts (US qt)	x 0.833	=	Imperial quarts (Imp qt)
US quarts (US qt)	x 0.946	= Litres (l)	x 1.057	=	US quarts (US qt)
Imperial gallons (Imp gal)	x 4.546	= Litres (l)	x 0.22	=	Imperial gallons (Imp gal)
Imperial gallons (Imp gal)	x 1.201	= US gallons (US gal)	x 0.833	=	Imperial gallons (Imp gal)
US gallons (US gal)	x 3.785	= Litres (l)	x 0.264	=	US gallons (US gal)

Mass (weight)

Ounces (oz)	x 28.35	= Grams (g)	x 0.035	=	Ounces (oz)
Pounds (lb)	x 0.454	= Kilograms (kg)	x 2.205	=	Pounds (lb)

Force

Ounces-force (ozf; oz)	x 0.278	= Newtons (N)	x 3.6	=	Ounces-force (ozf; oz)
Pounds-force (lbf; lb)	x 4.448	= Newtons (N)	x 0.225	=	Pounds-force (lbf; lb)
Newtons (N)	x 0.1	= Kilograms-force (kgf; kg)	x 9.81	=	Newtons (N)

Pressure

Pounds-force per square inch (psi; lbf/in²; lb/in²)	x 0.070	= Kilograms-force per square centimetre (kgf/cm²; kg/cm²)	x 14.223	=	Pounds-force per square inch (psi; lbf/in²; lb/in²)
Pounds-force per square inch (psi; lbf/in²; lb/in²)	x 0.068	= Atmospheres (atm)	x 14.696	=	Pounds-force per square inch (psi; lbf/in²; lb/in²)
Pounds-force per square inch (psi; lbf/in²; lb/in²)	x 0.069	= Bars	x 14.5	=	Pounds-force per square inch (psi; lbf/in²; lb/in²)
Pounds-force per square inch (psi; lbf/in²; lb/in²)	x 6.895	= Kilopascals (kPa)	x 0.145	=	Pounds-force per square inch (psi; lbf/in²; lb/in²)
Kilopascals (kPa)	x 0.01	= Kilograms-force per square centimetre (kgf/cm²; kg/cm²)	x 98.1	=	Kilopascals (kPa)
Millibar (mbar)	x 100	= Pascals (Pa)	x 0.01	=	Millibar (mbar)
Millibar (mbar)	x 0.0145	= Pounds-force per square inch (psi; lbf/in²; lb/in²)	x 68.947	=	Millibar (mbar)
Millibar (mbar)	x 0.75	= Millimetres of mercury (mmHg)	x 1.333	=	Millibar (mbar)
Millibar (mbar)	x 0.401	= Inches of water (inH₂O)	x 2.491	=	Millibar (mbar)
Millimetres of mercury (mmHg)	x 0.535	= Inches of water (inH₂O)	x 1.868	=	Millimetres of mercury (mmHg)
Inches of water (inH₂O)	x 0.036	= Pounds-force per square inch (psi; lbf/in²; lb/in²)	x 27.68	=	Inches of water (inH₂O)

Torque (moment of force)

Pounds-force inches (lbf in; lb in)	x 1.152	= Kilograms-force centimetre (kgf cm; kg cm)	x 0.868	=	Pounds-force inches (lbf in; lb in)
Pounds-force inches (lbf in; lb in)	x 0.113	= Newton metres (Nm)	x 8.85	=	Pounds-force inches (lbf in; lb in)
Pounds-force inches (lbf in; lb in)	x 0.083	= Pounds-force feet (lbf ft; lb ft)	x 12	=	Pounds-force inches (lbf in; lb in)
Pounds-force feet (lbf ft; lb ft)	x 0.138	= Kilograms-force metres (kgf m; kg m)	x 7.233	=	Pounds-force feet (lbf ft; lb ft)
Pounds-force feet (lbf ft; lb ft)	x 1.356	= Newton metres (Nm)	x 0.738	=	Pounds-force feet (lbf ft; lb ft)
Newton metres (Nm)	x 0.102	= Kilograms-force metres (kgf m; kg m)	x 9.804	=	Newton metres (Nm)

Power

Horsepower (hp)	x 745.7	= Watts (W)	x 0.0013	=	Horsepower (hp)

Velocity (speed)

Miles per hour (miles/hr; mph)	x 1.609	= Kilometres per hour (km/hr; kph)	x 0.621	=	Miles per hour (miles/hr; mph)

Fuel consumption*

Miles per gallon, Imperial (mpg)	x 0.354	= Kilometres per litre (km/l)	x 2.825	=	Miles per gallon, Imperial (mpg)
Miles per gallon, US (mpg)	x 0.425	= Kilometres per litre (km/l)	x 2.352	=	Miles per gallon, US (mpg)

Temperature

Degrees Fahrenheit = (°C x 1.8) + 32   Degrees Celsius (Degrees Centigrade; °C) = (°F - 32) x 0.56

It is common practice to convert from miles per gallon (mpg) to litres/100 kilometres (l/100km), where mpg x l/100 km = 282

Spare parts are available from many sources, including maker's appointed garages, accessory shops, and motor factors. To be sure of obtaining the correct parts, it will sometimes be necessary to quote the vehicle identification number. If possible, it can also be useful to take the old parts along for positive identification. Items such as starter motors and alternators may be available under a service exchange scheme – any parts returned should be clean.

Our advice regarding spare parts is as follows.

Officially appointed garages

This is the best source of parts which are peculiar to your car, and which are not otherwise generally available (eg, badges, interior trim, certain body panels, etc). It is also the only place at which you should buy parts if the vehicle is still under warranty.

Accessory shops

These are very good places to buy materials and components needed for the maintenance of your car (oil, air and fuel filters, light bulbs, drivebelts, greases, brake pads, tough-up paint, etc). Components of this nature sold by a reputable shop are of the same standard as those used by the car manufacturer.

Besides components, these shops also sell tools and general accessories, usually have convenient opening hours, charge lower prices, and can often be found close to home. Some accessory shops have parts counters where components needed for almost any repair job can be purchased or ordered.

Motor factors

Good factors will stock all the more important components which wear out comparatively quickly, and can sometimes supply individual components needed for the overhaul of a larger assembly (eg, brake seals and hydraulic parts, bearing shells, pistons, valves). They may also handle work such as cylinder block reboring, crankshaft regrinding, etc.

Tyre and exhaust specialists

These outlets may be independent, or members of a local or national chain. They frequently offer competitive prices when compared with a main dealer or local garage, but it will pay to obtain several quotes before making a decision. When researching prices, also ask what 'extras' may be added – for instance fitting a new valve and balancing the wheel are both commonly charged on top of the price of a new tyre.

Other sources

Beware of parts or materials obtained from market stalls, car boot sales or similar outlets. Such items are not invariably sub-standard, but there is little chance of compensation if they do prove unsatisfactory. In the case of safety-critical components such as brake pads, there is the risk not only of financial loss, but also of an accident causing injury or death.

Second-hand components or assemblies obtained from a car breaker can be a good buy in some circumstances, but his sort of purchase is best made by the experienced DIY mechanic.

Vehicle identification numbers

Note: *When new, the car is provided with a Car Pass (similar to a credit card) having all the vehicle's data recorded on a magnetic strip.*

Modifications are a continuing and unpublicised process in vehicle manufacture, quite apart from major model changes. Spare parts manuals and lists are compiled upon a numerical basis, the individual vehicle identification numbers being essential to correct identification of the component concerned.

When ordering spare parts, always give as much information as possible. Quote the car model, year of manufacture, body and engine numbers as appropriate.

The *Vehicle Identification Number (VIN)* is stamped on a plate riveted to the engine compartment front crossmember, behind the radiator. It is also stamped into the body floor panel between the driver's seat and the door sill panel; lift the flap in the carpet to see it **(see illustrations)**. On some non-UK models the plate may be attached to the front door frame.

The *Engine number* is stamped on the front left-hand side of the cylinder block.

The *Vehicle Identification Number (VIN)* is stamped on a plate riveted to the engine compartment front crossmember

The VIN is also stamped into the body floor panel next to the driver's seat

Whenever servicing, repair or overhaul work is carried out on the car or its components, observe the following procedures and instructions. This will assist in carrying out the operation efficiently and to a professional standard of workmanship.

Joint mating faces and gaskets

When separating components at their mating faces, never insert screwdrivers or similar implements into the joint between the faces in order to prise them apart. This can cause severe damage which results in oil leaks, coolant leaks, etc upon reassembly. Separation is usually achieved by tapping along the joint with a soft-faced hammer in order to break the seal. However, note that this method may not be suitable where dowels are used for component location.

Where a gasket is used between the mating faces of two components, a new one must be fitted on reassembly; fit it dry unless otherwise stated in the repair procedure. Make sure that the mating faces are clean and dry, with all traces of old gasket removed. When cleaning a joint face, use a tool which is unlikely to score or damage the face, and remove any burrs or nicks with an oilstone or fine file.

Make sure that tapped holes are cleaned with a pipe cleaner, and keep them free of jointing compound, if this is being used, unless specifically instructed otherwise.

Ensure that all orifices, channels or pipes are clear, and blow through them, preferably using compressed air.

Oil seals

Oil seals can be removed by levering them out with a wide flat-bladed screwdriver or similar implement. Alternatively, a number of self-tapping screws may be screwed into the seal, and these used as a purchase for pliers or some similar device in order to pull the seal free.

Whenever an oil seal is removed from its working location, either individually or as part of an assembly, it should be renewed.

The very fine sealing lip of the seal is easily damaged, and will not seal if the surface it contacts is not completely clean and free from scratches, nicks or grooves. If the original sealing surface of the component cannot be restored, and the manufacturer has not made provision for slight relocation of the seal relative to the sealing surface, the component should be renewed.

Protect the lips of the seal from any surface which may damage them in the course of fitting. Use tape or a conical sleeve where possible. Lubricate the seal lips with oil before fitting and, on dual-lipped seals, fill the space between the lips with grease.

Unless otherwise stated, oil seals must be fitted with their sealing lips toward the lubricant to be sealed.

Use a tubular drift or block of wood of the appropriate size to install the seal and, if the seal housing is shouldered, drive the seal down to the shoulder. If the seal housing is unshouldered, the seal should be fitted with its face flush with the housing top face (unless otherwise instructed).

Screw threads and fastenings

Seized nuts, bolts and screws are quite a common occurrence where corrosion has set in, and the use of penetrating oil or releasing fluid will often overcome this problem if the offending item is soaked for a while before attempting to release it. The use of an impact driver may also provide a means of releasing such stubborn fastening devices, when used in conjunction with the appropriate screwdriver bit or socket. If none of these methods works, it may be necessary to resort to the careful application of heat, or the use of a hacksaw or nut splitter device.

Studs are usually removed by locking two nuts together on the threaded part, and then using a spanner on the lower nut to unscrew the stud. Studs or bolts which have broken off below the surface of the component in which they are mounted can sometimes be removed using a stud extractor. Always ensure that a blind tapped hole is completely free from oil, grease, water or other fluid before installing the bolt or stud. Failure to do this could cause the housing to crack due to the hydraulic action of the bolt or stud as it is screwed in.

When tightening a castellated nut to accept a split pin, tighten the nut to the specified torque, where applicable, and then tighten further to the next split pin hole. Never slacken the nut to align the split pin hole, unless stated in the repair procedure.

When checking or retightening a nut or bolt to a specified torque setting, slacken the nut or bolt by a quarter of a turn, and then retighten to the specified setting. However, this should not be attempted where angular tightening has been used.

For some screw fastenings, notably cylinder head bolts or nuts, torque wrench settings are no longer specified for the latter stages of tightening, "angle-tightening" being called up instead. Typically, a fairly low torque wrench setting will be applied to the bolts/nuts in the correct sequence, followed by one or more stages of tightening through specified angles.

Locknuts, locktabs and washers

Any fastening which will rotate against a component or housing during tightening should always have a washer between it and the relevant component or housing.

Spring or split washers should always be renewed when they are used to lock a critical component such as a big-end bearing retaining bolt or nut. Locktabs which are folded over to retain a nut or bolt should always be renewed.

Self-locking nuts can be re-used in non-critical areas, providing resistance can be felt when the locking portion passes over the bolt or stud thread. However, it should be noted that self-locking stiffnuts tend to lose their effectiveness after long periods of use, and should then be renewed as a matter of course.

Split pins must always be replaced with new ones of the correct size for the hole.

When thread-locking compound is found on the threads of a fastener which is to be re-used, it should be cleaned off with a wire brush and solvent, and fresh compound applied on reassembly.

Special tools

Some repair procedures in this manual entail the use of special tools such as a press, two or three-legged pullers, spring compressors, etc. Wherever possible, suitable readily-available alternatives to the manufacturer's special tools are described, and are shown in use. In some instances, where no alternative is possible, it has been necessary to resort to the use of a manufacturer's tool, and this has been done for reasons of safety as well as the efficient completion of the repair operation. Unless you are highly-skilled and have a thorough understanding of the procedures described, never attempt to bypass the use of any special tool when the procedure described specifies its use. Not only is there a very great risk of personal injury, but expensive damage could be caused to the components involved.

Environmental considerations

When disposing of used engine oil, brake fluid, antifreeze, etc, give due consideration to any detrimental environmental effects. Do not, for instance, pour any of the above liquids down drains into the general sewage system, or onto the ground to soak away. Many local council refuse tips provide a facility for waste oil disposal, as do some garages. If none of these facilities are available, consult your local Environmental Health Department, or the National Rivers Authority, for further advice.

With the universal tightening-up of legislation regarding the emission of environmentally-harmful substances from motor vehicles, most vehicles have tamperproof devices fitted to the main adjustment points of the fuel system. These devices are primarily designed to prevent unqualified persons from adjusting the fuel/air mixture, with the chance of a consequent increase in toxic emissions. If such devices are found during servicing or overhaul, they should, wherever possible, be renewed or refitted in accordance with the manufacturer's requirements or current legislation.

OIL CARE
FOLLOW THE CODE
OIL BANK LINE
0800 66 33 66
www.oilbankline.org.uk

Note: It is antisocial and illegal to dump oil down the drain. To find the location of your local oil recycling bank, call this number free.

The jack supplied with the vehicle locates in the jacking points on the underside of the sills – see *Wheel changing* at the front of this manual. Ensure that the jack head is correctly engaged before attempting to raise the vehicle **(see illustration)**; this jack should only be used for changing the roadwheels. When carrying out any other kind of work, raise the vehicle using a hydraulic trolley jack, and always supplement the jack with axle stands positioned under the vehicle jacking points.

When using a trolley jack or axle stands, always position the jack head or axle stand head under, or adjacent to one of the relevant wheel changing jacking points under the sills. Use a block of wood between the jack or axle stand and the sill – the block of wood should have a groove cut into it, in which the welded flange of the sill will locate **(see illustration)**.

Do not attempt to jack the vehicle under the front crossmember, the sump, or any of the suspension components.

Never work under, around, or near a raised vehicle, unless it is adequately supported in at least two places.

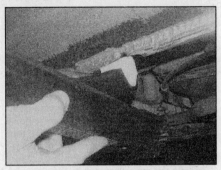

Using the jack supplied with the vehicle

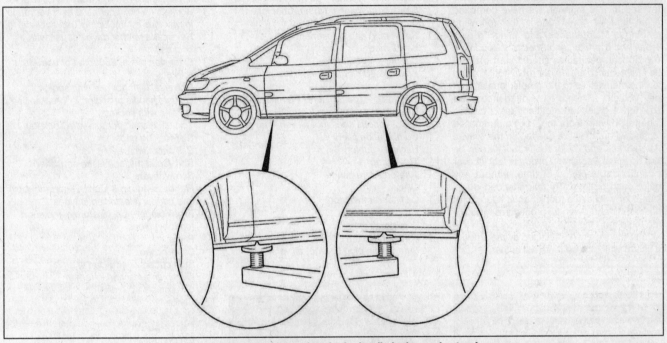

Front and rear jacking points for hydraulic jack or axle stands

Disconnecting the battery

Several systems fitted to the vehicle require battery power to be available at all times, either to ensure their continued operation (such as the clock) or to maintain control unit memories which would be erased if the battery were to be disconnected. Whenever the battery is to be disconnected therefore, first note the following, to ensure that there are no unforeseen consequences of this action:

a) First, on any vehicle with central locking, it is a wise precaution to remove the key from the ignition, and to keep it with you, so that it does not get locked in if the central locking should engage accidentally when the battery is reconnected.

b) If a security-coded audio unit is fitted, and the unit and/or the battery is disconnected, the unit will not function again on reconnecfion until the correct security code is entered. Details of this procedure, which varies according to the

unit fitted, are given in the vehicle owner's handbook. Ensure you have the correct code before you disconnect the battery. If you do not have the code or details of the correct procedure, but can supply proof of ownership and a legitimate reason for wanting this information, a Vauxhall dealer may be able to help.

c) The fuel system electronic control unit is of the 'self-learning' type, meaning that as it operates, it also monitors and stores the settings which give optimum engine performance under all operating conditions. When the battery is disconnected, these settings are lost and the ECU reverts to the base settings programmed into its memory at the factory. On restarting, this may lead to the engine running/idling roughly until the ECU has re-learned the optimum settings. This process is best accomplished by taking the vehicle on a road test (for approximately 15 minutes), covering all

engine speeds and loads, concentrating mainly in the 2500 to 3500 rpm region.

Devices known as 'memory-savers' (or 'code-savers') can be used to avoid some of the above problems. Precise details vary according to the device used. Typically, it is plugged into the cigarette lighter, and is connected by its own wires to a spare battery; the vehicle's own battery is then disconnected from the electrical system, leaving the memory-saver to pass sufficient current to maintain audio unit security codes and any other memory values, and also to run permanently-live circuits such as the clock.

⚠️ **Warning: Some of these devices allow a considerable amount of current to pass, which can mean that many of the vehicle's systems are still operational when the main battery is disconnected. If a memory saver is used, ensure that the circuit concerned is actually 'dead' before carrying out any work on it!**

Introduction

A selection of good tools is a fundamental requirement for anyone contemplating the maintenance and repair of a motor vehicle. For the owner who does not possess any, their purchase will prove a considerable expense, offsetting some of the savings made by doing-it-yourself. However, provided that the tools purchased meet the relevant national safety standards and are of good quality, they will last for many years and prove an extremely worthwhile investment.

To help the average owner to decide which tools are needed to carry out the various tasks detailed in this manual, we have compiled three lists of tools under the following headings: *Maintenance and minor repair*, *Repair and overhaul*, and *Special*. Newcomers to practical mechanics should start off with the *Maintenance and minor repair* tool kit, and confine themselves to the simpler jobs around the vehicle. Then, as confidence and experience grow, more difficult tasks can be undertaken, with extra tools being purchased as, and when, they are needed. In this way, a *Maintenance and minor repair* tool kit can be built up into a *Repair and overhaul* tool kit over a considerable period of time, without any major cash outlays. The experienced do-it-yourselfer will have a tool kit good enough for most repair and overhaul procedures, and will add tools from the *Special* category when it is felt that the expense is justified by the amount of use to which these tools will be put.

Maintenance and minor repair tool kit

The tools given in this list should be considered as a minimum requirement if routine maintenance, servicing and minor repair operations are to be undertaken. We recommend the purchase of combination spanners (ring one end, open-ended the other); although more expensive than open-ended ones, they do give the advantages of both types of spanner.

☐ *Combination spanners:*
  Metric - 8 to 19 mm inclusive
☐ *Adjustable spanner - 35 mm jaw (approx.)*
☐ *Spark plug spanner (with rubber insert) - petrol models*
☐ *Spark plug gap adjustment tool - petrol models*
☐ *Set of feeler gauges*
☐ *Brake bleed nipple spanner*
☐ *Screwdrivers:*
  Flat blade - 100 mm long x 6 mm dia
  Cross blade - 100 mm long x 6 mm dia
  Torx - various sizes (not all vehicles)
☐ *Combination pliers*
☐ *Hacksaw (junior)*
☐ *Tyre pump*
☐ *Tyre pressure gauge*
☐ *Oil can*
☐ *Oil filter removal tool*
☐ *Fine emery cloth*
☐ *Wire brush (small)*
☐ *Funnel (medium size)*
☐ *Sump drain plug key (not all vehicles)*

Repair and overhaul tool kit

These tools are virtually essential for anyone undertaking any major repairs to a motor vehicle, and are additional to those given in the *Maintenance and minor repair* list. Included in this list is a comprehensive set of sockets. Although these are expensive, they will be found invaluable as they are so versatile - particularly if various drives are included in the set. We recommend the half-inch square-drive type, as this can be used with most proprietary torque wrenches.

The tools in this list will sometimes need to be supplemented by tools from the *Special* list:

☐ *Sockets (or box spanners) to cover range in previous list (including Torx sockets)*
☐ *Reversible ratchet drive (for use with sockets)*
☐ *Extension piece, 250 mm (for use with sockets)*
☐ *Universal joint (for use with sockets)*
☐ *Flexible handle or sliding T "breaker bar" (for use with sockets)*
☐ *Torque wrench (for use with sockets)*
☐ *Self-locking grips*
☐ *Ball pein hammer*
☐ *Soft-faced mallet (plastic or rubber)*
☐ *Screwdrivers:*
  Flat blade - long & sturdy, short (chubby), and narrow (electrician's) types
  Cross blade – long & sturdy, and short (chubby) types
☐ *Pliers:*
  Long-nosed
  Side cutters (electrician's)
  Circlip (internal and external)
☐ *Cold chisel - 25 mm*
☐ *Scriber*
☐ *Scraper*
☐ *Centre-punch*
☐ *Pin punch*
☐ *Hacksaw*
☐ *Brake hose clamp*
☐ *Brake/clutch bleeding kit*
☐ *Selection of twist drills*
☐ *Steel rule/straight-edge*
☐ *Allen keys (inc. splined/Torx type)*
☐ *Selection of files*
☐ *Wire brush*
☐ *Axle stands*
☐ *Jack (strong trolley or hydraulic type)*
☐ *Light with extension lead*
☐ *Universal electrical multi-meter*

Sockets and reversible ratchet drive

Brake bleeding kit

Torx key, socket and bit

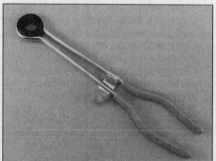

Hose clamp

Angular-tightening gauge

Special tools

The tools in this list are those which are not used regularly, are expensive to buy, or which need to be used in accordance with their manufacturers' instructions. Unless relatively difficult mechanical jobs are undertaken frequently, it will not be economic to buy many of these tools. Where this is the case, you could consider clubbing together with friends (or joining a motorists' club) to make a joint purchase, or borrowing the tools against a deposit from a local garage or tool hire specialist. It is worth noting that many of the larger DIY superstores now carry a large range of special tools for hire at modest rates.

The following list contains only those tools and instruments freely available to the public, and not those special tools produced by the vehicle manufacturer specifically for its dealer network. You will find occasional references to these manufacturers' special tools in the text of this manual. Generally, an alternative method of doing the job without the vehicle manufacturers' special tool is given. However, sometimes there is no alternative to using them. Where this is the case and the relevant tool cannot be bought or borrowed, you will have to entrust the work to a dealer.

- ☐ *Angular-tightening gauge*
- ☐ *Valve spring compressor*
- ☐ *Valve grinding tool*
- ☐ *Piston ring compressor*
- ☐ *Piston ring removal/installation tool*
- ☐ *Cylinder bore hone*
- ☐ *Balljoint separator*
- ☐ *Coil spring compressors (where applicable)*
- ☐ *Two/three-legged hub and bearing puller*
- ☐ *Impact screwdriver*
- ☐ *Micrometer and/or vernier calipers*
- ☐ *Dial gauge*
- ☐ *Stroboscopic timing light*
- ☐ *Dwell angle meter/tachometer*
- ☐ *Fault code reader*
- ☐ *Cylinder compression gauge*
- ☐ *Hand-operated vacuum pump and gauge*
- ☐ *Clutch plate alignment set*
- ☐ *Brake shoe steady spring cup removal tool*
- ☐ *Bush and bearing removal/installation set*
- ☐ *Stud extractors*
- ☐ *Tap and die set*
- ☐ *Lifting tackle*
- ☐ *Trolley jack*

Buying tools

Reputable motor accessory shops and superstores often offer excellent quality tools at discount prices, so it pays to shop around.

Remember, you don't have to buy the most expensive items on the shelf, but it is always advisable to steer clear of the very cheap tools. Beware of 'bargains' offered on market stalls or at car boot sales. There are plenty of good tools around at reasonable prices, but always aim to purchase items which meet the relevant national safety standards. If in doubt, ask the proprietor or manager of the shop for advice before making a purchase.

Care and maintenance of tools

Having purchased a reasonable tool kit, it is necessary to keep the tools in a clean and serviceable condition. After use, always wipe off any dirt, grease and metal particles using a clean, dry cloth, before putting the tools away. Never leave them lying around after they have been used. A simple tool rack on the garage or workshop wall for items such as screwdrivers and pliers is a good idea. Store all normal spanners and sockets in a metal box. Any measuring instruments, gauges, meters, etc, must be carefully stored where they cannot be damaged or become rusty.

Take a little care when tools are used. Hammer heads inevitably become marked, and screwdrivers lose the keen edge on their blades from time to time. A little timely attention with emery cloth or a file will soon restore items like this to a good finish.

Working facilities

Not to be forgotten when discussing tools is the workshop itself. If anything more than routine maintenance is to be carried out, a suitable working area becomes essential.

It is appreciated that many an owner-mechanic is forced by circumstances to remove an engine or similar item without the benefit of a garage or workshop. Having done this, any repairs should always be done under the cover of a roof.

Wherever possible, any dismantling should be done on a clean, flat workbench or table at a suitable working height.

Any workbench needs a vice; one with a jaw opening of 100 mm is suitable for most jobs. As mentioned previously, some clean dry storage space is also required for tools, as well as for any lubricants, cleaning fluids, touch-up paints etc, which become necessary.

Another item which may be required, and which has a much more general usage, is an electric drill with a chuck capacity of at least 8 mm. This, together with a good range of twist drills, is virtually essential for fitting accessories.

Last, but not least, always keep a supply of old newspapers and clean, lint-free rags available, and try to keep any working area as clean as possible.

Micrometers

Dial test indicator ("dial gauge")

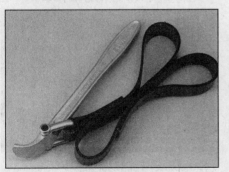
Strap wrench

Compression tester

Fault code reader

This is a guide to getting your vehicle through the MOT test. Obviously it will not be possible to examine the vehicle to the same standard as the professional MOT tester. However, working through the following checks will enable you to identify any problem areas before submitting the vehicle for the test.

Where a testable component is in borderline condition, the tester has discretion in deciding whether to pass or fail it. The basis of such discretion is whether the tester would be happy for a close relative or friend to use the vehicle with the component in that condition. If the vehicle presented is clean and evidently well cared for, the tester may be more inclined to pass a borderline component than if the vehicle is scruffy and apparently neglected.

It has only been possible to summarise the test requirements here, based on the regulations in force at the time of printing. Test standards are becoming increasingly stringent, although there are some exemptions for older vehicles.

An assistant will be needed to help carry out some of these checks.

The checks have been sub-divided into four categories, as follows:

1 Checks carried out **FROM THE DRIVER'S SEAT**

2 Checks carried out **WITH THE VEHICLE ON THE GROUND**

3 Checks carried out **WITH THE VEHICLE RAISED AND THE WHEELS FREE TO TURN**

4 Checks carried out on **YOUR VEHICLE'S EXHAUST EMISSION SYSTEM**

---

1 Checks carried out **FROM THE DRIVER'S SEAT**

Handbrake

☐ Test the operation of the handbrake. Excessive travel (too many clicks) indicates incorrect brake or cable adjustment.
☐ Check that the handbrake cannot be released by tapping the lever sideways. Check the security of the lever mountings.

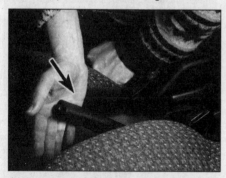

Footbrake

☐ Depress the brake pedal and check that it does not creep down to the floor, indicating a master cylinder fault. Release the pedal, wait a few seconds, then depress it again. If the pedal travels nearly to the floor before firm resistance is felt, brake adjustment or repair is necessary. If the pedal feels spongy, there is air in the hydraulic system which must be removed by bleeding.

☐ Check that the brake pedal is secure and in good condition. Check also for signs of fluid leaks on the pedal, floor or carpets, which would indicate failed seals in the brake master cylinder.
☐ Check the servo unit (when applicable) by operating the brake pedal several times, then keeping the pedal depressed and starting the engine. As the engine starts, the pedal will move down slightly. If not, the vacuum hose or the servo itself may be faulty.

Steering wheel and column

☐ Examine the steering wheel for fractures or looseness of the hub, spokes or rim.
☐ Move the steering wheel from side to side and then up and down. Check that the steering wheel is not loose on the column, indicating wear or a loose retaining nut. Continue moving the steering wheel as before, but also turn it slightly from left to right.
☐ Check that the steering wheel is not loose on the column, and that there is no abnormal

movement of the steering wheel, indicating wear in the column support bearings or couplings.

Windscreen, mirrors and sunvisor

☐ The windscreen must be free of cracks or other significant damage within the driver's field of view. (Small stone chips are acceptable.) Rear view mirrors must be secure, intact, and capable of being adjusted.

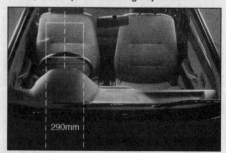

290mm

☐ The driver's sunvisor must be capable of being stored in the "up" position.

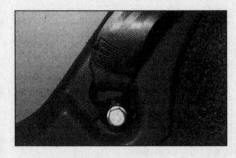

Seat belts and seats

Note: *The following checks are applicable to all seat belts, front and rear.*

☐ Examine the webbing of all the belts (including rear belts if fitted) for cuts, serious fraying or deterioration. Fasten and unfasten each belt to check the buckles. If applicable, check the retracting mechanism. Check the security of all seat belt mountings accessible from inside the vehicle.

☐ Seat belts with pre-tensioners, once activated, have a "flag" or similar showing on the seat belt stalk. This, in itself, is not a reason for test failure.

☐ The front seats themselves must be securely attached and the backrests must lock in the upright position.

Doors

☐ Both front doors must be able to be opened and closed from outside and inside, and must latch securely when closed.

2 Checks carried out WITH THE VEHICLE ON THE GROUND

Vehicle identification

☐ Number plates must be in good condition, secure and legible, with letters and numbers correctly spaced – spacing at (A) should be at least twice that at (B).

☐ The VIN plate and/or homologation plate must be legible.

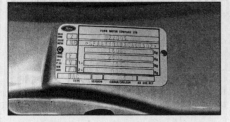

Electrical equipment

☐ Switch on the ignition and check the operation of the horn.

☐ Check the windscreen washers and wipers, examining the wiper blades; renew damaged or perished blades. Also check the operation of the stop-lights.

☐ Check the operation of the sidelights and number plate lights. The lenses and reflectors must be secure, clean and undamaged.

☐ Check the operation and alignment of the headlights. The headlight reflectors must not be tarnished and the lenses must be undamaged.

☐ Switch on the ignition and check the operation of the direction indicators (including the instrument panel tell-tale) and the hazard warning lights. Operation of the sidelights and stop-lights must not affect the indicators - if it does, the cause is usually a bad earth at the rear light cluster.

☐ Check the operation of the rear foglight(s), including the warning light on the instrument panel or in the switch.

☐ The ABS warning light must illuminate in accordance with the manufacturers' design. For most vehicles, the ABS warning light should illuminate when the ignition is switched on, and (if the system is operating properly) extinguish after a few seconds. Refer to the owner's handbook.

Footbrake

☐ Examine the master cylinder, brake pipes and servo unit for leaks, loose mountings, corrosion or other damage.

☐ The fluid reservoir must be secure and the fluid level must be between the upper (A) and lower (B) markings.

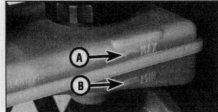

☐ Inspect both front brake flexible hoses for cracks or deterioration of the rubber. Turn the steering from lock to lock, and ensure that the hoses do not contact the wheel, tyre, or any part of the steering or suspension mechanism. With the brake pedal firmly depressed, check the hoses for bulges or leaks under pressure.

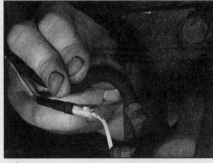

Steering and suspension

☐ Have your assistant turn the steering wheel from side to side slightly, up to the point where the steering gear just begins to transmit this movement to the roadwheels. Check for excessive free play between the steering wheel and the steering gear, indicating wear or insecurity of the steering column joints, the column-to-steering gear coupling, or the steering gear itself.

☐ Have your assistant turn the steering wheel more vigorously in each direction, so that the roadwheels just begin to turn. As this is done, examine all the steering joints, linkages, fittings and attachments. Renew any component that shows signs of wear or damage. On vehicles with power steering, check the security and condition of the steering pump, drivebelt and hoses.

☐ Check that the vehicle is standing level, and at approximately the correct ride height.

Shock absorbers

☐ Depress each corner of the vehicle in turn, then release it. The vehicle should rise and then settle in its normal position. If the vehicle continues to rise and fall, the shock absorber is defective. A shock absorber which has seized will also cause the vehicle to fail.

Exhaust system

☐ Start the engine. With your assistant holding a rag over the tailpipe, check the entire system for leaks. Repair or renew leaking sections.

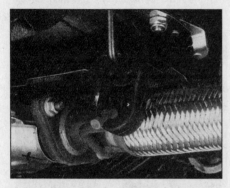

3 Checks carried out **WITH THE VEHICLE RAISED AND THE WHEELS FREE TO TURN**

Jack up the front and rear of the vehicle, and securely support it on axle stands. Position the stands clear of the suspension assemblies. Ensure that the wheels are clear of the ground and that the steering can be turned from lock to lock.

Steering mechanism

☐ Have your assistant turn the steering from lock to lock. Check that the steering turns smoothly, and that no part of the steering mechanism, including a wheel or tyre, fouls any brake hose or pipe or any part of the body structure.
☐ Examine the steering rack rubber gaiters for damage or insecurity of the retaining clips. If power steering is fitted, check for signs of damage or leakage of the fluid hoses, pipes or connections. Also check for excessive stiffness or binding of the steering, a missing split pin or locking device, or severe corrosion of the body structure within 30 cm of any steering component attachment point.

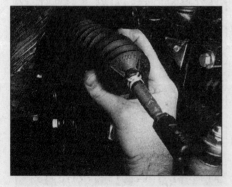

Front and rear suspension and wheel bearings

☐ Starting at the front right-hand side, grasp the roadwheel at the 3 o'clock and 9 o'clock positions and rock gently but firmly. Check for free play or insecurity at the wheel bearings, suspension balljoints, or suspension mountings, pivots and attachments.
☐ Now grasp the wheel at the 12 o'clock and 6 o'clock positions and repeat the previous inspection. Spin the wheel, and check for roughness or tightness of the front wheel bearing.

☐ If excess free play is suspected at a component pivot point, this can be confirmed by using a large screwdriver or similar tool and levering between the mounting and the component attachment. This will confirm whether the wear is in the pivot bush, its retaining bolt, or in the mounting itself (the bolt holes can often become elongated).

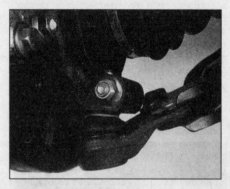

☐ Carry out all the above checks at the other front wheel, and then at both rear wheels.

Springs and shock absorbers

☐ Examine the suspension struts (when applicable) for serious fluid leakage, corrosion, or damage to the casing. Also check the security of the mounting points.
☐ If coil springs are fitted, check that the spring ends locate in their seats, and that the spring is not corroded, cracked or broken.
☐ If leaf springs are fitted, check that all leaves are intact, that the axle is securely attached to each spring, and that there is no deterioration of the spring eye mountings, bushes, and shackles.

☐ The same general checks apply to vehicles fitted with other suspension types, such as torsion bars, hydraulic displacer units, etc. Ensure that all mountings and attachments are secure, that there are no signs of excessive wear, corrosion or damage, and (on hydraulic types) that there are no fluid leaks or damaged pipes.
☐ Inspect the shock absorbers for signs of serious fluid leakage. Check for wear of the mounting bushes or attachments, or damage to the body of the unit.

Driveshafts (fwd vehicles only)

☐ Rotate each front wheel in turn and inspect the constant velocity joint gaiters for splits or damage. Also check that each driveshaft is straight and undamaged.

Braking system

☐ If possible without dismantling, check brake pad wear and disc condition. Ensure that the friction lining material has not worn excessively, (A) and that the discs are not fractured, pitted, scored or badly worn (B).

☐ Examine all the rigid brake pipes underneath the vehicle, and the flexible hose(s) at the rear. Look for corrosion, chafing or insecurity of the pipes, and for signs of bulging under pressure, chafing, splits or deterioration of the flexible hoses.
☐ Look for signs of fluid leaks at the brake calipers or on the brake backplates. Repair or renew leaking components.
☐ Slowly spin each wheel, while your assistant depresses and releases the footbrake. Ensure that each brake is operating and does not bind when the pedal is released.

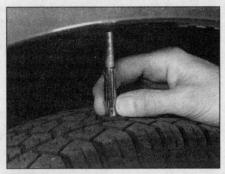

☐ Examine the handbrake mechanism, checking for frayed or broken cables, excessive corrosion, or wear or insecurity of the linkage. Check that the mechanism works on each relevant wheel, and releases fully, without binding.

☐ It is not possible to test brake efficiency without special equipment, but a road test can be carried out later to check that the vehicle pulls up in a straight line.

Fuel and exhaust systems

☐ Inspect the fuel tank (including the filler cap), fuel pipes, hoses and unions. All components must be secure and free from leaks.

☐ Examine the exhaust system over its entire length, checking for any damaged, broken or missing mountings, security of the retaining clamps and rust or corrosion.

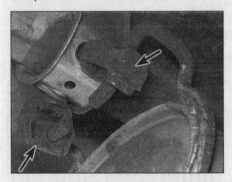

Wheels and tyres

☐ Examine the sidewalls and tread area of each tyre in turn. Check for cuts, tears, lumps, bulges, separation of the tread, and exposure of the ply or cord due to wear or damage. Check that the tyre bead is correctly seated on the wheel rim, that the valve is sound and properly seated, and that the wheel is not distorted or damaged.

☐ Check that the tyres are of the correct size for the vehicle, that they are of the same size and type on each axle, and that the pressures are correct.

☐ Check the tyre tread depth. The legal minimum at the time of writing is 1.6 mm over at least three-quarters of the tread width. Abnormal tread wear may indicate incorrect front wheel alignment.

Body corrosion

☐ Check the condition of the entire vehicle structure for signs of corrosion in load-bearing areas. (These include chassis box sections, side sills, cross-members, pillars, and all suspension, steering, braking system and seat belt mountings and anchorages.) Any corrosion which has seriously reduced the thickness of a load-bearing area is likely to cause the vehicle to fail. In this case professional repairs are likely to be needed.

☐ Damage or corrosion which causes sharp or otherwise dangerous edges to be exposed will also cause the vehicle to fail.

4 Checks carried out on YOUR VEHICLE'S EXHAUST EMISSION SYSTEM

Petrol models

☐ Have the engine at normal operating temperature, and make sure that it is in good tune (ignition system in good order, air filter element clean, etc).

☐ Before any measurements are carried out, raise the engine speed to around 2500 rpm, and hold it at this speed for 20 seconds. Allow the engine speed to return to idle, and watch for smoke emissions from the exhaust tailpipe. If the idle speed is obviously much too high, or if dense blue or clearly-visible black smoke comes from the tailpipe for more than 5 seconds, the vehicle will fail. As a rule of thumb, blue smoke signifies oil being burnt (engine wear) while black smoke signifies unburnt fuel (dirty air cleaner element, or other carburettor or fuel system fault).

☐ An exhaust gas analyser capable of measuring carbon monoxide (CO) and hydrocarbons (HC) is now needed. If such an instrument cannot be hired or borrowed, a local garage may agree to perform the check for a small fee.

CO emissions (mixture)

☐ At the time of writing, for vehicles first used between 1st August 1975 and 31st July 1986 (P to C registration), the CO level must not exceed 4.5% by volume. For vehicles first used between 1st August 1986 and 31st July 1992 (D to J registration), the CO level must not exceed 3.5% by volume. Vehicles first

used after 1st August 1992 (K registration) must conform to the manufacturer's specification. The MOT tester has access to a DOT database or emissions handbook, which lists the CO and HC limits for each make and model of vehicle. The CO level is measured with the engine at idle speed, and at "fast idle". The following limits are given as a general guide:
    At idle speed -
        CO level no more than 0.5%
    At "fast idle" (2500 to 3000 rpm) -
        CO level no more than 0.3%
    (Minimum oil temperature 60°C)

☐ If the CO level cannot be reduced far enough to pass the test (and the fuel and ignition systems are otherwise in good condition) then the carburettor is badly worn, or there is some problem in the fuel injection system or catalytic converter (as applicable).

HC emissions

☐ With the CO within limits, HC emissions for vehicles first used between 1st August 1975 and 31st July 1992 (P to J registration) must not exceed 1200 ppm. Vehicles first used after 1st August 1992 (K registration) must conform to the manufacturer's specification. The MOT tester has access to a DOT database or emissions handbook, which lists the CO and HC limits for each make and model of vehicle. The HC level is measured with the engine at "fast idle". The following is given as a general guide:
    At "fast idle" (2500 to 3000 rpm) -
        HC level no more than 200 ppm
    (Minimum oil temperature 60°C)

☐ Excessive HC emissions are caused by incomplete combustion, the causes of which can include oil being burnt, mechanical wear and ignition/fuel system malfunction.

Diesel models

☐ The only emission test applicable to Diesel engines is the measuring of exhaust smoke density. The test involves accelerating the engine several times to its maximum unloaded speed.

Note: *It is of the utmost importance that the engine timing belt is in good condition before the test is carried out.*

☐ The limits for Diesel engine exhaust smoke, introduced in September 1995 are:
Vehicles first used before 1st August 1979:
    Exempt from metered smoke testing, but must not emit "dense blue or clearly visible black smoke for a period of more than 5 seconds at idle" or "dense blue or clearly visible black smoke during acceleration which would obscure the view of other road users".
Non-turbocharged vehicles first used after 1st August 1979: 2.5m⁻¹
Turbocharged vehicles first used after 1st August 1979: 3.0m⁻¹

☐ Excessive smoke can be caused by a dirty air cleaner element. Otherwise, professional advice may be needed to find the cause.

Engine

- [ ] Engine fails to rotate when attempting to start
- [ ] Engine rotates, but will not start
- [ ] Engine difficult to start when cold
- [ ] Engine difficult to start when hot
- [ ] Starter motor noisy or excessively-rough in engagement
- [ ] Engine starts, but stops immediately
- [ ] Engine idles erratically
- [ ] Engine misfires at idle speed
- [ ] Engine misfires throughout the driving speed range
- [ ] Engine hesitates on acceleration
- [ ] Engine stalls
- [ ] Engine lacks power
- [ ] Engine backfires
- [ ] Oil pressure warning light illuminated with engine running
- [ ] Engine runs-on after switching off
- [ ] Engine noises

Cooling system

- [ ] Overheating
- [ ] Overcooling
- [ ] External coolant leakage
- [ ] Internal coolant leakage
- [ ] Corrosion

Fuel and exhaust systems

- [ ] Excessive fuel consumption
- [ ] Fuel leakage and/or fuel odour
- [ ] Excessive noise or fumes from the exhaust system

Clutch

- [ ] Pedal travels to floor – no pressure or very little resistance
- [ ] Clutch fails to disengage (unable to select gears)
- [ ] Clutch slips (engine speed increases, with no increase in vehicle speed)
- [ ] Judder as clutch is engaged
- [ ] Noise when depressing or releasing clutch pedal

Manual transmission

- [ ] Noisy in neutral with engine running
- [ ] Noisy in one particular gear
- [ ] Difficulty engaging gears
- [ ] Jumps out of gear
- [ ] Vibration
- [ ] Lubricant leaks

Driveshafts

- [ ] Vibration when accelerating or decelerating
- [ ] Clicking or knocking noise on turns (at slow speed on full-lock)

Braking system

- [ ] Vehicle pulls to one side under braking
- [ ] Noise (grinding or high-pitched squeal) when brakes applied
- [ ] Excessive brake pedal travel
- [ ] Brake pedal feels spongy when depressed
- [ ] Excessive brake pedal effort required to stop vehicle
- [ ] Judder felt through brake pedal or steering wheel when braking
- [ ] Pedal pulsates when braking hard
- [ ] Brakes binding
- [ ] Rear wheels locking under normal braking

Steering and suspension

- [ ] Vehicle pulls to one side
- [ ] Wheel wobble and vibration
- [ ] Excessive pitching and/or rolling around corners, or during braking
- [ ] Wandering or general instability
- [ ] Excessively-stiff steering
- [ ] Excessive play in steering
- [ ] Lack of power assistance
- [ ] Tyre wear excessive

Electrical system

- [ ] Battery will not hold a charge for more than a few days
- [ ] Ignition/no-charge warning light remains illuminated with engine running
- [ ] Ignition/no-charge warning light fails to come on
- [ ] Lights inoperative
- [ ] Instrument readings inaccurate or erratic
- [ ] Horn inoperative, or unsatisfactory in operation
- [ ] Windscreen/tailgate wipers inoperative, or unsatisfactory in operation
- [ ] Windscreen/tailgate washers inoperative, or unsatisfactory in operation
- [ ] Electric windows inoperative, or unsatisfactory in operation
- [ ] Central locking system inoperative, or unsatisfactory in operation

Introduction

The vehicle owner who does his or her own maintenance according to the recommended service schedules should not have to use this section of the manual very often. Modern component reliability is such that, provided those items subject to wear or deterioration are inspected or renewed at the specified intervals, sudden failure is comparatively rare. Faults do not usually just happen as a result of sudden failure, but develop over a period of time. Major mechanical failures in particular are usually preceded by characteristic symptoms over hundreds or even thousands of miles. Those components which do occasionally fail without warning are often small and easily carried in the vehicle.

With any fault-finding, the first step is to decide where to begin investigations. Sometimes this is obvious, but on other occasions, a little detective work will be necessary. The owner who makes half a dozen haphazard adjustments or replacements may be successful in curing a fault (or its symptoms), but will be none the wiser if the fault recurs, and ultimately may have spent more time and money than was necessary. A calm and logical approach will be found to be more satisfactory in the long run. Always take into account any warning signs or abnormalities that may have been noticed in the period preceding the fault – power loss, high or low gauge readings, unusual smells, etc – and remember that failure of components such as fuses or spark plugs may only be pointers to some underlying fault.

The pages which follow provide an easy-reference guide to the more common problems which may occur during the operation of the vehicle. These problems and their possible causes are grouped under headings denoting various components or systems, such as Engine, Cooling system, etc. The general Chapter which deals with the problem is also shown in brackets; refer to the relevant part of that Chapter for system-specific information. Whatever the fault, certain basic principles apply. These are as follows:

☐ *Verify the fault*. This is simply a matter of being sure that you know what the symptoms are before starting work. This is particularly important if you are investigating a fault for someone else, who may not have described it very accurately.

☐ *Do not overlook the obvious*. For example, if the vehicle will not start, is there fuel in the tank? (Do not take anyone else's word on this particular point, and do not trust the fuel gauge either) If an electrical fault is indicated, look for loose or broken wires before digging out the test gear.

☐ *Cure the disease, not the symptom*. Substituting a flat battery with a fully-charged one will get you off the hard shoulder, but if the underlying cause is not attended to, the new battery will go the same way. Similarly, changing oil-fouled spark plugs for a new set will get you moving again, but remember that the reason for the fouling (if it wasn't simply an incorrect grade of plug) will have to be established and corrected.

☐ *Do not take anything for granted*. Particularly, do not forget that a 'new' component may itself be defective (especially if it's been rattling around in the boot for months), and do not leave components out of a fault diagnosis sequence just because they are new or recently-fitted. When you do finally diagnose a difficult fault, you'll probably realise that all the evidence was there from the start.

Engine

Engine fails to rotate when attempting to start

☐ Battery terminal connections loose or corroded (see *Weekly checks*).
☐ Battery discharged or faulty (Chapter 5A).
☐ Broken, loose or disconnected wiring in the starting circuit (Chapter 5A).
☐ Defective starter solenoid or switch (Chapter 5A).
☐ Defective starter motor (Chapter 5A).
☐ Starter pinion or flywheel ring gear teeth loose or broken (Chapters 2 and 5A).
☐ Engine earth strap broken or disconnected (Chapter 5A).

Engine rotates, but will not start

☐ Fuel tank empty.
☐ Battery discharged (engine rotates slowly) (Chapter 5A).
☐ Battery terminal connections loose or corroded (see *Weekly checks*).
☐ Fuel injection system faulty (Chapter 4A).
☐ Stop solenoid faulty (Chapter 4A).
☐ Air in fuel system (Chapter 4A).
☐ Major mechanical failure (eg camshaft drive) (Chapter 2).

Engine difficult to start when cold

☐ Battery discharged (Chapter 5A).
☐ Battery terminal connections loose or corroded (see *Weekly checks*).
☐ Fuel injection system faulty (Chapter 4A).
☐ Pre-heating system fault (Chapter 5B).
☐ Low cylinder compressions (Chapter 2).

Engine difficult to start when hot

☐ Air filter element dirty or clogged (Chapter 1).
☐ Fuel injection system faulty (Chapter 4A).
☐ Low cylinder compressions (Chapter 2).

Starter motor noisy or excessively-rough in engagement

☐ Starter pinion or flywheel ring gear teeth loose or broken (Chapters 2 and 5A).
☐ Starter motor mounting bolts loose or missing (Chapter 5A).
☐ Starter motor internal components worn or damaged (Chapter 5A).

Engine starts, but stops immediately

☐ Blocked injector/fuel injection system fault (Chapter 4A).
☐ Faulty injector(s) (Chapter 4A).
☐ Air in fuel system (Chapter 4A).

Engine idles erratically

☐ Air filter element clogged (Chapter 1).
☐ Uneven or low cylinder compressions (Chapter 2).
☐ Camshaft lobes worn (Chapter 2).
☐ Timing belt incorrectly fitted (Chapter 2).
☐ Blocked injector/fuel injection system fault (Chapter 4A).
☐ Faulty injector(s) (Chapter 4A)

Engine misfires at idle speed

☐ Blocked injector/fuel injection system fault (Chapter 4A).
☐ Faulty injector(s) (Chapter 4A)
☐ Uneven or low cylinder compressions (Chapter 2).
☐ Disconnected, leaking, or perished crankcase ventilation hoses (Chapter 4B).

Engine misfires throughout the driving speed range

☐ Fuel filter choked (Chapter 1).
☐ Fuel pump faulty, or delivery pressure low (Chapter 4A).
☐ Fuel tank vent blocked, or fuel pipes restricted (Chapter 4).
☐ Faulty injector(s) (Chapter 4A)
☐ Uneven or low cylinder compressions (Chapter 2).
☐ Blocked injector/fuel injection system fault (Chapter 4A).

Engine hesitates on acceleration

☐ Blocked injector/fuel injection system fault (Chapter 4A).
☐ Faulty injector(s) (Chapter 4A)
☐ Incorrect injection pump timing (Chapter 4A)

Engine stalls

☐ Fuel filter choked (Chapter 1).
☐ Fuel tank vent blocked, or fuel pipes restricted (Chapter 4).
☐ Blocked injector/fuel injection system fault (Chapter 4A).
☐ Faulty injector(s) (Chapter 4A)
☐ Air in fuel system (Chapter 4A).

Engine lacks power

☐ Timing belt/chain incorrectly fitted or tensioned (Chapter 2).
☐ Fuel filter choked (Chapter 1).
☐ Uneven or low cylinder compressions (Chapter 2).
☐ Blocked injector/fuel injection system fault (Chapter 4A).
☐ Injection pump timing incorrect (Chapter 4A)
☐ Brakes binding (Chapters 1 and 9).
☐ Clutch slipping (Chapter 6).

Engine backfires

☐ Timing belt/chain incorrectly fitted or tensioned (Chapter 2).
☐ Blocked injector/fuel injection system fault (Chapter 4A).

Engine (continued)

Oil pressure warning light illuminated with engine running

- ☐ Low oil level, or incorrect oil grade (*Weekly checks*).
- ☐ Faulty oil pressure sensor (Chapter 5A).
- ☐ Worn engine bearings and/or oil pump (Chapter 2).
- ☐ High engine operating temperature (Chapter 3).
- ☐ Oil pressure relief valve defective (Chapter 2).
- ☐ Oil pick-up strainer clogged (Chapter 2).

Engine runs-on after switching off

- ☐ Excessive carbon build-up in engine (Chapter 2).
- ☐ High engine operating temperature (Chapter 3).
- ☐ Faulty stop solenoid (Chapter 4A).

Engine noises

Pre-ignition (pinking) or knocking during acceleration or under load

- ☐ Incorrect grade of fuel (Chapter 4).
- ☐ Excessive carbon build-up in engine (Chapter 2).
- ☐ Blocked injector/fuel injection system fault (Chapter 4A).

Whistling or wheezing noises

- ☐ Leaking exhaust manifold gasket or pipe-to-manifold joint (Chapter 4).
- ☐ Leaking vacuum hose (Chapters 4, 5 and 9).
- ☐ Blowing cylinder head gasket (Chapter 2).

Tapping or rattling noises

- ☐ Worn valve gear or camshaft (Chapter 2).
- ☐ Ancillary component fault (coolant pump, alternator, etc) (Chapters 3, 5, etc).

Knocking or thumping noises

- ☐ Worn big-end bearings (regular heavy knocking, perhaps less under load) (Chapter 2).
- ☐ Worn main bearings (rumbling and knocking, perhaps worsening under load) (Chapter 2).
- ☐ Piston slap (most noticeable when cold) (Chapter 2).
- ☐ Ancillary component fault (coolant pump, alternator, etc) (Chapters 3, 5, etc).

Cooling system

Overheating

- ☐ Insufficient coolant in system (*Weekly Checks*).
- ☐ Thermostat faulty (Chapter 3).
- ☐ Radiator core blocked, or grille restricted (Chapter 3).
- ☐ Electric cooling fan or thermostatic switch faulty (Chapter 3).
- ☐ Inaccurate temperature gauge sender unit (Chapter 3).
- ☐ Airlock in cooling system (Chapter 3).
- ☐ Expansion tank pressure cap faulty (Chapter 3).

Overcooling

- ☐ Thermostat faulty (Chapter 3).
- ☐ Inaccurate temperature gauge sender unit (Chapter 3).

External coolant leakage

- ☐ Deteriorated or damaged hoses or hose clips (Chapter 1).
- ☐ Radiator core or heater matrix leaking (Chapter 3).
- ☐ Pressure cap faulty (Chapter 3).

- ☐ Coolant pump internal seal leaking (Chapter 3).
- ☐ Coolant pump-to-block seal leaking (Chapter 3).
- ☐ Boiling due to overheating (Chapter 3).
- ☐ Core plug leaking (Chapter 2).

Internal coolant leakage

- ☐ Leaking cylinder head gasket (Chapter 2).
- ☐ Cracked cylinder head or cylinder block (Chapter 2).

Corrosion

- ☐ Infrequent draining and flushing (Chapter 1).
- ☐ Incorrect coolant mixture or inappropriate coolant type (see *Weekly checks*).

Fuel and exhaust systems

Excessive fuel consumption

- ☐ Air filter element dirty or clogged (Chapter 1).
- ☐ Fuel injection system faulty (Chapter 4A).
- ☐ Faulty injector(s) (Chapter 4A).
- ☐ Tyres under-inflated (see *Weekly checks*).

Fuel leakage and/or fuel odour

- ☐ Damaged or corroded fuel tank, pipes or connections (Chapter 4A).

Excessive noise or fumes from the exhaust system

- ☐ Leaking exhaust system or manifold joints (Chapters 1 and 4).
- ☐ Leaking, corroded or damaged silencers or pipe (Chapters 1 and 4).
- ☐ Broken mountings causing body or suspension contact (Chapter 1).

Clutch

Pedal travels to floor – no pressure or very little resistance

- ☐ Air in hydraulic system/faulty master or slave cylinder (Chapter 6).
- ☐ Faulty hydraulic release system (Chapter 6).
- ☐ Broken clutch release bearing or arm (Chapter 6).
- ☐ Broken diaphragm spring in clutch pressure plate (Chapter 6).

Clutch fails to disengage (unable to select gears)

- ☐ Air in hydraulic system/faulty master or slave cylinder (Chapter 6).
- ☐ Faulty hydraulic release system (Chapter 6).
- ☐ Clutch disc sticking on gearbox input shaft splines (Chapter 6).
- ☐ Clutch disc sticking to flywheel or pressure plate (Chapter 6).
- ☐ Faulty pressure plate assembly (Chapter 6).
- ☐ Clutch release mechanism worn or incorrectly assembled (Chapter 6).

Clutch slips (engine speed increases, with no increase in vehicle speed)

- ☐ Faulty hydraulic release system (Chapter 6).

- ☐ Clutch disc linings excessively worn (Chapter 6).
- ☐ Clutch disc linings contaminated with oil or grease (Chapter 6).
- ☐ Faulty pressure plate or weak diaphragm spring (Chapter 6).

Judder as clutch is engaged

- ☐ Clutch disc linings contaminated with oil or grease (Chapter 6).
- ☐ Clutch disc linings excessively worn (Chapter 6).
- ☐ Faulty or distorted pressure plate or diaphragm spring (Chapter 6).
- ☐ Worn or loose engine or gearbox mountings (Chapter 2).
- ☐ Clutch disc hub or gearbox input shaft splines worn (Chapter 6).

Noise when depressing or releasing clutch pedal

- ☐ Worn clutch release bearing (Chapter 6).
- ☐ Worn or dry clutch pedal pivot (Chapter 6).
- ☐ Faulty pressure plate assembly (Chapter 6).
- ☐ Pressure plate diaphragm spring broken (Chapter 6).
- ☐ Broken clutch friction plate cushioning springs (Chapter 6).

Manual transmission

Noisy in neutral with engine running

☐ Input shaft bearings worn (noise apparent with clutch pedal released, but not when depressed) (Chapter 7).*
☐ Clutch release bearing worn (noise apparent with clutch pedal depressed, possibly less when released) (Chapter 6).

Noisy in one particular gear

☐ Worn, damaged or chipped gear teeth (Chapter 7).*

Difficulty engaging gears

☐ Clutch faulty (Chapter 6).
☐ Worn or damaged gear linkage (Chapter 7).
☐ Incorrectly adjusted gear linkage (Chapter 7).
☐ Worn synchroniser units (Chapter 7).*

Jumps out of gear

☐ Worn or damaged gear linkage (Chapter 7).

☐ Incorrectly adjusted gear linkage (Chapter 7).
☐ Worn synchroniser units (Chapter 7).*
☐ Worn selector forks (Chapter 7).*

Vibration

☐ Lack of oil (Chapter 1).
☐ Worn bearings (Chapter 7).*

Lubricant leaks

☐ Leaking oil seal (Chapter 7).
☐ Leaking housing joint (Chapter 7).*
☐ Leaking input shaft oil seal (Chapter 7).*

Although the corrective action necessary to remedy the symptoms described is beyond the scope of the home mechanic, the above information should be helpful in isolating the cause of the condition, so that the owner can communicate clearly with a professional mechanic.

Driveshafts

Clicking or knocking noise on turns (at slow speed on full-lock)

☐ Worn outer constant velocity joint (Chapter 8).
☐ Lack of constant velocity joint lubricant, possibly due to damaged gaiter (Chapter 8).

Vibration when accelerating or decelerating

☐ Worn inner constant velocity joint (Chapter 8).
☐ Bent or distorted driveshaft (Chapter 8).

Braking system

Note: *Before assuming that a brake problem exists, make sure that the tyres are in good condition and correctly inflated, that the front wheel alignment is correct, and that the vehicle is not loaded with weight in an unequal manner. Apart from checking the condition of all pipe and hose connections, any faults occurring on the anti-lock braking system should be referred to a Vauxhall dealer for diagnosis.*

Vehicle pulls to one side under braking

☐ Worn, defective, damaged or contaminated front or rear brake pads/shoes on one side (Chapters 1 and 9).
☐ Seized or partially-seized front or rear brake caliper/wheel cylinder piston (Chapter 9).
☐ A mixture of brake pad/shoe lining materials fitted between sides (Chapter 9).
☐ Brake caliper or rear brake backplate mounting bolts loose (Chapter 9).
☐ Worn or damaged steering or suspension components (Chapters 1 and 10).

Noise (grinding or high-pitched squeal) when brakes applied

☐ Brake pad friction lining material worn down to audible warning sensor (Chapter 9).
☐ Brake pad/shoe friction lining material worn down to metal backing (Chapter 9).
☐ Excessive corrosion of brake disc or drum – may be apparent after the vehicle has been standing for some time (Chapter 9).
☐ Foreign object (stone chipping, etc) trapped between brake disc and shield (Chapter 9).

Excessive brake pedal travel

☐ Faulty rear drum brake self-adjust mechanism (Chapter 9).
☐ Faulty master cylinder (Chapter 9).
☐ Air in hydraulic system (Chapter 9).
☐ Faulty vacuum servo unit (Chapter 9).

Brake pedal feels spongy when depressed

☐ Air in hydraulic system (Chapter 9).

☐ Deteriorated flexible rubber brake hoses (Chapters 1 and 9).
☐ Master cylinder mountings loose (Chapter 9).
☐ Faulty master cylinder (Chapter 9).

Excessive brake pedal effort required to stop vehicle

☐ Faulty vacuum servo unit (Chapter 9).
☐ Faulty brake vacuum pump (Chapter 9).
☐ Disconnected, damaged or insecure brake servo vacuum hose (Chapters 1 and 9).
☐ Primary or secondary hydraulic circuit failure (Chapter 9).
☐ Seized brake caliper or wheel cylinder piston(s) (Chapter 9).
☐ Brake pads/shoes incorrectly fitted (Chapter 9).
☐ Incorrect grade of brake pads/shoes fitted (Chapter 9).
☐ Brake pads/shoe linings contaminated (Chapter 9).

Judder felt through brake pedal or steering wheel when braking

☐ Excessive run-out or distortion of brake disc(s) or drum(s) (Chapter 9).
☐ Brake pad/shoe linings worn (Chapter 9).
☐ Brake caliper or rear brake backplate mounting bolts loose (Chapter 9).
☐ Wear in suspension or steering components or mountings (Chapter 10).

Pedal pulsates when braking hard

☐ Normal feature of ABS – no fault

Brakes binding

☐ Seized brake caliper/wheel cylinder piston(s) (Chapter 9).
☐ Incorrectly-adjusted handbrake cable (Chapter 9).
☐ Faulty master cylinder (Chapter 9).

Rear wheels locking under normal braking

☐ Rear brake pad/shoe linings contaminated (Chapter 9).
☐ Rear brake proportioning valve faulty (Chapter 9).

Steering and suspension

Note: *Before diagnosing suspension or steering faults, be sure that the trouble is not due to incorrect tyre pressures, mixtures of tyre types, or binding brakes.*

Vehicle pulls to one side

- ☐ Defective tyre (see *Weekly checks*).
- ☐ Excessive wear in suspension or steering components (Chapters 1 and 10).
- ☐ Incorrect front wheel alignment (Chapter 10).
- ☐ Accident damage to steering or suspension components (Chapters 1 and 10).

Wheel wobble and vibration

- ☐ Front roadwheels out of balance (vibration felt mainly through the steering wheel) (Chapter 10).
- ☐ Rear roadwheels out of balance (vibration felt throughout the vehicle) (Chapter 10).
- ☐ Roadwheels damaged or distorted (Chapter 10).
- ☐ Faulty or damaged tyre (*Weekly Checks*).
- ☐ Worn steering or suspension joints, bushes or components (Chapters 1 and 10).
- ☐ Wheel bolts loose (Chapter 1 and 10).

Excessive pitching and/or rolling around corners, or during braking

- ☐ Defective shock absorbers (Chapters 1 and 10).
- ☐ Broken or weak coil spring and/or suspension component (Chapters 1 and 10).
- ☐ Worn or damaged anti-roll bar or mountings (Chapter 10).

Wandering or general instability

- ☐ Incorrect front wheel alignment (Chapter 10).
- ☐ Worn steering or suspension joints, bushes or components (Chapters 1 and 10).
- ☐ Roadwheels out of balance (Chapter 10).
- ☐ Faulty or damaged tyre (*Weekly Checks*).
- ☐ Wheel bolts loose (Chapter 10).
- ☐ Defective shock absorbers (Chapters 1 and 10).

Excessively-stiff steering

- ☐ Seized track rod end balljoint or suspension balljoint (Chapters 1 and 10).
- ☐ Broken or incorrectly adjusted auxiliary drivebelt – power steering (Chapter 1).

- ☐ Incorrect front wheel alignment (Chapter 10).
- ☐ Steering gear or column damaged (Chapter 10).

Excessive play in steering

- ☐ Worn steering column universal joint(s) (Chapter 10).
- ☐ Worn steering track rod end balljoints (Chapters 1 and 10).
- ☐ Worn steering gear (Chapter 10).
- ☐ Worn steering or suspension joints, bushes or components (Chapters 1 and 10).

Lack of power assistance

- ☐ Broken or incorrectly-adjusted auxiliary drivebelt – power steering (Chapter 1).
- ☐ Incorrect power steering fluid level (*Weekly Checks*).
- ☐ Restriction in power steering fluid hoses (Chapter 10).
- ☐ Faulty power steering pump (Chapter 10).
- ☐ Faulty steering gear (Chapter 10).

Tyre wear excessive

Tyres worn on inside or outside edges

- ☐ Tyres under-inflated (wear on both edges) (*Weekly Checks*).
- ☐ Incorrect camber or castor angles (wear on one edge only) (Chapter 10).
- ☐ Worn steering or suspension joints, bushes or components (Chapters 1 and 10).
- ☐ Excessively-hard cornering.
- ☐ Accident damage.

Tyre treads exhibit feathered edges

- ☐ Incorrect toe setting (Chapter 10).

Tyres worn in centre of tread

- ☐ Tyres over-inflated (*Weekly Checks*).

Tyres worn on inside and outside edges

- ☐ Tyres under-inflated (*Weekly Checks*).
- ☐ Worn shock absorbers (Chapter 10).

Tyres worn unevenly

- ☐ Tyres/wheels out of balance (Chapter 10).
- ☐ Excessive wheel or tyre run-out (Chapter 10).
- ☐ Worn shock absorbers (Chapters 1 and 10).
- ☐ Faulty tyre (*Weekly Checks*).

Electrical system

Note: For problems associated with the starting system, refer to the faults listed under 'Engine' earlier in this Section.

Battery will not hold a charge for more than a few days

- ☐ Battery defective internally (Chapter 5A).
- ☐ Battery electrolyte level low – where applicable (*Weekly Checks*).
- ☐ Battery terminal connections loose or corroded (*Weekly Checks*).
- ☐ Auxiliary drivebelt worn – or incorrectly adjusted, where applicable (Chapter 1).
- ☐ Alternator not charging at correct output (Chapter 5A).
- ☐ Alternator or voltage regulator faulty (Chapter 5A).
- ☐ Short-circuit causing continual battery drain (Chapters 5 and 12).

Ignition/no-charge warning light remains illuminated with engine running

- ☐ Auxiliary drivebelt broken, worn, or incorrectly adjusted (Chapter 1).
- ☐ Alternator brushes worn, sticking, or dirty (Chapter 5A).
- ☐ Alternator brush springs, weak or broken (Chapter 5A).
- ☐ Internal fault in alternator or voltage regulator (Chapter 5A).
- ☐ Broken, disconnected, or loose wiring in charging circuit (Chapter 5A).

Ignition/no-charge warning light fails to come on

- ☐ Warning light bulb blown (Chapter 12).
- ☐ Broken, disconnected, or loose wiring in warning light circuit (Chapter 12).
- ☐ Alternator faulty (Chapter 5A).

Lights inoperative

- ☐ Bulb blown (Chapter 12).
- ☐ Corrosion of bulb or bulbholder contacts (Chapter 12).
- ☐ Blown fuse (Chapter 12).
- ☐ Faulty relay (Chapter 12).
- ☐ Broken, loose, or disconnected wiring (Chapter 12).
- ☐ Faulty switch (Chapter 12).

Instrument readings inaccurate or erratic

Fuel or temperature gauges give no reading

- ☐ Faulty gauge sender unit (Chapters 3 and 4).
- ☐ Wiring open-circuit (Chapter 12).
- ☐ Faulty gauge (Chapter 12).

Fuel or temperature gauges give continuous maximum reading

- ☐ Faulty gauge sender unit (Chapters 3 and 4).
- ☐ Wiring short-circuit (Chapter 12).
- ☐ Faulty gauge (Chapter 12).

Horn inoperative, or unsatisfactory in operation

Horn operates all the time

- ☐ Horn contacts permanently bridged or horn push stuck down (Chapter 12).
- ☐ Horn cable-to-horn push earthed (Chapter 12).

Horn fails to operate

- ☐ Blown fuse (Chapter 12).
- ☐ Cable or cable connections loose, broken or disconnected (Chapter 12).
- ☐ Faulty horn (Chapter 12).

Horn emits intermittent or unsatisfactory sound

- ☐ Cable connections loose (Chapter 12).
- ☐ Horn mountings loose (Chapter 12).
- ☐ Faulty horn (Chapter 12).

Windscreen/tailgate wipers inoperative, or unsatisfactory in operation

Wipers fail to operate, or operate very slowly

- ☐ Wiper blades stuck to screen, or linkage seized or binding (*Weekly Checks* and Chapter 12).
- ☐ Blown fuse (Chapter 12).
- ☐ Cable or cable connections loose, broken or disconnected (Chapter 12).
- ☐ Faulty relay (Chapter 12).
- ☐ Faulty wiper motor (Chapter 12).

Wiper blades sweep over too large or too small an area of the glass

- ☐ Wiper arms incorrectly positioned on spindles (Chapter 12).
- ☐ Excessive wear of wiper linkage (Chapter 12).
- ☐ Wiper motor or linkage mountings loose or insecure (Chapter 12).

Wiper blades fail to clean the glass effectively

- ☐ Wiper blade rubbers worn or perished (*Weekly Checks*).
- ☐ Wiper arm tension springs broken, or arm pivots seized (Chapter 12).
- ☐ Insufficient windscreen washer additive to adequately remove road film (*Weekly Checks*).

Electrical system (continued)

Windscreen/tailgate washers inoperative, or unsatisfactory in operation

One or more washer jets inoperative

☐ Blocked washer jet (Chapter 12).
☐ Disconnected, kinked or restricted fluid hose (Chapter 12).
☐ Insufficient fluid in washer reservoir (*Weekly Checks*).

Washer pump fails to operate

☐ Broken or disconnected wiring or connections (Chapter 12).
☐ Blown fuse (Chapter 12).
☐ Faulty washer switch (Chapter 12).
☐ Faulty washer pump (Chapter 12).

Washer pump runs for some time before fluid is emitted from jets

☐ Faulty one-way valve in fluid supply hose (Chapter 12).

Electric windows inoperative, or unsatisfactory in operation

Window glass will only move in one direction

☐ Faulty switch (Chapter 12).

Window glass slow to move

☐ Regulator seized or damaged, or in need of lubrication (Chapter 11).
☐ Door internal components or trim fouling regulator (Chapter 11).
☐ Faulty motor (Chapter 11).

Window glass fails to move

☐ Blown fuse (Chapter 12).
☐ Faulty relay (Chapter 12).
☐ Broken or disconnected wiring or connections (Chapter 12).
☐ Faulty motor (Chapter 12).

Central locking system inoperative, or unsatisfactory in operation

Complete system failure

☐ Blown fuse (Chapter 12).
☐ Faulty relay (Chapter 12).
☐ Broken or disconnected wiring or connections (Chapter 12).
☐ Faulty motor (Chapter 11).

Latch locks but will not unlock, or unlocks but will not lock

☐ Faulty switch (Chapter 12).
☐ Broken or disconnected latch operating rods or levers (Chapter 11).
☐ Faulty relay (Chapter 12).
☐ Faulty motor (Chapter 11).

One solenoid/motor fails to operate

☐ Broken or disconnected wiring or connections (Chapter 12).
☐ Faulty motor (Chapter 11).
☐ Broken, binding or disconnected lock operating rods or levers (Chapter 11).
☐ Fault in door lock (Chapter 11).

A

ABS (Anti-lock brake system) A system, usually electronically controlled, that senses incipient wheel lockup during braking and relieves hydraulic pressure at wheels that are about to skid.

Air bag An inflatable bag hidden in the steering wheel (driver's side) or the dash or glovebox (passenger side). In a head-on collision, the bags inflate, preventing the driver and front passenger from being thrown forward into the steering wheel or windscreen.

Air cleaner A metal or plastic housing, containing a filter element, which removes dust and dirt from the air being drawn into the engine.

Air filter element The actual filter in an air cleaner system, usually manufactured from pleated paper and requiring renewal at regular intervals.

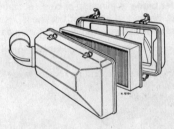

Air filter

Allen key A hexagonal wrench which fits into a recessed hexagonal hole.

Alligator clip A long-nosed spring-loaded metal clip with meshing teeth. Used to make temporary electrical connections.

Alternator A component in the electrical system which converts mechanical energy from a drivebelt into electrical energy to charge the battery and to operate the starting system, ignition system and electrical accessories.

Ampere (amp) A unit of measurement for the flow of electric current. One amp is the amount of current produced by one volt acting through a resistance of one ohm.

Anaerobic sealer A substance used to prevent bolts and screws from loosening. Anaerobic means that it does not require oxygen for activation. The Loctite brand is widely used.

Antifreeze A substance (usually ethylene glycol) mixed with water, and added to a vehicle's cooling system, to prevent freezing of the coolant in winter. Antifreeze also contains chemicals to inhibit corrosion and the formation of rust and other deposits that would tend to clog the radiator and coolant passages and reduce cooling efficiency.

Anti-seize compound A coating that reduces the risk of seizing on fasteners that are subjected to high temperatures, such as exhaust manifold bolts and nuts.

Asbestos A natural fibrous mineral with great heat resistance, commonly used in the composition of brake friction materials.

Asbestos is a health hazard and the dust created by brake systems should never be inhaled or ingested.

Axle A shaft on which a wheel revolves, or which revolves with a wheel. Also, a solid beam that connects the two wheels at one end of the vehicle. An axle which also transmits power to the wheels is known as a live axle.

Axleshaft A single rotating shaft, on either side of the differential, which delivers power from the final drive assembly to the drive wheels. Also called a driveshaft or a halfshaft.

B

Ball bearing An anti-friction bearing consisting of a hardened inner and outer race with hardened steel balls between two races.

Bearing The curved surface on a shaft or in a bore, or the part assembled into either, that permits relative motion between them with minimum wear and friction.

Bearing

Big-end bearing The bearing in the end of the connecting rod that's attached to the crankshaft.

Bleed nipple A valve on a brake wheel cylinder, caliper or other hydraulic component that is opened to purge the hydraulic system of air. Also called a bleed screw.

Brake bleeding Procedure for removing air from lines of a hydraulic brake system.

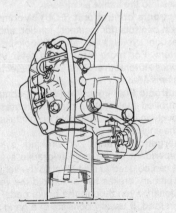

Brake bleeding

Brake disc The component of a disc brake that rotates with the wheels.

Brake drum The component of a drum brake that rotates with the wheels.

Brake linings The friction material which contacts the brake disc or drum to retard the vehicle's speed. The linings are bonded or riveted to the brake pads or shoes.

Brake pads The replaceable friction pads that pinch the brake disc when the brakes are applied. Brake pads consist of a friction material bonded or riveted to a rigid backing plate.

Brake shoe The crescent-shaped carrier to which the brake linings are mounted and which forces the lining against the rotating drum during braking.

Braking systems For more information on braking systems, consult the *Haynes Automotive Brake Manual*.

Breaker bar A long socket wrench handle providing greater leverage.

Bulkhead The insulated partition between the engine and the passenger compartment.

C

Caliper The non-rotating part of a disc-brake assembly that straddles the disc and carries the brake pads. The caliper also contains the hydraulic components that cause the pads to pinch the disc when the brakes are applied. A caliper is also a measuring tool that can be set to measure inside or outside dimensions of an object.

Camshaft A rotating shaft on which a series of cam lobes operate the valve mechanisms. The camshaft may be driven by gears, by sprockets and chain or by sprockets and a belt.

Canister A container in an evaporative emission control system; contains activated charcoal granules to trap vapours from the fuel system.

Canister

Carburettor A device which mixes fuel with air in the proper proportions to provide a desired power output from a spark ignition internal combustion engine.

Castellated Resembling the parapets along the top of a castle wall. For example, a castellated balljoint stud nut.

Castor In wheel alignment, the backward or forward tilt of the steering axis. Castor is positive when the steering axis is inclined rearward at the top.

Catalytic converter A silencer-like device in the exhaust system which converts certain pollutants in the exhaust gases into less harmful substances.

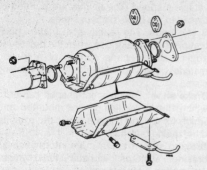

Catalytic converter

Circlip A ring-shaped clip used to prevent endwise movement of cylindrical parts and shafts. An internal circlip is installed in a groove in a housing; an external circlip fits into a groove on the outside of a cylindrical piece such as a shaft.

Clearance The amount of space between two parts. For example, between a piston and a cylinder, between a bearing and a journal, etc.

Coil spring A spiral of elastic steel found in various sizes throughout a vehicle, for example as a springing medium in the suspension and in the valve train.

Compression Reduction in volume, and increase in pressure and temperature, of a gas, caused by squeezing it into a smaller space.

Compression ratio The relationship between cylinder volume when the piston is at top dead centre and cylinder volume when the piston is at bottom dead centre.

Constant velocity (CV) joint A type of universal joint that cancels out vibrations caused by driving power being transmitted through an angle.

Core plug A disc or cup-shaped metal device inserted in a hole in a casting through which core was removed when the casting was formed. Also known as a freeze plug or expansion plug.

Crankcase The lower part of the engine block in which the crankshaft rotates.

Crankshaft The main rotating member, or shaft, running the length of the crankcase, with offset "throws" to which the connecting rods are attached.

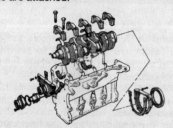

Crankshaft assembly

Crocodile clip See Alligator clip

D

Diagnostic code Code numbers obtained by accessing the diagnostic mode of an engine management computer. This code can be used to determine the area in the system where a malfunction may be located.

Disc brake A brake design incorporating a rotating disc onto which brake pads are squeezed. The resulting friction converts the energy of a moving vehicle into heat.

Double-overhead cam (DOHC) An engine that uses two overhead camshafts, usually one for the intake valves and one for the exhaust valves.

Drivebelt(s) The belt(s) used to drive accessories such as the alternator, water pump, power steering pump, air conditioning compressor, etc. off the crankshaft pulley.

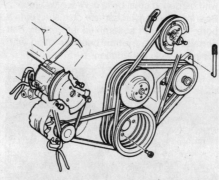

Accessory drivebelts

Driveshaft Any shaft used to transmit motion. Commonly used when referring to the axleshafts on a front wheel drive vehicle.

Drum brake A type of brake using a drum-shaped metal cylinder attached to the inner surface of the wheel. When the brake pedal is pressed, curved brake shoes with friction linings press against the inside of the drum to slow or stop the vehicle.

E

EGR valve A valve used to introduce exhaust gases into the intake air stream.

Electronic control unit (ECU) A computer which controls (for instance) ignition and fuel injection systems, or an anti-lock braking system. For more information refer to the *Haynes Automotive Electrical and Electronic Systems Manual*.

Electronic Fuel Injection (EFI) A computer controlled fuel system that distributes fuel through an injector located in each intake port of the engine.

Emergency brake A braking system, independent of the main hydraulic system, that can be used to slow or stop the vehicle if the primary brakes fail, or to hold the vehicle stationary even though the brake pedal isn't depressed. It usually consists of a hand lever that actuates either front or rear brakes mechanically through a series of cables and linkages. Also known as a handbrake or parking brake.

Endfloat The amount of lengthwise movement between two parts. As applied to a crankshaft, the distance that the crankshaft can move forward and back in the cylinder block.

Engine management system (EMS) A computer controlled system which manages the fuel injection and the ignition systems in an integrated fashion.

Exhaust manifold A part with several passages through which exhaust gases leave the engine combustion chambers and enter the exhaust pipe.

F

Fan clutch A viscous (fluid) drive coupling device which permits variable engine fan speeds in relation to engine speeds.

Feeler blade A thin strip or blade of hardened steel, ground to an exact thickness, used to check or measure clearances between parts.

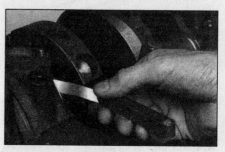

Feeler blade

Firing order The order in which the engine cylinders fire, or deliver their power strokes, beginning with the number one cylinder.

Flywheel A heavy spinning wheel in which energy is absorbed and stored by means of momentum. On cars, the flywheel is attached to the crankshaft to smooth out firing impulses.

Free play The amount of travel before any action takes place. The "looseness" in a linkage, or an assembly of parts, between the initial application of force and actual movement. For example, the distance the brake pedal moves before the pistons in the master cylinder are actuated.

Fuse An electrical device which protects a circuit against accidental overload. The typical fuse contains a soft piece of metal which is calibrated to melt at a predetermined current flow (expressed as amps) and break the circuit.

Fusible link A circuit protection device consisting of a conductor surrounded by heat-resistant insulation. The conductor is smaller than the wire it protects, so it acts as the weakest link in the circuit. Unlike a blown fuse, a failed fusible link must frequently be cut from the wire for replacement.

G

Gap The distance the spark must travel in jumping from the centre electrode to the side electrode in a spark plug. Also refers to the spacing between the points in a contact breaker assembly in a conventional points-type ignition, or to the distance between the reluctor or rotor and the pickup coil in an electronic ignition.

Adjusting spark plug gap

Gasket Any thin, soft material - usually cork, cardboard, asbestos or soft metal - installed between two metal surfaces to ensure a good seal. For instance, the cylinder head gasket seals the joint between the block and the cylinder head.

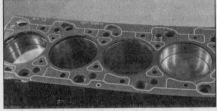

Gasket

Gauge An instrument panel display used to monitor engine conditions. A gauge with a movable pointer on a dial or a fixed scale is an analogue gauge. A gauge with a numerical readout is called a digital gauge.

H

Halfshaft A rotating shaft that transmits power from the final drive unit to a drive wheel, usually when referring to a live rear axle.

Harmonic balancer A device designed to reduce torsion or twisting vibration in the crankshaft. May be incorporated in the crankshaft pulley. Also known as a vibration damper.

Hone An abrasive tool for correcting small irregularities or differences in diameter in an engine cylinder, brake cylinder, etc.

Hydraulic tappet A tappet that utilises hydraulic pressure from the engine's lubrication system to maintain zero clearance (constant contact with both camshaft and valve stem). Automatically adjusts to variation in valve stem length. Hydraulic tappets also reduce valve noise.

I

Ignition timing The moment at which the spark plug fires, usually expressed in the number of crankshaft degrees before the piston reaches the top of its stroke.

Inlet manifold A tube or housing with passages through which flows the air-fuel mixture (carburettor vehicles and vehicles with throttle body injection) or air only (port fuel-injected vehicles) to the port openings in the cylinder head.

J

Jump start Starting the engine of a vehicle with a discharged or weak battery by attaching jump leads from the weak battery to a charged or helper battery.

L

Load Sensing Proportioning Valve (LSPV) A brake hydraulic system control valve that works like a proportioning valve, but also takes into consideration the amount of weight carried by the rear axle.

Locknut A nut used to lock an adjustment nut, or other threaded component, in place. For example, a locknut is employed to keep the adjusting nut on the rocker arm in position.

Lockwasher A form of washer designed to prevent an attaching nut from working loose.

M

MacPherson strut A type of front suspension system devised by Earle MacPherson at Ford of England. In its original form, a simple lateral link with the anti-roll bar creates the lower control arm. A long strut - an integral coil spring and shock absorber - is mounted between the body and the steering knuckle. Many modern so-called MacPherson strut systems use a conventional lower A-arm and don't rely on the anti-roll bar for location.

Multimeter An electrical test instrument with the capability to measure voltage, current and resistance.

N

NOx Oxides of Nitrogen. A common toxic pollutant emitted by petrol and diesel engines at higher temperatures.

O

Ohm The unit of electrical resistance. One volt applied to a resistance of one ohm will produce a current of one amp.

Ohmmeter An instrument for measuring electrical resistance.

O-ring A type of sealing ring made of a special rubber-like material; in use, the O-ring is compressed into a groove to provide the sealing action.

Overhead cam (ohc) engine An engine with the camshaft(s) located on top of the cylinder head(s).

Overhead valve (ohv) engine
An engine with the valves located in the cylinder head, but with the camshaft located in the engine block.

Oxygen sensor A device installed in the engine exhaust manifold, which senses the oxygen content in the exhaust and converts this information into an electric current. Also called a Lambda sensor.

P

Phillips screw A type of screw head having a cross instead of a slot for a corresponding type of screwdriver.

Plastigage A thin strip of plastic thread, available in different sizes, used for measuring clearances. For example, a strip of Plastigage is laid across a bearing journal. The parts are assembled and dismantled; the width of the crushed strip indicates the clearance between journal and bearing.

Plastigage

Propeller shaft The long hollow tube with universal joints at both ends that carries power from the transmission to the differential on front-engined rear wheel drive vehicles.

Proportioning valve A hydraulic control valve which limits the amount of pressure to the rear brakes during panic stops to prevent wheel lock-up.

R

Rack-and-pinion steering A steering system with a pinion gear on the end of the steering shaft that mates with a rack (think of a geared wheel opened up and laid flat). When the steering wheel is turned, the pinion turns, moving the rack to the left or right. This movement is transmitted through the track rods to the steering arms at the wheels.

Radiator A liquid-to-air heat transfer device designed to reduce the temperature of the coolant in an internal combustion engine cooling system.

Refrigerant Any substance used as a heat transfer agent in an air-conditioning system. R-12 has been the principle refrigerant for many years; recently, however, manufacturers have begun using R-134a, a non-CFC substance that is considered less harmful to the ozone in the upper atmosphere.

Rocker arm A lever arm that rocks on a shaft or pivots on a stud. In an overhead valve engine, the rocker arm converts the upward movement of the pushrod into a downward movement to open a valve.

Rotor In a distributor, the rotating device inside the cap that connects the centre electrode and the outer terminals as it turns, distributing the high voltage from the coil secondary winding to the proper spark plug. Also, that part of an alternator which rotates inside the stator. Also, the rotating assembly of a turbocharger, including the compressor wheel, shaft and turbine wheel.

Runout The amount of wobble (in-and-out movement) of a gear or wheel as it's rotated. The amount a shaft rotates "out-of-true." The out-of-round condition of a rotating part.

S

Sealant A liquid or paste used to prevent leakage at a joint. Sometimes used in conjunction with a gasket.

Sealed beam lamp An older headlight design which integrates the reflector, lens and filaments into a hermetically-sealed one-piece unit. When a filament burns out or the lens cracks, the entire unit is simply replaced.

Serpentine drivebelt A single, long, wide accessory drivebelt that's used on some newer vehicles to drive all the accessories, instead of a series of smaller, shorter belts. Serpentine drivebelts are usually tensioned by an automatic tensioner.

Serpentine drivebelt

Shim Thin spacer, commonly used to adjust the clearance or relative positions between two parts. For example, shims inserted into or under bucket tappets control valve clearances. Clearance is adjusted by changing the thickness of the shim.

Slide hammer A special puller that screws into or hooks onto a component such as a shaft or bearing; a heavy sliding handle on the shaft bottoms against the end of the shaft to knock the component free.

Sprocket A tooth or projection on the periphery of a wheel, shaped to engage with a chain or drivebelt. Commonly used to refer to the sprocket wheel itself.

Starter inhibitor switch On vehicles with an automatic transmission, a switch that prevents starting if the vehicle is not in Neutral or Park.

Strut See MacPherson strut.

T

Tappet A cylindrical component which transmits motion from the cam to the valve stem, either directly or via a pushrod and rocker arm. Also called a cam follower.

Thermostat A heat-controlled valve that regulates the flow of coolant between the cylinder block and the radiator, so maintaining optimum engine operating temperature. A thermostat is also used in some air cleaners in which the temperature is regulated.

Thrust bearing The bearing in the clutch assembly that is moved in to the release levers by clutch pedal action to disengage the clutch. Also referred to as a release bearing.

Timing belt A toothed belt which drives the camshaft. Serious engine damage may result if it breaks in service.

Timing chain A chain which drives the camshaft.

Toe-in The amount the front wheels are closer together at the front than at the rear. On rear wheel drive vehicles, a slight amount of toe-in is usually specified to keep the front wheels running parallel on the road by offsetting other forces that tend to spread the wheels apart.

Toe-out The amount the front wheels are closer together at the rear than at the front. On front wheel drive vehicles, a slight amount of toe-out is usually specified.

Tools For full information on choosing and using tools, refer to the *Haynes Automotive Tools Manual*.

Tracer A stripe of a second colour applied to a wire insulator to distinguish that wire from another one with the same colour insulator.

Tune-up A process of accurate and careful adjustments and parts replacement to obtain the best possible engine performance.

Turbocharger A centrifugal device, driven by exhaust gases, that pressurises the intake air. Normally used to increase the power output from a given engine displacement, but can also be used primarily to reduce exhaust emissions (as on VW's "Umwelt" Diesel engine).

U

Universal joint or U-joint A double-pivoted connection for transmitting power from a driving to a driven shaft through an angle. A U-joint consists of two Y-shaped yokes and a cross-shaped member called the spider.

V

Valve A device through which the flow of liquid, gas, vacuum, or loose material in bulk may be started, stopped, or regulated by a movable part that opens, shuts, or partially obstructs one or more ports or passageways. A valve is also the movable part of such a device.

Valve clearance The clearance between the valve tip (the end of the valve stem) and the rocker arm or tappet. The valve clearance is measured when the valve is closed.

Vernier caliper A precision measuring instrument that measures inside and outside dimensions. Not quite as accurate as a micrometer, but more convenient.

Viscosity The thickness of a liquid or its resistance to flow.

Volt A unit for expressing electrical "pressure" in a circuit. One volt that will produce a current of one ampere through a resistance of one ohm.

W

Welding Various processes used to join metal items by heating the areas to be joined to a molten state and fusing them together. For more information refer to the *Haynes Automotive Welding Manual*.

Wiring diagram A drawing portraying the components and wires in a vehicle's electrical system, using standardised symbols. For more information refer to the *Haynes Automotive Electrical and Electronic Systems Manual*.

Note: *References throughout this index are in the form - "Chapter number" • "Page number"*

Haynes Manuals – The Complete UK Car List

Title	Book No.
ALFA ROMEO Alfasud/Sprint (74 – 88) up to F *	0292
Alfa Romeo Alfetta (73 – 87) up to E *	0531
AUDI 80, 90 & Coupe Petrol (79 – Nov 88) up to F	0605
Audi 80, 90 & Coupe Petrol (Oct 86 – 90) D to H	1491
Audi 100 & A6 Petrol & Diesel (May 91 – May 97) H to P	3504
Audi A3 Petrol & Diesel (96 – May 03) P to 03	4253
Audi A3 Petrol & Diesel (June 03 – Mar 08) 03 to 08	4884
Audi A4 Petrol & Diesel (95 – 00) M to X	3575
Audi A4 Petrol & Diesel (01 – 04) X to 54	4609
Audi A4 Petrol & Diesel (Jan 05 – Feb 08) 54 to 57	4885
AUSTIN A35 & A40 (56 – 67) up to F *	0118
Mini (59 – 69) up to H *	0527
Mini (69 – 01) up to X	0646
Austin Healey 100/6 & 3000 (56 – 68) up to G *	0049
BEDFORD/Vauxhall Rascal & Suzuki Supercarry (86 – Oct 94) C to M	3015
BMW 1-Series 4-cyl Petrol & Diesel (04 – Aug 11) 54 to 11	4918
BMW 316, 320 & 320i (4-cyl)(75 – Feb 83) up to Y *	0276
BMW 3- & 5- Series Petrol (81 – 91) up to J	1948
BMW 3-Series Petrol (Apr 91 – 99) H to V	3210
BMW 3-Series Petrol (Sept 98 – 06) S to 56	4067
BMW 3-Series Petrol & Diesel (05 – Sept 08) 54 to 58	4782
BMW 5-Series 6-cyl Petrol (April 96 – Aug 03) N to 03	4151
BMW 5-Series Diesel (Sept 03 – 10) 53 to 10	4901
BMW 1500, 1502, 1600, 1602, 2000 & 2002 (59 – 77) up to S *	0240
CHRYSLER PT Cruiser Petrol (00-09) W to 09	4058
CITROEN 2CV, Ami & Dyane (67 – 90) up to H	0196
Citroen AX Petrol & Diesel (87- 97) D to P	3014
Citroen Berlingo & Peugeot Partner Petrol & Diesel (96 – 10) P to 60	4281
Citroen C1 Petrol (05 – 11) 05 to 11	4922
Citroen C2 Petrol & Diesel (03 – 10) 53 to 60	5635
Citroen C3 Petrol & Diesel (02 – 09) 51 to 59	4890
Citroen C4 Petrol & Diesel (04 – 10) 54 to 60	5576
Citroen C5 Petrol & Diesel (01 – 08) Y to 08	4745
Citroen C15 Van Petrol & Diesel (89 – Oct 98) F to S	3509
Citroen CX Petrol (75 – 88) up to F	0528
Citroen Saxo Petrol & Diesel (96 – 04) N to 54	3506
Citroen Xantia Petrol & Diesel (93 – 01) K to Y	3082
Citroen XM Petrol & Diesel (89 – 00) G to X	3451
Citroen Xsara Petrol & Diesel (97 – Sept 00) R to W	3751
Citroen Xsara Picasso Petrol & Diesel (00 – 02) W to 52	3944
Citroen Xsara Picasso (Mar 04 – 08) 04 to 58	4784
Citroen ZX Diesel (91 – 98) J to S	1922
Citroen ZX Petrol (91 – 98) H to S	1881
FIAT 126 (73 – 87) up to E *	0305
Fiat 500 (57 – 73) up to M *	0090
Fiat 500 & Panda (04 – 12) 53 to 61	5558
Fiat Bravo & Brava Petrol (95 – 00) N to W	3572
Fiat Cinquecento (93 – 98) K to R	3501
Fiat Grande Punto, Punto Evo & Punto Petrol (06 – 15) 55 to 15	5956
Fiat Panda (81 – 95) up to M	0793
Fiat Punto Petrol & Diesel (94 – Oct 99) L to V	3251
Fiat Punto Petrol (Oct 99 – July 03) V to 03	4066
Fiat Punto Petrol (03 – 07) 03 to 07	4746

Title	Book No.
Fiat Punto Petrol (Oct 99 – 07) V to 07	5634
Fiat X1/9 (74 – 89) up to G *	0273
FORD Anglia (59 – 68) up to G *	0001
Ford Capri II (& III) 1.6 & 2.0 (74 – 87) up to E *	0283
Ford Capri II (& III) 2.8 & 3.0 V6 (74 – 87) up to E	1309
Ford C-Max Petrol & Diesel (03 – 10) 53 to 60	4900
Ford Escort Mk I 1100 & 1300 (68 – 74) up to N *	0171
Ford Escort Mk I Mexico, RS 1600 & RS 2000 (70 – 74) up to N *	0139
Ford Escort Mk II Mexico, RS 1800 & RS 2000 (75 – 80) up to W *	0735
Ford Escort (75 – Aug 80) up to V *	0280
Ford Escort Petrol (Sept 80 – Sept 90) up to H	0686
Ford Escort & Orion Petrol (Sept 90 – 00) H to X	1737
Ford Escort & Orion Petrol (Sept 90 – 00) H to X	4081
Ford Fiesta Petrol (Feb 89 – Oct 95) F to N	1595
Ford Fiesta Petrol & Diesel (Oct 95 – Mar 02) N to 02	3397
Ford Fiesta Petrol & Diesel (Apr 02 – 08) 02 to 58	4170
Ford Fiesta Petrol & Diesel (08 – 11) 58 to 11	4907
Ford Focus Petrol & Diesel (98 – 01) S to Y	3759
Ford Focus Petrol & Diesel (Oct 01 – 05) 51 to 05	4167
Ford Focus Petrol (05 – 11) 54 to 61	4785
Ford Focus Diesel (05 – 11) 54 to 61	4807
Ford Focus Petrol & Diesel (11 – 14) 60 to 14	5632
Ford Fusion Petrol & Diesel (02 – 11) 02 to 61	5566
Ford Galaxy Petrol & Diesel (95 – Aug 00) M to W	3984
Ford Galaxy Petrol & Diesel (00 – 06) X to 06	5556
Ford Granada Petrol (Sept 77 – Feb 85) up to B *	0481
Ford Ka (96 – 08) P to 58	5567
Ford Ka Petrol (09 – 14) 58 to 14	5637
Ford Mondeo Petrol (93 – Sept 00) K to X	1923
Ford Mondeo Petrol & Diesel (Oct 00 – Jul 03) X to 03	3990
Ford Mondeo Petrol & Diesel (July 03 – 07) 03 to 56	4619
Ford Mondeo Petrol & Diesel (Apr 07 – 12) 07 to 61	5548
Ford Mondeo Diesel (93 – Sept 00) L to X	3465
Ford Transit Connect Diesel (02 – 11) 02 to 11	4903
Ford Transit Diesel (Feb 86 – 99) C to T	3019
Ford Transit Diesel (00 – Oct 06) X to 56	4775
Ford Transit Diesel (Nov 06 – 13) 56 to 63	5629
Ford 1.6 & 1.8 litre Diesel Engine (84 – 96) A to N	1172
HILLMAN Imp (63 – 76) up to R *	0022
HONDA Civic (Feb 84 – Oct 87) A to E	1226
Honda Civic (Nov 91 – 96) J to N	3199
Honda Civic Petrol (Mar 95 – 00) M to X	4050
Honda Civic Petrol & Diesel (01 – 05) X to 55	4611
Honda CR-V Petrol & Diesel (02 – 06) 51 to 56	4747
Honda Jazz (02 to 08) 51 to 58	4735
JAGUAR E-Type (61 – 72) up to L *	0140
Jaguar Mk I & II, 240 & 340 (55 – 69) up to H *	0098
Jaguar XJ6, XJ & Sovereign, Daimler Sovereign (68 – Oct 86) up to D	0242
Jaguar XJ6 & Sovereign (Oct 86 – Sept 94) D to M	3261
Jaguar XJ12, XJS & Sovereign, Daimler Double Six (72 – 88) up to F	0478
Jaguar X Type Petrol & Diesel (01 – 10) V to 60	5631
JEEP Cherokee Petrol (93 – 96) K to N	1943
LAND ROVER 90, 110 & Defender Diesel (83 – 07) up to 56	3017

Title	Book No.
Land Rover Discovery Petrol & Diesel (89 – 98) G to S	3016
Land Rover Discovery Diesel (Nov 98 – Jul 04) S to 04	4606
Land Rover Discovery Diesel (Aug 04 – Apr 09) 04 to 09	5562
Land Rover Freelander Petrol & Diesel (97 – Sept 03) R to 53	3929
Land Rover Freelander (97 – Oct 06) R to 56	5571
Land Rover Freelander Diesel (Nov 06 – 14) 56 to 64	5636
Land Rover Series II, IIA & III 4-cyl Petrol (58 – 85) up to C	0314
Land Rover Series II, IIA & III Petrol & Diesel (58 – 85) up to C	5568
MAZDA 323 (Mar 81 – Oct 89) up to G	1608
Mazda 323 (Oct 89 – 98) G to R	3455
Mazda B1600, B1800 & B2000 Pick-up Petrol (72 – 88) up to F	0267
Mazda MX-5 (89 – 05) G to 05	5565
Mazda RX-7 (79 – 85) up to C *	0460
MERCEDES-BENZ 190, 190E & 190D Petrol & Diesel (83 – 93) A to L	3450
Mercedes-Benz 200D, 240D, 240TD, 300D & 300TD 123 Series Diesel (Oct 76 – 85) up to C	1114
Mercedes-Benz 250 & 280 (68 – 72) up to L *	0346
Mercedes-Benz 250 & 280 123 Series Petrol (Oct 76 – 84) up to B *	0677
Mercedes-Benz 124 Series Petrol & Diesel (85 – Aug 93) C to K	3253
Mercedes-Benz A-Class Petrol & Diesel (98 – 04) S to 54	4748
Mercedes-Benz C-Class Petrol & Diesel (93 – Aug 00) L to W	3511
Mercedes-Benz C-Class (00 – 07) X to 07	4780
Mercedes-Benz E-Class Diesel (Jun 02 – Feb 10) 02 to 59	5710
Mercedes-Benz Sprinter Diesel (95 – Apr 06) M to 06	4902
MGA (55 – 62)	0475
MGB (62 – 80) up to W	0111
MGB 1962 to 1980 (special edition) *	4894
MG Midget & Austin-Healey Sprite (58 – 80) up to W *	0265
MINI Petrol (July 01 – 06) Y to 56	4273
MINI Petrol & Diesel (Nov 06 – 13) 56 to 13	4904
MITSUBISHI Shogun & L200 Pick-ups Petrol (83 – 94) up to M	1944
MORRIS Minor 1000 (56 – 71) up to K	0024
NISSAN Almera Petrol (95 – Feb 00) N to V	4053
Nissan Almera & Tino Petrol (Feb 00 – 07) V to 56	4612
Nissan Micra (83 – Jan 93) up to K	0931
Nissan Micra (93 – 02) K to 52	3254
Nissan Micra Petrol (03 – Oct 10) 52 to 60	4734
Nissan Primera Petrol (90 - Aug 99) H to T	1851
Nissan Qashqai Petrol & Diesel (07 – 12) 56 to 62	5610
OPEL Ascona & Manta (B-Series) (Sept 75 – 88) up to F *	0316
Opel Ascona Petrol (81 – 88)	3215
Opel Ascona Petrol (Oct 91 – Feb 98)	3156
Opel Corsa Petrol (83 – Mar 93)	3160
Opel Corsa Petrol (Mar 93 – 97)	3159
Opel Kadett Petrol (Oct 84 – Oct 91)	3196
Opel Omega & Senator Petrol (Nov 86 – 94)	3157
Opel Vectra Petrol (Oct 88 – Oct 95)	3158
PEUGEOT 106 Petrol & Diesel (91 – 04) J to 53	1882
Peugeot 107 Petrol (05 – 11) 05 to 11	4923
Peugeot 205 Petrol (83 – 97) A to P	0932

* Classic reprint

Title	Book No.
Peugeot 206 Petrol & Diesel (98 – 01) S to X	3757
Peugeot 206 Petrol & Diesel (02 – 09) 51 to 59	4613
Peugeot 207 Petrol & Diesel (06 – July 09) 06 to 09	4787
Peugeot 306 Petrol & Diesel (93 – 02) K to 02	3073
Peugeot 307 Petrol & Diesel (01 – 08) Y to 58	4147
Peugeot 308 Petrol & Diesel (07 – 12) 07 to 12	5561
Peugeot 405 Diesel (88 – 97) E to P	3198
Peugeot 406 Petrol & Diesel (96 – Mar 99) N to T	3394
Peugeot 406 Petrol & Diesel (Mar 99 – 02) T to 52	3982
Peugeot 407 Diesel (04 -11) 53 to 11	5550
PORSCHE 911 (65 – 85) up to C	0264
Porsche 924 & 924 Turbo (76 – 85) up to C	0397
RANGE ROVER V8 Petrol (70 – Oct 92) up to K	0606
RELIANT Robin & Kitten (73 – 83) up to A *	0436
RENAULT 4 (61 – 86) up to D *	0072
Renault 5 Petrol (Feb 85 – 96) B to N	1219
Renault 19 Petrol (89 – 96) F to N	1646
Renault Clio Petrol (91 – May 98) H to R	1853
Renault Clio Petrol & Diesel (May 98 – May 01) R to Y	3906
Renault Clio Petrol & Diesel (June 01 – 05) Y to 55	4168
Renault Clio Petrol & Diesel (Oct 05 – May 09) 55 to 09	4788
Renault Espace Petrol & Diesel (85 – 96) C to N	3197
Renault Laguna Petrol & Diesel (94 – 00) L to W	3252
Renault Laguna Petrol & Diesel (Feb 01 – May 07) X to 07	4283
Renault Megane & Scenic Petrol & Diesel (96 – 99) N to T	3395
Renault Megane & Scenic Petrol & Diesel (Apr 99 – 02) T to 52	3916
Renault Megane Petrol & Diesel (Oct 02 – 08) 52 to 58	4284
Renault Megane Petrol & Diesel (Oct 08 – 14) 58 to 64	5955
Renault Scenic Petrol & Diesel (Sept 03 – 06) 53 to 06	4297
Renault Trafic Diesel (01 – 11) Y to 11	5551
ROVER 216 & 416 Petrol (89 – 96) G to N	1830
Rover 211, 214, 216, 218 & 220 Petrol & Diesel (Dec 95 – 99) N to V	3399
Rover 25 & MG ZR Petrol & Diesel (Oct 99 – 06) V to 06	4145
Rover 414, 416 & 420 Petrol & Diesel (May 95 – 99) M to V	3453
Rover 45 / MG ZS Petrol & Diesel (99 – 05) V to 55	4384
Rover 618, 620 & 623 Petrol (93 – 97) K to P	3257
Rover 75 / MG ZT Petrol & Diesel (99 – 06) S to 06	4292
Rover 820, 825 & 827 Petrol (86 – 95) D to N	1380
Rover 3500 (76 – 87) up to E *	0365
SAAB 95 & 96 (66 – 76) up to R *	0198
Saab 90, 99 & 900 (79 – Oct 93) up to L	0765
Saab 900 (Oct 93 – 98) L to R	3512
Saab 9000 4-cyl (85 – 98) C to S	1686
Saab 9-3 Petrol & Diesel (98 – Aug 02) R to 02	4614
Saab 9-3 Petrol & Diesel (92 – 07) 52 to 57	4749
Saab 9-3 Petrol & Diesel (07-on) 57 on	5569
Saab 9-5 4-cyl Petrol (97 – 05) R to 55	4156
Saab 9-5 (Sep 05 – Jun 10) 55 to 10	4891
SEAT Ibiza & Cordoba Petrol & Diesel (Oct 93 – Oct 99) L to V	3571
Seat Ibiza & Malaga Petrol (85 – 92) B to K	1609
Seat Ibiza Petrol & Diesel (May 02 – Apr 08) 02 to 08	4889
SKODA Fabia Petrol & Diesel (00 – 06) W to 06	4376

Title	Book No.
Skoda Felicia Petrol & Diesel (95 – 01) M to X	3505
Skoda Octavia Petrol (98 – April 04) R to 04	4285
Skoda Octavia Diesel (May 04 – 12) 04 to 61	5549
SUBARU 1600 & 1800 (Nov 79 – 90) up to H *	0995
SUNBEAM Alpine, Rapier & H120 (68 – 74) up to N *	0051
SUZUKI SJ Series, Samurai & Vitara 4-cyl Petrol (82 – 97) up to P	1942
Suzuki Supercarry & Bedford/Vauxhall Rascal (86 – Oct 94) C to M	3015
TOYOTA Avensis Petrol (98 – Jan 03) R to 52	4264
Toyota Aygo Petrol (05 – 11) 05 to 11	4921
Toyota Carina E Petrol (May 92 – 97) J to P	3256
Toyota Corolla (Sept 83 – Sept 87) A to E	1024
Toyota Corolla (Sept 87 – Aug 92) E to K	1683
Toyota Corolla Petrol (Aug 92 – 97) K to P	3259
Toyota Corolla Petrol (July 97 0 Feb 02) P to 51	4286
Toyota Corolla Petrol & Diesel (02 – Jan 07) 51 to 56	4791
Toyota Hi-Ace & Hi-Lux Petrol (69 – Oct 83) up to A	0304
Toyota RAV4 Petrol & Diesel (94 – 06) L to 55	4750
Toyota Yaris Petrol (99 – 05) T to 05	4265
TRIUMPH GT6 & Vitesse (62 0 74) up to N *	0112
Triumph Herald (59 – 71) up to K *	0010
Triumph Spitfire (62 – 81) up to X *	0113
Triumph Stag (70 – 78) up to T *	0441
Triumph TR2, TR3, TR3A, TR4 & TR4A (52 – 67) up to F *	0028
Triumph TR5 & TR6 (67 – 75) up to P *	0031
Triumph TR7 (75 – 82) up to Y *	0322
VAUXHALL Astra Petrol (Oct 91 – Feb 98) J to R	1832
Vauxhall/Opel Astra & Zafira Petrol (Feb 98 – Apr 04) R to 04	3758
Vauxhall/Opel Astra & Zafira Diesel (Feb 98 – Apr 04) R to 04	3797
Vauxhall/Opel Astra Petrol (04 – 08)	4732
Vauxhall/Opel Astra Diesel (04 – 08)	4733
Vauxhall/Opel Astra Petrol & Diesel (Dec 09 – 13) 59 to 13	5578
Vauxhall/Opel Calibra (90 – 98) G to S	3502
Vauxhall Cavalier Petrol (Oct 88 0 95) F to N	1570
Vauxhall/Opel Corsa Diesel (Mar 93 – Oct 00) K to X	4087
Vauxhall Corsa Petrol (Mar 93 – 97) K to R	1985
Vauxhall/Opel Corsa Petrol (Apr 97 – Oct 00) P to X	3921
Vauxhall/Opel Corsa Petrol & Diesel (Oct 03 – Aug 06) 53 to 06	4617
Vauxhall/Opel Corsa Petrol & Diesel (Sept 06 – 10) 56 to 10	4886
Vauxhall/Opel Corsa Petrol & Diesel (00 – Aug 06) X to 06	5577
Vauxhall/Opel Frontera Petrol & Diesel (91 – Sept 98) J to S	3454
Vauxhall/Opel Insignia Petrol & Diesel (08 – 12) 08 to 61	5563
Vauxhall/Opel Meriva Petrol & Diesel (03 – May 10) 03 to 10	4893
Vauxhall/Opel Omega Petrol (94 – 99) L to T	3510
Vauxhall/Opel Vectra Petrol & Diesel (95 – Feb 99) N to S	3396
Vauxhall/Opel Vectra Petrol & Diesel (Mar 99 – May 02) T to 02	3930
Vauxhall/Opel Vectra Petrol & Diesel (June 02 – Sept 05) 02 to 55	4618

Title	Book No.
Vauxhall/Opel Vectra Petrol & Diesel (Oct 05 – Oct 08) 55 to 58	4887
Vauxhall/Opel Vivaro Diesel (01 – 11) Y to 11	5552
Vauxhall/Opel Zafira Petrol & Diesel (05 -09) 05 to 09	4792
Vauxhall/Opel 1.5, 1.6 & 1.7 litre Diesel Engine (82 – 96) up to N	1222
VW Beetle 1200 (54 – 77) up to S	0036
VW Beetle 1300 & 1500 (65 – 75) up to P	0039
VW 1302 & 1302S (70 – 72) up to L *	0110
VW Beetle 1303, 1303S & GT (72 – 75) up to P	0159
VW Beetle Petrol & Diesel (Apr 99 – 07) T to 57	3798
VW Golf & Jetta Mk 1 Petrol 1.1 & 1.3 (74 – 84) up to A	0716
VW Golf, Jetta & Scirocco Mk 1 Petrol 1.5, 1.6 & 1.8 (74 – 84) up to A	0726
VW Golf & Jetta Mk 1 Diesel (78 – 84) up to A	0451
VW Golf & Jetta Mk 2 Petrol (Mar 84 – Feb 92) A to J	1081
VW Golf & Vento Petrol & Diesel (Feb 92 – Mar 98) J to R	3097
VW Golf & Bora Petrol & Diesel (Apr 98 – 00) R to X	3727
VW Golf & Bora 4-cyl Petrol & Diesel (01 – 03) X to 53	4169
VW Golf & Jetta Petrol & Diesel (04 – 09) 53 to 09	4610
VW Golf Petrol & Diesel (09 – 12) 58 to 62	5633
VW LT Petrol Vans & Light Trucks (76 – 87) up to E	0637
VW Passat 4-cyl Petrol & Diesel (May 88 – 96) E to P	3498
VW Passat 4-cyl Petrol & Diesel (Dec 96 – Nov 00) P to X	3917
VW Passat Petrol & Diesel (Dec 00 – May 05) X to 05	4279
VW Passat Diesel (June 05 – 10) 05 to 60	4888
VW Polo Petrol (Nov 90 – Aug 94) H to L	3245
VW Polo Hatchback Petrol & Diesel (94 – 99) M to S	3500
VW Polo Hatchback Petrol & Diesel (00 – Jan 02) V to 51	4150
VW Polo Petrol & Diesel (02 – Sep 09) 51 to 59	4608
VW Polo Petrol & Diesel (Oct 09 – Jul 14) (59 to 14)	5638
VW Transporter 1600 (68 – 79) up to V	0082
VW Transporter 1700, 1800 & 2000 (72 – 79) up to V *	0226
VW Transporter (air cooled) Petrol (79 – 82) up to Y *	0638
VW Transporter (water cooled) Petrol (82 – 90) up to H	3452
VW T4 Transporter Diesel (90 – 03) H to 03	5711
VW T5 Transporter Diesel (July 03 – 14) 03 to 64	5743
VW Type 3 (63 – 73) up to M *	0084
VOLVO 120 & 130 Series (& P1800) (61 – 73) up to M *	0203
Volvo 142, 144 & 145 (66 – 74) up to N *	0129
Volvo 240 Series Petrol (74 – 93) up to K	0270
Volvo 440, 460 & 480 Petrol (87 – 97) D to P	1691
Volvo 740 & 760 Petrol (82 – 91) up to J	1258
Volvo 850 Petrol (92 – 96) J to P	3260
Volvo 940 Petrol (90 – 98) H to R	3249
Volvo S40 & V40 Petrol (96 – Mar 04) N to 04	3569
Volvo S40 & V50 Petrol & Diesel (Mar 04 – Jun 07) 04 to 07	4731
Volvo S40 & V50 Diesel (July 07 - 13) 07 to 13	5684
Volvo S60 Petrol & Diesel (01 – 08) X to 09	4793
Volvo S70, V70 & C70 Petrol (96 – 99) P to V	3573
Volvo V70 / S80 Petrol & Diesel (98 – 07) S to 07	4263
Volvo V70 Diesel (June 07 – 12) 07 to 61	5557
Volvo XC60 / 90 Diesel (03 – 12) 52 to 62	5630

* Classic reprint

CL 07.06.15

Preserving Our Motoring Heritage

< The Model J Duesenberg Derham Tourster. Only eight of these magnificent cars were ever built – this is the only example to be found outside the United States of America

Almost every car you've ever loved, loathed or desired is gathered under one roof at the Haynes Motor Museum. Over 300 immaculately presented cars and motorbikes represent every aspect of our motoring heritage, from elegant reminders of bygone days, such as the superb Model J Duesenberg to curiosities like the bug-eyed BMW Isetta. There are also many old friends and flames. Perhaps you remember the 1959 Ford Popular that you did your courting in? The magnificent 'Red Collection' is a spectacle of classic sports cars including AC, Alfa Romeo, Austin Healey, Ferrari, Lamborghini, Maserati, MG, Riley, Porsche and Triumph.

A Perfect Day Out

Each and every vehicle at the Haynes Motor Museum has played its part in the history and culture of Motoring. Today, they make a wonderful spectacle and a great day out for all the family. Bring the kids, bring Mum and Dad, but above all bring your camera to capture those golden memories for ever. You will also find an impressive array of motoring memorabilia, a comfortable 70 seat video cinema and one of the most extensive transport book shops in Britain. The Pit Stop Cafe serves everything from a cup of tea to wholesome, home-made meals or, if you prefer, you can enjoy the large picnic area nestled in the beautiful rural surroundings of Somerset.

> John Haynes O.B.E., Founder and Chairman of the museum at the wheel of a Haynes Light 12.

< Graham Hill's Lola Cosworth Formula 1 car next to a 1934 Riley Sports.

The Museum is situated on the A359 Yeovil to Frome road at Sparkford, just off the A303 in Somerset. It is about 40 miles south of Bristol, and 25 minutes drive from the M5 intersection at Taunton.
Open 9.30am - 5.30pm (10.00am - 4.00pm Winter) 7 days a week, *except Christmas Day, Boxing Day and New Years Day*
Special rates available for schools, coach parties and outings Charitable Trust No. 292048